Rand Morimoto
Michael Noel
Guy Yardeni
Chris Amaris
Andrew Abbate
Technical Edit by Ed Crowley

Microsoft® Exchange Server 2013

UNLEASHED

SAMS | 800 East 96th Street, Indianapolis, Indiana 46240 USA

Microsoft® Exchange Server 2013 Unleashed

ISBN-13: 978-0-672-33611-9
ISBN-10: 0-672-33611-1

Library of Congress Cataloging-in-Publication Data is on file.

Printed in the United States of America

First Printing November 2012

Trademarks

Warning and Disclaimer

Bulk Sales

Sams Publishing offers excellent discounts on this book when ordered in quantity for bulk purchases or special sales. For more information, please contact

U.S. Corporate and Government Sales
1-800-382-3419
corpsales@pearsontechgroup.com

For sales outside of the U.S., please contact

International Sales
international@pearsoned.com

Editor-in-Chief
Greg Wiegand

Executive Editor
Neil Rowe

Development Editor
Mark Renfrow

Managing Editor
Kristy Hart

Project Editor
Betsy Harris

Copy Editor
Karen Annett

Indexer
Heather McNeill

Proofreader
Dan Knott

Technical Editor
Ed Crowley

Editorial Assistant
Cindy Teeters

Cover Designer
Anne Jones

Compositor
Nonie Ratcliff

Contributing Writers
Pete Handley
Eva SooHoo

Contents at a Glance

Table of Contents

Part II Implementing and Transitioning to Exchange Server 2013

About the Authors

Rand Morimoto, Ph.D., MVP, MCITP, CISSP, has been in the computer industry for more than 30 years and has authored, coauthored, or been a contributing writer for dozens of books on Windows, Security, Exchange, BizTalk, and Remote and Mobile Computing. Rand is the president of Convergent Computing, an IT-consulting firm in the San Francisco Bay area that has been one of the key early adopter program partners with Microsoft, implementing the latest Microsoft technologies, including Microsoft Windows Server 2012, System Center 2012, Windows 8, Exchange Server 2013, SharePoint 2013, Office 365, and Azure cloud services in production environments more than 18 months before the initial product releases.

Michael Noel, MCITP, MVP, is an internationally recognized technology expert, best-selling author, and well-known public speaker on a broad range of IT topics. He authored multiple major industry books that have been translated into more than a dozen languages worldwide. Michael has presented at over 100 technical and business conferences in more than 50 countries around the world and on all seven continents, including the first ever IT conference in Antarctica. Currently a partner at Convergent Computing (www.cco.com) in the San Francisco Bay area, Michael's writing and extensive public-speaking experience across all seven continents leverage his real-world expertise in helping organizations realize business value from the information technology infrastructure.

Guy Yardeni, MCITP, CISSP, MVP, is an accomplished infrastructure architect, author, and overall geek-for-hire. Guy has been working in the IT industry for more than 15 years and has extensive experience designing, implementing, and supporting enterprise technology solutions. Guy is an expert at connecting business requirements to technology solutions and driving to successful completion the technical details of the effort while maintaining overall goals and vision. Guy maintains a widely read technical blog at www.rdpfiles.com and is a Windows MVP.

Chris Amaris, MCITP, MCTS, CISSP/ISSAP, CHS III, is the chief technology officer and cofounder of Convergent Computing. He has more than 20 years experience consulting for Fortune 500 companies, leading companies in the technology selection, design, planning, and implementation of complex information technology projects. Chris has worked with Microsoft Exchange Server since its original release in 1995. He specializes in messaging, security, performance tuning, systems management, and migration. Receiving his first Microsoft technologies certification in 1993, Chris is a current Microsoft Certified IT Professional (MCITP) with multiple Microsoft Certified Technology Specialist (MCTS) certifications in Microsoft technologies, a Certified Information Systems Security Professional (CISSP) with an Information System Security Architecture Professional (ISSAP) concentration, Certified Homeland Security (CHS III), a Novell CNE, a Banyan CBE, and a Certified Project Manager. Chris is also an author, writer, and technical editor for a number of IT books, including *Microsoft System Center 2012 Unleashed, Network Security for Government and Corporate Executives, Microsoft Exchange Server 2010 Unleashed,* and *Microsoft Windows Server 2012 Unleashed.*

Andrew Abbate enjoys the position of principal consultant and partner at Convergent Computing. With nearly 20 years of experience in IT, Andrew's area of expertise is understanding a business's needs and translating that to process and technologies to solve real problems. Having worked with companies from the Fortune Ten to companies of 10, Andrew has a unique perspective on IT and a grasp on "big picture" consulting. Andrew has also written nine industry books on varying technologies ranging from Windows to Security to Unified Communications and contributed to several others.

Dedication

I dedicate this book to Chip and Eduardo, as you look up to your two elder siblings, look to them for guidance and support, but always remember to carve your own path that is right for you... Achieve success through hard work, dedication, and determination!

—Rand Morimoto, Ph.D., MVP, MCITP, CISSP

This book is dedicated to my many wonderful nieces and nephews including Carrie, Zachary, Sophie, Joshua, Avery, Willow, River, and Aurora. I am truly blessed to be your Uncle, and I look forward to watching you all grow and flourish!

—Michael Noel, MCITP, MVP

I dedicate this book to my wonderful wife Allison who puts up with the insanity of writing these books and to my two daughters, Maya Aviv and Zoe Carmel who are the motivation and inspiration for the work.

—Guy Yardeni, MCSE, MCITP, CISSP

I dedicate this book to my wife Sophia, light of my life. And to my children, Michelle, Megan, Zoe, Zachary, and Ian, who give meaning to my life and work.

—Chris Amaris, MCITP, MCTS, CISSP/ISSAP, CHS III

This book is dedicated to my niece and nephew Nora and William. You guys remind me that there's much more to life than technology and work. You help keep me sane and grounded.

—Andrew Abbate, MCITP

Thanks to my wife, Juliet, and my children, E.J. and Jacob, for putting up with me ignoring them more than usual during my work on this book.

—Ed Crowley, BS-EECS, MBA, MVP, MCITP

Acknowledgments

Rand Morimoto, Ph.D., MVP, MCITP, CISSP WHEW, three books in one year; when I started out with the *System Center 2012 Unleashed* book, I had no idea how much work was still ahead of me. But with the *Windows Server 2012 Unleashed* book out in the marketplace and doing great, it's nice to wrap up the year with this book on Exchange Server 2013, a VERY exciting update to the Exchange platform!

A note of THANKS to the Wave 15 product team for all your support to our early adopter clients in helping us through our beta deployments to the final release of the code! It's hard to imagine the coordination and effort it takes to get a product like Exchange Server 2013 out the door with the complexity of cross-integration with SharePoint 2013, Lync 2013, and Office 2013 along with the evolution of the underlying Windows Server 2012 operating system.

I want to thank the team at Sams Publishing for turning this book around, yet again in record time! Thank you Neil, Mark, Betsy, Karen, and all the folks behind the scenes in making this happen!

I also wanted to thank the consultants at Convergent Computing and our early adopter clients who fiddle with these new technologies really early on and then take the leap of faith in putting the products into production to experience (and at times feel the pain) as we work through best practices. The early adopter experiences give us the knowledge and experience we need to share with all who use this book as their guide in their production environments based on the lessons learned.

To Kelly, Noble, Chip, and Eduardo, that's it for the year, no more book writing in the wee hours of the night and through the weekends! If you want to find me in the middle of the night, I won't be downstairs writing at the kitchen table, I'll be in that bed thing, ah, to get a full night's sleep! Remember to work hard at everything you do, as you've found so far, you can accomplish a lot when you put your mind to things!

Michael Noel, MCITP, MVP It seems so long ago that I was first introduced to Exchange Server. We were migrating 2,000 mailboxes off of a POP-based platform over to this brand-new Exchange 5.0 server running on an Alpha processor. My, how the product has changed over the years! It has evolved from a niche tool to the standard messaging platform for the vast majority of the world's organizations, and in the process has added some amazing capabilities that we in the industry could never have dreamed of. And here, over 15 years later, I'm still involved with the technology, having migrated literally over a million mailboxes to and from various versions of the product. Despite this, it is never easy to write new versions of these books, and I'm grateful to all who have helped along the way.

I'd like to especially thank lead author Rand Morimoto on this book, whom I've collaborated with on more than a dozen books over the past decade. His expertise and willingness to dig in and test different scenarios has ensured the integrity and usefulness of this volume over the years.

I'd also like to thank the many people who have attended my conferences and events over the past years, all around the world. I find it fascinating that we all live different lives in different cultures but are tied together with the same technical challenges that all IT workers worldwide face.

And last but not least, a huge thanks to my wonderful family for putting up with all of the book writing, public speaking, and late nights working in the lab. My wonderful wife Marina, thank you for everything, and thanks for putting up with the long nights! My beautiful daughter Julia, you will accomplish so much in life, and thanks for being you! I'd also like to thank my parents George and Mary, and my most amazing in-laws Val and Liza. I love all of you dearly!

Guy Yardeni, MCITP, CISSP I want to first and foremost thank Rand for the opportunity to join another book team and for the ridiculous amount of work he puts in to keep a group of authors moving ahead and focused on target.

I also want to thank the CCO contributing authors and technical editor for helping making this book as good as possible.

And another thanks to my family since they bear the brunt of my stress and craziness during the writing process. I couldn't have done this without you.

Chris Amaris, MCSE, MVP, CISSP I want to acknowledge Rand Morimoto for once again leading us to do that which is hard but rewarding. It was over a year ago that Rand outlined what was to be a yearlong marathon of writing. Rand inspired us, herded us, and put his shoulder to the wheel to help us. This endeavor would never have been a success without him. Huge thanks for all the support and for making this a reality!

I also want to acknowledge my family for their continued support: my wife Sophia, for keeping it all together and plying me with caffeine in many forms (cappuccinos, chocolate-covered espresso beans, Hong Kong milk tea, etc.). And to my children, Michelle, Megan, Zoe, Zachary, and Ian, for staying focused on their studies and keeping me young. To them, I say: "Word!"

Andrew Abbate, MCITP It seems like every year I tell myself "I'm not going to do a book this year" and yet each year, I'm trying to decide what to put in the acknowledgements of yet another book. At the risk of sounding like a broken record, I'd once again like to thank my coauthors for producing an excellent work and for being available to bounce ideas off of. A big thanks to the team at Pearson Education for turning another batch of my chicken scratch into a polished and professional book. And a big thanks to one of my peers, Mark Weinhardt, for having sparked my interest in Exchange many years ago. I'm also obligated under the terms of a bet to announce in a book that he's a better golfer than I.

We Want to Hear from You!

As the reader of this book, *you* are our most important critic and commentator. We value your opinion and want to know what we're doing right, what we could do better, what areas you'd like to see us publish in, and any other words of wisdom you're willing to pass our way.

We welcome your comments. You can email or write to let us know what you did or didn't like about this book—as well as what we can do to make our books better.

Please note that we cannot help you with technical problems related to the topic of this book.

When you write, please be sure to include this book's title and author as well as your name and email address. We will carefully review your comments and share them with the author and editors who worked on the book.

Email: consumer@samspublishing.com

Mail: Sams Publishing
ATTN: Reader Feedback
800 East 96th Street
Indianapolis, IN 46240 USA

Reader Services

Visit our website and register this book at informit.com/register for convenient access to any updates, downloads, or errata that might be available for this book.

Introduction

Microsoft Exchange Server is nearing its second decade in development, a product that shipped in the 1990s as an email system that at the time didn't even support integrated calendaring. With the release of Exchange Server 2013, Microsoft has come a *long* way in developing Exchange, not just to add more features and functions, but also to simply integrate several technologies into a common unified communications system. Exchange natively includes email, calendaring, contacts, tasks, voice mail, shared folders, and email archiving, and then tightly integrates with Microsoft Lync and SharePoint to include instant messages, web conferencing, videoconferencing, audio conferencing, document management, content management, and more.

Even though Exchange Server 2013 shipped at the end of 2012, the authors of this book have been fortunate enough to work with Exchange Server 2013 for more than a year in priority early adopter programs of the product and service offerings. The thing about being involved with a product so early on is that our first experiences with these products were without any documentation, Help files that provided guidance, or any shared experiences from others. We had to learn Exchange Server 2013 from experience, usually the hard way, but that has given us a distinct advantage of knowing the product forward and backward better than anyone could ever imagine. And we started to implement Exchange Server 2013 in production environments for a select group of our enterprise customers several months before the product release, gaining valuable experience in the implementation, migration, and cross-product integration that has led to the tips, tricks, and best practices included in this book.

So the pages of this book are filled with years of experience with Microsoft Exchange as well as many, many months of live production environment early adopter deployments that will hopefully help you design, plan, prototype, implement, migrate, administer, and support your Exchange environment.

This book is organized into six parts, each part focusing on core Exchange Server 2013 areas, with several chapters making up each part. The parts of the book are as follows:

- **Part I: Microsoft Exchange Server 2013 Overview**—This part provides an introduction to Exchange Server 2013 covering what's new, what's different, and how to successfully architect and plan the latest Exchange environments. This part of the book also covers strategies of addressing enterprise deployments of Exchange plus the inclusion of best practices in establishing a solid Active Directory, DNS, fabric, virtualization, and PKI security environment to support Exchange.
- **Part II: Implementing and Transitioning to Exchange Server 2013**—This part covers the implementation of Exchange Server 2013 from scratch, effectively an organization that may be new to Exchange or an organization looking to start all over again in building out Exchange after a merger or series of acquisitions suggest a clean implementation of Exchange makes the most sense. This part also includes transitioning from Exchange Server 2007 and 2010 to Exchange Server 2013, as well as high-availability designs for Exchange and new strategies in implementing public folders as well as proxy security using Threat Management Gateway (TMG).
- **Part III: Securing and Compliance in an Exchange Server 2013 Environment**—Security is on everyone's mind these days, so it was a major enhancement to Exchange Server 2013 to support better security of servers, messages, and message archives. This part of the book focuses on policy-based and content-enforced security using updates to Microsoft Active Directory Rights Management Services (RMS); built-in MailTips; the implementation of Microsoft Edge for antivirus and anti-malware; as well as integrated email archiving, retention, and eDiscovery.
- **Part IV: Exchange Administration, Management, Maintenance, and Optimization**—This part of the book is dedicated to the day-to-day administration of Exchange. This part includes content on the new Exchange Administration Center, using remoting, and role-based administration that may include core features in PowerShell. After you get Exchange Server 2013 in place and do the day-to-day administration, you end up spending time maintaining and supporting the Exchange environment. This includes descriptions of implementation best practices, including management and maintenance practices, Exchange environment optimization, backing up Exchange, implementation of external monitoring through System Center 2012 Operations Manager (SCOM), as well as documentation.
- **Part V: Platform Integration in an Exchange Server 2013 Environment**—Integration is key in this next wave of Microsoft Office server products, and tying together Exchange, SharePoint, and Unified Messaging are important for organizations looking to simplify communications into a consolidated platform. This part of the book covers Unified Messaging (voice mail) and SharePoint integration.

- **Part VI: Client Access to Exchange**—Another major enhancement in Exchange Server 2013 is its support for both Microsoft as well as non-Microsoft endpoint clients, including full Outlook clients for Windows in Office 2013 as well as full Outlook client support for Apple Mac users. In addition, for mobile users, Microsoft now includes the ability to support not only web-based client access using the age-old Outlook Web Apps (OWA) method of communications access, but now the ability to download apps for mobile phones to support a client-based access to Exchange from Microsoft and non-Microsoft mobile phone devices.

It is our hope that the real-world experience we have had in working with Exchange Server 2013 and our commitment to relaying to you information that will be valuable in your planning, implementation, and migration to an Exchange environment will help you get up to speed on the latest in core unified communications environment.

CHAPTER 1

Exchange Server 2013 Technology Primer

IN THIS CHAPTER

- What Is Exchange Server 2013?
- What's New in Exchange Server 2013?
- Exploring the New Exchange Administration Center (EAC)
- Architectural Changes in Exchange Server 2013
- Improvements in Exchange Server 2013 Relative to Security
- Improvements in Exchange Server 2013 Relative to eDiscovery and Retention
- Changes to Public Folders in Exchange Server 2013
- Introduction of Site Mailboxes in Exchange Server 2013
- Exchange Server 2013 as the Focal Point for Remote and Mobile Communications
- Integration with Lync 2013
- Improving Unified Messaging in Exchange Server 2013
- Making Exchange Server 2013 Extremely Reliable and Recoverable
- Improving Configuration, Administration, and Management Through the Exchange Management Shell
- Improving Performance Through Batch Moves and Processing
- Understanding Mail Flow in Exchange Server 2013
- Understanding the Importance of Active Directory for an Exchange Server 2013 Environment
- Installing and Transitioning to Exchange Server 2013
- Managing and Administering Exchange Server 2013

Microsoft Exchange Server 2013 is the latest release of the messaging and communications system from Microsoft built on the Windows operating system. This chapter introduces you to "What is Exchange Server 2013?" not just from the perspective of what's new in Exchange Server 2013 compared with previous versions, but also from the perspective of those who are new to Exchange. This chapter discusses the background of Exchange, the previous versions, and the general concepts of the Exchange messaging system, so that regardless of whether you are an Exchange Server 2007 or 2010 expert, or you are new to working with Exchange, you are prepared to dive into the remainder of this book on planning, testing, implementing, administering, managing, and supporting an Exchange Server 2013 environment.

What Is Exchange Server 2013?

At its core, Microsoft Exchange Server 2013 is an email, calendaring, and address book system that runs on a centralized Windows Server system. However, with the release of Exchange Server 2013, now the eighth major release of Exchange in the over 15-year history of the product, Microsoft has made significant improvements in the areas of global scalability, mobile and tablet client support, security, compliance, reliability, unified communications, and integration with SharePoint 2013 and Lync 2013. For those Exchange experts who are already very familiar with the product, you might choose to skip this section and jump to the "What's New in Exchange Server 2013" section to discover the latest and greatest in Exchange Server 2013.

So back to the basics of Exchange, with a centralized Exchange server holding mail messages, calendar appointments, contacts, and other user information, the Exchange environment provides a server-based storage of information. Users throughout the organization connect to the Exchange server from Microsoft Outlook, from a web browser, from a mobile phone or tablet system, or from a variety of other client systems to get access to their email and other information.

For larger organizations, multiple Exchange servers can be added to the environment hosting mailbox information of the users. Microsoft has split the roles of servers in an Exchange environment, where some servers are dedicated for antivirus and antispam filtering, and other servers are dedicated to client system connections throughout the organization. The "Architectural Changes in Exchange Server 2013" section discusses these roles in more detail.

Understanding the Evolution of Exchange

For those new to Microsoft Exchange, this section covers the history of the Exchange product line. Sometimes as a newcomer to a technology, it's hard to jump right into the technology because everyone working with the technology refers to previous versions without taking into consideration that some people might not remember what was in the last revision, or in the product a couple of revisions back. So, this section is intended to give you a little history of Exchange so that the version numbers and major notable features and functions make sense.

Exchange Server 4.0

The first version of Microsoft Exchange, despite the 4.0 designation, was Exchange Server 4.0. Some people ask, "What happened to Exchange Server 1.0, 2.0, and 3.0?" For a bit of trivia, prior to Exchange Server 4.0, Microsoft had MS-Mail 3.0 (and MS-Mail 2.0); prior to that, it was a product called Network Courier Mail that Microsoft bought in the early 1990s.

Microsoft Exchange Server 4.0 had nothing in common with MS-Mail 3.0; they were completely different products and different technologies. The first rollouts of Exchange Server 4.0 back in 1996 were on Windows NT Server 3.51, which anyone with old NT 3.x experience knows was a challenging operating system to keep fully operational. "Blue screens" in which the operating system would just lock up were common. Anything that caused a system error usually resulted in a blue screen, which meant that every patch, update, service pack addition, installation of antivirus software, and so on frequently caused complete server failures.

However, Exchange Server 4.0 was a major breakthrough, and organizations started to migrate from MS-Mail (or at that time cc:Mail was another popular mail system) to Exchange Server 4.0. One of the biggest reasons organizations were migrating to Exchange Server 4.0 was that in 1996, the Internet was just opening up to the public. The specifications for the World Wide Web had just been released. Organizations were connecting systems to the Internet, and one of the first real applications that took advantage of the Internet was Microsoft Exchange Server 4.0. Organizations were able to connect their Exchange Server 4.0 server to the Internet and easily and simply send and receive emails to anyone else with an Internet-connected email system. MS-Mail 3.0 at the time had a Simple Mail Transfer Protocol (SMTP) gateway; however, it worked more on a scheduled dial-up basis, whereas Exchange Server 4.0 had a persistent connection to, typically, Integrated Services Digital Network (ISDN) or 56-KB frame connections to the Internet. And with Windows NT 4.0 shipping and being a much more solid infrastructure to work from, Exchange Server 4.0 was much more reliable than MS-Mail was for centralized organizationwide email communications.

Exchange Server 5.0

Exchange Server 5.0 came out in 1997 and was built to run on Windows NT 4.0, which proved to add more reliability to the Exchange Server product. In addition, Exchange Server 5.0 supported the first version of Outlook that to this day has a similar mailbox folder concept with the Inbox, Sent Items, Calendar, Contacts, and other common folders duplicated by mail systems throughout the industry. With the support for the Microsoft Outlook (97) client, Exchange also included calendaring directly within the Exchange product. In Exchange Server 5.0, the calendaring product was Schedule+, which was an add-on to Exchange Server 4.0, meaning that a user's email and calendaring weren't tied together, so Exchange Server 5.0 tied email, calendaring, and address books all together. With a service pack to Exchange Server 5.0, Microsoft also released the first version of Outlook Web Access (OWA) so that those who accessed the new World Wide Web could get remote access to their email on Exchange. Back in 1997, this was a big thing as web mail was a new concept, and Exchange Server 5.0 had web mail built in to the messaging product.

Exchange Server 5.0 also had better third-party support for things such as fax gateways, unified voice mail add-in products, and document-sharing tools, leveraging shared public folders in Exchange. With better reliability, third-party product support, and a growing base of customers now migrating from MS-Mail and cc:Mail to Exchange, the Microsoft Exchange market share started to skyrocket.

Exchange Server 5.5

In 1998, Microsoft released Exchange Server 5.5, which until just a few years ago some organizations were still running in their networking environments because of its reliability and stability as an email system. With Exchange Server 5.5, Microsoft worked out the bugs and quirks of their first two revisions of the Exchange product, and significantly better integration occurred between email, calendar, contacts, and tasks than in previous releases of Exchange. Microsoft also expanded the support for a larger Exchange database used to store messages. So instead of being limited to 16GB of mail with earlier releases of Exchange, organizations could upgrade to the Enterprise Edition of Exchange Server 5.5 that provided more than 16GB of data storage. With larger storage capabilities, Exchange Server 5.5 greatly supported large corporate, government, and organizational messaging environments.

Along with Exchange Server 5.5, OWA was improved to provide a faster and easier-to-use web client. The concept of site connectors was expanded with Exchange Server 5.5 to provide a larger enterprise Exchange environment with distribution of administration, message routing, and multilanguage support.

Exchange 2000 Server

Exchange 2000 Server came out in 2000 right after the release of Windows 2000 Server and the first version of Microsoft Active Directory (AD). The biggest change in Exchange 2000 Server is that it used Active Directory for the Global Address List (GAL), instead of Windows NT having its list of network logon users and Exchange Server 5.5 having its own directory of email users. Active Directory combined a network and email user account into one single account, making the administration and management of Exchange much simpler. Exchange 2000 Server also went to an ActiveX version of the OWA client instead of a straight Hypertext Markup Language (HTML) version of the web access, thus providing users with drag-and-drop capabilities, pull-down bars, and other functionality that made the web access function much easier for remote users.

Exchange 2000 Server, which is required to run on top of Windows 2000 Server, became much more reliable than Exchange Server 5.5, which ran on top of Windows NT 4.0. However, because Exchange Server 5.5 can run on top of Windows 2000 Server, many organizations made the shift to Exchange Server 5.5 on top of Windows 2000 Server. These organizations also gained better performance and reliability, which is why many organizations did not migrate from Exchange Server 5.5. However, Windows 2000 Server provided Exchange 2000 Server a stable operating system platform from the beginning. Also by 2000, Novell's popularity was dramatically decreasing and organizations were migrating from Novell GroupWise to Exchange 2000 Server, so the Microsoft market share continued to grow.

Exchange Server 2003

Exchange Server 2003 was a major update to the Exchange messaging system that supported Active Directory. Although Exchange 2000 Server had Active Directory support, organizations found that Exchange Server 2003 on top of Active Directory 2003 provided a more reliable experience, better performance, and integration support between Exchange and AD. Exchange Server 2003 added mobility for users to synchronize their Pocket PC mobile devices to Exchange. In addition, OWA got yet another major face-lift mirroring the OWA interface with the normal Microsoft Office Outlook desktop client. With better remote support, Exchange Server 2003 became more than an office-based messaging system—it also greatly enhanced an organization's ability to provide remote and mobile users with email anytime and anywhere.

Exchange Server 2003, running on top of Windows Server 2003, took advantage of additional operating system enhancements, making Exchange Server 2003 an even more reliable and manageable messaging system. Windows Server 2003 clustering finally worked so that organizations that put Exchange Server 2003 on top of Windows Server 2003 were able to do active-active and active-passive clustering. In addition, clustering went from two-node clusters to four-node clusters, providing even more redundancy and recoverability.

Exchange Server 2003 also introduced the concept of a recovery storage group (RSG) that allowed an organization to mount an Exchange database for test and recovery purposes. Prior to Exchange Server 2003, an Exchange database could only be mounted on an Exchange server, typically with the exact same server name and for the sole purpose of making the database accessible to users. The recovery storage group in Exchange Server 2003 allowed an Exchange database from another Exchange server to be mounted in an offline manner so that the Exchange administrator can extract corrupt or lost messages, or possibly even have the database in a "ready mode" to allow for faster recovery of a failed Exchange server.

NOTE

The last supported direct transition path from Microsoft from Exchange Server 2003 was with the Exchange Server 2010 product in which a connector and transition tools enabled integration of Exchange Server 2003 and 2007 environments to coexist. Exchange Server 2013 does not support Exchange Server 2003 at all, and if an organization still has Exchange Server 2003 servers, it must either transition first to Exchange Server 2010 or export its mail out of Exchange Server 2003 before beginning the process of implementing Exchange Server 2013.

Exchange Server 2003 Service Pack 2

Although not a major release of Exchange, it is significant to note a major service pack for Exchange Server 2003, which is Exchange Server 2003 Service Pack 2 (SP2). Exchange Server 2003 Service Pack 1 (SPI) introduced cyclic redundancy check (CRC) error checking of the Exchange database. For 10 years, information written to Exchange was done without error checking, so prior to 2005, Microsoft Exchange had a bad reputation for having corruption in its databases any time the databases got too large. Early Exchange administrators are likely familiar with the utilities EDBUtil and ISInteg that were used regularly to fix database corruption. Those utilities are, for the most part, not used anymore because error correction repairs are performed in real time to the Exchange databases. With the release of Exchange Server 2003 SP1, error checking brought Exchange to a whole new world in better reliability.

Exchange Server 2003 SP2 added to the reliability and security of Exchange by introducing support for SenderID message integrity checks as well as enhanced journaling of messages that captured a copy of messages in Exchange and locked the original copies of the messages in a tamperproof database that allowed for better support for regulatory compliance auditing and message integrity.

Exchange Server 2003 SP2 also added in direct push for mobile devices so that instead of having a Windows Mobile or Pocket PC device constantly "pull" messages down from Exchange, Exchange Server 2003 SP2 pushes messages to mobile devices, thus preventing constant polling by the mobile device, which increases battery life and enables Exchange and mobile devices to remain synchronized in real time.

Exchange Server 2007

Exchange Server 2007 was released in 2007 and changed the direction of Exchange in several ways. Exchange Server 2007 completely eliminated the concept of routing groups being separate from Active Directory sites. Prior to Exchange Server 2007, organizations would have both Active Directory sites and Exchange routing groups, and in most organizations they were identical and effectively required separate parallel configuration.

Exchange Server 2007 eliminated the separate routing group and instead looked to Active Directory's sites and services to identify the subnets of various sites, and used the routing topology specified in Active Directory to move email along the same path and route as Active Directory replication.

Exchange Server 2007 also eliminated the Exchange Bridgehead server as a role that simply routed mail from Bridgehead server to Bridgehead server. The Bridgehead server evolved to the Hub Transport server in Exchange Server 2007 where every piece of email goes through. The Hub Transport server could be seen as a major central point of failure because every inbound, outbound, or even user-to-user email must pass through a Hub Transport server. However, because every piece of mail goes through the Hub Transport server, policies and rules can be set so that every email message can be filtered so that a single policy can be applied to not only Hub Transport to Hub Transport messages, but also even messages between users with mailboxes on the same Exchange server.

Outlook Web Access in Exchange Server 2007 was also dramatically improved being more than 95% feature complete with the full 32-bit version of Outlook. Web users have full control over mailbox rules and out-of-office rules, access to digitally rights managed content, and both provision and deprovision of their Windows Mobile devices within the OWA interface.

And finally, one of the major improvements in Exchange Server 2007 is the introduction of continuous replication, a major enhancement in mail system redundancy. Prior to Exchange Server 2007, a user's mailbox was on only one server. If that server failed or if the database was corrupt, a third-party solution needed to be leveraged to minimize Exchange system outage. The most common method for fast database recovery was the use of storage area network (SAN) snapshots. Exchange Cluster Continuous Replication (CCR) provided organizations with a primary and secondary copy of the Exchange database. If the primary database failed, the secondary copy of the database automatically came online within 20–30 seconds, the user's Outlook 2007 reconnected to the new server automatically, and the user never knew that the primary Exchange server had failed. And unlike many third-party solutions in the past that didn't gracefully fail back to the primary server, Exchange Server 2007's CCR failed back to the primary server just as it failed forward, providing organizations with a clean, high-availability solution.

Exchange Server 2007 Service Pack 1

Exchange Server 2007 Service Pack 1 was released late in 2007 and was seen by many as the first real version of Exchange Server 2007 with the addition of key components for the product version. Exchange Server 2007 SP1 enabled the access of public folders in OWA, something that many organizations could not upgrade to in the initial Exchange Server 2007 release because OWA users needed access to their public folders. Exchange Server 2007 SP1 also included Standby Continuous Replication (SCR) that provided a second-tier replication of Exchange databases. Where Exchange CCR provided a primary and secondary copy of the Exchange databases using instant failover clustering technology, SCR allowed for a replica of the Exchange databases to be created to a remote site with replication occurring in a 20-minute delayed manner. SCR provided organizations the capability to replicate information across a wide area network (WAN) to potentially an offsite data center.

Along the lines of high availability and disaster recovery came the concept of a stretched or geo-cluster in Exchange where Exchange Server 2007 SP1 could be installed on top of Windows Server 2008 that provided a geographically distributed cluster to split the Exchange CCR replicated data. With the Exchange CCR cluster split across a WAN link, if a primary server (and now site) failed, the secondary CCR cluster server would immediately become available for users to automatically reconnect to their mail. Stretch clusters for CCR provided not only high availability for mail, but also disaster recovery in a single solution.

Exchange Server 2010

Exchange Server 2010 is the most recent release of Exchange prior to the current Exchange Server 2013. Exchange Server 2010 took the technological enhancements introduced in Exchange Server 2007 and further extended the capabilities in terms of performance, reliability, and scalability. Most notable in Exchange Server 2010 was the introduction of database availability groups, or DAGs, for storage. Where Exchange Server 2007 introduced an online primary and secondary copy of mail across mailboxes with Cluster Continuous Replication, Exchange Server 2010 provided up to 16 copies of a user's mailbox that could be situated on servers within a database or across multiple sites. With multiple copies of a user's mailbox on multiple servers around the world, true high availability and disaster recovery has been achieved. High availability and redundancy has been so improved that many organizations no longer back up their Exchange servers as data is available and replicated for real-time redundancy.

Additionally with Exchange Server 2010, Outlook Web Access was not only renamed Outlook Web App to match the Office Apps concept, but closer feature parity between OWA and the traditional Outlook client was achieved. Users are able to access their email either through a full client or from a web client and be able to have full access to emails, calendars, contacts, mailbox rules, mobile phone management, and the like. Many organizations only provide Outlook through OWA when offline folders are not required, eliminating the need to deploy and support client software.

Behind the scenes to Exchange Server 2010 were also significant improvements in reliability such as the inclusion of a worker thread that defragmented the Exchange database as well as the ability for Exchange writes to be sequential to the Exchange database (instead of random writes to disk) that drastically improved overall performance for Exchange. With sequential reads of defragmented disks, Exchange Server 2010 performed 30% to 40% more efficiently for organizations, which allowed for greater density of users per Exchange server and virtually eliminated the concept of *database maintenance* that was a crux of Exchange in the first decade of its existence.

And by the year 2010, the use of mobile phones and tablet devices became common endpoint platforms with users desiring access from more than just a desktop or Web console. As such, Exchange Server 2010 provided full connectivity to Exchange from multiple endpoint platforms as well as voice prompt enabled Exchange so that a user could call into Exchange and navigate her mailbox, access calendar appointments, listen to messages that are text to speech converted for audio listening, and even have voice mail messages converted from voice to text for text-based viewing of voice messages.

Exchange Server 2010 integrated the world of voice mail, email, desktop access, and mobile access into the common platform.

While the list can go on with advancements made in Exchange Server 2010, to wrap up the content on Exchange Server 2010, the enhancements to email retention, archiving, and eDiscovery search were significant in Exchange Server 2010. Organizations were able to eliminate third-party archiving products and rely solely on Exchange Server 2010 for the long-term storage and compliance support for messaging. Users not only have primary mailboxes in Exchange, but also have email archives where data can be stored both from a data management perspective (eliminating the need for users to have multiple personal store (PST) files spread around with old mail messages stored) and also from the ability of the organization to implement and enforce data retention for legal compliance reasons. Exchange Server 2010 enabled eDiscovery of content stored in users' mailboxes with the ability to query message content, extract messages, and put mailboxes on litigation hold to prevent users from purposely or accidentally deleting legal message evidence.

You'll find Exchange Server 2013 extends *all* of these core enhancements introduced in Exchange Server 2010, further improving users' experiences in their messaging, voice, content, and information management systems.

Office 365

Office 365 is Microsoft's cloud-based Exchange Server, SharePoint, and Lync offering. As much as Office 365 is not in direct line with the Exchange on-premise offering, it is a parallel branch of Exchange Server worth noting. Office 365 was released in 2011 and provided organizations the option of setting up and implementing Exchange Server 2010 on-premise or pay a monthly fee for Exchange Server 2010 mailboxes hosted by Microsoft.

Through frequent updates of Office 365 by Microsoft, the cloud-based offering mirrored the features and capabilities of the on-premise Exchange Server. By early 2012, Microsoft releaseed a Hybrid mode of Office 365 that provided very tight integration between Exchange Online in the cloud and Exchange Server 2010 Service Pack 2 on-premise. Organizations were able to have users split between on-premise Exchange and Office 365 whether the hybrid was during a migration process, the hybrid was temporary during, for example, an acquisition of an organization, or the strategy of the organization to have core administration users access Exchange on-premise and field workers or temporary workers on Office 365.

Office 365 continues to evolve, and with Exchange Server 2013 again provides an onpremise Exchange Server 2013 environment as well as a cloud-based version of Exchange Server.

Exchange Server 2013 on 64-Bit Hardware

As with Exchange Server 2010, the Exchange Server 2013 product only comes in an x64-bit version. Exchange Server 2013 requires either Windows Server 2008 R2 or Windows Server 2012 (both x64-bit only operating systems) to run as the core operating system. Although Exchange Server 2013 requires Windows x64-bit to run the Exchange Server software, an organization can still run 32-bit Windows Server 2003 domain controllers and global catalog servers throughout the environment. Just the Exchange Server 2013 servers need to run x64-bit.

One of the biggest problems with earlier versions of Exchange on a 32-bit platform is the support for only 4GB of memory on an Exchange server. Just a few years ago, no one thought 4GB of RAM was a limitation. However, with Exchange and the amount of messaging transactions an organization can send and receive, what is required for an Exchange server to process far exceeded the memory space available in just 4GB of RAM. Because the processing of messages, write transactions to disk, logging for rollback recoverability, and the addition of spam and virus protection takes away from available memory in the system, 4GB would be used up quite quickly.

To compensate for the lack of available memory in 32-bit Exchange, Microsoft Exchange Server 2003 and prior depended heavily on caching transactions to disk. As an example, for an organization with 5,000 users on an Exchange Server 2003 server in a large enterprise, the Exchange Server 2003 server would have 4GB of RAM and need about 100GB of disk storage to have as available spool memory. In very large enterprises with tens of thousands of users, the Exchange servers could easily take up 500GB of disk space for spooling.

With 64-bit Windows and its support for 8TB of RAM memory, an Exchange Server 2013 server with 5,000 users now needs 32GB of RAM, but can do with just 5GB or less of spool disk space. Not only does the additional RAM eliminate the need for hundreds of gigabytes of spool disk space, the additional memory allows an Exchange Server 2013 server to support three to six times as many users per server, and provides a 50% to 80% increase in system efficiency of transactions.

Likewise, the 64-bit operating system also has proven to provide better support for significantly larger Exchange EDB databases. Most organizations wouldn't think of having an Exchange 2000 Server or Exchange Server 2003 database greater than 80GB to 100GB in size; however, with a 64-bit operating system, Exchange Server 2013 supports databases that easily run in the hundreds of gigabyte and even multiple terabyte sizes.

This means that organizations need to make sure their server hardware is x64-bit. Most organizations have been buying x64-bit hardware for the past three to four years anyway because many hardware vendors stopped shipping 32-bit hardware years ago. The benefit of x64-bit hardware is that you can still run 32-bit software on the hardware until such time that you want to just install 64-bit software on the systems.

NOTE

Organizations with volume licensing agreements with Microsoft do not need to purchase or upgrade their Windows licenses from 32-bit to 64-bit. A Windows server license is a Windows server license, so regardless of whether the system is 32-bit or 64-bit, the organization's server licenses remain the same.

What's New in Exchange Server 2013?

Exchange Server 2013, being the eighth major release of the Exchange Server product, adds to the existing technology base that the most recent version of Exchange (Exchange Server 2010) provides. Exchange administrators familiar with Exchange Server 2007 and 2010 will find that Exchange Server 2013 is about 70% to 80% the same; however, the 20% to 30% that is different is drastically different and requires some relearning of the changes.

What's the Same Between Exchange Server 2007/2010 and Exchange Server 2013?

The core infrastructure of Exchange Server 2013 is basically the same as Exchange Server 2007 and 2010. Microsoft continues to use the Jet EDB database as the main database store. Some time ago, it was rumored that Microsoft would rewrite Exchange to run off SQL Server; however, neither Exchange Server 2013 nor versions coming out from Microsoft in the foreseeable future will change the basic EDB database structure.

Exchange Server 2013 still has the concept of a Mailbox server where EDBs are stored, and where user mailbox data resides. An Exchange server can have multiple Exchange databases running on the system, and multiple Exchange servers can reside in an environment for both scalability as well as redundancy.

Users can use the Microsoft Outlook client and can access Exchange using OWA, as shown in Figure 1.1, for browser-based access, as well as synchronize with Exchange from their mobile and tablet systems.

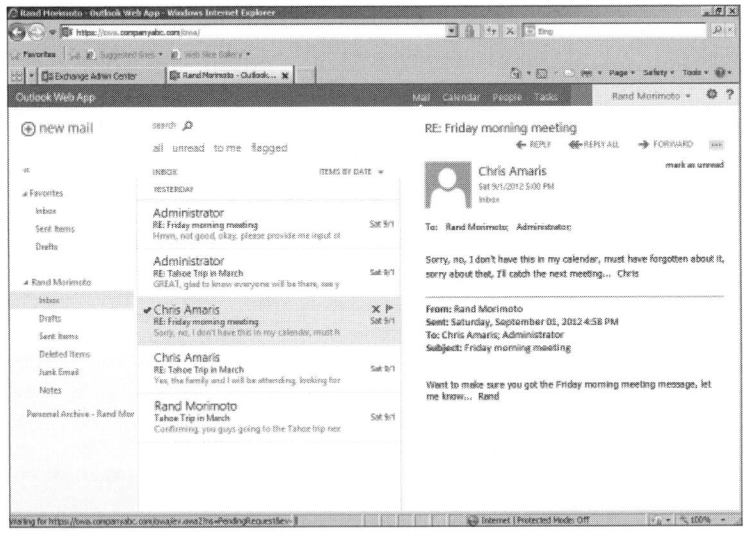

FIGURE 1.1 Outlook Web App in Exchange Server 2013.

Exchange Server 2013 still uses the VSSBackup application programming interface (API) to freeze the state of the Exchange database to perform a backup of the Exchange database.

One of the most important things that the users of an Exchange Server 2013 environment who get moved from Exchange Server 2007 or 2010 to Exchange Server 2013 will notice is nothing new or different from the end-user standpoint, assuming you keep the same Outlook client that the user has been using. A transition from Exchange Server 2007 and 2010 to Exchange Server 2013 does not require an upgrade to the Outlook 2013 client. Effectively, the user's mailbox is moved from an old server to a new server, and the user still has the exact same look, feel, and functionality as he had with Exchange Server 2007 and 2010. This relatively seamless cutover of user mailboxes, covered in Chapter 7, "Transitioning from Exchange Server 2007/2010 to Exchange Server 2013," minimizes user interruption as part of the transition process. Users will notice enhanced features with the new OWA, and even more enhancements if/when their systems are upgraded to Outlook 2013.

What's Missing in Exchange Server 2013 That Was in Previous Versions?

A common question that is asked is "What is missing in Exchange Server 2013 that was in previous versions of Exchange?" Although the balance of this section of the chapter covers the new features—which could arguably be said to be missing because they have drastically changed—this portion of the chapter focuses on things that are completely gone or do not exist in Exchange Server 2013.

For administrators, the biggest change is the Exchange Management Console (EMC) is completely gone. No more graphical user interface (GUI)–based administration; however, that doesn't mean that administrators are stuck with just PowerShell in the Exchange Management Shell (EMS) environment. What Microsoft has done is expand the Exchange Control Panel (ECP) from Exchange Server 2010 into the new Exchange Administration Center (EAC).

The Exchange Administration Center allows the administrator a web-based access to everything the administrator used EMC for before. The administrator can create and manage user mailboxes, manage Exchange servers, manage public folders, create send and receive connectors, perform eDiscovery tasks, and the like. More details on EAC can be found in the section "Exploring the New Exchange Administration Center (EAC)."

For administrators more familiar with Exchange Server 2007 than the most recent Exchange Server 2010, the concept of the storage group has been removed. With Exchange Server 2007, when an organization implemented Cluster Continuous Replication, each database had to be in its own storage group. With database recoverability as an important topic in Exchange Server 2010 and 2013 in which all databases should have a replica, the need for storage groups was removed in Exchange Server 2010, and Exchange Mailbox servers simply have databases on them.

Relative to Exchange databases, the STM database that was in Exchange Server 2007 has been removed, so Exchange Server 2010 and 2013 are now back to just the EDB database as it was in Exchange 2000 Server and prior versions. Rather than completely removing the STM database, Microsoft incorporated the streaming data technology into the new EDB database, so instead of having two databases for each mailbox and trying to reconcile the storage of information within those two databases, the combined mailbox database is now the standard.

From an administration standpoint, the concept of administrative groups and routing groups has been completely removed. Administrative groups were introduced with Exchange 2000 Server as a method of grouping together users to identify who would manage and administer groups of mailboxes. Administrative groups were brought forward from Exchange Server 5.5 where administration was done based on sites connected by site connectors. In Exchange Server 2013 (as in Exchange Server 2007 and 2010), administration is now completely consolidated into an enterprise view of users and mailboxes. The administration of the users and mailboxes is handled as delegated rights of administrators, not by a group of users and servers. So, rather than grouping together servers and users into special containers, an administrator is merely assigned rights to manage specific users, mailboxes, servers, or preexisting containers.

As noted in the preceding paragraph, routing groups have also been removed. Rather than having to group servers by routing groups, Exchange Server 2010 (and continued in Exchange Server 2013) no longer has separate routing groups within Exchange. Instead, Exchange uses sites from Active Directory Sites and Services to determine organizational sites and the routing of message communications to those sites.

With Exchange Server 2013, Microsoft has also eliminated the support of communicating directly with Exchange via remote procedure calls (RPC). Users now access Exchange Server 2013 through Hypertext Transfer Protocol (HTTP), Hypertext Transfer Protocol Secure (HTTPS), Post Office Protocol 3 (POP3), or Internet Message Access Protocol (IMAP). By eliminating RPC, Microsoft has simplified the number of client protocols needed to be supported and managed by the Exchange Server 2013 Client Access server, which in turn has helped Microsoft improve the reliability and scalability of Exchange Server 2013 in a geo-global implemented environment.

With the release of Exchange Server 2007, Microsoft had noted that public folders were going to be deemphasized, which basically means they would be going away in a future version of Exchange. What you will find is when you install Exchange Server 2013 from scratch, public folders are not created at all. You need to manually add public folders to a Mailbox server and extend public folder access from the server system. During a transition, if the organization has public folders, they will continue to operate in Exchange Server 2013. So as much as Microsoft has stated that public folders are being deemphasized, they are still completely and fully supported in Exchange Server 2013, and because of the prevalent use of public folders in enterprises, it would seem that public folders will continue to be in Exchange for the foreseeable future. Public folder databases have undergone a radical change, however, now using mailboxes in mailbox databases, which is described in more detail later in this chapter and in Chapter 9, "Public Folders." Microsoft has created excellent hooks between Exchange Server 2013 and SharePoint 2013 that allow a user to click on what used to be a folder for public folders, but instead a SharePoint share is rendered in the user's Outlook or OWA screen. More details on this concept can be found later in the section on "Introduction of Site Mailboxes in Exchange Server 2013." You can do pretty much everything you were able to do with public folders with SharePoint 2013—and then some. More on SharePoint integration with Exchange Server 2013 is covered in Chapter 20, "Integrating Exchange with SharePoint Site Mailboxes, Enterprise Search, and More."

Exploring the New Exchange Administration Center (EAC)

As mentioned in the previous section, Microsoft completely did away with the Exchange Management Console in place of the Exchange Administration Center, or EAC. EAC works just like OWA. An administrator uses a web browser and types in the uniform resource locator (URL) with /ecp at the end instead of accessing OWA with a /owa at the end. So after typing https://{*owa address*}/ecp, the administrator sees a screen similar to what is shown in Figure 1.2.

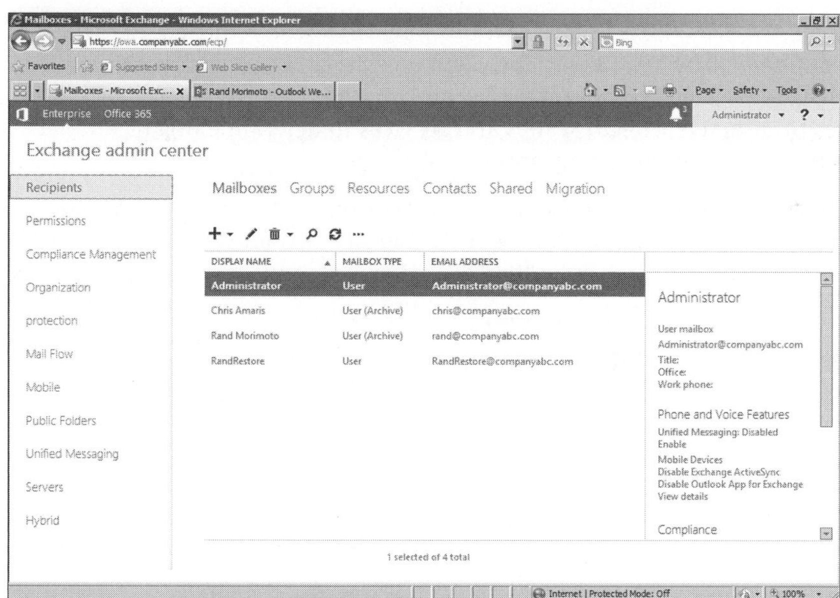

FIGURE 1.2 The new Exchange Administration Center (EAC).

NOTE

The /ecp for the Exchange Administration Center refers to the old Exchange Control Panel (ECP) that was introduced in earlier versions of Exchange. At some point, Microsoft may change the URL for access to the EAC, but for now, the URL includes ecp at the end.

The benefit of the Exchange Administration Center is that it no longer requires installing the 64-bit Exchange Management Console program along with the .NET Framework, Active Directory Domain Services remote admin tools, and everything else that was needed to administer Exchange. Now, an administrator can be anywhere, and as long as the administrator has access to Outlook Web App, the administrator can also access the Exchange Administration Center. For the longtime Exchange administrator, think about it: No more having to remote into a server, using Remote Desktop Protocol (RDP) to access a server—just log on from any web browser to perform administration tasks.

The administration tasks in EAC include everything from creating and managing Exchange recipients to creating Active Directory distribution lists, creating send and receive connectors for mail routing, managing the public folder hierarchy, checking for anti-malware traps, creating new Exchange databases, failing over database availability groups, doing eDiscovery, and so on.

The Exchange Administration Center is available for users to manage their personal mailbox settings such as user-specific content like mobile phone numbers, photos, OWA settings, and the like. So the EAC serves as a tool for user Exchange settings, Exchange-related Active Directory settings, and Exchange administration tasks.

More on the Exchange Administration Center is covered in Chapter 13, "Administering an Exchange Server 2013 Environment."

Architectural Changes in Exchange Server 2013

The architecture of Exchange Server 2013 has undergone significant changes. Most users will *never* see or know these changes were made other than hopefully better performance and reliability. The core of the changes made were to simplify Exchange Server 2013 and make it more geo-redundant, scalable, and ultimately more reliable.

Specifically, with Exchange Server 2013, Microsoft eliminated the Hub Transport role and the Unified Messaging role, so the core roles are now the Client Access server and the Mailbox server (MBX) roles. The Client Access server (CAS) no longer does data rendering; the role just focuses on authentication, redirection, and proxy. The Mailbox server role now includes Client Access protocols, Hub Transport services, mailbox databases, and Unified Messaging services.

Because the Client Access server role is drastically simplified to just support HTTP, HTTPS, POP, and IMAP client protocols with no requirement for session affinity between the CAS and MBX roles, Exchange Server 2013 now has better failover and the ability to do simple Level 4 load balancing.

CAS and MBX servers no longer need to be geographically close to one another, whereas in the past, the two roles needed to be on the same subnet with high-speed connectivity because of the amount of data transferred between the two servers and the dependence on split roles shared between the two servers. As such, the CAS role can now be geo-centralized with MBX servers distributed to various sites in the enterprise. In addition, with the elimination of integrated components between the CAS and the MBX servers, the requirement of identical patch levels between CAS and MBX servers is no longer a dependency. Organizations can patch and update CAS and MBX servers in a pattern and manner that makes sense to the organization, greatly providing better flexibility in updating an Exchange environment, and greatly improving the uptime of Exchange. Server configuration and server optimization are covered in Chapter 2, "Understanding Core Exchange Server 2013 Design Plans," and in Chapter 15, "Optimizing an Exchange Server 2013 Environment."

Another significant improvement in Exchange Server 2013 is the simplification of the namespace used in Exchange. Instead of having the seven names used in Exchange Server 2010 and requiring large and sometimes expensive Subject Alternative Name (SAN) certificates, Exchange Server 2013 can use as few as two names in the environment. In fact, the Mailbox server has a self-signed certificate automatically assigned to it on installation that is trusted by the Client Access server. Because the MBX role is no longer exposed directly to the endpoint client, the public or trusted root certificate only needs to reside on the Client Access server. The relationship between the CAS and MBX can remain a self-signed certificate, again, a movement to simplify certificate management in the Exchange Server 2013 environment.

Specific to Exchange Server 2013 certificate management, the management of certificates is part of the Exchange Administration Center through the Certificate Management Wizard shown in Figure 1.3. More details on certificates and certificate management are covered in Chapter 5, "Integrating Certificate-Based Public Key Infrastructure (PKI) in Exchange Server 2013."

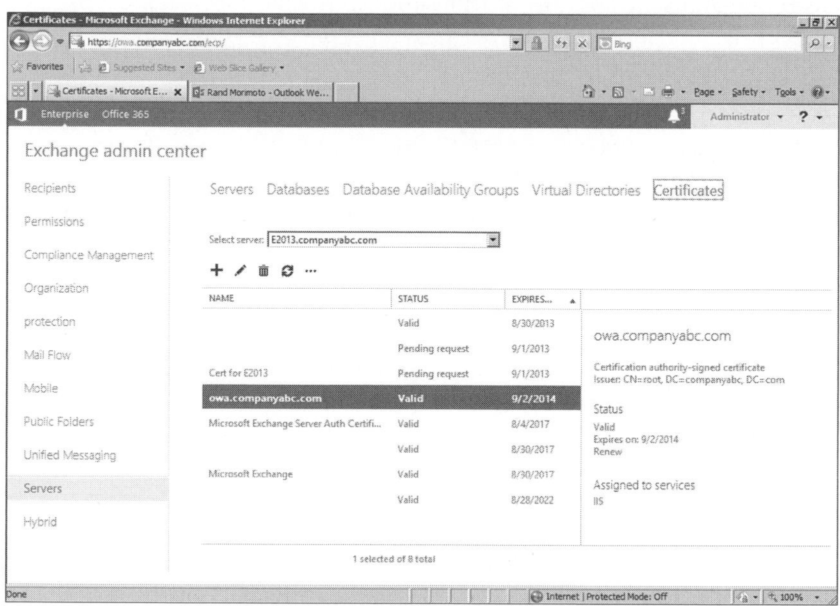

FIGURE 1.3 Certificate management in Exchange Server 2013.

Improvements in Exchange Server 2013 Relative to Security

One of the improvement goals Microsoft has had with all of its products over the past few years has been to constantly improve the security in the products. More recently with all of the regulatory compliance laws and policies being implemented, Microsoft has focused a lot of security enhancements to address privacy, information archiving, and compliance support. The release of Exchange Server 2007, 2010, and 2013 has been no different—Microsoft added in several new enhancements in the areas of security and compliance support.

One of the additions in Exchange Server 2007 was the creation of an Edge Transport server role that supplements the traditional Exchange database server as a system in the Exchange organization environment. Whereas the Exchange database server holds user data, the Edge Transport server is dedicated to provide the first line of defense relative to virus and spam blocking. Organizations with Exchange have had servers in their demilitarized zone (DMZ) typically as SMTP relay servers that collect messages, perform antivirus and antispam filtering, and route the messages internal to the organization. However, most of the message relay servers in the DMZ have typically had no tieback to Exchange, so when messages come in for email addresses for individuals who don't even exist in the organization, the DMZ mail relays didn't really have a way to know, so they blindly processed antispam and antivirus checks, and then forwarded messages on to the Exchange server. The Exchange server would realize when individuals did not exist and would bounce or delete the message. This meant that the Exchange server would still have to process hundreds if not thousands or tens of thousands of invalid messages.

Another major enhancement in Exchange Server 2007 was the addition of the Hub Transport server. For many, the Hub Transport server merely replaces the Bridgehead server that handled routing in earlier versions of Exchange. However, the Hub Transport server that was in Exchange Server 2007 and 2010 has now been replaced as simply a Hub Transport service in Exchange Server 2013. The service runs on the Exchange Mailbox server and acts as the focal point for policy compliance. Policies can be configured in Exchange Server 2013 so that after a message is filtered for spam and viruses, the message goes to the policy server to be assessed whether the message meets or fits into any regulated message policy, and appropriate actions are taken. The same is true for outbound messages, that the messages go to the policy server, the content of the message is analyzed, and if the message is determined to meet specific message policy criteria, the message can be routed unchanged, or the message might be held or modified based on the policy. As an example, an organization might want any communications referencing a specific product code name or a message that has content that looks like private health information, such as a Social Security number, date of birth, or health records of an individual, to be held so that encryption can be enforced on the message before it continues its route. Exchange Server 2013 adds built-in capabilities to support policies specific to personally identifiable information as well that is key to many privacy regulations as well as payment card industry data security for organizations that use credit cards as part of their transactions. More details on the role of policy compliance are in Chapter 10, "Understanding Exchange Policy Enforcement Security."

Policies in Exchange Server 2013 are more than just internal policies that identify messages in transit or at rest in the Exchange environment, but also policies that protect the leakage of protected content outside of the organization. Data leakage protection, or DLP, is addressed both as the built-in policies components of Exchange Server 2013 as well as further enhanced by Microsoft's Rights Management Services (RMS) that actively encrypts and protects content.

For organizations leveraging Outlook 2013 as the endpoint client for users, Microsoft has expanded the MailTips feature that was introduced in Outlook 2010 with PolicyTips in Outlook 2013. PolicyTips analyzes email messages and provides recommendations and guidance how the message applies to organizational policies.

Not new to Exchange Server 2013, but key in an organization's effort to maintain security and privacy of information is the ability to encrypt email messages and content at the client level. Exchange Server 2013 encrypts content between the Exchange Server 2013 server and an Outlook 2013 client by default, and provides full support for certificate-based Public Key Infrastructure (PKI) encryption of mail messages. More details on client-level security and encrypted email are covered in Chapter 5.

Improvements in Exchange Server 2013 Relative to eDiscovery and Retention

Beyond compliance policies, message encryption, and data leakage protection are simple processes like message retention and eDiscovery search of content within Exchange. Exchange Server 2013 includes extensive enhancements in discovery and retention. Exchange Server 2013 continues to support email archiving that was introduced in Exchange Server 2010. Content can be archived and retained based on retention tags, shown in Figure 1.4; whether the retention is set for one year, seven years, or infinite, Exchange Server 2013 provides the ability to retain message content.

In addition, Exchange Server 2013 introduces the ability of an organization to search for information across both the mailbox and the user's archive at the same time, something that with Exchange Server 2010, a query had to be done once against the user's mailbox and then separately against the user's archive. Unified search in Exchange Server 2013 can then be set to preserve the results of the query for immediate export or for immediate content hold.

Content hold in Exchange Server 2013 can be set using policies or can automatically be applied as time-based holds, where content is prevented from deletion based on a time factor. And Exchange Server 2013 continues to support litigation hold that locks a mailbox from having content permanently deleted from the mailbox for future search and reporting.

Lastly, Microsoft has included FAST Search as the default search engine for Exchange Server 2013; FAST Search is the common search tool for Exchange Server 2013, SharePoint 2013, and Lync 2013 and provides administrators the ability to search for content from a single tool.

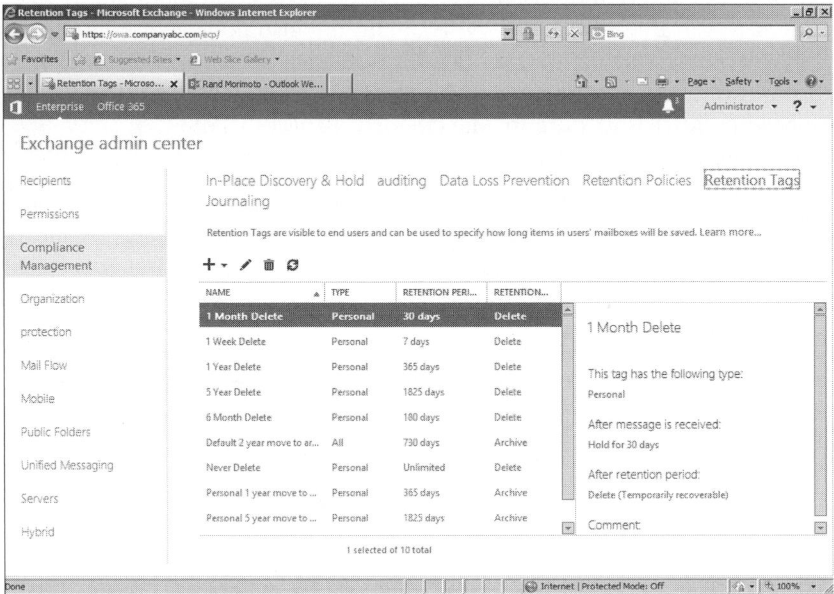

FIGURE 1.4 Retention tags in Exchange Server 2013.

This content and more is covered in Chapter 12, "Designing and Implementing Message Archiving, Retention, and eDiscovery."

Changes to Public Folders in Exchange Server 2013

Years back, it was rumored that public folders were going to go away, but in Exchange Server 2013, not only are public folders still alive and kicking, but Microsoft has also improved how public folders are managed.

Public folders in Exchange Server 2013 are no longer a monolithic hierarchy in a separate public folder database. Public folders are now a series of mailboxes tied together by a common directory. Although viewed as if they are public folders, the content is actually mailbox content. Thus, administrators have the ability to leverage database availability group replication of the public folder mailboxes and utilize the ability to have high availability and disaster recovery of public folders handled just like mailboxes.

Public folders are no longer treated separately or differently than normal mailbox databases, so administration tools, management tools, policies, replication, and all tasks done with mailboxes can be applied to the new public folders. Public folders are managed within the Exchange Administration Center, as shown in Figure 1.5.

The only disadvantage in the new Exchange Server 2013 public folder system is that the public folders are no longer multimastered, meaning that a copy of the public folder no longer exists on multiple Exchange public folder servers across the enterprise. The administrator has to determine to which Exchange server a public folder is homed. Users in that location have local access to the public folder. Users in other locations can access the public folder, but their access will be across the WAN instead of to a local replica. Most organizations have not found this change to be a dramatic problem as most organizations have public folders that are specific to a unique site; however, some organizations have leveraged public folders for the ability to have live copies of public folders in each and every site that a public folder database resides. Some reengineering may need to be done to address public folders in certain environments.

More on public folders is covered in Chapter 9.

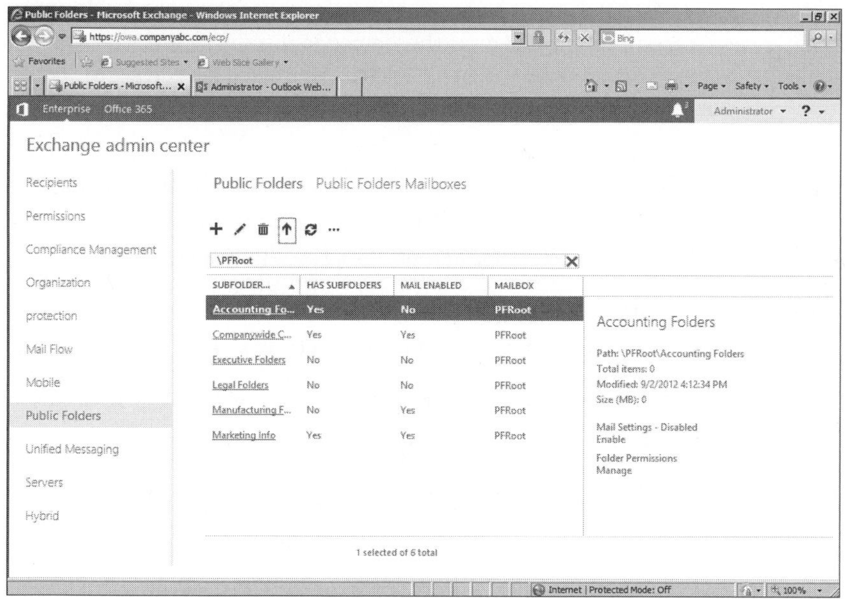

FIGURE 1.5 Public folder administration within the Exchange Administration Center.

Introduction of Site Mailboxes in Exchange Server 2013

With the proliferation of SharePoint in most business environments, Microsoft is providing better integration between SharePoint 2013 and Exchange Server 2013. Exchange Server 2013 introduces site mailboxes. Site mailboxes are nothing more than document libraries and containers within SharePoint 2013 that are accessible through the Outlook Web App and Outlook 2013 interface.

Users can still access the SharePoint folders within SharePoint; however, by linking the SharePoint folders as site mailboxes in Exchange Server 2013, users can simply access SharePoint without having to toggle or launch a separate browser screen.

Site mailboxes are covered in detail in Chapter 20.

Exchange Server 2013 as the Focal Point for Remote and Mobile Communications

One of the big focuses for Microsoft for Exchange Server 2013 was to have better support for mobile phones and tablets. Until now, mobile devices used client software that was built in to the mobile phone, whether that was the mail app that came with the Apple iPhone or iPad, or the mail client that came with Android or Blackberry. With Exchange Server 2013, Microsoft is providing direct support for mobile devices through an extension of Outlook Web App.

With HTML5, Outlook Web App supports offline storage of OWA content, so a device that that has a browser that supports HTML5, such as Internet Explorer 10, Safari 5.1, Chrome 18, or the like, not only can access OWA, but when the device is disconnected, the user can still read, respond, and queue up messages. Microsoft has addressed screen form factor as well as finger touch support in OWA, providing a single OWA server multiple ways to provide OWA content.

In fact, there are three OWA modes supported, one which supports three columns that is the OWA that most organizations are familiar with for full desktops and laptops. Microsoft also provides a two-column mode that is optimized for tablet systems. OWA recognizes tablet devices and can format OWA to the two-column mode, or by adding the /?layout=twide to the end of the OWA string (like https://{*servername*}/owa/?layout=twide), the user of the tablet device (e.g., Windows 8 tablet, Windows Surface, iPad, Android tablet, Slate) will see a two-column screen similar to what is shown in Figure 1.6.

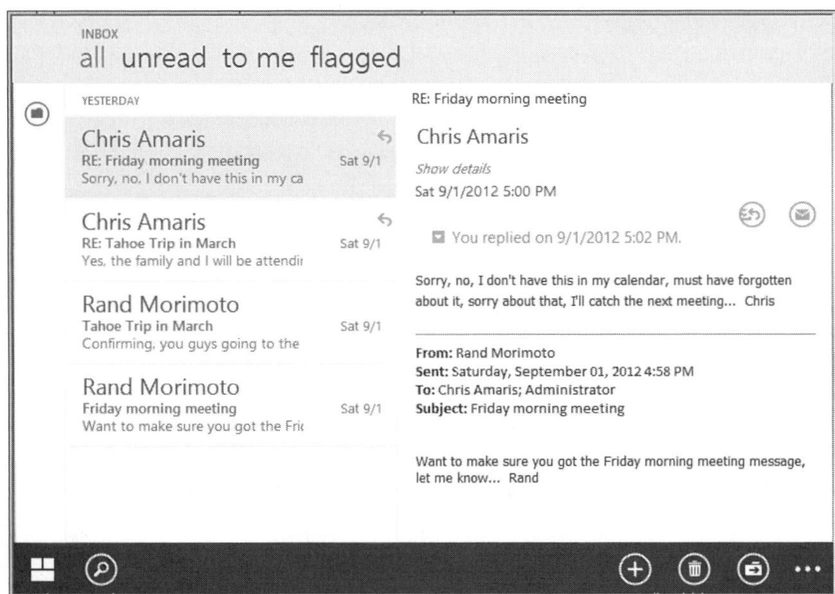

FIGURE 1.6 OWA in a "wide" format for mobile phones.

The third mode is a single column mode that is optimized for mobile phones. Because mobile phones typically do not have a wide surface screen, having a single column off OWA provides a better viewing experience. By adding the /?layout=tnarrow to the end of the OWA string (like https://{*servername*}/owa/?layout=tnarrow), the user will get a narrow view of OWA similar to what is shown in Figure 1.7.

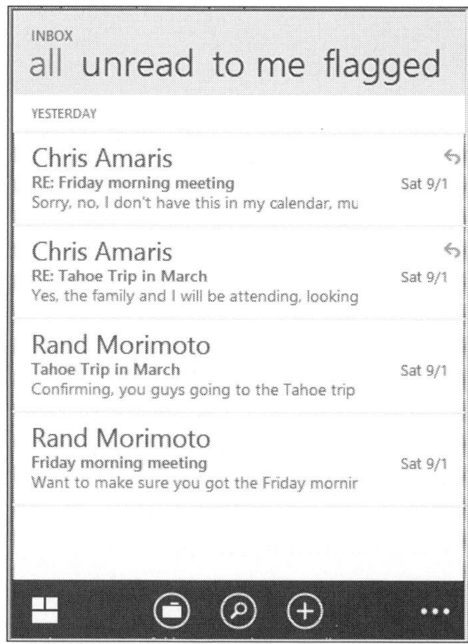

FIGURE 1.7 OWA in a "narrow" format for tablets.

Despite the column form factor, whether one, two, or three columns, it is still hitting the exact same OWA server, with no special servers, configurations, or programming required. And with HTML5 support for offline access, users can cache their email messages on their mobile devices or tablets. In addition, because HTML5 is universal, the endpoint can be an Apple Mac, iPad, Android phone, or other device with HTML5 support.

Additionally in OWA for Exchange Server 2013, Microsoft has embedded the concept of apps. OWA 2013 comes with default apps such as Bing Maps, Suggested Appointments, and Action Items with the ability for third-party development of apps for OWA. Apps activate Exchange Server 2013 for additional functionality; as an example, the Bing Maps app provides Bing Maps to automatically be displayed and accessible within email messages. If someone sends you an address, a click or tap of the address opens up Bing Maps to display the map of the address as well as other information about the site.

Organizations using Exchange Server 2013 have found the new OWA so feature complete that when users are remote, they only use OWA as their method to check and manage their messages. More on OWA in Exchange Server 2013 is covered in Chapter 22, "Leveraging the Capabilities of the Outlook Web App (OWA) Client."

Integration with Lync 2013

With the release of Exchange Server 2013, Microsoft also has SharePoint 2013 and Lync 2013 that make up the rest of the Office 2013 servers family of products. With the parallel development of the 2013 server products, there's tie-in together between the servers. Already covered earlier in this chapter were the site mailboxes that are the integration between SharePoint 2013 and Exchange Server 2013. For Lync 2013 integration, organizations will find that Lync 2013 uses Exchange for the contact store. Instead of having separate contacts for Lync and separate contacts for Exchange, a shared contacts list stored in Exchange simplifies the identification of individuals for users.

In addition, Lync content is archived in Exchange Server 2013, which is an extension of how "conversations" in Lync 2010 are saved in a Conversation History folder in Exchange that tracks IM communications, tracks incoming and outgoing phone calls in Lync, and identifies and logs missed communications within the Conversation History folder.

Microsoft is also supporting OAuth for authentication, a standard used heavily by public cloud providers that allows for authentication as a service and user impersonation when permitted, similar to how Facebook identities and LinkedIn identities are shared across platforms.

Improving Unified Messaging in Exchange Server 2013

One of the major improvements to Exchange Server 2010 was the updates to Unified Messaging. Unified Messaging is the capability for Exchange Server 2013 to be the voice mail server for an organization. Rather than having a separate voice mail system connected to the organization's phone system, Exchange can be integrated into the phone system to be able to take messages on incoming calls, and the messages are stored in the user's Exchange mailbox for playback from the phone or by accessing the message from within Outlook, from within OWA, or from a mobile device.

Unified Messaging is not new to Exchange; in fact, many organizations, including Cisco, Avaya, Shortel, and others, have had voice mail to Exchange add-ons for years. Key to Microsoft's Unified Messaging is that it is tightly integrated in Exchange, requires no installation of special software, leverages existing Exchange high-availability and failover capabilities, and is not affected by patches or updates to Exchange. With Exchange Server 2013, Microsoft has eliminated the dedicated Unified Messaging server role and has folded the Unified Messaging service right within the Exchange Server 2013 Mailbox server role.

With the UM service built right in to the Exchange Mailbox server, the only other service outside of the Mailbox server is the UM Call Router service, which is installed on the Exchange Client Access server. The UM Call Router proxies incoming calls. Being integrated directly with Exchange Server 2013, Microsoft now provides improved CallerID lookup, where CallerID in Exchange Server 2010 and prior looked only at the default

Contacts folder. Now with Exchange Server 2013, contact lookup is extended to look at other contact folders in Exchange as well.

One of the benefits of Unified Messaging in Exchange from any vendor is the concept of a single data store for inbound email messages and voice mail messages. Rather than checking Outlook for emails, and calling into a phone voice mail system for voice messages, having all messages go in to Exchange provides a single point of message control. A single point for message access allows Exchange Server 2013 to provide anywhere access to all messages, whether it is from an Outlook client, from OWA, or from a Windows Mobile device.

Unified Messaging is significant in Exchange Server 2013 because it is the foundation that Microsoft has built upon that provides unified communications across its entire product line. Microsoft has been tightly integrating instant messaging (IM), Voice over IP (VoIP) telephone integration, videoconferencing, data conferencing, and so forth into a complete, centralized communications system. With Exchange Server 2013, Microsoft has standardized on the Unified Communications Managed API (UCMA) v4.0 instead of the older v2.0 used in Exchange Server 2010. UCMA v4.0 utilizes the same version of the speech engine for text to speech (TTS) and automatic speech recognition (ASR) so that the call attendant, call router, text to speech, voice mail conversation to text are all utilizing the same API set. UCMA v4.0 also provides improvements to grammar generation and language improvements.

Microsoft has introduced several new products to the marketplace, including Lync 2013 and SharePoint 2013, that integrate technologies together in a unified communications backbone. Exchange Server 2013 is the core to the unified communications strategy that Microsoft is setting forth because Exchange is the point of connection for email, contacts, remote access, mobile access, and, now, voice communications.

More information on Unified Messaging and the capabilities provided out of the box from Microsoft on Unified Messaging is in Chapter 19, "Designing and Configuring Unified Messaging in Exchange Server 2013."

Making Exchange Server 2013 Extremely Reliable and Recoverable

In addition to security and mobility as core areas in which Microsoft has invested heavily for all of its products, Microsoft has added significant improvements in making Exchange Server 2013 more reliable and more recoverable. As messaging has become critical to business communications, Exchange Server 2013 becomes an important component in making sure an organization can effectively communicate between employees as well as from employees to customers, to vendors, to business partners, and to the public. Add voice communications into the new Exchange unified communications strategy, and it becomes even more important that Exchange Server 2013 is extremely reliable.

With Exchange Server 2013, Microsoft expanded the database availability group (DAG) continuous replication technology that effectively allows Exchange to hold up to

16 copies of a user's mailbox information. In the past, Exchange only had one copy of a user's mailbox sitting in an Exchange database. In the event that the database holding the user's information became corrupt or the server holding the user's information failed, the way to get the user's mailbox back up and running was to typically restore the data to another server. Several hardware and software utility vendors have created snapshot technologies that replicate a user's mailbox information to another server; however, as much as the user's data can be available on another system in another site, the user's Outlook client was still pointing to the old Exchange server where the mailbox used to reside. So, as much as the data was available, business continuity couldn't continue until the user's Outlook profile was changed to redirect the user to the new location of the data.

With Exchange Server 2010 and 2013, Microsoft has eliminated single copy clusters, local continuous replication, Cluster Continuous Replication, and standby continuous replication in place of an updated DAG replication technology. DAGs still use log shipping as the method of replication of information between servers. Log shipping means that the 1-MB log files that note the information written to an Exchange server are transferred to other servers, and the logs are replayed on that server to build up the content of the replica system from data known to be accurate. If during a replication cycle a log file does not completely transfer to the remote system, individual log transactions are backed out of the replicated system and the information is re-sent. Unlike bit-level transfers of data between source and destination used in SANs or most other Exchange database replication solutions, if a system fails, bits don't transfer, and Exchange has no idea what the bits were, what to request for a resend of data, or how to notify an administrator what file or content the bits referenced. Microsoft's implementation of log shipping provides organizations a clean method of knowing what was replicated and what was not.

In addition, because log shipping is done with small 1-MB log files, Exchange Server 2013 replication can be conducted over relatively low-bandwidth connections. Dependent on the amount of data written to an Exchange server, a T1 line can potentially be used to successfully keep a source and destination replica server up to date. Other uses of the DAG include staging the replication of data so that a third or fourth copy of the replica resides offline in a remote data center so that instead of having the data center actively be a failover destination, the remote location can be used to simply be the point where data is backed up to tape, or a location where data can be recovered if a catastrophic enterprise environment failure occurs. More details on continuous backup are covered in Chapter 8, "Implementing and Supporting a Highly Available Exchange Server 2013 Environment."

Another major point about having data come live on a remote system is to redirect a user's Outlook clients to the location of his or her data. With Outlook 2010 and Outlook 2013, shown in Figure 1.8, Microsoft no longer hard-codes the Mailbox server name to the user's Outlook profile, but rather has the user connect to the CAS with merely the user's logon name and password, and the CAS parses Active Directory and Exchange and directs the user's Outlook client to the appropriate server that is currently hosting the user's mailbox. This automatic swap over at the client level provides the business continuity functionality that is needed in a server failover scenario.

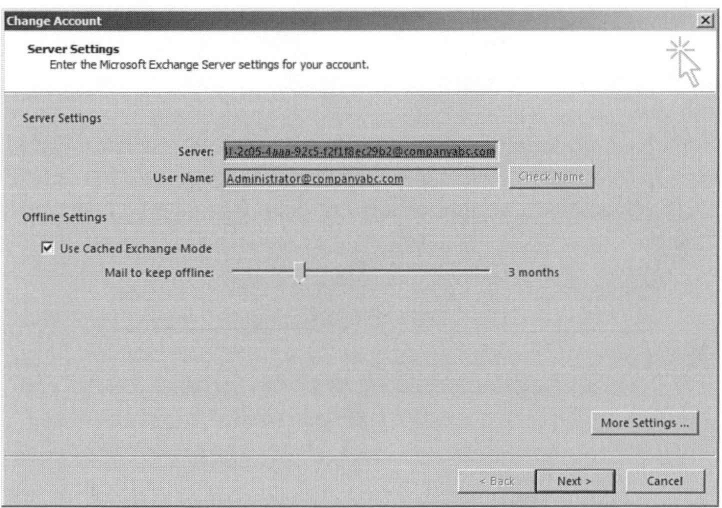

FIGURE 1.8 Outlook 2013 profile setting.

Improving Configuration, Administration, and Management Through the Exchange Management Shell

Improved in Exchange Server 2013 is a command-line shell known as Exchange Management Shell, or EMS. The command-line shell, shown in Figure 1.9, provides an administrator the ability to configure, administer, and manage an Exchange Server 2013 server environment using text commands instead of solely a GUI. In fact with Exchange Server 2013, the Exchange Administration Center is nothing more than a front end to the Exchange Management Shell. Every EAC check box or pull-down function executes an EMS script in the back end. Experience with Exchange Server 2013 has shown that only 80% to 90% of an administrator's tasks can be done through the Exchange Administration Center; however, on a regular basis, the Exchange administrator has to do things through the scripted interface because an EAC option does not exist. Throughout this book, the various chapters relating to administrative tasks note the EMS text command that needs to be run to perform specific tasks.

Exchange administrators have found that the EMS is very easy to use for day-to-day tasks. For example, tasks such as adding mailboxes or moving mailboxes used to require dozens of key clicks but can now be scripted and simply cut/pasted into the EMS tool to be executed. As an example, a common task is moving a mailbox to a different database. Through the graphical management console, the task would take dozens of key clicks to move the mailboxes of a group of users. With EMS, it just takes a simple command such as:

```
Get-mailbox -server SERVER1 | move-mailbox -targetdatabase
"SERVER2\Mailbox Database 1"
```

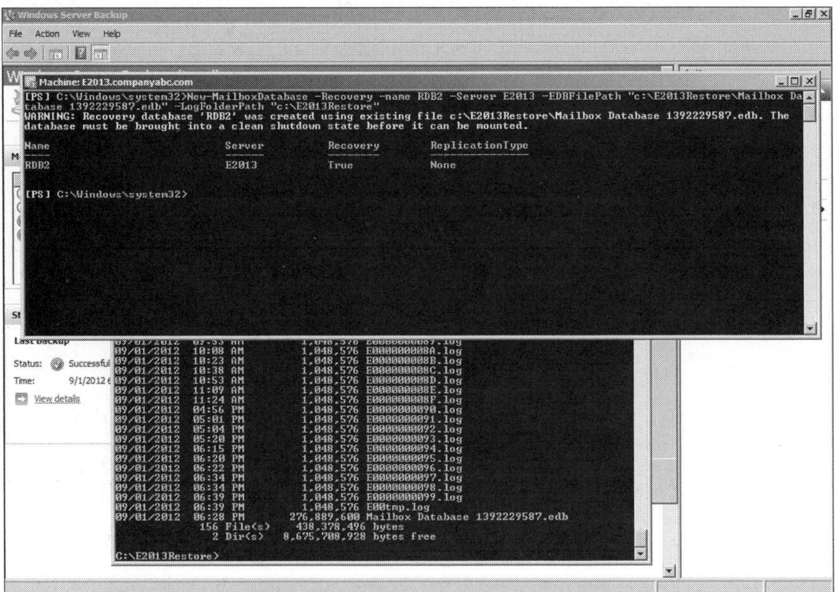

FIGURE 1.9 Sample Exchange Management Shell interface.

By creating a library of commands, an administrator can just search and replace words such as server names, usernames, or other object data; replace it in the command-line script; and then paste the script into EMS to have it execute. EMS is not only a necessity to do many tasks that are not available from the GUI, but it also makes administering and managing Exchange Server 2013 much easier for redundant tasks or for complex tasks that can be cut and pasted from a script library.

Although EMS was included as early as the release of Exchange Server 2007, the execution of commands in EMS typically had to be initiated from the server in which the command was executed. With Exchange Server 2013 and the use of PowerShell 3.0 remoting technologies, an EMS command can be executed on one server with the effect taking place on another remote server.

Improving Performance Through Batch Moves and Processing

For Exchange Server 2013 and the movement of mailboxes, whether it is between servers or in a migration scenario from on-premise to the cloud, Exchange Server 2013 leverages batch move processes. Exchange Server 2013 provides the movement of multiple mailboxes in large batches. In addition, email notifications can be generated during the move process providing updates on move status, success, and failures.

Exchange Server 2013 also provides automatic prioritization and automatic retry of batch moves so that during the batch move process, a block of mailboxes can be prioritized for moves, and if any mailbox fails to move, an automatic retry is initiated. In addition, primary and archive mailboxes can be moved together or separately; in previous versions of Exchange, the movement of primary and archive mailboxes could not be queued together, creating a challenge in moving mailboxes when the user and all of his data was not automatically moved at the same time.

These improvements are not obvious to many administrators until the administrator is in the middle of a transition and has a lot of mailboxes and a lot of users waiting for their mail to be moved. This is a great improvement in Exchange Server 2013 that helps in the overall operation of Exchange.

Understanding Mail Flow in Exchange Server 2013

As introduced previously in this chapter, Exchange Server 2013 has three server roles, the Edge Transport server, the Client Access server, and the Mailbox server. While Exchange Server 2007 and Exchange Server 2010 had two additional roles (Hub Transport server role and Unified Messaging role), this consolidation in Exchange Server 2013 actually improves Exchange operational efficiencies. You might think that spreading out the roles would be faster and more efficient; however, the end effect was that having too many roles caused a lot of communications traffic between the roles to process information, and it made administration management significantly more difficult.

The three roles work together in managing the routing of messages in and out of the Internet and between users within an organization. This section of the chapter covers how messages route within the organization to clarify the mail flow in various situations.

How Messages Get to Exchange from the Internet

To follow the flow of messages in an Exchange Server 2013 environment with all of the various server roles, the following flow occurs:

1. An incoming message from the Internet first goes to the Edge Transport server.
2. The Edge Transport server performs first-level recipient validation as well as spam and virus filtering. The message is then passed on to the Exchange Server 2013 Mailbox server.
3. The Mailbox server is running the Hub Transport service that performs compliance content assessment and then looks at the internal routing for messages and either keeps the messages if the message is destined to a mailbox stored on the server, or forwards the message to another Mailbox server running the Hub Transport service where the mailbox for the message is destined.
4. The Mailbox server places the incoming message into the user's mailbox and notifies the user that a message has arrived.

5. The user launches Outlook, OWA, a mobile device, or another client system and connects to the Client Access server. The Client Access server confirms the destination point of the user's mailbox and provides the user access to his or her mailbox data.

6. In parallel, if a voice mail message comes in for a user, the Unified Messaging service that is running on the Exchange Mailbox server processes the incoming voice message, and then takes the message and places the voice message into the user's mailbox residing on the Mailbox server for the recipient.

How Messages Route Within an Internal Exchange Environment

Internal messages are routed through Exchange in a similar manner. The process for a mail user to send a message to another mail user in the organization or to the Internet is as follows:

1. A message is created by a user in Outlook, on his or her mobile device, on OWA, or in other client message systems where the user is connected to the Client Access server.

2. The message is stored on the user's Mailbox server as an Outbox message and once sent, a copy is stored in the user's Sent Items folder on the Mailbox server.

3. The Mailbox server then sends the message to a Hub Transport service that is running on the Mailbox server; the Hub Transport service performs compliance content assessment and then looks at the internal routing for messages and either keeps the message if the destination mailbox resides on the server, or forwards the message to another Hub Transport service running on another Mailbox server.

4. For internal messages, the Mailbox server places the incoming message into the user's mailbox and notifies the user that a message has arrived.

5. The message recipient launches Outlook, OWA, his or her mobile device, or another client system and connects to the Client Access server. The Client Access server confirms the destination point of the user's mailbox and provides the user access to his or her mailbox data.

Understanding the Importance of Active Directory for an Exchange Server 2013 Environment

Unlike earlier versions of Exchange (like Exchange 2000 Server and Exchange Server 2003) that leveraged Active Directory but still had separate components specific to routing of messages or separate administration roles, Exchange Server 2013 does not rely on many of the Exchange-specific functions and instead relies primarily on Active Directory as the source for configuration information. With Exchange Server 2013, the directory provides the sole source for users, administrative roles, sites, server locations, and security functions. With this reliance on Active Directory, an Exchange Server 2013 environment needs to have a very reliable and properly configured Active Directory.

The Role of the Directory in an Exchange Server 2013 Environment

The directory in Active Directory is leveraged by Exchange Server 2013 to not only act as the lookup point for users' email addresses and contact information, but to also act as an authoritative directory to validate users within the organization. When messages come in from the Internet, rather than being processed for spam and virus filtering, a message is first checked to see if the recipient even exists in the environment. If the recipient is not in Active Directory, the message is quarantined or deleted completely, eliminating the task of processing messages for nonexistent recipients that could take up to 60%, 70%, and even 80% of a server's processing time if the messages were processed instead of quickly disregarded.

Active Directory works in conjunction with Active Directory Application Mode, or ADAM, using a tool called EdgeSync on an Exchange Server 2013 Edge Transport server to move a portion of Active Directory to the edge in an encrypted, secure manner. In addition, Active Directory is leveraged by the Hub Transport service on the Mailbox servers to process rules for compliance and regulatory content assessment. Using Active Directory user, group, organizational unit, site, domain, and forest level rules, content can be assessed and filtered at the Hub Transport service level.

The Role of Domain Name System (DNS) for Internal and External Message Routing

Exchange Server 2013 no longer maintains a separate message routing table nor does it provide a lookup table for servers within an Exchange environment. Rather, Exchange Server 2013 simply uses DNS to determine name resolution and to identify servers and destination points from which to communicate. Unlike previous versions of Exchange that could still communicate using NetBIOS naming and Windows Internet Naming Service (WINS), Exchange Server 2013 solely depends on DNS. With the dependence on DNS in Exchange message transport and communications, it is extremely important that DNS is configured properly. More information on DNS is presented in Chapter 4, "Understanding Network Services and Active Directory Domain Controller Placement for Exchange Server 2013."

The Role of Sites in Exchange Server 2013

Exchange Server 2013 no longer has separate routing rules like routing groups found in Exchange Server 2003 for information on proper routing of messages within an Exchange environment. Rather, Exchange Server 2013 uses Active Directory Sites and Services to determine how to route messages and to determine the most efficient route to transport messages within an organization. With the dependence on Active Directory Sites and Services in Exchange message transport and routing, it is extremely important that Active Directory Sites and Services be configured properly.

Installing and Transitioning to Exchange Server 2013

With an overview on what Exchange is and what is new in Exchange Server 2013, organizations usually turn to understanding how to plan, implement, or transition to Exchange

Server 2013 and how to administer, manage, and support the environment on an ongoing basis.

Installing Exchange Server 2013 from Scratch

Some organizations choose to install Exchange Server 2013 from scratch. This might occur for an organization that is new to email, or at least new to Exchange. This is common for an organization that had a different email platform, such as Lotus Notes, Novell GroupWise, or a sendmail/POP3/IMAP messaging system. Other times organizations implement Exchange from scratch is when an organization undergoes a major merger and consolidation and is better off creating the new environment from scratch rather than trying to consolidate or modify an existing environment. Note that after installing Exchange Server 2013 from scratch, you will not be able to install earlier versions of Exchange into the organization.

Whatever the case might be, this book begins with design planning and implementation preparation tasks in Chapter 2. This is a good chapter for any size organization to plan and prepare for Exchange, including tips, tricks, and best practices specific to large enterprise environments.

After a design plan has been identified, Chapter 6, "Installing and Configuring the Basics of Exchange Server 2013 for a Brand-New Environment," helps the implementer of Exchange walk through the steps of installing Windows Active Directory and Exchange Server 2013 and configure the basic server roles as necessary.

Transitioning to Exchange Server 2013

As opposed to a migration, which means moving between two separate Exchange forests or from a different email system to Exchange, a transition is an upgrade from an earlier version of Exchange within the same Active Directory forest.

For an organization that has an existing Exchange environment, the organization would likely transition to Exchange Server 2013. The Exchange transition path is pretty limited. You cannot transition directly from Exchange Server 2003 or earlier directly into Exchange Server 2013. The only supported migrations from Microsoft are transitions from Exchange Server 2007 and Exchange Server 2010 to Exchange Server 2013. Furthermore, there is no support to perform an in-place upgrade of any Exchange server to Exchange Server 2013.

So because of this limited support, the process of transitioning to Exchange Server 2013 is drastically simplified. There are specific tips, tricks, and best practices created in transitioning from Exchange Server 2007 and Exchange Server 2010 to Exchange Server 2013 that help an organization more reliably and more effectively perform its transition. The steps for transition are outlined in Chapter 7.

Managing and Administering Exchange Server 2013

After an Exchange Server 2013 environment has been properly designed and implemented, the administrators of the organization need to be able to jump in and begin managing and administering the messaging environment. Because Exchange Server

2013 is more than just email message boxes and calendars, there is more to manage and administer. Chapter 13 goes through the top administrative tasks performed by Exchange administrators, such as adding users, deleting users, moving mailboxes, adding users to distribution lists, and so on. These tasks can now be performed both from the Exchange Administration Center and from the Exchange Management Shell command-line interface.

With Exchange Server 2013, a handful of ongoing management and maintenance tasks have proven to be important in keeping the Exchange environment operational. These management and maintenance tasks are covered in Chapter 14, "Exchange Server 2013 Management and Maintenance Practices." The tasks include daily, weekly, and monthly maintenance routines intended to keep Exchange operational on an ongoing basis.

Monitoring Exchange Using System Center 2012 Operations Manager (SCOM)

Part of any best practice in network systems management is to monitor servers and services to ensure that the system is operating properly, and to provide proactive alerts if something is no longer operating. Chapter 17, "Using Microsoft System Center Operations Manager to Monitor Exchange Server 2013," covers the SCOM product used to monitor and alert on Exchange Server 2013 activities. There is a dedicated Exchange Server 2013 management pack that provides specific monitoring functions for Exchange Server 2013.

Summary

This chapter highlighted the new features, functions, migration tools, and management utilities in Exchange Server 2013 that will help administrators take advantage of the capabilities of the new messaging system. An upgrade to Exchange Server 2013 is more than just a simple upgrade from one messaging system to another, but should take into account the new ways Exchange Server 2013 will be leveraged as the depository for more than just email messages, but also voice and mobile communications.

Planning and implementing a new implementation or an upgrade to Exchange Server 2013 is an opportunity for the organization to make Exchange Server 2013 a highly reliable and fully recoverable communications infrastructure environment. The new capabilities of Exchange Server 2013 allow an organization to change the way users access the system remotely; improve security both in the background and at the client; and have the tools available to maintain, manage, and recover from a disaster.

The steps to proper planning and successful implementation are highlighted throughout this book, with tips, tricks, and best practices noted throughout the chapters.

Best Practices

The following are best practices from this chapter:

- Spend a moment to understand what is new in Exchange Server 2013 and how the focal point of Exchange Server 2013 as the infrastructure foundation for unified communications requires a rethinking of the current architecture and ultimate redesign of an organization's Exchange environment.

- Plan for the implementation of Exchange Server 2013 by reviewing the architecture recommendations for a basic Exchange configuration environment as well as recommendations for larger enterprises covered in Chapter 2.
- Use the step-by-step installation procedures for implementing Exchange Server 2013 covered in Chapter 6.
- Use the step-by-step transition process covered in Chapter 7 to properly plan a transition from Exchange Server 2007 and/or Exchange Server 2010.
- Consider using the new Outlook Web App 2013 not only as a web browser client, but possibly as the primary mail client.
- Leverage the Outlook Anywhere functionality to enable remote, full-client Outlook connectivity to Exchange Server 2013 without the need to implement virtual private networks (VPNs) or other secured connection systems.
- Implement the DAG technology covered in Chapter 8 to create a more redundant Exchange environment for fast and fully supported recovery of Exchange mailboxes.
- Test the mailbox recovery process highlighted in Chapter 8 to ensure that if you need to recover from mailbox deletion or corruption, you have successfully tested the functionality.
- For better Exchange server management, administration, and reporting, review Chapters 13 and 14 on tips and techniques for managing and administering Exchange Server 2013.
- Leverage Microsoft System Center 2012 Operations Manager to better proactively monitor and respond to Exchange Server 2013 operational problems before the problems impact users.
- To minimize spam and unwanted messaging, enable Exchange Server 2013 Edge Transport servers to perform front-line filtering.
- Consider using the Exchange Server 2013 built-in remote and mobile capabilities for mobile phones and tablet devices for the communication of messages, calendars, and contacts.
- Review existing enterprise configurations for network settings that can be modified or reconfigured with an upgrade to Exchange Server 2013.

CHAPTER 2

Understanding Core Exchange Server 2013 Design Plans

IN THIS CHAPTER

- Planning for Exchange Server 2013
- Understanding AD Design Concepts for Exchange Server 2013
- Determining Exchange Server 2013 Placement
- Configuring Exchange Server 2013 for Maximum Performance and Reliability
- Securing and Maintaining an Exchange Server 2013 Implementation

The fundamental capabilities of Microsoft Exchange Server 2013 are impressive. Improvements to security, reliability, and scalability enhance an already road-tested and stable Exchange Server platform. Along with these impressive credentials comes an equally impressive design task. Proper design of an Exchange Server 2013 platform will do more than practically anything to reduce headaches and support calls in the future. Many complexities of Exchange Server might seem daunting, but with a full understanding of the fundamental components and improvements, the task of designing the Exchange Server 2013 environment becomes manageable.

This chapter focuses specifically on the Exchange Server 2013 components required for design. Key decision-making factors influencing design are presented and tied into overall strategy. All critical pieces of information required to design Exchange Server 2013 implementations are outlined and explained. Enterprise Exchange Server design and planning concepts are expanded in Chapter 3, "Architecting an Enterprise-Level Exchange Server 2013 Environment."

Planning for Exchange Server 2013

Designing Exchange Server used to be a fairly simple task. When an organization needed email and the decision was made to go with Exchange Server, the only real decision to make was how many Exchange servers were needed. Primarily, organizations really needed only email and eschewed any "bells and whistles."

Exchange Server 2013, on the other hand, takes messaging to a whole new level. No longer do organizations require only an email system, but they now require a high level of system availability and resilience and other messaging and unified communications functionality. After the productivity capabilities of an enterprise email platform have been demonstrated, the need for more productivity improvements arises. Consequently, it is wise to understand the integral design components of Exchange Server before beginning a design project.

The Evolution of Exchange Server 2013

Exchange Server 2013 is the evolution of a product that has consistently been improving over the years from its roots. Since the Exchange 5.x days, Microsoft has released dramatic improvements with the 2000 and 2003 versions of the product. Microsoft then followed upon the success of Exchange Server 2003 with some major architectural changes with Exchange Server 2007 and Exchange Server 2010. This latest version, Exchange Server 2013, uses a similar architecture to both Exchange Server 2007 and 2010, but adds further improvements in key areas and simplifies others.

The major areas of improvement in Exchange Server 2013 include many of the concepts and technologies introduced in Exchange Server 2007 and Exchange Server 2010 but expand upon them and include additional improvements. Key areas improved upon in Exchange Server 2013 architecture include the following:

- **Simplified and streamlined role architecture**—Exchange Server 2013 simplifies the roles that were introduced in Exchange Server 2007 and Exchange Server 2010, collapsing the Transport roles and Unified Messaging roles into the Mailbox and Client Access Server (CAS) roles, simplifying architecture and providing for design options that were previously unavailable, such as the ability to separate CAS and Mailbox servers geographically. In addition, CAS servers are now stateless, which allows them to be used by any type of load balancer.
- **Database availability groups (DAGs)**—The Exchange Server 2007 concept of Cluster Continuous Replication (CCR) was replaced with a concept called database availability groups in Exchange Server 2010. DAGs, as they are known, remain available in Exchange Server 2013, and allow a copy of an Exchange Server mailbox database to exist in up to 16 locations within an Exchange Server organization.
- **Transport and access improvements**—All client access continues to be funneled through the CAS role in an organization, which allows for improvements in client access and limited end-user disruption during mailbox moves and maintenance.
- **Integrated archiving capabilities**—Exchange Server 2013 users and administrators have the ability to archive messages for the purpose of cleaning up a mailbox of old messages, as well as for legal reasons for applying a retention policy on key

messages. Users can simply drag and drop messages into their archive folders, or a policy or rule can be set to have messages automatically moved to the archive folder.

- **"Access anywhere" improvements**—Microsoft has focused a great deal of Exchange Server 2013 development time on new access methods for Exchange Server, including a greatly enhanced Outlook Web App (OWA) that works with Microsoft and a variety of third-party browsers, Microsoft ActiveSync improvements, Unified Messaging built in, and Outlook Anywhere enhancements. Having these multiple access methods greatly increases the design flexibility of Exchange Server because end users can access email via multiple methods.
- **Protection and compliance enhancements**—Exchange Server 2013 now has antispam and anti-malware protection built in natively, protecting end users from malicious content. Compliance policies can also be more easily created.
- **Admin tools improvements and Exchange PowerShell scripting**—Introduced as the primary management tool for Exchange Server 2007, Exchange Server 2013 improves upon PowerShell capabilities and adds additional PowerShell applets and functions. The main graphical user interface (GUI) has also been moved to a Metro UI–style Web console that is accessed through the CAS role. Finally, new split permissions models can be created, which allows Active Directory (AD) and Exchange administrators to have completely separate admin models.

It is important to incorporate the concepts of these improvements into any Exchange Server design project because their principles often drive the design process.

Reviewing Exchange Server and Operating System Requirements

Exchange Server 2013 has some specific requirements, both hardware and software, that must be taken into account when designing. These requirements fall into several categories:

- Hardware
- Operating system
- Active Directory
- Exchange Server version

Each requirement must be addressed before Exchange Server 2013 can be deployed.

Reviewing Hardware Requirements

It is important to design Exchange Server hardware to scale out to the user load, which is expected for at least three years from the date of implementation. This helps retain the value of the investment put into Exchange Server. Specific hardware configuration advice is offered in later sections of this book.

Reviewing Operating System (OS) Requirements

Exchange Server 2013 is optimized for installation on Windows Server 2008 R2 with Service Pack 1 (SP1) or Windows Server 2012. These versions of Windows provide the basis for many of the improvements in Exchange Server 2013. The specific compatibility matrix, which indicates compatibility between Exchange Server versions and operating systems, is illustrated in Table 2.1.

TABLE 2.1 Exchange Server Version Compatibility

Version	Windows 2000 Server	Windows Server 2003	Windows Server 2003 R2	Windows Server 2008	Windows Server 2008 R2	Windows Server 2012
Exchange 2000 Server	Yes	No	No	No	No	No
Exchange Server 2003	Yes	Yes	Yes	No	No	No
Exchange Server 2007	No	Yes*	Yes*	Yes*	Yes*	No
Exchange Server 2010	No	No	No	Yes*	Yes*	Yes*
Exchange Server 2013	No	No	No	No	Yes*	Yes*

** 64-bit editions only supported*

Understanding Active Directory Domain Services (AD DS) Requirements

Exchange Server originally maintained its own directory. With the advent of Exchange 2000 Server, however, the directory for Exchange Server was moved to Microsoft Active Directory Domain Services, the enterprise directory system for Windows. This gave greater flexibility and consolidated directories but at the same time increased the complexity and dependencies for Exchange Server. Exchange Server 2013 uses the same model but requires specific AD functional levels and domain controller specifics to run properly.

Exchange Server 2013, while requiring an AD forest in all deployment scenarios, has certain flexibility when it comes to the type of AD it uses. It also provides for new capabilities to completely separate domain administrative rights from Exchange rights, a new feature that will be well appreciated by those organizations that have those administrative duties separated.

From an AD DS design perspective, it is possible to deploy Exchange Server in the following scenarios:

- **Single forest**—The simplest and most traditional design for Exchange Server is one where Exchange Server is installed within the same forest used for user accounts. This design also has the least amount of complexity and synchronization concerns to worry about.

- **Resource forest**—The Resource forest model in Exchange Server 2013 involves the deployment of a dedicated forest exclusively used for Exchange Server itself, and the only user accounts within it are those that serve as a placeholder for a mailbox. These user accounts are not logged on to by the end users, but rather the end users are given access to them across cross-forest trusts from their particular user forest to the Exchange Server forest. More information on this deployment model can be found in Chapter 4, "Understanding Network Services and Active Directory Domain Controller Placement for Exchange Server 2013."

- **Multiple forests**—Different multiple forest models for Exchange Server are presently available, but they do require a greater degree of administration and synchronization. In these models, different Exchange Server organizations live in different forests across an organization. These different Exchange Server organizations are periodically synchronized to maintain a common Global Address List (GAL). More information on this deployment model can also be found in Chapter 4.

It is important to determine which design model will be chosen before proceeding with an Exchange Server deployment because you cannot rename a domain that contains an Exchange server and cannot move an Exchange server to another domain.

Outlining Exchange Server Version Requirements

As with previous versions of Exchange Server, there are separate Enterprise and Standard versions of the Exchange Server 2013 product. The Standard Edition supports all Exchange Server 2013 functionality with the exception of the fact that it is limited to no more than five databases on a single server.

NOTE

Unlike many of the other previous versions of the software, Microsoft provides only a single set of media for Exchange Server 2013. When installed, server version can be set by simply entering a license key. A server can be upgraded from the Trial version to Standard or Enterprise or from Standard to Enterprise. Downgrading the version is not supported.

Scaling Exchange Server 2013

Exchange 2000 Server originally provided the basis for servers that could easily scale out to thousands of users in a single site, if necessary. Exchange Server 2003 further improved the situation by introducing Messaging Application Programming Interface (MAPI) compression and RPC over HTTP. Exchange Server 2007 and Exchange Server 2010 and their 64-bit architecture allowed for even further scalability and reduced I/O levels. Finally, Exchange Server 2013 and the separation of client traffic to load-balanced client access servers enable the client tier to be much more scalable than with previous versions.

Site consolidation concepts enable organizations that might have previously deployed Exchange servers in remote locations to have those clients access their mailboxes across wide area network (WAN) links or dial-up connections by using the enhanced Outlook or OWA clients. This solves the problem that previously existed of having to deploy Exchange servers and global catalog (GC) servers in remote locations, with only a handful of users, and greatly reduces the infrastructure costs of setting up Exchange Server.

Having Exchange Server 2013 Coexist with an Existing Network Infrastructure

In a design scenario, it is necessary to identify any systems that require access to email data or services. For example, it might be necessary to enable a third-party monitoring application to relay mail off the Simple Mail Transfer Protocol (SMTP) engine of Exchange Server so that alerts can be sent. Identifying these needs during the design portion of a project is subsequently important.

Identifying Third-Party Product Functionality

Microsoft built specific hooks into Exchange Server 2013 to enable third-party applications to improve upon the built-in functionality provided by the system. For example, built-in support for antivirus scanning, backups, and Unified Messaging exist right out of the box, although functionality is limited without the addition of third-party software. The most common additions to Exchange Server implementation are the following:

- Antivirus (though it is important to note that Exchange Server 2013 now has these features built in)
- Backup
- Phone/PBX/Unified Messaging integration
- Fax software
- Archiving software

Understanding AD Design Concepts for Exchange Server 2013

After all objectives, dependencies, and requirements have been mapped out, the process of designing the Exchange Server 2013 environment can begin. Decisions should be made in the following key areas:

- AD DS design
- Exchange server placement
- Global catalog placement
- Client access methods

Understanding the AD DS Forest

Because Exchange Server 2013 relies on the Windows Server 2008 AD DS for its directory, it is therefore important to include AD DS in the design plans. In many situations and AD implementations, whether based on Windows Server 2003, Windows Server 2008, or Windows Server 2012, AD DS already exists in the organization. In these cases, it is necessary only to plan for the inclusion of Exchange Server into the existing forest.

NOTE

Exchange Server 2013 has several key requirements for AD. First, all domains and the forest must be at least in Windows Server 2003 functional levels. Second, it requires that at least one domain controller in each site that includes Exchange Server be at least Windows Server 2003 Service Pack 2 (SP2), Windows Server 2008, Windows Server 2008 R2, or Windows Server 2012.

If an AD DS structure is not already in place, a new AD DS forest must be established for Exchange to be installed into. Designing the AD DS forest infrastructure can be complex, and can require nearly as much thought into design as the actual Exchange Server configuration itself. Therefore, it is important to fully understand the concepts behind AD DS before beginning an Exchange Server 2013 design.

In short, a single instance of AD DS consists of a single AD DS forest. A forest is composed of AD DS trees, which are contiguous domain namespaces in the forest. Each tree is composed of one or more domains, as illustrated in Figure 2.1.

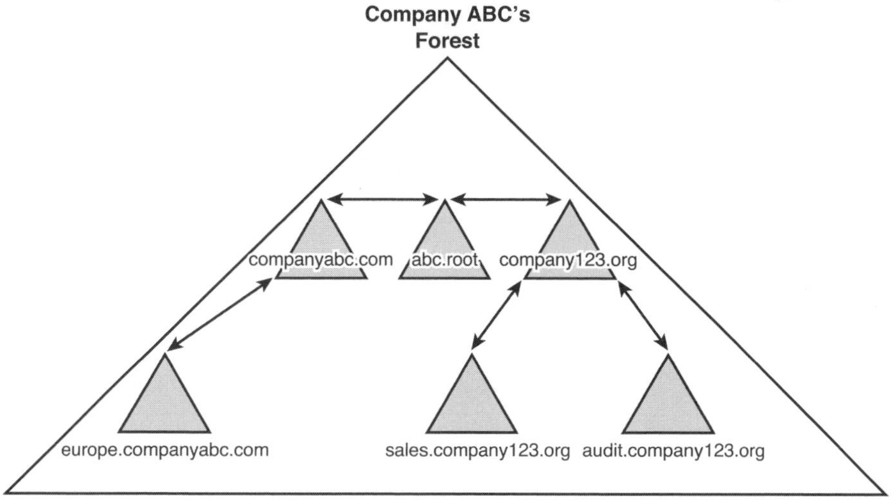

FIGURE 2.1 Multitree AD DS forest design.

Certain cases exist for using more than one AD DS forest in an organization:

- **Political limitations**—Some organizations have specific political reasons that force the creation of multiple AD DS forests. For example, if a merged corporate entity requires separate divisions to maintain completely separate information technology (IT) infrastructures, more than one forest is necessary.
- **Security concerns**—Although the AD DS domain serves as a de facto security boundary, the ultimate security boundary is effectively the forest. In other words, it is possible for user accounts in a domain in a forest to hack into domains within the same forest if they know what they are doing. Although these types of vulnerabilities are not common and are difficult to do, highly security-conscious organizations should implement separate AD DS forests or organizational units with delegated rights.
- **Application functionality**—A single AD DS forest shares a common directory schema, which is the underlying structure of the directory and must be unique across the entire forest. In some cases, separate branches of an organization require that certain applications, which need extensions to the schema, be installed. This might not be possible or might conflict with the schema requirements of other branches. These cases might require the creation of a separate forest, though this particular scenario is particularly discouraged.
- **Exchange-specific functionality (resource forest)**—In certain circumstances, it might be necessary to install Exchange Server 2013 into a separate forest to enable Exchange Server to reside in a separate schema and forest instance. An example of this type of setup is an organization with two existing AD DS forests that creates a third forest specifically for Exchange Server, called a resource forest, and uses cross-forest trusts to assign mailbox permissions.

The simplest designs often work the best. The same principle applies to AD DS design. The designer should start with the assumption that a simple forest and domain structure will work for the environment. However, when factors such as those previously described create constraints, multiple forests can be established to satisfy the requirements of the constraints.

Understanding the AD Domain Structure

After the AD DS forest structure has been chosen, the domain structure can be laid out. As with the forest structure, it is often wise to consider a single domain model for the Exchange Server 2013 directory. In fact, if deploying Exchange Server is the only consideration, this is often the best choice.

There is one major exception to the single domain model: the placeholder domain model. The placeholder domain model has an isolated domain serving as the root domain in the forest. The user domain, which contains all production user accounts, would be located in a separate domain in the forest, as illustrated in Figure 2.2.

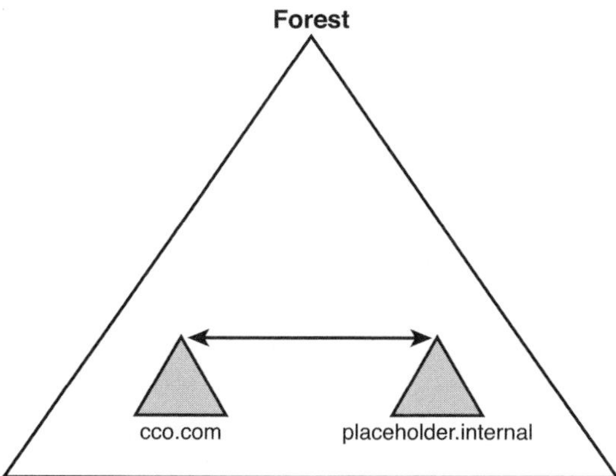

FIGURE 2.2 The placeholder domain model.

The placeholder domain structure segregates high-level schema-access accounts into a completely separate domain from the regular user domain. Access to the placeholder domain can be audited and restricted to maintain tighter control on the critical schema. The downside to this model, however, is the fact that the additional domain requires a separate set of domain controllers, which increases the infrastructure costs of the environment. In general, this makes this domain model less desirable for smaller organizations because the trade-off between increased cost and less security is too great. This is a model that was once commonly deployed by organizations before it became apparent that the domain is not an effective security boundary.

Reviewing AD DS Infrastructure Components

Several key components of AD must be installed within an organization to ensure proper Exchange Server 2013 and AD DS functionality. In smaller environments, many of these components can be installed on a single machine, but all need to be located within an environment to ensure server functionality.

Outlining the Domain Name System (DNS) Impact on Exchange Server 2013 Design

In addition to being tightly integrated with AD DS, Exchange Server 2013 is joined with the Domain Name System (DNS). DNS serves as the lookup agent for Exchange Server 2013, AD, and most new Microsoft applications and services. DNS translates common names into computer-recognizable IP addresses. For example, the name `www.cco.com` translates into the IP address of `12.155.166.151`. AD DS and Exchange Server 2013 require that at least one DNS server be made available so that name resolution properly occurs.

Given the dependency that both Exchange Server 2013 and AD DS have on DNS, it is an extremely important design element.

Reviewing DNS Namespace Considerations for Exchange Server

Given Exchange Server 2013's dependency on DNS, a common DNS namespace must be chosen for the AD DS structure to reside in. In multiple tree domain models, this could be composed of several DNS trees, but in small organization environments, this normally means choosing a single DNS namespace for the AD DS domain.

There is a great deal of confusion between the DNS namespace in which AD DS resides and the email DNS namespace in which mail is delivered. Although they are often the same, there is no reason that the two namespaces have to be the same. When Exchange Server is first installed, the AD domain is chosen as the default SMTP domain, but that can be changed. For example, CompanyABC's AD DS structure is composed of a single domain named `abc.internal`, and the email domain to which mail is delivered is `companyabc.com`. The separate namespace, in this case, was created because someone believed that it reduced the security vulnerability of maintaining the same DNS namespace both internally and externally (published to the Internet).

Likewise, there is no necessary relationship between the Active Directory user principal name (UPN) that can be used for user logon and the SMTP email address, but using the same for both makes it easier for users.

For simplicity, CompanyABC could have chosen `companyabc.com` as its AD DS namespace. This choice increases the simplicity of the environment by making the AD DS logon UPN and the email address the same. For example, the user Pete Handley is `pete@companyabc.com` for logon and `pete@companyabc.com` for email. This option is the choice for many organizations because the need for user simplicity often trumps the higher security.

Optimally Locating Global Catalog Servers

Because all Exchange Server directory lookups use AD, it is vital that the essential AD global catalog information is made available to each Exchange server in the organization. For many small offices with a single site, this simply means that it is important to have a full global catalog server available in the main site where there are Exchange servers.

The global catalog is an index of the AD DS database that contains a partial copy of its contents. All objects within the AD DS tree are referenced within the global catalog, which enables users to search for objects located in other domains. Not every attribute of each object is replicated to the global catalogs, only those attributes that are commonly used in search operations, such as first name and last name. Exchange Server 2013 uses the global catalog for the email-based lookups of names, email addresses, and other mail-related attributes.

NOTE

Exchange Server 2013 cannot make use of Windows Server 2008 Read-Only Domain Controllers (RODCs) or Read-Only Global Catalog (ROGC) servers, so be sure to plan for full GCs and domain controllers (DCs) for Exchange Server.

Because full global catalog replication adds bandwidth usage to the standard domain controller replication, it is important to design a site structure to reflect the available WAN link capacity. If a sufficient amount of capacity is available, a full global catalog server can be deployed. If, however, capacity is limited, universal group membership caching can be enabled to reduce the bandwidth load.

Determining Exchange Server 2013 Placement

Previous versions of Exchange Server essentially forced many organizations into deploying servers in sites with relatively few users. With the concept of site consolidation in more recent versions of Exchange, smaller numbers of Exchange servers can service clients in multiple locations, even if they are separated by slow WAN links. For small and medium-sized organizations, this essentially means that fewer servers are required. In addition, Exchange Server 2013 introduces new consolidated server role concepts, which should be understood so that the right server can be deployed in the right location.

Understanding Exchange Server 2013 Server Roles

Exchange Server 2013 firmed up the server role concept outlined with Exchange Server 2007 and 2010 and simplified them. Before Exchange Server 2007, server functionality was based on how a server was used rather than the components that were installed, such as referring to an Exchange server as a front-end, bridgehead, or back-end server. In reality, there was no official terminology that was used for Exchange server roles; these terms evolved through common use. Exchange Server 2007 and 2010 introduced new roles that were very specific, but Microsoft found that most clients were seldom deploying all of those roles on separate servers and were combining them together, especially the Hub Transport and Client Access Server roles.

Microsoft has combined server roles in Exchange Server 2013, but more for technical rather than usage reasons. The server roles included in Exchange Server 2013 include the following:

- **Client Access Server**—The CAS role allows for client connections via nonstandard methods such as OWA, Exchange ActiveSync, Post Office Protocol 3 (POP3), and Internet Message Access Protocol (IMAP). Exchange Server 2013 also forces MAPI traffic and effectively all client traffic through the CAS layer. CAS servers in Exchange Server 2013 are also completely stateless, so they can be load-balanced for redundancy purposes using any number of load-balancing technologies, including simple solutions such as DNS Round Robin (though this is not recommended). As with the other server roles, the CAS role can coexist with other roles for smaller organizations with a single server, for example.
- **Mailbox server**—The Mailbox server role is intuitive; it acts as the storehouse for mail data in users' mailboxes and down-level public folders if required. All connections to the mailbox servers are proxied through the CAS servers. The Mailbox server role also handles the previous Hub Transport and Unified Messaging capabilities that were separate roles in the past.
- **Edge Transport server**—The Edge Transport server is unchanged from Exchange Server 2010, providing a gateway for SMTP traffic for message hygiene and recipient filtering. Note that the RTM version of Exchange Server 2013 does not support a 2013 server being installed with the Edge Transport role, though it does support existing Exchange Server 2010 Edge Transport servers. This is expected to be remedied in later releases of Exchange Server.

The first two roles can be installed on a single server or on multiple servers. For smaller organizations, a single server holding all Exchange Server roles is sufficient. For larger organizations, a more complex configuration might be required. For more information on designing large and complex Exchange Server implementations, see Chapter 4.

Understanding Environment Sizing Considerations

In some cases with very small organizations, the number of users is small enough to warrant the installation of all AD DS and Exchange Server 2013 components on a single server. This scenario is possible, as long as all necessary components—DNS, a global catalog domain controller, and Exchange Server 2013—are installed on the same hardware. In general, however, it is best and highly recommended to separate AD DS and Exchange Server onto separate servers wherever possible.

Identifying Client Access Points

At its core, Exchange Server 2013 essentially acts as a storehouse for mailbox data. Access to the mail within the mailboxes can take place through multiple means, some of which might be required by specific services or applications in the environment. A good understanding of what these services are and if and how your design should support them is warranted.

Outlining Full Outlook Client Access

The "heavy" client of Outlook is in its latest 2013 version and has gone through a significant number of changes, both to the look and feel of the application and to the back-end mail functionality. The look and feel has been streamlined based on Microsoft research and customer feedback. The latest Outlook client, Outlook 2013, uses the Office Ribbon introduced with Office 2007 to improve the client experience. Outlook connects to Exchange CAS servers, improving the scalability of the environment.

In addition to MAPI compression, Outlook 2013 expands upon Outlook's ability to run in cached mode, which automatically detects slow connections between client and server and adjusts Outlook functionality to match the speed of the link. When a slow link is detected, Outlook can be configured to download only email header information. When emails are opened, the entire email is downloaded, including attachments if necessary. This drastically reduces the amount of bits across the wire that is sent because only those emails that are required are sent across the connection.

The Outlook client is the most effective and full-functioning client for users who are physically located close to an Exchange server. With the enhancements in cached mode functionality, however, Outlook can also be effectively used in remote locations. When making the decision about which client to deploy as part of a design, you should keep these concepts in mind.

Accessing Exchange Server with OWA

The OWA client in Exchange Server 2013 has been enhanced and optimized for performance and usability. There is now less difference between the full-functioning client and

OWA. The most recent improvement is the ability to take OWA content offline and work on a cached version of a mailbox from an offline browser. Also new is updated support for non-Microsoft browsers, such as Firefox, Safari, and Chrome.

Using Exchange ActiveSync (EAS)

Exchange ActiveSync (EAS) support in Exchange Server 2013 allows a mobile client, such as an iPhone, Android phone, iPad, Android tablet, or Windows Phone device, to synchronize with the Exchange server, allowing for access to email from a handheld device.

Understanding the SMTP

The SMTP is the standard protocol for Internet email delivery. SMTP is built in to Exchange servers and is used by Exchange Server systems for relaying mail messages from one system to another, similar to the way that mail is relayed across SMTP servers on the Internet.

By default, Exchange Server 2013 uses DNS to route messages destined for the Internet out of the Exchange Server topology. If, however, a user wants to forward messages to a smart host before they are transmitted to the Internet, a Send connector can be so configured.

Using Outlook Anywhere (Previously Known as RPC over HTTP)

One very effective and improved client access method to Exchange Server 2013 is known as Outlook Anywhere. This technology was previously referred to as RPC over HTTP(S). This technology enables standard Outlook 2013/2010/2007 access using a protocol that firewalls typically allow to pass. The Outlook client encapsulates Outlook RPC packets into HTTP or HTTPS packets and sends them across standard web ports (80 and 443), where they are then extracted by the Exchange Server 2013 system. Outlook Anywhere also obviates the need for a virtual private network (VPN) connection for Outlook connectivity to the Exchange server.

Configuring Exchange Server 2013 for Maximum Performance and Reliability

After decisions have been made about AD design, Exchange server placement, and client access, optimization of the Exchange server itself helps ensure efficiency, reliability, and security for the messaging platform.

Designing an Optimal Operating System Configuration for Exchange Server

As previously mentioned, Exchange Server 2013 only operates on the Windows Server 2008 R2 with SP1 or Windows Server 2012 operating systems. The Standard Edition of Windows Server 2008 is sufficient for Exchange servers when the server is not a member of a DAG.

NOTE

Contrary to popular misconception, the Enterprise Edition of Exchange Server can be installed on the Standard Edition of the operating system, and vice versa. Choose the version of each based on the requirements.

Working with Multiple Exchange Server Databases

Exchange Server 2013 database availability groups allow for multiple databases to be installed across multiple servers and to have multiple versions of those databases in more than one location. It also has the following advantages:

- **Reduce database restore time**—Smaller databases take less time to restore from tape, so it may make more sense to deploy a larger quantity of smaller databases. This concept can be helpful if there is a group of users who require quicker recovery time (such as management). All mailboxes for this group might then be placed in a separate database to provide quicker recovery time in the event of a server or database failure.
- **Provide for separate mailbox limit policies**—Each database can be configured with different mailbox storage limits. For example, the standard user database could have a 200-MB limit on mailboxes, and the management database could have a 500-MB limit.
- **Mitigate risk by distributing user load**—By distributing user load across multiple databases, the risk of losing all user mail connectivity is reduced. For example, if a single database failed that contained all users, no one would be able to mail. If those users were divided across three databases, however, only one third of those users would be unable to mail in the event of a database failure.

Monitoring Design Concepts with System Center Operations Manager 2012

The enhancements to Exchange Server 2013 do not stop with the improvements to the product itself. New functionality has been added to the Exchange Management Pack for System Center Operations Manager that enables OpsMgr to monitor Exchange servers for critical events and performance data. The OpsMgr Management Pack is preconfigured to monitor for Exchange Server–specific information and to enable administrators to proactively monitor Exchange servers. More information is presented in Chapter 17, "Using Microsoft System Center Operations Manager to Monitor Exchange Server 2013."

Securing and Maintaining an Exchange Server 2013 Implementation

One of the greatest advantages of Exchange Server 2013 is its emphasis on security. Along with Windows Server, Exchange Server 2013 was developed during and after the Microsoft Trustworthy Computing initiative, which effectively put a greater emphasis on security over new features in the products. In Exchange Server 2013, this means that the OS and the application were designed with services "Secure by Default."

With Secure by Default, all nonessential functionality in Exchange Server must be turned on if needed. This is a complete change from earlier Microsoft practice, which had all services, add-ons, and options turned on and running at all times, presenting much larger security vulnerabilities than was necessary. Designing security effectively becomes much easier in Exchange Server 2013 because it now becomes necessary only to identify components to turn on, as opposed to identifying everything that needs to be turned off.

Patching the Operating System Using Windows Software Update Services

Although Windows Server presents a much smaller target for hackers, viruses, and exploits by virtue of the Secure by Default concept, it is still important to keep the OS up to date against critical security patches and updates. Currently, two approaches can be used to automate the installation of server patches. The first method involves configuring the Windows Server Automatic Updates client to download patches from Microsoft and install them on a schedule. The second option is to set up an internal server to coordinate patch distribution and management. The solution that Microsoft supplies for this functionality is known as Windows Software Update Services (WSUS).

WSUS enables a centralized server to hold copies of OS patches for distribution to clients on a preset schedule. WSUS can be used to automate the distribution of patches to Exchange Server 2013 servers, so that the OS components will remain secure between service packs. WSUS might not be necessary in smaller environments, but can be considered in medium-sized to large organizations that want greater control over their patch management strategy.

Summary

Exchange Server 2013 offers a broad range of functionality and improvements to messaging and is well suited for organizations of any size. With proper thought for the major design topics, a robust and reliable Exchange Server email solution can be put into place that will perfectly complement the needs of any organization.

When Exchange Server design concepts have been fully understood, the task of designing the Exchange Server 2013 infrastructure can take place.

Best Practices

The following are best practices from this chapter:

- Use DAGs to distribute multiple copies of all mailboxes to multiple locations, taking advantage of high availability and disaster recovery capabilities that are built in to Exchange Server 2013.
- Separate the Exchange Server log and database files onto separate physical volumes.

- Plan for a Windows Server 2003 forest functional level and at least one Windows Server 2003 SP2 or later domain controller in each site that will run Exchange Server.
- Integrate a backup strategy into Exchange Server design.
- Install at least two global catalog servers in the same site as any Exchange server.
- Keep the OS and Exchange Server up to date through service packs and software patches, either manually or via Windows Software Update Services.
- Keep the AD DS design simple, with a single forest and single domain, unless a specific need exists to create more complexity.
- Identify the client access methods that will be supported and match them with the appropriate Exchange Server 2013 technology.
- Monitor DNS functionality closely in the environment on the AD DS domain controllers.

CHAPTER 3

Architecting an Enterprise-Level Exchange Server 2013 Environment

IN THIS CHAPTER

Microsoft Exchange Server 2013 was designed to accommodate the needs of multiple organizations, from the small businesses to large, multinational corporations. In addition to the scalability features present in previous versions of Exchange Server, Exchange Server 2013 offers more opportunities to scale the back-end server environment to the specific needs of any group.

This chapter addresses specific design guidelines for midsize to large enterprise organizations. Throughout the chapter, specific examples of enterprise organizations are presented and general recommendations are made. This chapter assumes a base knowledge of design components that can be obtained by reading Chapter 2, "Understanding Core Exchange Server 2013 Design Plans."

Designing Active Directory for Exchange Server 2013

Active Directory (AD) is a necessary and fundamental component of any Exchange Server 2013 implementation. That said, organizations do not necessarily need to panic about setting up Active Directory in addition to Exchange Server, as long as a few straightforward design steps are followed. The following areas of Active Directory must be addressed to properly design and deploy Exchange Server 2013:

- Forest and domain design
- AD site and replication topology layout
- Domain controller and global catalog placement
- Domain name system (DNS) configuration

Understanding Forest and Domain Design

Because Exchange Server 2013 uses Active Directory Domain Services (AD DS) for its underlying directory structure, it is necessary to link Exchange Server with a single AD DS forest.

In many cases, an existing AD DS forest and domain structure is already in place in organizations considering Exchange Server 2013 deployment. In these cases, Exchange Server can be installed on top of the existing AD environment, and no additional AD DS design decisions need to be made. It is important to note that Exchange Server 2013 requires that the AD DS forest be at least at Windows Server 2003 functional level and also requires that at least one Windows Server 2003 SP2 or later global catalog is installed in each AD DS site in which Exchange servers reside. Finally, the schema master for the forest must be Windows Server 2003 SP2 or later.

In some cases, there might not be an existing AD DS infrastructure in place, and one needs to be deployed to support Exchange Server. In these scenarios, design decisions need to be made for the AD DS structure in which Exchange Server will be installed. In some specific cases, Exchange Server might be deployed as part of a separate forest by itself, as illustrated in Figure 3.1. This model is known as the Exchange Resource Forest model. This is sometimes the case in an organization with multiple existing AD forests.

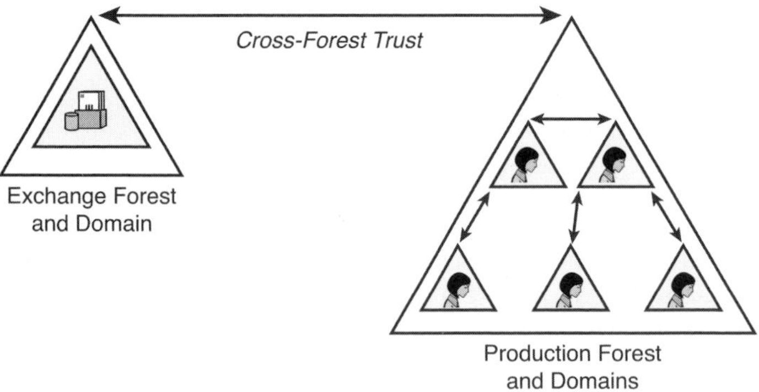

FIGURE 3.1 Understanding the Exchange Resource Forest model.

In any case, AD should be designed with simplicity in mind. A single-forest, single-domain model, for example, solves the needs of many organizations. If Exchange Server itself is all that is required of AD DS, this type of deployment is the best practice to consider.

NOTE

The addition of Exchange Server 2013 into an Active Directory forest requires an extension of the AD forest's Active Directory schema.

Considerations for this factor must be taken into account when deploying Exchange Server onto an existing AD forest.

Outlining AD DS Site and Replication Topology Layout

AD DS sites should mirror existing network topology. Where there are pools of highly connected AD DS domain controllers, for example, AD DS sites should be created to optimize replication. Smaller organizations have the luxury of a simplified AD DS site design. In general, the number of sites is small—or, in most cases, composed of a single physical location. Midsize and larger organizations might require the creation of multiple AD DS sites to mirror the wide area network (WAN) connectivity of the organization.

Exchange Server 2013 no longer uses a separate replication mechanism (routing groups) from AD DS, and Exchange Server replication takes place within the context of Active Directory sites. This makes proper AD DS site topology creation a critical component of an Exchange Server deployment.

Reviewing Domain Controller and Global Catalog Placement Concepts

In small or midsize organizations, you have effectively two options regarding domain controller placement. The first option involves using the same physical server for domain controller and Exchange Server duties. This option is feasible, though not recommended, for smaller organizations if budget constraints preclude the addition of more than one server. This type of deployment strategy is not feasible for midsize and enterprise organizations, however, and the domain controller functions should be separated onto dedicated systems.

Configuring DNS

Because AD DS and Exchange Server are completely dependent on DNS for lookups and overall functionality, configuring DNS is an important factor to consider. As a common AD DS best practice, DNS is installed on the domain controller(s), which enables the creation of Active Directory–integrated DNS zones. AD–integrated zones enable DNS data to be stored in AD with multiple read/write copies of the zone available for redundancy purposes. Although using other non-Microsoft DNS for AD DS is supported, it is not recommended.

The main decision regarding DNS layout is the decision about the namespace to be used within the organization. The DNS namespace is the same as the AD DS domain information, and it is difficult to change later. The two options in this case are to configure DNS to use either a published, external namespace that is easy to understand, such as `cco.com`, or an internal, secure namespace that is difficult to hack in to, such as `cconet.internal`. In general, the more security-conscious an organization, the more often the internal namespace will be chosen. This, however, is a dated concept.

Creating a split-brain DNS architecture, where the same DNS zone is used internally as well as externally, such as companyabc.com, is strongly recommended because it will greatly simplify the creation and management of Secure Sockets Layer (SSL) certificates because few public certificate authorities will add internal domains to certificates. In a split-brain arrangement, hostnames are entered in DNS to point to internal IP addresses, while the same entries in external DNS point to the Internet addresses. The external DNS zone needs only to contain hosts that are referenced from outside the network.

Determining Hardware and Software Components

Justifying hardware and software purchases is often a difficult task for organizations of any size. It is, therefore, important to balance the need for performance and redundancy with the available funds in the budget, and, thus, deploy the optimal Exchange Server hardware and software configuration.

Unlike some of the older versions of Exchange Server, Exchange Server 2013 requires the use of 64-bit capable systems, so it is critical to order the appropriate equipment when deploying Exchange Server 2013 systems.

Designing Server Number and Placement

Exchange Server scales very well to a large number of mailboxes on a single machine, depending on the hardware chosen for the Exchange server. Subsequently, Exchange Server 2013 is optimal for organizations that want to limit the amount of servers that are deployed and supported in an environment.

Some of the older versions of Exchange Server required a local Exchange presence in each office location, as they didn't support cross-WAN mailbox access very efficiently. Exchange Server 2013, on the other hand, expands upon the concept of site consolidation, introduced in Exchange Server 2003. This concept enables smaller sites to use the Exchange servers in the larger sites through the more efficient bandwidth usage present in Outlook 2007 and Outlook 2003 and other mobile technologies. It also allows for the previously unheard of scenario of separating out Client Access servers from their equivalent Mailbox servers in situations where it makes sense to have those roles in separate geographical locations.

Providing for Server Redundancy and Optimization

The ability of the Exchange server to recover from hardware failures is more than just a "nice-to-have" feature. Many server models come with an array of redundancy features, such as multiple fans and power supplies and mirrored disk capabilities. These features incur additional costs, however, so it is wise to perform a cost-benefit analysis to determine what redundancy features are required. Midsize and larger organizations should seriously consider robust redundancy options, however, because the increased reliability and uptime is often well worth the up-front costs.

Exchange Server 2013 further expands the redundancy options with the concept of database availability groups (DAGs), which enable a mailbox database to reside in up to 16 different locations at one time. This allows for unprecedented levels of redundancy and frees the architect from the requirement of focusing heavily on server-level redundancy because the loss of a single server is no longer a catastrophic event.

One of the most critical but overlooked performance strategies for Exchange Server is the concept of separating the Exchange Server logs and database onto separate physical drive sets. Because Exchange Server logs are very write-intensive, and the database is read-intensive, having these components on the same disk set would degrade performance. Separating these components onto different disk sets, however, is the best way to get the most out of Exchange Server.

Reviewing Server Memory and Processor Recommendations

Exchange Server is a resource-hungry application that, left to its own devices, will consume a good portion of any amount of processor or memory that is given to it. The amount of processors and random access memory (RAM) required should reflect the budgetary needs of the organization. In general, midsize and larger organizations should consider multiprocessor servers and greater amounts of RAM—16GB or 32GB or more. This helps increase the amount of mailboxes that can be homed to any particular server.

Outlining Server Operating System Considerations

The base operating system (OS) for Exchange Server, Windows Server, comes in two versions, Enterprise and Standard. Some midsize and larger organizations could deploy the Enterprise Edition of the Windows Server product, namely for clustering support for database availability groups. If this functionality is not required, the Standard Edition of the OS is sufficient.

Designing Exchange Server Roles in an Exchange Server Environment

Exchange Server 2013 was designed to be resilient and be able to adapt to a wide variety of deployment scenarios. Part of this design revolves around the concept that individual servers can play one or more roles for an organization. Each of these roles provides for specific functionality that is commonly performed by Exchange servers, such as the Mailbox server or Client Access server (CAS). You'll also immediately note that the Unified Messaging and Hub Transport roles have been retired, as their functionality has been rolled up into the CAS and Mailbox roles.

Central to the understanding of Exchange Server 2013 and how to design and architect it is the understanding of these individual roles. During the design process, understanding server roles is central to proper server placement.

The individual server roles in Exchange Server 2013 are as follows:

- Mailbox server role
- Client Access server role

Each of these roles is described in more detail in the subsequent sections.

Planning for the Mailbox Server Role

The Mailbox server role is the central role in an Exchange Server topology as it is the server that stores the actual mailboxes of the user. Therefore, Mailbox servers are often the most critical for an organization, and are given the most attention.

With the Enterprise Edition of Exchange Server, a Mailbox server can hold anywhere from one to thousands of databases on it. Each of the databases are theoretically unlimited in size, although it is wise to keep an individual database limited to 100GB or less for performance and recovery scenarios.

NOTE

In large organizations, a single server or a cluster of servers is often dedicated to individual server roles. That said, a single server can also be assigned other roles, such as the Client Access server role, in the interest of consolidating the number of servers deployed.

Planning for the Client Access Server Role

The Client Access server role in Exchange Server is the role that controls access to mailboxes from all clients, including the full version of Outlook. It is the component that controls access to mailboxes via the following mechanisms:

- Outlook Web App (OWA)
- Exchange ActiveSync
- Outlook Anywhere (formerly RPC over HTTP), which is now Outlook's preferred connection method now that MAPI RPC is gone
- Post Office Protocol 3 (POP3)
- Internet Message Access Protocol (IMAP4)
- The Exchange Administration Center (EAC) that is used to administer Exchange mailboxes and settings
- Exchange Web Services provides support to Outlook 2011 for Mac, Entourage 2008 Web Services Edition, and other similar client and application software

In addition, CAS systems also handle the following two special services in an Exchange Server topology:

- **Autodiscover service**—The Autodiscover service allows clients to determine their synchronization settings (such as Mailbox server and so on) by entering in their Simple Mail Transfer Protocol (SMTP) address and their credentials. It is supported across standard OWA connections.
- **Availability service**—The Availability service is the replacement for free/busy functionality in Exchange Server 2000/2003. It is responsible for making a user's calendar availability visible to other users making meeting requests.

Client Access servers in Exchange Server 2013 are the only way that clients can access their mailbox in Exchange Server 2013, which differs from previous versions of Exchange Server that required direct access to Mailbox servers. By separating client traffic to a load-balanced array of CAS servers, Exchange Server architects have more flexibility in design and failover; using concepts such as DAGs becomes easier and more efficient.

Finally, the CAS role has been made to be completely stateless in this version of Exchange, which means that architects have the flexibility to use software-based load balancing, hardware-based load balancing, or even potentially simple solutions, such as DNS Round Robin. That said, it's still not very effective to use concepts like DNS Round Robin, and a good hardware-based load balancer is required, though it is no longer required to use session-based affinity (stickiness) for the traffic.

Understanding a Sample Deployment Scenario

A better understanding of Exchange Server roles can be achieved by looking at sample deployment scenarios that utilize these roles. For example, Figure 3.2 illustrates a large enterprise deployment of Exchange Server that takes advantage of all of the unique server roles.

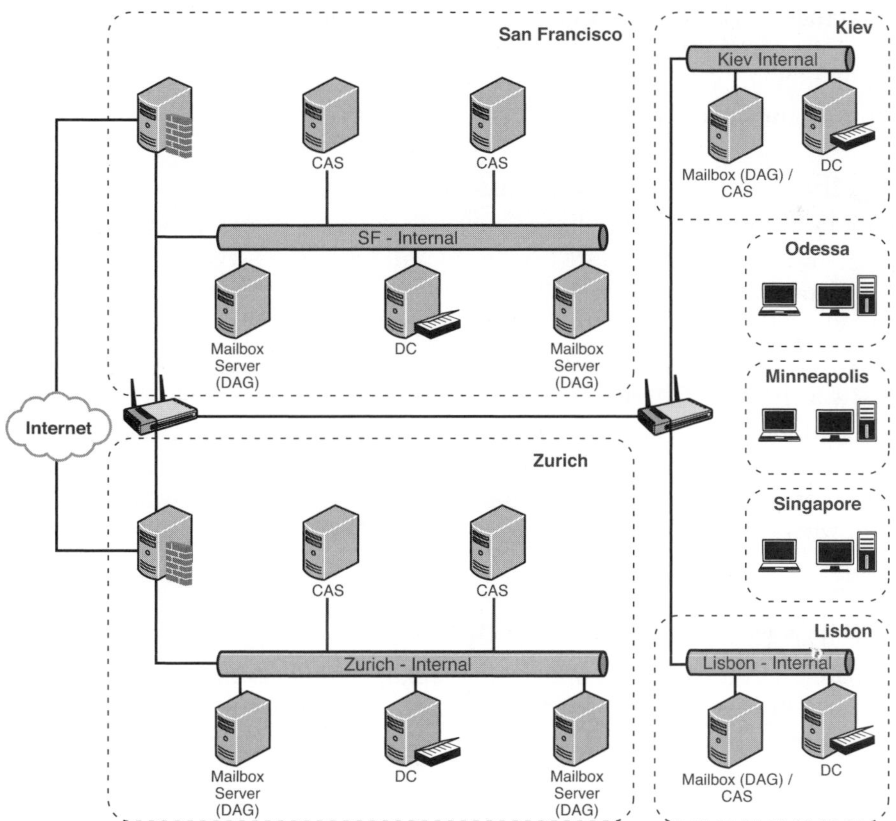

FIGURE 3.2 Examining an Enterprise Exchange Server deployment.

In this design, the following key deployment features are illustrated:

- DAGs are distributed across multiple Mailbox servers, with at least three copies of each mailbox database across the organization.
- Mailbox servers automatically distribute mail between the two major sites in San Francisco and Zurich.
- Medium-sized sites such as Kiev and Lisbon make use of combined CAS/Mailbox server systems.
- Dedicated Client Access servers are set up in the two main sites, to provide for client access mechanisms in those sites.
- Smaller sites, such as Minneapolis, Odessa, and Singapore, have their mailboxes hosted in the two hub locations and use the Client Access servers with Outlook Anywhere to access their mailboxes remotely.

Designing Exchange Server Infrastructure

After AD DS and the physical OS has been chosen and deployed, the Exchange Server infrastructure can be set up and optimized for the specific needs of the organization. With these needs in mind, you can do several things to optimize an Exchange Server 2013 setup, as detailed in the following sections.

Determining the Exchange Server Version

When installing Exchange Server, the choice of Exchange Server version needs to be made. As with Windows Server, there are two versions of Exchange Server, Standard and Enterprise. The Standard Edition enables all Exchange Server 2013 functionality except that it does not allow for more than five mailbox databases on a server.

Determining Exchange Server Database Layout

As previously mentioned, the Enterprise Edition of Exchange Server enables the concept of multiple databases, up to a maximum of 100 per server. This enables a greater amount of design freedom and gives administrators more flexibility. This type of flexibility is even more important when designing infrastructures that include multiple copies of a single database.

Outlining Exchange Server Recovery Options

Deploying Exchange Server requires considerable thought about backup and recovery solutions. Because Exchange Server is a live, active database, special considerations need to be taken into account when designing the backup strategy for email.

Microsoft designed Exchange Server 2013 to use the backup application programming interfaces (APIs) from Windows Server 2008. These APIs support the Volume Shadow Copy Service, which enables Exchange Server databases to be backed up through creation of a "shadow copy" of the entire disk at the beginning of the backup. The shadow copy is then used for the backup, so that the production disk is not affected.

NOTE

The Windows Server 2003/2008 backup utility can be used to back up Exchange Server using the traditional online backup approach although with limited features. Volume Shadow Copy requires a third-party solution that has been written to support the Windows Server 2003/2008 backup and restore APIs. Microsoft also offers enterprise Exchange Server backup using the System Center Data Protection Manager (DPM) product.

For more information on backup and recovery options, see Chapter 16, "Backing Up the Exchange Server 2013 Environment."

Considering Exchange Server Antivirus and Antispam Design

Viruses are a major problem for all organizations today. Email is especially vulnerable because it is typically unauthenticated and insecure. Consequently, design of an Exchange Server implementation should include consideration for antivirus options.

Spam, unsolicited email, has become another major headache for most organizations. In response to this, Exchange Server 2013 has some built-in antispam functionality that enables email messages to contain a spam rating. This helps determine which emails are legitimate, and can be used by third-party antispam products as well.

Microsoft's anti-malware, antispam, and antivirus engine, previously known as Forefront Protection for Exchange, has now been included natively in Exchange Server, and can be turned on or off as needed.

Monitoring Exchange Server

Email services are required in many organizations. The expectations of uptime and reliability are increasing, and end users are beginning to expect email to be as available as phone service. Therefore, the ability to monitor Exchange Server events, alerts, and performance data is optimal.

Exchange Server 2013 is an organism with multiple components, each busy processing tasks, writing to event logs, and running optimization routines. You can monitor Exchange Server using one of several methods, the most optimal being System Center Operations Manager (SCOM) 2012. SCOM 2012 is essentially a monitoring, alerting, and reporting product that gathers event information and performance data and generates reports about Microsoft servers. An Exchange Server–specific management pack for SCOM contains hundreds of prepackaged counters and events for Exchange Server 2013. Use of the management pack is ideal in midsize and larger environments to proactively monitor Exchange Server.

Although close monitoring of multiple Exchange servers is best supported through the use of SCOM, this might not be the most ideal approach for smaller organizations because SCOM is geared toward medium and large organizations. Exchange Server monitoring for small organizations can be accomplished through old-fashioned approaches, such as manual reviews of event log information, performance counters using perfmon, and simple Simple Network Management Protocol (SNMP) utilities to monitor uptime.

Integrating Client Access into Exchange Server 2013 Design

Although the Exchange server is a powerful systems component, it is only half the equation for an email platform. The client systems compose the other half, and are a necessary ingredient that should be carefully determined in advance.

Outlining Client Access Methods

Great effort has been put into optimizing and streamlining the client access approaches available in Exchange Server 2013. Not only have traditional approaches such as the Outlook client been enhanced, but support for nontraditional access with POP3 and IMAP clients is also available. The following options exist for client access with Exchange Server 2013:

- **Outlook MAPI**—Traditional MAPI access remains but is available only over Outlook Anywhere (see its description later in this list), which enables Outlook clients to communicate through any CAS server, not just a specific client access array. Outlook versions that support access to Exchange Server 2013 servers are limited to the 2007, 2010, and 2013 versions of Outlook.
- **Outlook Web App (OWA)**—The Outlook Web App (OWA) client is now nearly indistinguishable from the full Outlook client, and includes new features such as offline access support.
- **ActiveSync**—ActiveSync provides for synchronized access to email from a handheld device, such as a Pocket PC, Windows Mobile, iPhone, or other ActiveSync enabled device. It allows for real-time send and receive functionality to and from the handheld through the use of push technology.
- **Outlook Anywhere**—Outlook Anywhere (previously known as RPC over HTTP) is a method by which a full Outlook client can dynamically send and receive messages directly from an Exchange server over a Hypertext Transfer Protocol (HTTP) or Hypertext Transfer Protocol Secure (HTTPS) web connection. This allows for virtual private network (VPN)–free access to Exchange Server data, over a secured HTTPS connection.
- **Post Office Protocol 3 (POP3)**—POP3 is a legacy protocol that is supported in Exchange Server 2013. POP3 enables simple retrieval of mail data via applications that use the POP3 protocol. Mail messages, however, cannot be sent with POP3 and must use the SMTP engine in Exchange Server. By default, POP3 is not turned on and must be explicitly activated.
- **Internet Message Access Protocol (IMAP)**—Legacy Interactive Mail Access Protocol (IMAP) access to Exchange Server is also available, which can enable an Exchange

server to be accessed via IMAP applications, such as some UNIX mail clients. As with the POP3 protocol, IMAP support must be explicitly turned on.

Each organization will have individual needs that determine which client or set of clients will be supported. In general, the full Outlook client offers the richest messaging experience with Exchange Server 2013, but many of the other access mechanisms, such as Outlook Web App, are also valid. The important design consideration is identifying what will be supported, and then enabling support for that client or protocol. Any methods that will not be supported should be disabled or left turned off for security reasons.

Summary

Exchange Server 2013 offers a broad range of functionality and improvements to messaging and is well suited for organizations of any size. With proper thought into the major design topics, a robust and reliable Exchange Server email solution can be put into place that will perfectly complement the needs of organizations of any size.

In short, Exchange Server easily scales up to support thousands of users on multiple servers, and it also scales down very well. Single Exchange server implementations can easily support hundreds of users, even those that are scattered in various locations. This flexibility helps establish Exchange Server as the premier messaging solution for organizations of any size.

Best Practices

The following are best practices from this chapter:

- Try to create an AD DS design that is as simple as possible. Expand the directory tree with multiple subdomains and forests at a later date only if absolutely necessary.
- Even if the organization has high bandwidth between sites, create a site to better control replication and traffic between sites.
- Highly consider the use of DAGs that enable a mailbox to exist in up to 16 locations at one time. Consider a design approach that focuses on a DAG as a primary redundancy mechanism.
- Minimize the number of servers needed by consolidating services into as few systems as possible; however, after systems have been consolidated, take the leftover spare systems and create redundancy between systems.

CHAPTER 4

Understanding Network Services and Active Directory Domain Controller Placement for Exchange Server 2013

IN THIS CHAPTER

- Domain Name System and Its Role in Exchange Server 2013
- Outlining the Types of DNS Servers
- Examining DNS Components
- Using DNS to Route SMTP Mail in Exchange Server 2013
- Understanding DNS Requirements for Exchange Server 2013
- Configuring DNS to Support Exchange Servers
- Troubleshooting DNS Problems
- Global Catalog and Domain Controller Placement
- Examining the Role of Domain Controllers in AD
- Defining the Global Catalog
- Exploring Microsoft Exchange Active Directory Topology Service
- Understanding AD Functionality Modes and Their Relationship to Exchange Groups

With Microsoft Exchange relying on Active Directory and domain name system (DNS) to function, it is important for an organization to make sure that critical networking services are configured and operating properly and that domain controllers have been deployed and configured to adequately support the environment. Exchange Server 2013 has removed its reliance on NetBIOS and Windows Internet Naming Service (WINS) for its networking services and is now very dependent upon the successful operation of Active Directory and DNS. This chapter covers best practices for the design, implementation, and validation that Windows networking services and Active Directory are working properly in an Exchange Server 2013 environment.

Domain Name System and Its Role in Exchange Server 2013

For computer systems to communicate with each other, whether you are talking about a local area network (LAN), a wide area network (WAN), or the Internet, they must have the ability to identify one another using some type of name resolution. Several strategies have been developed over the years, but the most reliable one to date (and the current industry standard) is the use of a DNS.

Accurate name resolution is critical in a mail environment as well. For a message to reach its destination, it might pass through several systems that need to know where it came from and where it is going.

Even Lightweight Directory Access Protocol (LDAP) queries for local mailbox users require the DNS client to be properly configured and functioning on your Exchange Server 2013 servers.

This first half of this chapter details how DNS interacts with Exchange Server 2013 and offers troubleshooting techniques and best practices to ensure the system functions properly. The second half of this chapter covers the proper placement and optimized configuration of Active Directory services for the successful operation of Exchange Server 2013.

Domain Name System Defined

The Internet, as well as most home and business networks, rely on Internet Protocol (IP) addresses to allow computers to connect to one another. If we had to remember the IP addresses of every website, server, workstation, and printer that we connect to on a daily basis, it would be very difficult to accomplish anything!

The domain name system, commonly abbreviated as DNS, is a hierarchical, distributed database used to resolve, or translate, domain and host names to IP addresses. Using DNS, users, computers, and applications that query DNS can specify remote systems by fully qualified domain names (FQDNs).

DNS is the primary method for name resolution for the Microsoft Windows Server platforms. DNS is also a requirement for deploying Active Directory (AD), though Active Directory is not a requirement for deploying DNS. That being said, in a Microsoft Windows environment, integrating DNS and Active Directory enables DNS servers to take advantage of the security, performance, and fault-tolerance capabilities designed into Active Directory.

Using DNS

DNS is composed of two components: clients and servers. Servers store information about specific components.

When a DNS client needs to contact a host system, it first attempts to do so by using local resources. The client first checks its local cache, which is created by saving the results of previous queries. Items in the local cache remain until one of three things occurs:

- The Time to Live (TTL) period, which is set on each item, expires.
- The client runs the `ipconfig /flushdns` command.
- The DNS client is shut down.

Next, the client attempts to resolve the query using the local hosts file, which, on Windows systems, is located in the `%systemroot%\system32\drivers\etc` directory. This file is used to manually map host names to IP addresses, and remains in place even if the system is rebooted.

Finally, if the client is unable to resolve the query locally, it forwards the request to the first DNS server in the list in the network configuration that responds for resolution. The DNS server attempts to resolve the client's query as detailed next:

- If the query result is found in any of the zones for which the DNS server is authoritative, the server responds to the host with an authoritative answer.
- If the result is in the zone entries of the DNS server, the server checks its own local cache for the information.

If the DNS server is unable to resolve the query, it forwards the request to other DNS servers, sending what is known as a recursive query. The server forwards to other servers that are listed as "forwarders," or to one of a set of servers configured in the DNS server's "Root Hints" file.

The DNS query is forwarded through communications channels on the Internet until it reaches a DNS server that is listed as being authoritative for the zone listed in the query. That DNS server then sends back a reply—either an "affirmative," with the IP address requested, or a "negative" stating that the host in question could not be resolved.

Understanding Who Needs DNS

Not all situations require the use of DNS. There are other name resolution mechanisms that exist besides DNS, some of which come standard with the operating system (OS) that companies deploy. Although not all scenarios have the requirement of a complex name resolution structure, DNS makes life easier by managing name servers in a domain sometimes with little overhead.

In the past, an organization with a standalone, noninterconnected network could get away with using only host files or WINS to provide NetBIOS-to-IP address name translation. Some very small environments could also use broadcast protocols such as NetBEUI to provide name resolution. In modern networks, however, DNS becomes a necessity, especially in Active Directory environments.

Outlining the Types of DNS Servers

DNS is an integral and necessary part of any Windows Active Directory implementation. In addition, it has evolved to be the primary naming service for UNIX operating systems and the Internet. Because of Microsoft's decision to make Windows 2000 Server, Windows Server 2003, and Windows Server 2012 Internet-compatible, DNS has replaced WINS as the default name resolution technology. Microsoft followed Internet Engineering Task Force (IETF) standards and made its DNS server compatible with other DNS implementations.

Examining UNIX BIND DNS

Many organizations have significant investment in UNIX DNS implementations. Microsoft Exchange heavily relies on Active Directory, and Active Directory heavily relies on DNS. Microsoft Active Directory can coexist and use third-party DNS implementations as long as they support active updates and Service (SRV) records. In some cases, organizations choose not to migrate away from the already implemented UNIX DNS environment; instead, they coexist with Microsoft DNS. Companies using UNIX DNS for Microsoft AD clients should consider the following:

- The UNIX DNS installation should be at least 8.1.2.
- For incremental zone transfers, the UNIX DNS implementation should be at least 8.2.1.

Examining DNS Compatibility Between DNS Platforms

In theory, DNS clients should be able to query any DNS server. Active Directory, however, has some unique requirements. Clients that authenticate to Active Directory look specifically for server resources, which means that the DNS server has to support SRV records. In Active Directory, DNS clients can dynamically update the DNS server with their IP address using Dynamic DNS. It is important to note that Dynamic DNS is not supported by all DNS implementations.

NOTE

In a mixed DNS environment, Microsoft specifically recommends using Microsoft DNS server as the primary DNS server for clients, with other DNS servers set up as forwarders or secondary zone servers. This is because Microsoft clients natively support dynamic registration and lookups against Microsoft DNS.

Examining DNS Components

As previously mentioned, name servers, or DNS servers, are systems that store information about the domain namespace. Name servers can have either the entire domain namespace or just a portion of the namespace. When a name server only has a part of the domain namespace, the portion of the namespace is called a zone.

DNS Zones

There is a subtle difference between zones and domains. All top-level domains, and many domains at the second and lower levels, are broken into zones—smaller, more manageable units by delegation. A zone is the primary delegation mechanism in DNS over which a particular server can resolve requests. Any server that hosts a zone is said to be authoritative for that zone, with the exception of stub zones, defined later in the chapter.

A name server can have authority over more than one zone. Different portions of the DNS namespace can be divided into zones, each of which can be hosted on a DNS server or group of servers.

Forward Lookup Zones

A forward lookup zone is created to do forward lookups on the DNS database, resolving names to IP addresses and resource information.

Reverse Lookup Zones

A reverse lookup zone performs the opposite operation as the forward lookup zone. IP addresses are matched up with a common name in a reverse lookup zone. This is similar to knowing the phone number but not knowing the name associated with it. Reverse lookup zones must be manually created, and do not exist in every implementation. Reverse lookup zones are primarily populated with Pointer (PTR) records, which serve to point the reverse lookup query to the appropriate name.

TIP

It is good practice for the Simple Mail Transfer Protocol (SMTP) mail server to have a record in the Internet-facing reverse lookup DNS zone. Spam control sites check for the existence of this record. It is possible to have outbound mail rejected as spam if the site does not have a PTR record for the Mail Exchange (MX) entry in the DNS reverse lookup zone.

Active Directory–Integrated Zones

A Windows Server 2008 or Windows 2012 DNS server can store zone information in two distinct formats: Active Directory–integrated or standard text file. An Active Directory–integrated zone is an available option when the DNS server is installed on an Active Directory domain controller. When a DNS zone is installed as an Active Directory zone, the DNS information is automatically updated on other server AD domain controllers with DNS by using Active Directory's multimaster update techniques. Zone information stored in the Active Directory allows DNS zone transfers to be part of the Active Directory replication process secured by Kerberos authentication.

Primary Zones

In traditional (non–Active Directory–integrated) DNS, a single server serves as the master DNS server for a zone, and all changes made to that particular zone are done on that particular server. A single DNS server can host multiple zones, and can be primary for one and secondary for another. If a zone is primary, however, all requested changes for that particular zone must be done on the server that holds the master copy of the zone. As illustrated in Figure 4.1, `companyabc.com` is set up on `DC1` as an Active Directory–integrated primary zone. However, `DC1` also holds a secondary zone copy of the `amaris.org` zone.

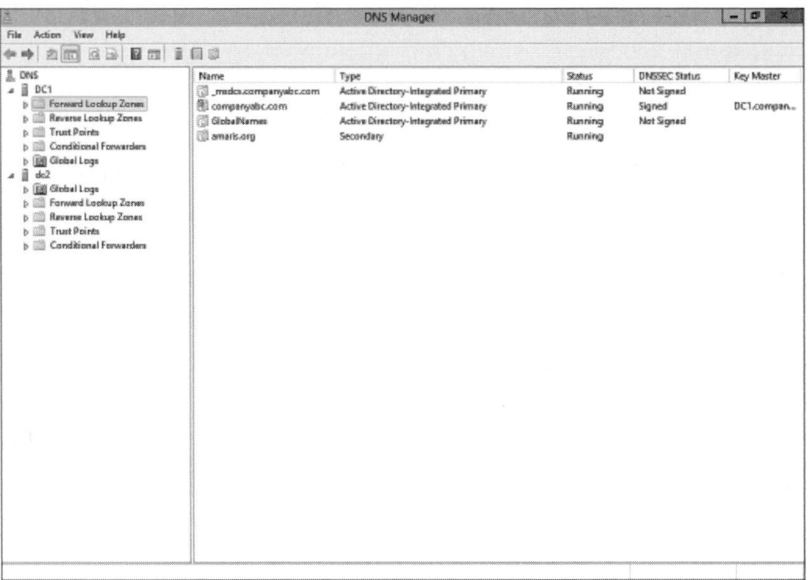

FIGURE 4.1 DNS primary and secondary zones.

Creating a new primary zone manually is a fairly straightforward process. The following procedure outlines the creation of a standard zone for the `companyabc.com` DNS namespace:

1. Open the DNS Manager.
2. Navigate to DNS, <Servername>, Forward Lookup Zones.
3. Right-click Forward Lookup Zones, and choose New Zone.
4. Click Next on the Welcome screen.
5. Select Primary Zone from the list of zone types available. Also, determine if the zone will be stored in Active Directory. If not, uncheck the Store the Zone in Active Directory check box. Click Next to continue.
6. If the zone is Active Directory–integrated, then the replication scope needs to be selected. The replication can be to all DNS servers in the forest, all DNS servers in the domain, or just to the domain controllers in the domain for Windows 2000 Server compatibility.
7. Type the name of the primary zone to be created, and click Next.
8. If creating a primary zone, enter the zone filename or accept the default.
9. Determine whether dynamic updates will be allowed in this zone. By default, Allow Only Secure Dynamic Updates is selected if the zone is Active Directory–integrated, or Do Not Allow Dynamic Updates if a primary zone. Click Next to continue.
10. Click Finish on the Summary page to create the zone.

Secondary Zones

A secondary zone is established to provide redundancy and load balancing for the primary zone. Secondary zones are not necessary if the zone has been set up as the Active Directory–integrated zone because the zone will be replicated to all domain controllers in the domain. With secondary zones, each copy of the DNS zone database is read-only; however, because all record keeping is done on the primary zone copy. A single DNS server can contain several zones that are primary and several that are secondary. The zone creation process is similar to the one outlined in the preceding section on primary zones, but with the difference being that the zone is transferred from an existing primary server.

Stub Zones (Delegated Zones)

A stub zone is a zone that contains no information about the members in a domain but simply serves to forward queries to a list of designated name servers for different domains. A stub zone contains only Name server (NS), Start of Authority (SOA), and glue records. Glue records are A records that work in conjunction with a particular NS record to resolve the IP address of a particular name server. A server that hosts a stub zone for a namespace is not authoritative for that zone.

A stub zone effectively serves as a placeholder for a zone that is authoritative on another server. It allows a server to forward queries that are made to a specific zone to the list of name servers in that zone.

DNS Queries

The primary function of DNS is to provide name resolution for requesting clients, so the query mechanism is one of the most important elements in the system. Two types of queries are commonly made to a DNS database: recursive and iterative.

Recursive Queries

Recursive queries are most often performed by resolvers, or clients that need to have a specific name resolved by a DNS server. Recursive queries are also accomplished by a DNS server if forwarders are configured to be used on a particular name server. A recursive query asks whether a particular record can be resolved by a particular name server. The response to a recursive query is either negative or positive.

Iterative Queries

Iterative queries ask a DNS server to either resolve the query or make a best-guess referral to a DNS server that might contain more accurate information about where the query can be resolved. Another iterative query is then performed to the referred server and so on until a result, positive or negative, is obtained.

DNS Replication or Zone Transfer

Copying the DNS database from one server to another is accomplished through a process known as a zone transfer. Zone transfers are required for any zone that has more than one name server responsible for the contents of that zone. The mechanism for zone transfer varies, however, depending on the version of DNS and whether the zone is Active Directory–integrated.

Primary-Secondary (Master-Slave) (RW-RO)

The primary name server holds the authoritative copy of the zone. For redundancy and load sharing, a secondary or slave name server should be set up. The DNS name resolution does not care if it is dealing with a primary or secondary server.

The main difference between the primary and secondary server is where the data comes from. Primary servers read it from a text file, and the secondary server loads it from another name server over the network via the zone transfer process. A slave name server is not limited to loading its data from a primary master name server; a slave server can load a zone from another slave server.

A big advantage of using a secondary name server over multiple primary name servers is that only one set of DNS databases needs to be maintained because all secondary name servers are read-only (RO) databases. All updates to the zone file have to be done at the server holding the primary zone file.

AD-Integrated Replication

One of the most significant changes from Windows Server 2000 to Windows Server 2012 is the location where the zone file is stored in Active Directory. Windows Server 2012 Active Directory–integrated zones are stored in the application partition, whereas in Windows 2000 Server the zones were part of the global catalog (GC). This change in the location of the zone file reduces cross-forest replication traffic because the application partition is unique to each domain.

DNS Resource Records

In the DNS hierarchy, objects are identified through the use of resource records (RRs). These records are used for basic lookups of users and resources within the specified domain and are unique for the domain in which they are located. Because DNS is not a flat namespace, multiple identical RRs can exist at different levels in a DNS hierarchy.

Start of Authority Records

The SOA record indicates that this name server is the best source for information within the zone. An SOA record is required for each zone. In a non-Active Directory–integrated zone, the server referenced by the SOA record maintains and updates the zone file.

The SOA record also contains other useful information, such as the latest serial number for the zone file, the email address of the responsible person for the zone, and the TTL.

Host Records

A host (A) record is the most common form of DNS records; its data is an Internet address in a dotted decimal form (for example, `10.32.1.132`). There should be only one A record for each address of a host.

Name Server Records

NS records indicate which servers are available for name resolution for that zone. All DNS servers are listed as NS records within a particular zone. When slave servers are configured for the zone, they will have an NS record as well.

Mail Exchange Records

An MX record specifies a mail forwarder or delivery server for SMTP servers. MX records are the cornerstone of a successful Internet mail routing strategy.

One of the advantages of a DNS over hosts files is its support for advanced mail routing. Hosts files allowed only attempts to deliver mail to the host's IP address. If that failed, they could either defer the delivery of the message and try again later or bounce the message back to the sender. DNS offers a solution to this problem, by allowing the setup of backup mail server records.

The MX record defines the email domain, that is, the part to the right of the @ symbol in the email address. In Figure 4.2, `microsoft.com` has a single mail server (mail.messaging.microsoft.com), with the priority of `10`. Note that the single DNS host name resolves to two different IP addresses, which will be issued in a round-robin fashion for load balancing and fault tolerance.

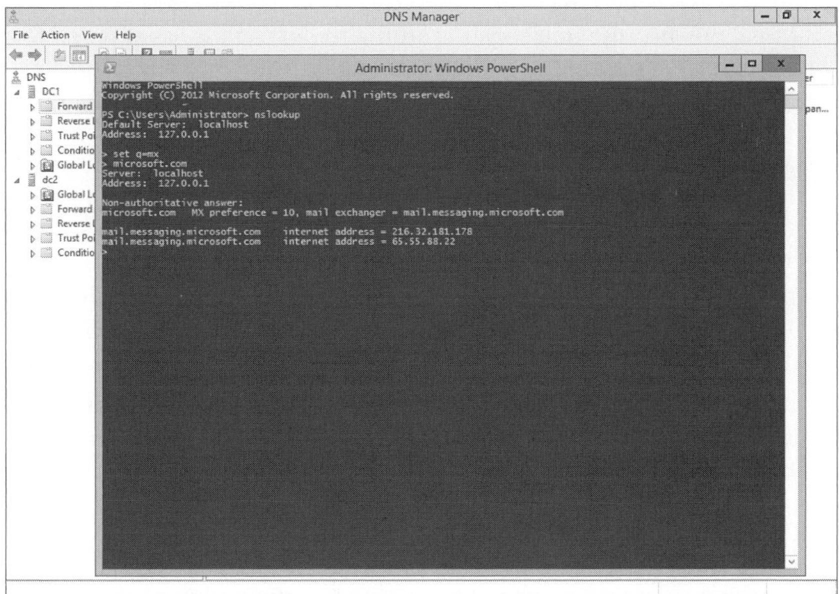

FIGURE 4.2 `Microsoft.com` mail server entry.

The preference value associated with an MX record determines the order in which a mailer uses a record. The preference value of an MX record is important only in relation to the other servers for the same domain. Mail servers attempt to use the MX record with the lower number first; if that server is not available, they try to contact the server with a higher number, and so on.

MX record preferences can also be used for load sharing. When several mail hosts have the same preference number associated with them, a sender can choose which mail server to contact first.

Mail routing based on preference numbers sounds simple enough, but there are major caveats that mail administrators have to understand. When troubleshooting mail routing problems, administrators use the following concepts to pinpoint the problem.

Mail routing algorithms based on preference numbers can create routing loops in some situations. The logic in mail servers helps circumvent this problem:

```
Companyabc.com  IN    MX   10    m1.companyabc.com
Companyabc.com  IN    MX   20    m2.companyabc.com
Companyabc.com  IN    MX   30    m3.companyabc.com
```

Using this example, if a message is sent from a client to `Bob@companyabc.com` from an email address outside of `companyabc.com`, the sending mail server looks up the receiving mail server for `companyabc.com` based on the MX records set up for that domain. If the first mail server with the lowest priority is down (`m1.companyabc.com`), the mail server attempts to contact the second server (`m2.companyabc.com`). `m2` tries to forward the message to `m1.companyabc.com` because that server is on the top of the list based on preferences. When `m2` notices that `m1` is down, it tries to contact the second server on the list, (itself), creating a routing loop. If `m2` tries to send the message to `m3`, `m3` tries to contact `m1`, then `m2`, and then itself, creating a routing loop. To prevent these loops from happening, mail servers discard certain addresses from the list before they decide where to send a message. A mailer sorts the available mail host based on preference number first, and then checks the canonical name of the domain name on which it's running. If the local host appears as a mail exchange, the mailer discards that MX record and all MX records with the same or higher preference value. In this example, `m2` does not try to send mail to `m1` and `m3` for final delivery.

The second common mistake administrators have to look out for with an MX record is the alias name. Most mailers do not check for alias names; they check for canonical names. Unless an administrator uses canonical names for MX records, there is no guarantee that the mailer will find itself, which could result in a mail loop.

Hosts listed as mail exchangers must have A records listed in the zone so that mailers can find address records for each MX record and attempt mail delivery.

Another common mistake when configuring mail hosts is the configuration of the hosted domain local to the server. Internet service providers (ISPs) and organizations commonly host mail for several domains on the same mail server. As mergers and acquisitions happen, this situation becomes more common. The following MX record illustrates that the mail server for `companyabc.com` is really the server `mail.companyisp.com`:

```
companyabc.com IN MX 10 mail.companyisp.com
```

Unless `mail.companyisp.com` is set up to recognize `companyabc.com` as a local domain, it tries to relay the message to itself, creating a routing loop and resulting in the following error message:

```
554 MX list for companyabc.com points back to mail.companyisp.com
```

In this situation, if `mail.companyisp.com` was configured not to relay messages to unknown domains, it would refuse delivery of the mail.

Service (SRV) Records

SRV records are RRs that indicate which resources perform a particular service. Domain controllers in Active Directory are referenced by SRV records that define specific services, such as the global catalog, LDAP, and Kerberos. SRV records are relatively new additions to DNS and did not exist in the original implementation of the standard. Each SRV record contains information about a particular functionality that a resource provides. For example, an LDAP server can add an SRV record indicating that it can handle LDAP requests for a particular zone. SRV records can be very useful for Active Directory because domain controllers can advertise that they can handle GC requests.

NOTE

Because SRV records are a relatively new addition to DNS, they are not supported by several down-level DNS implementations, such as UNIX BIND 4.1 and NT 4.0 DNS. It is, therefore, critical that the DNS environment that is used for Windows Server 2012 Active Directory has the capability to create SRV records. For UNIX BIND servers, version 8.1.2 or higher is required.

Alias Records

A canonical name (CNAME) record represents a server alias or allows any one of the member servers to be referred to by multiple names in DNS. The record redirects queries made to the A record for the particular host. CNAME records are useful when migrating servers, and for situations in which friendly names, such as `mail.companyabc.com`, are required to point to more complex, server-naming conventions, such as `sfoexch01.companyabc.com`.

CAUTION

Though DNS entries for MX records can be pointed to CNAME host records, doing so is not advised and is not a Microsoft recommended best practice. Increased administrative overhead and the possibility of misrouted messages can result. Microsoft recommends that mail/DNS administrators always link MX records to fully qualified principal names or domain literals. For further details, see Microsoft Knowledge Base Article #153001 at http://support.microsoft.com/kb/153001/.

Other Records

Other, less common forms of records that might exist in DNS have specific purposes, and there might be cause to create them. The following is a sample list, but it is by no means exhaustive:

- **AAAA**—Maps a standard IP address into a 128-bit IPv6 address. This type of record becomes more prevalent as IPv6 is adopted.
- **ISDN**—Maps a specific DNS name to an Integrated Services Digital Network (ISDN) telephone number.
- **KEY**—Stores a public key used for encryption for a particular domain.
- **RP**—Specifies the responsible person for a domain.
- **WKS**—Designates a particular well-known service.
- **MB**—Indicates which host contains a specific mailbox.

Multihomed DNS Servers

For multihomed DNS servers, an administrator can configure the DNS service to selectively enable and bind only to IP addresses that are specified using the DNS console. By default, however, the DNS service binds to all IP interfaces configured for the computer.

This can include the following:

- Any additional IP addresses configured for a single network connection.
- Individual IP addresses configured for each separate connection where more than one network connection is installed on the server computer.
- For multihomed DNS servers, an administrator can restrict DNS service for selected IP addresses. When this feature is used, the DNS service listens for and answers only DNS requests that are sent to the IP addresses specified on the Interface tab in the Server properties.

By default, the DNS service listens on all IP addresses and accepts all client requests sent to its default service port (UDP 53 or TCP 53 for zone transfer requests). Some DNS resolvers require that the source address of a DNS response be the same as the destination address that was used in the query. If these addresses differ, clients could reject the response. To accommodate these resolvers, you can specify the list of allowed interfaces for the DNS server. When a list is set, the DNS service binds sockets only to allowed IP addresses used on the computer.

In addition to providing support for clients that require explicit bindings to be used, specifying interfaces can be useful for other reasons:

- If an administrator does not want to use some of the IP addresses or interfaces on a multihomed server computer
- If the server computer is configured to use a large number of IP addresses and the administrator does not want the added expense of binding to all of them

When configuring additional IP addresses and enabling them for use with the Windows Server 2012 DNS server, consider the following additional system resources that are consumed at the server computer:

- DNS server performance overhead increases slightly, which can affect DNS query reception for the server.
- Although Windows Server 2012 provides the means to configure multiple IP addresses for use with any of the installed network adapters, there is no performance benefit for doing so.
- Even if the DNS server is handling multiple zones registered for Internet use, it is not necessary or required by the Internet registration process to have different IP addresses registered for each zone.
- Each additional address might only slightly increase server performance. In instances when a large overall number of IP addresses are enabled for use, server performance can be degraded noticeably.
- In general, when adding network adapter hardware to the server computer, assign only a single primary IP address for each network connection.
- Whenever possible, remove nonessential IP addresses from existing server TCP/IP configurations.

Using DNS to Route SMTP Mail in Exchange Server 2013

The primary protocol for sending email on the Internet today is known as Simple Mail Transfer Protocol, or SMTP. SMTP has been used for quite some time in UNIX and Linux environments, and has been incorporated into Active Directory as an alternative transport mechanism for site traffic.

Domains that want to participate in electronic mail exchange need to set up MX record(s) for their published zone. This advertises the system that will handle mail for the particular domain, so that SMTP mail will find the way to its destination.

Understanding SMTP Mail Routing

After the World Wide Web, email is arguably the second most widely used TCP/IP and Internet application today. SMTP defines a set of rules for addressing, sending, and receiving mail between systems. As a result of a user mail request, the SMTP sender establishes a two-way connection with the SMTP receiver. The SMTP receiver can be either the ultimate destination or an intermediate (mail gateway). The SMTP sender generates commands that are replied to by the receiver. All this communication takes place over TCP port 25. When the connection is established, a series of commands and replies are exchanged between the client and server. This connection is similar to a phone conversation, and the commands and responses are equivalent to verbal communication.

NOTE

In various implementations, there is a possibility of exchanging mail between the TCP/IP SMTP mailing system and the locally used mailing systems. These applications are called mail gateways or mail bridges. Sending mail through a mail gateway may alter the end-to-end delivery specification because SMTP guarantees delivery only to the mail gateway host, not to the real destination host, which is located beyond the TCP/IP network. When a mail gateway is used, the SMTP end-to-end transmission is host-to-gateway, gateway-to-host, or gateway-to-gateway; the behavior beyond the gateway is not defined by SMTP.

Examining Client DNS Use for Exchange

Before users can access their mailboxes on an Exchange server, they must be authenticated. Authentication requires a DNS lookup to locate a domain controller on which the users' accounts can be authenticated.

Clients normally cannot deliver messages directly to destination mail hosts. They typically use a mail server to relay messages to destinations. Using SMTP, clients connect to a mail server, which first verifies that the client is allowed to relay through this server, and then accepts the message destined for other domains.

A client uses DNS to resolve the name of a mail server. For example, when configuring an Outlook mail client to connect to an Exchange server, only the short name and not the FQDN is used to connect to the server. The short name is resolved by DNS to the FQDN of the Exchange server to which the client is connected.

Understanding DNS Requirements for Exchange Server 2013

In Active Directory, all client logons and lookups are directed to local domain controllers and GC servers through references to the SRV records in DNS. Each configuration has its DNS and resource requirements. Exchange relies on other servers for client authentication and uses DNS to find those servers. In an Active Directory domain controller configuration, on the other hand, the Exchange server also participates in the authentication process for Active Directory.

Using DNS in Exchange Server 2013

As has been stated, Active Directory and DNS access are vital to an Exchange implementation. It is critical that the host records for all Exchange Server 2013 servers be properly registered and configured in the DNS server for the Active Directory forest. Clients, as well as other servers, will use DNS to locate and communicate with Exchange Server 2013 servers.

Any computer acting in one of the Exchange Server 2013 organizational server roles must be a domain member and registered in DNS. The three server roles are as follows:

- Edge Transport
- Client Access server
- Mailbox server

All server roles, with the exception of the Edge Transport, can be deployed on a single server.

Configuring Edge Transport Server DNS Settings

For the Edge Transport server(s), which reside in the perimeter network, to communicate with the Hub Transport servers in your Exchange environment, they must be able to locate each other using host name resolution. This is accomplished by creating host records in a forward lookup zone on the internal DNS server that each server is configured to query, or by editing the local hosts file for each server.

Before installing the Edge Transport server role, you have to configure a DNS suffix for the server name. After you have installed the Edge Transport server role, the server name cannot be changed.

To complete this task, you must log on to the Edge Transport server as a user who is a member of the local Administrators group.

To use Windows Control Panel to configure the DNS suffix, complete the following steps:

1. Open Windows Control Panel.
2. Double-click on System to open the System page.
3. Click Advanced System Settings to open the System Properties dialog box.
4. Click the Computer Name tab.
5. Click Change.
6. On the Computer Name Changes page, click More.
7. In the Primary DNS Suffix of This Computer field, type a DNS domain name and suffix for the Edge Transport server.

DNS and SMTP RFC Standards

In 1984, the first DNS architecture was designed. The result was released as RFC 882 and 883. These were superseded by RFC 1034 (Domain Names—concepts and facilities) and 1035 (Domain Names—implementation and specification), the current specifications of the DNS. RFCs 1034 and 1035 have been improved by many other RFCs, which describe fixes for potential DNS security problems, implementation problems, best practices, and performance improvements to the current standard.

RFCs 2821 and 2822 define SMTP, which replaced the earlier versions of RFCs 821 and 822.

SMTP Mail Security, Virus Checking, and Proxies

Spamming and security issues are daily concerns for email administrators. As the Internet grows, so too does the amount of spam that mail servers have to confront. Unwanted messages not only can take up a lot of space on mail servers, but can also carry dangerous payloads or viruses. Administrators have to maintain a multilayered defense against spam and viruses.

There are several security areas that have to be addressed:

- Gateway security to control access to the mail server delivering messages to/from the Internet
- Mail database security where messages are stored
- Client mail security where messages are opened and processed

Gateway security is a primary concern for administrators because a misconfigured gateway can become a gateway used by spammers to relay messages. Unauthenticated message relay is the mechanism spammers rely on to deliver their messages. When a server is used for unauthenticated message relay, it not only puts a huge load on server resources, but also might get the server placed on a spam list. Companies relying on spam lists to control their incoming mail traffic refuse mail delivered from servers listed in the database; therefore, controlling who can relay messages through the mail relay gateway is a major concern.

Application-level firewalls such as Microsoft ForeFront Threat Management Gateway (TMG) allow mail proxying on behalf of the internal mail server. Essentially, mail hosts trying to connect to the local mail server have to talk to the proxy gateway, which is responsible for relaying those messages to the internal server. Going one step further, these proxy gateways can also perform additional functions to check the message they are relaying to the internal host or to control the payload passed along to the internal server.

This configuration is also helpful in stopping dangerous viruses from being spread through email. For example, dangerous scripts could potentially be attached to email, which could execute as soon as the user opens the mail. A safe configuration allows only permitted attachment types to pass through. Even those attachments have to pass virus checking before they are passed to an internal mail server.

The following process describes how one server contacts another server to send email messages that include virus checking:

1. The sender contacts its SMTP gateway for message delivery.
2. The SMTP gateway looks up the MX record for the recipient domain, then looks up the A record, and establishes communication with the host at the IP address specified in the A record. The application proxy acting as the SMTP server for the recipient's domain receives the message. Before the recipient gateway establishes communication with the sender gateway, it can check whether the sender SMTP

gateway is listed on any known spam lists. If the server is not located on any spam lists, communication can resume and the message can be accepted by the proxy server.

3. The application proxy forwards the message for virus checking.
4. After virus checking, the mail is routed back to the application proxy.
5. Mail is delivered to the internal SMTP gateway.
6. The recipient picks up the mail message.

NOTE

Application proxy and virus or spam checking might be done within the same host. In that case, steps 2–5 are done in one step without having to transfer a message to a separate host.

Third-party products can be used for virus checking not only at the gateway level, but also directly on an Exchange email database. Database-level scans can be scheduled to run at night when the load is lower on the server; real-time scans can perform virus checking in real time before any message is written to the database.

The final checkpoint for any multilayered virus protection is on the workstation. The file system and the email system can be protected by the same antivirus product. Messages can be scanned before a user is able to open the message or before a message is sent.

Protecting email communications and message integrity puts a large load on administrators. Threats are best dealt with using a multilayered approach from the client to the server to the gateway. When each step along the way is protected against malicious attacks, the global result is a secure, well-balanced email system.

The Edge Transport Server's Role in Antivirus and Antispam Protection

In Exchange Server 2007, the introduction of the Edge Transport server role was brought about by the increased need to protect organizations from unwanted message traffic. The Edge Transport server is designed to provide improved antivirus and antispam protection for the Exchange environment. This server role also applies policies to messages in transport between organizations. The Edge Transport server role is deployed outside the Active Directory forest in the perimeter network and can be deployed as a smart host and SMTP relay server for an existing Exchange Server 2013 organization.

Actually, you can add an Edge Transport server to any existing Exchange environment without making any other organizational changes or upgrading the internal Exchange servers. There are no preparation steps needed in Active Directory to install the Edge Transport server.

For additional protection, Microsoft Forefront for Exchange Server 2010 can be used on the Edge Transport 2010 role to provide a more robust anti-malware defense.

SMTP Server Scalability and Load Balancing

In a larger environment, administrators might set up more than one SMTP server for inbound and/or outbound mail processing. Windows Server 2012 and Exchange Server 2013 provide a very flexible platform to scale and balance the load of SMTP mail services. DNS and Network Load Balancing (NLB) are key components for these tasks.

Administrators should not forget about hardware failover and scalability. Multinetwork interface cards are highly recommended. Two network cards can be teamed together for higher throughput, can be used in failover configuration, or can be load-balanced by using one network card for front-end communication and another for back-end services, such as backup.

Network design can also incorporate fault tolerance by creating redundant network routes and by using technologies that can group devices together for the purpose of load balancing and delivery failover. Load balancing is the process where requests can be spread across multiple devices to keep individual service load at an acceptable level.

Using NLB, Exchange Server SMTP processes can be handed off to a group of servers for processing, or incoming traffic can be handled by a group of servers before it gets routed to an Exchange server. The following example outlines a possible configuration for using NLB in conjunction with Exchange.

DNS, in this example, has been set up to point to the name of the NLB cluster IP address. Externally, the DNS MX record points to a single mail relay gateway for `companyabc.com`. Exchange Server uses smart host configuration to send all SMTP messages to the NLB cluster. The NLB cluster is configured in balanced mode where the servers share equal load. Only port 25 traffic is allowed on the cluster servers. This configuration would offload SMTP mail processing from the Exchange servers because all they have to do is to pass the message along to the cluster for delivery. They do not need to contact any outside SMTP gateway to transfer the message. This configuration allows scalability because when the load increases, administrators can add more SMTP gateways to the cluster. This setup also addresses load balancing because the NLB cluster is smart enough to notice whether one of the cluster nodes has failed or is down for maintenance. An additional ramification of this configuration is that message tracking will not work beyond the Exchange servers.

NOTE

Administrators should not forget about the ramifications of antivirus and spam checking software with NLB. These packages in Gateway mode can also be used as the SMTP gateway for an organization. In an NLB clustered mode, an organization would need to purchase three sets of licenses to cover each NLB node.

A less used but possible configuration for SMTP mail load balancing uses DNS to distribute the load between multiple SMTP servers. This configuration, known as DNS round-robin, does not provide as robust a message routing environment as the NLB solution.

Configuring DNS to Support Exchange Servers

Because DNS is already required and integrated with Active Directory before Exchange Server is installed, most companies already have a robust DNS environment in place. Exchange by itself accesses DNS servers to find resources on the local network, such as global catalog servers and domain controllers. It also uses DNS to search for MX records of other domains.

External DNS Servers for the Internet

The external DNS server for Exchange (or any other mail system) is responsible for giving out the correct MX and A records for the domain for which it is authoritative. Administrators should take security precautions regarding who can change these records—and how. Intentionally or accidentally changing these records can result in undelivered mail.

Most companies let their ISP host the external DNS entries for their domain. ISPs provide internal administrators with methods of managing DNS entries for their domain. In some cases, it has to be done over the phone, but normally a secure web interface is provided for management. Although this setup is convenient and ISPs usually take care of load balancing and redundancy, some companies opt to host their own zone records for the Internet. In this case, companies have to host their own DNS server in-house with the ISP responsible only for forwarding all requests to their DNS server. When hosting an external DNS server, in-house administrators have to think about security issues and DNS configuration issues.

Internal DNS Servers for Outbound Mail Routing

Exchange SMTP gateways are responsible for delivering mail to external hosts. As with any name process involving resolving names to IP addresses, DNS plays a major part in successful mail delivery.

Exchange can route mail to outbound destinations two ways. One is by using smarthosts to off-load all processing of messages destined to other domains. As seen in the previous section, an NLB cluster can be used to route Internet mail to its final destination.

The second way is the default, with Exchange Server 2013 taking care of delivering messages to other domains. In this scenario, Exchange queries DNS servers for other domains' MX records and A records for address resolution.

Troubleshooting DNS Problems

Troubleshooting is part of everyday life for administrators. DNS is no exception to this rule. Therefore, understanding how to use the following tools to troubleshoot DNS not only helps avoid mistakes when configuring DNS-related services, but also provides administrators with a useful toolbox to resolve issues.

Using Event Viewer to Troubleshoot

The first place to look for help when something is not working, or appears to not be working, is the system logs. With Windows Server 2012, the DNS logs are conveniently located directly in the DNS MMC console. Parsing this set of logs can help the administrator troubleshooting DNS replication issues, query problems, and other issues.

For more advanced event log diagnosis, administrators can turn on Debug Logging on a per-server basis. Debugging should be turned on only for troubleshooting because log files can fill up fast. To enable Debug Logging, follow these steps:

1. Open the DNS Manager.
2. Right-click on the server name, and choose Properties.
3. Select the Debug Logging tab.
4. Check the Log Packets for Debugging check box.
5. Configure any additional settings as required, and click OK.

Turn off these settings after the troubleshooting is complete.

Troubleshooting Using the `ipconfig` Utility

The `ipconfig` utility is used not only for basic TCP/IP troubleshooting, but can also be used to directly resolve DNS issues. These functions can be invoked from the command prompt with the correct flag, detailed as follows:

- **ipconfig /displaydns**—This command displays all locally cached DNS entries. This is also known as the DNS resolver cache.
- **ipconfig /flushdns**—This switch can be used to save administrators from a lot of headaches when troubleshooting DNS problems. This command flushes the local DNS cache. The default cache time for positive replies is 1 day; for negative replies, it is 15 minutes.
- **ipconfig /registerdns**—This flag informs the client to automatically reregister itself in DNS, if the particular zone supports dynamic zone updates.

NOTE

Client-side DNS caching is configurable in the Registry via the following key:

```
\\HKLM\System\CurrentControlSet\Services\Dnscache\Parameters
MaxCacheEnrtyTtlLimit = 1 (default = 86400)
NegativeCacheTime = 0 (default = 300)
```

These DWORD values need to be created. The first entry overwrites the TTL number in the cached address to 1 second, essentially disabling the local cache. The second entry changes the negative cache from 15 minutes to 0, essentially disabling the negative cache facility.

Monitoring Exchange Using Performance Monitor

Performance Monitor is a built-in, often overlooked utility that enables a great deal of insight into issues in a network. Many critical DNS counters can be monitored relating to queries, zone transfers, memory use, and other important factors.

Using `nslookup` for DNS Exchange Lookup

In both Windows and UNIX environments, `nslookup` is a command-line administrative tool for testing and troubleshooting DNS servers. Simple query structure can provide powerful results for troubleshooting. A simple query contacts the default DNS server for the system and looks up the inputted name.

To test a lookup for `www.companyabc.com`, type

```
nslookup www.companyabc.com
```

at the command prompt. `nslookup` can also be used to look up other DNS resource types—for example, an MX or SOA record for a company. To look up an MX record for a company type, use the following steps, as illustrated in Figure 4.3:

```
Administrator: Command Prompt - nslookup
Microsoft Windows [Version 6.1.7601]
Copyright (c) 2009 Microsoft Corporation.  All rights reserved.

C:\Users\administrator>nslookup
Default Server:  dc1.companyabc.com
Address:  10.1.1.10

> set query=mx
> cco.com
Server:  dc1.companyabc.com
Address:  10.1.1.10

Non-authoritative answer:
cco.com MX preference = 100, mail exchanger = judge.cco.com
cco.com MX preference = 10, mail exchanger = exedge.cco.com

judge.cco.com   internet address = 12.222.165.253
exedge.cco.com  internet address = 12.222.165.157
> _
```

FIGURE 4.3 `nslookup` MX query.

1. Open a command prompt instance.
2. Type **`nslookup`** and press Enter.
3. Type **`set query=mx`** (or simply **`set q=mx`**), and press Enter.
4. Type **`cco.com`** and press Enter.

An MX record output not only shows all the MX records that are used for that domain, their preference number, and the IP address they are associated with, but it also shows the name server for the domain.

By default, `nslookup` queries the local DNS server the system is set up to query. Another powerful feature of `nslookup` is that it can switch between servers to query. This feature enables administrators to verify that all servers answer with the same record as expected. For example, if an organization is moving from one ISP to another, it might use this technique because the IP addresses for its servers might change during the move. The DNS change takes an administrator only a few minutes to do, but replication of the changes through the Internet might take 24 to 72 hours. During this time, some servers might still use the old IP address for the mail server. To verify that the DNS records are replicated to other DNS servers, an administrator can query several DNS servers for the answer through the following technique:

1. Open a command prompt instance.
2. Type `nslookup` and press Enter.
3. Type `server <server IP address>` for the DNS server you want to query.
4. Type `set query=mx` (or simply `set q=mx`), and press Enter.
5. Type `cco.com` and press Enter.

Repeat from step 3 for other DNS servers.

`nslookup` can also help find out the version of BIND used on a remote UNIX DNS server. An administrator might find it useful to determine which version of BIND each server is running for troubleshooting purposes. To determine this, the following steps must be performed:

1. From the command line, type `nslookup`, and then press Enter.
2. Type `server <server IP address>` for the IP address of the DNS server queried.
3. Type `set class=chaos` and then press Enter.
4. Type `set type=txt` and then press Enter.
5. Type `version.bind` and then press Enter.

If the administrator of the BIND DNS server has configured the server to accept this query, the BIND version that the server is running is returned. As previously mentioned, the BIND version must be 8.1.2 or later to support SRV records.

Troubleshooting with DNSLINT

DNSLINT is a Microsoft Windows utility that helps administrators diagnose common DNS name resolution issues. The utility is not installed by default on Windows servers and has to be downloaded from Microsoft. Microsoft Knowledge Base Article #321045 found at http://support.microsoft.com/kb/321045 contains the link to download this utility.

When this command-line utility runs, it generates a Hypertext Markup Language (HTML) file in the directory it runs from. It can help administrators with Active Directory troubleshooting and also with mail-related name resolution and verification. Running `DNSLINT /d <domain_name> /c` tests DNS information as known on authoritative DNS servers for the domain being tested; it also checks SMTP, Post Office Protocol version 3 (POP3), and Internet Message Access Protocol (IMAP) connectivity on the server. For the complete options for this utility, run `DNSLINT /?`.

Using `dnscmd` for Advanced DNS Troubleshooting

The `dnscmd` utility is essentially a command-line version of the MMC DNS console. Installed natively with Windows Server 2012, this utility enables administrators to create zones, modify zone records, and perform other vital administrative functions. To install the support tools, run the support tools setup from the Windows Server 2003 CD (located in the `\support\tools` directory). You can view the full functionality of this utility by typing `DNSCMD /?` at the command line.

Global Catalog and Domain Controller Placement

When deploying Exchange Server 2013 in your environment, Active Directory is a critical component. Exchange Server 2013 uses the Active Directory directory service to store and share directory information with Microsoft Windows.

If you have already deployed Active Directory into your environment, it is important that you have a solid understanding of your existing implementation and how Exchange will fit into your structure. If you have not deployed AD, you need to design the environment with your Exchange environment in mind.

In addition, you need to evaluate your organization's administrative model, as the marriage of Exchange Server 2013 and AD allows you to administer Exchange along with the operating system.

When integrating Exchange Server 2013 and Active Directory, the placement of domain controllers and global catalog servers is paramount; without proper placement of these key items, your Exchange environment will not be able to perform optimally.

The remainder of this chapter discusses these items and offers troubleshooting techniques for directory access problems. In addition, best-practice recommendations are offered for the placement of domain controllers and global catalog servers.

Understanding Active Directory Structure

AD is a standards-based LDAP directory service developed by Microsoft that stores information about network resources and makes it accessible to users and applications, such as Exchange Server 2013. Directory services are vital in any network infrastructure because they provide a way to name, locate, manage, and secure information about the resources contained.

The Active Directory directory service provides single-logon capability and a central repository for the information for your entire organization. User and computer management are greatly simplified, and network resources are easier than ever to access.

In addition, Active Directory is heavily utilized by Exchange, and stores all of your Exchange attributes: email addresses, mailbox locations, home servers, and a variety of other information.

Exploring AD Domains

An Active Directory domain is the main logical boundary of Active Directory. In a standalone sense, an AD domain looks very much like a Windows NT domain. Users and computers are all stored and managed from within the boundaries of the domain. However, several major changes have been made to the structure of the domain and how it relates to other domains within the Active Directory structure.

Domains in Active Directory serve as a security boundary for objects and contain their own security policies. For example, different domains can contain different password policies for users. Keep in mind that domains are a logical organization of objects and can easily span multiple physical locations. Consequently, it is no longer necessary to set up multiple domains for different remote offices or sites because replication concerns can be addressed with the proper use of Active Directory sites, which are described in greater detail later in this chapter.

Exploring AD Trees

An Active Directory tree is composed of multiple domains connected by two-way transitive trusts. Each domain in an Active Directory tree shares a common schema and global catalog. The transitive trust relationship between domains is automatic, which is a change from the domain structure of NT 4.0, wherein all trusts had to be manually set up. The transitive trust relationship means that because the `asia` domain trusts the root `companyabc` domain, and the `europe` domain trusts the `companyabc` domain, the `asia` domain also trusts the `europe` domain. The trusts flow through the domain structure.

Exploring AD Forests

Forests are a group of interconnected domain trees. Implicit trusts connect the roots of each tree into a common forest.

The overlying characteristics that tie together all domains and domain trees into a common forest are the existence of a common schema and a common global catalog. However, domains and domain trees in a forest do not need to share a common namespace. For example, the domains `microsoft.com` and `msnbc.com` could theoretically be part of the same forest, but maintain their own separate namespaces (for obvious reasons).

NOTE

Each separate instance of Exchange Server 2013 requires a completely separate AD forest. In other words, AD cannot support more than one Exchange organization in a single forest. This is an important factor to bear in mind when examining AD integration concepts.

The domain is not an ironclad security boundary between domains in a forest because a domain administrator who knows what he is doing can grant himself rights on other domains in the forest. This security hole has diminished the justification for creating multidomain forests. Delegated organizational units can actually provide better compartmentalized security.

Understanding AD Replication with Exchange Server 2013

An understanding of the relationship between Exchange and Active Directory is not complete without an understanding of the replication engine within AD itself. This is especially true because any changes made to the structure of Exchange must be replicated across the AD infrastructure.

Active Directory replaced the concept of Primary Domain Controllers (PDCs) and Backup Domain Controllers (BDCs) with the concept of multiple domain controllers that each contains a master read/write copy of domain information. Changes that are made on any domain controller within the environment are replicated to all other domain controllers in what is known as multimaster replication.

Active Directory differs from most directory service implementations in that the replication of directory information is accomplished independently from the actual logical directory design. The concept of Active Directory sites is completely independent from the logical structure of Active Directory forests, trees, and domains. In fact, a single site in Active Directory can actually host domain controllers from different domains or different trees within the same forest. This enables the creation of a replication topology based on your WAN structure, and your directory topology can mirror your organizational structure.

From an Exchange point of view, the most important concept to keep in mind is the delay that replication causes between when a change is made in Exchange and when that change is replicated throughout the entire AD structure. The reason for these types of discrepancies lies in the fact that not all AD changes are replicated immediately. This concept is known as replication latency. Because the overhead required in immediately replicating change information to all domain controllers is large, the default schedule for replication is not as often as you might want. To immediately replicate changes made to Exchange or any AD changes, use the following procedure:

1. Open the Active Directory Sites and Services tool.
2. Drill down to Sites, sitename, Servers, servername, NTDS Settings. The server name chosen should be the server you are connected to, and from which the desired change should be replicated.
3. Right-click each connection object and choose Replicate Now, as illustrated in Figure 4.4.

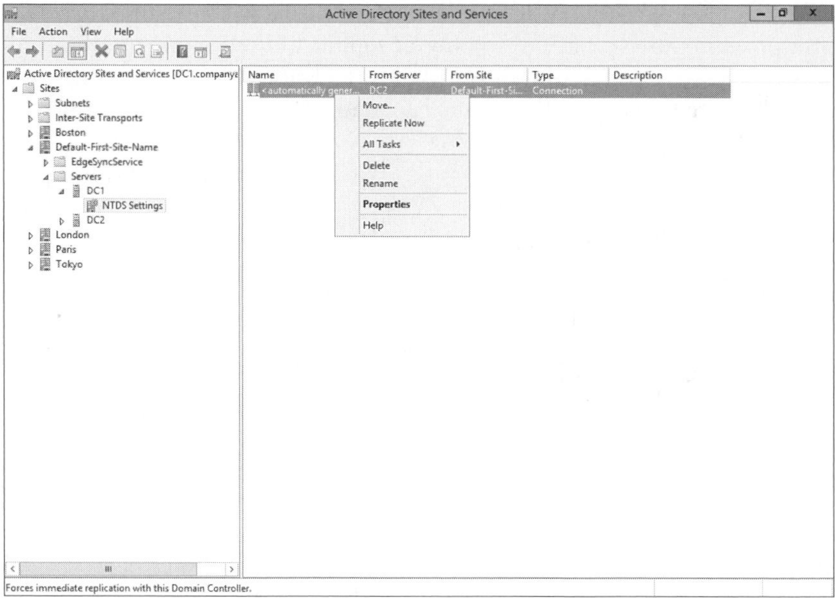

FIGURE 4.4 Forcing AD replication.

Examining the Role of Domain Controllers in AD

Even before the existence of Active Directory, Exchange has relied on domain controllers to authenticate user accounts. With the advent of Active Directory, this has not changed. Exchange still relies on domain controllers to provide all authentication services. To provide optimal logon authentication response times, the proper placement of domain controllers is crucial.

Examining Domain Controller Authentication in Active Directory

To understand how Exchange manages security, an analysis of Active Directory authentication is required. This information aids in troubleshooting the environment, as well as in gaining a better understanding of Exchange Server 2013 as a whole.

Each object in Exchange, including all mailboxes, can have security directly applied for the purposes of limiting and controlling access to those resources. For example, a particular administrator might be granted access to control a certain set of Exchange servers, and users can be granted access to mailboxes. What makes Exchange particularly useful is that security rights can be assigned not only at the object level, but also at the attribute level. This enables granular administration, by allowing tasks such as a Telecom group being able to modify only the phone number field of a user, for example.

When a user logs on to a domain, the domain controller performs a lookup to ensure a match between the username and password. If a match is made, the client is then authenticated and given the rights to gain access to resources.

Because the domain controllers provide users with the permission to access the resources, it is important to provide local access to domain controllers for all Exchange servers. If a local domain controller became unavailable, for example, users would be unable to authenticate to their mailboxes in Exchange, effectively locking them out.

Determining Domain Controller Placement with Exchange Server 2013

Because Exchange relies on the security authentication performed by Active Directory domain controllers, the placement of these domain controllers becomes critical to the overall performance of your messaging environment. If a domain controller cannot be reached in a reasonable amount of time, access to messages and network resources is delayed.

At a minimum, at least one Active Directory domain controller must be within close proximity to any Exchange server to ensure speedy authentication for local users and mailboxes. Additional Active Directory domain controllers can be implemented to provide increased performance in heavily utilized sites or to provide redundancy in the event of a domain controller failure.

For organizations with a high concentration of Exchange servers and clients, a significant demand for directory services can negatively impact all aspects of network performance. The presence of other applications and services that require authentication, directory services, or directory replication can cause your Exchange performance to suffer. A current best practice to avoid these pitfalls is to create a dedicated Active Directory site, with dedicated domain controllers and global catalog servers. By segmenting a Service Delivery Location (SDL) into multiple Active Directory sites, you can separate the directory traffic generated by Exchange servers and Microsoft Outlook clients from other directory service traffic.

In addition, you can deploy more than one Active Directory domain controller in close proximity to users for user authentication. This enables the distribution of domain controller tasks and builds redundancy into the design. Because each Microsoft Windows Server 2012 domain controller is a multimaster, in the event of a failure of one domain controller, others are able to continue to function and allow uninterrupted authentication.

Defining the Global Catalog

The global catalog is an index of the Active Directory database that stores a full replica of all objects in the directory for its host domain, and a partial replica of all objects contained in the directory of every domain in the forest. In other words, a global catalog contains a replica of every object in Active Directory, but with a limited number of each object's attributes.

Global catalog servers, often referred to as GCs, are Active Directory domain controllers that house a copy of the global catalog. A global catalog server performs two key roles:

- Provides universal group membership information to a domain controller when a logon process is initiated

- Enables finding directory information regardless of which domain in the forest contains the data

Access to a global catalog server is necessary for a user to authenticate to the domain. If a global catalog is not available when a user initiates a network logon process, the user is only able to log on to the local computer, and cannot access network resources.

With such an important role to play, it is a common practice to locate at least one global catalog server in each physical location, as it is referenced often by clients and by applications such as Exchange.

Understanding the Relationship Between Exchange Server 2013 and the AD Global Catalog

In the past, an Exchange server could continue to operate by itself with few dependencies on other system components. Because all components of the mail system were locally confined to the same server, downtime was an all-or-nothing prospect. The segregation of the directory into Active Directory has changed the playing field somewhat. In many cases, down-level clients no longer operate independently in the event of a global catalog server failure. Keep this in mind, especially when designing and deploying a domain controller and global catalog infrastructure.

NOTE

Because Outlook clients and Exchange can behave erratically if the global catalog they have been using goes down, it is important to scrutinize which systems receive a copy of the global catalog. In other words, it is not wise to set up a GC/DC on a workstation or substandard hardware, simply to off-load some work from the production domain controllers. If that server fails, the effect on the clients is the same as if their Exchange server failed.

Understanding Global Catalog Structure

The global catalog is an oft-misunderstood concept with Active Directory. In addition, design mistakes with global catalog placement can potentially cripple a network, so a full understanding of what the global catalog is and how it works is warranted.

As mentioned earlier, Active Directory was developed as a standards-based LDAP implementation, and the AD structure acts as an X.500 tree. Queries against the Active Directory must, therefore, have some method of traversing the directory tree to find objects. This means that queries that are sent to a domain controller in a subdomain need to be referred to other domain controllers in other domains in the forest. In large forests, this can significantly increase the time it takes to perform queries.

In Active Directory, the global catalog serves as a mechanism for improving query response time. The global catalog contains a partial set of all objects (users, computers, and other AD objects) in the entire AD forest. The most commonly searched attributes are stored and replicated in the global catalog (that is, first name, username, email address). By storing a read-only copy of objects from other domains locally, full tree searches across the entire forest are accomplished significantly faster. So, in a large forest, a server that holds a copy of the global catalog contains information replicated from all domains in the forest.

Using Best Practices for Global Catalog Placement

All users accessing Exchange resources should have fast access to a global catalog server. At least one global catalog server must be installed on each domain that contains an Exchange server; however, to achieve the best performance in larger organizations, additional global catalog servers should definitely be considered.

As a starting point, per site, there should be a 4:1 ratio of Exchange processor cores to global catalog server 32-bit processor cores. So, if you have four Exchange servers, each with four processors, you should have four processors running your global catalog servers. For global catalog servers with 64-bit processor cores, there should be an 8:1 ratio of Exchange processor cores to global catalog server 64-bit processor cores when there is sufficient memory in to cache the entire Active Directory database (DIT file). Of course, Exchange Server 2013 processor cores are always 64-bit.

Bear in mind, however, that increased global catalog server usage, very large Active Directory implementations, or the use of extremely large distribution lists might necessitate more global catalog servers.

Promoting a Domain Controller to a Global Catalog

Although any domain controller can easily be promoted to a global catalog server, the promotion can have a significant impact on network operations and performance while the topology is updated and the copy of the catalog is passed to the server.

The procedure to promote a domain controller to a global catalog server is as follows:

1. Open the Active Directory Sites and Services tool.
2. In the console tree, double-click Sites, double-click the name of the site, and then double-click Servers.
3. Double-click the target domain controller.
4. In the details pane, right-click NTDS Settings, and then click Properties.
5. On the General tab, click to select the Global Catalog check box, as shown in Figure 4.5.
6. Click OK to finalize the operation.

FIGURE 4.5 Making a domain controller a global catalog server.

Verifying Global Catalog Creation

When a domain controller receives the orders to become a global catalog server, there is a period of time when the GC information replicates to that domain controller. Depending on the size of the global catalog, this could take a significant period of time. To determine when a domain controller has received the full subset of information, use the `repadmin` utility in Windows Server 2012. The `repadmin` utility indicates which portions of the AD database are replicated to different domain controllers in a forest and how recently they have been updated.

`Repadmin` enables an administrator to determine the replication status of each domain naming context in the forest. The command is `repadmin /showrepl <server name>`. Because a global catalog server should have a copy of each domain naming context in the forest, determine the replication status of the new GC with `repadmin`. For example, the fully replicated global catalog server in Figure 4.6 contains the default naming contexts, such as Schema, Configuration, and DnsZones, in addition to domain naming contexts for all domains. In this example, the `companyabc.com` domain has been replicated successfully to the DC2 domain controller.

Global Catalog and Outlook in Exchange Server 2013

In Exchange Server 2003 and Exchange Server 2007, Outlook clients would make direct calls to global catalog servers. This made them susceptible to failure or demotion of domain controllers with global catalogs. In many cases, the failure of a global catalog server would require the restart of all Outlook clients that were using it for lookups.

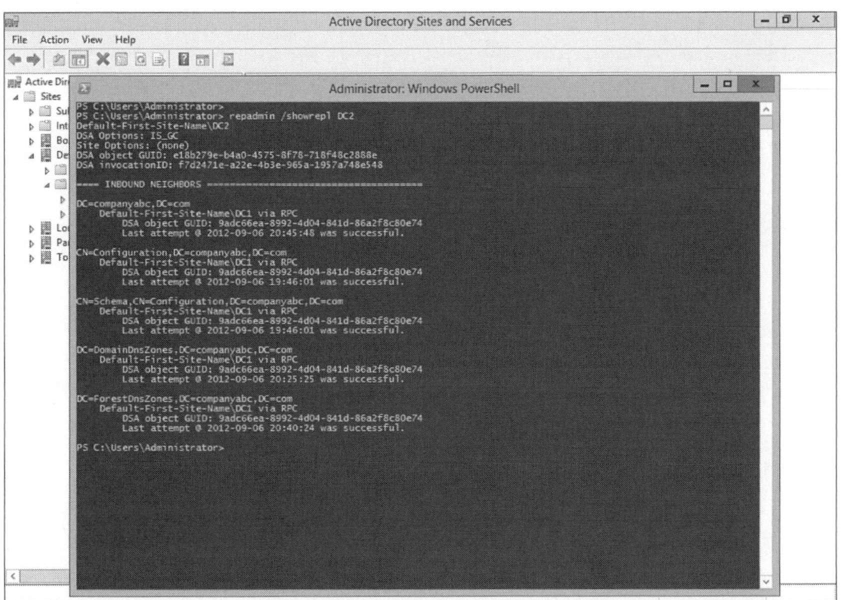

FIGURE 4.6 `Repadmin` GC creation verification.

In Exchange Server 2013, the Outlook client access to the directory has been changed. Outlook clients communicate with the RPC Client Access Service on a Client Access server. This service proxies the global catalog lookups for the Outlook clients rather than having them query the global catalog directly. This reduces the direct dependency of Outlook clients on the global catalog, allowing for better scalability and faster recovery if a global catalog failure occurs.

Understanding Universal Group Caching for AD Sites

Windows Server 2012 Active Directory enables the creation of AD sites that cache universal group membership. Any time a user uses a universal group, the membership of that group is cached on the local domain controller and is used when the next request comes for that group's membership. This also lessens the replication traffic that would occur if a global catalog was placed in remote sites.

One of the main sources of replication traffic is group membership queries. In Windows 2000 Server Active Directory, every time clients logged on, their universal group membership was queried, requiring a global catalog to be contacted. This significantly increased logon and query time for clients that did not have local global catalog servers. Consequently, many organizations had stipulated that every site, no matter the size, have a local global catalog server to ensure quick authentication and directory lookups. The downside of this was that replication across the directory was increased because every site would receive a copy of every item in the entire AD, even though only a small portion of those items would be referenced by an average site.

Universal group caching solved this problem because only those groups that are commonly referenced by a site are stored locally, and requests for group replication are limited to the items in the cache. This helps limit replication and keep domain logons speedy.

The universal group caching capability is established on a per-site basis, through the following technique:

1. On the domain controller, open the Active Directory Sites and Services tool.
2. Navigate to Sites, sitename.
3. Right-click NTDS Site Settings, and choose Properties.
4. Check the Enable Universal Group Membership Caching check box, as shown in Figure 4.7.
5. Click OK to save the changes.

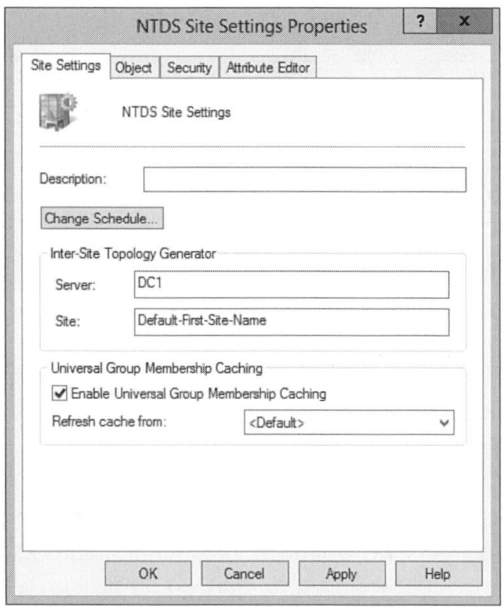

FIGURE 4.7 Universal group caching.

NOTE

Universal group (UG) caching is useful for minimizing remote-site replication traffic and optimizing user logons. Universal group caching does not replace the need for local global catalog servers in sites with Exchange servers, however, because it does not replace the use of the GC port (3268), which is required by Exchange. UG caching can still be used in remote sites without Exchange servers that use the site consolidation strategies of Exchange Server previously mentioned.

Exploring Microsoft Exchange Active Directory Topology Service

The relationship that Exchange Server 2013 has with Active Directory is complex and often misunderstood. Because the directory is no longer local, a special service was written for Exchange to access and process information in AD. Understanding how this service works is critical for understanding how Exchange interacts with AD.

Understanding Microsoft Exchange Active Directory Topology Service

Microsoft Exchange Active Directory Topology service is one of the most critical services for Exchange Server 2013. The Microsoft Exchange Active Directory Topology service is used to discover current Active Directory topology and direct Exchange to various AD components. The service dynamically produces a list of published AD domain controllers and global catalog servers and directs Exchange resources to the appropriate AD resources.

In addition to simple referrals from Exchange to AD, Microsoft Exchange Active Directory Topology service intelligently detects global catalog and domain controller failures, and directs Exchange to failover systems dynamically, reducing the potential for downtime caused by a failed global catalog server. Microsoft Exchange Active Directory Topology service also caches LDAP queries made from Exchange to AD, speeding up query response time in the process.

On start of the Exchange Server 2013 services, the Microsoft Exchange Active Directory Topology service queries Active Directory and determines which domain controllers and global catalogs are available. It also chooses one as the configuration domain controller. A 2081 event in the application event log is generated. Microsoft Exchange Active Directory Topology service then polls the Active Directory every 15 minutes to identify changes to site structure, domain controller placement, or other structural changes to Active Directory. A 2080 event in the application event log is generated each time. By making effective use of LDAP searches and global catalog port queries, domain controller and global catalog server suitability is determined. Through this mechanism, a single point of contact for the Active Directory is chosen and maintained, which is known as the configuration domain controller.

Determining the Microsoft Exchange Active Directory Topology Service Roles

Microsoft Exchange Active Directory Topology service lists identified domain controllers on the Exchange server properties page and identifies servers belonging to either of two groups:

- **Domain Controller Servers Being Used by Exchange**—Domain controllers that have been identified by Microsoft Exchange Active Directory Topology service to be fully operational are shown here.
- **Global Catalog Servers Being Used by Exchange**—Global catalog servers are shown here.

4

A third role was visible on the properties page in Exchange Server 2003; however, it is not in the same location in Exchange Server 2013. The third role is the following:

- **Configuration domain controller**—A single AD domain controller is chosen as the configuration domain controller to reduce the problems associated with replication latency among AD domain controllers. In other words, if multiple domain controllers were chosen to act as the configuration domain controller, changes Exchange makes to the directory could conflict with each other. The configuration domain controller role is transferred to other local domain controllers in a site every 8 hours.

To determine the default configuration domain controller, view the Event Viewer application log and search for Event ID 2081. The results of the `Microsoft Exchange Active Directory Topology service` query are listed here as well, as shown in Figure 4.8.

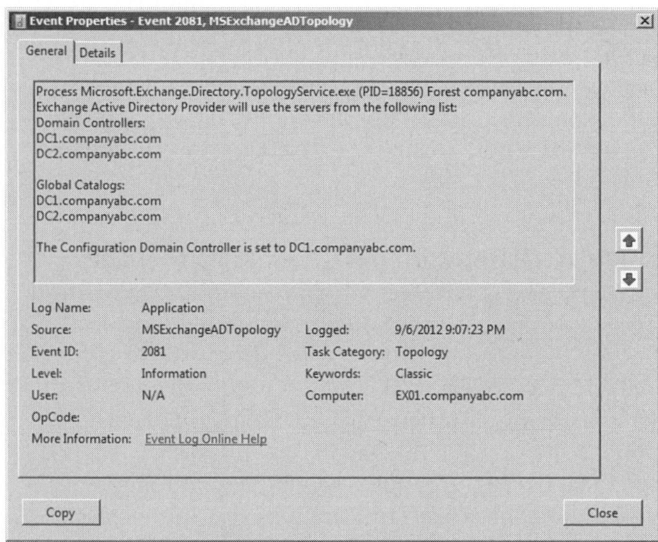

FIGURE 4.8 Identifying the default configuration domain controller.

In addition, the default configuration domain controller can be changed to one of your choice by performing the following steps:

1. Open the Exchange Management Shell.
2. Enter the command **Get-ADServerSettings | fl**. This shows the current default preferred domain controller (DefaultPreferredDomainController).
3. To change the preferred domain controller, enter the command **Set-ADServerSettings -PreferredServer <server name>**, as shown in Figure 4.9, to manually select the configuration domain controller.

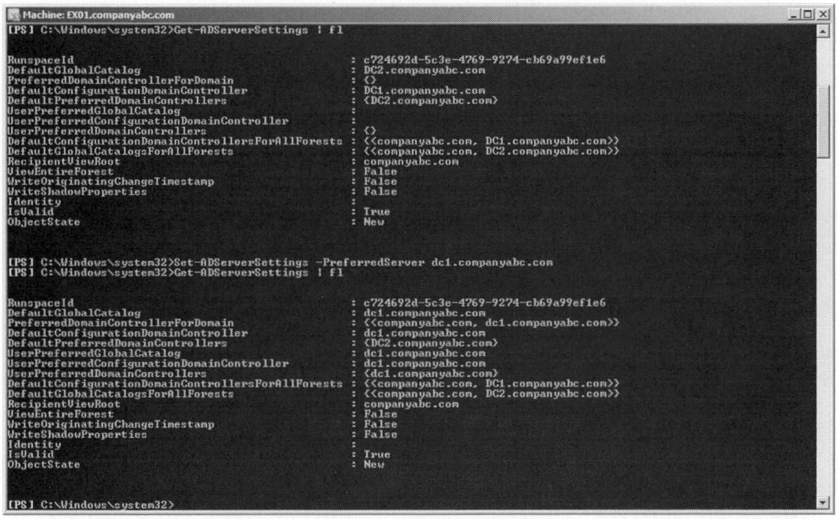

```
Machine: EX01.companyabc.com
[PS] C:\Windows\system32>Get-ADServerSettings | fl

RunspaceId                                         : c724692d-5c3e-4769-9274-cb69a99ef1e6
DefaultGlobalCatalog                               : DC2.companyabc.com
PreferredDomainControllerForDomain                 : {}
DefaultConfigurationDomainController               : DC1.companyabc.com
DefaultPreferredDomainControllers                  : {DC2.companyabc.com}
UserPreferredGlobalCatalog                         :
UserPreferredConfigurationDomainController         :
UserPreferredDomainControllers                     : {}
DefaultConfigurationDomainControllersForAllForests : {<companyabc.com, DC1.companyabc.com>}
DefaultGlobalCatalogsForAllForests                 : {<companyabc.com, DC2.companyabc.com>}
RecipientViewRoot                                  : companyabc.com
ViewEntireForest                                   : False
WriteOriginatingChangeTimestamp                    : False
WriteShadowProperties                              : False
Identity                                           :
IsValid                                            : True
ObjectState                                        : New


[PS] C:\Windows\system32>Set-ADServerSettings -PreferredServer dc1.companyabc.com
[PS] C:\Windows\system32>Get-ADServerSettings | fl

RunspaceId                                         : c724692d-5c3e-4769-9274-cb69a99ef1e6
DefaultGlobalCatalog                               : dc1.companyabc.com
PreferredDomainControllerForDomain                 : {<companyabc.com, dc1.companyabc.com>}
DefaultConfigurationDomainController               : dc1.companyabc.com
DefaultPreferredDomainControllers                  : {DC2.companyabc.com}
UserPreferredGlobalCatalog                         : dc1.companyabc.com
UserPreferredConfigurationDomainController         : dc1.companyabc.com
UserPreferredDomainControllers                     : {dc1.companyabc.com}
DefaultConfigurationDomainControllersForAllForests : {<companyabc.com, DC1.companyabc.com>}
DefaultGlobalCatalogsForAllForests                 : {<companyabc.com, DC2.companyabc.com>}
RecipientViewRoot                                  : companyabc.com
ViewEntireForest                                   : False
WriteOriginatingChangeTimestamp                    : False
WriteShadowProperties                              : False
Identity                                           :
IsValid                                            : True
ObjectState                                        : New


[PS] C:\Windows\system32>
```

FIGURE 4.9 Viewing and changing domain controllers and global catalog servers used by Exchange.

4

Understanding AD Functionality Modes and Their Relationship to Exchange Groups

The most recent versions of Exchange Server, as well as Active Directory, were designed to break through the constraints that had limited previous Exchange implementations. However, realistically, it was understood that the products would have to maintain a certain level of compatibility with previous NT domains and Exchange Server 5.5 organizations. After all, not all companies have the resources to completely replace their entire network and messaging infrastructure at once. This requirement stipulated the creation of several functional modes for AD and Exchange that allow backward compatibility, while necessarily limiting some of the enhanced functionality—at least for the duration of the migration/upgrade process. Several of the limitations of the AD functional modes in particular impact Exchange Server 2013, specifically Active Directory group functionality. Consequently, a firm grasp of these concepts is warranted.

Understanding Windows Group Types

Groups in Windows Server 2012 come in two flavors: security and distribution. In addition, groups can be organized into different scopes: machine local, domain local, global, and universal. It might seem complex, but the concept, once defined, is simple.

Defining Security Groups

The type of group that most administrators are most familiar with is the security group. A security group is primarily used to apply permissions to resources, enabling multiple users to be administered more easily. For example, users in the Sales Department can be added as members to the Sales Department security group, which would then be given permission to specific resources in the environment. When a new member is added to the Sales Department, instead of modifying every resource that the department relies on, you can simply add the new member to the security group and the appropriate permissions would be inherited by the new user. This concept should be familiar to anyone who has administered down-level Windows networks, such as NT or Windows 2000 Server.

Defining Distribution Groups

The concept of distribution groups as it exists in Windows Server 2012 was first introduced in Windows 2000 Server with the deployment of Active Directory. Essentially, a distribution group is a group whose members are able to receive mail messages that are sent to the group. Any application that has the capability of using Active Directory for address book lookups can use this functionality in Windows Server 2012.

NOTE

Distribution groups can be used to create email distribution lists that cannot be used to apply security. However, if separation of security and email functionality is not required, you can make security groups mail-enabled just as with distribution groups.

Outlining Mail-Enabled Security Groups in Exchange Server 2013

With the introduction of Exchange into an Active Directory environment came a new concept: mail-enabled groups. These groups are essentially security groups that are referenced by an email address, and can be used to send SMTP messages to the members of the group. This type of functionality becomes possible only with the inclusion of Exchange 2000 Server or greater, and Exchange actually extends the forest schema to enable Exchange-related information, such as SMTP addresses, to be associated with each group.

Most organizations will find that the use of mail-enabled security groups will satisfy the majority of their group requirements. For example, a single group called Marketing, which contains all users in that department, could also be mail-enabled to allow users in Exchange to send emails to everyone in the department.

Explaining Group Scope

Groups in Active Directory work the way that previous group structures, particularly in Windows NT, have worked, but with a few modifications to their design. As mentioned earlier, group scope in Active Directory is divided into several groups:

- **Machine local groups**—Machine local groups, also known as local groups, previously existed in Windows NT 4.0 and can theoretically contain members from any trusted location. Users and groups in the local domain, as well as in other trusted domains and forests can be included in this type of group. However, local groups allow resources only on the machine they are located on to be accessed, which greatly reduces their usability.

- **Domain local groups**—Domain local groups are essentially the same as local groups in Windows NT, and are used to administer resources located only on their own domain. They can contain users and groups from any other trusted domain and are typically used to grant access to resources for groups in different domains.
- **Global groups**—Global groups are on the opposite side of domain local groups. They can contain only users in the domain in which they exist, but are used to grant access to resources in other trusted domains. These types of groups are best used to supply security membership to user accounts who share a similar function, such as the sales global group.
- **Universal groups**—Universal groups can contain users and groups from any domain in the forest, and can grant access to any resource in the forest. With this added power comes a few caveats: First, universal groups are available only in Windows 2000, 2003, 2008, or 2012 AD Native mode domains. Second, all members of each universal group are stored in the global catalog, increasing the replication load. Universal group membership replication has been noticeably streamlined and optimized in Windows Server 2012, however, because the membership of each group is incrementally replicated.

Universal groups are particularly important for Exchange environments. For example, when migrating from Exchange Server 5.5 to later versions of Exchange, the Exchange Server 5.5 distribution lists were converted into universal groups for the proper application of public folder and calendaring permissions. An AD domain that contains accounts that have security access to Exchange Server 5.5 mailboxes must be in AD Native mode before performing the migration. This is because the universal groups are made as universal security groups, which are only available in AD Native mode.

Mail-enabled groups should be universal groups for full Exchange function, especially in multiple-domain forests.

Functional Levels in Windows Server 2012 Active Directory

Active Directory was designed to be backward compatible. This helps to maintain backward compatibility with Windows NT domain controllers. Four separate functional levels exist at the domain level in Windows Server 2003 and Windows Server 2012, and five separate functional levels exist at the forest level:

- **Windows 2000 Server Native**—Installed into a Windows 2000 Server Active Directory that is running in Windows 2000 Server Native mode, Windows Server 2003 runs itself at a Windows Server 2000/2003 functional level. Only Windows 2000 Server and Windows Server 2003 domain controllers can exist in this environment.

- **Windows Server 2003**—Functionality on this level opens the environment to features such as schema deactivation, domain rename, domain controller rename, and cross-forest trusts. To get to this level, first all domain controllers must be updated to Windows Server 2003, Windows Server 2008, or Windows Server 2012. Only after this can the domains, and then the forest, be updated to Windows Server 2003 functionality.
- **Windows Server 2008**—Windows Server 2012 functionality is the eventual goal of all Windows Server 2008 Active Directory implementations. Functionality on this level opens the environment to features such as Distributed File System (DFS) replication of SYSVOL, Advanced Encryption Standard (AES) support for Kerberos, last interactive logon information, and finer-grained password policies. To get to this level, first all domain controllers must be updated to Windows Server 2008 or higher. Only after this can the domains, and then the forest, be updated to Windows Server 2008 functionality.
- **Windows Server 2008 R2**—Functionality at this level adds authentication mechanism assurance, which supports advanced identity management. Only Windows Server 2008 R2 or Windows Server 2012 domain controllers are supported.
- **Windows Server 2012**—No additional features are added at this level, but only Windows Server 2012 domain controllers are supported. This serves to ensure that older domain controllers are not joined to the forest.

NOTE

Beginning with Exchange Server 2003 Service Pack 1 (SP1), Microsoft extended the ability to perform domain rename on an Active Directory forest that was previously extended for Exchange. Before SP1, it was not possible to rename an AD domain within a forest that contained Exchange.

As previously mentioned, it is preferable to convert AD domains into at least Windows 2000 Server Native mode or Windows Server 2003 Functional mode before migrating Exchange Server 5.5 servers that use those domains. The universal group capabilities that these modes provide for make this necessary. And if possible, upgrade all domain controllers to Windows Server 2012 and raise the functional level to Windows Server 2012 Functional mode.

To change domain and forest functional levels in Active Directory to the highest level for Windows Server 2012, follow these steps:

1. Open Active Directory Domains and Trusts tool.
2. In the left scope pane, right-click your domain name, and select Raise Domain Functional Level.
3. Click on the Available Domain Functional Level option, select Windows Server 2012, and then choose Raise.

4. At the warning screen, click OK, and then click OK again to complete the task.
5. Repeat the steps for all domains in the forest.
6. Perform the same steps on the forest root, except this time click Raise Forest Functional Level, and follow the prompts.

After the domains and the forest have been upgraded, the Functional mode will indicate Windows Server 2012, as shown in Figure 4.10.

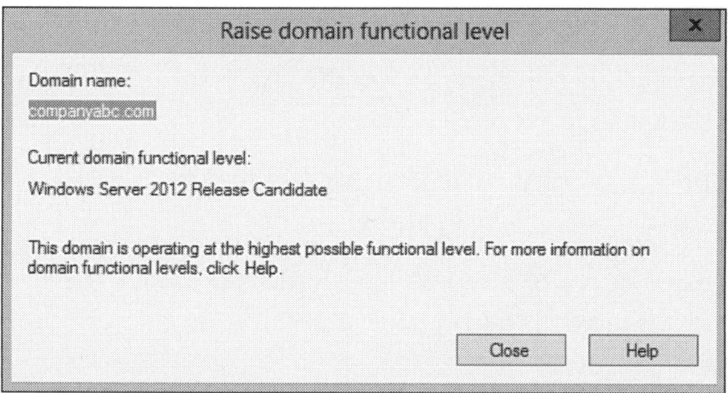

FIGURE 4.10 Windows Server 2012 forest functional level.

Summary

Exchange Server 2013 is a complicated, but extremely powerful messaging tool. With the scalability and performance enhancements comes an increased degree of interdependence with other system components, most notably the DNS and the global catalog. Access to the global catalog and AD domain controllers is critical and cannot be overlooked. A good Exchange deployment plan takes these factors into account.

Best Practices

The following are best practices from this chapter:

- Use Microsoft Windows Server 2008/2012 DNS for client AD name resolution whenever possible. If not possible, ensure that the UNIX BIND version is 8.1.2 or higher to support SRV records.
- Administrators should set up redundant name resolution servers in the event that one server fails.
- Use caching-only DNS servers to help leverage load and minimize zone transfer traffic across WAN links.
- Make any DNS implementations compliant with the standard DNS character set so that zone transfers are supported to and from non–Unicode-compliant DNS

implementations, such as UNIX BIND servers. This includes a–z, A–Z, 0–9, and the hyphen (-) character.

- Set up multiple MX records for all mail servers for redundancy, but only if a secondary server is available. ISPs usually function as a secondary mail relay gateway for the hosted domain.
- It is wise to segregate inbound and outbound SMTP traffic from direct exposure to the Internet by deploying an SMTP smarthost in the demilitarized zone (DMZ) of the firewall.
- Promote or demote global catalog servers and domain controllers during off-hours.
- Use Exchange Server 2013 site consolidation concepts to reduce the total number of deployed Exchange servers and global catalog servers.
- Place at least one GC in close network proximity to any major service (such as Exchange Server 2013) that requires use of the global catalog (3268) port.
- Deploy enough global catalog processor cores to support the deployed Exchange Server 2013 processor cores. Consider deploying 64-bit global catalog processor cores to increase the ratio.
- Ensure that the AD domain is in Windows Server 2008 Functional mode or higher before migrating to Exchange Server 2013.
- Do not use substandard hardware for global catalog servers, as a simple hardware failure can affect Outlook clients.
- Consider the use of universal group caching for domain controllers in sites without local Exchange servers.

CHAPTER 5

Integrating Certificate-Based Public Key Infrastructure (PKI) in Exchange Server 2013

IN THIS CHAPTER

- Understanding Public Key Infrastructure
- Server Certificates in Exchange Server 2013
- Installing a Windows Certification Authority Server
- Securing an Exchange Server 2013 Server
- Securing an IIS Web Server
- Implementing Secured Email Communications with Exchange Server 2013
- Using Outlook to Send and Receive Digitally Signed and Encrypted Emails

Exchange Server 2013 uses certificates to secure much of the internal and external traffic. This provides out-of-the-box secured communications for all Exchange Server 2013 transmissions, which prevents both snooping on and tampering with messages sent and received by the systems. Clients can also use certificates to sign and encrypt messages so that they are protected even in storage. Proper issuance of all these certificates and integration with a Public Key Infrastructure (PKI) is important to the security and administration of the Exchange Server 2013 environment.

This chapter compares the various certificate types that you can use with Exchange Server 2013, which server components use certificates, and how to choose the certificates to use with the components. In addition, the chapter covers how to request, install, and maintain these certificates.

This chapter also covers email encryption in which the actual email message from a sender is encrypted so that someone trying to intercept the message will not have the ability to read the message because of the encryption on the message itself.

This chapter focuses on certificate-based encryption of messages, including the creation of a certificate server and the installation of certificates within the Microsoft Outlook client software.

Understanding Public Key Infrastructure

Because Microsoft Exchange Server 2013 resides on a Microsoft Windows Server system, administrators can rely heavily on the technology of the underlying operating system in their efforts to implement a secure messaging environment.

Microsoft Windows Server 2003, 2008, 2008 R2, and 2012 allow for the use of PKI, which enables an administrator to exchange information with strong security and easy administration across both internal and external networks. PKI is an extensible infrastructure used to provide certificate-based services by combining digital certificates, registration authorities, and certificate authorities that can be used to provide authentication, authorization, nonrepudiation, confidentiality, and verification. A certificate authority (CA) is a digital signature of the certificate issuer.

PKI implementations are widespread and are becoming a critical component of modern networks. Windows Server fully supports the deployment of various PKI configurations, ranging from very simplistic to extremely complex. Entire books have been written on the subject of implementing PKI, but this chapter endeavors to give administrators a basic understanding of the subject and show how PKI can be used to help secure their Exchange Server environments.

Certificate Services in Windows Server

Windows Server (2003, 2008, 2008 R2, 2012) includes a built-in CA known as Certificate Services. Certificate Services can be used to create certificates and subsequently manage them and is responsible for ensuring their validity. Certificate Services can also be used to trust external PKIs, such as a third-party PKI, to expand services and secure communication with other organizations.

The type of CA that you install and configure depends on the purpose or purposes of the Active Directory Certificate Services (AD CS) role in Windows Server 2008, 2008 R2, and 2012 can be installed as one of the following CA types:

- **Enterprise root CA**—The enterprise root CA is the most trusted CA in an organization and, if utilized, should be installed before any other CA. All other CAs are subordinate to an enterprise root CA. Enterprise root CAs store certificates in Active Directory (AD) by default.
- **Enterprise subordinate CA**—An enterprise subordinate CA must get a CA certificate from an enterprise root CA and can then issue certificates to all users and computers in the enterprise. These types of CAs are often used for load balancing of an enterprise root CA. More important, using subordinates provides stronger security for the PKI.
- **Stand-alone root CA**—A stand-alone root CA is the root of a hierarchy that is not related to the enterprise domain information, and, therefore, certificates are not stored in AD. Multiple stand-alone CAs can be established for particular purposes.

- **Stand-alone subordinate CA**—A stand-alone subordinate CA receives its certificate from a stand-alone root CA and can then be used to distribute certificates to users and computers associated with that stand-alone CA.

A Windows Server PKI can also be either online or offline based on the level of security that is required in the organization.

TIP

An enterprise root CA is the most versatile CA in Windows Server because it integrates tightly with AD and offers more certificate services. All domain members trust the enterprise CA, and the enterprise CA can be used for autoenrollment of certificates to domain members. If you're unsure as to what CA to use, choose an enterprise root or subordinate CA for use with messaging. Most important, however, is that with any PKI there must be careful planning and design.

PKI Planning Considerations

Any PKI implementation requires thorough planning and design, as noted earlier. Possible planning and design considerations include the following:

- Multinational legal considerations, including creation and standardization of a formal Certificate Practice Statement (CPS)
- Policies and procedures for issuing, revoking, and suspending certificates
- PKI hardware identification and standardization, including employee badge integration
- Determination of CA hierarchy administration model
- Creation of a redundant CA infrastructure based on geographical location
- Policies and procedures for creation of CAs as subordinates and policy enforcers within a greater hierarchy, including qualified subordination and cross-certification
- Policies and procedures for creation of registration authorities (RAs) and their placement within the CA hierarchy
- CA trust strategies
- Policies and procedures for maintaining the CA as a 24×7×365 operation (24 hours a day, 7 days a week, 365 days a year)
- Policies and procedures for key and certificate management, including, but not limited to, key length, cryptographic algorithms, certificate lifetime, certificate renewal, storage requirements, and more
- Policies and procedures for securing the PKI

5

- Published plans for providing high availability and recoverability
- Policies and procedures for integrating the CA with Lightweight Directory Access Protocol (LDAP) and/or Active Directory
- Policies and procedures for integrating with existing applications
- Policies and procedures for security-related incidents (for example, bulk revocation of certificates)
- Policies and procedures for delegation of administrative tasks
- Standards for PKI auditing and reporting
- Policies and procedures for change control
- Standards for key length and expiration of certificates
- Policies and procedures for handling lost certificates (that is, smart card)
- Policies and procedures for safe distribution of the CA public key to end users
- Policies and procedures for enrollment (for example, autoenrollment, stations, and so forth)
- Policies and procedures for incorporating external users and companies
- Procedures for using certificate templates

As you can see from this list, implementing PKI is not to be taken lightly. Even if the organization is implementing PKI just for enhanced Exchange Server 2013 messaging functionality, the considerations should be planned and designed.

Fundamentals of Private and Public Keys

Encryption techniques can primarily be classified as either symmetrical or asymmetrical. Symmetrical encryption requires that each party in an encryption scheme hold a copy of a private key that is used to encrypt and decrypt information sent between the two parties. One shortcoming of the private key encryption method is that the private key must somehow be transmitted from one party to the other, without it being intercepted and used to decrypt the information.

Asymmetrical encryption uses a combination of two keys that are mathematically related to each other. The first key, known as the private key, is kept closely guarded and is used to encrypt the information. The second key, known as the public key, can be used to decrypt the information. The integrity of the public key is ensured through certificates. The asymmetric approach to encryption ensures that the private key does not fall into the wrong hands and only the intended recipient is able to decrypt the data.

Understanding Certificates

A certificate is essentially a digital document issued by a trusted central authority that is used by the authority to validate a user's identity. Central, trusted authorities such as

Symantec/VeriSign are widely used on the Internet to ensure that software that is being downloaded from Microsoft, for example, is actually originating from Microsoft, and is not, in fact, a virus in disguise.

Certificates can be used for multiple functions, including but not limited to the following:

- Secure email
- Web-based authentication
- IP Security (IPSec)
- Secure web-based communications
- Code signing
- Certification hierarchies

Certificates are signed using information from the subject's public key and the CA. Items such as the originator's name, email address, and others can be used.

Certificate Templates

Certificates have multiple functions, and, therefore, multiple types of certificates are available to meet the need. One certificate might be used to sign code, whereas another is used to provide support for secure email. In this one-to-one relationship, a certificate is used for a single purpose. Certificates can also have a one-to-many relationship in which one certificate is used for multiple purposes.

TIP

One of the best examples of a certificate that uses a one-to-many relationship is the user certificate. By default, a user certificate provides support for user authentication, secure email, and the Encrypting File System (EFS).

Windows Server contains a large number of certificates, each with an assigned set of settings and purposes. In essence, certificates can be categorized into six different functional areas:

- **Server authentication**—These certificates are used to authenticate servers to clients and servers to other servers. These are the type used by Exchange Server 2013 servers.
- **Client authentication**—These certificates are used to provide client authentication to servers or server-side services.
- **Secure email**—Utilizing these certificates, users can digitally sign and encrypt email messages. These are the type used by Outlook clients.

- **Encrypting File System**—These certificates are used to encrypt and decrypt files using EFS.
- **File recovery**—These certificates are used for recovering encrypted EFS files.
- **Code signing**—These certificates can sign content and applications. Code signing certificates help users and services verify the validity of code.

Manual Encrypted Communications Using Outlook

Specific to this chapter, encryption is used for email communications to allow users to send and receive secured communications. An encryption system is built in to Exchange Server that allows users within an Exchange Server environment to send email messages to other users within their Exchange Server environment in an encrypted manner. The problem with the default encryption in Exchange Server is that it does not provide encryption outside of the company's Exchange Server environment. So, most organizations do not use the built-in email encryption in Exchange Server, but rather use a more standard method of encrypted communications built on the PKI standard.

You have several methods of providing encrypted communications between users within and external to a Microsoft Exchange Server and Outlook email system. Users can each get a certificate from an organization such as Symantec/VeriSign and perform encrypted communications. Or, an organization can purchase an enterprise license of Pretty Good Privacy (PGP) that provides encryption between users and organizations also using PGP email security. In this example, the use of individual Symantec/VeriSign certificates is noted.

In this case, a user who wants to encrypt messages between himself and someone else needs to get an individual email certificate and install that certificate in his Microsoft Outlook email client software. In this example using Symantec, the user would go to http://www.symantec.com/verisign/digital-id and for approximately $25 per year, both individuals wanting to conduct secured communications can purchase a certificate. The individuals share the public portion of their certificates with the other individuals and they can now send encrypted messages back and forth.

To acquire a certificate, do the following:

1. Go to a certificate provider such as Symantec, and sign up and purchase a digital ID: http://www.symantec.com/verisign/digital-id.
2. Follow the instructions to download and install the certificate in your Outlook client.
3. Have the individual you want to communicate with do the same.

This process of purchasing, downloading, and installing a certificate needs to be done only once per year.

NOTE

If you use multiple computers, you need to install the certificate on each machine on which you run the Outlook client to be able to send and receive encrypted email messages.

After you have downloaded and installed the certificate on your computer, you need to configure Outlook to support the certificate. To do so, do the following:

1. Launch Outlook.
2. For Outlook 2007, choose Tools, Trust Center, and then click Email Security. For Outlook 2010, choose File, Options, Trust Center, Trust Center Settings, E-mail Security. For Outlook 2013, choose File, Options, Trust Center, Trust Center Settings, Email Security.
3. Click the Settings button.
4. In the Security Settings Name text box, type **`Email Encryption`**. Using the Cryptographic Format list arrow, choose S/MIME. Check the Default Security Setting for This Cryptographic Message Format and the Default Security Settings for All Cryptographic Messages check boxes.
5. Next to the Signing Certificate box, click Choose.
6. From the Select Certificate page, select the certificate that was previously installed and click OK.
7. Using the Hash Algorithm list arrow, choose SHA1. Using the Encryption Algorithm list arrow, choose 3DES.
8. Check the Send These Certificates with Signed Messages check box.
9. Click OK to apply these settings, and then click OK again.

The Outlook client is now ready to send signed and encrypted emails. Individual users, depending on how computer savvy they are, might have difficulties signing up, downloading, and installing the certificate, and then configuring Outlook to send emails. In addition, because the certificates are individual based, *each* individual user has to do this process himself every year and for every system on which he conducts email communications.

This process can be completely automated and transparent to the user with a little administrative work. As you will see in the section "Implementing Secured Email Communications with Exchange Server 2013," the issuance of certificates and the configuration of the user's Outlook client can be completed automatically using autoenrollment of certificates as well as using Group Policy Objects in Windows Server Active Directory.

Server Certificates in Exchange Server 2013

Exchange Server 2013 uses certificates extensively to protect the confidentiality and integrity of communications. Certificates facilitate the use of industry-standard Secure Sockets Layer (SSL) and Transport Layer Security (TLS) protocols to secure communications by Exchange Server in a flexible manner using Open Standards. These protocols are native to the Internet as well, allowing easy transition and transport of services over the Internet and intranet.

Components Using Certificates

Key Exchange Server 2013 server components use certificates to authenticate and to encrypt communications. Components that use certificates include the following:

- **SMTP**—The Simple Mail Transfer Protocol (SMTP) component in Exchange Server 2013 uses certificates to encrypt and authenticate SMTP traffic between Hub Transport servers and Edge Transport servers, between partner organizations, and for opportunistic TLS.
- **EdgeSync Synchronization**—Certificates encrypt the LDAP communications between the Hub Transport and Edge Transport servers.
- **Unified Messaging**—Certificates encrypt the SMTP traffic from the Unified Messaging (UM) server to the Hub Transport servers, IP gateways, and Lync servers.
- **Autodiscover**—The Hypertext Transfer Protocol Secure (HTTPS) traffic between the Client Access server (CAS) and the client are encrypted with certificates.
- **POP3/IMAP4**—The Post Office Protocol 3 (POP3) and the Internet Message Access Protocol 4 (IMAP4) protocols are encrypted and authenticated with certificates via SSL and TLS to improve the security.
- **Outlook Anywhere**—Certificates are used to secure the Outlook Anywhere Hypertext Transfer Protocol (HTTP) communications from the CAS to the client.
- **Outlook Web App**—Certificates secure the Outlook Web App HTTP communications from the CAS to the client.
- **ActiveSync**—Certificates secure the Exchange ActiveSync HTTP communications from the CAS to the client.
- **Exchange Web Services**—Certificates are used to secure the HTTPS traffic between Outlook for free/busy data, to set the out-of-office configuration, and to secure communication between Outlook 2011 for Mac and the Exchange server.
- **Offline Address Book**—Certificates secure the Web Service through which the Offline Address Book is downloaded by Outlook clients.

Many of these services are client facing, and all the services can be externally facing as well, creating potential risks to the confidentiality of the services. Certificates enable the services to be protected with advanced encryption to ensure their privacy. In general, a single certificate can be used for most, if not all, of the services.

Self-Signed Versus Public Versus Private Certificates

The difference between self-signed, public, and private certificates is simply their issuing source. If issued and signed by the owner of the certificate, they are self-signed certificates. If issued by a public CA, they are public certificates. If issued by a private CA, they are private certificates. The difference is all in the level of trust that third parties can place in the certificates.

Public certificates are the gold standard of certificates. The public CAs that issue these certificates are trusted by most operating systems and browsers, which means they trust the certificates issued by the CAs. Examples of public CAs include Symantec/VeriSign, Thawte, Digicert, and Go Daddy. Using a public certificate is usually easy, but a cost is charged by the public CA for the certificate, and that cost can be substantial depending on the issuer. Because certificates have expiration dates, this is a recurring cost every time the certificate is renewed.

Private certificates are issued by private CAs. A private CA can be created on a number of platforms, including Windows Server 2003, 2008, 2008 R2, and 2012. Certificates issued by these private CAs have no cost. However, these private CAs are not trusted by default by the operating systems and browsers, so the certificates issued by these private CAs are not trusted either. This can lead to annoying pop-up warnings or even failed applications. These can be circumvented by adding the private CA to the list of trusted CAs on the specific computers and deploying a Public Key Infrastructure (PKI), which can be a significant administrative overhead that is proportional to the number of PCs and mobile devices that use email. Root certificates can be automatically distributed via Group Policy to PCs that are domain joined, but non-domain-joined machines and mobile devices are more complicated to support.

Self-signed certificates are issued by the computer using the certificate, which does not require any additional PKI infrastructure, because the computer maintains its own certificate. This enables an application such as Exchange Server 2013 to reap the benefits of certificates on installation without having to go through the additional configuration steps to acquire a certificate from a CA. And there is no cost or infrastructure requirement. However, this is the least trusted and least secure of certificates because there is no third party, public or private, vouching for the certificate, so this method is even more difficult to administer than the private CA method.

The server components covered in the previous section all install by default in a protected mode (that is, using SSL/TLS) using self-signed certificates. These default self-signed certificates can be replaced as needed.

Choosing Certificates in Exchange Server 2013

Exchange Server 2013 can use any of the three types of X.509 certificates to encrypt a communications channel. However, how the other end of the communications channel views the certificate that is presented by Exchange Server 2013 is a major factor in which type to use. When the two endpoints, for example the Exchange Server 2013 server and a client, negotiate the security of the communications channel, the Exchange Server 2013 certificate is presented to the client. If the client does not trust the CA that issued the

Exchange Server 2013 certificate, the communications might fail or the user is prompted with a warning.

By default, Exchange Server 2013 issues self-signed certificates on installation. Self-signed certificates can be used for external communications but are not recommended on a long-term basis. Self-signed certificates are the best option for internal communications, such as for Unified Messaging or EdgeSync services.

It is recommended to use self-signed certificates for internal SMTP communications between Exchange servers.

NOTE

Self-signed certificates that are created by Exchange Server expire in one year. The internal components that rely on the default self-signed certificates continue to operate even if the self-signed certificates have expired. However, when the self-signed certificates have expired, events are logged in Event Viewer. It is a best practice to renew the self-signed certificates before they expire.

You should use internal CA or public certificates for internal communications, including the following:

- Between servers running Hub Transport services
- Between servers running the Hub Transport and Edge Transport services
- For EdgeSync communications
- For Unified Messaging communications
- For internal only Client Access server communications

Public certificates typically have a cost associated with their use but are trusted by all the communications channel endpoints like the clients. This ensures that when the Exchange Server 2013 presents a public certificate during the negotiation of the communications channel, the client accepts it without question if the client has the root certificate installed.

You should use public certificates for external client access communications, which are the following:

- POP3 and IMAP4
- Outlook Web App
- Outlook Anywhere
- Exchange ActiveSync
- Autodiscover
- SMTP

Using public certificates enables users to access services from a wide array of locations, such as home systems, Internet kiosks, and other companies' systems without any certificate issues due to the nearly ubiquitous trust of the major public CAs.

Nearly all current clients have the major certificate authorities' root certificates installed automatically. If you are considering using a certificate from a lesser-known certificate authority, you should verify that your client devices have the required root certificates installed.

Private certificates fall into an interesting area for Exchange Server 2013. Private certificates are identical to public certificates, except that the clients must be configured to trust the issuing CA. This means inserting the private CA root certificate into the client's Trusted Certificate Authority container. When this is done, the client trusts all certificates issued by the private CA just as if it were a public CA.

Using private certificates enables administrators to forego the cost of public certificates with some administrative effort. This is most effective if users access the Exchange Server 2013 services from relatively few locations in which there is a measure of administrative control, such as mobile domain members or home systems. Domain members automatically trust an enterprise CA via Active Directory, so no configuration is needed. The home users can be given instructions or scripts that configure the home systems to trust the private CA. This is not effective with locations such as Internet kiosks in which the users have no local control.

Names in Certificates

Certificates are used as a mechanism to validate something such as a computer, user, or application. For users, the "subject" name of the certificate is the user's name and his or her email address. For Exchange Server 2013 servers, the subject is the server name. In an X.509 certificate, the Subject field contains the identity in the format CN = <subject name>. For example, the Exchange Server 2013 EX1 server self-issued certificate will have CN=EX1 or CN=ex.companyabc.com in the Subject field. A user named Chris Amaris from Company ABC might have an autoenrolled certificate with CN = Chris Amaris and E = chrisa@companyabc.com to designate the email address of the subject. Note that the Subject field can contain only one CN reference.

However, multiple DNS names for a single server can be quite common; owa.companyabc.com, autodiscover.companyabc.com, smtp.companyabc.com, and imap.companyabc.com might all reference different services on an Exchange Server 2013 server supporting Hub Transport and Client Access server roles. A server might also be referenced by its NetBIOS name (for example, EX1) or by its fully qualified domain name (for example, EX1.companyabc.com). When a receiving application examines the certificate to verify the identity of the server, it might not find the name for the server in the certificate Subject field and fail authentication. These naming dichotomies cannot be represented with only the Subject name.

To address this, there are three name types of X.509 certificates:

- Single Name Certificates
- Unified Communications Certificates
- Wildcard Certificates

These certificates are the same X.509 certificates but have different fields within the certificate populated in different ways. Public CAs charge different amounts depending on how the fields are populated. And some private CAs and some public CAs won't issue certain types of certificates. Operating systems and applications might or might not support all usages of these certificates, so care must be taken in how they are deployed.

Single name certificates contain only one subject name in the Subject field and are the default certificate name type. All certificates must contain at least one name. These certificates are supported by all platforms and applications.

Unified Communications Certificates (UCCs) have one or more names in the Subject Alternative Name (SAN) field of the X.509 certificate, typically in the format DNS Name=<subject name>. When examining the certificate, the receiving application matches names in both the Subject field and in the Subject Alternative Name field. Exchange Server 2013 issues self-signed SAN certificates by default. For example, the Exchange Server 2013 EX1 server self-issued certificate is a SAN certificate and will have CN = EX1 in the Subject field and DNS Name=EX1 and DNS Name=EX1.companyabc.com in the Subject Alternative Name field. SAN certificates are supported by most modern public CAs, operating systems, and applications.

Rather than adding each subject name into the SAN field of the certificate, it is convenient to have the certificate represent all potential subject names. This simplifies configuration and avoids the need to reissue certificates if additional names are added later. Wildcard certificates use the asterisk character (*) to designate all possible subject names rather than list the names specifically. For example, rather than having a certificate with multiple individual names like ex1, ex1.companyabc.com, owa.companyabc.com, and mail.companyabc.com, the certificate can be issued with a single wildcard subject name *.companyabc.com that'll match all names for any host name the server will operate as. Wildcard certificate support is being adopted slowly by operating systems, clients, and applications. There is no common agreement on how to match wildcard certificates to names, which is hindering the progress on adoption.

Wildcard certificates are supported by Exchange Server 2013, Outlook, Outlook Anywhere, Windows Mobile, and Outlook Web App.

However, special configuration is sometimes needed on the Exchange Server 2013 server to support wildcard certificates. For example, if wildcard certificates are used on an Exchange Server 2013 CAS server, the `set-OutlookProvider` cmdlet must be run to enable the Autodiscover service to function properly. The command for Company ABC using a wildcard certificate would be `set-OutlookProvider -Identity EXPR -CertPrincipalName msstd:*companyabc.com`.

To illustrate the emerging support for wildcard certificates, some older mobile device and PC operating systems and/or mail clients do not support wildcard certificates out of the box and receive a certificate error when accessing an Exchange Server 2013 CAS server that's configured with a wildcard certificate. Special configuration may be able to make it work. As an example, for earlier releases of Outlook 2007, to configure Outlook 2007 to support a wildcard certificate issued to companyabc.com, execute the following on the Outlook 2007 client:

1. In Outlook 2007, on the Tools menu, click Account Settings.
2. Select the Microsoft Exchange Account Name and then click Change.
3. Click the More Settings button.
4. Select the Connection tab and click the Exchange Proxy Settings button.
5. Select the Connect Using SSL Only check box.
6. Select the Only Connect to Proxy Servers That Have This Principal Name in Their Certificate check box, and then in the box that follows, enter **`msstd:*.companyabc.com`**.
7. Click OK twice.
8. Click Next.
9. Click Finish.
10. Click Close.

Close Outlook and open it again to have the setting take effect. The certificate error will no longer be present.

In general, choosing SAN certificates is the safest and most widely supported certificate name type. Wildcard certificates are a good option if the public CA supports them and additional configuration and testing time are allocated.

It is important to note that in an environment that supports split-brain DNS, where the same DNS domain name, for example companyabc.com, is used for resolving host names both internally and externally, a UCC certificate with just one SAN can work just fine. In this case, the CN is the single OWA/ActiveSync/Outlook Anywhere hostname, for example, webmail.companyabc.com, and the SAN is autodisocover.companyabc.com (where companyabc.com is the email domain). All OWA access would have to use the uniform resource locator (URL) https://webmail.companyabc.com/owa, and you would probably want to configure HTTP Redirect so that users who try to use http://webmail/owa are redirected to the proper host name so that they do not get certificate warnings in their browsers.

5

Installing a Windows Certification Authority Server

The manual processes noted in the previous section showed what is involved in manually enabling security in a Windows and Exchange Server environment. Beyond the complexity for users having to perform critical system tasks to enable and access secured information, the security provided by these manual methods is not even that good. A simple compromise of a shared key can invalidate the security of files, access systems, and secured communications. The better method is to use a certificate-based security system using encryption to provide a significantly higher level of security. In addition, by automating the process, users do not have to be involved in the encryption, transport, or communications between their laptop or desktop, and the network.

This section covers the creation of a basic CA server system that issues certificates and the process known as autoenrollment of certificates that automatically issues certificates to users and computers in a Microsoft Active Directory environment.

NOTE

This section assumes that you have a Windows Server 2008, 2008 R2, or 2012 system that has been fully patched with the latest service pack and updates, and that the server is connected to a Microsoft Active Directory environment. If you are creating this system in a limited lab environment, the certificate server can be added on the same server system as the global catalog server so that a single domain controller and certificate server can be used.

Installing Active Directory Certificate Services

To install AD CS on Windows Server 2008 R2 (and very similar for Windows Server 2012), determine which server will serve as the root CA, keeping in mind that it is highly recommended that this be a dedicated server and also recommended that it be physically secured and shut off for most of the time to ensure integrity of the certificate chain. It is important to note that an enterprise CA cannot be shut down; however, when a stand-alone root with a subordinate enterprise CA is deployed, the stand-alone root can be shut down. If the strategy of having a stand-alone root with a subordinate enterprise CA is taken, the root CA must first be created and configured, and then an enterprise subordinate CA must then be created.

In smaller scenarios, a PKI infrastructure consisting of a single server that is an enterprise root CA can be provisioned, though in many cases, those smaller organizations might still want to consider a stand-alone root and a subordinate enterprise CA. For the single enterprise root CA scenario, however, the following steps can be taken to provision the CA server:

CAUTION

After AD CS is installed onto a server, the name of that server and the domain status of that server cannot change. Also, the server name must not change while it is a CA.

1. Open Server Manager.
2. Select Roles and then click Add Roles.
3. Click Next at the Before You Begin page.
4. Select the Active Directory Certificate Services check box and click Next.
5. On the Introduction to Active Directory Certificate Services page, click Next.
6. On the Select Role Services page, choose which role services will be required. A base install will need only the Certificate Authority role. Click Next to continue.
7. On the Specify Setup Type page, select Enterprise and then click Next.
8. On the Set Up Private Key page, select Create a New Private Key and then click Next.
9. On the Configure Cryptography for CA page, accept the defaults and then click Next.
10. On the Configure CA Name page, enter a common name of your choice, change the distinguished name suffix if you have a need to, and then click Next.
11. On the Set Validity Period page, change the validity period if you want and then click Next.
12. On the Configure Certificate Database page, change the database and log locations if you want and then click Next.
13. On the Confirm Installation Sections page, click Install.

For Windows Server 2012, the process is similar for the installation of the role services, whereas on Windows Server 2012 the Select role service page looks similar to what is shown in Figure 5.1; however, the process to create a certificate is slightly different. The following process is used to generate a certificate from a Windows Server 2012 Certification Authority service:

1. When the installation is complete, click the Configure Active Directory Certificate Services on the Destination Server link.
2. If needed, click Change to change the credentials, and then click Next.
3. Select the Certificate Authority role service to be configured and click Next.
4. Select whether to install an Enterprise (integrated with AD DS) CA or a Stand-alone CA on the subsequent page. In this example, we are installing a domain-based enterprise root CA. Click Next to continue.
5. On the CA Type page, choose the CA type, as shown in Figure 5.2. In this case, we are installing a root CA on the server. Click Next to continue.

FIGURE 5.1 Installing AD CS.

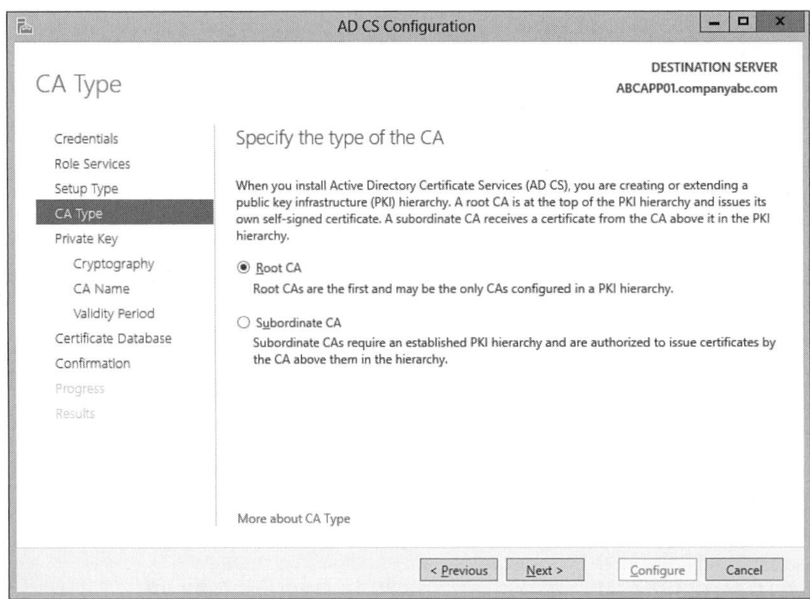

FIGURE 5.2 Specifying a CA type.

6. On the following Private Key page, you can choose whether to create a new private key from scratch or reuse an existing private key from a previous CA implementation. In this example, we create a new key. Click Next to continue.

7. On the Cryptography for CA page, enter the private key encryption settings, as shown in Figure 5.3. Normally, the defaults are fine, but there might be specific needs to change the Cryptographic Service Provider (CSP), key length, or other settings. Click Next to continue.

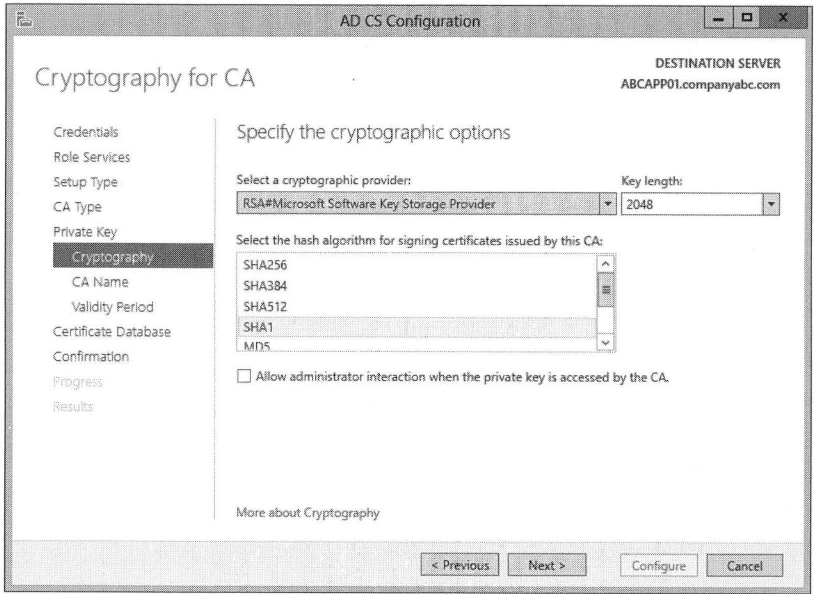

FIGURE 5.3 Choosing cryptography settings.

8. Choose a common name that will be used to identify the CA. Remember that this name will appear on all certificates issued by the CA. In this example, we enter the common name **`CompanyABC-CorpCA`**. Click Next to continue.

9. Set the validity period for the certificate that will be installed on this CA server. If this is a root CA, the server will have to reissue the certificate chain after the expiration period has expired. In this example, we choose a five-year validity period, though many production scenarios will have a 20-year CA created for the root. Click Next to continue.

10. Specify a location for the certificate database and log locations, and click Next to continue.

11. Review the configuration selections on the Confirmation page, as shown in Figure 5.4, and click Configure.

12. Click Close when the wizard is complete.

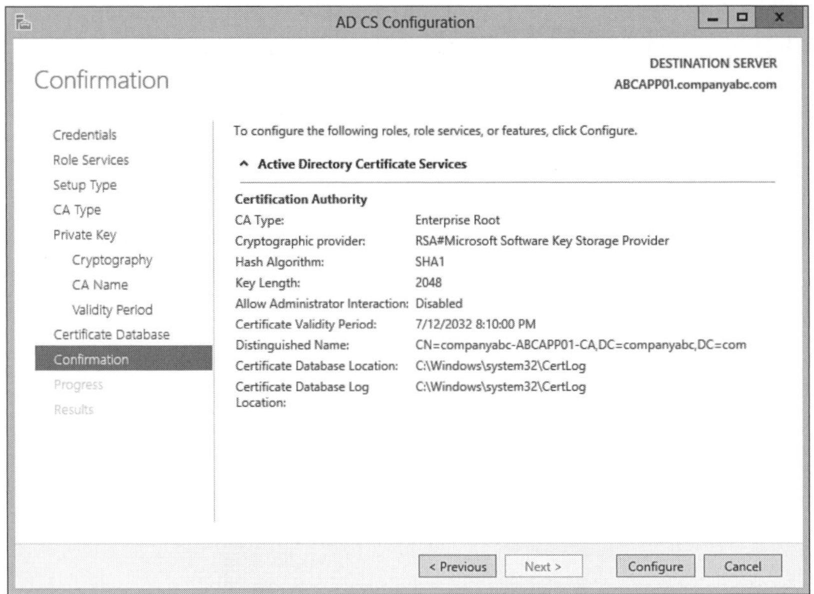

FIGURE 5.4 Reviewing AD CS installation options.

After you install AD CS, you can install additional CAs as subordinate CAs, and administration of the PKI can be performed from the Certification Authority console. (From the Server Manager Tools menu, choose Certification Authority.)

NOTE

For Exchange Server 2013, while the installation of a Certification Authority server noted previously is followed for the creation of Active Directory managed certificates, the issuing of certificates for Exchange Server 2013 uses the Exchange Certificate Wizard.

Securing an Exchange Server 2013 Server

Exchange Server 2013 uses certificates to identify servers in communications between one another, in providing secured HTTPS access to Outlook Web App, in encrypting email messages between users, and the like. Because of the heavy use of certificates in Exchange Server, it is important to create certificates and apply certificates to servers as part of the security process.

Creating a Certificate for Exchange Server 2013 Using the Exchange Certificate Wizard

The process of generating and applying certificates in Exchange Server 2013 is most commonly done through the Exchange Certificate Wizard built in to the Exchange Administration Center because of how well it simplifies the process.

In the Exchange Administration Center, an Exchange administrator can view, renew, create, and apply certificates for all Exchange servers in the environment.

Viewing Certificates in the Exchange Administration Center

An Exchange administrator can view existing certificates in the Exchange Administration Center. This helps the administrator know whether the certificates currently applied are self-signed, private, or public certificates; when the certificates will expire and other certificate status information. To view existing certificates in the Exchange Administration Center, do the following:

1. As an Exchange administrator, log on to the Exchange Administration Center with the URL https://servername.domain.com/ecp (e.g., https://ex01.companyabc.com/ecp).
2. Click the Servers option on the left side of the screen, and then click Certificates, which results in a view similar to the one shown in Figure 5.5.

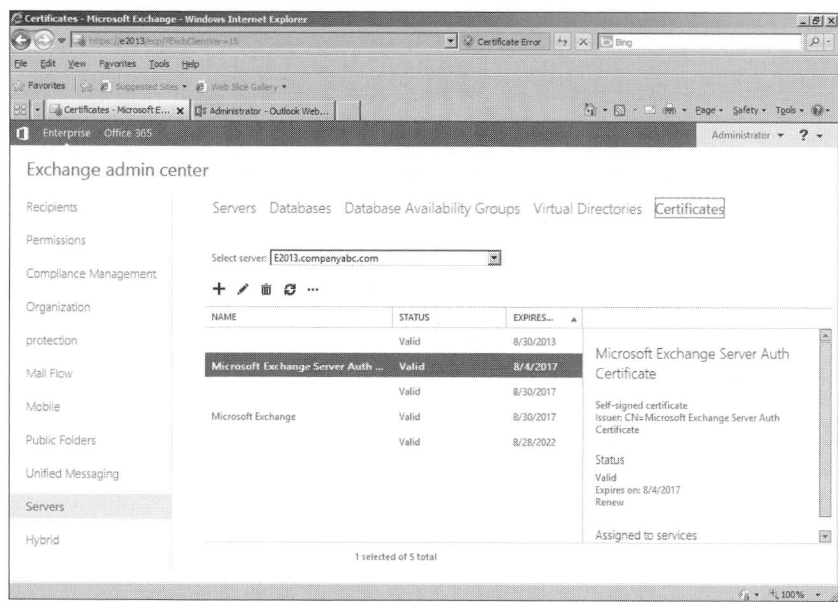

FIGURE 5.5 Navigating and viewing certificates.

3. By clicking on each of the certificates, the administrator can see the issuer of the certificate or whether the certificate is self-signed. The details also show the services to which the certificate is assigned, such as IMAP, POP, SMTP, IIS, UM, Federation, or UMCallRouter.

Creating a New Certificate in the Exchange Administration Center

The creation of a certificate for Exchange is handled as a combination between the Exchange Administration Center and the process of your certificate authority, whether that is a public CA or a private CA. To create and install a certificate from a private Microsoft Certification Authority server, do the following:

1. Log on to the Exchange Administration Center and navigate to the Certificates tab of the Servers section as noted previously.
2. Click the + button in the middle of the Certificates screen to start the process of creating a new certificate for Exchange.
3. Choose to Create a Request for a Certificate from a Certificate Authority and then click Next.
4. For the friendly name of the certificate, this is the name you want to identify your certificate. It can be anything that will help you identify the certificate among other certificates in the certificate store, such as "Certificate for E2013." Then click Next.
5. If you are going to create a wildcard certificate, select the Request a Wildcard Certificate and enter the Root domain; otherwise just click Next.

NOTE

Generally, wildcard certificates are imported into the server instead of requested and issued through this process.

6. Choose an Exchange Server 2013 server holding the Client Access role on which to store the certificate by clicking Browse and selecting the server, and then click Next.
7. For the domains you want to be included in your certificate, you have several options. This would be the URLs for access such as owa.companyabc.com, smtp.companyabc.com, or pop3.companyabc.com. In some cases, the URL may be the same if you don't care that POP3 users access webmail.companyabc.com or email is routed to webmail.companyabc.com. However, most organizations give different services different names so that it is easier and more consistent for access, for example, webmail.companyabc.com, imap.companyabc.com, pop3.companyabc.com, and smtp.companyabc.com. Scroll through the list of access services, select a service, click the Edit icon (depicted by a pencil), and enter in the URLs you want associated with the access service. Be sure to remove or change URLs you do not want as well. When all of the access services are edited as desired, click Next.

NOTE

The default values that are populated in this wizard are taken from the settings of the various virtual directories' `InternalUrl` and `ExternalUrl` properties, so it is a best practice to properly configure these before creating the certificate.

NOTE

It is not strictly necessary to provide a domain for every access service as long as all the domains you are planning to use are specified in at least one access service.

NOTE

When associating names to access services, as much as it might make sense to have multiple names, for example, owa.companyabc.com, pop3.companyabc.com, imap.companyabc.com, if you use a public certification authority provider, the provider will commonly increase the cost for each name embedded in a certificate. So if you pay $500 per year for the certificate for owa.companyabc.com, it could cost $1,000 per year for the certificate if you want owa.companyabc.com and pop3.companyabc.com, or $1,500 if you want owa.companyabc.com, pop3.companyabc.com, and imap.companyabc.com. Therefore, it is important to verify how your certification authority provider charges for Subject Alternative Name certificates. Pricing varies; some certificate issuers give you a minimum number of SANs, for example five, for the same price as one, so you may have some flexibility in your name selection.

NOTE

For the Autodiscover service, keep the autodiscover using the autodiscover.domainname, for example autodiscover.companyabc.com, where *companyabc.com* is the email address domain, because Outlook and mobile devices look for that specific name. This fully qualified domain name is commonly used for both internal and external access.

8. This next page shows all of the fully qualified domain name names that will be requested as part of the Subject Alternative Name. Validate that all of the names are included, and then click Next.
9. Enter in your Organization Name, Department Name, Country/Region Name, City/Locality, and State/Province as requested. If you are using a public certification authority, you need to make sure these names match exactly as your CA provider has your organization on file. If you even abbreviate a name, the CA provider will typically reject the certificate request. The easiest thing to do is check the properties of an existing certificate issued by the provider to see how these fields are entered in other generated certificates. When filled in, click Next.
10. Specify where you want the certificate request stored (such as `\\e2013\c$\Certificates\E2013.req`), and then click Finish.

You will notice that the request you have entered shows up in the certificate list as a Pending request.

The next step is to request the certificate authority to issue the certificate request. For public CAs, you need to follow the instructions of the CA provider. Typically, a CA administrator in your organization will have a Web Portal that they would log in to, upload the certificate request that was just created, an approval process is conducted, and the certificate is generated and returned.

For organizations using Microsoft Certification Authority, the process to issue the certificate through the Microsoft CA is as follows:

1. As a Certification Authority administrator, run the Web Request Website for the CA server, typically http://caserver.domain.com/certsrv, for example https://ca01/certsrv.
2. Click Request a Certificate.
3. Click Advanced Certificate Request.
4. Click Submit a Certificate Request By Using a Base-64-Encoded CMC.
5. On the Submit a Certificate Request or Renewal Request page, in the Saved Request box, paste in the contents of the certificate request you made from the Exchange Administration Center. For Certificate Template, choose Web Server. The page should look like what is shown in Figure 5.6. Click Submit.

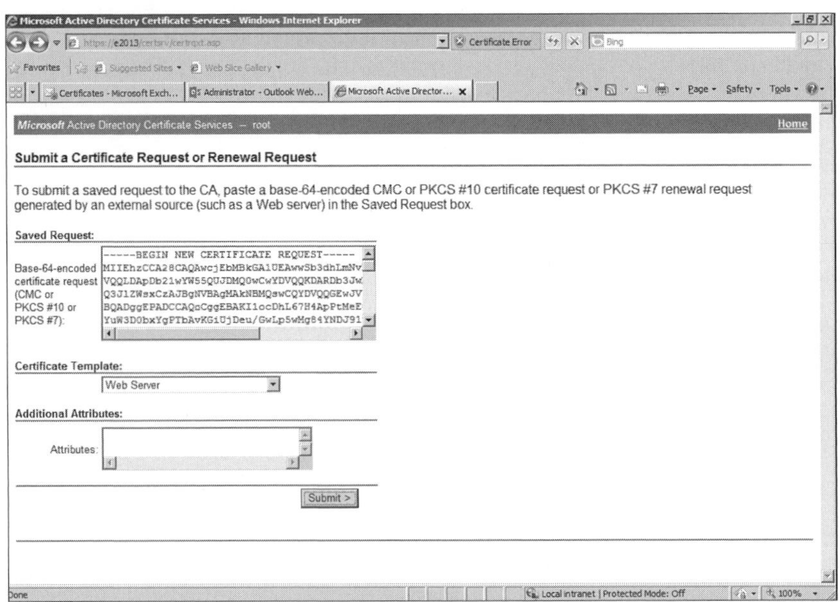

FIGURE 5.6 Preparing for the generation of an Exchange certificate.

6. On the Certificate Issued page, click Download Certificate and then save the certificate to a location to which you can then import the certificate to Exchange to complete the process, such as `C:\Certificates\E2013.cer`.

With the certificate issued by either the public CA or by the Microsoft Certification Authority, the next step is to complete the certificate request. This is completed in the Exchange Administration Center. Do the following:

1. Log on to the Exchange Administration Center and navigate to the Certificates tab of the Servers section.
2. Click the certificate that is "Pending Request" that was requested earlier in the process and for which you have just completed the process of getting a certificate.
3. Click Complete in the details pane on the right.
4. When prompted to specify the filename for the completed certificate request, specify the UNC path to file that was generated from the CA, for example, `\\e2013\c$\Certificates\E2013.cer`, and click OK.

Assigning the Certificate to Services

With the certificate request completed, the next step is to associate Exchange services to the certificate, such as associating IIS (OWA), SMTP, UM, IMAP, POP3, and so on. The process is to do the following:

1. Log on to the Exchange Administration Center and navigate to the Certificates tab of the Servers section.
2. Select the certificate that was just generated and then click the Properties icon that looks like a pencil.
3. Click the Services option in the left side of the window.
4. Click to select the services to which to assign this certificate, for example, IIS (OWA), UM, IMAP, POP3, and then click Save.

If you selected SMTP and are warned whether to overwrite the existing default SMTP certificate, click OK. The existing self-signed SMTP certificate will continue to work.

The final step is to make sure to add the Exchange names to DNS, either going into your DNS server or submitting a request to your DNS administrator to add in the names created in the previous step, for example owa.companyabc.com, pop3.companyabc.com, and autodiscover.companyabc.com.

Renewing Certificates in the Exchange Administration Center

As noted previously in this chapter, it is important to renew self-signed certificates before they expire, as well as make sure that public and private certificates are renewed before users get a certificate error when accessing their email or messages are transferred to the Exchange environment. To renew a certificate, the procedure is exactly the same as outlined in the creation of the certificate but instead of clicking + to create a new certificate, you would click Renew in the details of the certificate. This initiates the process to have a certificate created, and the process is as outlined throughout this section on the creation of a certificate for Exchange.

Exporting and Importing the Certificate

If you have multiple servers in the CAS array, you should use the same certificate for both. To export an Exchange certificate and import it into another server, follow these steps.

1. In the Exchange Control Panel, choose Servers, then Certificates, and select the server which has the certificate you want to export; in this case, choose the one you just created in the previous step.
2. In the list of certificates, select the certificate you created and then click the ellipses More icon in the toolbar, and then click Export Exchange Certificate.
3. Enter the UNC patch to the export location, for example, `\\E2013\C$\Certificates\E2013.pfx`, enter a password for the file, and then click OK.
4. Back in the Servers, Certificates screen, click the ellipses "More" icon, and then click Import Exchange Certificate.
5. Enter the UNC patch to the location of the file you just exported, for example, `\\E2013\C$\Certificates\E2013.pfx`, enter the password for the file, and then click OK.
6. Click the + icon.
7. Select the servers into which to import the certificate, click Add, and then click OK.
8. Click Finish.
9. Assign services to the certificate by following the procedure in the earlier section "Assigning the Certificate to Services."

Creating SSL Certificate Through PowerShell

If you want to get an SSL certificate issued for an Exchange Server 2013 server and prefer to use PowerShell to generate the certificate request and apply the certificate to Exchange, the process can be done completely through PowerShell. The process and commands are as follows:

1. On the Exchange server that you want an SSL certificate generated for, run the Exchange Management Shell (EMS).
2. Run the PowerShell command:

```
New-ExchangeCertificate -GenerateRequest -SubjectName
" CN=webmail.companyabc.com,OU=CompanyABC,O=IT,C=US,S=California,L=San
Francisco" -DomainName autodiscover.companyabc.com,legacy.companyabc.com
-PrivateKeyExportable $true > c:\Certificates\e2013cert.req
```

   where CN is the website FQDN, OU is the name of your company or organization, O is the department or organizational component, C is the two-letter country code, S is the state or province spelled out, and L is the locality or city. The `DomainName` parameter is a list of the SANs to be added to the certificate, which does not need to include the CN. The path after the pipe symbol is the text file path to which the request is written.

NOTE

The CN should be the primary FQDN used for OWA and Web Services.

3. Submit the request file to your Certification Authority provider who will return with a CER (certificate) file that you will then import into Exchange. If you are using a Microsoft Certification Authority, the process would follow the certification authority certification generation process in the previous section on "Creating a Certificate for Exchange Server 2013 Using the Exchange Certificate Wizard."
4. With the returned certificate file, run the following PowerShell command in EMS replacing the path with the path to your issued certificate:

```
Import-ExchangeCertificate -FileData ([Byte[]]$(Get-Content -Path
C:\Certificates\E2013.cer -Encoding Byte -ReadCount 0))
```

   The output you'll see on screen will include a "thumbprint." Copy the thumbprint to the Clipboard (the easiest way is to click the orange EMS icon in the upper left of the EMS screen and choose Edit, Mark, highlight the thumbprint test, click the upper-right EMS icon again, and do an Edit, Copy).
5. To assign the certificate to services, enter the following PowerShell command, replacing the thumbprint with the one you copied to the Clipboard:

```
Enable-ExchangeCertificate -Thumbprint
DF2F5B145805F77D3EC04F49514A8F474F33E0DD -services IMAP,POP,IIS,SMTP
```

6. Enter `Y` to confirm replacement of the SMTP certificate.

The certificate generated by Exchange, sent to the certification authority certifier, returned to the organization, and then imported will be the active certificate for the server.

Securing an IIS Web Server

This section covers the implementation of certificates on general Internet Information Services (IIS) Web Services in a Windows environment. This would be used for an IIS Web Server, intranet server, or a general-purpose secured business server. This section does not apply to securing Exchange Server 2013 services. A certificate is assigned to the public-facing server so that the endpoint knows that they are hitting a valid server in the organization's environment. On the other side of the secured connection is the user logging on and authenticating to a server to validate that the user is who he says he is. It is this two-way interaction of communications that ensures the user and the destination server can be validated by one another.

IIS Authentication

Authentication is a process that verifies that users are who they say they are. IIS supports a multitude of authentication methods, including the following:

5

- **Anonymous authentication**—Users can establish a connection to the website without providing credentials.
- **Active Directory client certificate authentication**—Users can establish a connection by using their Active Directory client certificate for authentication.
- **ASP.NET impersonation**—Users can utilize an impersonation context other than the ASP.NET account.
- **Windows authentication**—This authentication method can be integrated with Active Directory. As users log on, the hash value of the password is sent across the wire instead of the actual password.
- **Digest authentication**—Similar to Integrated Windows authentication, a hash value of the password is transmitted. Digest authentication requires a Windows Server domain controller to validate the hash value.
- **Basic authentication**—Basic authentication sends the username and password over the wire in clear-text format unless combined with SSL-based protection (HTTPS). Without HTTPS, this authentication method offers little security to protect against unauthorized access by itself.
- **Forms authentication**—Users are redirected to a secure page where they enter their credentials. After they have been authenticated, they are redirected back to the page they originally requested.

In IIS, these authentication methods can be enabled under the Authentication feature page, as illustrated in Figure 5.7. You can view this window by selecting the feature under the IIS section at the server, site, or virtual directory level.

NOTE

For Exchange Server, you generally configure Authentication settings in Exchange and not directly in IIS. Again, this is covered in the section "Creating a Certificate for Exchange Server 2013 Using the Exchange Certificate Wizard."

Auditing Web Services

Windows Server auditing can be applied to websites to record attempts (successful and unsuccessful) to log on, gain unauthorized access to service accounts, modify or delete files, and execute restricted commands. These events can be viewed through Event Viewer. It's also important to monitor IIS logs in conjunction with audited events to determine how, when, and if external users are trying to gain unauthorized access.

Using SSL Certificates

SSL encryption preserves user and content integrity and confidentiality so that communications between a client and the web server, containing sensitive data such as passwords or credit card information, are protected. SSL is based on the PKI X.509 security standards that protect communication by encrypting data before being transmitted.

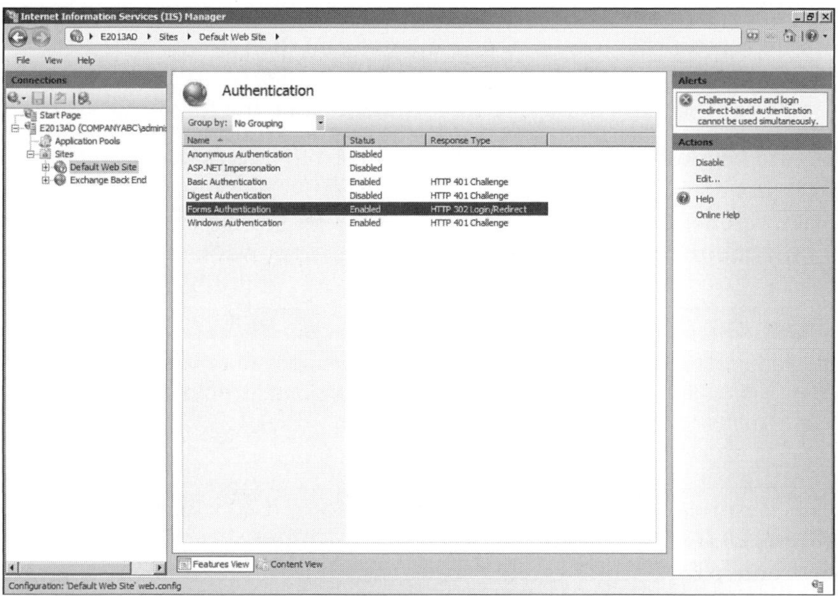

FIGURE 5.7 Authentication feature page.

Earlier versions of IIS supported SSL, and IIS 8 is no different. IIS 8, however, introduces significant improvements to the use of SSL for securing websites, especially when it comes to scalability.

The use of certificates with IIS can serve three primary purposes, although they are typically used to encrypt connections:

- **SSL server authentication**—This allows a client to validate a server's identity. SSL-enabled client software can use a PKI to check whether a server's certificate is valid and has been issued by a trusted certificate authority (CA).
- **Client authentication**—This allows a server to validate a client's identity. IIS can validate that a client's certificate is valid as well as check whether the certificate is from a trusted CA. Client authentication is not normally deployed in conjunction with Exchange Server because of the complexity of deployment.
- **Encrypting SSL connections**—The most common reason for deploying certificates is for SSL-based encrypting of all traffic for a given website or virtual directory. This provides a high degree of confidentiality and security.

From an IIS perspective, SSL can be applied to an entire website, directories, or specific files within the website. SSL configuration can be done through IIS Manager.

The high-level steps for using certificates and SSL consist of the following: The first step is to obtain a certificate. The second step is to create an HTTPS binding for a specific site that needs to be encrypted. The final step is to configure SSL settings for a site, application, or physical directory.

To use SSL on a website, a certificate must first be requested and then installed. The request can be created to obtain a certificate either from an external, trusted CA or from an internal PKI. The types of server requests available in IIS include the following:

- **Create Certificate Request**—This option is typically used for creating a certificate request, which will be submitted to a trusted CA. The certificate's distinguished name properties, cryptographic service provider, and bit-length information are entered into a file and then submitted to a public CA for approval.

TIP

When creating the certificate request to a public CA, it is recommended to use 2048 (the default) or higher as the bit length. Keep in mind that higher bit lengths enforce stronger security; however, a greater length can decrease performance.

- **Create Domain Certificate**—A domain certificate request is used when providing a request to an internal certificate authority. Typically, the internal certificate authority would be an enterprise certificate authority associated with the company's Active Directory domain. This approach reduces the cost of purchasing third-party certificates and also simplifies the certificate deployment.
- **Create Self-Signed Certificate**—The final option available when creating a certificate request is to use a self-signed certificate. This method is usually only used for maintaining certificates for a testing environment because the certificates are not from a trusted CA.

This example illustrates the procedures to create a domain-based certificate request. To complete this task, this example requires an internal CA running within your domain. To create a domain-based certificate request, follow these steps:

1. Launch IIS Manager.
2. In the Connections pane, highlight the IIS server that will request an Internet Server Certificate.
3. In the Feature view, double-click the Server Certificates element.
4. In the Actions pane, select Create Domain Certificate.
5. On the Distinguished Name Properties page, specify the required information for the certificate, as displayed in Figure 5.8. The Common Name is typically the fully qualified domain name (FQDN) of the URL users will use to connect to the website (for example, intranet.companyabc.com). Click Next to continue.

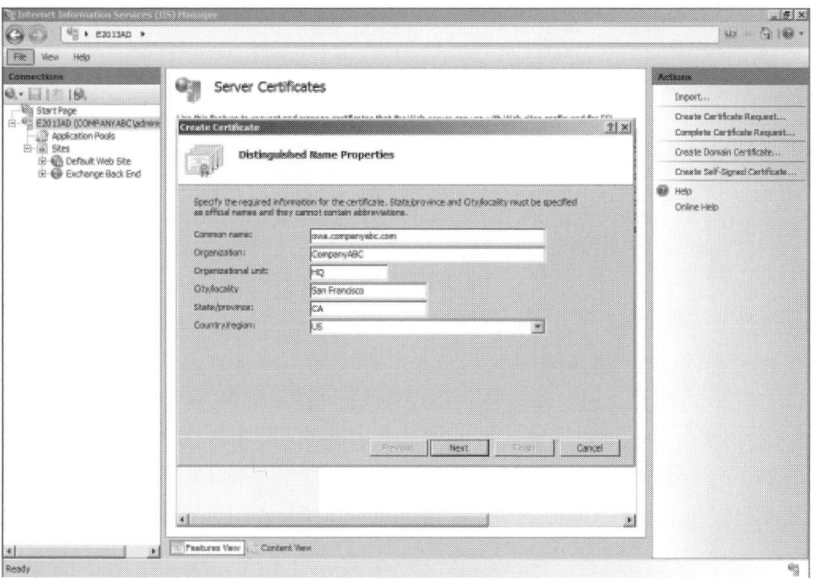

FIGURE 5.8 Creating a domain-based certificate request.

6. Because this is a domain-based certificate request, the next page presented is the Online Certificate Authority. Specify the online certificate authority that will accept the request by clicking Select, selecting the CA from a list, and then entering a friendly name for the certificate. Click Finish to finalize the request.

Binding the SSL Certificate to the IIS Web Server

When this process has been completed, the certificate resides on the Server Certificates page and can be viewed by selecting it and clicking View Task in the Actions pane. Once the certificate is installed, the next step in the process is to bind the Internet server certificate for the desired website and enable SSL. To do this, follow these steps:

1. Open IIS Manager and select the website for which the certificate will be used.
2. In the Actions pane, select Bindings to launch the Site Bindings configuration page.
3. In the Edit Site Bindings dialog box, click Add.
4. In the Add Site Binding dialog box, select the HTTPS option from the Type drop-down menu, assign an IP address, and verify the port is 443, as shown in Figure 5.9.

NOTE

The port number does not necessarily have to be 443. If port 443 is in use for a different website, another port number, such as 444 or 4433 might be used. Of course, the website has to be opened specifying the port number when the default 443 is not used, as in https://intranet.companyabc.com:444.

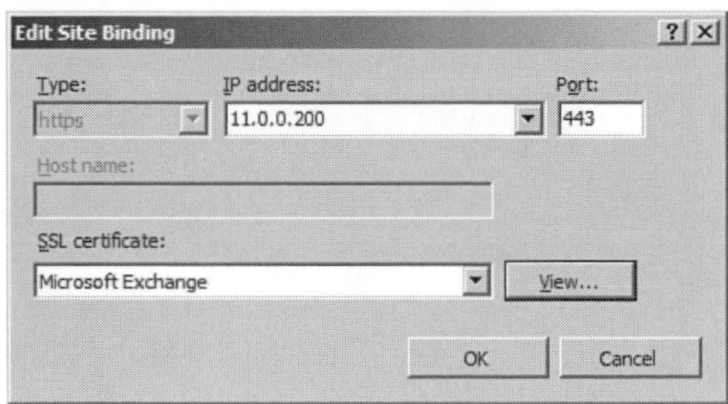

FIGURE 5.9 Editing SSL site binding.

5. Select an SSL certificate, such as the one that was created in the preceding section. You can view the certificate selected by clicking the View button. Click OK to return to the Site Bindings dialog box.

6. Click Close in the Site Bindings dialog box to finalize the binding process.

Configuring SSL Settings for IIS Site

The final process when configuring a site to utilize SSL is to configure the SSL settings for the site, application, physical directory, or virtual directory. To configure SSL settings on the default website, follow these steps:

1. In IIS Manager, navigate to the website.
2. Double-click the SSL Settings icon in Features view.
3. On the SSL Settings page, enable the Require SSL option.
4. The final setting is to configure whether to accept, ignore, or require client certificates. Choose the appropriate Client Certificates option, and click Apply in the Actions pane to save the changes, as shown in Figure 5.10.

Creating SSL Certificates with Subject Alternative Names Using Autoenrollment of a Domain Certificate Server

One of the things commonly done in Exchange is to create SSL certificates with multiple names in the certificate like owa.companyabc.com, autodiscover.companyabc.com, legacy.companyabc.com, and the like. In the previous process of creating a domain certificate, only a single URL name was allocated in the certificate. To create a single certificate that is installed on a server with multiple names, commonly called a certificate with Subject Alternative Names, or a SAN Cert, in an environment with a Microsoft Certification Authority server, do the following:

1. On a Windows server connected to the domain where the Microsoft Certification Authority server is present and logged in as an administrator with rights to manage the Certification Authority server, run `MMC.exe` (Start, Run MMC.exe or in Windows 2012 Metro, Run, MMC.exe).

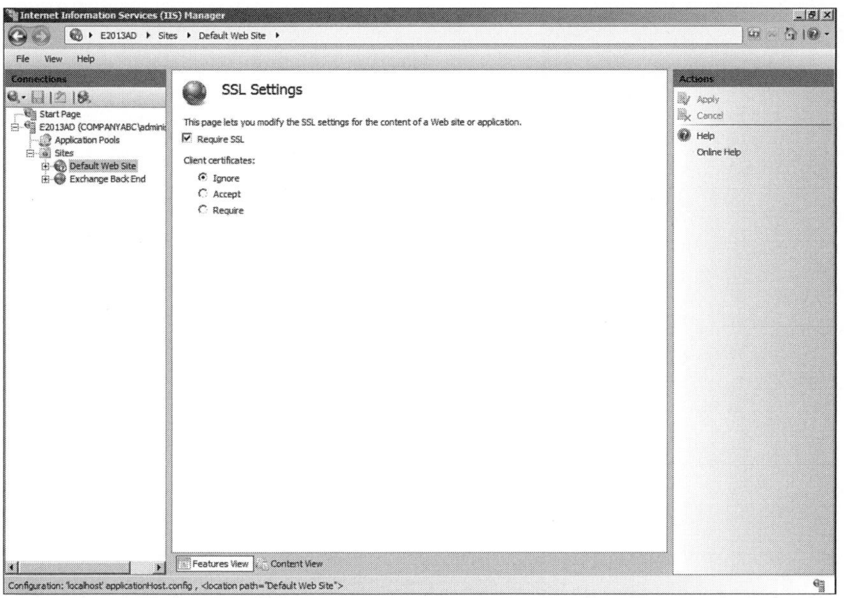

FIGURE 5.10 Configuring properties on the SSL Settings feature page.

2. In the MMC console, choose File, Add/Remove Snap-in, select Certificate Templates, and then click Add.
3. While still in the MMC console, click Certificates, and then click Add. When prompted for "This Snap-in Will Always Manage Certificates For," choose Computer Account, and then click Next. For "Select the Computer You Want This Snap-in to Manage," click Local Computer, assuming you are on the Certification Authority server, and then click Finish.
4. While still in the MMC console, click Certification Authority, and then click Add. For "Select the Computer You Want This Snap-in to Manage," click Local Computer, assuming you are on the Certification Authority server, and then click Finish.
5. Click OK to have all three certificate add-ins available on your MMC console.
6. Click Certificate Templates, which shows a list of templates available on the system, right-click Web Server and choose Duplicate Template, select Windows Server 2003 Enterprise, and then click OK.
7. For this new template, enter the following:
    a. On the General tab, for Template Display Name, enter in `Template for SAN Web Server`.
    b. On the General tab, check the Publish Certificate in Active Directory check box, so that the General tab page looks something similar to Figure 5.11.

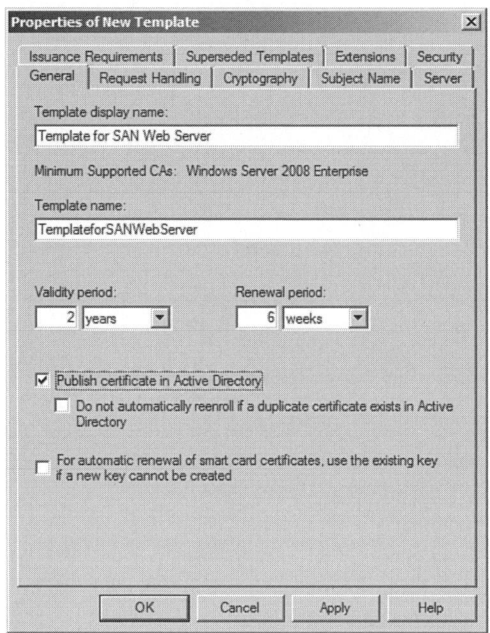

FIGURE 5.11 Configuring a template for SAN certificate.

- **c.** On the Request Handling tab, select the Allow Private Key to Be Exported check box.
- **d.** On the Security tab, make sure the administrator or a group containing the administrators has the Enroll permission check box enabled.

8. Click OK to save the new template.
9. Click the Certification Authority snap-in option on the left pane of the MMC and expand the tree, then right-click the Certificate Templates, and choose New, Certificate Template to Issue.
10. Scroll down and choose the new template created, the "Template for SAN Web Server," and then click OK.
11. Click the Certificates snap-in option on the left pane of the MMC and expand the tree.
12. Expand the Personal container, then right-click the Certificates container and choose All Tasks, Request New Certificate.
13. Click Next on the welcome page and at the Certificate Enrollment page, select the Active Directory Enrollment Policy, and click Next.
14. On the Certificate Enrollment page, choose the Template for SAN Web Server, which you created, click Details, and your screen will be similar to what is shown in Figure 5.12.

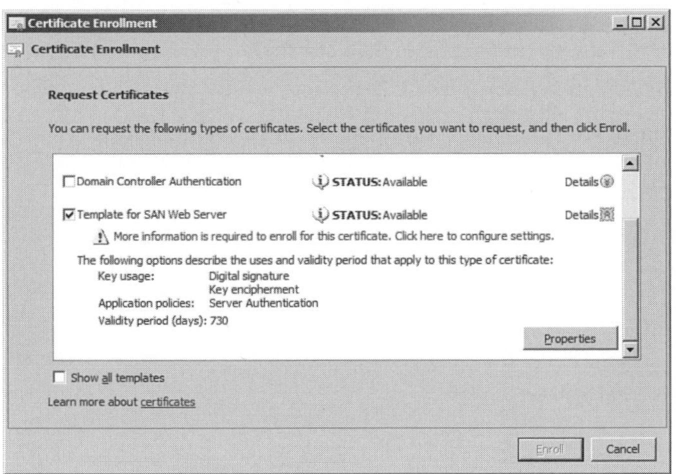

FIGURE 5.12 Selecting the template to issue a certificate.

15. Click Properties and then for Certificate Properties, do the following:

   a. On the Subject tab, for Subject Name, for the Type Common Name, under the value, enter in the primary DNS name that the Exchange server will be known as (like owa.companyabc.com), and then click Add.

   b. On the Subject tab, for Subject Name, for the Type Organization, under the value, enter in the name of the company of the Exchange organization (like CompanyABC), and then click Add.

   c. On the Subject tab, for Subject Name, for the Type Organizational Unit, under the value, enter in the organizational unit of the Exchange organization (like Corp), and then click Add.

   d. On the Subject tab, for Subject Name, for the Type Locality, under the value, enter in the name of the city for the organization (like San Francisco), and then click Add.

   e. On the Subject tab, for Subject Name, for the Type State, under the value, enter in name of the state of the Exchange organization (like CA), and then click Add.

   f. On the Subject tab, for Subject Name, for the Type Country, under the value, enter in the two-letter country code of the Exchange organization (like US), and then click Add.

   g. On the Subject tab, for Alternate Name, for the Type DNS, under the value, enter in the first alternate name for the certificate (like autodiscover.companyabc.com), and then click Add.

h. On the Subject tab, for Alternate Name, for the Type DNS, under the value, enter in the second alternate name for the certificate (like legacy.companyabc.com), and then click Add.

i. Repeat until you get all of the Subject Alternative Names entered with the Subject tab looking similar to Figure 5.13.

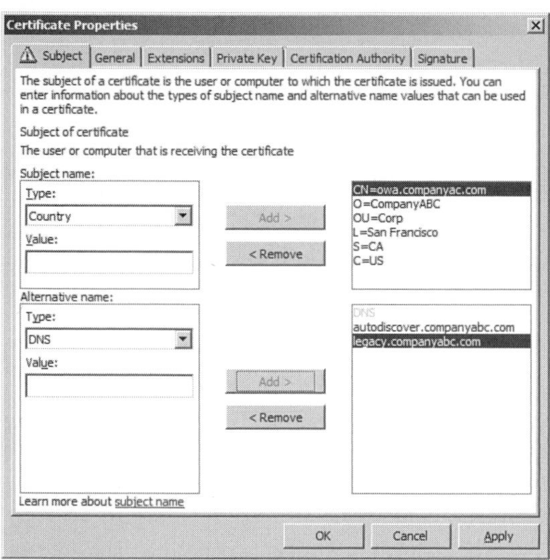

FIGURE 5.13 Subject tab for the SAN certificate.

j. On the General tab, under Friendly Name, enter in a name that will remind you what this certificate is for (such as IIS Web Cert for Main Servers), and then click OK.

16. Click Enroll to have the certificate issued by the Windows Certification of Authority server.

Implementing Secured Email Communications with Exchange Server 2013

Separate from certificates on the server are the certificates used to securely communicate between users and Exchange servers. Encrypted email communications can be sent by manually configuring certificates as covered earlier in this chapter, or by enabling the autoenrollment of certificates for emails that are issued to users via Group Policy. Email encryption can be automated to the point where users are effectively issued certificates, the certificates are automatically installed, and the user can immediately begin to send and receive messages using encrypted communications.

If you have completed the following steps for the autoenrollment of certificates for a user, the certificate will automatically work for Exchange Outlook encryption.

Note that Exchange Server 2013 provides opportunistic TLS encryption, which essentially means that the Exchange Server 2013 servers encrypt mail with outside organizations if possible. The requirement is that the outside organization supports the STARTTLS command. This is described in RFC 3207, "SMTP Service Extension for Secure SMTP over TLS," and is supported by a number of mail systems in addition to Exchange Server 2013. This encrypts only email between the servers, leaving the messages in the users' Inboxes unencrypted. This protects the confidentiality of the email while traveling over the Internet.

NOTE

Opportunistic TLS encryption and the support for the STARTTLS command have been a huge leap forward in the security of intercompany email communications. In the past, most communications between companies were sent in clear text and completely unprotected, unless the companies spent considerable time and effort to coordinate to secure their email communications. Now, it just happens automatically using the STARTTLS command.

Opportunistic TLS does not protect the confidentiality of the email while it is traveling from the user's desktop to the server, while stored on the server, or when traveling from the receiving user's server to his or her desktop. Also, there is no guarantee that the email will be encrypted if the opportunistic TLS fails because the email is then transmitted unencrypted. To ensure that the email is truly secure end-to-end during the transmissions and storage, the following procedures must be followed.

Configuring Exchange Server User Certificates Using Autoenrollment

After Certificate Services has been installed on the system, the administrator of the network can issue certificates to users and computers. However, rather than manually generating and issuing certificates, the best practice is to have the certificate server automatically issue certificates to users and computers in Active Directory. This is known as autoenrollment of certificates.

Autoenrollment of certificates requires the following processes to be followed:

1. A certificate template needs to be created.
2. The template needs to be added to the certification authority server.
3. A group policy needs to be created to automatically deploy the certificate to the user or computer.

With autoenrollment of certificates, rules are created that define which certificates should be issued to a user or computer. As an example, a rule can be created to create the autoenrollment of a certificate that allows a user to have his certificates automatically created for the encryption of data files. With autoenrollment of encrypted files, the user can simply save files to a shared location, and the files stored in the location will be encrypted.

To have certificates automatically installed for the Exchange Server users in Active Directory, do the following:

1. On the certificate server, launch the Certificate Template Microsoft Management Console (MMC) by clicking Start, Run, typing **`mmc.exe`** in the Open text box, and then clicking OK.
2. Click File and click Add/Remove Snap-in.
3. Select Certificate Templates and then click Add.
4. Click OK.
5. Click the Certificate Templates folder.
6. Right-click the Exchange User template, select Duplicate Template, select Windows Server 2003 Enterprise, and click OK.
7. In the Template Display Name text box, type **`AutoEnroll Exchange User`**.
8. Make sure the Publish Certificate in Active Directory and the Do Not Automatically Reenroll if a Duplicate Certificate Exists in Active Directory check boxes are both checked. The screen should look similar to Figure 5.14.

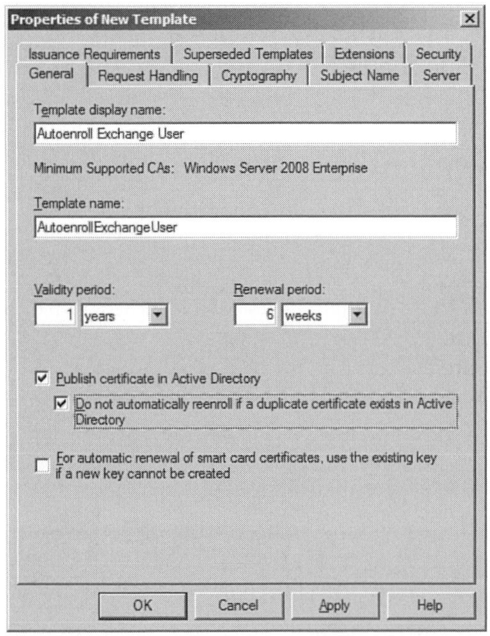

FIGURE 5.14 Creating an AutoEnroll Exchange User template.

9. Select the Subject Name tab.
10. Select Build from this Active Directory Information, and for Subject Name format, select Common Name. For Include E-Mail Name in the Subject Name, select the E-mail Name check box.
11. Click the Request Handling tab.
12. In the Purpose pull-down, select Signature and Encryption.
13. Click the Security tab.
14. Highlight the Authenticated Users Name and select the check boxes in the Allow column for the Read, Enroll, and Autoenroll permissions for the Authenticated Users.
15. Click OK.

Adding the Template to the Certificate Server

After an autoenroll Exchange Server user template has been created, the template needs to be added to the certificate server and distributed to users. You can do this by completing the following steps:

1. Launch the Certification Authority MMC by clicking Start, Administrative Tools, and then Certification Authority.
2. Expand the Certification Authority folder.
3. Expand the folder for your certificate server.
4. Right-click the Certificate Templates folder, and select New, Certificate Template to Issue.
5. Highlight the AutoEnroll Exchange User template, and then click OK.

NOTE

This step of adding the AutoEnroll Exchange User template you created earlier adds this new template to the certificate server. The AutoEnroll User template allows user certificates to be issued automatically through Group Policy.

Creating a Group Policy to Distribute User Certificates

The next step for autoenrollment is to create a group policy that can then distribute certificates to the users' laptops and desktops automatically. This is done by creating a group policy and having the group policy distribute the certificates created in the previous step. To create this group policy, do the following:

1. Launch the Server Manager and expand the Features, Group Policy Management, Forest, and then Domains.

2. Right-click the domain name of the network (such as companyabc.com), and choose Create a GPO in This Domain and Link It Here.
3. Enter the name Exchange AutoEnrollment Group Policy Object and click OK.
4. Select the domain and in the right pane, right-click the new GPO, and select Edit.
5. Under the User Configuration container, expand the Policies, Windows Settings folder.
6. Expand the Security Settings folder and then click to select the Public Key Policies folder. You see an Object Type named Certificate Services Client - Auto-Enrollment, as shown in Figure 5.15.

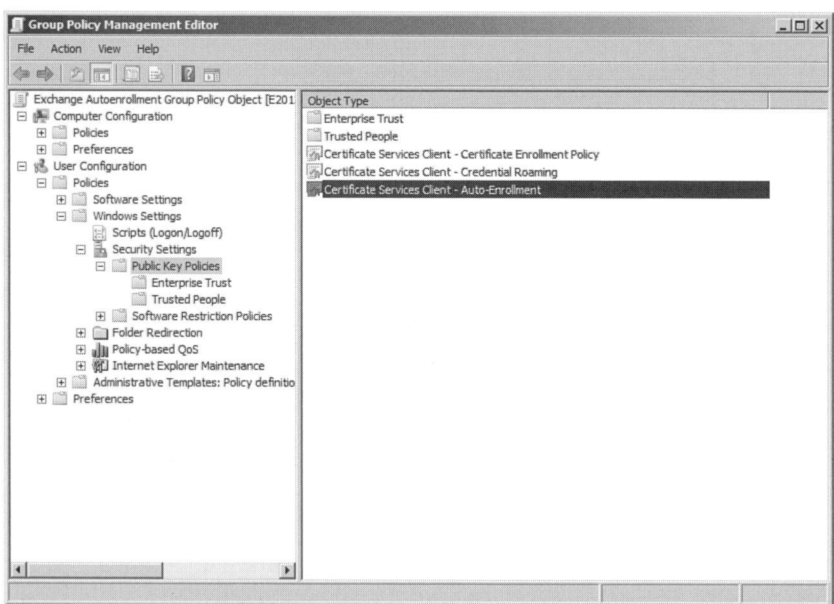

FIGURE 5.15 Expanding folders to access the Autoenrollment Settings object.

7. Right-click the Certificate Services Client - Auto-Enrollment object, and select Properties on the shortcut menu.
8. If needed, set the Configuration Model to Enabled.
9. Check the Renew Expired Certificates, Update Pending Certificates, and Remove Revoked Certificates check box and check the Update Certificates That Use Certificate Templates check box. Then click OK.

Validating That Certificates Are Working Properly

The autoenrollment of user certificates has now been configured for all users who log on to the domain. To validate that certificates are working properly, do the following:

1. From a Windows workstation, log on to the domain.
2. Launch the Certificates MMC by clicking Start, Run, typing `mmc.exe` in the Open text box, and then clicking OK.
3. Click File, Add/Remove Snap-in, select the Certificates snap-in, and then click Add.
4. Assuming you logged on as the user for whom you want to verify that certificates are working, choose My User Account, and then click Finish.
5. Click OK.
6. Expand the Certificates – Current User folder.
7. Expand the Personal folder and click to highlight the Certificates folder.
8. You should have a Secure Email certificate created by the Autoenroll Exchange User certificate template, as shown in Figure 5.16.

FIGURE 5.16 Exchange Server user certificate added to the user's Certificates folder.

If the Exchange Server user certificate has not pushed to the user's Certificates container, you can easily add the certificate by doing the following:

1. From a Windows workstation, log on to the domain.
2. Launch the Certificates MMC by clicking Start, Run, typing `mmc.exe` in the Open text box, and then clicking OK.
3. Click File, Add/Remove Snap-in, select the Certificates snap-in, and then click Add.

4. Assuming you logged on as the user for whom you want to verify that certificates are working, choose My User Account, and then click Finish.
5. Click OK.
6. Right-click the Certificates – Current User folder, choose All Tasks, Automatically Enroll and Retrieve Certificates, and then click Next to begin the wizard.
7. Click Next at the Before You Begin screen.
8. Highlight AutoEnroll Exchange User, and then click Next.
9. Click Next to accept the defaults on the Friendly Name and Description page.
10. Click Finish.

Using Outlook to Send and Receive Digitally Signed and Encrypted Emails

After the Windows Server and Exchange Server 2013 environments have been set up to support a certificate-based infrastructure, the next step is to launch the Outlook client to confirm that certificates are working in the environment, and to then send and receive digitally signed and encrypted messages.

When discussing email security, you need to consider two primary questions:

- How do you know the message truly came from the suspected source?
- How do you know the message has not been intercepted or tampered with?

Both of these questions can be answered by the use of digital signatures and encryption. Digital signatures provide authentication, nonrepudiation, and data integrity, whereas encryption keeps message contents confidential.

In an Exchange Server environment, both of these solutions can be provided by using Secure/Multipurpose Internet Mail Extensions (S/MIME).

Utilizing S/MIME with Microsoft Outlook allows you to do the following:

- **Digitally sign a message to prove the identity of the sender**—S/MIME is the only option supported in Outlook to digitally sign a message. Although a message protected with Information Rights Management (IRM), covered in Chapter 10, “Understanding Exchange Policy Enforcement Security,” can prevent a message from being tampered with, IRM protection is more limited because there is no authority to verify the identity of the sender. Furthermore, with IRM, the Outlook user interface does not show information about the identity of the sender like it does when using S/MIME.
- **Protect messages from unauthorized users**—By utilizing encryption, messages are not sent in clear text. It is possible for attackers to monitor network traffic and intercept network traffic, but by encrypting the message, you can prevent them from

gathering usable data. This protection is especially important for email sent over the Internet, as that is where point-to-point encryption is most valuable and where interoperability standards are most important.

Protecting your messages with S/MIME signatures and encryption is primarily used when users send or receive messages outside of your organization's boundaries, as they are no longer protected by the corporate firewall.

Fundamentals of Digital Signatures and Encryption

The primary purpose of S/MIME is to provide digital signatures and encryption. S/MIME is a small subset of PKI, which addresses a much wider array of security-related capabilities. For instance, PKI supports smart cards, Secure Sockets Layer (SSL), user certificates, and much more.

The International Telecommunication Union (ITU), based in Geneva, Switzerland, has a Telecommunication Standardization Sector (ITU-T) that coordinates standards for telecommunications. X.509 is an ITU-T standard for PKI that specifies (among other things) standard formats for public key certificates and a certification path validation algorithm. Originally issued in 1988, this standard has been revised twice over the years, and Version 3 (the current version) defines the format for certificate extensions used to store information regarding the certificate holder and to define certificate usage.

In short, X.509 is a digital certificate standard that defines the format of the actual certificate used by S/MIME.

The certificate identifies information about the certificate's owner and includes the owner's public key information. X.509 is the industry standard digital certificate and is, by far, the most widely used. PKI products such as Microsoft's Certificate Services (included in Windows Server 2008) adhere to this standard and generate X.509 digital certificates to be used with S/MIME-capable clients.

The Signing Process

When a message sender elects to sign a message, a process is completed where a numerical value is calculated based on the number of set bits in the message. Enclosing the numerical value, known as a checksum, with the original message allows the recipient to apply the same formula to the message.

The random checksum acts as the digital signature, sometimes called a digital ID. This signature is then encrypted using the user's private signing key. The user then sends the message to the recipient, and the message has three components: the message in plain text, the sender's X.509 digital certificate, and the digital certificate.

Upon receipt of the message, the recipient checks its certificate revocation list (CRL) to determine if the sender's certificate has been revoked. If it is found on the CRL, the recipient is warned that the sender's certificate has been revoked.

If the certificate is not on the revocation list, the digital signature is decrypted with the sender's public signing key (which is included in the digital certificate). The recipient's client then generates the checksum based on the plain text message and compares it with the digital signature.

If the checksum generated by the recipient does not match the one generated by the sender, the recipient knows that the message has been garbled or tampered with.

The Encryption Process

When a user elects to encrypt a message, the client generates a random bulk encryption key that is used to encrypt the contents of the message. The bulk encryption key is then encrypted using the recipient's public key. This is known as a lockbox. If the message has multiple recipients, individual lockboxes are created, one for each recipient, using his or her own public encryption key. However, the content of each is still the same bulk signing key. This process prevents the client from having to encrypt the message separately for each recipient, while ensuring the contents remain secure.

For this process to work, the sender must have a copy of the recipient's digital certificate. The certificate can be retrieved from either the Global Address List (GAL) or the sender's Contact list. The digital certificate contains the recipient's public encryption key, which is used to create the lockbox for the bulk encryption key.

When the message is received, the recipient uses his or her private encryption key to decrypt the lockbox, exposing the bulk encryption key that was used to encrypt the original message. The bulk encryption key is then used to decrypt the message.

This process sounds complicated, but it is actually very straightforward—the message is encrypted and needs a key to be decrypted. The key is sent with the message, but it is encrypted itself with the recipient's public key—so, only the intended recipient is able to unlock the key and, in turn, unlock the message.

NOTE

For Exchange Server 2003 Service Pack 1 (SP1) and higher, antivirus software using the Virus Scanning API (VSAPI) 2.5 can scan digitally signed or encrypted messages. This includes Exchange Server 2007, Exchange Server 2010, and Exchange Server 2013.

Making Sure Outlook Acknowledges the Certificate

After autoenrollment has issued a certificate to the user and the user has confirmed the certificate has been successfully received, you can confirm that Microsoft Outlook recognizes the certificate for encrypted communications. To do so, do the following:

1. Launch Outlook.
2. For Outlook 2007, choose Tools, Trust Center, and then click Email Security. For Outlook 2010, choose File, Options, Trust Center. For Outlook 2013, choose Tools, Options, Trust Center, Trust Center Settings, and then click Email Security.
3. Click the Trust Center Settings button.

Under Security Settings Name is the email certificate that enables you to send and receive signed and encrypted communications.

4. Click OK and then click OK again to continue.

Outlook automatically detects the correct autoenrolled certificate and configures Outlook to use the certificate for signing and encrypting email.

Sending a Digitally Signed Email

With the email certificate installed, you can now begin the process of sending and receiving encrypted emails. However, to complete the process, you need to communicate with someone who also has a certificate to send and receive encrypted emails. Email encryption requires both the sender and the receiver to have valid certificates.

The easiest process for setting up encrypted email communications is to send a user a digitally signed email with a copy of your public key certificate attached. With a digitally signed email and a copy of your public key, the recipient can then add your certificate to his or her address book and can then reply to the message sending you his or her public key. After you have exchanged public keys, you can send and receive encrypted emails.

The process for sending a person a digitally signed email with your public key is as follows:

1. Launch Microsoft Outlook.
2. Create a new email message.
3. Enter in the recipient's email address that you want to communicate with in the To field, and enter in a subject such as "`Initial Email for Secured Communications`."
4. For the body of the message, you might want to enter in text such as "`Here is an email message that will help us initiate secured communications. I am attaching a copy of my certificate for you to install; please reply to the message with a copy of your certificate.`"

NOTE

Writing a message in the body of the email might not be necessary; however, in this day and age of spam filters, if you just send a message with your digital signature and an attachment of your public key, the message will frequently be quarantined in the recipient's spam filter. So, it is best to write a few words describing what you are doing as part of the message.

5. On the Options tab at the top of the page, select Sign and ensure that it is highlighted. To see what settings this affects, you can click the arrow at the bottom of the Options box, and then click the Security Settings button.
6. The Add Digital Signature to This Message and Send This Message as Clear Text Signed check boxes should already be selected.

7. After selecting the Change Settings button, you should see that the Send These Certificates with Signed Messages check box is already selected. If it is not, select the box so that your certificate is sent with the message, and then click OK.
8. Click OK and then click Close.
9. Click Send to send the message.

Your message will now be sent to the recipient with a copy of your key in a digitally signed email message. When the recipient opens the message, an error will likely appear that says "There are problems with the signature. Click the signature button for details." This message is because the certificate being received is from a domain with which the recipient has not communicated in a secured or encrypted manner in the past.

After confirming that you indeed sent the message and deciding to trust your certificate, the recipient should do the following:

1. Click the yellow warning icon on the right side of the email message; a warning dialog box opens.
2. Because you (the recipient) have confirmed the validity of the sender, click Trust.
3. A message box opens that warns and prompts that the recipient is trusting the sender. Click Yes to accept the trust.
4. Close and reopen the email. The error no longer appears, and the digital signature is confirmed.

Your certificate has now been installed on the recipient's system; the recipient now needs to send you his or her certificate so you can follow the exact same procedures to install his or her certificate on your system.

Sending Encrypted Email Messages

After you have exchanged certificates, you can now send and receive fully encrypted email messages with another individual. To do so, complete the following steps:

1. Launch Microsoft Outlook.
2. Create a new email.
3. Enter in the recipient's email address in the To field, and enter in a subject such as "`Encrypted Email Message.`"
4. For the body of the message, you might want to enter in text such as "`Here is an email message that should now be encrypted. Please let me know if you successfully receive this message.`"
5. On the Options tab at the top of the page, select Encrypt and ensure that it is highlighted. To see what settings this affects, you can click the arrow at the bottom of the Options box, and then click the Security Settings button.

6. The Encrypt Message Contents and Attachments check box should be selected. Click OK, and then click Close.
7. Click Send to send the message.

The recipient will receive an encrypted copy of your message. This process not only works within Microsoft Outlook within an organization, but also works the same way when you want to send and receive encrypted messages to individuals outside of your organization. If the recipient is also running Microsoft Outlook, the process to install your certificate into his or her address book is the same as described previously. If the recipient is using a different email system, he or she might need to detach the certificate, save it, and manually save the certificate into his or her address book.

Summary

The goal of this chapter was to provide step-by-step procedures that can be followed for the creation of a certificate server, creating the appropriate templates and certificates for users, and having certificates automatically issued to users and computers so that a certificate-based encryption system can be easily implemented in an environment.

When implementing security features in a network environment, it is important to look beyond the security of the computers alone. The data that travels between these computers is often more vulnerable than the data stored on the computers themselves. By implementing security methods such as certificate-based encryption to protect the information contained in the emails, administrators are taking one more step toward a well-rounded security solution.

Best Practices

The following are best practices from this chapter:

- Implement a Public Key Infrastructure solution within your environment that meets your organization's security needs.
- For environments requiring additional security measures, consider implementing smart cards to use in addition to ordinary network passwords.
- Set up autoenrollment of certificates on Windows Server to automatically generate certificates for users who have an Active Directory user account.
- Replace self-signed certificates with private or public certificates to properly identify Exchange servers as authenticated servers with trusted authorities.
- Use the Certificate Wizard in Exchange to generate requests and apply certificates in Exchange Server 2013.
- Use a Unified Communications Certificate (UCC) with Subject Alternative Names (SANs) for most Exchange Server 2013 environments.

- Use group policies to push user certificates to users to minimize the administrative overhead of having users manually download certificates and install the certificates in their Outlook application themselves.
- Utilize digital signatures and encryption in your messaging environment by implementing S/MIME for your Microsoft Outlook clients.
- Use public certificates for client-facing components.
- Maintain a self-signed certificate with the server's NetBIOS name for SMTP as required by Exchange's internal server-to-server communication.
- Test to make sure certificates are working by sending a digital signature first, and then validate the complete successful exchange of keys by sending and receiving fully encrypted messages.

CHAPTER 6

Installing and Configuring the Basics of Exchange Server 2013 for a Brand-New Environment

IN THIS CHAPTER

- Understanding the Exchange Server 2013 Server Roles
- Understanding the Prerequisites for Exchange Server 2013
- Understanding High Availability and Site Resilience in Exchange Server 2013
- Exchange Server 2013 Hardware Requirements
- Understanding the Active Directory Requirements for Exchange Server 2013
- Understanding Role Based Access Control
- Planning Your Exchange Server 2013 Installation
- Deploying Active Directory from Scratch
- Preparing Your Environment for Exchange Server 2013
- Installing Exchange Server 2013
- Finalizing the Deployment

Installing an Exchange Server is like taking a hike through the woods. If you have a map and can accurately follow the directions, you can quickly and safely arrive at your destination. If you get lost in the process (or try to "wing it"), you might or might not reach your destination, but even if you do, it is likely that you will take a lot longer and travel over more challenging roads.

To those who have worked with Exchange Server 2010 in the past, the Exchange Server 2013 Installation Wizard will seem familiar. The wizard walks the administrator through the installation of updates, checks for the necessary prerequisites and allows for the selection of specific server roles for deployment. However, the installation wizard does *not* cover all twists and turns. There are steps that must be taken to prepare the Active Directory (AD) environment and steps that must be taken to prepare the underlying operating system on the server you are installing on.

This chapter focuses on the installation process for a new Microsoft Exchange Server 2013 server in a typical configuration. In addition, this chapter assumes that the supporting infrastructure and server operating system do not exist and includes instructions on how to install Windows servers, Active Directory, supporting configuration settings, and the Exchange Server 2013 prerequisites from scratch.

Understanding the Exchange Server 2013 Server Roles

As with Exchange Server 2010, Exchange Server 2013 has various roles that can be installed on the server to perform specific functions. With Exchange Server 2010, there were five major server roles. The original design intent dating back to Exchange Server 2007 was to allow the roles to be modular where they could reside on a single server (for small environments) or be distributed to multiple servers throughout an organization.

However, even as the roles evolved in Exchange Server 2010, the reality was that they remained tightly coupled, presenting real-world restrictions on how they could be distributed on servers geographically. With the goal of improving hardware utilization, deployment simplicity, cross-version interoperability, and failure isolation, which can serve self-hosted small organizations to Office 365, Microsoft invested in a major re-architecture of Exchange to realign the roles into the following two (primary) roles:

- Client Access server role
- Mailbox server role

NOTE

The third role for Exchange Server 2013 is the Edge Transport role, covered in Chapter 11, "Exchange Edge Including Antispam/Anti-Malware Protection for Exchange." For now, the Edge Transport role runs on Exchange Server 2010 and is not a direct Exchange Server 2013 role.

Client Access Server Role—Providing User Connectivity and Mail Routing

The Exchange Server 2013 Client Access servers assume the roles formerly handled by the Exchange Server 2010 Client Access and Hub Transport roles. The Client Access servers are responsible for accepting connections from clients and proxy requests to the back-end Mailbox servers. Like the front-end servers found in Exchange Server 2003, Client Access servers manage connectivity via Outlook Web App (OWA) and ActiveSync, and like the Client Access servers in Exchange Server 2007, they also manage connectivity from Post Office Protocol (POP) and Internet Message Access Protocol (IMAP) users. Exchange Server 2010 Client Access servers added the ability to also manage Messaging Application Programming Interface (MAPI) (such as Outlook) client connectivity. In a pure Exchange Server 2010 environment, clients never had to connect directly to their Mailbox servers—all connectivity was to the Client Access server. The Exchange Server 2013 Client Access servers perform authentication, redirection, and proxy services for all clients, such as Microsoft Office Outlook, Outlook Web App, mobile devices, Simple Mail Transfer Protocol (SMTP), and POP, as well as accepting and delivering mail from and to other mail hosts on the Internet.

Client Access servers can be organized into Client Access server arrays. By taking responsibility for managing these additional connections, Client Access servers allow Mailbox servers to focus on their primary role—processing messaging requests.

Mailbox Server Role—What It's All About

The Mailbox server role is the core role within Exchange Server 2013. Mailbox servers host the servers that contain mailboxes, mail-enabled objects such as contacts and distribution lists, as well as public folder data. In Exchange Server 2013, the public folders architecture uses mailboxes to store both the hierarchy and public folder content. Public folder databases have been eliminated. High availability for the hierarchy and content mailboxes can be provided through database availability groups (DAGs).

The Mailbox server runs two Transport services. The Hub Transport service routes emails within the organization and provides connectivity between the Front End Transport service, hosted by the Client Access server, and the Mailbox Transport service. The Mailbox Transport service routes email messages between the Hub Transport service and the mailbox database.

In addition, the Mailbox server role includes the Unified Messaging service.

Understanding the Prerequisites for Exchange Server 2013

The prerequisites that are needed will depend on the Exchange role installed on the server. Before installing Exchange Server 2013, the administrator should become familiar with the prerequisites for each of the server roles. This section covers the prerequisites for the implementation of Exchange Server 2013 in a Windows networking environment.

Active Directory Infrastructure

Exchange Server 2013 relies on an Active Directory infrastructure to do its job. AD Sites and Services, domain name system (DNS), global catalog (GC) servers, domain controllers—all must be in place and configured properly for Exchange Server to function well.

The importance of each of these services, and the steps to deploy them, are explained in greater detail later in the chapter.

Windows Server 2008 R2—64-Bit All the Way

From inception through Exchange Server 2003, Exchange Server was always a 32-bit application. Although this technology was able to handle the needs of organizations in the past, organizations today have more demanding messaging requirements.

In a world with ever-increasing message traffic, the need for highly available systems that allow access from multiple client technologies, through the Internet, and through continuous synchronization with wireless devices resulted in the desire for increased productivity through increased performance.

To address these growing needs, Microsoft released a 64-bit version of its Exchange Server 2007 server for production environments. Although Microsoft still produced a 32-bit version of the product, it was intended primarily for nonproduction environments.

With Exchange Server 2010, 32-bit support went away; likewise Exchange Server 2013 is only being released in a 64-bit version.

By utilizing 64-bit architecture, Exchange Server has significantly enhanced processor and memory utilization. This ensures higher performance gains, the ability to handle an ever-increasing volume of messages, the capability of supporting more users per server, and more simultaneously connected mail clients. This last item is critical as more and more organizations take advantage of the capabilities of OWA and ActiveSync.

The Exchange Server 2013 application can only be installed on Windows Server 2012, Windows Server 2008 R2 Standard or Enterprise Editions with Service Pack 1 (SP1) (or later), or Windows Server 2008 R2 Datacenter RTM or later operating systems. However, if you plan on having the Mailbox server be a member of a DAG, you must use the Enterprise or Datacenter Edition. Windows 2008 Server R2 SP1 Standard Edition does not support the Windows Clustering feature required for DAGs.

Microsoft .NET Framework 4.5

Microsoft .NET Framework is a Microsoft Windows component that allows the ability to build, deploy, and run Web Services and other applications. The .NET Framework is a key offering from Microsoft, and most new applications created for the Windows platform rely on it in one way or another.

.NET Framework 4.5 builds on the features added in previous releases, provides core new features and improvements, and adds a number of new features to support .NET for Metro style Apps, portable class libraries, parallel computing, networking, Windows Presentation Foundation, Windows Communication Foundation, and Windows Workflow Foundation.

Windows Server 2012 ships with the .NET Framework 4.5 already installed; however, on Windows Server 2008 R2 SP1 servers, .NET Framework 4.5 must be installed separately. Exchange Server 2013 requires .NET Framework 4.5.

Windows Management Framework 3.0

Windows Management Framework 3.0 contains Windows PowerShell v3, Windows Management Instrumentation (WMI), and Windows Remote Management (WinRM). Windows Management Framework 3.0 is included with Windows Server 2012 and does not need to be installed separately as with Windows Server 2008 R2 SP1. Windows Management Framework 3.0 can be downloaded and installed from the Internet, and instructions on how to do so are included later in this chapter.

Windows PowerShell v3

Administrators who are familiar with Exchange Server 2007 or 2010 have most likely had some experience with Windows PowerShell. For many, the implementation of PowerShell addressed one of the most glaring shortcomings of older Windows installations—the lack of a usable command-line interface for performing administrative tasks.

PowerShell is an extensible command-line shell and scripting language from Microsoft that integrates with the .NET Framework to allow administrators to perform just about any task in an Exchange environment from a command line. From simple to complex, scripts can be written using the PowerShell scripting language to save administrators from time-consuming and repetitive tasks.

Although some have found the PowerShell scripting language to be difficult to learn and challenging to implement, few who have seen the results of this product being put into action can complain about the results.

Windows PowerShell v3 introduces several new features to PowerShell v2 that extend its capabilities, including the following:

- **Workflows**—Workflows allow running of long-running activities in sequence or in parallel to perform more extensive and complex management tasks. Workflows are repeatable, interruptible, and recoverable.
- **Robust sessions**—Windows PowerShell v3 sessions automatically recover from network failures and interruptions. Disconnected sessions can be reconnected from a different computer without interrupting running tasks.
- **Scheduled jobs**—Schedule jobs to run regularly or as triggered by an event.
- **Delegated administration**—Delegated administration allows setup of commands with a delegated set of credentials that can be run by users with limited permissions.
- **Simplified language syntax**—Commands and script syntax now appear more like natural language.

Windows Management Instrumentation (WMI)

WMI is the infrastructure for accessing management data and operations on Windows operating systems. WMI scripts and applications can be used to supply management data to operating system components and other Windows-based products or automate administrative tasks on remote computers. WMI in Windows Management Framework 3.0 supports an extended Windows PowerShell semantics application programming interface (API), allowing the ability to write Windows PowerShell cmdlets in native code.

Windows Remote Management 2.0 (WinRM)

The Exchange Management Shell is a command-line interface that enables you to manage your Microsoft Exchange organization without having to rely on a graphical user interface (GUI).

WinRM 2.0 is the transport mechanism that enables your local version of Windows PowerShell to connect to remote Exchange servers, whether that server is in the next rack or across the country. Utilizing WinRM 2.0, administrators can manage servers, devices, and applications throughout their organizations from a single management server.

Microsoft Unified Communications Managed API 4.0, Core Runtime 64-Bit

The Unified Communications Managed API (UCMA) provides a managed-code multilayer platform for developers to implement communication- and collaboration-enabled middle tier services that work with Microsoft Lync Server.

Microsoft Office 2010 Filter Pack 64-Bit and Service Pack 1

The Microsoft Filter Pack contains a series of IFilters that allow search services to index specific file type contents. The filters are intended for the use of the Microsoft search services. Service Pack 1 is a roll-up of all previously released updates that contain security, performance, and stability updates.

Understanding High Availability and Site Resilience in Exchange Server 2013

In Exchange Server 2007, Microsoft introduced new technologies that allowed organizations to deploy their Exchange environments with improved availability. Known as Continuous Replication, this technology was offered in three flavors—Local Continuous Replication (LCR), Cluster Continuous Replication (CCR), and Standby Continuous Replication (SCR).

Although these options were a significant improvement over previous technologies, organizations found that the technologies were challenging to implement, as they required a significant amount of time and experience to deploy. This was largely due to the fact that some parts of the technology were owned by the Windows operating system, and some parts were owned by Exchange Server.

Exchange Server 2010 built on these technologies and combined the onsite data replication features of CCR with the offsite data replication features of SCR. This combination of technologies is known as a DAG. This architecture is designed to provide recovery from disk-level, server-level, and site-level failures. Although Exchange Server 2013 also uses DAGs and mailbox database copies, Microsoft has enhanced the high-availability platform, using the Exchange Information Store and the Extensible Storage Engine (ESE) for improved availability, easier management, and reduced costs. These improvements include the following:

- **Managed Store**—A newly rewritten Information Store process that works with the Microsoft Exchange Replication service to manage mailbox databases
- **Managed Availability**—Tightly integrated internal monitoring and recovery-oriented features to help prevent failures, proactively restore services, initiate server failovers automatically, and send administrator alerts
- **Support for multiple databases per disk**—Ability to support a mix of active and passive database copies on the same disk to allow greater disk utilization efficiencies

- **Unified namespace for site resilient configurations**—Ability to have a unified namespace across multiple Active Directory sites for resilient configuration

Exchange Server 2013 Hardware Requirements

Recommended hardware requirements for Exchange Server 2013 servers vary depending on factors such as the server roles and anticipated loads; however, Microsoft maintains a list of minimum hardware requirements to install Exchange Server 2013. For the latest list of requirements, go to http://technet.microsoft.com and search for "Exchange 2013 System Requirements."

Table 6.1 shows the minimum and recommended hardware requirements for Exchange Server 2013, as stated by Microsoft.

NOTE

These hardware requirements from Microsoft are the bare minimum and should not be used in best-practice scenarios. In addition, hardware requirements can change because of features and functionality required by the company. For example, the implementation of Unified Messaging voice mail services or clustering on an Exchange Server 2013 server can require more memory. See Chapter 15, "Optimizing an Exchange Server 2013 Environment," for more tips and best practices on sizing the server for your environment.

TABLE 6.1 Minimum Hardware Requirements

Hardware	Minimum Requirements
Processor	X64 architecture-based computer with Intel Processor that supports Intel 64 Technology (formerly known as Intel EM64T). AMD processor that supports AMD64 platform. Note: Intel Itanium IA64 processors are *not* supported.
Memory	Client Access server—Minimum: 2GB. Maximum: 16GB. **Recommended:** 2GB per core (8GB Minimum, 16GB Maximum). Mailbox server—Minimum: 2GB. Maximum: 64GB. **Recommended:** 2GB plus 2–4MB per mailbox. Multiple Roles (combinations of Client Access and Mailbox server roles)—Minimum: 4GB. Maximum: 64GB. **Recommended:** 8GB plus 2–4MB per mailbox.
Disk space	At least 1.2GB on the disk where Exchange Server 2013 will be installed. An additional 500MB for each Unified Messaging language pack that will be installed. 200MB on the system drive. At least 500MB on the disk that stores the message queue databases on an Edge Transport server.

Understanding the Active Directory Requirements for Exchange Server 2013

An AD infrastructure running on Windows Server 2012, Windows Server 2008 R2 Standard or Enterprise, or Windows Server 2008 Standard or Enterprise must be in place before an organization can deploy Exchange Server 2013. Exchange Server depends on the services provided by AD to successfully function, and the design and implementation of the AD environment can have an enormous impact on the success of the Exchange Server deployment. Mistakes made in the planning or implementation of AD can be costly and difficult to correct later.

If AD is already deployed, it is important that the team designing the Exchange Server infrastructure have a solid understanding of the existing AD environment. Organizations with an AD infrastructure already in place need to evaluate how Exchange Server can fit into their environments. If AD has not been deployed, the organization or team designing Exchange Server needs to plan its implementation with a thought as to what their messaging infrastructure will look like.

This section is designed to give a basic understanding of the AD infrastructure required to support an Exchange Server 2013 implementation. Many facets are involved when planning a production AD infrastructure—forest model, domain model, group policies, and delegation of administration to name a few, and the information needed to design an AD infrastructure from end to end is beyond the scope of this book.

Some of the AD factors that should be considered when deploying Exchange Server 2013 include the following:

- Global catalog server placement
- AD Sites and Services
- Forest and domain functional levels
- Flexible Single Master Operations role placement
- Permissions needed to install Exchange
- Bandwidth and latency in the network

NOTE

For in-depth guidance on designing, implementing, and maintaining an AD infrastructure, refer to *Windows Server 2008 Unleashed*, by Sams Publishing (ISBN: 0-672-32930-1); *Windows Server 2008 R2 Unleashed*, by Sams Publishing (ISBN: 0-672-33092-X); or *Windows Server 2012 Unleashed*, by Sams Publishing (ISBN: 0-672-33622-7).

Global Catalog Server Placement

As was the case in Exchange 2000 Server through Exchange Server 2010, Exchange Server 2013 requires a global catalog infrastructure to function. The global catalog maintains an index of the Active Directory database for objects within its domain. In addition, it stores partial copies of data for all other domains within a forest.

Just as important, Exchange Server relies on global catalog servers to resolve email addresses for users within the organization. Failure to contact a global catalog server causes emails to bounce, as the recipient's name cannot be resolved.

Sizing a global catalog infrastructure and server placement is discussed in depth later in this chapter in the section titled "Establishing a Proper Global Catalog Placement Strategy."

Active Directory Sites and Services

In Exchange Server 2003 and earlier, Exchange Server utilized a dedicated routing topology for transporting messages throughout the organization. Beginning with Exchange Server 2007, Microsoft redesigned the product to be a *site-aware* application. This continues in Exchange Server 2013.

Site-aware applications are able to determine what site they (and other servers) belong to by querying Active Directory. The site attribute of all Exchange Server objects is maintained by the Microsoft Exchange Active Directory Topology Service. In addition, Exchange Server 2013 servers utilize site membership to identify which domain controllers and global catalog servers should be utilized to process Active Directory queries.

The Exchange Server 2013 servers utilize Active Directory site membership as follows:

- **Client Access servers**—When a Client Access server receives a connection request from a user, it contacts AD to determine which Mailbox server houses the user's mailbox and which site that server belongs to. If the Mailbox server is in a different site, the connection may be redirected to a more suitable Client Access server in the same site as the Mailbox server, if one exists. Otherwise, the Client Access server proxies the request to the Mailbox server that houses the currently active copy of the database that contains the user's mailbox.
- **Mailbox servers**—The Mailbox servers use Lightweight Directory Access Protocol (LDAP) to access recipient, server, and organization information from AD.

Forest and Domain Functional Levels

With each new edition of the Windows Server and Exchange Server operating systems, new functionalities are introduced. Some of these enhancements require that the Active Directory infrastructure be upgraded before you can take advantage of the new capabilities. At times, these capabilities cannot be implemented until all domain controllers in an environment have been upgraded to the same level.

To support this, Active Directory has forest and domain functional levels that determine what enhancements are enabled or disabled. By raising the functional level of an environment, new functionalities are enabled. By maintaining an older functional level, interoperability with older domain controllers is supported.

Forest Functional Levels

Windows Server 2003 supports three forest functional levels:

- **Windows 2000 Native**—Required while any Windows 2000 Server domain controllers remain in your forest. Supports domain controllers running Windows NT 4.0, Windows 2000 Server, and Windows Server 2003.
- **Windows Server 2003 Interim**—A special functional level only implemented during Windows NT 4.0 to Windows Server 2003 upgrades.
- **Windows Server 2003**—All DCs in the forest must be running Windows Server 2003, and all domains in the forest must be at the Windows Server 2003 domain functional level before you can raise your forest functional level to Windows Server 2003.

Windows Server 2008 supports three forest functional levels:

- **Windows 2000 Native**—Supports Windows 2000 Server, Windows Server 2003, and Windows Server 2008 domain controllers
- **Windows Server 2003**—Allows for a mix of Windows Server 2003 and Windows Server 2008 functional level domains
- **Windows Server 2008**—Ensures all domain controllers in the forest are running Windows Server 2008 and all domains have been raised to the Windows Server 2008 domain functional level

Windows Server 2012 supports three forest functional levels:

- **Windows Server 2003**—Allows for a mix of Windows Server 2003 and Windows Server 2008 functional level domains
- **Windows Server 2008**—Ensures all domain controllers in the forest are running Windows Server 2008 and all domains have been raised to the Windows Server 2008 domain functional level
- **Windows Server 2012**—Ensures all domain controllers in the forest are running Windows Server 2012 and all domains have been raised to the Windows Server 2012 domain functional level

NOTE

To install Exchange Server 2013, the Active Directory forest functional level *must* be Windows Server 2003 or higher.

Windows 2000 Native and Windows Server 2003 Interim modes are *not* supported.

Domain Functional Levels

Windows Server 2008 supports three domain functional levels:

- **Windows 2000 Native**—Allows domain controllers running Windows Server 2008 to interact with domain controllers running either Windows Server 2008, Windows Server 2003, or Windows 2000 Server
- **Windows Server 2003**—Supports an environment composed of a mixture of Windows Server 2003 and Windows Server 2008 domain controllers
- **Windows Server 2008**—Only available after all domain controllers in a domain are running Windows Server 2008

Windows Server 2012 supports three domain functional levels:

- **Windows Server 2003**—Supports an environment composed of a mixture of Windows Server 2003 and Windows Server 2008 domain controllers
- **Windows Server 2008**—Supports an environment composed of a mixture of Windows Server 2008 and Windows Server 2012 domain controllers
- **Windows Server 2012**—Only available after all domain controllers in a domain are running Windows Server 2012

NOTE

To install Exchange Server 2013, the Active Directory domain functional level *must* be Windows Server 2003 or higher for each domain in the Active Directory forest that will house an Exchange Server 2013 server.

Windows 2000 Mixed, Windows 2000 Native, and Windows Server 2003 Interim modes are *not* supported.

Understanding Flexible Single Master Operations Roles

Active Directory uses a multimaster replication scheme for replicating directory information between domain controllers; however, certain domain and enterprisewide operations are not well suited for a multimaster model. Some services are better suited to a single master operation to prevent the introduction of conflicts while an Operations Master is offline. These services are referred to as Operations Master or Flexible Single Master Operations (FSMO) roles.

FSMO roles can be either forestwide or domainwide. The forestwide roles consist of the schema master and the domain naming master. The domainwide roles consist of the Relative ID (RID) master, the Primary Domain Controller (PDC) emulator, and the infrastructure master. A brief description of each is as follows:

- **Schema master**—Maintains all modifications to the schema throughout the Active Directory forest, as no other domain controller is allowed to write to the schema. The schema determines what types of objects are permitted in the forest and the attributes of those objects.

- **Domain naming master**—Maintains a list of the names of all domains in the forest and is required to add any new domains (or to remove existing ones).
- **RID master**—Allocates security RIDs to domain controllers to assign to new AD security users, groups, or computer objects. RIDs are the part of the security identifier (SID) that identifies an account or group within a domain. The RID master also manages objects moving between domains.
- **PDC emulator**—Processes all password changes in the domain. If a user logon attempt fails due to a bad password, the request is forwarded to the PDC emulator to check the password against the most recent one. This allows a user to log on immediately after a password change instead of having to wait for that change to replicate throughout the Active Directory.
- **Infrastructure master**—Maintains security identifiers, globally unique identifiers (GUIDs), and DNS for objects referenced across domains. This role is also responsible for ensuring that cross-domain group-to-user references are correctly maintained.

When designing the FSMO role placement of an Active Directory environment, the following best practices should be considered:

- If a domain has only one domain controller, that domain controller holds all the domain roles. However, this configuration is not recommended (even for smaller organizations), as it creates a single point of failure.
- The schema master and domain naming master should be placed on the same domain controller in the root or placeholder domain. This server can (and should) also be configured as a global catalog server.
- Place the RID master and PDC emulator roles on the same domain controller. If the load on this server justifies separating the roles, place them on domain controllers in the same domain and AD site and ensure the two domain controllers are direct replication partners of each other.
- As a general rule, the infrastructure master should be deployed on a domain controller that is *not* also a global catalog server. This domain controller should have a direct connection to a GC server, preferably in the same Active Directory site. Global catalog servers hold a partial replica of every object in the forest and the infrastructure master, when placed on a global catalog server, will never update anything as it does not contain any references to objects that it does not hold. There are two exceptions to this rule:

    - **Single domain forest**—In a forest with a single AD domain, there are no phantoms and the infrastructure master has no work to do. In this case, the infrastructure master can be placed on any domain, including those that are also global catalog servers.
    - **Multidomain forests where *every* domain controller is a global catalog server**—When *every* domain controller in a domain that is part of a

multidomain forest is configured as a global catalog server, there are no phantoms or work for the infrastructure master to do. The infrastructure master can be placed on any domain controller in the domain.

NOTE

As stated by Microsoft, to install Exchange Server 2013, the schema master must be running Windows Server 2003 with SP2 or later.

In addition, in each Active Directory site where you plan to install Exchange Server 2013, you must have at least one global catalog server that meets the same criteria.

Understanding How DNS and AD Namespace Are Used in Exchange Server 2013

The first step in the actual design of the AD structure is the decision on a common DNS namespace that AD will occupy. AD revolves around (and is inseparable from) DNS, and this decision is one of the most important ones to make. The namespace chosen can be as straightforward as companyabc.com, for example, or it can be more complex. Multiple factors must be considered, however, before this decision can be made. Is it better to register an AD namespace on the Internet and potentially expose it to intruders, or is it better to choose an unregistered, internal namespace? Is it necessary to tie in multiple namespaces into the same forest? These and other questions must be answered before the design process can proceed.

Impact Forests Have on an Exchange Server 2013 Design

An AD forest and an Exchange Server organization are tightly integrated. Exchange Server relies on AD as its directory repository for mailboxes, mail-enabled objects, Exchange servers, and much more. An AD forest can only host a single Exchange organization, and an Exchange organization can only span one AD forest.

It is recommended that a single AD forest should be utilized to minimize complexity and administration when designing and implementing a company's Exchange Server implementation. However, there will be times when a single AD forest will not meet the company's business, security, or political requirements.

If multiple AD forests are necessary to satisfy the company's requirements, it must be decided on which forest the Exchange organization will be hosted. It is possible to have Exchange Server reside in a single forest, a dedicated resource forest, or to implement multiple Exchange organizations in multiple forests.

The Role of a Domain in Exchange Server 2013

After the AD forest structure has been laid out, the domain structure can be contemplated. Unlike the forest structure, an Exchange Server 2013 organization can span multiple domains within the forest if needed. Therefore, a user mailbox, Exchange server, or other Exchange object can reside in any domain within the forest where Exchange Server 2013 has been deployed. A company can plan its domain model structure (single domain model or multiple domain model) based on its business and security requirements without a direct negative impact to the Exchange Server 2013 design.

Although a single domain model is often considered due to its simplicity, some organizations prefer the Placeholder Domain. The Placeholder Domain model has an isolated domain serving as the root domain in the forest. The user domain, which contains all production user accounts, would be located in a separate domain in the forest, as illustrated in Figure 6.1.

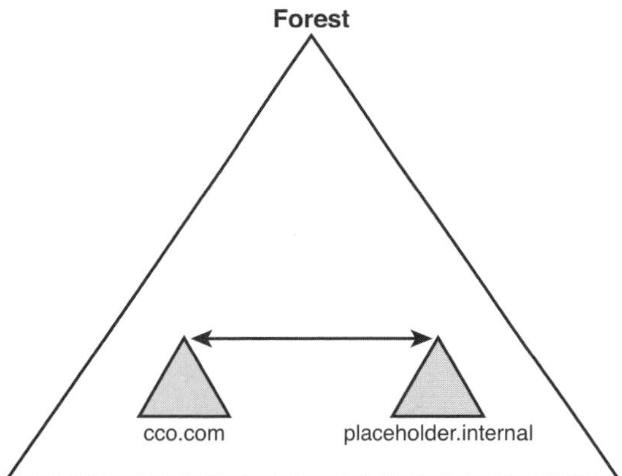

FIGURE 6.1 The placeholder domain model.

The placeholder domain structure increases security in the forest by segregating high-level schema-access accounts into a completely separate domain from the regular user domain. Access to the Placeholder Domain can be audited and restricted to maintain tighter control on the critical schema. A downside to this model, however, is that it requires a separate set of domain controllers, which increases the infrastructure costs of the environment. Smaller organizations may have a difficult time justifying the extra infrastructure costs to provide the increased security, but whenever the budget allows, this model should be considered.

Planning a Proper Sites and Services Architecture

As stated earlier, as with its predecessors, Exchange Server 2007 and Exchange Server 2010, Exchange Server 2013 has the ability to natively utilize Active Directory Sites and Services for routing mail, rather than having to implement and maintain an independent routing topology using connectors. For more information on coexistence of Exchange Server 2013 with legacy versions, refer to Chapter 7, "Transitioning from Exchange Server 2007/2010 to Exchange Server 2013."

Administrators should be aware of the best practices for designing a proper Sites and Services architecture to support Exchange Server 2013. From a high-level perspective, within AD it is necessary for administrators to create sites, allocate subnets to sites, and then create site links between sites for communication to occur.

Active Directory Sites

The basic unit of AD replication is known as the site. Not to be confused with physical sites or Exchange Server sites, the AD site is simply a group of domain controllers connected by high-speed network connections. Each site is established to more effectively replicate directory information across the network. In a nutshell, domain controllers within a single site will, by default, replicate more often than those that exist in other sites. The concept of the site constitutes the centerpiece of replication design in AD.

Associating Subnets with Sites

In most cases, a separate instance of a site in AD physically resides on a separate subnet from other sites. This idea stems from the concept that the site topology most often mimics, or should mimic, the physical network infrastructure of an environment.

In AD, sites are associated with their respective subnets to allow for the intelligent assignment of users to their respective domain controllers. For example, consider the design shown in Figure 6.2.

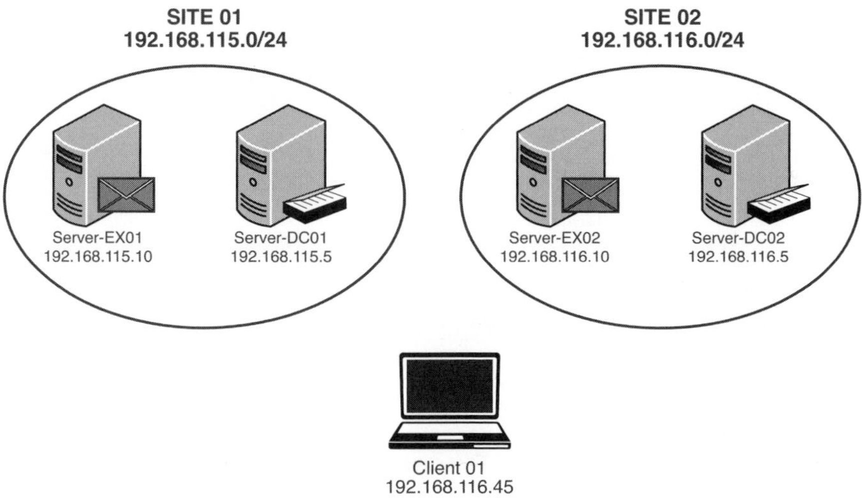

FIGURE 6.2 Sample Exchange Server and Client site assignment.

In this example, Server-EX01 is a physical member of the 192.168.115.0/24 subnet. Server-EX02 and Client01 are both members of the 192.168.116.0/24 subnet. Based on the subnets, Server-EX01 will automatically be assigned to the domain controller Server01 in SITE01, and Server-EX02 and Client01 will be assigned to the domain controller in SITE02.

Using Site Links

By default, the creation of two sites in AD does not automatically create a connection linking the two sites. This type of functionality must be manually implemented by the creation of a *site link*.

A site link is essentially a connection that joins together two sites and allows for replication traffic to flow from one site to another. Multiple site links can be set up and should normally follow the wide area network (WAN) lines of your organization. Multiple site links also assure redundancy so that if one link goes down, replication traffic has an alternate path.

Site link replication schedules can be modified to fit the requirements of your organization. If, for example, the WAN link is saturated during the day, a schedule can be established to replicate information at night. This functionality allows you to easily adjust site links to the needs of any WAN design.

Exchange Server 2013 and Site Membership

After the AD site topology has been created, including adding the appropriate subnets to sites and creating site links between sites, an administrator can now take Exchange Server placement into consideration.

Similar to AD domain controllers, Exchange Server 2013 servers will be associated with sites in AD based on their IP address and subnet mask. As stated earlier, there should be at least one domain controller/global catalog server residing in each site that an Exchange Server 2013 server resides.

For more information on creating an Exchange Server routing topology, refer to Chapter 3, "Architecting an Enterprise-Level Exchange Server 2013 Environment."

NOTE

If an AD infrastructure already exists prior to the design of the Exchange Server 2013 environment, there might be a need to make changes to the AD routing topology to support the Exchange routing requirements.

Establishing a Proper Global Catalog Placement Strategy

Another area of importance is the design and placement of global catalog servers within the environment. The importance of the global catalog server cannot be overstated. The global catalog is used for the address list that users see when they are addressing a message and by Exchange servers every time a message is delivered. If a global catalog server is not available, the recipient's address will not resolve when users address a message, and the message cannot be delivered.

There should be at least one global catalog server in every AD site that contains an Exchange Server 2013 server. The recommendation from Microsoft is as follows:

If Active Directory is running on a 32-bit system, the recommendation is 4:1—for every four processor cores in your Mailbox servers, you should have one processor core in a global catalog server. For example, if you have two Mailbox servers, each with dual quad-core processors, that is 16 processor cores. You should have at least 4 processor cores worth of global catalog computing, so 1 quad core server, or 2 dual-core servers should do the trick.

If Active Directory is running on a 64-bit system, the recommended ratio is 1:8. However, you must have enough memory installed on the server to cache the entire Active Directory database in memory. To confirm the size of your Active Directory database, look at the size of the `%WINDIR%\NTDS\NTDS.DIT` file.

For optimization, plan on having a global catalog server close to the clients to provide efficient address list access. Making all domain controller servers global catalog servers is recommended for an organization that has a single AD domain model and a single site. Otherwise, for multidomain models, all domain controllers can be configured as global catalog servers *except* for the domain controller hosting the Infrastructure Master FSMO role.

NOTE

It is a best practice to have a minimum of at least two global catalog servers within an AD infrastructure.

Understanding Role Based Access Control

Exchange Server 2013 uses the *Role Based Access Control* (RBAC) permissions model on the Mailbox and Client Access server roles. As with Exchange Server 2010, Exchange Server 2013 provides predefined roles, role groups, and role assignment policies to facilitate the assignment of permissions to administrators and users.

Using RBAC allows you to easily control what your administrators and users can (and cannot) access. Rather than applying permissions directly to user accounts, the permissions are applied directly to the role. To facilitate assigning multiple roles to administrators, Exchange Server 2013 includes role groups. Role groups can contain Active Directory users, universal security groups, and other role groups. Roles assigned to a role group grant permissions to all members of the role group.

In addition, role assignments can be "scoped" to include only specific resources within the organization. The role (and the permissions associated with it) allows certain tasks to be accomplished, while the role scope determines what resources can be administered.

The RBAC model role groups consist of the following:

- **Management role**—A container for grouping management role entries.
- **Management role entries**—A cmdlet (including parameters) that is added to a management role. This process grants rights to manage or view the objects associated with that cmdlet.

- **Management role assignment**—The assignment of a management role to a particular user or a universal security group. This grants the user (or the members of the security group) the ability to perform the management role entries in the management role that they are assigned to.
- **Management role scope**—Scopes are used to target the specific object or objects that the management role assignment is allowed to control. A management role scope can include servers, organizational units, filters on server or recipient objects, and more.

As described by Microsoft, this process allows complete control of the *who* (management role assignment), the *what* (management role and management role entries), and the *where* (management role scope) in the security model.

Role Based Access Control is *not* used on Edge Transport servers, as these servers are designed to sit outside the domain.

Exchange Server 2013 provides several built-in management role groups that cannot be modified, nor can the management role entries be configured on them. However, the *scope* of the built-in management roles can be modified.

The following built-in management role groups are included by default in Exchange Server 2013:

- **Organization Management**—Administrators assigned to this role group have administrative access to the entire Exchange Server 2013 organization, and can perform almost any task against any Exchange Server 2013 object, with some exceptions, such as the Discovery Management role. Even if a task can only be completed by another role, members of the Organization Management role group have the ability to add themselves to any other role.

  As this role group is very powerful, it is recommended that it only be assigned to users who are responsible for organizational-level administration. Changes made by this role can potentially impact the entire Exchange organization.
- **View-Only Organization Management**—Members of this role group can view the properties of any object in the Exchange organization but cannot modify the properties of any object.

  This role group is useful for personnel who need to be able to view the configuration of objects within the environment but who do not need the ability to add new or modify existing objects.
- **Recipient Management**—Administrators assigned to this role group have the ability to create or modify Exchange Server 2013 recipients within the organization.
- **UM Management**—Administrators assigned to this role group can manage features in the Exchange Server 2013 organization such as Unified Messaging (UM) server configuration, UM properties on mailboxes, UM prompts, and UM auto attendant configuration.

- **Help Desk**—Members of this role group can view and modify the Microsoft Office Outlook Web App options of any user in the organization, such as the user's display name, address, and phone number. However, it does not include options that aren't available in Outlook Web App options, such as modifying the size of mailboxes or configuring the mailbox database.
- **Hygiene Management**—Members of this role group can configure the antivirus and antispam features of Exchange Server 2013.
- **Records Management**—Administrators assigned to this role group have the ability to configure compliance features, including transport rules, message classifications, retention policy tags, and others.

  This role group is often assigned to administrators or members of an organization's Legal Department who need the ability to view and modify compliance features in an organization.
- **Discovery Management**—Administrators assigned to this role group have the ability to perform searches of mailboxes in the Exchange organization for data that meets specific criteria and can also configure legal holds on mailboxes.
- **Public Folder Management**—Member of this role group can manage Exchange Server 2013 public folders.
- **Server Management**—Administrators assigned to this role group can configure Unified Messaging, client access, server-specific configuration of transport, and mailbox features, such as database copies, certificates, transport queues and Send connectors, virtual directories, and client access protocols.
- **Delegated Setup**—Members of this role group have the ability to deploy servers running Exchange Server 2013 that have been provisioned by a member of the Organization Management role group.
- **Compliance Management**—Administrators assigned to this role group have the ability to configure and manage Exchange compliance settings in accordance with their organization's policy.

If the Exchange Server 2013 built-in role groups don't match the job functions of the organization's administrators, role groups can be created and customized.

NOTE

Membership in the Organization Management role group should be limited to personnel who have advanced knowledge of the Exchange Server operating system and your particular network environment.

Exchange Server 2013 also provides role assignment policies to control the settings that users can configure on their personal mailboxes and distribution groups. The policies can control the users' ability to change their display name, contact information, membership in distribution groups, or voice mail settings. Mailboxes are assigned a default role assignment policy if an alternative role assignment policy is not specified.

The Exchange Administration Center (EAC) can be used to manage role groups and role assignment policies.

Planning Your Exchange Server 2013 Installation

Before installing Exchange Server, you should review the following chapters earlier in this book:

- Chapter 1, "Exchange Server 2013 Technology Primer," covers what is new in Exchange Server 2013 and differences between the available versions.
- Chapter 2, "Understanding Core Exchange Server 2013 Design Plans."
- Chapter 3, "Architecting an Enterprise-Level Exchange Server 2013 Environment," addresses the planning and design of an Exchange Server 2013 implementation for a small, medium, or large enterprise organization.

From these chapters, you will learn the industry best practices and recommendations for planning and deploying Exchange Server 2013.

Installing Exchange Server 2013 in a Test Environment

To reduce risks, prevent end-user downtime, and minimize the exposure of the production environment, it is typically recommended that the first implementation of Exchange Server 2013 be conducted in an isolated test lab rather than being installed into a production environment.

Having a test environment isolates functional errors so that if there are any problems they will not be injected into the existing production environment. In addition, the test environment acts as a "Proof of Concept" for the new Exchange Server 2013 design.

Occasionally, organizations attempt to repurpose their test environments into their production environment. Administrators should be cautious, as "shortcuts" are sometimes taken in the lab—the use of evaluation copies of software and/or underpowered hardware may work flawlessly in the lab, but transitioning the equipment to production results in inadequate performance and unnecessary downtime.

Production equipment should be rebuilt and deployed from scratch, not moved from a test environment.

Prototyping an Exchange Server 2013 Installation

Some of the steps an organization should go through when considering to build a test Exchange Server environment include the following:

- Building Exchange Server 2013 in a lab
- Testing email features and functionality

- Reviewing Exchange Server 2013 server roles
- Verifying design configuration
- Testing failover and recovery
- Selecting to install on physical hardware or virtual machines

Much of the validation and testing should occur during the testing process. It is much easier, for example, to test a disaster recovery rebuild of Exchange Server in an exclusive test environment than it is to do so in a production environment, where production servers or users could accidentally be impacted.

In addition, testing application compatibility in a lab environment can be much more effective than attempting to do so in a production environment, where you might suddenly find business-critical third-party fax, voice mail, or paging software nonfunctional.

Other items to test and confirm in your lab environment include the following:

- **Sites and Services Configuration**—Ensure replication is completed as expected.
- **Role Based Access Control**—Ensure the proposed security settings allow proper user and administrative access.

Building an Exchange Server 2013 prototype test lab can be a costly affair for companies that want to simulate a large, global implementation. For companies with a global presence where it is necessary to provide messaging services for thousands of employees, in multiple sites throughout the world, mirroring their production site can prove a daunting task. However, without successfully prototyping the installation, upgrade strategy, and application compatibility before they move forward in production, they cannot be assured that the deployment will go smoothly.

The cost of building a lab of this magnitude using physical servers can be prohibitive; there can be AD domain controllers, Exchange Server 2007 and 2010 servers, and application servers. The cost of building the lab could eat up a large part of the overall budget allocated to the project.

However, with the improvements in server virtualization, companies can significantly lower the costs associated with the prototype phase. Server virtualization enables multiple virtual operating systems to run on a single physical machine, while remaining logically distinct with consistent hardware profiles. For further cost savings, the hardware utilized for the virtual lab can be purchased with an eye toward reutilization in the production environment once the prototype phase is complete.

Upgrading from Previous Versions of Microsoft Windows

Many organizations already have an existing directory structure in place. It is great if a company has the opportunity to implement a new Windows Server 2008 R2 or Windows

Server 2012 AD environment from scratch; however, this is not usually possible for environments with previous versions of Exchange Server deployed.

When upgrading an existing Active Directory infrastructure, the deployment plan should be carefully thought out and tested before implementation in the production environment.

Deploying Active Directory from Scratch

Before installing Exchange Server 2013, there must be an existing Active Directory environment to support it. The environment must have at least one domain controller running either Windows Server 2008 Standard or Enterprise, Windows Server 2008 R2 Standard or Enterprise, or Windows Server 2012. The following sections focus on the steps needed to install an Active Directory environment on a Windows Server 2008 R2 platform from scratch. This example can be followed in a lab environment to prepare it for the deployment of Exchange Server 2013.

This sample deployment will consist of a single site and single domain controller, as might be found in a small organization. The steps we will deploy include the following:

- Installing the Windows Server 2008 R2 with SP1 operating system
- Promoting a Windows Server 2008 R2 SP1 Server to a domain controller
- Configuring Active Directory Sites and Services
- Configuring a global catalog server

Installing the Windows Server 2008 R2 SP1 Operating System

Microsoft Exchange servers rely heavily on the Active Directory environment they are installed in.

For those experienced with installing previous versions of the Windows Server operating system, most of the concepts covered in this section will feel very familiar. The installation of Windows Server 2008 R2 SP1 is straightforward, and takes approximately 30 minutes to an hour to complete. The following procedure is based on installing Windows Server from the standard media provided by Microsoft. Many hardware manufacturers include special installation instructions and procedures specific to their hardware platform, but the concepts should be roughly the same.

For our test lab, we will install Windows Server 2008 R2 SP1 Enterprise Edition on two machines. One will be promoted later in the chapter to a domain controller. The other will have the Exchange Server 2013 software installed on it.

To install Windows Server 2008 R2 SP1 (Standard or Enterprise Edition), perform the following steps:

1. Insert the Windows Server 2008 R2 SP1 DVD into the DVD drive.
2. Power up the server and let it boot to the DVD-ROM drive. If there is currently no operating system on the hard drive, it automatically boots into the DVD-ROM-based setup.
3. Select the Language to Install, the Time and Currency Format, and the Keyboard or Input Method you want to install. When ready, click Next to continue.
4. Click Install Now.
5. Select which version of the Windows Server 2008 R2 operating system you want to install. For this example, we will be installing Windows Server 2008 R2 Enterprise (Full Installation) on a 64-bit platform. When ready, click Next to continue.
6. Review the Microsoft Software License Terms, click the I Accept the License Terms check box, and click Next to continue.
7. Select Custom (Advanced) to install a clean copy of Windows.
8. Select the physical disk on which Windows will be installed and click Next to continue.

   The server will begin the installation process, rebooting several times during the process.
9. A default user account called Administrator will be created, but you will have to set the password for this account. When prompted with "The User's Password Must Be Changed Before Logging on the First Time," click OK to continue.
10. Enter the new password for the Administrator account in both the New Password and Confirm Password fields, and then click the arrow to continue. When prompted with "Your Password Has Been Changed," click OK.

Once the installation process has completed, there will be an Initial Configuration Tasks screen. Perform the steps in the Provide Computer Information section as follows.

Setting the Time Zone

To set the server time zone, follow these steps:

1. Click Set Time Zone. On the Date and Time tab, review the current Date, Time, and Time zone settings and configure them as needed.
2. If desired, up to two additional clocks can be configured for additional time zones with customized display names. If you want to display more than one clock, select the Additional Clocks tab and configure them.
3. By default, Windows Server 2008 R2 servers are configured to automatically synchronize with time.windows.com. The server is configured to synchronize once a week. If you need to change the source of your time updates, you can click the Internet Time tab. This process changes when servers are joined to the domain.
4. Click OK to return to the Initial Configuration Tasks screen.

Configuring Networking

Windows Server 2008 R2 has a completely redesigned implementation of the TCP/IP protocol stack, which is known as the *Next Generation TCP/IP stack*. This updated functionality applies to both Internet Protocol version 4 (IPv4) and Internet Protocol version 6 (IPv6).

1. Click Configure Networking, double-click the Local Area Network Connection icon, and then click Properties.
2. Double-click the Internet Protocol Version 4 (TCP/IPv4) option and input appropriate values for the IP Address, Subnet Mask, Default Gateway, and Preferred DNS Server for your environment.
3. Click OK to save your changes.
4. Perform the same steps to configure the Internet Protocol version 6 (TCP/IPv6).
5. Save all settings and exit the Configure Networking utility.
6. Launch Internet Explorer and confirm Internet connectivity. Adjust your network settings if necessary to allow the computer access to the Internet.

Providing the Computer Name and Domain

Each computer on a Windows network and in Active Directory must have a unique computer name. This name, known as the NetBIOS name, allows users, resources, and other computers to contact this computer on the network.

A standard NetBIOS name is limited to 15 characters and should only consist of letters (A–Z, a–z), digits (0–9), and hyphens (-). For example, companyabc-dc is a standard computer name, but companyabc_dc is nonstandard. Although the implementation of a DNS server will allow you to use nonstandard computer names and still find the resources in your environment, servers as critical as domain controllers and Exchange servers should only use standard computer names.

To configure the computer name and domain, follow these steps:

1. Click Provide Computer Name and Domain. If you have already closed your Initial Configuration Tasks screen, you can click Start, right-click Computer, select Properties; then, under Computer Name, Domain, and Workgroup Settings, click Change Settings.
2. On the Computer Name tab, click Change.
3. Under Computer Name, enter the computer name for this machine, and then click OK to continue.
4. Acknowledge that you must restart your computer to apply these changes by clicking OK, and then click Close.
5. When prompted with "You Must Restart Your Computer to Apply These Changes," click Restart Now.

Enabling Automatic Updating and Feedback

Windows Server allows you the option of automatically applying updates as they are released from Microsoft. Although this option may be a good idea for some applications, most organizations require change control procedures before updating servers as business critical as domain controllers and Exchange servers.

1. Click Enable Automatic Updating and Feedback. Although the first option, Enable Windows Automatic Updating and Feedback, states that it is "recommended," in this author's opinion, that setting is *not* recommended for domain controllers or Exchange servers. Instead, click Manually Configure Settings.

2. Under Windows Automatic Updating, click Change Setting. Set the automatic updates according to your organization's policies. The author recommends selecting either Download Updates but Let Me Choose Whether to Install Them or Check for Updates but Let Me Choose Whether to Download and Install Them. In addition, the author recommends Give Me Recommended Updates the Same Way I Receive Important Updates, as shown in Figure 6.3.

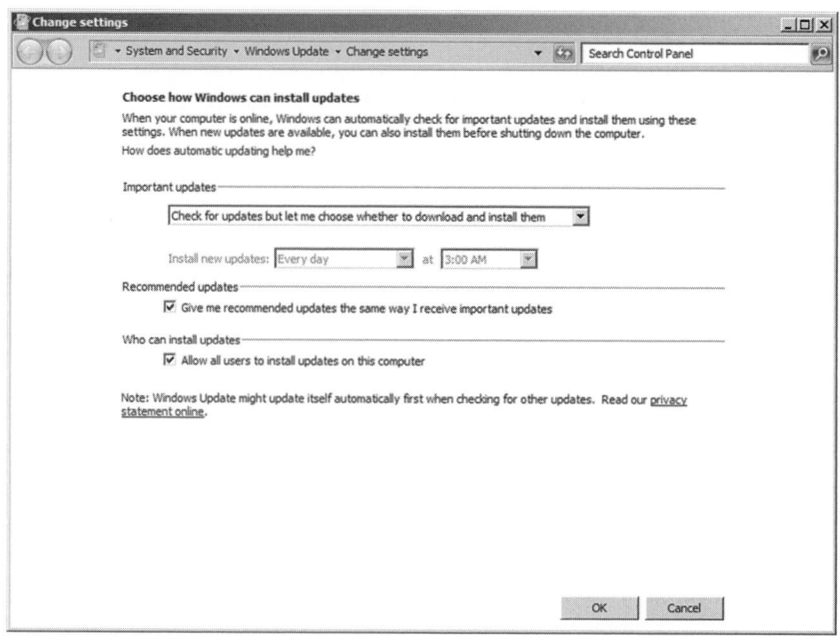

FIGURE 6.3 Configuring automatic updates.

3. When ready, click OK to continue.

4. Review the Windows Error Reporting and Customer Experience Improvement Program settings. The author recommends the default settings, as shown in Figure 6.4. When finished, click Close to continue.

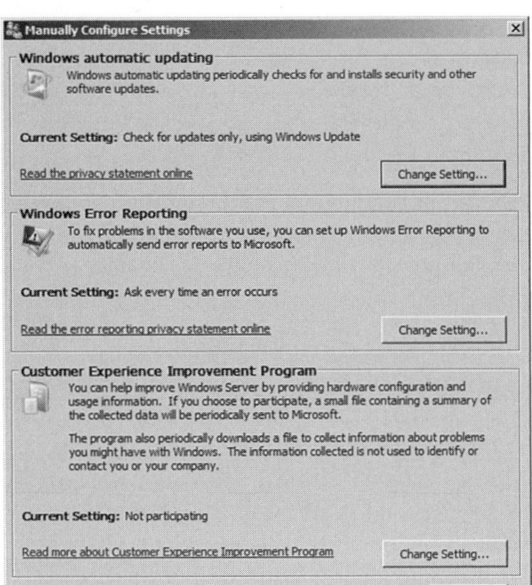

FIGURE 6.4 Configuring Windows Error Reporting and Customer Experience Improvement Program.

5. Click Download and Install Updates. If prompted to install new Windows Update Software, click Install Now. As part of the installation process, the Windows Updates application will automatically close and reopen and begin checking for updates.
6. At this point, you can either view the important and optional updates that are available and select which ones to install or simply click Install Updates to automatically download and install the selected updates.
7. Accept any license agreements and click Finish to begin installing available updates. Monitor the installation, as you may have additional prompts from the installation process. When finished, if a restart is required, click Restart Now.
8. When the server has rebooted, log on again and return to the Download and Install Updates section.
9. Click Find Out More for Get Updates for Other Microsoft Products.
10. From the Microsoft Update site, place a check mark in the I Agree to the Terms of Use for Microsoft Update check box and click Next.
11. Select Use Current Settings and click Install. If prompted to install new Windows Update Software, click Install Now.
12. When complete, your server now checks for updates for all Microsoft products on the server (such as Exchange Server), and not just for the standard Windows updates. Close all windows to finish.

This concludes the installation of the base operating system for both the domain controller and the Exchange Server 2013 server.

Promoting a Windows Server 2008 R2 Server to a Domain Controller

As previously stated, in this example we are creating a new Active Directory environment, creating a new forest and domain, and installing a new domain controller in that domain. This is accomplished by using the Active Directory Domain Services Installation Wizard.

To set up the domain controller, follow these steps:

1. The Installation wizard can be started from the Add Roles option on the Initial Configuration Tasks screen, but the easiest way is simply to kick off the wizard from a command prompt. To do so, from the Start menu, select Run, type **`DCPROMO`** in the text box, and then click OK. This installs the Active Directory Domain Services binaries and starts the Installation Wizard.

2. When the wizard starts, select Use Advanced Mode Installation and click Next.

NOTE

There were many improvements in the Active Directory Domain Services Installation Wizard in Windows Server 2008. Although all of these improvements are available by default, some of the wizard pages will appear only if the administrator selects Use Advanced Mode Installation.

Advanced mode installation can also be selected by running the `DCPROMO` command with the `/ADV` switch (`dcpromo /adv`).

3. On the Operating System Compatibility screen, read the information and then click Next.

4. At the Choose a Deployment Configuration screen, for our purposes, we select Create a New Domain in a New Forest and click Next. Other available options enable you to modify an existing forest by adding a new domain controller in a new or existing domain.

5. Enter the fully qualified domain name (FQDN) of the Forest Root Domain and click Next. For our example, we use **`companyabc.lab`**.

6. Enter the Domain NetBIOS name. A suggested default name is suggested for you, derived from the Forest Root Domain name in the previous step. In our example, the suggested domain name is **`COMPANYABC`**. When you have the domain name entered, click Next.

7. Set the Forest Functional Level. For our purposes, set the level to Windows Server 2003, as Exchange Server 2013 requires at least Windows Server 2003 or higher. If you are certain your environment will not contain any Windows Server 2003 domain controllers in the future, you can set it to Windows Server 2008. For our test installation, we select Windows Server 2003 and click Next to continue.

8. Set the Domain Functional Level. As above, we will select Windows Server 2003 and click Next.

9. Microsoft recommends that you install DNS server on the first domain controller, and requires that this server be a global catalog. Leave the default settings and click Next to continue. Electing to install Microsoft DNS on the new domain controller will also modify the server's TCP/IP properties to use the new DNS installation for name resolution.

10. If your computer has any IP addresses (either IPv4 or IPv6) that are assigned by a DHCP server, you will receive a notice that static IP addresses should be assigned to all network adapters. Check your IP settings and continue when ready.

11. If no authoritative parent DNS zone exists, you will receive the warning shown in Figure 6.5.

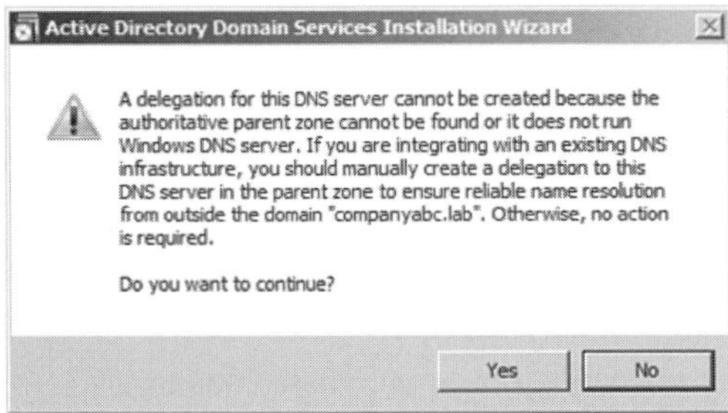

FIGURE 6.5 DNS installation error message.

In our example, we are not integrating with an existing DNS infrastructure, so we will simply click Yes to continue.

12. Depending on your server configuration design, select the location where the AD databases will be located. Using the Browse buttons, select the locations for your Database, Log Files, and SYSVOL folders. When ready, click Next.

NOTE

When configuring AD database locations, make sure that your server hardware configuration plan takes recoverability and performance into account.

For best performance, install the AD databases on a separate hard disk than the server operating system and server page file.

For best recoverability, use disk fault tolerance such as RAID or disk mirroring for the AD databases.

13. Assign a password to the Directory Services Restore Mode Administrator account. This account is used in the event that you have to start the domain controller in Directory Services Restore Mode. This password should be a strong password, containing a combination of uppercase and lowercase letters, numbers, and special characters. The password should be documented and stored in a secure location. Enter the Directory Services Restore Mode Administrator password and click Next.
14. Review the selections you have made. In the future, when creating additional domain controllers that will be similar to one another, you can export the settings to an "answer file" that you can use for future unattended installations. If you need to make any changes, use the Back button to go to the section you want to change, and then use the Next button to return you to the review screen. When ready, click Next to continue.
15. The Installation Wizard now installs DNS and the Active Directory Domain Services. When the installation has completed, click Finish to close the wizard, and then click Restart Now to restart the server.

When the server has rebooted, log on to the new domain. Your default administrator account will now be a domain administrator, and the password is the same. Take the time to review the server's Event Viewer application and system logs to identify any errors or potential problems with your installation before continuing.

Configuring Active Directory Sites and Services

As previously stated, for Exchange Server 2013 to successfully deliver mail, it relies heavily on Active Directory Sites and Services to determine what site particular servers belong to.

After the AD domain controller has been installed, it is necessary to configure Sites and Services to support the future Exchange Server deployment. In our example, we are going to configure two sites for a future installation of Exchange servers in two locations. We cover how to rename the default first site and how to create the second site from scratch.

Changing Site Properties

To change the AD Default-First-Site-Name, follow these steps:

1. On the domain controller, select Start, Administrative Tools, Active Directory Sites and Services.
2. Click the plus sign (+) to expand the Sites tree.
3. Right-click Default-First-Site-Name in the left pane of the console, and then click Rename.
4. Enter a name, and then press Enter, which changes the default site name to your custom site name. In our sample lab, we will use `FredericksburgVA`.

Creating a New Active Directory Site

To create a new site in AD, follow these steps:

1. On the domain controller, open AD Sites and Services.
2. Click the plus sign (+) to expand the Sites tree.
3. Right-click Sites in the left pane of the console, and then click New and Site.
4. Enter the new site name in the New Object-Site dialog box. In this example, we will use `SunnyvaleCA`.
5. Click to highlight DEFAULTIPSITELINK, and then click OK.
6. Review the Active Directory Domain Services message box (shown in Figure 6.6) and ensure the configuration was successful, and then click OK.

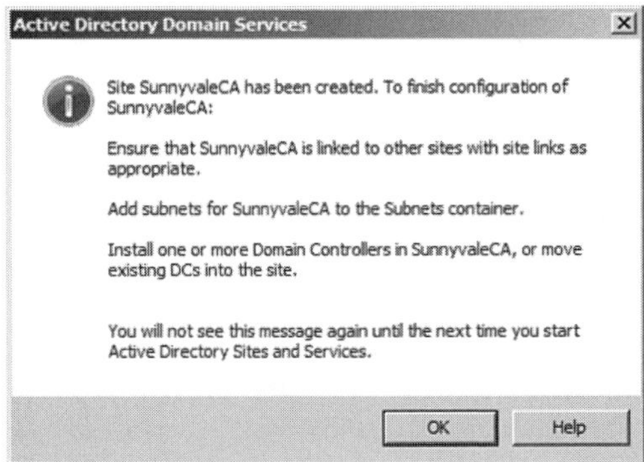

FIGURE 6.6 Active Directory Domain Services message box.

In AD, sites are associated with their respective subnets to allow for the intelligent assignment of users to their respective domain controllers.

To create a new subnet and associate it with a site, follow these steps:

1. Open AD Sites and Services.
2. Click the plus sign (+) to expand the Sites tree.
3. Right-click Subnets and choose New and Subnet.
4. Enter the address prefix using network prefix notation. This requires the address and the prefix length, where the prefix length shows the number of fixed bits in the subnet. The example shown in Figure 6.7 uses the 192.168.80.0/24 subnet, providing us with a Class C (255.255.255.0) subnet. Next, select a site to associate with the subnet and click OK.

Perform the same steps to create a second subnet and associate it with the second site.

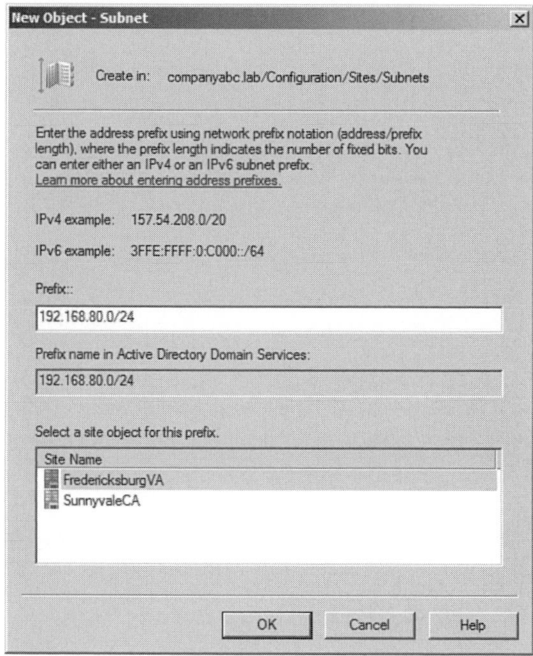

FIGURE 6.7 Associate a subnet to a site.

Configuring a Global Catalog Server

By default, the first domain controller in a domain is automatically configured as a global catalog server. Any additional domain controllers need to be configured manually.

To configure or verify that a domain controller is a global catalog server, follow these steps:

1. Open AD Sites and Services.
2. Click the plus sign (+) to expand the Sites tree.
3. Expand the desired site name, the Servers folder, and then the server object.
4. Right-click the NTDS Settings object, and then click Properties.
5. On the General tab, ensure the Global Catalog check box is marked if you want the server to be a global catalog server (as illustrated in Figure 6.8). When ready, click OK.

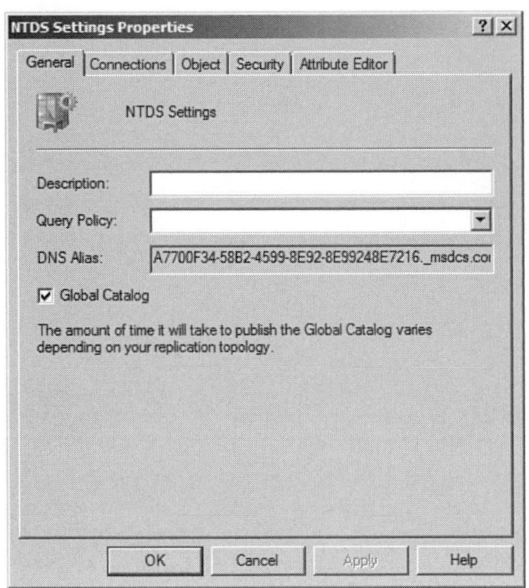

FIGURE 6.8 Configuring a global catalog server.

Preparing Your Environment for Exchange Server 2013

Before deploying Exchange Server 2013, there are several steps that *must* be done, and several more that are highly recommended.

Performing an Active Directory Health Check

This is a step that is highly recommended, especially if AD is not being set up from scratch (as it is in our scenario). The existing AD environment should be validated to ensure it is functioning correctly. Because Exchange Server relies so heavily on Active Directory, an extensive health check utilizing tools such as DCDiag, NetDiag, and Replication Monitor can help identify any underlying problems that will impact the installation or performance of Exchange Server. A combination of Windows Server 2003 and Windows Server 2008 support tools can be utilized for these tasks.

For detailed instructions on performing an AD health check, see the Digital ShortCut titled "Performing an AD Health Check" (Sams Publishing, ISBN: 0-7686-6842-5), which can be purchased and downloaded from http://www.samspublishing.com/bookstore/product.asp?isbn=0768668425.

Granting the Appropriate Permissions

To install Exchange Server 2013, you must make sure the domain account you will be using is a member of the following groups: Domain Admins, Enterprise Admins, and Schema Admins.

To do so, perform the following steps:

1. On the domain controller, from the Start menu, select Administrative Tools, then Active Directory Users and Computers.
2. Right-click the domain and click Find. Enter the name of the account that you will be using to install Exchange Server 2013 and click Find Now.
3. Double-click the user account and select the Member Of tab.
4. Click Add. In the Enter the Object Names to Select field, type **`Enterprise Admins; Domain Admins; Schema Admins`** (separated by semicolons as shown). Click Check Names to ensure all group names are resolved, and then click OK. Ensure all three groups show in the Member Of section and click Apply. Click OK to exit the screen.

Installing the Base Operating System on Your Exchange Server

Exchange Server 2013 can be installed on Windows Server 2008 R2 Standard or Enterprise with SP1, Windows Server 2008 R2 Datacenter RTM or later, or Windows Server 2012 operating systems. Although either Standard or Enterprise can be used, the Enterprise version is required for some of the more advanced Exchange Server features such as DAGs.

Perform the following steps to deploy and join the Exchange server to the domain:

1. Install Windows Server 2008 R2 with Service Pack 1 on your Exchange server by following the installation procedures earlier in this chapter in the section titled "Installing the Windows Server 2008 R2 SP1 Operating System." Do *not* continue with promoting the server to a domain controller.
2. On the TCP/IPv4 settings of your new Exchange server configure your domain controller/DNS server as the preferred DNS server.
3. From the Initial Configuration Tasks screen, click Provide Computer Name and Domain.
4. On the Computer Name tab, click Change.
5. In the Member Of section, select the Domain option button and type the name of the domain you created. In our example, this is **`companyabc`**. Click OK to continue.
6. When prompted, enter the administrator name and password for your domain and click OK.
7. When prompted with "Welcome to the companyabc Domain," click OK; then click OK again to acknowledge that the computer must be restarted. Close all open windows and, when prompted, click Restart Now.
8. After the computer restarts, from the logon screen, click Switch User; then click Other User and enter the domain administrator credentials in the following format: *domain\administrator*, where *domain* is the name of your domain, and *administrator* is the administrative account for that domain.

Preparing Internet Explorer to Accept ActiveX Downloads

The default security settings of Windows Server 2008 R2, combined with the default security settings of Internet Explorer 8.0, can result in some real challenges when attempting to download the prerequisite applications for Exchange Server. To ease the process, perform the following settings.

1. On the new Exchange server, log on with your domain administrative account.
2. Right-click the Internet Explorer icon and click Run as Administrator. Ensure you have Internet connectivity by bringing up an Internet website. If you do not, troubleshoot your network settings and resolve any issues before continuing.
3. In Internet Explorer, select Tools, and then Internet Options. Select the Security tab and then the Trusted Sites icon, and click Sites.
4. In the Add This Website to the Zone field, type `https://connect.microsoft.com` and click Add. Then type `https://download.microsoft.com` and click Add. When finished, click Close.
5. Click the Internet icon and click Custom Level. Under the ActiveX Controls and Plug-Ins section, change Download Signed ActiveX Controls to Prompt (Recommended).
6. Click OK and click Yes in response to the warning; then click OK again and exit Internet Explorer.

Installing Required Windows Roles and Features

There are several additional operating system components that are prerequisites for all Exchange Server 2013 roles. In addition, there are specific prerequisites that are required for each of the individual roles.

To determine what prerequisites are needed for each role, review the Exchange Server 2013 Prerequisites document on Microsoft TechNet. You can find this by going to http://technet.microsoft.com and searching for "Exchange 2013 Prerequisites."

The following components are required for a server that will contain the Client Access and Mailbox server roles:

- Web-Server
- Web-ISAPI-Ext
- Web-Metabase
- Web-Lgcy-Mgmt-Console
- Web-Basic-Auth
- Web-Digest-Auth
- Web-Windows-Auth
- Web-Dyn-Compression
- NET-HTTP-Activation
- RPC-over-HTTP-proxy
- Desktop-Experience
- NET-Framework
- RSAT-Clustering
- RSAT-Web-Server

- WAS-Process-Model
- Web-Asp-Net
- Web-Client-Auth
- Web-Dir-Browsing
- Web-Http-Errors
- Web-Http-Logging
- Web-Http-Redirect
- Web-Http-Tracing
- Web-ISAPI-Filter
- Web-Mgmt-Console
- Web-Mgmt-Service
- Web-Net-Ext
- Web-Request-Monitor
- Web-Stat-Compression
- Web-Static-Content
- Web-WMI

To install these roles, perform the following steps:

1. Log on with your domain administrator account. Run Windows PowerShell as an administrator.
2. Run the following command to load the Server Manager module:

   ```
   Import-Module ServerManager
   ```

3. Run the following command to install the required roles and features:

   ```
   Add-WindowsFeature Desktop-Experience, NET-Framework, NET-HTTP-Activation,
   RPC-over-HTTP-proxy, RSAT-Clustering, RSAT-Web-Server, WAS-Process-Model,
   Web-Asp-Net, Web-Basic-Auth, Web-Client-Auth, Web-Digest-Auth,
   Web-Dir-Browsing, Web-Dyn-Compression, Web-Http-Errors, Web-Http-Logging,
   Web-Http-Redirect, Web-Http-Tracing, Web-ISAPI-Ext, Web-ISAPI-Filter,
   Web-Lgcy-Mgmt-Console, Web-Metabase, Web-Mgmt-Console, Web-Mgmt-Service,
   Web-Net-Ext, Web-Request-Monitor, Web-Server, Web-Stat-Compression,
   Web-Static-Content, Web-Windows-Auth, Web-WMI
   ```

   When complete, you should see Success: True.

4. Upon completion, close all open windows and restart the server.

Installing the Prerequisites

After installing the additional roles and features, there are some software applications that must be installed on the server before you can run the Exchange Setup Wizard. Except as noted in the following, these applications must be installed regardless of which server role you are going to install. Install the following applications in the order shown:

Installing Microsoft .NET Framework 4.5

Windows Server 2012 includes .NET Framework 4.5. Therefore, this section can be skipped for a Windows Server 2012 installation. To install .NET Framework 4.5, follow these steps:

1. Log on to the server with your domain administrative account.
2. Download the .NET Framework 4.5 directly through the Microsoft Download Center.
3. Navigate to the directory containing the downloaded file. Double-click the downloaded file to start the install. When prompted with "Do You Want to Run This File?" click Run.
4. Accept the license terms by clicking I Have Read and Accept the License Terms. Click Install to start the installation.
5. Click Finish when complete.

Installing Windows Management Framework 3.0 (KB2506143)

This section can be skipped for a Windows Server 2012 installation. To install Windows Management Framework 3.0, follow these steps:

1. Log on to the server with your domain administrative account.
2. Download the correct Windows Management Framework package for your operating system and architecture directly through the Microsoft Download Center.
3. Navigate to the directory containing the downloaded file. Double-click the downloaded file to start the install. When prompted with "Do You Want to Install the Following Windows Software Update?" click Yes.
4. Accept the license terms by clicking I Accept to start the installation.
5. Once completed, click Restart Now.

Installing Microsoft Unified Communications Managed API 4.0, Core Runtime 64-Bit

To install the Unified Communications Managed API 4.0, follow these steps:

1. Log on to the server with your domain administrative account.
2. Download the Microsoft Unified Communications Managed API 4.0, Core Runtime 64-bit directly through the Microsoft Download Center.
3. Navigate to the directory containing the downloaded file. Double-click the downloaded file to start the install. When prompted with "Do You Want to Run This File?" click Run.
4. From the Microsoft Unified Communications Managed API 4.0, Runtime Wizard, click Next.
5. Accept the license terms by clicking I Have Read and Accept the License Terms. Click Install to start the installation.
6. Click Finish when complete.

Installing the Microsoft Office 2010 Filter Pack 64-Bit

This section is required only for Exchange Server 2013 servers that will have the Mailbox server role installed. To install the Microsoft Office 2010 Filter Pack 64-Bit, follow these steps:

1. Log on to the server with your domain administrative account.
2. Download the Microsoft Office 2010 Filter Pack directly through the Microsoft Download Center.
3. Navigate to the directory containing the downloaded file. Double-click the downloaded file to start the install. When prompted with "Do You Want to Run This File?" click Run.
4. From the Welcome screen, click Next.
5. Accept the license terms by clicking I Accept the Terms in the Licensing Agreement. Click Next to start the installation.
6. When complete, click OK to exit the installation.

Installing Service Pack 1 for Microsoft Office Filter Pack 2010 (KB2460041) 64-Bit Edition

This section is required only for Exchange Server 2013 servers that will have the Mailbox server role installed. To install Service Pack 1, follow these steps:

1. Log on to the server with your domain administrative account.
2. Download the Service Pack 1 for Microsoft Office Filter Pack 2010 (KB2460041) directly through the Microsoft Download Center.
3. Navigate to the directory containing the downloaded file. Double-click the downloaded file to start the install. When prompted with "Do You Want to Run This File?" click Run.
4. From the Microsoft Software License Terms screen, click Click Here to Accept the Microsoft Software License Terms and click Continue.
5. When complete, click OK to exit the installation.

Installing Windows Identity Foundation (KB974405)

This section can be skipped for a Windows Server 2012 installation. To install Windows Identity Foundation, follow these steps:

1. Log on to the server with your domain administrative account.
2. Download Windows Identity Foundation directly through the Microsoft Download Center.
3. Navigate to the directory containing the downloaded file. Double-click the downloaded file to start the install.

4. When prompted with "Do You Want to Install the Following Windows Software Update?" click Yes.
5. Accept the license terms by clicking I Accept to start the installation.
6. When complete, click Close to exit the installation.

Installing the Hot Fix to Enable the Association Cookie/GUID That Is Used by RPC over HTTP (KB2619234)

This section can be skipped for a Windows Server 2012 installation. To install the hot fix, follow these steps:

1. Log on to the server with your domain administrative account.
2. Open Internet Explorer and go to www.support.microsoft.com. Search for KB2619234. Select the hot fix.
3. On the Microsoft Support page for the hot fix, click Hotfix Download Available. On the Terms and Conditions screen, click I Accept.
4. Click the Select box for the Windows 7/Windows Server 2008 R2 SP1, Fix381274. Enter your email, confirm your email, and type the characters shown in the Picture. Click Request Hotfix.
5. Navigate to your email, locate the email with the hot fix, and follow the instructions for downloading the hot fix.
6. Navigate to the directory containing the downloaded file. Double-click the downloaded file to start the install. When prompted with "Do You Want to Run This File?" click Run.
7. Click Continue on the Microsoft Self-Extractor screen. Select a folder where the files can be extracted and click OK. Click OK when the files are unzipped successfully.
8. Navigate to the folder where the file was extracted. Double-click the file to start the install. When prompted "Do You Want to Install the Following Windows Software Update?" click Yes.
9. Once completed, click Restart Now.

Installing Updates for Microsoft Security Advisory: Insecure Library Loading Could Allow Remote Code Execution (KB2533623)

NOTE

This hot fix may already be installed if you have configured Windows Update to install Security Updates.

This section can be skipped for a Windows Server 2012 installation. To install this hot fix, follow these steps:

1. Log on to the server with your domain administrative account.
2. Open Internet Explorer and go to www.support.microsoft.com. Search for KB2533623. Select Microsoft Security Advisory: Insecure Library Loading Could Allow Remote Code Execution.
3. On the Validation Required screen, click Continue.
4. Look for the Internet Explorer Information Bar. When prompted with "This Website Wants to Install the Following Add-On: 'Windows Genuine Advantage' from Microsoft Corporation," click Install.
5. When prompted "Do You Want to Install this Software?" click Install.
6. On the hot fix download screen, click Download.
7. Save the file to a local folder.
8. Double-click the downloaded file to start the install. When prompted with "Do You Want to Install the Following Windows Software Update?" click Yes.
9. Once completed, click Restart Now.

Installing the Active Directory Services Remote Management Tools

These steps allow an administrator to perform the schema and domain preparation commands from your Windows Server 2008 server.

To install the Active Directory Services Remote Management Tools, follow these steps:

1. Log on with your domain administrator account. Open Windows PowerShell as an administrator.
2. Run the following command:

   ```
   Add-WindowsFeature RSAT-ADDS
   ```

   Upon completion, you see four warnings in yellow stating "You Must Restart This Server to Finish the Installation."
3. After you have successfully installed the Role Administration Tools and the Active Directory Domain Services Tools, close all open windows and restart the server as instructed.

Preparing the Active Directory Forest, Domain, and Exchange Organization

Before you can install Exchange Server, the schema and domain must be prepared.

Preparing the Schema

To prepare the Active Directory schema, follow these steps:

1. From the Exchange server, log on with your administrative account. This account must be a member of the Schema Admins and Enterprise Admins groups.
2. Copy the contents of your Exchange Server 2013 installation media to a directory on a local drive, such as `c:\E2k13Install`.
3. Open a Command Prompt window as an administrator, change to the drive and directory that holds your Exchange Server 2013 installation media and run the following command:

```
Setup /PrepareSchema /IAcceptExchangeServerLicenseTerms
```

NOTE

Depending on how you obtain the media for Exchange Server 2013, you may need to copy the installation media to a local drive and run the setup from that local drive. If you do not, your installation may result in the following error:

```
An error occurred while copying the file d:\\en\Setup\ServerRoles\Common
\en\Details Templates Editor.msc. The error code was 5.
```

If you did not copy the installation media locally and you receive this error, delete the contents of the `c:\%windir%\temp` file, copy the media locally, and run the command again.

4. When completed, the screen should look like the one shown in Figure 6.9.

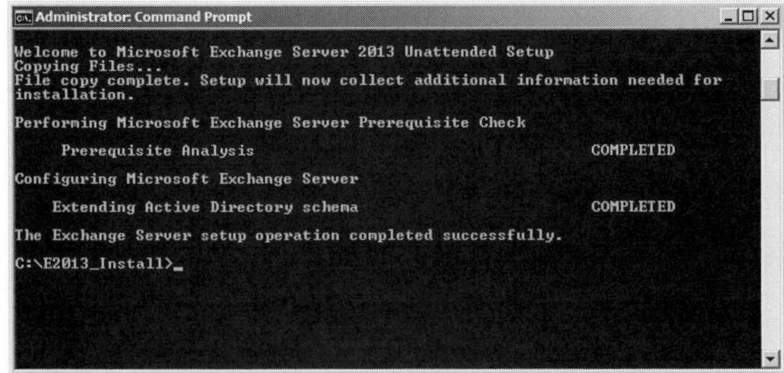

FIGURE 6.9 Preparing the Active Directory schema.

5. When finished, leave your Command Prompt window open and continue with the next section.

Preparing the Active Directory and Organization

To prepare the Active Directory and Organization, follow these steps:

1. From the Exchange server, log on with your administrative account. This account must be a member of the Enterprise Admins and Domain Admins groups.

2. From an administrator-enabled command prompt, change to the drive and directory that holds your Exchange Server 2013 installation media and run the following command:

```
Setup /PrepareAD /OrganizationName:ORGNAME
/IAcceptExchangeServerLicenseTerms
```

where ORGNAME is the organization name for your environment. In our lab, we are using TestLab as the organization name, so the command will look like this:

```
Setup /PrepareAD /OrganizationName:TestLab
/IAcceptExchangeServerLicenseTerms
```

3. When completed, the screen should look like the one shown in Figure 6.10.

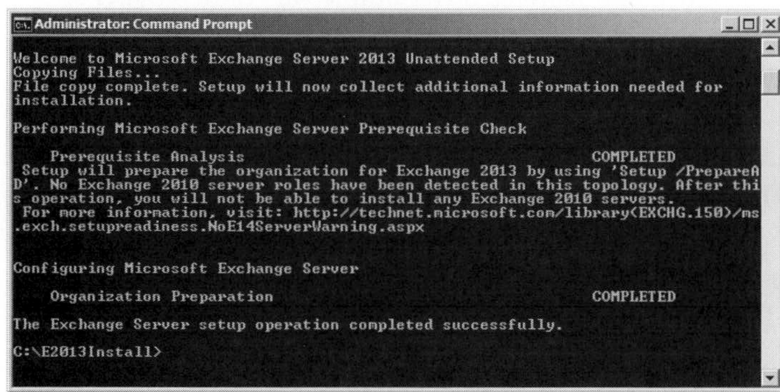

FIGURE 6.10 Preparing the Active Directory and creating the organization.

4. When finished, leave your Command Prompt window open and continue with the next section.

Preparing the Domain

To prepare the domain, follow these steps:

1. From the Exchange server, log on with your administrative account. This account must be a member of the Enterprise Admins and Domain Admins groups.

2. From an administrator-enabled command prompt, change to the drive and directory that holds your Exchange Server 2013 installation media and run the following command:

```
Setup /PrepareDomain /IAcceptExchangeServerLicenseTerms
```

3. When finished, close the command prompt.

NOTE

If you have multiple domains in your forest, you can prepare all of them by specifying `/PrepareAllDomains` instead of `/PrepareDomain`.

Installing Exchange Server 2013

Although the installation of all the Active Directory components, prerequisites, operating system components, updates, and hot fixes might seem to have taken forever, we are now finally ready to kick off the Exchange Server 2013 installation.

Installing Exchange Server 2013 from the GUI Interface

Utilizing the Exchange Server 2013 Installation Wizard is a simple way of deploying an Exchange server. The GUI interface is extremely intuitive and makes the installation a snap. To install Exchange Server using the Installation Wizard, perform the following tasks:

1. Log on with your domain administrator account. From your Exchange Server 2013 installation media, run the Exchange Installation Wizard (`d:\setup.exe`, for example).
2. On the Check for Updates screen, select Connect to Internet and Check for Updates and then click Next.
3. On the Copying Files and Initializing Setup screens, the program copies required files and prepares the system for installation.
4. After reviewing the information on the Introduction screen, click Next to continue.
5. On the License Agreement screen, select I Accept the Terms in the License Agreement and click Next to continue.
6. On the Recommended Settings screen, select Don't Use Recommended Settings. It is the author's opinion that these settings on domain controllers and Exchange servers should be configured manually after the installation is completed. Click Next to continue.
7. On the Server Role Selection screen, select the roles to be installed. In our test environment, we are installing the Client Access and Mailbox server roles (as well as the Exchange Management Tools), so we select the Mailbox and Client Access roles. Click Next to continue.
8. On the Installation Space and Location screen, review the path for the Exchange Server installation. If you are not installing the Exchange Server application to the default location, click Browse to select the installation directory. Click Next to continue.
9. If the schema, AD, and/or domain preparation steps were not completed previously, the Exchange Organization screen requires the name of the Exchange organization.

This screen also allows the option of selecting the Active Directory split permissions security model for large organizations. For the lab, enter `Test Lab` for the Organization, leave the check box blank, and click Next.

10. On the Malware Protection Settings screen, select whether you want to disable malware scanning. The default is No. Click Next to continue.
11. On the Readiness Checks screen, if the Prerequisite Analysis completes without finding any errors, click Install to continue. If errors are identified, follow the instructions on the screen to resolve issues. Retry the setup when errors have been remedied.
12. On the Completion screen, review the results of the installation. Ideally, you should see Setup Completed, as shown in Figure 6.11. Click Finish. Restart the server to complete the installation.

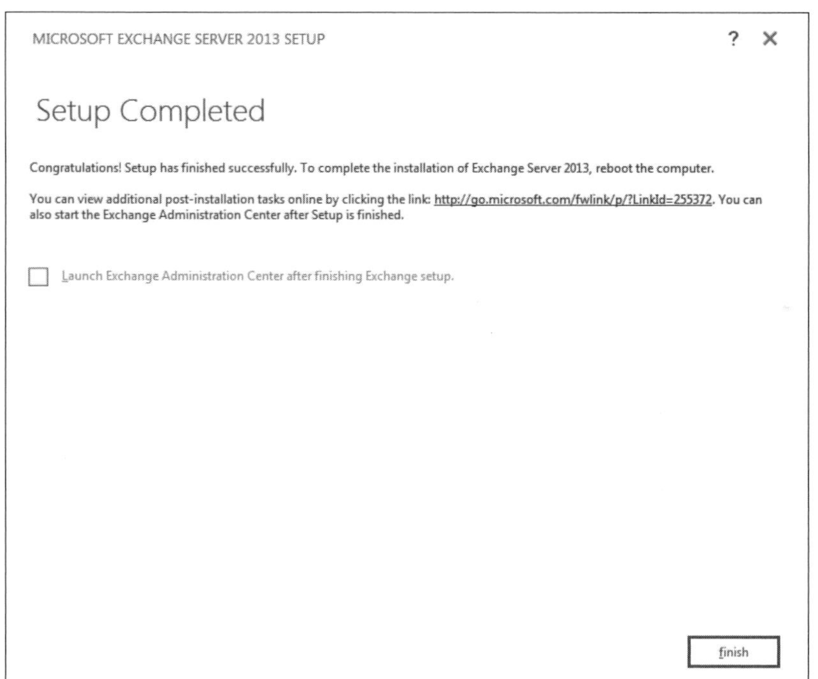

FIGURE 6.11 Completion screen reporting setup has completed.

Installing Exchange Server 2013 from the Command Prompt

In several situations (such as the deployment of an Exchange server in a remote location), administrators would prefer to install Exchange Server 2013 from the command prompt.

To do so, perform the following steps:

1. From an administrator-enabled command prompt, change to the drive and directory that contains your installation media.
2. Run the following command:

```
Setup.exe /mode:<setup mode> /roles:<roles to install> [/OptionalParameters]
```

For our purposes, we will simply run the following command:

```
Setup.exe /mode:Install /Roles:ClientAccess,Mailbox
/IAcceptExchangeServerLicenseTerms
```

The optional parameters cover all of the various configuration possibilities, including the organization name, target directory, source directory, default database name, and others.

All optional parameters can be viewed from the command line by typing:

```
Setup.exe /help:install
```

Finalizing the Deployment

After completing the installation of the Exchange Server software, several tasks should be completed to ensure the installation completed successfully. These include the following:

- Exchange Server 2013 postinstallation tasks
- Review Exchange Server installation logs
- Review the Event Viewer for errors and warnings
- Verify server roles were successfully installed

Exchange Server 2013 Postinstallation Tasks

After the Exchange installation has completed, open the Exchange Administration Center and perform the Exchange Server 2013 postinstallation tasks.

- Create a Send connector.
- Add additional accepted domains.
- Configure the default email address policy.
- Configure a Secure Sockets Layer (SSL) certificate.
- Configure external uniform resource locators (URLs).
- Configure Outlook Anywhere authentication methods.

Reviewing Exchange Server Installation Logs

After the first Exchange Server 2013 server installation is complete, administrators should review the installation logs located on the root drive of the installation path selected. The typical location of the installation log file is `C:\ExchangeSetupLogs`.

The log files contain all the details pertaining to the installation of the Exchange server throughout the process.

Reviewing the Event Viewer for Errors and Warnings

After an administrator has verified the installation logs for any anomalies and determined the implementation is a success, it is beneficial to review the Windows Event Viewer logs.

The application event log can contain both positive and negative Exchange Server information about the installation. The Exchange Server events can consist of information, warning, and critical errors. The application event log can be found by launching the Event Viewer included with Windows Server 2008 R2.

Verifying Server Roles Were Successfully Installed

Another recommended postinstallation task is to verify that the appropriate server roles were installed. This can be conducted by running the `get-ExchangeServer |fl` command from within the Exchange Management Shell. Look at the "ServerRole" header to determine what roles are installed on the server.

Summary

The installation of Exchange Server 2013 is a relatively simple process, thanks to the Exchange Server Installation Wizard. However, the key to a successful deployment is proper planning—administrators should know exactly what they are deploying before they begin, and the plan should be confirmed in a test environment before deployment.

A solid understanding of the prerequisites, testing the installation process, and carefully following the installation steps confirmed during the testing phase is critical to a smooth and error-free deployment.

Best Practices

The following are best practices from this chapter:

- Carefully review and complete all prerequisites before attempting to install Exchange Server 2013. The trial-and-error method is time consuming and frustrating. Proper planning before execution will greatly increase the chance of an error-free installation.
- Download and store all prerequisite installation files needed for Exchange Server 2013 so that as you install more servers, you do not have to download all the files again.

- Use virtual servers when creating a test lab to simulate large production implementations and to minimize hardware costs.
- For small organizations, it is probably reasonable to install the Mailbox and Client Access roles on the same server.
- Perform a health check on Active Directory before installing Exchange Server 2013 to make sure that AD is working properly.
- Check hardware requirements for servers to allocate the right amount of memory and processors for the size and capacity of the Exchange server environment.
- Monitor and check the performance optimization of Exchange and add memory and processors to properly optimize an Exchange Server 2013 server.
- Before installing Exchange Server 2013 into a production environment, it is beneficial to prototype the design in a test environment.
- To install Exchange Server 2013, the Active Directory forest functional level *must* be Windows Server 2003 or higher.
- Install the Telnet Client on Exchange servers. It is an essential Exchange administrator tool for troubleshooting mail flow issues.

CHAPTER 7

Transitioning from Exchange Server 2007/2010 to Exchange Server 2013

IN THIS CHAPTER

In this day and age, most organizations already have some form of email in their environment. Some have been using Microsoft Exchange Server since its infancy, some have only recently started to use it, and others have used other messaging platforms. In many of these cases, these organizations may decide to transition to the latest Microsoft messaging offering, Exchange Server 2013. That said, a transition is a fundamental change in infrastructure, and it is important to understand fully how an organization can transition to the new version.

This chapter makes a differentiation between *migrations* and *transitions* to Exchange Server 2013. Microsoft defines a transition as moving between one version of Exchange to a later one, whereas a migration is a move from a different vendor's messaging platform to Exchange Server 2013 or between two separate Exchange organizations. This chapter focuses on Exchange Server 2013 transitions. Covered are transition scenarios from Exchange Server 2007 directly to Exchange Server 2013, and transition scenarios from Exchange Server 2010 directly to Exchange Server 2013. Transitions from earlier versions of Exchange directly to Exchange Server 2013 are not supported.

The focus of this chapter is on the free tools available from Microsoft, and the process involved in using the tools based on tips, tricks, and lessons learned from previous transitions leveraging the built-in tools from Microsoft. This chapter does not cover migration from non-Microsoft messaging platforms, only transitions from Exchange Server 2007 and Exchange Server 2010 to Exchange Server 2013. Areas where the two migration paths differ are noted when they exist, as Microsoft handles a 2007–2013 migration differently than a 2010–2013 one.

High-Level Guide for Transition from Exchange Server 2007/2010 to Exchange Server 2013

Although this chapter explains the transition process in detail, this first section gives a high-level overview of the process to help conceptualize it. Specific details on each step are provided in subsequent sections of the chapter. This list can later be used as a checklist for the actual transition process.

Differences in Migration from Exchange Server 2007 and Exchange Server 2010 to Exchange Server 2013

Transitioning from Exchange Server 2007 to Exchange Server 2013 is very similar in principle to an Exchange Server 2010 to Exchange Server 2013 migration, though there are a few key differences. These differences are as follows:

- Exchange Server 2013 Outlook Web App (OWA) servers can proxy a mailbox on an Exchange Server 2010 OWA server but cannot do so for a 2007 mailbox. 2007 mailboxes need to be presented with a referral to the 2007 OWA server, requiring a second logon.
- Exchange Server 2013 servers show up as servers within the Exchange Management Console in Exchange Server 2010 but do not in Exchange Server 2007. They can still be used as mailbox migration targets from the 2013 side, however.

It is noted throughout the chapter where the transition process differs. If it is not noted, it can be assumed that the same process is utilized as is with a 2010 migration.

High-Level Steps to Transition

Ultimately, a transition to Exchange Server 2013 from Exchange Server 2007/2010 is not a terribly complex endeavor. In principle, the migration paths are similar as well, though a few key differences do exist between the two.

Simply put, it requires the following fundamental steps:

1. Upgrade all Exchange servers to Exchange Server 2007 Service Pack 3 RU8 or Exchange Server 2010 Service Pack 3 so they can understand Exchange Server 2013 functionality.
2. Prepare a Windows Server (2008 R2 Service Pack 1 [SP1] or 2012) server for the first Exchange Server 2013 server.
3. Install any necessary prerequisites (WWW for Client Access server [CAS] role, .NET Framework 4.5, Windows Management Framework 3.0, Unified Communications

Managed API 4.0, and Windows Identity Foundation 64-bit). Also install the Active Directory Domain Services (AD DS) tools to be able to upgrade the server.

4. Run setup on the Exchange Server 2013 server, upgrade the schema, and prepare the forest and domains. (Setup runs all in one step, or separate at the command line.)
5. Install the Exchange Server 2013 role servers and configure per 2013 design. Validate functionality.
6. Create new certificates for Exchange Server 2013 using the End to End Certificate Wizard in the Exchange Administration Center (EAC). Be sure to include a legacy namespace for old OWA clients that haven't been migrated yet to Exchange Server 2013.
7. Transfer OWA, ActiveSync, and Outlook Anywhere traffic to new CAS servers and validate using the Remote Connectivity Analyzer.
8. Transfer inbound and outbound mail traffic to the 2013 SMTP Connectors.
9. Configure Databases (database availability group [DAG] if needed).
10. Create public folder mailboxes on Exchange Server 2013 servers to replace the existing public folder hierarchy (if required).
11. Move mailboxes to Exchange Server 2013 using the Move Mailbox Wizard or PowerShell.
12. Transfer all public folder replicas to Exchange Server 2013 public folder store(s) and cutover public folders when replication is complete.
13. Delete public and private Information Stores from Exchange Server 2007/2010 server(s).
14. Uninstall all Exchange Server 2007/2010 servers.

For more information on specifics for each of these steps, refer to subsequent sections of this chapter.

Understanding How to Transition to Exchange Server 2013

Before getting too far into the tools and process of transitioning to Exchange Server 2013, it is important to understand, from a high level, the strategy on how to transition to Exchange Server 2013. The transition strategy could be as simple as effectively moving everything from Exchange Server 2007/2010 straight in to Exchange Server 2013 without making drastic modifications. Or, it could mean a very complex Exchange environment restructuring is performed as part of the transition process.

It is not required to completely restructure Exchange as part of the transition. In fact, if an Exchange Server 2007/2010 environment is working fine today, then just a simple transition is all that is required. The reason this book even addresses organizational restructuring as a potential option is that over the years with mergers, acquisitions, downsizing, or business changes, many organizations have Exchange structures that are not appropriate for the ongoing needs of an organization. Possibly, the organizational structure worked fine for years for the organization; however, a redesign is now needed because of a change in how the organization does business. These types of changes can make the transition process more complex as are transitions that take place from a messaging system other than Exchange Server 2007/2010. Some of the transition changes are things that could take place before or after the transition to Exchange Server 2013. This chapter itself covers the general process of transitioning to Exchange Server 2013.

Organizations that are currently running on Exchange Server 2003 will need to completely upgrade first to either Exchange Server 2007 or Exchange Server 2010, removing all Exchange Server 2003 servers from the organization before they can directly migrate to Exchange Server 2013 on-premises. This is not the case if migrating to Exchange Online, however, which supports a direct Exchange Server 2003 migration using tools that Microsoft uses for the process.

Simple Transition from Exchange Server 2007/2010 to Exchange Server 2013

For organizations that have a working Exchange Server 2007/2010 environment that is happy with the architecture and operation of their Exchange environment and simply want to move to Exchange Server 2013, the transition process is a relatively simple and methodical process. In a condensed format, the process involves replacing Exchange Server 2007/2010 Hub Transport (HT), CAS, Unified Messaging (UM), and Mailbox servers with Exchange Server 2013 CAS role systems, adding new Exchange Server 2013 Mailbox servers, and moving the mailboxes from the old server, or servers, to the new server, or servers. It's not quite that simple, however, because there are several preparation steps that need to be conducted, a handful of test procedures that can assist the organization in the event of a transition failure that requires rolling back during the transition process.

Restructuring Exchange as Part of the Transition to Exchange Server 2013

For organizations that have undergone business changes since the installation of Exchange Server, or that have an Exchange environment that is not architected properly for the current and near-future business environment of the organization, they might choose to restructure Exchange as part of their transition to Exchange Server 2013. The restructuring can occur with Exchange Server 2007/2010 prior to the transition, the restructuring can occur during the Exchange Server 2013 transition, or the restructuring can occur after Exchange Server 2013 has been put in place.

The deciding factor on when the restructure occurs depends on the effort involved to perform the restructuring. Some organizations will consolidate servers as part of their restructuring process. This is a simple process that can usually be done during the transition where, for example, several Exchange Server 2007/2010 Mailbox servers are consolidated into a smaller number of Exchange Server 2013 Mailbox servers. As mailboxes are moved from the old Exchange to the new Exchange, they can be moved from multiple systems to a single system. This restructuring is easy to do as part of the transition process.

Some transition processes are more complex, for example, if the organization wants to completely collapse remote site servers and bring all of the servers into a centralized Exchange environment model. From an Exchange perspective, collapsing sites is one of the restructuring options that can be done as part of the transition; however, the challenge is typically trying to move large amounts of email over a wide area network (WAN) connection. If a remote site has tens or hundreds of gigabytes or even terabytes of mail data, it is unrealistic to transition that amount of mail over a WAN connection as part of a transition process. In many cases, the actual server, hard drives of the server, or backup of the databases are physically brought into the centralized data center, and the data is copied in the data center. Although a logistical shuffle to physically move servers or data during the transition process, this is not an insurmountable process when trying to move large sets of data across a slow WAN link connection.

The more complex restructuring model is required when an organization wants to add some sites, remove some sites, consolidate other sites, and completely redo sites that already exist. The choice of when to do the changes depends on the length and scope of the Exchange transition. If the scope and goal of the transition are to do the restructuring in the Exchange transition project, plan the process and proceed with a restructuring of Exchange as part of the transition to Exchange Server 2013. However, if the restructuring would be nice to have, but is not significant to the scope of the project, you might choose to consolidate servers and transition to Exchange Server 2013, and then perform the restructuring after Exchange Server 2013 has been installed.

Transitioning to a Brand-New Exchange Server 2013 Organization

Another method for transitioning to Exchange Server 2013 is one where a brand-new Active Directory forest and Exchange Server 2013 organization is built from scratch, and then data is moved into the new Exchange environment. An organization might choose to use this method if there are significant problems with its existing Exchange Server 2007/2010 environment, or if the configuration of its existing Exchange environment is not ideally suited for Exchange Server 2013. This turns the transition into a migration, which is guaranteed to be substantially more complex and likely to cause problems users would not experience in a transition. In few scenarios would this be a recommended option because of the added complexity of cross-forest migrations. In general, cleaning up an existing Active Directory and Exchange environment is less complex than creating a new organization.

When building a new Exchange Server 2013 environment, users and groups can be migrated to the new domain and mailboxes moved using PowerShell or the Exchange Administration Center. Indeed, the migration process can help to streamline this process more than was possible in the past, allowing for Outlook profiles to be automatically moved over. It is important to note that anyone with offline stores or Cached-mode Exchange configurations will need to completely rebuild his or her offline Outlook databases.

In addition, with a clean installation of Exchange Server 2013, the organization will not be able to add back in an Exchange Server 2007/2010 or Exchange Server 2007 system. Old Exchange server versions are only supported in an Exchange Server 2013 environment that was transitioned from the old version to the new version of Exchange. When Exchange Server 2013 is installed from scratch, none of the legacy backward-compatibility tools are installed or configured to work.

So, a brand-new Exchange Server 2013 installation is a drastic move for an organization that already has Exchange Server 2007/2010. If the organization can do one of the transition methods and then clean up the model after migration, it would be easier to perform the transition.

Transitioning from Exchange Server 5.5, Exchange 2000 Server, or Exchange Server 2003

A transition from any version of Exchange prior to Exchange Server 2007 directly to Exchange Server 2013 is not supported and requires a transition first to Exchange Server 2007 or Exchange Server 2010. After successfully transitioning to Exchange Server 2007/2010, the organization can then execute the subsequent transition to Exchange Server 2013. For more information on performing an Exchange Server 5.5 or Exchange Server 2003 to Exchange Server 2007/2010 transition, refer to the Sams Publishing volumes *Microsoft Exchange Server 2007 Unleashed* or *Microsoft Exchange Server 2010 Unleashed*.

Migrating from Lotus Notes, Novell GroupWise, and SendMail

The migration scenarios to Exchange involve an organization with an existing non-Exchange environment, such as Lotus Notes, Novell GroupWise, or an IMAP platform. A migration from a non-Microsoft Exchange messaging platform is not covered in this chapter. The process of migrating from a non-Exchange environment is one that requires tools to transition user email, calendars, contacts, shared folders, and other information stored in the old email system to Exchange Server 2013. This type of migration usually starts with the installation of a completely clean Exchange Server 2013 environment in which user data is then migrated into the new environment. If Microsoft tools are used for these types of migrations, they must be performed first to Exchange Server 2007/2010, and then subsequently transitioned to Exchange Server 2013 as the Microsoft offerings for migrating from these platforms to Exchange Server 2013 are either weak or nonexistent. Many organizations look to third-party companies to fill this niche, or migrate first to Exchange Server 2007/2010 before transitioning to Exchange Server 2013.

Transitions Involving a Limited Number of Servers

Beyond just transitioning from one version of messaging to Exchange Server 2013, the destination environment of Exchange Server 2013 can depend on the size and architectural structure of the resulting Exchange Server 2013 environment. For a small organization, the destination Exchange environment could be a single server where the various Exchange Server 2013 roles are all on a single system. If there is no need to add additional server systems to the environment, then having a limited number of servers and placing server roles on a single system is easy to do.

The Client Access and Mailbox server roles of Exchange Server 2013 can all be placed on a single server; however, if the organization wants to add an Edge Transport role server to the organization, the Edge Transport server needs to be on a separate server. As of the date of this book's publication, there is not an Exchange Server 2013 Edge Transport role, but an Exchange Server 2010 Edge Transport role server in an Exchange Server 2013 organization.

Transitions Involving a Distributed Server Strategy

For larger organizations, the various server roles will likely be applied to systems dedicated to a particular server role for purposes of performance and scalability. In many cases, a larger organization will already have existing roles for UM, HT, CAS, and/or Mailbox servers. In these larger environments, assuming that separate servers will be retained, the Exchange Server 2013 server roles will replace the existing Exchange Server 2007/2010 server systems with a similar distribution of server systems, with the understanding that Exchange Server further simplifies these roles.

When transitioning to an Exchange Server 2013 environment with individual servers, the process of transitioning involves the following:

1. Transition the Client Access server roles first, and transition Internet-facing sites before transitioning non-Internet facing sites.
2. Install Exchange Server 2013 Mailbox role servers.
3. Move transport connectors to Exchange Server 2013 Mailbox role servers.
4. Next, move mailboxes to new Exchange Server 2013 Mailbox role servers.
5. Move UM functionality to Exchange Server 2013 Mailbox servers.

Coexistence in a Mixed Exchange Environment

During the coexistence between Exchange Server 2007/2010 and Exchange Server 2013, an administrator needs to be mindful which administration tool to use for which function. This is a confusing task because some functions, such as those related to the Edge Transport role, no longer exist in Exchange Server 2013 and require the administrator to go back to the Exchange Management Console in Exchange Server 2007/2010 to perform tasks. This is why the shorter the coexistence between Exchange Server 2007/2010 and Exchange Server 2013, the better.

The following list discusses some of the administrative tasks that need consideration for environments where Exchange Server 2007 or 2010 is coexisting with Exchange Server 2013:

- Exchange Server 2013 mailboxes must be managed with the Exchange Administration Center found in Exchange Server 2013. Many objects in Exchange

Server 2013 are not exposed in Exchange Server 2007/2010, and if mailboxes are created in Exchange Server 2007/2010 for an Exchange Server 2013 user, certain objects will not be provisioned.

- Mailboxes on Exchange Server 2007/2010 must be created using the Exchange Server 2007 or 2010 Management Console.
- The Exchange Server 2013 Administration Center can be used on Exchange Server 2007/2010 mailboxes for nearly all functions. So, as long as the mailbox has been created with the Exchange System Manager tool, thereafter the mailbox can be managed or administered from either tool.
- Public folders must be managed from the Exchange Server 2007/2010 side until they are cutover, after which they can only be managed from the Exchange Administration Center.

Deploying a Prototype Lab for the Exchange Server 2013 Transition Process

Regardless of the method that is chosen to transition Exchange, care should be taken to test design assumptions as part of a comprehensive prototype lab. A prototype environment can help simulate the conditions that will be experienced as part of the transition process. Establishing a functional prototype environment also can help reduce the risk associated with transitions. In addition to traditional approaches for creating a prototype lab, which involves restoring from backups, several techniques exist to replicate the current production environment to simulate transition.

Creating Temporary Prototype Domain Controllers to Simulate Transition

Construction of a prototype lab to simulate an existing Exchange infrastructure is not particularly complicated but requires thought in its implementation. Because an exact copy of the Active Directory is required, the most straightforward way of accomplishing this is by building a new domain controller in the production domain and then isolating that domain controller in the lab to create a mirror copy of the existing domain data. Domain name system (DNS) and global catalog information should be transferred to the server when in production, to enable continuation of these services in the testing environment.

NOTE

You should keep several considerations in mind if planning this type of duplication of the production environment. First, when the temporary domain controller is made into a global catalog server, the potential exists for the current network environment to identify it as a working global catalog server and refer clients to it for directory lookups. When the server is brought offline, the clients would experience connectivity issues. For these reasons, it is good practice to create a temporary domain controller during off hours.

A major caveat to this approach is that the system must be completely separate, with no way to communicate with the production environment. This is especially the case because the domain controllers in the prototype lab respond to requests made to the production domain, authenticating user and computer accounts and replicating information. Prototype domain controllers should never be added back into a production environment.

Seizing Operations Master (OM) Roles in the Lab Environment

Because Active Directory is a multimaster directory, any one of the domain controllers can authenticate and replicate information. This factor is what makes it possible to segregate the domain controllers into a prototype environment easily. There are several different procedures that can be used to seize the OM (also referred to as Flexible Single Master Operations [FSMO]) roles. One approach uses the `ntdsutil` utility, as follows:

1. Open a command prompt by selecting Start, Run, typing **`cmd`** in the Open text box, and then clicking OK.

> **CAUTION**
>
> Remember, this procedure should only be performed in a lab environment or in disaster recovery situations. Never perform it against a running production domain controller unless the intent is to forcibly move OM roles.

2. Type **`ntdsutil`** and press Enter.
3. Type **`roles`** and press Enter.
4. Type **`connections`** and press Enter.
5. Type **`connect to server SERVERNAME`** (where *SERVERNAME* is the name of the target Windows Server 2003/2008/2012 domain controller that will hold the OM roles), and press Enter.
6. Type **`quit`** and press Enter.
7. Type **`seize schema master`** and press Enter.
8. Click Yes at the prompt asking to confirm the OM change.
9. Type **`seize domain naming master`** and press Enter.
10. Click Yes at the prompt asking to confirm the OM change.
11. Type **`seize pdc`** and press Enter.
12. Click OK at the prompt asking to confirm the OM change.
13. Type **`seize rid master`** and press Enter.
14. Click OK at the prompt asking to confirm the OM change.
15. Type **`seize infrastructure master`** and press Enter.

16. Click OK at the prompt asking to confirm the OM change.
17. Exit the Command Prompt window.

After these procedures have been run, the domain controllers in the prototype lab environment will control the OM roles for the forest and domain, which is necessary for additional transition testing.

NOTE

Although the temporary domain controller procedure just described can be very useful toward producing a copy of the AD environment for a prototype lab, it is not the only method that can accomplish this. The AD domain controllers can also be restored via the backup software's restore procedure. A third option—which is often easier to accomplish but is somewhat riskier—is to break the mirror on a production domain controller, take that hard drive into the prototype lab, and install it in an identical server. This procedure requires the production server to lose redundancy for a period of time while the mirror is rebuilt, but is a "quick-and-dirty" way to make a copy of the production environment. This process can also be performed on a virtual snapshot of a domain controller if running on virtual servers.

Validating and Documenting Design Decisions and Transition Procedures

The actual transition process in a prototype lab should follow, as closely as possible, any design decisions made regarding an Exchange Server 2007/2010 implementation. It is ideal to document the steps involved in the process so that they can be used during the actual implementation to validate the process. The prototype lab is not only an extremely useful tool for validating the transition process, but it can also be useful for testing new software and procedures for production servers.

The chosen transition strategy can be effectively tested in the prototype lab at this point. Follow all transition steps as if they were happening in production.

Migrating to a Brand-New Exchange Server 2013 Environment

One of the options to get to Exchange Server 2013 is to build a brand-new Exchange Server 2013 environment and then move or import any existing data into the new Exchange environment.

This scenario is typically limited to organizations that might have one of the following environments:

- An organization that is migrating from a completely non-Microsoft environment where a brand-new Exchange Server 2013 is installed, and then data from the old non-Microsoft messaging system is migrated to the new Exchange Server 2013 environment

- An organization that is undergoing a drastic business change that dictates the need to start from scratch with a new Exchange Server 2013 configuration such as a merger of two companies with a third company emerging that has a completely different business name and organizational structure

This scenario is not expanded on further in this chapter as the migration process really mirrors that of a brand-new installation of Exchange Server 2013 (covered in Chapter 6, "Installing and Configuring the Basics of Exchange Server 2013 for a Brand-New Environment") with the process of importing old data, if desired, into the new environment.

Planning Your Transition

The planning process in transitioning from an environment that has Exchange Server 2007/2010 to Exchange Server 2013 involves ensuring that the existing environment is ready for a transition, and that the hardware necessary to accept the transitioned server roles is compatible with Exchange Server 2013. The planning process to Exchange Server 2013 proceeds using the following path:

1. Review Chapter 2, "Understanding Core Exchange Server 2013 Design Plans," to become familiar with terminology used in Exchange Server 2013 design architecture.
2. Confirm that you want to do a one-to-one transition of servers from Exchange Server 2007/2010 to Exchange Server 2013 (that is, Exchange Server 2007/2010 CAS servers become Exchange Server 2013 Client Access servers, and Exchange Server 2007/2010 Mailbox servers become Exchange Server 2013 Mailbox servers). Also, note that any existing Hub Transport servers have their functionality replaced by Exchange Server 2013 Mailbox servers.

NOTE

As part of this transition, you can do server consolidation by moving mailboxes from multiple servers to fewer servers and transition from shared storage cluster mailbox servers to servers running Exchange Server 2013 DAGs. These variations just need to be slipped in to the transition plan. For implementation of Client Access servers, see Chapter 6. For implementation of DAG, see Chapter 8, "Implementing and Supporting a Highly Available Exchange Server 2013 Environment."

3. Select the proper version of Exchange Server 2013 in which you will be implementing Exchange Server 2013 on, whether it is the Standard Edition or the Enterprise Edition of the server software.

CHOOSING BETWEEN STANDARD AND ENTERPRISE EDITIONS

The Exchange Server 2013 Standard Edition is the basic messaging server version of the software. The Standard Edition supports five databases and has full support for web access, mobile access, and server recovery functionality. The Standard Edition is a good version of Exchange to support a messaging system for a small organization, or as a dedicated Client Access server for a larger environment. Many small and medium-sized organizations find the capabilities of the Standard Edition sufficient for most messaging server services, and even large organizations use the Standard Edition for message routing servers or as the primary server in a remote office. The Standard Edition meets the needs of effectively any environment wherein a server with a limited database storage capacity is sufficient.

The Exchange Server 2013 Enterprise Edition is focused at server systems that require more Exchange messaging databases. With support for up to 100 databases per server, the Enterprise Edition of Exchange Server 2013 is the appropriate version of messaging system for organizations that have a lot of mailboxes or a lot of mail storage, and for an organization that wants to set up clustering for higher reliability and redundancy of the Exchange environment.

4. The next step is to acquire the appropriate hardware necessary to implement the new Exchange Server 2013 environment.
5. Confirm that all of the current Exchange Server 2007/2010 servers are at the service pack and update rollup level that is compatible with Exchange Server 2013.
6. Validate that add-ons and utilities used in the existing Exchange Server 2007/2010 environment are compatible with Exchange Server 2013 or upgraded to support Exchange Server 2013. This includes products like BlackBerry services, Cisco Unity voice mail services, tape backup software, and so on.

NOTE

If a software program is not compatible with Exchange Server 2013, many times you can keep the software operating on an older Exchange Server 2007/2010 server, and transition the rest of the environment to Exchange Server 2013. This can typically be done for gateway tools that route information in to or out of an Exchange environment.

7. Test the transition process in a lab environment to confirm all of the steps necessary in transitioning to Exchange Server 2013. The test transition is covered in the next section.

Testing the Transition Process

Part of any transition best practice is to perform the transition in a test lab prior to performing the transition in a real production environment. The test lab allows the person performing the transition to test and validate assumptions. Effectively, if it works in the lab, you have a higher level of confidence that it will work in the production environment. At a minimum, after walking through the transition process, you will understand the steps necessary to perform the transition, become familiar with the steps, work through problems if they arise, and correct problems so that if or when they happen in the production transition you will already be prepared for the necessary action. In addition, testing the transition process provides you with a timeline to know how long it will likely take to transition the databases into the Exchange Server 2013 environment.

The test lab creation process is covered in detail earlier in this chapter in the section "Deploying a Prototype Lab for the Exchange Server 2013 Transition Process." This section addresses getting a copy of an Active Directory global catalog (GC) server and seizing the roles to make this GC replica the master global catalog for the lab environment. This section also addresses getting a copy of the current Exchange Server 2007/2010 server data into the lab.

Key to the test lab process is to validate the operation of your third-party add-ons, utilities, backup software, and so on to confirm that all of the components in your current Exchange environment will successfully transition to Exchange Server 2013. Take this chance to confirm whether you need to download any patches or hot fixes from the third-party product vendors, and whether you can simply reinstall the third-party products on an Exchange Server 2013 server, or whether you need to keep a legacy Exchange Server 2007/2010 server in your environment to maintain backward compatibility for a while.

When the lab is ready, you can run through the processes outlined in the following step-by-step sections to confirm that the processes outlined work as planned in your transition environment. Again, make note of all problems you run in to and document the work-arounds you come up with in the lab so that when you get into the production transition, you will have step-by-step notes on how to work through problems that come up. And also keep track of how long it takes processes to complete so you are prepared for how long the production transition process will take to complete.

Backing Up Your Production Environment

When you are ready to perform the transition in your production environment, you need to have a complete backup of the critical components that you will be working on just in case you need to roll back your environment. The expectation is that if your test lab replicated as much of your production environment as possible, then there should be no surprises in your production transition. However, as a best practice, make a backup of your Active Directory global catalog server, all of your Exchange servers, and all of the servers that interoperate with Exchange, such as gateway systems or replicated directory servers.

It is also a best practice to turn off any replication to other environments during the transition process, such as Forefront Identity Manager (previously named ILM, MIIS, IIFP, and MMS), or other directory synchronization tools.

Preparing the Exchange Server 2013 Server with the Windows Server OS

Each Exchange Server 2013 server in the new environment needs to have Windows Server 2008 R2 with SP1 or Windows Server 2012 Standard or Enterprise Edition installed on the system. The Exchange Server 2013 should also be joined to the expected Active Directory domain.

Preparing Exchange Server 2007/2010

Whether you are performing this transition in a lab environment or in production, after performing a backup of your production environment, the first step in the transition process is to update every Exchange Server 2010 server in the organization with Service Pack 3, as shown in Figure 7.1, and every Exchange Server 2007 server with Service Pack 3 and Update Rollup 8. After all servers have been updated, you must then extend the Active Directory schema for Exchange Server 2013. This readies Active Directory and Exchange Server 2007/2010 to integrate Exchange Server 2013 in the existing Exchange environment. This is necessary because during the transition process, or potentially in a long-term coexistence between Exchange Server 2007/2010 with Exchange Server 2013, the old and new environments need to support each other.

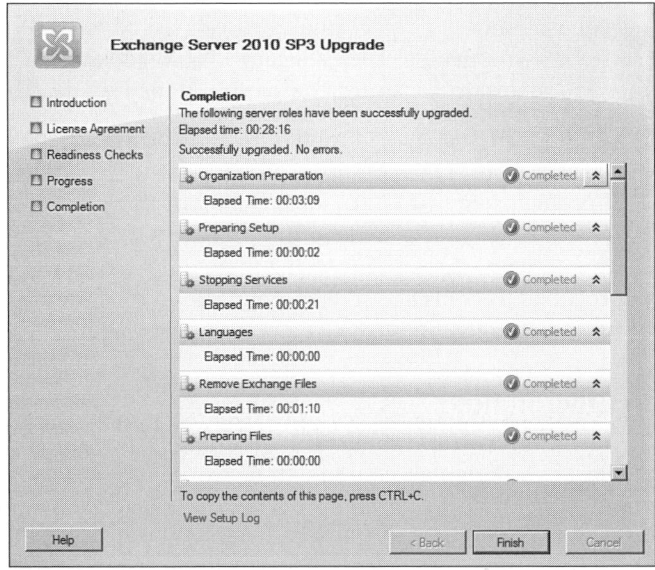

FIGURE 7.1 Upgrading existing Exchange Server 2010 servers with Service Pack 3.

The first time Exchange Server 2013 setup is run in an existing Exchange organization, it runs a set of prerequisite checks against the AD forest and the organization itself. If all prerequisites are satisfied, the setup utility allows an administrator to prepare the forest, domain, and existing Exchange organization for Exchange Server 2013. Administrators will see a dialog box similar to what is shown in Figure 7.2, which indicates that once setup proceeds, it will modify the Active Directory schema and extend it with the new Exchange Server 2013 schema. The user logged in to the server when running this update will need be in the Schema Administrators and Enterprise Administrators group for the forest.

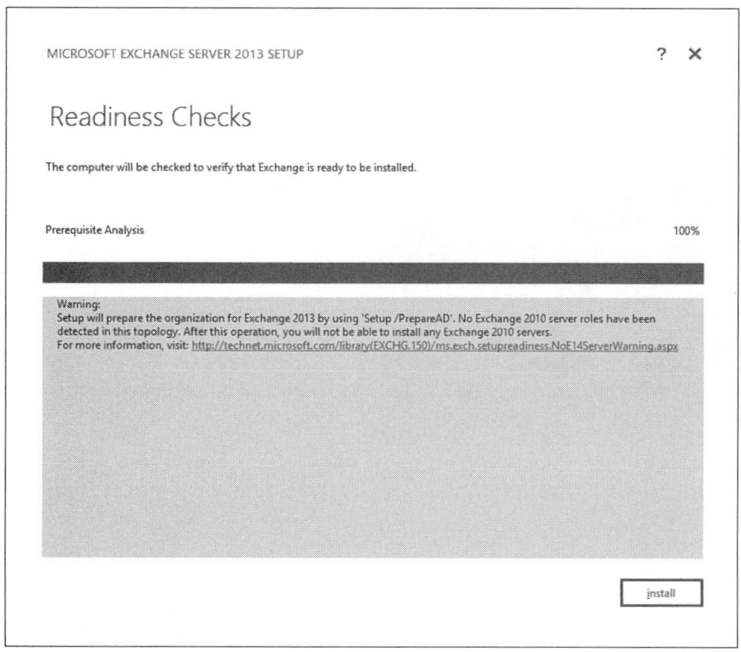

FIGURE 7.2 Running Organization prerequisite checks before the Exchange Server 2013 schema upgrade.

NOTE

An Active Directory schema update is no minor task, and should be fully tested in the prototype lab environment in advance. The account running setup must also be an Enterprise Admin and Schema Admin for the forest, as well as an Exchange Full Administrator for the organization. If there are separate accounts for these roles, the schema upgrade portion of the installation can be run from the command prompt using the `setup.exe /prepareAD` switch.

Installing Exchange Server 2013 on a Server

The overall process for installing Exchange Server 2013 is outlined in Chapter 6. For the purposes of a transition, after the schema has been upgraded, setup can commence on the Exchange Server 2013 servers that will replace the existing servers. This may be part of the same step, or it can be separated if using the `setup.exe /PrepareAD` option.

For example, Mailbox and Client Access servers can be installed from the command line using the following syntax:

```
Setup.exe /mode:install /roles:clientaccess /IAcceptExchangeServerLicenseTerms
Setup.exe /mode:install /roles:mailbox /IAcceptExchangeServerLicenseTerms
```

Or, both roles can be installed using the shorthand format, simply using the `/r:MB,CA` format illustrated in Figure 7.3.

```
Administrator: Command Prompt - setup /r:CA,MB /IAcceptExchangeServerLicenseTerms
Copying Files...
Languages
Management tools
Mailbox Server Role Component 1
Mailbox Server Role Component 2
Mailbox Server Role Component 3
Mailbox Server Role Component 4
Client Access Server Role Component 1
Client Access Server Role Component 2

Performing Microsoft Exchange Server Prerequisite Check

    Configuring Prerequisites                              COMPLETED
    Prerequisite Analysis                                  COMPLETED

Configuring Microsoft Exchange Server

    Preparing Setup                                        COMPLETED
    Stopping Services                                      COMPLETED
    Copying Exchange Files                                 COMPLETED
    Language Files                                         COMPLETED
    Restoring Services                                     COMPLETED
    Language Configuration                                 COMPLETED
    Exchange Management Tools                              COMPLETED
    Mailbox Role Component 1                               3%
```

FIGURE 7.3 Installing Exchange Server 2013 into an existing organization for the transition.

Continue to install new Exchange Server 2013 servers.

NOTE

One of the key differences between Exchange Server 2007 to 2013 transitions and Exchange Server 2010 to 2013 transitions is that the new servers now show up in the Exchange Server 2010 Management Console, as shown in Figure 7.4. The Exchange Server 2007 Management Console keeps the servers separate even though they are still potential targets for mailbox and public folder migrations.

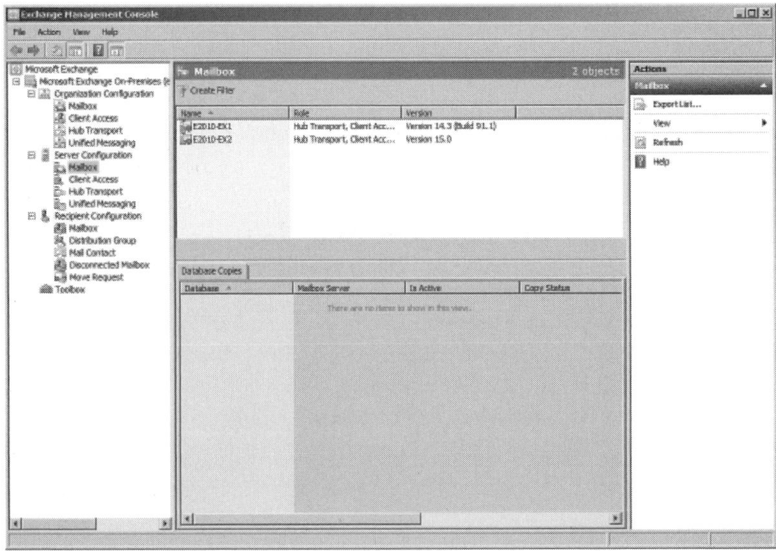

FIGURE 7.4 Viewing an Exchange Server 2013 server within the Exchange Server 2010 Management Console.

Creating Certificates for Exchange Server 2013

After the new servers have been installed into the Exchange organization, it will be required to replace legacy certificates with new Secure Sockets Layer (SSL) certificates. Exchange Server 2013 Exchange Administration Center includes a wizard known as the End to End Certificate Wizard, which can be used to automatically generate the certificate requests and prepare them to be sent to third-party certificate authorities. The certificates in Exchange can then be easily managed within the EAC, as shown in Figure 7.5.

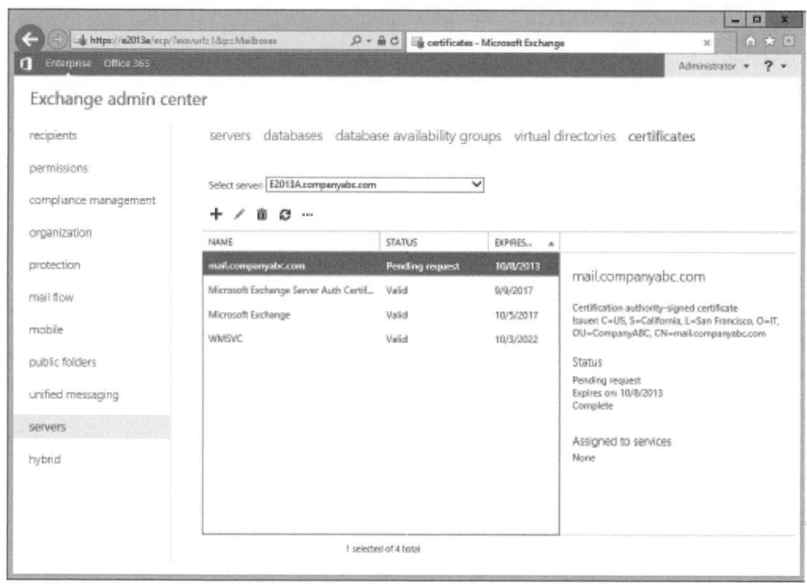

FIGURE 7.5 Using the EAC to manage certificates.

Although Mailbox servers have self-signed certificates installed out of the box, it is recommended to create external certificates for use on the CAS servers. The wizard will help you with this process, but it effectively involves adding the names of the CAS arrays to the certificate as Subject Alternative Names (SANs). In addition, a legacy uniform resource locator (URL) will be required for any mailboxes accessing OWA that have not been moved yet to Exchange Server 2013. This name can be any other URL, but the name legacy.companyabc.com is often chosen. Other records such as autodiscover.companyabc.com and the OWA namespace are added using the wizard and automatically applied to the CAS array(s).

Microsoft also recommends the following best practices in regard to these certificates:

- Use split-brain DNS for the Exchange host names, so that the fully qualified domain name (FQDN) is the same for OWA for both internal and external clients.

- It is generally not necessary to list machine host names in the certificate, instead list the load-balanced names and configure all internal and external URLs in the virtual directories to use those names instead of machine names.
- Minimize the number of certificates and SAN names in a certificate to those that will actually be used.

Once certificates have been installed, you can test access to Exchange Server 2013 OWA and legacy access for older mailboxes. The new certificates must then be implemented and cutover to before continuing with the migration.

Moving Mailboxes

After the new Exchange Server 2013 server(s) have been installed into an existing Exchange Server 2007/2010 organization, the movement of mailboxes from an old Exchange back-end server to a new Exchange Server 2013 Mailbox server is as a mailbox move. A new service called the Mailbox Replication Service (MRS) has been created for Exchange Server 2013 to handle this process and can be invoked from the Exchange Administration Center, as shown in Figure 7.6. This tool allows for administrators to stage the mailbox moves in batches.

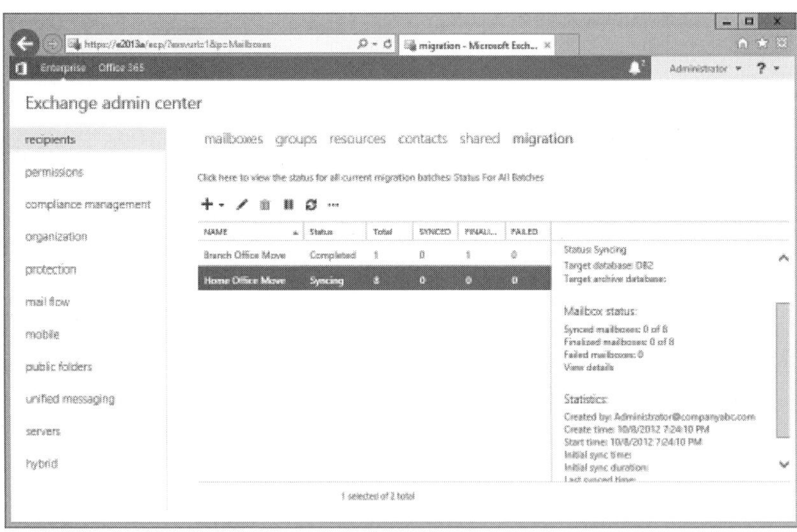

FIGURE 7.6 Moving mailboxes using the EAC.

Alternatively, mailboxes can be moved at the command prompt using the `New-MoveRequest` cmdlet, as shown in Figure 7.7.

The first mailbox to be moved should be an administrator mailbox or one that is created for the migration. This mailbox can also simply be created on the 2013 side. This will allow you to log in to the new Exchange Administration Center through the Web console.

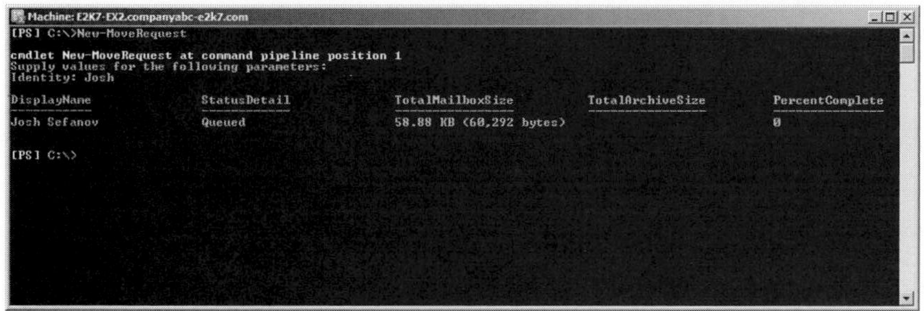

FIGURE 7.7 Moving mailboxes in PowerShell.

The move time will vary based on the amount of data to be moved, and the bandwidth between the source and destination server. This is something that should be tested in the lab to determine whether all of the mailboxes desired to be moved at any one time can be accomplished in the time available.

Replicating Public Folders from Exchange Server 2007/2010 to Exchange Server 2013

The final stage of a transition to Exchange Server 2013 involves the movement of public folders from their legacy structure on Exchange Server 2007/2010 to the new Public Folder Mailbox architecture that is used in Exchange Server 2013.

NOTE

Not all organizations may be using public folders in Exchange Server 2007/2010 as they are optional components. If your organization does not have public folders, these steps can be skipped.

The first step to public folder migration is to analyze the existing public folder hierarchy and data size. Microsoft has included a PowerShell tool to assist with this called `PublicFoldertoMailboxMapGenerator.ps1`, which can be invoked to determine how the existing public folder hierarchy should be created within the new Public Folder Mailbox approach.

As shown in Figure 7.8, start by exporting out the hierarchy to a comma-separated values (CSV) file from the Exchange Server 2007/2010 server, then use `PublicFoldertoMailboxMapGenerator.ps1` script to create a Folder to Mailbox mapping file that will be used in later steps.

Next, switch to the Exchange Server 2013 server and create the public folder database(s) that are listed in the CSV file. You can rename the Public Folder names in the file if you like, as the tool creates very generic names. Just be sure that the name listed in the CSV file is the same as the mailbox or mailboxes you created, as shown in Figure 7.9.

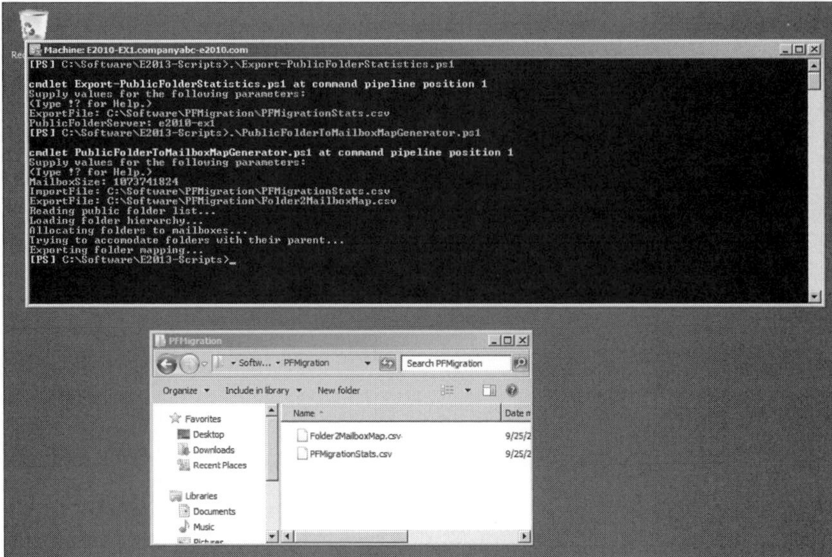

FIGURE 7.8 Step 1 in the Public Folder migration process: Collecting info on the existing public folder hierarchy.

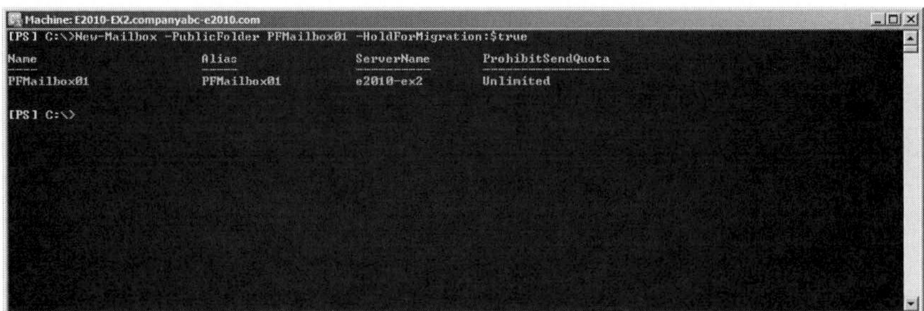

FIGURE 7.9 Step 2 in the Public Folder migration process: Creating the PF mailbox on the Exchange Server 2013 server.

Following the creation of the mailboxes for the public folders, you can start the incremental synchronization process by issuing a `New-PublicFolderMigrationRequest` command on the Exchange Server 2013 server, as shown in Figure 7.10.

Depending on the size of your public folders, this may take a very long time to complete. Run the following command to check on the status of the Public Folder copy:

```
Get-PublicFolderMigrationRequest | Get-PublicFolderMigrationRequestStatistics
-IncludeReport | Format-List
```

A status of *AutoSuspended* means that all content has been copied.

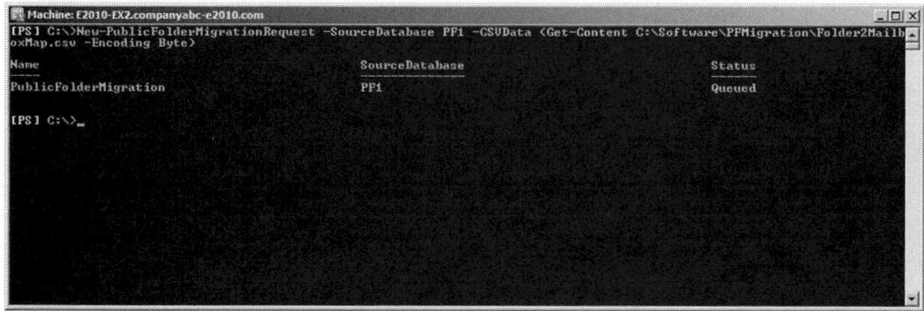

FIGURE 7.10 Step 3 in the Public Folder migration process: Starting incremental synchronization of the PF content.

At this point, users in Exchange Server 2007/2010 can still access and change public folders on the source side. Once all mailboxes have been moved to Exchange Server 2013, or at least all that use public folders, you will need to lock access to legacy public folders to prepare for the final migration. Using the following command, illustrated in Figure 7.11, will do this. Be sure to run it on an Exchange Server 2007/2010 server:

```
Set-OrganizationConfig -PublicFoldersLockedForMigration:$true
```

FIGURE 7.11 Step 4 in the Public Folder migration process: Locking the source public folders in preparation for migration.

From the target Exchange Server 2013 side, you can then finalize the migration by running the following two commands, shown in Figure 7.12:

```
Set-PublicFolderMigrationRequest -Identity \PublicFolderMigration
-PreventCompletion:$false
Resume-PublicFolderMigrationRequest -Identity \PublicFolderMigration
```

The public folders should then be fully migrated. Validate that all the data is there by checking item count, sizes, and so forth on both source and target. Once validated, you can remove public folders from the source environment.

7

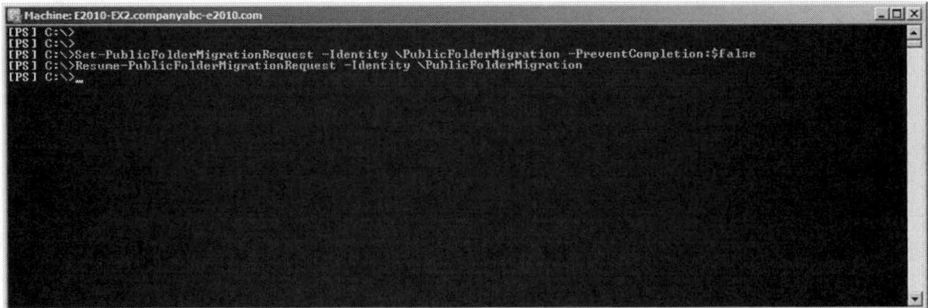

FIGURE 7.12 Step 5 in the Public Folder migration process: Finalizing the migration.

Cleaning Up the Exchange Server 2007/2010 Environment

After a new Exchange Server 2013 server is added to the network to functionally replace an old Exchange Server 2007/2010 server and all mailboxes and public folders have been removed, there comes a time when the old server or servers should be removed.

Rather than simply removing or disconnecting an old Exchange server from the network, it is important to uninstall Exchange from the old server system. The uninstall process doesn't just remove the Exchange software off the hard drive of the system; it performs the very important task of properly removing that Exchange server from Active Directory.

After all mailboxes, public folder replicas, and connectors have been moved off an old Exchange Server 2007/2010 system, the server can be retired and removed from service. The easiest and most straightforward approach to this is to uninstall the Exchange Server 2007/2010 component via the Add/Remove Programs applet in Windows. To perform this operation, do the following:

1. On the legacy Exchange server, select Start, Control Panel.
2. Double-click Uninstall Program.
3. Select Microsoft Exchange Server (2007 or 2010), as shown in Figure 7.13 and click Uninstall.
4. Click Next at the Welcome screen.
5. Under Action, select Remove from the drop-down box, and click Next to continue.
6. At the Summary screen, click Next to continue. The Exchange server will then be uninstalled.
7. Repeat the process for any additional Exchange Server 2007/2010 servers.

Upon removal of the last Exchange Server 2007/2010 server, the environment should be completely void of any Exchange Server 2007/2010 functionality. There is no Native Exchange Server 2013 mode. The removal of the last Exchange Server 2007/2010 routing group clears legacy mail routing that is no longer needed in Exchange Server 2013.

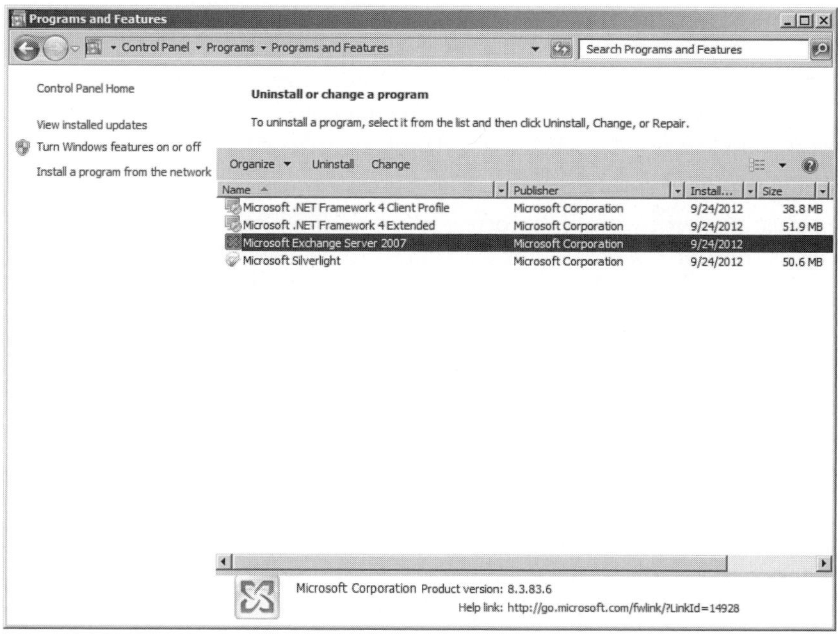

FIGURE 7.13 Removing legacy Exchange Server components.

Summary

A transition to Exchange Server 2013 is relatively straightforward, provided the proper thought goes into execution of the tasks required. Effectively, the process merely involves adding Exchange Server 2013 servers to an existing Exchange Server 2007 or 2010 environment, and moving server roles and mailbox data to the new servers. This chapter covered several other prerequisite processes along with tips and tricks needed to have a higher success factor in the transition process. With proper thought put into how to make the process seamless, a transition from Exchange Server 2007/2010 to Exchange Server 2013 can be made relatively painless.

Best Practices

The following are best practices from this chapter:

- Use the high-level transition checklists from the beginning of this chapter as a guide to the transition process.
- Key to a successful transition to Exchange Server 2013 is to properly plan and test the transition process to ensure all data as well as server role functions have a successful transition to the new environment. See Chapters 2 and 3 of this book on design and architecture best practices prior to performing a transition to Exchange Server 2013.

- Because Exchange Server 2013 does not support certain Exchange Server 2007/2010 functions, an Exchange Server 2007/2010 server may need to exist in the organization after the transition or until that functionality is no longer required. This is especially the case for the Edge Transport role, which is not yet supported directly on Exchange Server 2013.
- Before transitioning to Exchange Server 2013, the Active Directory schema needs to be updated. Test this process in a prototype lab in advance of the transition. The account that runs this portion of the setup will need to be a member of the Schema Administrators and Enterprise Administrators group in the AD DS forest.
- Being that Microsoft does not provide a direct transition from Exchange Server 2003 or earlier to Exchange Server 2013, the organization should plan its transition from Exchange Server 2003 to Exchange Server 2010 as a separate intermediate step before transitioning to Exchange Server 2013.
- Test the transition process in a lab environment before implementing the transition in production. A test transition confirms that all data successfully transitions to the new environment (that is, there is no mailbox corruption that can halt the transition process). In addition, by running through the process in a lab, you gain experience on the transition process and gain a good sense of how long it will take to complete the transition at the time of the live transition.
- Install an Exchange Server 2013 Client Access Server role first, and then at least one Mailbox role system because both servers are required for the remote PowerShell that the Exchange Server 2013 management tools need to work properly.
- Use the Certificate Wizard to create the certificates required for Exchange Server 2013.
- Use load-balanced names instead of machine names in the certificates and configure all virtual directories' `InternalURL` and `ExternalURL` properties with URLs with those load-balanced names.
- Use the Batch Move utility in the Exchange Administration Center to move large groups of mailboxes to Exchange Server 2013.
- Do not finish the migration of public folders until all mailboxes have been moved to Exchange Server 2013.
- Keep in mind that if a brand-new Exchange Server 2013 environment is implemented as a clean installation of Exchange, it must be noted that a clean Exchange Server 2013 environment cannot have Exchange Server 2007/2010 servers added in to the new Exchange Server 2013 organization. Related to this, if Exchange Server 2013 is installed directly into an Exchange Server 2010 organization that has never had Exchange Server 2007 in place, no Exchange Server 2007 servers can be added after the fact, or vice versa.

CHAPTER 8

Implementing and Supporting a Highly Available Exchange Server 2013 Environment

IN THIS CHAPTER

- ▶ Understanding Windows Failover Clustering
- ▶ Understanding Database Availability Groups
- ▶ Deploying a Database Availability Group
- ▶ Comparing and Contrasting DAG Versus CCR/SCR/SCC
- ▶ Load Balancing in Exchange Server 2013
- ▶ Software Load Balancing in Windows

As companies become increasingly dependent on email for communications and collaboration, the concept of high availability has become a requirement. To address this need, Microsoft introduced database availability groups (DAGs) back in Exchange Server 2010 to replace Cluster Continuous Replication (CCR) and Standby Continuous Replication (SCR) which were available in Exchange Server 2007. Exchange Server 2013 retains DAGs with the expected improvements in performance and configuration. DAGs allow an administrator to replicate a database to as many as 16 geographically dispersed Mailbox servers. The identity of the mail server no longer needs to be maintained by the cluster resources and moves back and forth between the cluster nodes. In Exchange Server 2013, although the overall server roles have changed, ultimately DAGs stay pretty much the same. Database availability groups still allow the Client Access server (CAS) tier to make decisions about which copy of the back-end data should be accessed. If a failure were to occur on the "preferred" copy of the mailbox database, another copy would be selected based on a series of criteria, including index health, copy queues, and replay queues. In this way, mailbox redundancy scales beyond the two copies offered by CCR and was improved to as many as 16 copies. Although SCR previously allowed an administrator to store mailbox replicas in more than two places, the recovery via SCR was always a manual process, whereas DAG is an automatic occurrence among a subset of servers as defined by the administrator. This ability to replicate and automatically attach to a valid copy of the data has tremendous implications for today's email administrators ranging from simple geographic redundancy all the way to fundamentally changing the way storage for Exchange Server is designed. Having so many potential copies of mailbox data, coupled with mailbox retention policies, could completely eliminate the need for nightly backups for Exchange Server data. Do note, however, that these new abilities come with a price. Replication, while efficient, still requires bandwidth. Replicating daily Exchange Server 2013 traffic to as many as 16 wide area network (WAN)–attached locations will eat up a significant amount of bandwidth and must be planned for appropriately. It also eats up a fair amount of storage as each DAG member has an independent copy of the database.

Windows Network Load Balancing (WNLB) is as important as ever in the Exchange Server 2013 world because it allows various services such as Messaging Application Programming Interface (MAPI), Post Office Protocol 3 (POP3), Internet Message Access Protocol 4 (IMAP4), or Outlook Anywhere to enjoy redundancy as well. As Exchange Server 2013 has further improved the Outlook Web App (OWA) and ActiveSync experiences, email administrators can expect an increase in the number of users that access OWA and ActiveSync for remote access to their email. As such, the ability to load-balance web-based services becomes even more critical. Hardware load balancing is still supported and it is interesting to note that with the changes in logic to what a Client Access server does, it is no longer necessary to deploy expensive Layer 7 load balancers. Exchange Server 2013 is load-balanced at Layer 4 now.

This chapter further details these new functions and offers advice on how best to utilize them. Step-by-step installation and configuration instructions are included where appropriate.

Understanding Windows Failover Clustering

Windows Failover Clustering, in the context of Exchange Server 2013 DAGs, is a Majority Node Set cluster. This is to say that decisions made within the cluster require a majority of the nodes to vote the same way.

In an Exchange Server 2013 DAG cluster with an even number of nodes, it is important to add a file share witness (FSW) server so the cluster ends up with an odd number of nodes. At first, this might not be intuitive, but consider the case where there is an even number of nodes. Let's say, for example, that a DAG is deployed with six members, three in each site. If there were a WAN failure between the two sites, each site would be left with three nodes and, thus, three out of six votes. Because neither site would have a majority, neither side could make decisions within the cluster. An example of such a decision would be the decision to activate a replica copy of a database. At first, this seems bad, but in reality, it's done intentionally. This is done to prevent a situation called "split-brain syndrome." This is a situation where two groups of nodes within a cluster both think that they should activate their resources. If this were to happen, there would be divergent versions of the databases that exist in both sites that could never be brought back into sync with one another. If one was picked as "better" by the administrator and the "lesser" copy deleted and reseeded with the better copy, it would still result in a loss of email content, which is generally considered unacceptable. For this reason, Microsoft recommends the use of a file share witness to always serve as the tiebreaker. Three out of six plus the file share witness is a majority, and, thus, the site that could reach the FSW would have sufficient votes to activate its copies of the databases. The site with only three of six nodes without the file share witness wouldn't. The FSW is not actually a voter—it is referenced only when there is an even number of nodes, of which exactly half are able to communicate with each other.

In some situations, this can create a difficult situation when dealing with n+1 capacity at a primary site with disaster recovery nodes at another site. Recall the earlier example with three nodes in site A and three nodes in site B. Assume that databases are distributed such that there is always n+1 capacity in the primary location. If a Mailbox server fails, there is still an alternate copy available in the primary site. Let's also assume that in this example, there is an FSW available in the primary site. Now let's imagine that the WAN fails and the two sites are orphaned from each other. Because the primary site has three of the six voters plus the file share witness to break the tie, it's able to continue running. Now let's see what happens when we lose a server in this situation in the primary site. Even though there is a second copy of each database in the primary data center, the loss of a node drops the number of voters from three of six to only two of six, and all databases dismount because there is no longer a node majority. What happened? We planned for n+1 capacity in the main site and configured an FSW to create an odd number of nodes and now the loss of a single server has wiped out all of Exchange Server 2013 until the WAN is restored? Yes. However, if you need coverage in even this grim scenario, there is still a way.

In a DAG cluster, any server with the Mailbox server role installed is a voter. In the example with six Mailbox servers and an FSW, we can have at most three of six voters in the primary site if the WAN fails plus the FSW to break the tie, but what if we stack the deck in our favor? Consider the CAS servers. If they are hardware load balanced, we could simply add the Mailbox server role to a pair in the primary site and not create any databases on them. Now the voter count is eight instead of six, and a minimum of four plus the FSW is required for majority. In the primary site, there are now five of eight voters plus the FSW. If the WAN were to fail, there would still be five voters in the primary site. If we were to lose a Mailbox server, which our n+1 configuration protects against by having multiple copies of the database in the primary site, we still have four of eight voters plus the FSW, and the cluster remains running happily.

Understanding Database Availability Groups

A database availability group is a group of up to 16 Exchange Server 2013 Mailbox servers that replicate mailbox data to each other and that can perform automated recovery as the mailbox database level in the event of a hardware, storage, or network failure. They utilize a subset of Windows Server 2008 or 2012 Failover Clustering in order to monitor each other's health. This allows them to determine which node should be primary for a given database.

Although a database availability group isn't a cluster in the traditional sense, it does utilize some of the functions of Windows Server 2008/2012 clustering in order to track system availability. One of the components required for this function is a file share witness. Administrators familiar with Exchange Server 2007 may recall that a file share witness acts like a voting node in a cluster, specifically a Majority Node Set cluster. This allows a cluster to have as few as two traditional nodes with the FSW acting like a tiebreaker. This allows the cluster to achieve a majority if a node were to fail. Were there only two voting nodes total, the majority of two is two, so only one being up and running wouldn't constitute a majority and it wouldn't be able to make cluster-related decisions. The cluster only utilizes the FSW when doing so will bring the total number of voters to an odd number. This is to prevent the possibility of a split-brain scenario if a WAN failure were to occur, effectively splitting the cluster in half. By always having an odd number, it's impossible for both groups of nodes to think they have majority and both activate.

To understand database availability groups and how they work, it's important to understand the various technologies that are involved with making this work. DAGs have the following attributes:

- They require Windows Server Failover Clustering.
- They allow for database portability.
- They use log shipping for data replication.
- They support Shadow Redundancy.
- They can be incrementally reseeded.
- There are no storage groups.

Although Exchange Server 2013 DAGs aren't built on a traditional Windows cluster, DAGs do take advantage of parts of Windows Server 2008/2012 Failover Clustering to establish a heartbeat among them and to monitor the availability of each other. Unlike earlier versions of Exchange Server, Exchange Server 2013 does not require the administrators to manage resources at the cluster level through Failover Clustering tools. The installation of Failover Clustering features and the management of failover clustering is handled entirely "under the covers" by Exchange Server 2013.

Database portability is a concept that was introduced in Exchange Server 2007. In short, it effectively uncoupled the Exchange server's identity from the security settings on the mailbox database. This allowed an Exchange Server 2007 server to host a mailbox database that was originally owned by a different server. In versions of Exchange Server prior to 2007, this concept didn't exist, and as a result, recovering mailbox databases on new servers was a rather painful exercise. In Exchange Server 2013, this concept is what allows multiple Exchange Server 2013 Mailbox servers to be effectively authoritative for the same mailbox database information.

NOTE

Because a single mailbox database can be replicated across multiple servers, it is required by Exchange Server 2013 that all mailbox databases be created with unique names. In Exchange Server 2007 and earlier, it was acceptable to reuse a database name because they were always referenced by Server name\Storage Group name\Database name, which made them unique within the Exchange Server organization. In Exchange Server 2013, this is not the case as a replica could potentially have a name conflict with a local database.

Log Shipping Replication was introduced into Exchange Server 2007 with the creation of Clustered Continuous Replication and later employed in Standby Continuous Replication. The same base technology is used to replicate mailbox database transactions between members of a database availability group. This replication has been improved in terms of resiliency and recovery through the introduction of Shadow Redundancy and Incremental Reseeding.

Shadow Redundancy is the name given to a new process that was introduced in Exchange Server 2010. Similar to the Transport Dumpster function in Exchange Server 2007, wherein a message that was sent via a Hub Transport server was saved for a period of time in case it needed to be re-sent after a CCR or SCR failover, Shadow Redundancy ensures that a message is not deleted from a transport database until after it's received a confirmation of receipt from the next hop. If the next hop doesn't confirm receipt, the message is resubmitted for delivery. This is especially useful in high-traffic environments where large numbers of messages are potentially "in flight" on a Hub Transport server. If that server was to fail and the messages not sent to their next hop, the Mailbox server would detect this and resubmit the unconfirmed messages to another available Hub Transport server. Should those messages later become available through a "fix" of the failed Hub Transport, the destination would recognize them as duplicates and suppress them from the target mailbox.

Incremental Reseeding is another function of Exchange Server 2013 that is further improved over the version introduced in Exchange Server 2010 that reduces the impact of replicating mailbox data to a database that was offline for a period of time. In Exchange Server 2007, if a CCR or SCR replica was too far out of sync, the only solution was to delete the database and start replication from scratch. This resulted in potentially hundreds of gigabytes of data being replicated to get the database back to a point where it could accept and process log files. During this time, the databases were no longer redundant, and the mailbox data was at risk. With Incremental Reseeding, the out-of-sync database is compared with the source database and only the necessary updates are sent to the database to bring it back to a level where replication can resume normally. This greatly reduces the time taken to reseed a database and thus reduces the windows of exposure for the mailbox data. As database sizes increase, this function becomes more and more important.

The last piece of database availability groups was the removal of the concept of a storage group from Exchange Server 2010, which is still the case in Exchange Server 2013. In Exchange Server 2007, any of the replication technologies required that the system be configured with only one database per storage group. Log files for all databases within a storage group were grouped together and recovery of a database read the log files from this storage group. In Exchange Server 2010 and Exchange Server 2013 DAGs, because the databases are no longer associated with a specific server, the need to manage by storage group was removed. Databases are now associated with the DAG instead.

NOTE

Database replication within a DAG is only supported between Mailbox servers with less than 250ms of round-trip latency. As such, it's important to be aware of the typical latency between sites that might potentially house replicas of your mailbox data. Although physics tells us that electricity can travel the circumference of the earth in around 135ms, network-induced latency as well as indirect paths can make this number significantly higher.

Deploying a Database Availability Group

Deployment of a DAG is a fairly straightforward process, but it does have several steps that must occur in the correct order. By becoming familiar with the requirements and the process, the implementation should be fairly uneventful.

Because a DAG doesn't require a Windows Server 2008/2012 cluster to be prebuilt, the instructions will assume that the administrator has already built a basic Exchange Server 2013 Mailbox server. For detailed instructions on building an Exchange Server 2013 Mailbox server, see Chapter 6, "Installing and Configuring the Basics of Exchange Server 2013 for a Brand-New Environment."

Requirements for DAG

You will need two or more servers that are capable of supporting the Exchange Server 2013 Mailbox server role. You don't need shared storage with a DAG because the transactions are shipped to the replicas and applied locally. This allows up to 16 independent databases and sets of log files on up to 16 different servers with independent media. You will want to follow the same standards as you would with a normal Mailbox server in terms of database sizes and hardware specifications to support your anticipated user load.

To set up a DAG, you need the following:

- Two or more servers running Windows Server 2008, Enterprise Edition/Datacenter Edition or any version of Windows Server 2012
- Two network interfaces per server are strongly recommended for high-availability sites
- Exchange Server 2013 Standard or Enterprise Edition
- One file share witness per DAG when there are an even number of nodes, and recommended even for odd-number-node configurations in the event an additional DAG member is added

Microsoft recommends using a Client Access server for the file share witness because it will be installed first according to standard installation practice, and it will have all the permissions properly configured so that Exchange Setup can automatically create the file share witness on it. You may join Mailbox servers running Exchange Server 2013 Standard Edition into a DAG, but you will be limited to a total of five active and passive database copies, including archive and journal databases, public folder databases, and recovery databases on any Mailbox server; so, except for test lab situations, most DAG implementations will employ the Enterprise Edition of Exchange.

Creating the DAG Via the Graphical User Interface (GUI)

Once the Exchange Server Mailbox servers are prepared, they can be joined into a new database availability group by performing the following steps:

1. Point a web browser at a front-end server/ecp, for example, https://exchangefe-01.companyabc.com/ecp.
2. When prompted, enter domain\name and the password of an account with Organization Admin rights. Click Sign In.
3. When the Exchange Administration Center (EAC) launches, click Servers in the left pane to see a list of servers, as shown in Figure 8.1.

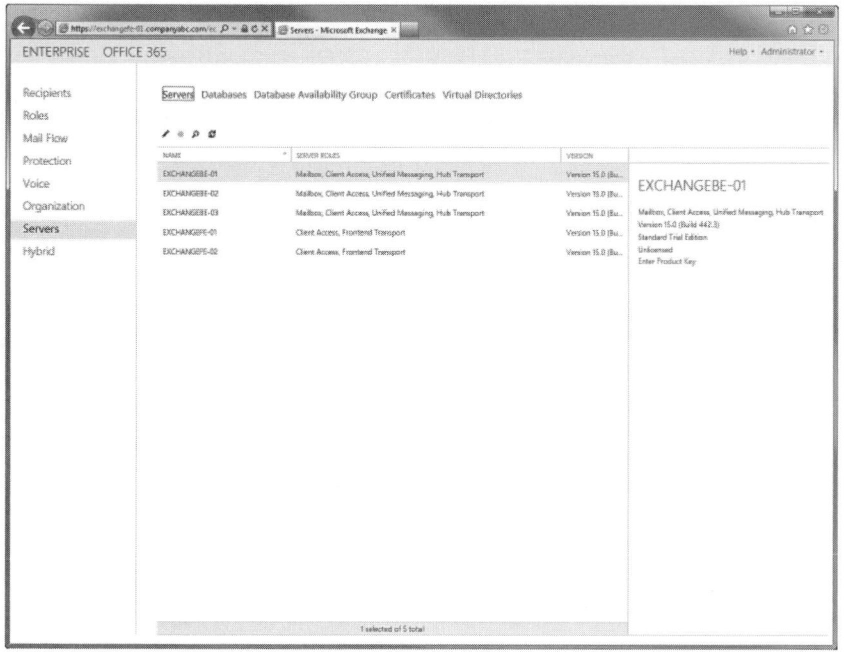

FIGURE 8.1 Viewing the servers in the EAC.

4. In the upper menu, click Database Availability Group.

5. Click the + icon to create a new DAG.

6. When the New Database Availability Group window appears, enter a Database Availability Group Name, Witness Server, Witness Directory, and Database Availability Group IP Address, as shown in Figure 8.2, and click Save. Make sure to click the + icon after typing the IP address.

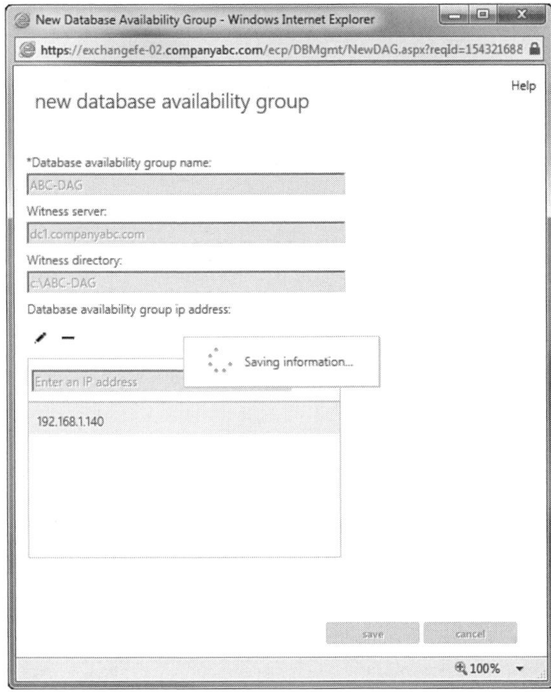

FIGURE 8.2 Creating a new DAG.

7. Once the DAG object is created, click the Manage Membership button.

8. Click Add (+), select one or more servers, click Add ->, click OK, and then click Save.

At this point, the Failover Cluster services will be installed on the selected nodes, and they will join the DAG. Should this step fail, ensure that the Trusted Installer group has rights to the file share witness and that the Exchange-related services are started on all Exchange servers that are to be added to the DAG.

When the database availability group is created, a computer object is created in Active Directory to represent the failover cluster virtual network name account. If a DAG is going to be re-created with the same name, it is necessary to disable or delete this computer account or the process will error out and fail.

Renaming Exchange Server 2013 Databases

Once the DAG is created, administrators will notice that each node in the DAG cluster already had a database created. Most administrators will not want to utilize the default naming scheme for databases and will want to rename them and update their path based on that name. This task can be performed with the following steps:

1. Point a web browser at a front-end server/ecp, for example, https://exchangefe-01.companyabc.com/ecp.
2. When prompted, enter domain\name and the password of an account with Organization Admin rights. Click Sign In.
3. When the EAC launches, click Servers in the left pane to see a list of servers.
4. In the upper menu, click Databases.
5. Click the database you plan to rename and click the Edit icon, which looks like a small pencil.
6. When the Mailbox Database window appears, as shown in Figure 8.3, set the name to the value you want and click Save.

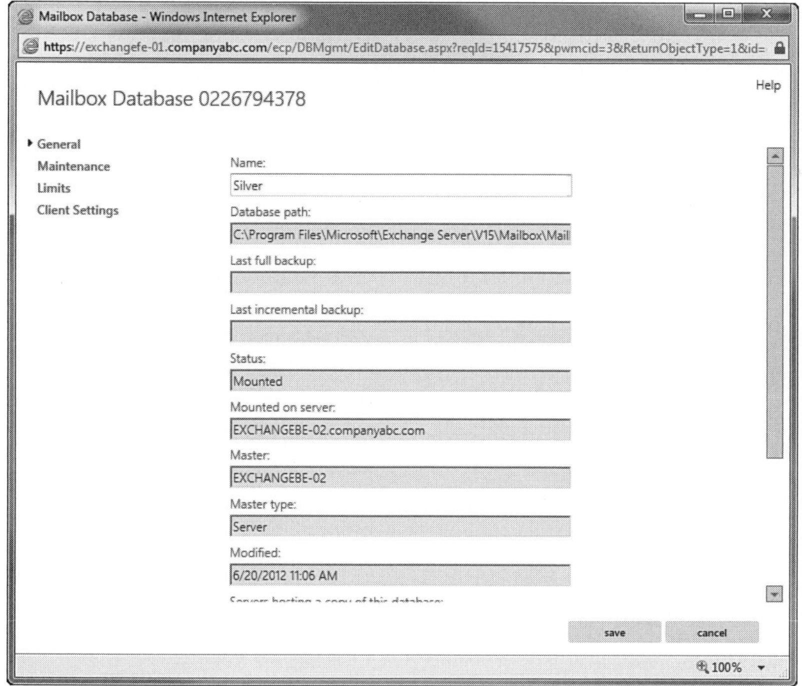

FIGURE 8.3 Renaming the database.

7. With the renamed database selected, click the ellipsis (...) and click Dismount. Confirm the desire to dismount by clicking Yes.

NOTE

It is not necessary to dismount the database prior to moving its path; the operation will dismount the database before moving it and remount it after completion.

8. Launch the Exchange Management Shell from the system hosting the database that was renamed.
9. Type the following: **`Move-DatabasePath -db DBName -EdbFilePath newpath.`**

   For example, **`Move-DatabasePath -db Silver -EdbFilePath "C:\Program Files\Microsoft\Exchange Server\V15\Mailbox\Silver\Silver.edb" -LogFolderPath "C:\Program Files\Microsoft\Exchange Server\V15\Mailbox\Silver"`**
10. Type **`Y`** to confirm each action or type **`A`** to confirm all related actions.
11. Return to ECP and select the recently moved database. Click the ellipsis and choose Mount.

Alternately, the database could be mounted via Exchange Management Console with the command:

```
Mount-Database Silver
```

Adding Database Copies

Once the databases have been created, administrators will want to add copies of those databases to other DAG members to provide availability in the sense that there are redundant copies of the database that can be activated if the primary copy becomes unavailable. Typically, you would strive for at least two copies of a given database in the primary data center and at least one additional copy in a remote data center. This provides for local high availability along with geographic disaster recovery capabilities.

To add database copies, follow these steps:

1. Point a web browser at a front-end server/ecp, for example, https://exchangefe-01.companyabc.com/ecp.
2. When prompted, enter domain\name and the password of an account with Organization Admin rights. Click Sign In.
3. When the EAC launches, click Servers in the left pane to see a list of servers.
4. In the upper menu, click Databases.
5. Click the button for Add Database Copy.

6. When the Add Mailbox Database Copy window appears, click Browse and select a Mailbox server to receive the copy. Assign an Activation Preference Number, optionally add a Replay Lag Time (Days), and optionally check the box to postpone seeding. Click Save.

This updates the GUI to show the list of additional replicas, as shown in Figure 8.4.

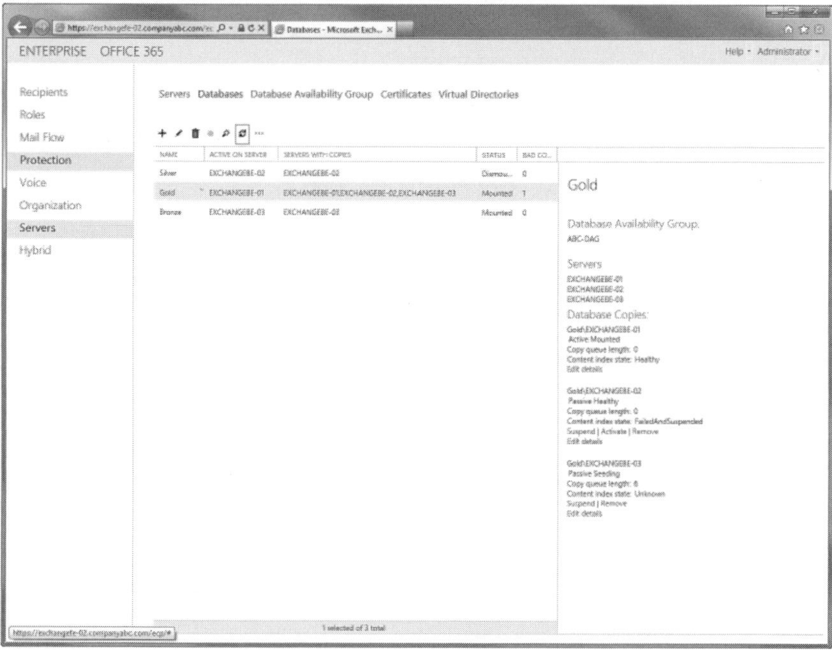

FIGURE 8.4 Adding a DAG replica.

Removing Database Copies

Should an administrator find himself retiring servers or reducing capacity in some way, it might be necessary to remove database copies. For example, if a node were going to be down for an extended period of time, rather than just suspend the copy and let log files build up (as Exchange Server 2013 can't delete logs that still need to be copied to a replica), the administrator might remove the copy from the server that will be unavailable. This task can be performed with the following steps:

1. Point a web browser at a front-end server/ecp, for example, https://exchangefe-01.companyabc.com/ecp.

2. When prompted, enter domain\name and the password of an account with Organization Admin rights. Click Sign In.

3. When the EAC launches, click Servers in the left pane to see a list of servers.
4. In the upper menu, click Databases.
5. Click the database from which you want to remove a copy.
6. In the far right pane, look for the copy you want to remove. Click the link for Remove.
7. When the warning appears, click Yes to indicate that you are sure that you want to remove the database copy.

The Databases interface will immediately update to reflect the change in "Servers with Copies" for that database.

Suspending and Reseeding a Database

In the event that a replica of a mailbox database should become out of sync with the primary copy, it becomes necessary to reseed the database to resume the replication of log files. There are a few situations that can cause the need to sync the databases:

- Bringing a replica back online after extended downtime
- Corruption of log files
- Corruption of a database
- An extended WAN outage

The easiest way to determine if a database needs to be resynchronized is to look at its current replication status. This can be viewed with the following steps:

1. Point a web browser at a front-end server/ecp, for example, https://exchangefe-01.companyabc.com/ecp.
2. When prompted, enter domain\name and the password of an account with Organization Admin rights. Click Sign In.
3. When the EAC launches, click Servers in the left pane to see a list of servers.
4. In the upper menu, click Databases.
5. Look at the Bad Copy Count to determine if any copy is in an unhealthy state.
6. Click a database that has a Bad Copy Count of 1 or higher and look at the details of the copies in the far-right pane. This shows the state they are in.

Administrators who are more comfortable with the Exchange Management Shell can use the cmdlet:

```
Get-MailboxServer | Get-MailboxDatabaseCopyStatus
```

Simply running `Get-MailboxDatabaseCopyStatus` will only return status for the server it was run from. Other helpful queries are:

```
Get-MailboxServer | Get-MailboxDatabaseCopyStatus | where {($_.CopyQueueLength
-gt "20")}
Get-MailboxServer | Get-MailboxDatabaseCopyStatus | where {($_.status -ne
"Healthy") -and ($_.status -ne "Mounted")}
```

The first example shows all databases with a Copy Queue of 20 or more log files. The second example shows databases that are neither mounted nor healthy.

NOTE

If you have a large number of mailbox databases, take advantage of PowerShell to do your work for you by utilizing filtered queries to return only the information you are interested in.

If the database is found to be in a failed state, it can be reseeded in the following manner:

1. Point a web browser at a front-end server/ecp, for example, https://exchangefe-01.companyabc.com/ecp.
2. When prompted, enter domain\name and the password of an account with Organization Admin rights. Click Sign In.
3. When the EAC launches, click Servers in the left pane to see a list of servers.
4. In the upper menu, click Databases.
5. Select the database that will be reseeded.
6. In the right pane, find the copy you will be reseeding and click the link to Suspend the Database.
7. When prompted, click OK to indicate that you are sure you want to suspend replication.
8. In the right pane, find the copy you will be reseeding and click the link to Update the Database.
9. Click Browse and select the source server for seeding. This should be a server that has a healthy copy of the database to be reseeded. Click OK.
10. Click Save.
11. When the process is complete, click Finish.

The database will be reseeded from the source server.

The same process of suspending and updating the database copy can be performed via PowerShell:

```
Suspend-MailboxDatabaseCopy -Identity DBName\MailboxServer -SuspendComment
"reason for suspending"
Update-MailboxDatabaseCopy -Identity DBName\MailboxServer -SourceServer
SourceServerName
```

[with the option of `-DatabaseOnly` or `-CatalogOnly` if only one is out of sync]

For example, to suspend database `Gold` on `ExchangeBE-01` you could use:

```
Suspend-MailboxDatabaseCopy -Identity Gold\ExchangeBE-01 -SuspendComment
"on hold for disk maintenance"
```

To reseed only the database and not the index on database `Gold` on server `ExchangeBE-01` using `ExchangeBE-02` as the source:

```
Update-MailboxDatabaseCopy -Identity Gold\ExchangeBE-01 -SourceServer
ExchangeBE-02 -DatabseOnly
```

Creating the DAG Via Exchange Management Shell

Many Exchange Server administrators have embraced the Exchange Management Shell as the preferred tool for configuration. Doing things via the shell has many advantages. The primary advantage being that it is very easy to script configuration and deployment, which ensures that all systems are configured correctly and that no human error has occured while following a set of directions. To create a DAG via the Exchange Management Shell, perform the following steps:

1. Launch the Exchange Management Shell.
2. Type **`New-DatabaseAvailabilityGroup-Name name -WitnessDirectory DirectoryPath -WitnessServer Server -DatabaseAvailabilityGroupIpAddresses IPAddresses`**

   For example, **`New-DatabaseAvailabilityGroup-Name Dag-ABC -WitnessDirectory c:\FSW-FileShareWitnessShare -WitnessServer Hotspare -DomainController Coldspare`**.

Adding Nodes to the DAG Via Exchange Management Shell

When the database availability group has been created via Exchange Management Shell, the same shell can be used to add members to the DAG via the following steps:

1. Launch the Exchange Management Shell.
2. Type **`Add-DatabaseAvailabilityGroupServer -Identity DAGName -MailboxServer firstnode`**.

   For example, **`Add-DatabaseAvailabilityGroupServer -Identity Dag-ABC -MailboxServer ExchangeBE-02`**.

3. Add any additional nodes with the same command; simply replace the name of the node to be added.

Adding a Database Copy to a DAG Via Exchange Management Shell

With the database availability group configured and functional, you can add database copies to DAG members by following these steps:

1. Launch the Exchange Management Shell.
2. Type `Add-MailboxDatabaseCopy-Identity DatabaseName -MailboxServer ReplicaServer-ActivationPreference number`.

   For example, `Add-MailboxDatabaseCopy-Identity Gold -MailboxServer ExchangeBE-03 -ActivationPreference 3`.

Monitoring the Health of DAG Replication

When a database availability group has been established and replicas added to it, it is useful for administrators to be able to check on the health of the replication. Should this replication fail for any reason, the sooner an administrator can be aware of it, the better his or her chance is to fix the replication before a reseed becomes necessary.

The health of the replication can be checked in two ways, through the GUI by using the Exchange Administration Center or from the command line by using the Exchange Management Shell.

To check the health of a replica via the GUI, follow these steps:

1. Point a web browser at a front-end server/ecp, for example, https://exchangefe-01.companyabc.com/ecp.
2. When prompted, enter domain\name and the password of an account with Organization Admin rights. Click Sign In.
3. When the EAC launches, click Servers in the left pane to see a list of servers.
4. In the upper menu, click Databases.
5. View the Bad Copy Count column.

Additional status information is available by clicking the Edit Details link in the far-right pane. This status includes the following:

- Content Index State
- Status
- Copy Queue Length
- Replay Queue Length
- Error Messages

- Latest Available Logtime
- Last Inspected Logtime
- Last Copied Logtime
- Last Replayed Logtime
- Activation Preference Number
- Relay Lag Time (Days)

This information can be useful in determining the cause of replication problems and to provide an overall snapshot of database health.

To perform a similar task in Exchange Management Shell, perform the following steps:

1. Launch Exchange Management Shell.
2. Type **`Get-MailboxDatabaseCopyStatus -Server ReplicaServer`**.

   For example, **`Get-MailboxDatabaseCopyStatus -Server Exchangebe-01`**.

This shows the current status of the replication and will show the Copy Queue Length and the Replay Queue Length. This makes it easy to see if a copy is in sync or if not, how far behind it is.

There are several advantages to querying the replication status via the Exchange Management Shell. For example, at first the output from the command would seem to suggest that there is less information available than what is shown by the GUI. This is actually not the case. If you were to pipe the output of `Get-DatabaseCopyStatus` to a formatted list, you would find that there are 77 parameters that are tracked by this command.

```
Get-MailboxDatabaseCopyStatus -Identity Gold\Exchangebe-01 | FL
```

This can be exceptionally useful when you need to query a large number of systems for any errors. By querying all of your Mailbox servers and filtering out just ones where a particular parameter is returning a specific status, you can quickly find all servers matching those criteria.

For example, an administrator might want to generate a real-time report showing all Mailbox servers that have a database status of `Failed = true`. This can be written fairly easily in Exchange Management Shell:

```
del c:\users\Administrator \Documents\FailedState.csv
$mailboxservers = Get-MailboxServer
Foreach ($server in $mailboxservers)
{
$var=Get-MailboxDatabaseCopyStatus -server $server | where {$_.Failed -match
"True"}
$status=$Var.Failed
```

```
$ID=$Var.Databasename
$log=$var.LastCopiedLogTime
Add-content c:\users\Administrator\Documents\FailedState.csv "$server,$ID,
$Status, $Log"}
```

This produces a list showing replica servers that have one or more databases in a Failed state. It shows specifically which databases are in that Failed state and show the time stamp of the last log that was shipped. This type of a script could be scheduled to run hourly to allow for an up-to-date view of replication across the whole environment.

Moving the Active Copy of the Database

When, in the course of administrator events, it becomes necessary for you to perform maintenance on a member of a database availability group, it might be necessary to move the active copy of a given database from one server to another. Although taking down a node that is currently the active copy causes the second priority node to activate, the process is cleaner and smoother if it is initiated intentionally.

Given that the active copy of the database is effectively the source of replication, it is important to consider that the site holding a given copy of the database will experience an increase in bandwidth usage if there are multiple copies of a database distributed across the environment. As such, it is recommended to move the active copy to a well-connected site whenever possible.

To activate a replica copy of a mailbox database, perform the following steps:

1. Point a web browser at a front-end server/ecp, for example, https://exchangefe-01.companyabc.com/ecp.
2. When prompted, enter domain\name and the password of an account with Organization Admin rights. Click Sign In.
3. When the EAC launches, click Servers in the left pane to see a list of servers.
4. In the upper menu, click Databases.
5. Click the database you want to move.
6. In the right pane, find the passive copy you want to activate and click the Activate link.
7. When the warning appears, click Yes, and the move will commence, as shown in Figure 8.5.
8. When the move is completed, click OK.

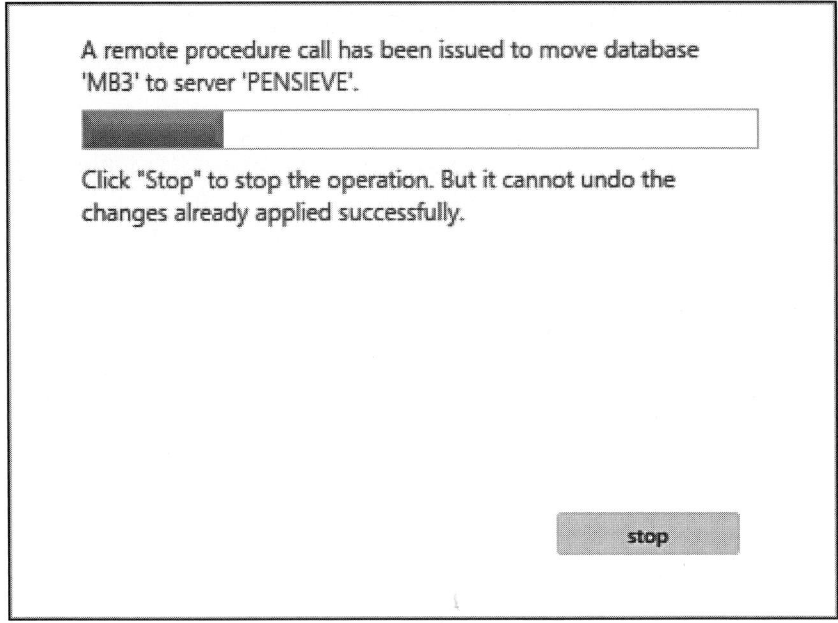

A remote procedure call has been issued to move database 'MB3' to server 'PENSIEVE'.
Click "Stop" to stop the operation. But it cannot undo the changes already applied successfully.
stop

FIGURE 8.5 Active Database copy.

The same process can be done entirely from the Exchange Management Shell as well by following these steps:

1. Launch the Exchange Management Shell.
2. Type **`Move-ActiveMailboxDatabase DBName -ActivateOnServer MailboxServer`**.
3. When prompted, enter **`A`** to accept all confirmations.

For example:

```
Move-ActiveMailboxDatabase Gold -ActivateOnServer ExchangeBE-01
```

Should you need to move a database to a copy whose index isn't current, add the `-SkipClientExperienceChecks` to the `Move-ActiveMailboxDatabase` cmdlet. This skips the check for index health.

If you want to move all active copies off of a particular Mailbox server, for example if you want to apply a service pack or rollup hot fix, then use the following command:

```
Move-ActiveMailboxDatabase -Server ExchangeBE-01
```

NOTE

It is of value to point out that when the active copy status is moved from one host to another, several things happen automatically. Replication from the active copy to replicas automatically resumes from the new source, and Client Access servers automatically connect to the copy of the database that is now active. OWA clients might see a small hiccup in service, stating that their mailbox is not mounted, but simply refreshing the browser reconnects the session.

Changing Priorities on Replicas of Mailbox Databases

As an Exchange Server 2013 environment grows and evolves, you might want to alter the initial distribution of mailbox database replicas in terms of the preferred replacement if a failure occurs. For example, an environment may start off with an active copy of a database in San Francisco with a replica copy in an office in New York. Sometime down the road, a new office, say in Denver, might be brought online. Based on latency, it might be more desirable for Denver to be the secondary site for San Francisco rather than New York. Denver could be added as a replica using the steps shown earlier in this chapter and it would default to being third in the list of preferred replicas. To change this replica to preference 2, simply follow these steps:

1. Point a web browser at a front-end server/ecp, for example, https://exchangefe-01.companyabc.com/ecp.
2. When prompted, enter domain\name and the password of an account with Organization Admin rights. Click Sign In.
3. When the EAC launches, click Servers in the left pane to see a list of servers.
4. In the upper menu, click Databases.
5. Click the database whose priorities are to be changed.
6. In the right pane, find the copy you want to alter and click the Edit Details link.
7. Find the drop-down near the bottom of the window labeled Activation Preference Number, as shown in Figure 8.6.
8. Click the down arrow and select the new preference value.
9. Click Save.

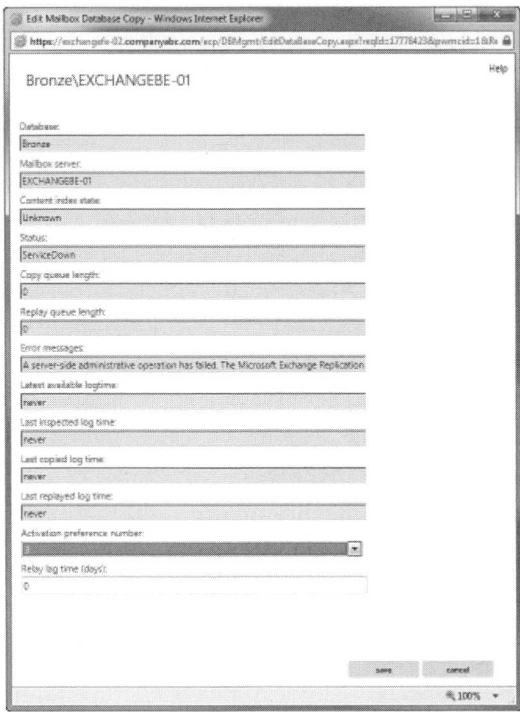

FIGURE 8.6 Editing the database details.

The same change can be performed via the Exchange Management Shell by using the following steps:

1. Launch the Exchange Management Shell.
2. Type **`Set-mailboxDatabaseCopy -Identity DBName\ServerName -ActivationPreference PreferenceNumber`**.

   For example, **`Set-MailboxDatabaseCopy-Identity Silver\Exchangebe-03 -ActivationPreference 3`**.

This would take the copy of the database called `Silver` that was living on Exchange DAG member `Exchangebe-03` and alter its priority to 3. All activation preferences must be consecutive—you cannot assign a preference value of 4 to a database when there are only three copies. When you assign a preference value, the preference values of other copies are automatically adjusted as necessary.

NOTE

Although logic would dictate that setting a database activation preference to 3 would make it the third choice for activation, this isn't actually the case. When a database fails and a copy needs to be activated, Exchange evaluates several factors to determine which copy could be brought up the fastest. This means that factors like Index State and Replay

Queue Length are more important than preference number. Preference number is only used if 10 other checks result in all copies being equally viable for activation. As such, it's important to use concepts like activation policies to prevent a remote copy from being activated ahead of a local copy.

Hardware Considerations for Database Availability Group Members

With the evolutionary changes that come with Exchange Server 2013, there is a noticeable shift in recommendations around hardware that should be used to support Exchange Server, especially in the area of database availability groups.

Administrators who were familiar with Cluster Continuous Replication in Exchange Server 2007 will immediately see the parallels between DAG and CCR. CCR introduced, and DAG continues to show, the benefits of direct attached storage for Exchange Server. Older versions of Exchange Server required very high levels of I/O to be provided for users to get good performance. Similarly, older versions of Exchange Server were dependent on shared storage to allow for redundancy at the mailbox level. DAG creates a situation in which there is no requirement to share any storage whatsoever across the nodes that form a DAG. This means that DAG members are free to utilize direct attached storage. This, coupled with the changes in architecture within Exchange Server 2013 that further lower I/O requirements through the use of larger blocks of data being transferred, further reduce the need for high-performance disk subsystems.

Although it might seem logical that replica copies of databases might consume far less resources than active copies, it is generally true that replica copies work the storage nearly as much because they must play in all the changes made to the active database copies from the logs that are shipped to them.

Another factor that heavily influenced the hardware used for Exchange Server in the past was the requirements around localized redundancy and fault tolerance. Traditionally, Exchange servers were built with multiple sets of disks for the operating system, the database files, and the transaction logs. The logic was that by mirroring the operating system, the administrator could protect against a server failure due to a failed hard drive. Similarly, logs were always kept separate from the databases so that if a database failed, the data could be restored from a backup and the current log files could be replayed to bring the database back to a current state. In a database availability group, the Exchange Server Mailbox servers become a disposable resource. Not unlike domain controllers in Active Directory, there is very little need to ever restore a failed DAG member, as long as at least one other DAG member exists with a replica of the mailbox databases. The administrator simply installs a fresh Exchange Server 2013 Mailbox server and adds it to the appropriate DAG and then adds that server to the list of replicas for the databases that were previously hosted in that site. The data is replicated, and the level of redundancy and fault tolerance is restored to its previous state.

Based on this ability to quickly and easily replace a lost DAG member, the requirements around local redundancy are effectively removed. Money that previously would have been used to purchase multiple disks and very high-performance disks can now be used to instead purchase commodity hardware to act as an additional DAG member with replicas of databases. Microsoft has gone as far as to recommend building Mailbox servers with no RAID whatsoever when using four or more database copies, including an offsite copy. The redundancy is effectively moved from the storage layer to the application layer.

When planning for the hardware to deploy an Exchange Server 2010 environment, keep in mind that the old CCR model of active/passive is no longer a limiting factor in your planning. For example, in Exchange Server 2007, if you were to build high availability for a site, you would have to build a CCR pair where one system was active for all its users and the other system sat by just dealing with replication. Site redundancy was usually accomplished with the use of SCR copies that would be difficult and time consuming to deploy in an emergency.

In a database availability group, this one-for-one relationship isn't necessarily a requirement. Imagine a three-site DAG where each host is running at 66% capacity. Each site has 10 databases that are active copies and each site is replicated to each other site. In the event of a failure, rather than having all 10 databases fail over to a single site, a clever administrator might have set 5 of the databases to priority 2 in site B and priority 3 in site C with the other 5 set to priority 3 in site B and priority 2 in site C. In this scenario, the 66% load is spread evenly to the other two sites, resulting in each site capable of handling the load. This level of granularity in determining where loads will go in the case of a failure is exactly what Exchange Server 2007 administrators were wishing for.

This concept can be carried further in the case of smaller sites that are replicated to a centralized disaster recovery site. Although an environment might have a dozen sites with, for example, 500 users each, the administrator doesn't necessarily build his or her disaster recovery site to handle 6,000 users. If, by some terrible series of events, all 12 sites suffered simultaneous failures, the odds of all 6,000 users being able to access their email would be very low. The administrator might instead plan the capacity from a performance standpoint to handle, for example, 2,000 users, but build the storage to replicate the mailboxes for all 6,000 users.

In older versions of Exchange Server, supporting 6,000 users required a fair amount of spindles on the disk subsystem. Exchange Server 2003, for example, recommended about 0.75 disk I/O per second per user. With a 6,000 user load, this meant about 4,500 I/O per sec. Given that a typical 10,000rpm disk can provide 110 I/O at an acceptable disk latency (under 20ms), it required 41 disks to provide this level of performance. If an administrator needed the storage to be redundant, and most did, this requirement jumped to 82 disks to provide the I/O in a RAID 0+1 configuration. It was in these days that SAN reigned supreme, as it was otherwise unrealistic to present 82 disks to an Exchange server. In Exchange Server 2013, the I/O requirement is more like 0.1 I/O per sec per user, due to the larger transfer block size and the amount of data that is cached. The cache of mailbox information is significantly larger due to the ability to access large amounts of memory, made possible by the 64-bit architecture. In this scenario, the same 6,000 users would require 600 I/O per sec, which could be provided by six spindles. Assuming the administrator was planning to replicate the data via a database availability group, the local requirement would literally be for six disks, in RAID 0. The cost of a SAN plus the 82 disks minus the costs of the six local disks would more than cover the price of a second server with six disks to provide the replica. It becomes easy to see that Exchange Server 2013 has the potential to be a much lower cost to deploy and become a much faster return on investment.

The logical extension of the reduction in resources required to support Exchange Server 2013 in a database availability group model is the concept of virtualization for the hosts. Depending on your level of trust and expertise with virtualization, it might make sense to initially virtualize one set of the replicas to gain knowledge and trust in managing a virtualized environment and for those who have already headed down a path of virtualization, all the roles in Exchange Server 2013 are very good candidates for virtualization, especially with the hypervisor improvements made in Windows Server 2012.

Perhaps the simplest point to take away from this discussion is that the old days of needing identical hardware across all cluster nodes is no longer the case. Database availability groups, while loosely dependent on Windows clustering services, have no requirements for the hardware to be identical, or even similar for that matter. Mixing and matching levels of performance, processor architecture, and storage types are completely supported. Just make sure a given system has enough performance to perform its primary job and to take over any additional loads that you're planning it to be redundant for.

Older versions of Exchange, including Exchange Server 2010, often suffered from odd utilization patterns. CAS and Hub Transport servers tended to be processor heavy and light on memory usage. Mailbox servers were low CPU load and high memory. With the architectural changes to Exchange Server 2013 where rendering and content logic have been moved to the Mailbox server role, servers make much better use of their physical or virtual resources, resulting in a more balanced load profile.

NOTE

Administrators who are considering virtualization of very large Exchange Server 2013 servers should be aware of performance issues surrounding non-uniform memory access (NUMA) boundaries. The short version is that host system memory divided by the number of processor cores is the size of a NUMA boundary on that system. Guest virtual machines that are allocated memory larger than a single NUMA boundary will suffer a performance loss compared with a virtual system whose memory allocation is equal to or smaller than a NUMA boundary.

Dedicating a Network to Log Shipping for DAG Replication

Many companies that run Exchange Server have invested in very high-performance WAN connections. Multiprotocol label switching (MPLS) networks have become something of a corporate standard due to their performance and stability. The drawback to these high-speed MPLS networks is often the cost. Although bandwidth has become steadily more affordable, the connections and high bandwidth is nonetheless a large portion of most IT groups' budgets. Many companies have moved toward a strategy of utilizing the high-performance MPLS network for servicing end users and have moved their replication to lower-cost networks, such as IPSec or VPN tunnels running across the Internet. Environments who run these multitiered networks will likely want to take advantage of Exchange Server 2013's capability to specify a network to be used for DAG replication.

In Exchange Server 2007, an administrator had to create additional network interfaces as cluster resources and associate them with each cluster group and then utilize host files so that the CCR or SCR targets always resolved their sources by the dedicated replication interfaces. Exchange Server 2013 makes this significantly easier by allowing an administrator to define a database availability group network.

To create a database availability group network via the GUI, follow these steps:

1. Point a web browser at a front-end server/ecp, for example, https://exchangefe-01.companyabc.com/ecp.
2. When prompted, enter domain\name and the password of an account with Organization Admin rights. Click Sign In.
3. When the EAC launches, click Servers in the left pane to see a list of servers.
4. In the upper menu, click Database Availability Group.
5. Click the DAG for which you are adding a network.
6. Click the New DAG Network button (fourth from the left).
7. When the window appears, enter a Database Availability Group Network Name, a Description, and click the + icon to add a subnet, as shown in Figure 8.7.
8. Click Save.

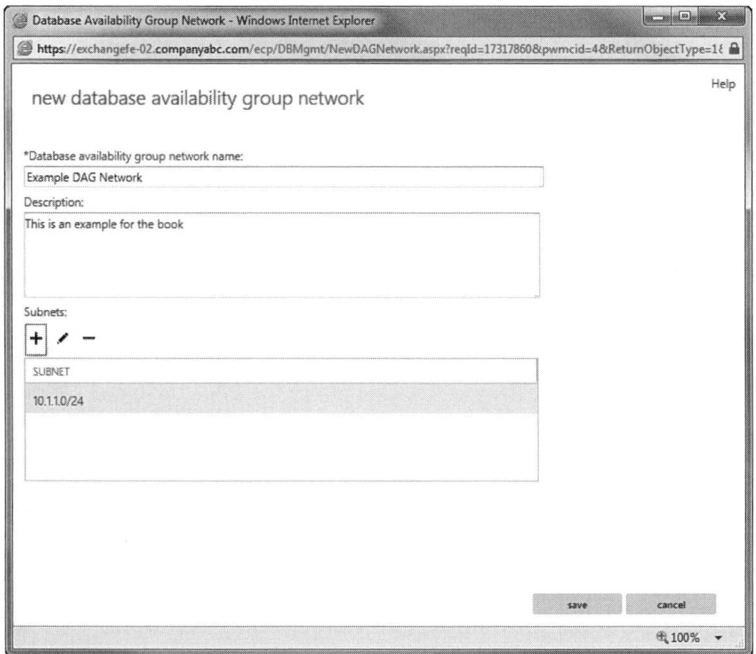

FIGURE 8.7 Configuring a DAG replication network.

If the DAG is configured for automatic network configuration, this will need to be disabled to add the additional network. This can be done with this command:

```
Set-DatabaseAvailabilityGroup -Identity DAGName -ManualDAGNetworkConfiguration
$true
```

or by editing the DAG object in the GUI and checking the Configure the Database Group Network Manually check box.

Once created, the new DAG network will appear in the database availability group pane. From here, you can view its details, disable its replication, or remove it.

To create a database availability group network via the Exchange Management Shell, follow these steps:

1. Launch the Exchange Management Shell.
2. Type **`New-DatabaseAvailabilityGroupNetwork -DatabaseAvailabilityGroup DAG -Name DAGNet -Description "description" -Subnets "#.#.#.#/#" -ReplicationEnabled:$true`**.

   For example, **`New-DatabaseAvailabilityGroupNetwork -DatabaseAvailabilityGroup ABC-DAG -Name DAGNetworkSFtoNY -Description "dedicated replication network via IPSec tunnel from SF to NY" -Subnets "192.168.1.0/24" -ReplicationEnabled:$true`**.

It is generally unnecessary to add DAG networks because all networks on the computer should show up as a DAG network, and you will just use `Set-DatabaseAvailabilityGroupNetwork` to configure whether it is to be used for replication. Note that configuring a DAG network with `ReplicationEnabled` set to `$False` doesn't prohibit it from being used as a replication network; the network may be used for replication traffic if no other replication network is available. The switch configures a preference, not a requirement.

You may find it necessary to configure iSCSI and backup networks using a command like the following:

```
Set-DatabaseAvailabilityGroupNetwork -Identity DAGNetwork05 -IgnoreNetwork $True
```

8

Using DAG to Provide a "Tiered Services" Model

One of the limitations of Cluster Continuous Replication in Exchange Server 2007 was that you didn't have any level of granularity in which content got replicated. It was really an all-or-nothing configuration. Database availability groups give you the ability to determine which database should be replicated and how often. This allows an administrator to create an interesting tiered services model that allows her to establish parameters around classes of mailboxes.

For example, an administrator might want to replicate all mailboxes locally to allow for simplified maintenance windows. The administrator can simply alter a replica to be the current active copy and perform maintenance on the previously active copy. When that maintenance is completed, the administrator can optionally reactivate the previous replica, after it's had a chance to get back into sync. This is likely to be a common scenario as it accomplishes redundancy and allows for quick maintenance without incurring a lot of overhead expense. Local area network (LAN) bandwidth isn't much of a concern in most environments, and the total cost to provide this level of convenience and protection is simply an additional server and its associated licenses.

In more advanced environments, there may be a requirement to replicate mailbox data offsite to protect against a failure of an entire site or perhaps even an entire geographic region. In some cases, this need for geographic redundancy may really only be appropriate for specific types of users. Although managers and executives may have a requirement for nearly 100% mailbox availability, it might not be required for resource mailboxes or for part-time workers or perhaps for factory floor users whose jobs aren't dependent on email access. For these types of situations, administrators can take advantage of the granularity of database availability groups to set different replication rules for different databases. By organizing users into databases by job types, an administrator can easily increase the number of replicas for specific groups to provide the level of protection he or she needs without incurring the overhead of having to replicate an entire server.

Comparing and Contrasting DAG Versus CCR/SCR/SCC

For administrators coming from an Exchange Server 2007 environment looking to upgrade to Exchange Server 2013, it may prove useful to compare and contrast database availability groups with existing replication technologies that they might already be familiar with.

Way back in Exchange Server 2003, the only clustering option available was Single Copy Cluster. Exchange Server 2003 could withstand a hardware failure of a Mailbox server because another node in the cluster could take over the identity and host the Exchange Virtual Server. DAG provides a similar ability to recover from a failed server though it does so without the need for a shared identity or the limitations of shared storage.

Exchange Server 2007 brought about the concept of Cluster Continuous Replication, which, like SCC, provided protection against the failure of a server. It did so by sharing the identity between two hosts. It surpassed SCC by providing two copies of the Exchange Server mailbox database, which protected Exchange Server from a storage failure or a database corruption. DAG utilizes the same log shipping and replay process that was introduced by CCR to perform its replication of mailbox databases. Many of the same concepts such as `Suspend-StorageGroupCopy` and `Update-StorageGroupCopy` are still present and accomplish essentially the same tasks. The names have been updated to reflect the fact that the storage group is no longer the root of the replication but instead it occurs at the database layer. As readers may recall, storage groups no longer exist in Exchange Server 2010 or Exchange Server 2013 as the databases belong to the database availability group or to the Exchange organization. Administrators with experience in maintaining a CCR environment will likely have an easy transition to DAGs.

Exchange Server 2007 also offered Standby Continuous Replication, which while similar to CCR, didn't utilize a shared identity. It used the same log shipping and replay technologies to keep a remote Exchange Server 2007 in sync with the primary copy of data, but it was up to the client to make a determination about where the mailbox was currently located. The other drawback to SCR as opposed to CCR was that SCR required an administrator to make complicated manual changes to the systems in order to bring up a remote copy of the mailbox database. DAG made an important improvement by moving the logic for finding the active copy of the database from the client to the Client Access servers. In this manner, clients that could not previously redirect themselves based on information in Active Directory can now successfully connect to their mailbox when the primary copy is moved to another location. Like SCR, DAG doesn't need to share the identity of the server as the middle tier of this application architecture is able to determine that automatically.

Backing Up a Database Availability Group

While Chapter 16, "Backing Up the Exchange Server 2013 Environment," covers this concept in more detail, there are some interesting implications of database availability groups in the area of backing up Exchange Server 2013. Exchange Server 2013 provides a hook for VSS-based backup via third-party applications or via System Center Data Protection Manager. That said, consider the possibility that with database availability groups and an appropriate retention policy, it might not be necessary to backup Exchange Server 2013 at all.

Consider, for example, an environment with a written policy that "no email shall be retained for more than 30 days in a backup." For companies that don't have specific regulatory requirements for mail retention, this is actually a fairly common situation. Now imagine that Exchange Server 2013 mailbox databases are configured with retention of 30 days. This is to say that a user can use Outlook to "undelete" a message that has cleared the Deleted Items folder for up to 30 days. This means that the only thing a backup needs to protect against is a failure of the database or the storage, as accidental deletions are covered for up to 30 days. By definition, DAG is providing a remote backup that is an independent copy of the mailbox database. This means that if the active database copy was corrupted or if there was a hardware or storage failure of the active copy, the best copy of the mailbox database would automatically take over and there would be no loss of messages. Similarly, because there are multiple replicas of the mailbox databases, there would really never be a situation in which it was necessary to restore a mailbox database. Not unlike a domain controller, an administrator would simply build a new one and let it replicate with the other copies.

This ability to replicate rather than restore replicas offers an interesting possibility. In older versions of Exchange Server, an administrator could restore a Mailbox server to current by restoring an older database from tape and replaying the log files, assuming the log files were still available on the system. This is why it was always critical to store the log files separately from the databases. In an Exchange Server 2013 DAG, there is no need to restore from tape and replay logs, which raises the question, why bother to maintain log files?

An administrator could configure the environment to have three or more DAG nodes and enable circular logging for the Exchange Server databases. This would eliminate the need to perform log truncations, which is one of the primary reasons that backups are run in Exchange Server 2007 and older environments.

For longer-term backups, the administrator could dismount the databases on an inactive DAG replica and simply copy those files to another location. Now there would be a point-in-time backup that could be stored long term. The administrator could even use something like Single Mailbox Recovery tool from NetApp to mount the `.edb` file directly and recover individual messages without even having to put it back onto Exchange Server.

A similar option would be to snapshot the storage if the administrator were using a SAN to host the Exchange Server 2013 data and that SAN supported snapshots.

There was a time not long ago when administrators would think one crazy for suggesting that they stop backing up their email environment, but in today's competitive market, hosted email solutions stopped doing traditional backups a long time ago as the huge cost savings allowed them to be extremely competitive in pricing their services. As an Exchange administrator, your biggest competitor is the hosted email provider. By being aware of options and keeping costs low, it's easier to justify keeping email services in house.

Load Balancing in Exchange Server 2013

Load balancing in Exchange Server 2013 is quite different than it was in any previous version of Exchange. In the past, load balancing required the client to maintain session state to the front end or Client Access server. This meant that Layer 7 load balancing was required. The popular ways to achieve this were to either use Windows Network Load Balancing, also referred to as software load balancing, or to implement dedicated third-party hardware-based load balancers. It is generally accepted that hardware load balancing is higher performance, but it comes with a higher cost. Hardware load balancers that operate at Layer 7 can range from $1,500 to as high as $25,000, whereas software load balancing is effectively free because it's included in Windows.

The other important factor that influenced the choice of hardware versus software load balancing is the fact that DAGs utilize Windows Failover Clustering, and that is incompatible with Windows Network Load Balancing. This is to say that you can either software cluster or software load balance, but not both. This is a common reason for why CAS/HT was typically separated from mailboxes in Exchange Server 2010.

With the architectural changes in Exchange Server 2013, all that matters is that any protocol request find any CAS anywhere in the organization and the CAS logic will put the client in contact with the Mailbox server with the active copy of the database that hosts the user. This means that moving back and forth across various CAS servers isn't an issue. This allows administrators to use much less-expensive load-balancing technologies because there is no need to maintain session state. This means that administrators could use something as simple as DNS Round Robin with very short Time to Live (TTL) values and that would be enough to provide redundancy across multiple front-end servers.

This concept can be taken one step further to allow remote users to utilize a single namespace and yet still take the most efficient path to their mailbox in a situation with multiple entry points. So as long as they hit a CAS, they will be given the appropriate path to their active mailbox database.

Software Load Balancing in Windows

Both Windows Server 2008 and 2012 provide a high-availability technology called Windows Network Load Balancing. WNLB clusters provide high network performance and availability by balancing client requests across several server systems. When the client load increases, WNLB clusters can easily be scaled out by adding more nodes to the WNLB configuration, to maintain an acceptable client response time to client requests.

Using WNLB offers administrators the ability to leverage two dynamic features: First, to implement WNLB clusters, no proprietary hardware is required and WNLB clusters can be implemented and configured through Windows management interfaces fairly easily and quickly.

WNLB clusters are most effectively used to provide front-end support for web applications, virus scanning, and Simple Mail Transfer Protocol (SMTP) gateways. Because they are a very effective solution when used for web application functionality, WNLB technology is a very effective solution for front-end access to Exchange OWA and terminal servers maintaining Exchange Server client software.

WNLB clusters can grow to 32 nodes, and if larger cluster farms are necessary, the Microsoft Application Center server can be considered as an option for server platform support, along with technologies such as domain name system (DNS) round-robin to meet larger client access demands.

NOTE

It is somewhat unfortunate that Microsoft refers to both Windows Failover Clusters and Windows Network Load Balance clusters as "clusters" because it makes it very easy to confuse the two. Windows Failover Cluster is a cluster in the sense that applications can move back and forth between nodes and carry their identity with them. WNLB clusters simply respond to traffic on load-balanced ports based on a decision made within the group. All nodes are balanced to do the same job and, thus, their requirements are much less stringent.

8

WNLB Modes and Port Configuration Overview

WNLB offers two modes of load balancing. Choosing one over the other is typically determined by what the network infrastructure can support. Those two modes are Unicast and Multicast. In Unicast mode, clients and servers maintain a one-to-one relationship when communicating. In Multicast mode, servers respond by broadcasting a single, multicast address, which clients attach to when accessing information such as websites. WNLB groups configured in Unicast mode will have a tendency to flood the switch to which they are connected, as the switch will need to pass traffic to all ports to be sure that all potential WNLB nodes see the requests. If you plan to utilize Unicast mode WNLB, it is recommended to place the WNLB hosts onto their own virtual local area network (VLAN) to limit the scope of this broadcast traffic. Systems configured with Multicast mode will likely require minor changes to be made to the network switches to bind the virtual media access control (MAC) address in the address resolution protocol (ARP) tables and to define which ports should be forwarded traffic destined for that MAC address. Systems configured in Multicast mode should have two or more network interface cards (NICs) installed to be properly supported.

For example, on a Cisco switch running Internetwork Operating System (IOS), to configure a WNLB group with a virtual MAC address of 00-1D-60-18-83-83 and an IP address of 10.1.1.100, use the following code:

```
Arp 10.1.1.100 001D.6018.8383
Mac-address-table static 001D.6018.8383 vlan 1 interface fa4/5 fa5/5
```

where the VLAN value matches the VLAN assigned to the ports to which the WNLB hosts are attached. Similarly, the "interface" should reference the ports to which the WNLB hosts are attached.

Another option when configuring WNLB with OWA is the ability to define the ports in which WNLB cluster members will respond to client requests. This option is effective for the scenario because administrators can restrict and allow access to ports such as Hypertext Transfer Protocol (HTTP) port 80 and Secure Sockets Layer (SSL) port 443.

WNLB Installations

One of the first steps when configuring WNLB cluster nodes in Windows Server 2008 is the installation of Network Load Balancing as a feature. In Windows Server 2008, this isn't turned on by default and must be installed via the following steps:

1. From the Start menu, right-click Computer and choose Manage, as shown in Figure 8.8.
2. In the left pane, click Features.
3. In the right pane, click Add Features, as shown in Figure 8.9.
4. Check the box for Network Load Balancing and click Next.
5. Confirm the installation selections and click Install.
6. When the installation is completed, click Close.
7. Repeat these steps for all nodes of the WNLB group.

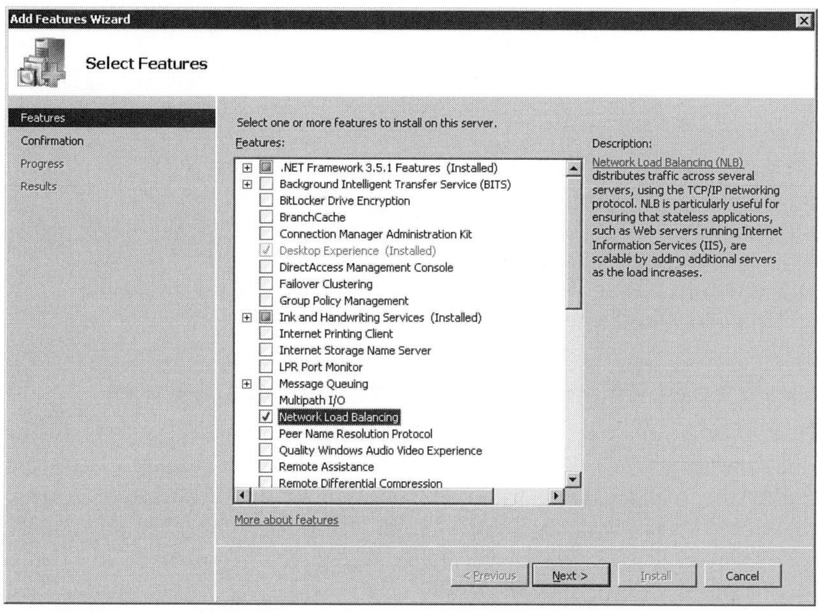

FIGURE 8.8 Managing Windows Server 2008 features.

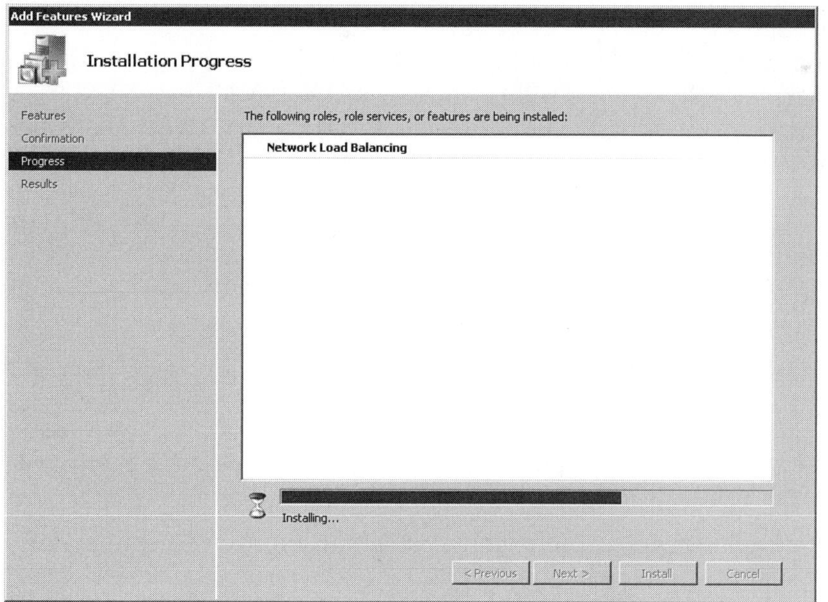

FIGURE 8.9 Installing WNLB as a feature.

8

If one prefers to perform this task from PowerShell, you can enter the following commands:

```
Import-Module ServerManager
Add-WindowsFeature NLB
```

Next is the configuration of the NICs in each server. A configuration of network cards can be completed using the WNLB Manager and the TCP/IP properties of each node's network interface. One other option for configuring NICs is the command-line tool `nlb.exe`. This utility enables administrators to configure TCP/IP properties on WNLB cluster nodes remotely and through the command line.

Configuring Network Load Balancing with Client Access Servers

Using the WNLB Manager is the simplest method in configuring Client Access servers into a load-balanced cluster configuration. When using the Network Load Balancing Manager, all information regarding the WNLB cluster and load-balancing TCP/IP addresses is added dynamically to each cluster node when configured. Using the WNLB Manager also simplifies the tasks of adding and removing nodes by enabling administrators to use the NetBIOS name or TCP/IP address to identify nodes.

TIP

To effectively manage WNLB clusters on remote servers, install and configure two NICs on the local WNLB Manager system.

In the following example, WNLB services will be implemented to provide support with two separate OWA servers. This scenario assumes that each OWA server (Client Access server) has already been installed and configured and is functioning.

To begin, configure the network cards for each OWA system that you plan to configure in the WNLB cluster:

1. Log on to the local console of a WNLB node using an account with local Administrator privileges.
2. Select Start, right-click Network, and choose Properties.
3. In the tasks list, click Manage Network Connections.
4. Ensure that the WNLB network adapter is configured without a default gateway and to not register the hostname in DNS.
5. In Advanced Network settings, ensure that the public NIC is listed higher in priority (above) the WNLB NIC.
6. If you will be using Multicast clustering operation mode, then enter the following command in a command window opened as administrator, where "NLB" is the name of the load-balanced NIC.

   ```
   NETSH interface ipv4 set int "NLB" forwarding=enabled
   ```

7. Repeat this process on all nodes that will participate in this WNLB group.

TIP

It is a good practice to rename each network card so you can easily identify it when configuring interfaces and troubleshooting problems.

After Network Load Balancing has been enabled on each node, it is time to configure the WNLB rules. This is most easily configured via the Network Load Balancing Manager. To configure the WNLB hosts, perform these steps:

1. Log on to the local console of a WNLB node using an account with local Administrator privileges.
2. From the Start menu, click Run and type **`nlbmgr.exe`**.
3. From the Cluster menu, click New, as shown in Figure 8.10.

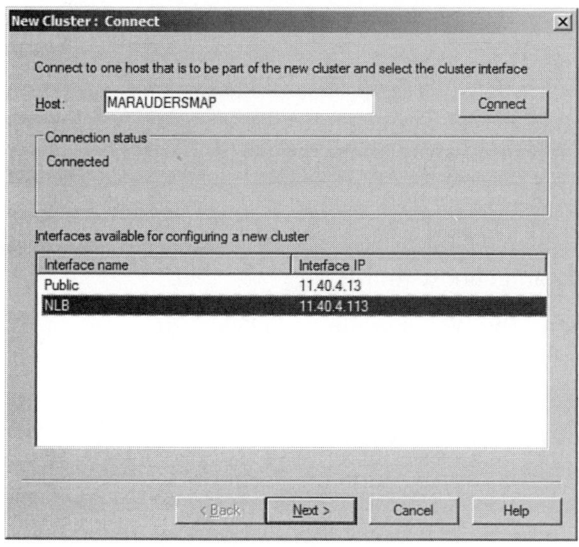

FIGURE 8.10 Creating a WNLB cluster.

4. Enter the name of one of the hosts that will form the WNLB group and click Connect.
5. Highlight the interface that will be used for WNLB and click Next.
6. Set the Priority (this acts as a unique identifier) to a unique value for the WNLB group and click Next. Generally, you may leave this at 1.
7. Click Add, enter the IP address and subnet mask to be used for Exchange connectivity, and then click OK. Click Next.

8

8. Enter the fully qualified domain name (FQDN) for Exchange connectivity. Set the Cluster Operation Mode to the mode desired. Click Next.
9. Highlight the defined port rule and click Edit. Set the port range to the range needed (e.g., 443 to 443). Click OK.

   Note: It's perfectly fine to keep the default of all ports load-balanced.
10. If additional ports need to be load-balanced, such as SMTP, IMAP, or POP for making non-MAPI client access fault tolerant, click Add and repeat step 9.
11. Click Finish.
12. Add an A record to DNS with the Exchange connectivity name and IP address.

NOTE

A Windows Server 2008 host that has the Windows Cluster services installed cannot be a member of a WNLB group. This means that a DAG member, while capable of running the CAS and/or HT roles, cannot load-balance those roles.

Additional CAS servers can be added to the WNLB group by following these steps at any time:

1. Log on to the local console of a WNLB node using an account with local Administrator privileges.
2. From the Start menu, click Run and type **`nlbmgr.exe`**.
3. Right-click the existing WNLB group and choose Add Host.
4. Type in the name of the host to add to the WNLB group and click Add.
5. Click Finish.

Validate that the state of the clustered WNLB system is listed in the WNLB Manager as Started, and close the Manager to complete the configuration of additional servers.

Summary

As you have seen in this chapter, Microsoft has improved several different methods of providing high availability and disaster recovery with a single unified solution. By disassociating mailbox database from storage groups and instead associating them with database availability groups, Microsoft has further improved the flexibility around high availability and disaster recovery. The limitation of CCR in terms of being required to replicate an entire server has been bypassed by DAG and the ability to replicate database by database and, in fact, to configure replications differently for different mailbox databases. Microsoft has given administrators enough granularity to finally configure their Exchange Server implementation specifically for their own unique needs. DAG does an excellent job of replacing both CCR and SCR by providing for the best of both worlds—the ability to automatically fail mailbox services from one host to another without the complexity and limitations of a traditional Windows cluster.

Microsoft has also opened up a whole new world of options for Exchange Server backups by introducing an environment that could conceivably operate without any backups whatsoever. By replicating the mailbox database information to multiple geographic locations and by avoiding log generation through the use of circular logging, Exchange Server 2013 database availability groups, combined with prudent deleted item retention, could eliminate the need for traditional backups. Taking a replica offline to simply copy the databases in an acquiesced state would still allow an administrator to maintain a long-term copy of Exchange Server 2013 in the way that was traditionally performed by tape backups.

By changing load-balancing requirements from Layer 7 to Layer 4, Microsoft has greatly simplified the way in which front-end servers are load-balanced. By removing the session state requirements and writing the Client Access server logic such that reaching any CAS will get the user to the correct Mailbox server, Microsoft has made it easier and more economical than ever to provide redundant services and to effectively provide geographic affinity without the costs associated with geographic traffic management.

Although some might wonder why Microsoft deprecated Cluster Continuous Replication and Standby Continuous Replication, you can easily see how those two technologies evolved into database availability groups and can hopefully see the inherent advantages to this technology. Exchange Server administrators are highly encouraged to consider the implementation of database availability groups in their Exchange Server 2013 deployments to provide the levels of high availability and disaster recovery that are demanded by modern businesses. As companies become more and more dependent on email and calendaring, Microsoft continues to raise the bar to make Exchange Server more resilient and easier to manage than ever.

Best Practices

The following are best practices from this chapter:

- Install an additional NIC in DAG member nodes to properly support Windows clustering.
- Ensure that hardware is chosen to not only support its dedicated load, but to also take over additional loads when it's acting as a replica for other master copies of a mailbox database.
- Base your disk subsystem primarily on storage, as the performance requirements have dropped drastically.
- Always plan for a sufficient amount of TCP/IP addresses in advance to support current and future cluster needs.
- Do not try to use both clustering and WNLB on the same computer; it is unsupported by Microsoft because of potential hardware-sharing conflicts between MSCS and WNLB.

- Always plan for the additional WAN traffic created by adding another DAG replica that isn't on the local LAN.
- To avoid unwanted failover, power management should be disabled on each of the cluster nodes, both in the motherboard BIOS and in the power applet in Control Panel.
- Thoroughly test failover and failback mechanisms after the configuration is complete and before assigning users to a database availability group.
- Make sure that mailbox databases have unique names.
- When utilizing load balancing, make sure to only load-balance the ports necessary. This avoids the possibility of network-related issues when talking to Active Directory.
- Be sure to regularly monitor replicate between DAG nodes to ensure that replication is healthy.
- Periodically test the move of master status between various copies of mailbox database groups to ensure that the data is valid and the cluster is working correctly.
- Utilize Datacenter Activation Coordination mode to prevent unexpected failovers between data centers. Take the approach of automatic failover within a data center for HA and manual failover between data centers for DR.

CHAPTER 9

Public Folders

IN THIS CHAPTER

From the earliest version of Microsoft Exchange, the platform was designed and built to be much more than an email platform. Advanced communication features, such as mobile client support, server-side rule processing, built-in support for encryption and digital signing, instant messaging support, and a feature-rich client, Microsoft Outlook, have been extended with sophisticated collaboration features. Shared mailboxes and calendars, a unified address book, and calendar free/busy searches are just some of the collaboration features that have made Exchange Server a leading collaboration tool for more than 15 years.

Of all the collaboration tools provided in Exchange Server, public folders are possibly the most powerful and beneficial. Public folders have been used in almost every organization as part of Exchange Server. The seamless client support provided through Microsoft Outlook or a browser-based client has made them a part of every user's workday and a core part of many vital business processes.

To fully realize the benefits provided by public folders, this chapter provides an overview of the mechanisms and advantages provided by public folders. Approaches to planning a public folder architecture are discussed as well as a detailed review of implementing public folders. For organizations with legacy public folder repositories or cloud-based requirements, a variety of migration scenarios for public folders is also outlined. Finally, processes and tools to support the public folder structure are provided.

Understanding Public Folders

As with most technology implementations, it is important to fully understand public folders before embarking on introducing them into an environment. Specifically, it is important to be familiar with public folder benefits and features as well as common use cases.

Positioning the public folder implementation for success involves using public folders in cases in which they excel and selecting other solutions for problems that are not a good fit for public folders. A thorough effort focused on developing a good grasp of the component and defining expected use cases is the first step of any implementation.

History of Public Folders

Since their introduction in 1996, public folders have undergone many changes, but their core functionality, including built-in replication, support for custom forms, and an intuitive client interface have been features of public folders since the very early versions. As part of Exchange Server versions 4.0, 5.0, and 5.5, public folders were a unique collaboration tool with few competitors that were a vital business tool for many organizations.

With the introduction of Active Directory and Exchange Server 2000, public folders were enhanced with the support for multiple folder trees, a feature that was dropped later because of its lack of usefulness. As for many other aspects of the product, Exchange Server 2003 was a significant step forward with integration with Windows security groups, a built-in migration tool, and improved administration controls over replication and reorganization.

Exchange Server 2007 brought a new direction for public folders with a Microsoft announcement that public folders were being deprecated and would not be included in future versions. For the first time, public folders were made an optional component for the installation by replacing the system public folders with Exchange services. The release to manufacturing (RTM) release of Exchange Server 2007 included limited support for public folders and no graphical administration interface, but administration did benefit greatly from the introduction of PowerShell to the Exchange Server platform.

The release of Service Pack 1 for Exchange Server 2007 responded to widespread customer dissatisfaction by partially reversing the deprecation decision and improved the situation with expanded support for public folders. A new graphical management interface was introduced along with support for public folders in Outlook Web Access (OWA) and Exchange Web Services (EWS).

Even with the improved client and administration interfaces, using public folders in the enterprise was further complicated by the need for nonclustered public folder servers in organizations that take advantage of high availability with Cluster Continuous Replication (CCR). Fortunately, Exchange Server 2010 resolved this issue by introducing a new high-availability mechanism called database availability groups that once again allow public folder replication to coexist with database replication.

Exchange Server 2010 also provided improvements to the management interface of public folders and a full integration of public folders into the roles-based administration model that's part of the platform. Altogether, the last few sets of improvements seem to indicate that Microsoft has shifted its strategy for public folders to one that supports the component for the use cases for which it is ideal.

Modern Public Folders

This brings us to the current version, Exchange Server 2013. Public folders undergo another major transformation as a component of Exchange Server 2013 with major changes to the architecture, underlying storage, and replication. These changes will hopefully help ensure the continuing existence of public folders for the next few years but will also require a change in the way public folders are used, designed, and implemented.

Public folders in Exchange Server 2013 are stored within special-purpose mailboxes in regular mailbox databases. The public folder hierarchy is stored in each public folder mailbox with one mailbox hosting a read/write copy and the rest hosting a read-only replica. The public folder mailbox hosting the read/write copy is called the master public folder mailbox and is typically the first public folder mailbox created. There can only be one master mailbox at any one time, but the role can be transferred to another public folder mailbox as needed. The more common and frequent read operations can be performed using any of the public folder mailboxes, whereas the typically less-frequent changes to the hierarchy are performed using the mailbox with the read/write copy.

The use of mailbox storage and replication technology for public folders means that public folder architecture can now be managed, migrated, and monitored using the relevant mailbox commands and management tools. Management and administration of public folders themselves have not changed and neither has client software access and end-user experience.

The new architecture also impacts migration plans and processes as data must be migrated from the existing public folder databases to public folder mailboxes within mailbox databases. Migrations are handled like mailbox moves with seamless access during the migration process, except that the final cutover operation must be executed for all public folders at the same time. This cutover mechanism, along with the fact that only users with Exchange Server 2013 mailboxes can access Exchange Server 2013 public folders, does require careful planning and execution for public folder upgrades and migrations. More information about migrations, including step-by-step instructions, is provided later in this chapter.

An unfortunate side effect of the magnitude of the change in architecture is that Exchange Server 2013 does not include support for public folders with OWA. Support for public folders in OWA is expected with Service Pack 1 for Exchange 2013.

A more welcome side effect of the new mailbox database architecture is the newly introduced support for public folders as part of Microsoft's cloud email services: Office 365 and Exchange Online.

Benefits and Use Cases of Public Folders

As with most tools, public folders are well suited to solve certain problems and poorly suited to solve others. Understanding the use cases public folders were designed to solve is a key step in creating an effective public folder system. In fact, much of the frustration many organizations have experienced with implementations of public folders is due to the attempt to use public folders to address a use case for which it is ill suited.

The use cases for which public folders were designed and work very well include the following:

- **Public email**—General mailboxes that are monitored and managed by multiple users, for example careers@companyabc.com, postmaster@companyabc.com, or helpdesk@companyabc.com, make good candidates for public folders. Using a public folder for this purpose makes it simple to assign permissions and very easy for users to read emails, send emails, and manage the folder.
- **Public announcements**—Email data that is managed by few and consumed by many is a good fit for public folders. Some examples include internal bulletin boards, IT outage announcements, and even a suggestion box. Public folders are prominent in Outlook and easy for most users to see and access.
- **Distribution list archiving**—For many distribution lists, it can be useful to create a repository for all mail sent to the distribution list. Change management distribution lists, sensitive distribution lists, and notification lists would all benefit from a historical record that all members could search and review but none could modify or delete.

As Microsoft strives to provide an alternative for public folders using SharePoint Server, there are several use cases that can be addressed using either public folders or SharePoint server:

- **Discussion forums**—Forums can be served well by public folders but as the membership and volume of items grows, it is better to migrate the discussions to a platform with structured storage and advanced indexing such as SharePoint Server.
- **Group calendaring**—Basic calendar collaboration, typically with few editors and many consumers, is a good fit for public folders. Use cases such as a department vacation calendar, corporate "important dates" calendars, or project milestones are a good fit. Again, as the volume of data grows or as requirements are introduced, for advanced access to the data as well as integration with other data sources, SharePoint Server becomes a better solution.
- **Group contacts**—Shared contacts lists are also a good use case for public folders. They are typically relatively small from a data perspective and the public folder integration with email is especially useful for solutions such as internal directories, IT vendor lists, or project contact sheets. If advanced operations on the contact list or members are needed, SharePoint Server will likely be a worthwhile tool to consider.

Several commonly used uses for public folders are typically not a good fit and are often better served by other solution categories, such as document management systems, content management systems, and so on. These use cases include the following:

- **Document management**—Key features for a document management system include advanced management and indexing of files and a flexible, sophisticated metadata and classification mechanism. Public folders–based document management, while easy to implement and use, does not provide these features and is very unwieldy as the data volume grows. Until Exchange Server 2013, the multimaster nature of public folders is counter to the needs of document management systems to protect documents from multiple simultaneous edits. SharePoint Server provides these functions along with an excellent user experience.
- **Line-of-business applications**—Early in the days of Exchange Server and public folders, the forms mechanism used by public folders and Microsoft Outlook provided an industry-leading solution for line-of-business applications. Today's technology provides better solutions for line-of-business application requirements, including SharePoint Server. Due to a lack of structured storage, integration features, and advanced presentation mechanisms, public folders are not well suited for this function.
- **Team collaboration**—An effective tool for sharing information and managing efforts between team members is a necessity for most organizations. Due to the need to consolidate different types of data and integrate with external systems, SharePoint Server is a much better solution than public folders for team collaboration. The flexible and customizable user interface of SharePoint further cements its suitability for this purpose.

Planning a Public Folder Environment

The task of planning the public folder environment is an important one to complete before implementation begins. It is significantly more disruptive and costly to make fundamental changes to the environment after it has been implemented. In addition, a good planning exercise should produce a document that can be used to reach consensus on the structure prior to deployment as well as an initial documentation of the environment.

Even in the case of a migration from an existing public folder environment, careful planning is a good idea. First and foremost, the changes in the architecture for public folders necessitate a redesign of the infrastructure supporting public folders. In addition, a migration project is often the best time to validate the existing structure and make required changes to the topology, permission model, or storage configuration.

Hardware planning considerations are identical to those used for Exchange private mailbox data. For more information about allocating hardware appropriately for Exchange servers, see Chapter 2, "Understanding Core Exchange Server 2013 Design Plans," and Chapter 3, "Architecting an Enterprise-Level Exchange Server 2013 Environment."

Designing the Content

There are two separate facets of public folders that need to be carefully planned and subjected to a review process prior to implementation: the content model and the infrastructure.

The content model includes the structure of folders and subfolders starting with the top level. The model also includes permissions to content for end users as well as administrators; configuration or settings, such as quotas and delivery options; and, finally, identification of customization requirements, such as forms or third-party application integration. It is important to design and implement the top-level structure initially so that the ability to create top-level folders can be restricted to very few.

Typically, organization structures for public folders use geography and/or departments to organize data. In addition to making it easier for users to find content, the structure also facilitates delegation of public folder administration to users and/or IT Department staff who are responsible for specific departments or locations. A sample structure is shown in Figure 9.1.

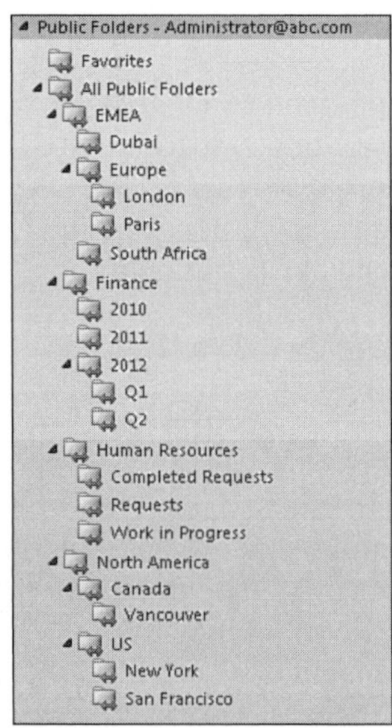

FIGURE 9.1 Planning a department- or location-based public folder structure.

Along with the structure itself, permissions to the folder and content must be determined as well as any applicable quotas and delivery options. Finally, for each folder, it must be decided if the folder will accept content submissions via email.

Designing the Infrastructure

The final step of the design process involves a design of the public folder infrastructure. This is where the changes to the public folder database component introduced in

Exchange Server 2013 have the most impact. In this step, the placement of each public folder within public folder mailboxes must be determined. The location of the primary (routinely active) copy and secondary (active during availability events) copies must be identified. Finally, required administrative permissions to the public folder structure and locations should be identified and documented.

As a result of storing public folders in mailboxes and mailbox databases, public folders now work with a single-master model as opposed to the previous multimaster model. This means that instead of having multiple copies of public folders, which can all be used to access content (as was the case with Exchange Server 2010 and earlier), with Exchange Server 2013 public folders, only one of the copies is active at any one time. As a result, geographical placement of public folders can be very important to ensure acceptable performance of public folders for end users.

Three scenarios will be reviewed in the remainder of this section to provide examples for how these concepts can be used to design a public folder infrastructure. The first scenario focuses on a fully centralized Exchange environment, the second on a fully distributed Exchange environment, and the final on a hybrid Exchange environment.

Centralized Exchange Environment

A centralized environment is one where all Exchange services are provided to users via servers located in a single data center. This definition is limited to active data and, therefore, does not preclude a disaster recovery data center with passive or "warm" copies of the data.

In this type of environment, the design is relatively simple as all data is stored on mailboxes in the central data center. The number and placement of mailboxes need only take maximum sizes and storage into account as distance from the end users is not a variable.

Distributed Exchange Environment

A distributed environment is one where all Exchange services are provided to users via servers located in their geographical location so that end-user systems always have a fast, local area network (LAN)–based, connection to their Exchange server. In this scenario, data use is also distributed geographically with minimal to no public folder content sharing between locations.

In this scenario, public folders would be distributed according to the usage with folders located on the same Exchange servers as the mailboxes of the users who use them. Secondary copies would be located in other locations for disaster recovery purposes. This topology ensures the fastest performance for users but requires servers and administration of Exchange resources in each location.

Hybrid Exchange Environment

The final and most common scenario is one where some public folder data usage is contained to a location while other data is shared globally throughout the organization. Also in this scenario, Exchange resources are distributed regionally with data centers on each continent that service messaging and public folder data.

In this scenario, as shown in a diagram in Figure 9.2, public folders data is separated into regional data and global data. Regional data is hosted in the data center closest to the end-user mailboxes while global public folder data is centralized in the data center with the highest bandwidth capacity. In this scenario, users access some data over a high-performance link but must still traverse a potentially slower link to access globally shared data.

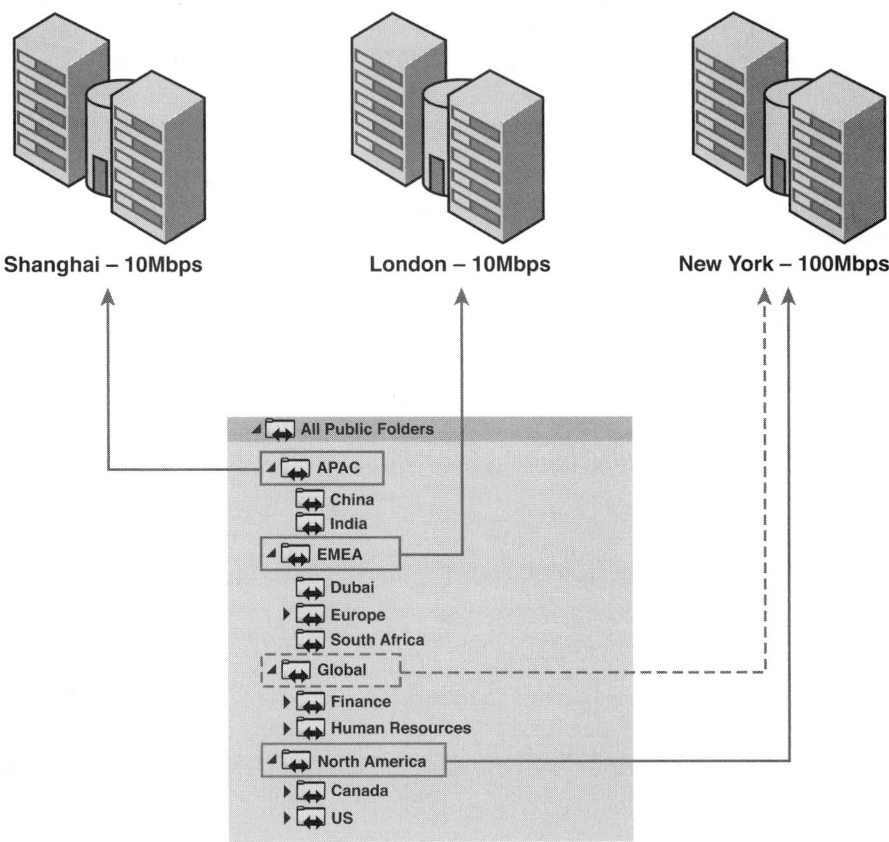

FIGURE 9.2 Designing a hybrid model public folder infrastructure.

Implementing a Public Folder Environment

The implementation of the public folder environment is simple once the design is finalized. The process itself includes preparation steps for required databases followed by the creation and securing of each required public folder. Due to the repetitive nature of the task, you are advised to create and use PowerShell-based commands to ensure an error-free implementation and record the steps taken.

Preparing the Environment

The new mailbox database–based architecture of public folders simplifies the implementation process. First the mailbox database structure must be established based on the planning guidelines provided previously. Databases containing public folder mailboxes are no different than other databases and are created using the `New-MailboxDatabase` commands.

For example, the following commands would create two mailbox databases used for data for the Asia Pacific region and create copies on two Exchange servers, ABCEX1 and ABCEX2, that are members of the same database availability group (DAG):

```
New-MailboxDatabase USDB1 -Server ABCEX1 -EdbFilePath D:\USDB1\USDB1.edb
-LogFolderPath D:\USDB1
Mount-Database USDB1
Add-MailboxDatabaseCopy USDB1 -MailboxServer ABCEX2

New-MailboxDatabase EUDB1 -Server ABCEX2 -EdbFilePath D:\EUDB1\EUDB1.edb
-LogFolderPath D:\EUDB1
Mount-Database EUDB1
Add-MailboxDatabaseCopy EUDB1 -MailboxServer ABCEX1
```

For more detailed information about creating and configuring databases and database availability groups, see Chapter 6, "Installing and Configuring the Basics of Exchange Server 2013 in a Brand-New Environment," and Chapter 8, "Implementing and Supporting a Highly Available Exchange Server 2013 Environment."

Once the databases are created and distributed correctly, public folder mailboxes can be created and configured to support the creation or migration of public folders and associated data.

To create the mailbox using the Exchange Administration Center, do the following:

1. Open the console by navigating to https://*servername*/ecp.
2. Log in to the Exchange Administration Center using an administrative account.
3. Select the Public Folders workspace and the Public Folder Mailboxes configuration area.
4. Click on the plus (+) symbol to create a new public folder mailbox, as shown in Figure 9.3.
5. Enter a name for the public folder mailbox, in this example, **`NAPF1`**.
6. Click the Browse buttons to select an organizational unit and database for the mailbox. In this example, use the USDB1 database. The organizational unit will contain a disabled user account associated with the mailbox.
7. Repeat the process to create the mailbox **`EMEAPF1`** on database EUDB1.

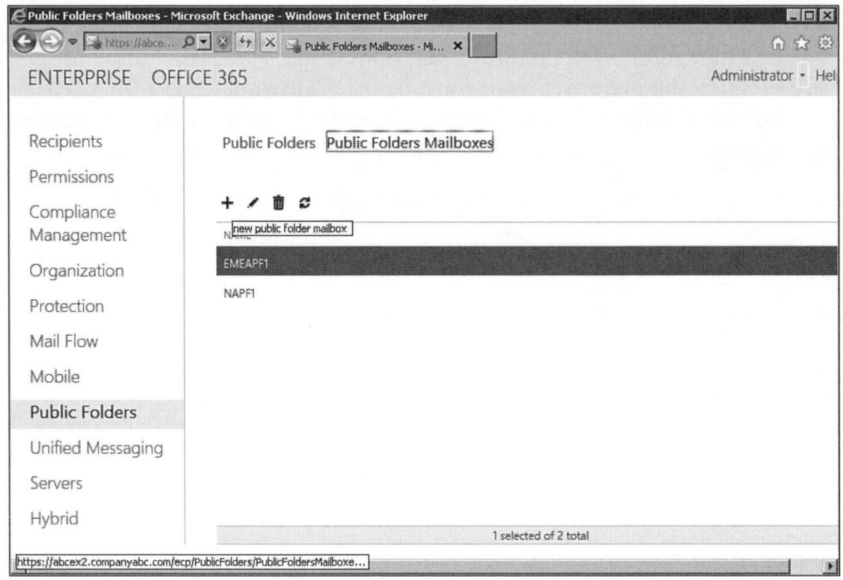

FIGURE 9.3 Creating a public folder mailbox.

When working with PowerShell to manage modern public folders, even though the process uses familiar mailbox management commands, there are added parameters to support public folders. To accomplish the same task using PowerShell, execute the command as shown in the following examples:

```
New-mailbox -Name NAPF1 -Database USDB1 -PublicFolder -OrganizationalUnit
"OU=Public Folder Databases,DC=companyabc,DC=com"
New-Mailbox -Name EMEAPF1 -Database EUDB1 -PublicFolder -OrganizationalUnit
"OU=Public Folder Databases,DC=companyabc,DC=com"
```

Add the `-HoldForMigration` switch when creating public folder mailboxes in a mixed Exchange Server 2010 environment during the interoperability phase.

Creating Public Folders

The public folder mailboxes can then be used to store public folders and public folder trees. The process of creating the public folders can be performed using several tools, including Exchange Administration Center, Microsoft Outlook, and Exchange Management Shell.

To create a new folder using the Exchange Administration Center, execute the following steps:

1. Open the console by navigating to https://*servername*/ecp.
2. Log in to the console using an administrative account.

3. Select the Public Folders workspace and the Public Folders configuration area.
4. Click on the plus (+) symbol to create a new public folder.
5. Enter a name for the root-level public folder, in this example, **`Human Resources`**.
6. Click the newly created public folder name to change the level of the user interface, as shown in Figure 9.4.
7. Repeat the process to create subfolders under the Human Resources root folder.

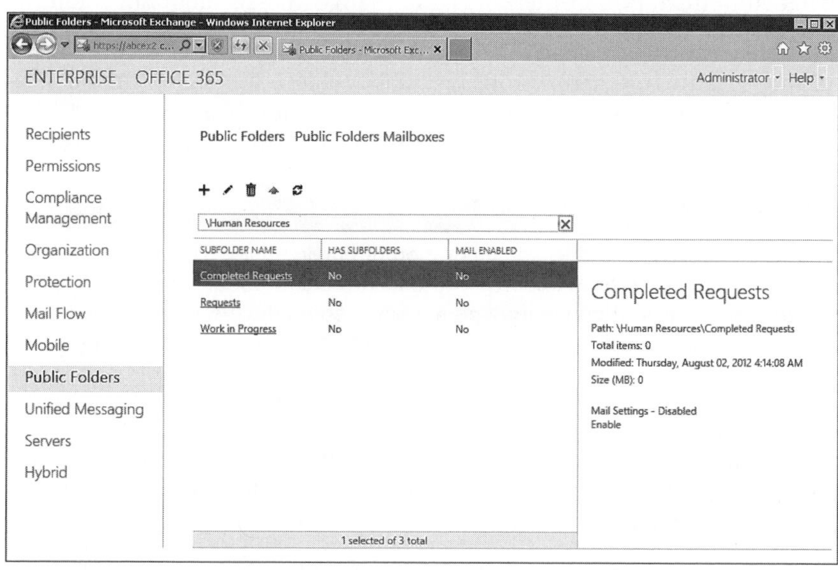

FIGURE 9.4 Navigating folders in order to create a subfolder.

Obviously, this process can become quite tedious and time consuming if many public folders are needed. In practice, most public folders are created either by users with a mail client such as Microsoft Outlook or using PowerShell. Also, you cannot control the public folder mailbox into which a root folder is created using the Exchange Administration Center; you can do that only in the Exchange Management Shell.

To create a sample public folder structure for the Human Resources Department in the NAPF1 mailbox, execute the following commands:

```
New-PublicFolder -Name "Human Resources" -Path \ -Mailbox NAPF1
New-PublicFolder -Name "Requests" -Path "\Human Resources"
New-PublicFolder -Name "Completed Requests" -Path "\Human Resources"
New-PublicFolder -Name "Work in Progress" -Path "\Human Resources"
```

Securing Public Folders

A critical component of planning and deploying a public folder infrastructure is the configuration of permissions for each public folder. Based on the purpose of the public folder, it is important to make sure that only authorized users can see, modify, or delete the data within a public folder. To support these requirements, public folders include their own security mechanism, which parallels that of mailbox folders.

Just like other public folder management tasks, the management, configuration, or public folder permissions can be accomplished using a messaging client such as Microsoft Outlook, the Exchange Administration Center, or the Exchange Management Shell administrative interface.

However, before starting to configure permissions on public folders, it is important to understand the available permission levels and how those permissions can be applied so that the overall structure can be planned and deployed to meet business requirements.

NOTE

It is common in many organizations to see administration of public folders delegated to departmental users. In these cases, it is important to educate users about the approved security model and the mechanics of configuring permissions correctly. It is also important to audit public folder usage and permissions in these cases to ensure compliance and optimal performance.

Permissions for public folders can be configured; 10 individually selectable permissions accommodate folder visibility, read access, modify access, deletions, and subfolder creation. The specific rights are as follows:

- **Read Items**—Gives the user the right to read items within the designated public folder.
- **Create Items**—Gives the user the right to create new items within the designated public folder.
- **Edit Own Items**—Gives the user the right to edit items that the user has created or owns within the designated public folder.
- **Delete Own Items**—Gives the user the right to delete items that the user has created or owns within the designated public folder.
- **Edit All Items**—Gives the user the right to edit all items within the designated public folder.
- **Delete All Items**—Gives the user the right to delete all items within the designated public folder.
- **Create Subfolders**—Gives the user the right to create subfolders within the designated public folder.

- **Folder Owner**—Gives the user the owner right on the designated public folder, including the ability to see, move the folder, and create a subfolder. This right does not give the rights to read, modify, delete, or create items within the folder.
- **Folder Contact**—Configures the user as the contact for the designated public folder, an administrative designation that does not provide any specific rights to the folder or contained items.
- **Folder Visible**—Gives the user the right to view the public folder but not to read or modify items within the folder.

To facilitate common use cases, the rights are organized into nine roles, each of which is a predefined combination of rights. The following list of roles can be used to simplify rights configuration and assignment and their associate permissions:

- **None**—Folder Visible
- **Owner**—Create Items, Read Items, Folder Owner, Folder Contact, Create Subfolders, Edit Owned Items, Delete Owned Items, Edit All Items, Delete All Items, Folder Visible
- **Publishing Editor**—Create Items, Read Items, Create Subfolders, Edit Owned Items, Delete Owned Items, Edit All Items, Delete All Items, Folder Visible
- **Editor**—Create Items, Read Items, Edit Owned Items, Delete Owned Items, Edit All Items, Delete All Items, Folder Visible
- **Publishing Author**—Create Items, Read Items, Edit Owned Items, Delete Owned Items, Folder Visible, Create Subfolders
- **Author**—Create Items, Read Items, Edit Owned Items, Delete Owned Items, Folder Visible
- **Nonediting Author**—Create Items, Read Items, Folder Visible
- **Reviewer**—Read Items, Folder Visible
- **Contributor**—Create Items, Folder Visible

Configuring permissions can be done quickly using PowerShell; for example, these commands accomplish the following goals:

- Assign the Publishing Editor role to members of the Human Resources Department to the Human Resources folder and subfolders.
- Assign all domain users the Contributor role to the Human Resource\Requests folder.

- Assign all domain users the Folder Visible right to the Human Resources folder to allow them to navigate to the Requests folder.

```
Get-PublicFolder "\Human Resources" -Recurse | Add-PublicFolderClientPermission
-User "COMPANYABC\Human Resources" -AccessRights PublishingEditor
Add-PublicFolderClientPermission "\Human Resources" -User "COMPANYABC\Domain
Users" -AccessRights FolderVisible
Add-PublicFolderClientPermission "\Human Resources\Requests" -User
"COMPANYABC\domain Users" -AccessRights Contributor
```

The commands listed allow all users to submit human resources requests and allow members of the Human Resources Department to service those requests using public folders.

PowerShell commands can also be used to view or remove existing public folder permissions as follows:

```
Get-PublicFolderClientPermission "\Human Resources\Requests"
Remove-PublicFolderClientPermission "\Human Resources\Requests" -User
"companyabc\domain users"
```

The same actions can be performed using Microsoft Outlook by following this process:

1. Open the Outlook client.
2. Select the Folder list workspace.
3. Expand the Public Folders container.
4. Expand the All Public Folders container.
5. Navigate to the public folder that needs to be edited, right-click it, and select Properties.
6. Select the Permissions tab and make the required changes, as shown in Figure 9.5.
7. Repeat the process to assign the required rights.

The previous permission management provides granular and detailed control over rights and permissions to the public folder and public folder data, but in cases of full administrative control over the entire public folder environment, an existing role group can be used.

Granting full control is managed using the predefined Public Folder Management role group, which is created by default in the Microsoft Exchange Security Groups root OU in the forest root domain. Membership in the group grants full rights for all public folders and the public folder hierarchy.

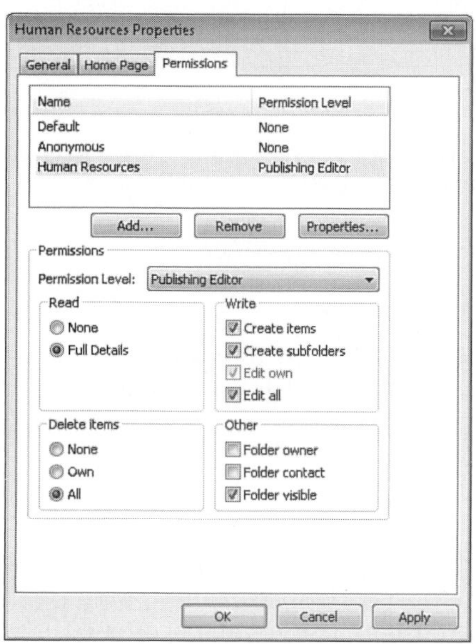

FIGURE 9.5 Configuring public folder permissions using Microsoft Outlook.

Managing Public Folders

To further extend the functionality of public folders and enable specific use cases and scenarios, several properties and operations are available through the Exchange Administration Center as well as the Exchange Management Shell. In addition to the mechanisms available to manage the behavior and content of public folders themselves, tools are also available to manage the public folder structure, including data replication and hierarchy.

Managing Public Folder Settings

Many commonly used scenarios for public folders require public folders to receive content using email. Public folders for shared email address (such as info@, career@, support@, etc.), those that are members of a distribution list and group calendars, all require an email address. An email address for public folders is not assigned by default to public folders because they are not by default mail-enabled.

Mail-enabling public folders can be accomplished using the Exchange Management Shell and the following command:

```
Enable-MailPublicFolder "\Human Resources"
```

To combine some of the commands to enable several folders, use one of the following commands:

9

```
Get-PublicFolder "\Human Resources"  -Recurse | Enable-MailPublicFolder
Get-PublicFolder "\" -Recurse | Where {$_.Name -like "Re*"} |
Enable-MailPublicFolder
```

To assign a specific email address to a mail-enabled public folder, use a command similar to the following:

```
Set-MailPublicFolder -Identity "\Human Resources"  -EmailAddresses
SMTP:hr@companyabc.com -EmailAddressPolicyEnabled $False
```

The operation can be reversed, removing all email addresses from the public folder and can be completed using the `Disable-MailPublicFolder` command. For example:

```
Disable-MailPublicFolder "\Human Resources\Requests"
```

To avoid the confirmation prompt, add this universal parameter:

```
Disable-MailPublicFolder "\Human Resources\Requests" -Confirm:$false
```

Although folders can't be mail-enabled or mail-disabled using the user interface–based Exchange Administration Center, their state can be monitored using the console with the following process:

1. Open the console by navigating to https://*servername*/ecp.
2. Log in to the console using an administrative account.
3. Select the Public Folders workspace and the Public Folders configuration area.
4. Select appropriate folders to navigate to the relevant folder.
5. Review the value of the Mail Enabled property, as shown in Figure 9.6.

Another common requirement is the need to define public folder storage quotas. Quotas allow administrators to limit public folder growth as well as predict public folder mailbox size for storage allocation and cost-effective management.

The quota configuration is similar to private mailbox limits with the following properties available:

- `IssueWarningQuota`—Once the folder has surpassed the specified size, owners will be issued a warning. This setting can be configured individually on a folder or inherited from organizational policies.
- `ProhibitPostQuota`—Once the folder has surpassed the specified size, all users will be issued a warning when using the folder and items can no longer be posted to the folder. This setting can be configured individually on a folder or inherited from organizational policies.
- `MaxItemSize`—This parameter specifies the maximum size for an item posted to the folder. Larger items will be rejected. This setting can be configured individually on a folder or inherited from organizational policies.

- `AgeLimit`–Content within the folder that is older than the age specified in the parameter is automatically deleted. This parameter is useful for bulletin boards, announcements, and other folders that need content pruned automatically. This setting can be configured individually on a folder or inherited from organizational policies.

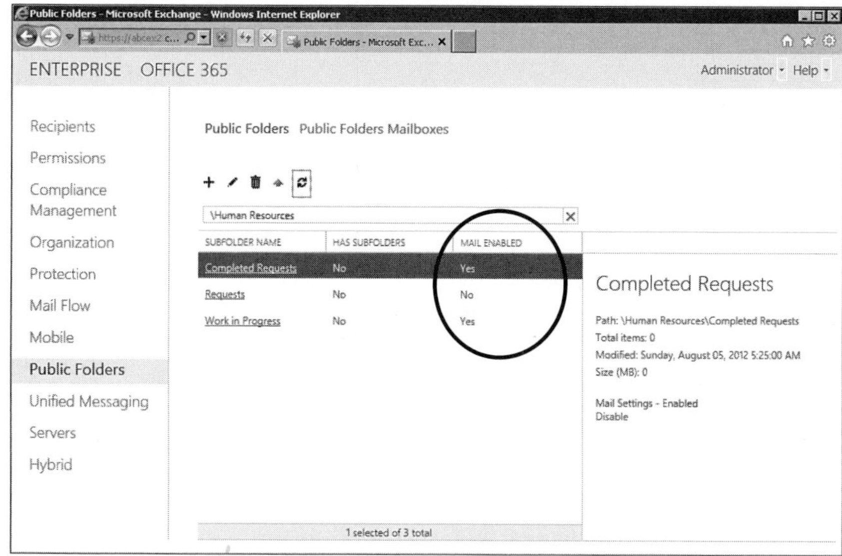

FIGURE 9.6 Identifying mail-enabled folders.

Quotas properties can be configured using the following process:

1. Open the console by navigating to https://*servername*/ecp.
2. Log in to the console using an administrative account.
3. Select the Public Folders workspace and the Public Folders configuration area.
4. Select appropriate folders to navigate to the relevant folder.
5. Select the relevant folder and click the pencil-shaped Edit button.
6. Select the Limits tab from the list on the left.
7. Adjust quota values as needed; clearing the Use Organization Quota check box allows configuration of explicit values, as shown in Figure 9.7.

When using PowerShell to configure size quotas, use the following scale designations:

- **MB**—Megabytes
- **GB**—Gigabytes
- **TB**—Terabytes

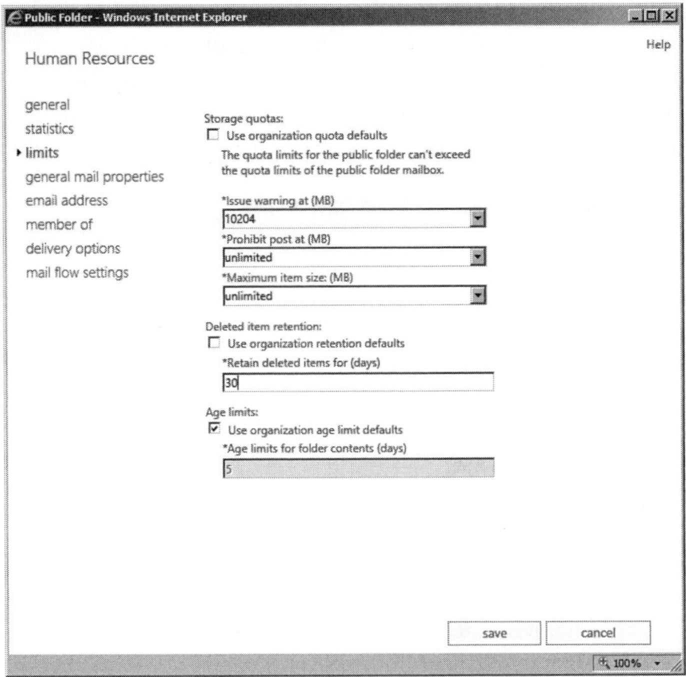

FIGURE 9.7 Configuring public folder quotas.

For example, to configure an `IssueWarningQuota` of 10GB on the Human Resources public folder and inherit the `ProhibitPostQuota` and `MaxItemSize` values from the organization, issue the following command:

```
Set-PublicFolder "\Human Resources" -IssueWarningQuota 10GB -ProhibitPostQuota
unlimited -MaxItemSize unlimited
```

Also on the Limits page is the Deleted Item Retention setting for the public folder. This setting controls the number of days that deleted items are retained for recovery. As with the quota settings, this setting can be configured individually on a folder or inherited from organizational policies.

Retention can be configured using PowerShell with the following command (for 30 days in this example):

```
Set-publicfolder "\Human Resources" -RetainDeletedItemsFor 30
```

Mail-enabled public folders support the configuration of several other properties, many of which are common Exchange Server recipient properties. These settings are organized in the following tabs:

- **General Mail Properties**—This tab contains properties that control the identity of the folder, including the folder's Alias and Display Name.

Also on this tab is the ability to manage custom properties for the public folder and hide the folder from the address book.

- **Email Addresses**—This tab allows the administrator to manage email addresses for the public folder, which is typically used to add email addresses to the ones assigned by organizational address policies. Public folders can also be excluded from automatic address generation based on policy, commonly used in cases of duplicate addresses.
- **Member Of**—As with all other recipients and other objects, this tab controls group membership for the public folder. Public folders can be members of distribution groups, managed through this tab, and used frequently for distribution list archiving.
- **Delivery Options**—This tab allows administrators to configure users who are able to send mail as the public folder and on behalf of the public folder. Both of these options allow users who manage the public folder to respond to emails and have the response come from the public folder.

  In the case of Send on Behalf Of, there is a clear indication of both the public folder and the sending user. When using the Send As section, the email appears to come from the public folder with no indication of the user, as shown in Figure 9.8. This is often used for common service addresses, such as HelpDesk@, Resume@, and info@.

  A final delivery option allows a copy of all email sent to the public folder to be forwarded to another recipient.

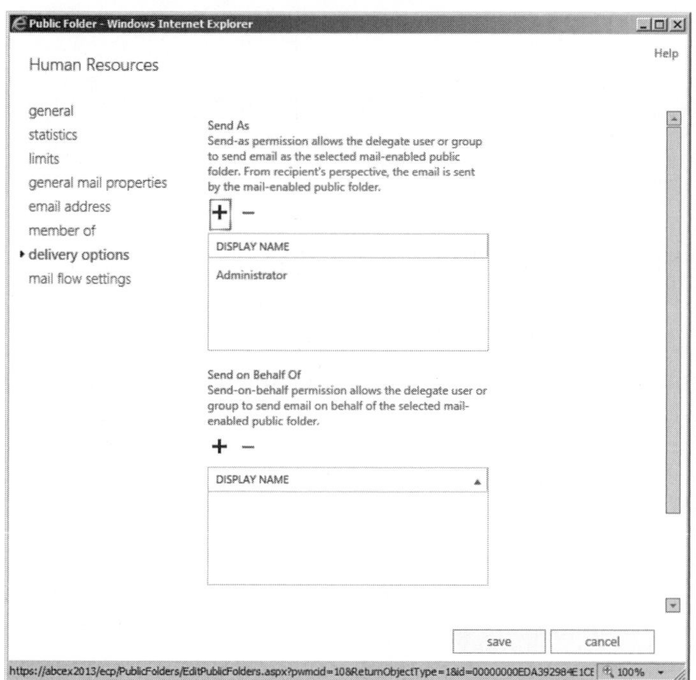

FIGURE 9.8 Granting users the Send As right to the public folder.

- **Mail Flow Settings**—This final tab includes options for message size and delivery restrictions, including limiting who can and can't send messages to the public folder, as shown in Figure 9.9. A very useful option on this page is the Require That All Senders Are Authenticated check box. This is commonly used for mail-enabled folders that should only be used by internal staff as it prevents Internet email from reaching the public folder.

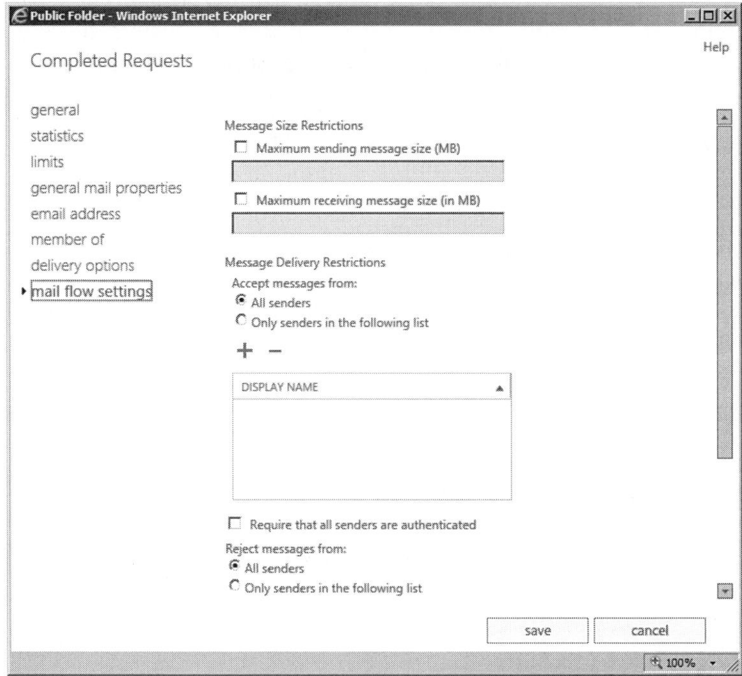

FIGURE 9.9 Blocking a public folder from anonymous (Internet-based) email.

Managing the Public Folder Infrastructure

Several tools and operations are also available to manage the structure of public folders, including the databases themselves, database replication, public folder hierarchy, and mailbox distribution of public folders. Understanding and mastering these processes is vital to managing a public folder environment and to adjusting the environment as the needs of the organization change.

Many of the infrastructure operations are new to Exchange Server 2013 due to the new public folder storage and replication mechanisms. Also as a result of these changes, many of the tools and mechanisms are identical with the ones used to manage user mailboxes within databases.

As public folders grow or content evolves, it is often necessary to move public folders between mailboxes. Common reasons include balancing the storage among multiple mailboxes to prevent a single mailbox from getting too large, relocating a public folder to a database that is centered in another geographical location, or adjusting the storage tier used by the public folder.

Moving a public folder requires Exchange Management Shell and the `New-PublicFolderMoveRequest` cmdlet. As an example, use the following command to move the folder Human Resources to public folder mailbox EMEANPF1:

```
New-PublicFolderMoveRequest -Folders "\Human Resources" -TargetMailbox EMEANPF1
```

As is evident from the cmdlet name, the move is submitted using the command and executed in the background on one of the Exchange servers. The move can be monitored using the `Get-PublicFolderMoveRequest` and `Get-PublicFolderMoveRequestStatistics` commands, as shown in Figure 9.10.

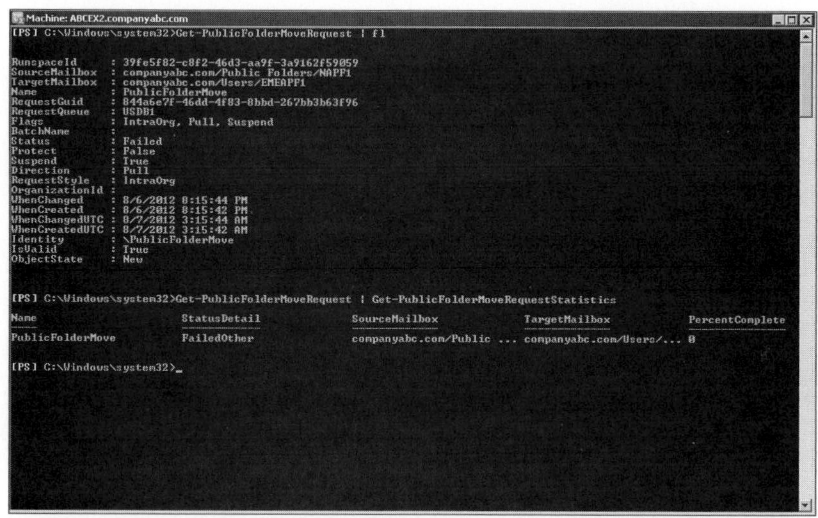

FIGURE 9.10 Monitoring public folder move requests.

When the move is completed, the request must be removed before another request can be submitted. The request can be removed using the `Remove-PublicFolderMoveRequest` cmdlet.

9

As public folders are placed in databases, especially database clusters, known as database availability groups, it can be very helpful to monitor replication traffic and ensure that high availability and disaster recovery processes are in place and healthy. Because the new public folder infrastructure allows for only one usable copy of the content, replication monitoring is no longer needed to ensure that all users are accessing current data.

Reviewing the status of database replication within a database availability group can be performed using the following commands:

```
Test-ReplicationHealth
Get-MailboxDatabaseCopyStatus
```

For more information about configuration and monitoring replication for database availability groups, see Chapter 8.

One component of modern public folders still retains a separate replication mechanism for the hierarchy, which is stored in each public folder mailbox. The master public folder mailbox, typically the first public folder mailbox created, contains the only read/write copy and every other public folder mailbox contains a read-only copy.

This architecture ensures that client can easily locate a copy of the hierarchy close to them for common read operations. In the event of a database failure that renders the master public folder mailbox unavailable, a manual process can be used to designate a new master copy for the hierarchy.

Migrating Public Folders

Another side effect of the new public folder architecture is evident when examining the migration process. The migration process for upgrading Exchange Server 2010–based public folder databases to Exchange Server 2013 public folder mailboxes is more complex than in the recent past. The process does not support a mixed deployment. All users access public folder data from a single system.

The high-level process includes several preparation steps. After preparation is complete, public folder data is synchronized from Exchange Server 2010 to Exchange Server 2013 until the migration is ready for the final transition. At that point, data in public folders is locked to prevent access in preparation to finalize the migration. After the migration is finalized, public folder access is available through Exchange Server 2013.

The following steps are executed to complete the process:

1. Perform migration preparation steps.
2. Create migration files.
3. Create public folder mailboxes.
4. Synchronize public folder data.
5. Lock down source folders.
6. Finalize the migration.
7. Validate migrated data.

During the first four steps, all client access is made to the Exchange Server 2010 public folder databases.

Perform Migration Preparation Steps

Several steps are required and recommended to migrate an Exchange Server 2010 public folder environment to Exchange Server 2013. The steps include technical prerequisites as well as steps designed to minimize risks, provide validation, and facilitate rollback if needed. It is, therefore, a good idea to follow the entire process and take your time to ensure no data is lost.

Preparation steps for the Exchange Server 2010 environment are as follows:

- Migrate all users to Exchange Server 2013 because Exchange Server 2010 mailboxes cannot access public folders hosted on Exchange Server 2013.
- Upgrade all Exchange Server 2010 servers to Service Pack 3 and the latest update rollup.
- Complete a successful full backup of all public folder databases.
- Capture the structure, statistics, and rights using the following commands. For the second command, disregard the error about not being able to find "\".

```
Get-PublicFolder -Recurse | ft Identity,ParentPath,MailEnabled,MaxItemSize,
OriginatingServer -Auto | Out-File c:\scripts\Exchange2010PFReport.txt
Get-PublicFolder -Recurse | Get-PublicFolderStatistics | ft Name,ItemCount,
TotalItemSize,OwnerCount,CreationTime,FolderPath -Auto | Out-File
c:\scripts\Exchange2010PFReport.txt -Append
Get-PublicFolder -Recurse | Get-PublicFolderClientPermission | fl
Identity,User,AccessRights | Out-File c:\scripts\Exchange2010PFReport.txt
-Append
```

  This information will be used to validate the migration after completion.

- Confirm that there are no remnants of previous migrations using the following command:

```
Get-OrganizationConfig | FL PublicFoldersLockedforMigration,
PublicFolderMigrationComplete
```

  Both properties should be False.

Preparation steps for the Exchange Server 2013 environment are as follows. These steps are required only if you have been testing migrations of public folders before starting this procedure. Perform these steps on the Exchange Server 2013 server:

- Clear any remnants of previous public folder migration requests using the following command on the Exchange Server 2013 server:

```
Get-PublicFolderMigrationRequest | Remove-PublicFolderMigrationRequest
-Confirm:$false
Remove any existing public folders or public folder Get-Mailbox
-PublicFolder |Remove-Mailbox -PublicFolder -Confirm:$false
```


Create Migration Files

The first step of the migration after preparation is complete is to use provided scripts to generate two comma-delimited, or separated (CSV), files for the migration: the public folder statistics files and the public folder to mailbox mapping file. The scripts can be found in the script directory on an Exchange Server 2013 server, by default `C:\Program Files\Microsoft\Exchange Server\V15\Scripts`. After the scripts are copied to the Exchange Server 2010 server, the following commands will generate these files when executed on the Exchange Server 2010 SP3 server:

```
.\Export-PublicFolderStatistics.ps1 <ExportFileName> <PublicFolderSourceServerFQDN>
.\PublicFolderToMailboxMapGenerator.ps1 <MaxMailboxSize> <StatisticsFileName>
<ExportFileName>
```

For example:

```
Cd \scripts
.\Export-PublicFolderStatistics.ps1 C:\Scripts\FolderStatistics.csv
ex1.companyabc.com
.\PublicFolderToMailboxMapGenerator.ps1 5GB C:\Scripts\FolderStatistics.csv
C:\Scripts\FolderToMailboxMap.csv
```

NOTE

The first parameter of the `PublicFolderToMailboxMapGenerator` script specifies the maximum desired mailbox size for a public folder mailbox (in bytes). You can use the standard size suffixes, as shown in the previous example. It is recommended to leave room for growth. Depending on the anticipated pace of growth across public folders, it is recommended to start with a mailbox size that is 50% to 75% of the desired size.

Sample output for both scripts is shown in Figures 9.11 and 9.12. Once generated, the mapping file can be edited to reflect organizational requirements and approved designs.

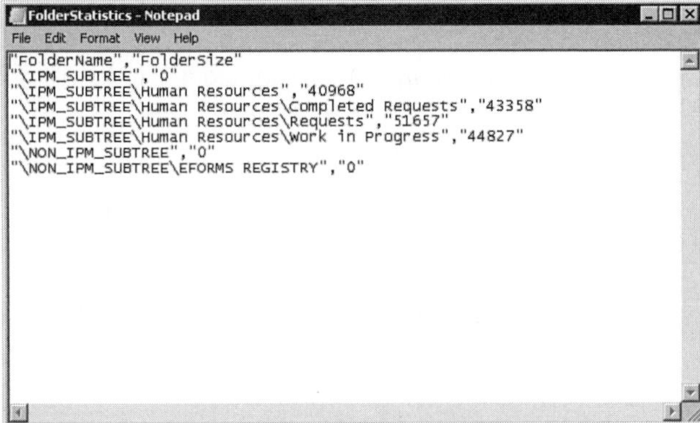

FIGURE 9.11 Public folder statistics export file.

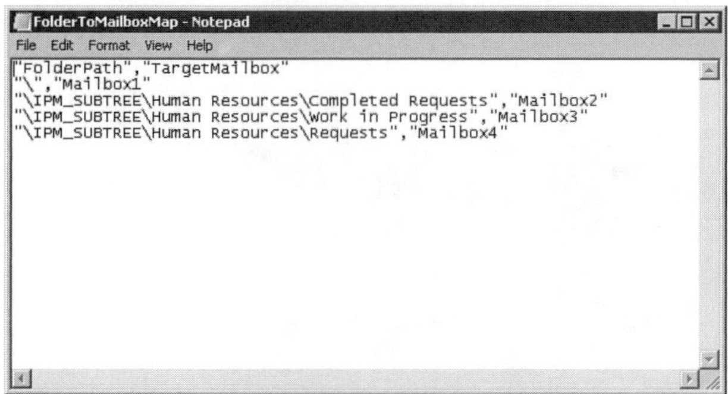
FolderToMailboxMap - Notepad
File Edit Format View Help
"FolderPath","TargetMailbox"
"\","Mailbox1"
"\IPM_SUBTREE\Human Resources\Completed Requests","Mailbox2"
"\IPM_SUBTREE\Human Resources\Work in Progress","Mailbox3"
"\IPM_SUBTREE\Human Resources\Requests","Mailbox4"

FIGURE 9.12 Public folder mapping file.

Create Public Folder Mailboxes

Based on the output of the public folder to mailbox script, the public folder mailboxes on Exchange Server 2013 must now be created. Create all the public folder mailboxes specified in the CSV file. This can be completed using PowerShell or the Exchange Administration Center. For this example, the following commands will do the trick:

```
New-Mailbox Mailbox1 -Database USDB1 -PublicFolder -HoldForMigration:$true
New-Mailbox Mailbox2 -Database USDB1 -PublicFolder -HoldForMigration:$true
New-Mailbox Mailbox3 -Database USDB1 -PublicFolder -HoldForMigration:$true
New-Mailbox Mailbox4 -Database USDB1 -PublicFolder -HoldForMigration:$true
```

NOTE

Make sure to specify the database that has the geographical configuration for this specific public folder or public folder tree based on the design plan created earlier.

Synchronize Public Folder Data

With the infrastructure ready, the initial synchronization can be started by initiating the migration request using the `New-PublicFolderMigrationRequest` cmdlet. The cmdlet requires the name of the source database and the CSV mapping file.

Continuing with the sample migration scenario, the command to submit and start the request (after the mapping file is copied to the Exchange Server 2013 server) is as follows:

```
New-PublicFolderMigrationRequest -SourceDatabase USDB1 -CSVData (Get-Content
C:\Scripts\FolderToMailboxMap.csv -Encoding Byte)
```

Allow time for the synchronization to finish and review status using the `Get-PublicFolderMigrationRequestStatistics` command, as shown in this example:

```
Get-PublicFolderMigrationRequest | Get-PublicFolderMigrationRequestStatistics
-IncludeReport | Format-List
```

The output of this command can be used to identify and troubleshoot errors, as shown in Figure 9.13.

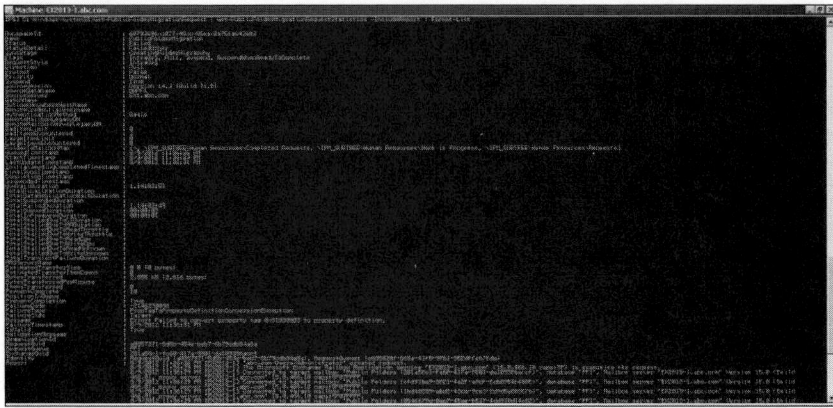

FIGURE 9.13 Detailed report for public folder migration request. (Figure not intended to be read in detail.)

The synchronization process has completed successfully when the status is reported as AutoSuspended. As indicated by the status, the process is automatically suspended at the conclusion of the synchronization to allow the administrator to lock down the source folders before final cutover.

The request process can be executed multiple times to allow testing of the target data and validating of the migration and to reduce the time required for the final cutover, which includes a final synchronization. Subsequent requests will only migrate data changed since the previous migration. Enter the following command to resume the suspended job to perform a delta synchronization:

```
Resume-PublicFolderMigrationRequest \PublicFolderMigration
```

Lock Down Source Folders and Finalize the Migration

The final series of steps is the only portion of the process that involves interruption to access to public folders. To ensure that the data transfer is complete before directing users to the Exchange Server 2013 copies of the public folders, access to the source data must be locked and a final data transfer initiated.

To lock down access to Exchange Server 2010 public folders, execute the following command, which will log out all users from the public folder databases:

```
Set-OrganizationConfig -PublicFoldersLockedForMigration:$true
```

Wait for the replication topology to replicate this change to all public folder databases and execute the following commands on the Exchange Server 2013 server to complete the migration:

```
Set-PublicFolderMigrationRequest \PublicFolderMigration -PreventCompletion:$false
Resume-PublicFolderMigrationRequest \PublicFolderMigration
```

These commands will require some time to complete a final data synchronization and then enable access to the Exchange Server 2013 public folders. Run the following command and wait until the Status shows Complete:

```
Get-PublicFolderMigrationRequest
```

To verify the data on the Exchange Server 2013 side, use the same commands executed during the preparation steps:

```
Get-PublicFolder -Recurse | ft Identity,ParentPath,MailEnabled,MaxItemSize-Auto |
Out-File C:\scripts\Exchange2013PFReport.txt
Get-PublicFolder -Recurse | Get-PublicFolderStatistics | ft Name,ItemCount,
TotalItemSize,OwnerCount,CreationTime,FolderPath -Auto | Out-File
C:\scripts\Exchange2013PFReport.txt -Append
Get-PublicFolder -Recurse | Get-PublicFolderClientPermission | fl Identity,
User,AccessRights | Out-File C:\scripts\Exchange2013PFReport.txt -Append
```

The output file can then be compared with the file generated from the Exchange Server 2010 servers.

NOTE

Keep in mind that depending on how much time has passed since the source statistics were collected, the more chance there is of variation in the statistics, especially folder size and number of items. To make validation easier, generate a statistics and configuration dump from the source system immediately prior to the cutover steps.

Contingency Rollback

In the event of an issue with the migration process, the cutover can be reversed by running the following command on the Exchange Server 2010 server:

```
Set-OrganizationConfig -PublicFoldersLockedForMigration:$False
-PublicFolderMigrationComplete:$False
```

This command can result in a data loss because changes to the public folders on the Exchange Server 2013 servers are not replicated back and are lost.

Before attempting the migration again, clean out the Exchange Server 2013 system using the steps listed in the preparation section earlier in this chapter.

Summary

Public folders have an important component of Exchange Server since the early version and after a couple of versions where the component was marginalized and almost deprecated, Exchange Server 2013 brings a new investment in public folders. With the upgrade of public folder databases and infrastructure, public folders now perform better, are easier to manage, and continue to deliver benefits for a long time. In addition, the new storage architecture allows Microsoft to bring public folder use to the hosted Exchange offering, Exchange Online as part of Office 365.

These changes do require administrators to relearn public folder architecture and administration, and take care to plan, design, implement, and migrate data carefully, taking into account the new advantages and limitations of modern public folders.

As organizations migrate to Exchange Server 2013 mailbox-based public folders, administrators may determine that some instances of public folders should be converted to team mailboxes or SharePoint lists and libraries. The resulting structure, if designed and executed correctly, should provide a significant improvement with each component leveraged to accentuate its strengths and minimize its weaknesses. In addition, a well-designed environment using all the appropriate technologies should provide scalable, available, secure data storage for advanced collaboration data for years to come. The solution will also be flexible enough to address future needs of the organization as they arise.

This chapter provided detailed information about the new enhancements added to modern public folders and how to leverage the new components to design an appropriate public folder structure. Procedures and commands were presented to support the implementation, securing, and configuration of public folders in accordance with the design. And finally, the process to migrate legacy public folders into the environment was discussed.

Best Practices

The following are best practices from this chapter:

- Carefully review existing public folder environments in line with changes to the architecture.
- Migrate all user mailboxes to Exchange Server 2013 before starting the public folder migration.
- Design the public folder architecture with careful consideration of current and future geographical topology.
- Fully examine and understand the changes to public folders before attempting to design the Exchange Server 2013 environment.
- Define and validate security and access requirements before and after the implementation.
- Consider the use of public folder quotas to control and manage the storage allocation for public folders.
- For public folder access using OWA, wait for Service Pack 1 for Exchange Server 2013.

- Use the commands listed in the "Migrating Public Folders" section to record and document your public folder architecture.
- Leverage the mechanisms provided by database availability groups (DAGs) to provide high availability and disaster recovery for public folders.
- Mail-enable public folders that require content submission via email.
- Leverage PowerShell for comprehensive and automated public folder administration.
- Validate user and administrator requirements carefully before implementing public folder security.
- Adhere to the principle of least privilege when designing and implementing public folder security.
- Delegate management of public folder content to power users who understand the content requirements.
- Manage and restrict the maximum size of public folder mailboxes to prevent unmanageable mailboxes and poor performance.

CHAPTER 10

Understanding Exchange Policy Enforcement Security

IN THIS CHAPTER

- What Is Enterprise Policy Management in Exchange Server 2013?
- Understanding Relevant Governmental Regulations for Policy Enforcement
- Using Transport Agents in Exchange Server 2013
- Understanding the Hub Transport Agents in Exchange Server 2013
- Understanding Transport Agent Policies on the Edge
- Creating Messaging Records Retention Policies
- Utilizing Rights Management Services for Policy Enforcement
- Exchange Server 2013 Client-Level Security Enhancements
- Protecting Against Spam
- Securing Outlook Web App

In the past decade, organizations have become more and more aware of the need to gain greater control over the content that traverses through the systems. In the past, these types of considerations were not given much thought, and email was pretty much open for all users to send whatever they wanted, both internally and externally.

Over time, as specific high-profile court cases over email content have taken place and governmental regulations such as the Health Insurance Portability and Accountability Act (HIPAA) and Sarbanes-Oxley Act have been enforced, organizations have begun to take note that they need to establish policies to control their messaging environments.

Exchange Server 2013 provides for robust integrated support of enterprise policy enforcement, allowing organizations to apply restrictions to mail messages, limiting content that can be sent and creating a framework in which specific retention policies can be created.

This chapter focuses on the Exchange Server 2013 capabilities in this space. The role that governmental policies such as HIPAA and Sarbanes-Oxley play in forming these policies is described. Specific information on policy enforcement using Transport Rule agents and Messaging Records Management are outlined and explained. In addition, best practices for organizations looking to use Exchange Server 2013 for policy management are defined.

What Is Enterprise Policy Management in Exchange Server 2013?

The technologies built in to Exchange Server 2013 provide support for Enterprise Policy Management as a built-in component of Exchange. Microsoft integrated Enterprise Policy Management into Exchange as a direct result of the changes in the marketplace that required that certain types of communications such as email be controlled, managed, secured, and audited to levels previously unattainable without third-party products.

Enterprise Policy Management in Exchange Server 2013 is effectively composed of several components, each providing a different layer in the management space. These components are defined as follows:

- **Messaging Records Management (MRM)**—Messaging Records Management in Exchange Server 2013 defines retention settings for individual mail folders within mailboxes.
- **Journaling**—Exchange Server 2013 journaling allows for mailbox-specific archiving of all communications sent to or from specific users, allowing organizations to comply with strict retention policies stipulated by governmental regulations.
- **Edge Transport rules**—Exchange Server 2013 has the ability to apply policies and rules at the edge layer, protecting an organization from spam, spyware, undesired corporate information leakage, and other undesirable emails.
- **Hub Transport rules**—Exchange Server 2013 also allows for specific transport rules, which are run against all traffic sent through the Hub Transport service (Microsoft Exchange Transport service; "Hub" does not appear in the actual service name).
- **Address rewriting**—Edge Transport servers in Exchange Server 2013 can implement a policy to rewrite all of the outgoing Simple Mail Transfer Protocol (SMTP) domain names within a company to a single domain name, thus ensuring consistency with corporate policies.
- **Disclaimers**—Disclaimer policies also run on Edge servers and are created to allow a corporate disclaimer to be appended to the end of every outgoing mail message.
- **Rights Management Services**—Exchange Server 2013 integrates directly with Active Directory Rights Management Services (AD RMS), allowing rights-protected encrypted emails to be sent across forest boundaries.

Each of these components is described in more detail in later sections of this chapter. In addition, step-by-step guides for deploying best-practice policies are defined.

Understanding Relevant Governmental Regulations for Policy Enforcement

Multiple governmental and industry regulations have direct consequences for messaging platforms within organizations. Security systems within an organization can be based on proprietary standards; however, as organizations have the need to securely exchange information with other entities, the need to have information systems built on standards becomes crucial. Security standards enable organizations to not only store and transmit information within the enterprise in a secure manner, but to also securely exchange information with other entities.

A universal security standard requires the creation of common criteria for a secured environment, the adoption of the standard by an accepted standards organization, the acceptance of the standard by organizations, and the implementation of the standard in enterprise transactions.

There are many initiatives to create security standards. Some of these standards include ISO/IEC 27002, HIPAA, and provisions of the Gramm-Leach-Bliley Act. These initiatives, and how they relate to Exchange Server 2013 Policy Management, are detailed in the subsequent sections of this chapter.

Understanding the ISO/IEC 27002 Security Standard

ISO/IEC 27002 is "a comprehensive set of controls comprising best practices in information security." It is an internationally recognized generic information security standard. ISO/IEC 27002 is based on BS7799-1 and has existed in various forms for a number of years.

ISO/IEC 27002 is organized into 12 major sections, each covering a different topic or area:

- Risk Assessment
- Security Policy
- Organization of Information Security
- Asset Management
- Human Resources Security
- Physical and Environment Security
- Communications and Operations Management
- Access Control
- Information Systems Acquisition, Development, and Maintenance
- Information Security Incident Management
- Business Continuity Management
- Compliance

The first step toward ISO/IEC 27002 certification is to comply with the standard itself. This is a good security practice in its own right, but it is also the longer-term status adopted by a number of organizations that require the assurance of an external measure, yet do not want to proceed with an external or formal process immediately.

In either case, the method and rigor enforced by the standard can be put to good use in terms of better management of risk. It is also being used in some sectors as a market differentiator, as organizations begin to quote their ISO/IEC 27002 status within their individual markets and to potential customers.

Understanding the Health Insurance Portability and Accountability Act of 1996 (HIPAA)

HIPAA is the acronym for the Health Insurance Portability and Accountability Act of 1996. When HIPAA was enacted in 1996, it had two major purposes. One was to allow employees to change jobs while maintaining health-care coverage. The second was to ensure that health-care providers maintain the confidentiality of patient information.

With respect to the portability of insurance, a few decades ago, people stayed in one or two jobs throughout a whole career. In those days, people had no need for HIPAA because their jobs were stable and their employee benefits were retained by a single or limited number of providers. However, in the past decade in a time when jobs and even careers are constantly changing, HIPAA provides the continuity of health insurance even through job changes and unemployment.

The original act was unclear and led to much confusion in the health-care industry specifically with how to comply with HIPAA, so several revisions to HIPAA were enacted along with clarification documents.

Early Provisions of HIPAA

The initial actions of HIPAA were clarified and implemented related to consumer rights to health-care coverage. HIPAA increased an individual's ability to get health coverage for himself and his dependents. It also lowered an employee's chance of losing existing health-care coverage, through a job change or unemployment. HIPAA also helped employees buy health insurance coverage on their own if they lost coverage under an employer's group health plan and have no other health coverage available.

Among its specific protections, HIPAA limited the use of preexisting condition exclusions and prohibited group health plans from discriminating by denying coverage or charging employees extra for coverage based on their individual or family member's past or present poor health. HIPAA provided guarantees to employers or individuals who purchased health insurance so they could renew the coverage regardless of any health conditions of individuals covered under the insurance policy.

HIPAA, however, does not require employers to offer or pay for health coverage to their employees nor does it guarantee health coverage for all workers. HIPAA also does not control the amount that an insurer can charge for coverage nor require group health plans to offer specific benefits. Other provisions do not require an employer or insurer to offer the same level of health-care coverage as a previous provider nor eliminate all use of preexisting condition exclusions.

Later Provisions of HIPAA

After the early provisions for HIPAA relative to consumer rights to health care were defined and implemented, the focus of HIPAA turned to the accountability aspects of the act. The focus areas were standards for transactions and code sets, privacy of patient information, and security of information.

HIPAA Transaction and Code Sets

The rules for Transactions and Code Sets (TCS) were published in the middle of 2000 and have since been modified several times. Key to the transaction and code sets are rules that provide provisions applicable to electronic data transaction standards. The transaction and code sets standardize the electronic exchange of information (transactions) between trading partners.

The HIPAA Code Set Regulations establish a uniform standard of data elements used to document reasons why patients are seen and the procedures performed during health-care encounters.

HIPAA specified administrative codes set for use in conjunction with certain transactions and HIPAA eliminated local codes.

The Need for Privacy of Health-Care Information

The American public began to register serious concerns about the privacy and security of health records in the early 1990s. Breaches of health privacy, such as press disclosures of individuals' HIV status, network hacking incidents, and misdirected patient emails fueled this concern. When HIPAA was passed in 1996, it included a mandate for standards that would ensure the security and integrity of health information that is maintained or transmitted electronically. A Notice of Proposed Rulemaking (NPRM) on security was published by the U.S. Department of Health and Human Services DHHS in 1998.

The security rule focused on both external and internal security threats and vulnerabilities. Threats from "outsiders" include breaking through network firewalls, email attacks through interception or viruses, compromise of passwords, posing as organization "insiders," computer viruses, and modem number prefix scanning. These activities can result in denial of service, such as the disruption of information flow by "crashing" or overloading critical computer servers. The outsider might steal and misuse proprietary information, including individual health information. Attacks can also affect the integrity of information, by corrupting data that is being transmitted.

Internal threats are of equal concern, and are far more likely to occur according to many security experts. Organizations must protect against careless staff or others who are unaware of security issues, and curious or malicious insiders who deliberately take advantage of system vulnerabilities to access and misuse personal health information.

The rule is intended to set a minimum level or "floor" of security. Organizations can choose to implement safeguards that exceed the HIPAA standards—and, in fact, might find that their business strategies require stronger protections. Covered entities are required to do the following:

- Assess potential risks and vulnerabilities.
- Protect against threats to information security or integrity and against unauthorized use or disclosure.
- Implement and maintain security measures that are appropriate to their needs, capabilities, and circumstances.
- Ensure compliance with these safeguards by all staff.

Central to HIPAA security is the tenet that information security must be comprehensive. No single policy, practice, or tool can ensure effective overall security. Cultural and organizational issues must be addressed, as well as technological and physical concerns. The safeguards that make up HIPAA-mandated security focus on protecting "data integrity, confidentiality, and availability" of individually identifiable health information through the following:

- **Administrative procedures**—Documented, formal practices to manage the selection and execution of security measures
- **Physical safeguards**—Protection of computer systems and related buildings and equipment from hazards and intrusion
- **Technical security services**—Processes that protect and monitor information access
- **Technical security mechanisms**—Processes that prevent unauthorized access to data that is transmitted over a network

These regulations established standards for all health plans, clearinghouses, and storage of health-care information to ensure the integrity, confidentiality, and availability of electronic protected health information.

HIPAA Privacy

Starting in 2003, health-care providers and health plans were required to be in compliance with the HIPAA privacy regulation. HIPAA took critical steps in ensuring that sensitive personal health information can be shared for core health activities, with safeguards in place to limit the inappropriate use and sharing of patient data to require that privacy and security be built in to the policies and practices of health-care providers, plans, and others involved in health care.

The U.S. Department of Health and Human Services (DHHS) had addressed the concerns with new privacy standards that set a national minimum of basic protections. Congress recognized that advances in electronic technology could erode the privacy of health information. Consequently, Congress incorporated into HIPAA provisions that mandate an adoption of federal privacy protections for certain individually identifiable health information.

The HIPAA Privacy Rule (Standards for Privacy of Individually Identifiable Health Information) provided the first national standards for protecting the privacy of health information. The Privacy Rule regulates how certain entities, called covered entities, use and disclose certain individually identifiable health information, called protected health information (PHI). PHI is individually identifiable health information that is transmitted or maintained in any form or medium (for example, electronic, paper, oral), but excludes certain educational records and employment records. Among other provisions, the Privacy Rule provides for the following:

- Gives patients more control over their health information
- Sets boundaries on the use and release of health records
- Establishes appropriate safeguards that the majority of health-care providers and others must achieve to protect the privacy of health information
- Holds violators accountable with civil and criminal penalties that can be imposed if they violate patients' privacy rights
- Strikes a balance when public health responsibilities support disclosure of certain forms of data
- Enables patients to make informed choices based on how individual health information can be used
- Enables patients to find out how their information can be used and what disclosures of their information have been made
- Generally limits release of information to the minimum reasonably needed for the purpose of the disclosure
- Generally gives patients the right to obtain a copy of their own health records and request corrections
- Empowers individuals to control certain uses and disclosures of their health information

DHHS recognized the importance of sharing PHI to accomplish essential public health objectives and to meet certain other societal needs (for example, administration of justice and law enforcement). Therefore, the Privacy Rule expressly permits PHI to be shared for specified public health purposes. For example, covered entities can disclose PHI, without individual authorization, to a public health authority legally authorized to collect or receive the information for the purpose of preventing or controlling disease, injury, or disability [45 CFR § 164.512(b)]. Further, the Privacy Rule permits covered entities to make disclosures that are required by other laws, including laws that require disclosures for public health purposes. Thus, the Privacy Rule provides for the continued functioning of the U.S public health system.

HIPAA Implications for Exchange Messaging Environments

The most important implication that HIPAA requirements have on an Exchange messaging environment is regarding data security. Organizations subject to HIPAA regulations must demonstrate that they are taking significant precautions against confidential patient data being compromised, lost, or stolen. This includes the transmission of this type of data across a medium such as email.

Exchange Server 2013 can help organizations become HIPAA compliant through the use of enterprise policies that define which email data needs to be encrypted, thus securing the transmission of protected data. Information on how to set up these policies is presented in upcoming sections of this chapter.

Understanding the Gramm-Leach-Bliley Act

Information that many would consider private—including bank balances and account numbers—is regularly bought and sold by banks, credit card companies, and other financial institutions. The Gramm-Leach-Bliley Act (GLBA), which is also known as the Financial Services Modernization Act of 1999, provides limited privacy protections against the sale of the private financial information of consumers. In addition, the GLBA codifies protections against pretexting, the practice of obtaining personal information through false pretenses.

The GLBA primarily sought to "modernize" financial services—that is, end regulations that prevented the merger of banks, stock brokerage companies, and insurance companies. The removal of these regulations, however, raised significant risks that these new financial institutions would have access to an incredible amount of personal information, with no restrictions upon its use. Prior to GLBA, the insurance company that maintained health records was distinct from the bank that held the mortgage on a consumer's house or the stockbroker who traded a person's stock. After these companies merged, however, they had the ability to consolidate, analyze, and sell the personal details of their customers' lives. Because of these risks, the GLBA included three simple requirements to protect the personal data of individuals: First, banks, brokerage companies, and insurance companies must securely store personal financial information. Second, they must advise consumers of their policies on sharing of personal financial information. Third, they must give consumers the option to opt out of some sharing of personal financial information.

Privacy Protections Under the GLBA

The GLBA's privacy protections only regulate financial institutions—businesses that are engaged in banking, insuring, stocks and bonds, financial advice, and investing.

First, these financial institutions, regardless of whether they want to disclose the personal information of individuals, must develop precautions to ensure the security and confidentiality of customer records and information, to protect against any anticipated threats or hazards to the security or integrity of such records, and to protect against unauthorized access to or use of such records or information that could result in substantial harm or inconvenience to any customer.

Second, financial institutions are required to provide consumers with a notice of their information-sharing policies when the individual first becomes a customer, and annually thereafter. That notice must inform the consumer of the financial institutions' policies on disclosing nonpublic personal information (NPI) to affiliates and nonaffiliated third parties, disclosing NPI after the customer relationship is terminated, and protecting NPI. *Nonpublic personal information* means all information on applications to obtain financial services (credit card or loan applications), account histories (bank or credit card), and the fact that an individual is or was a customer. This interpretation of NPI makes names, addresses, telephone numbers, Social Security numbers, and other data subject to the GLBA's data-sharing restrictions.

Third, the GLBA gives consumers the right to opt out from a limited amount of NPI sharing. Specifically, a consumer can direct the financial institution to not share information with unaffiliated companies.

Consumers have no right under the GLBA to stop sharing of NPI among affiliates. An affiliate is any company that controls, is controlled by, or is under common control with another company. The individual consumer has absolutely no control over this kind of "corporate family" trading of personal information.

Several exemptions under the GLBA can permit information sharing over the consumer's objection. For instance, if a financial institution wants to engage the services of a separate company, it can transfer personal information to that company by arguing that the information is necessary to the services that the company will perform. A financial institution can transfer information to a marketing or sales company to sell new products (different stocks) or jointly offered products (cosponsored credit cards). After this unaffiliated third party has an individual's personal information, it can share the information with its own "corporate family." However, the company itself cannot likewise transfer the information to further companies through this exemption.

In addition, financial institutions can disclose information to credit reporting agencies, to financial regulatory agencies, as part of the sale of a business, to comply with any other laws or regulations, or as necessary for a transaction requested by the consumer.

Fourth, financial institutions are prohibited from disclosing, other than to a consumer reporting agency, access codes or account numbers to any nonaffiliated third party for use in telemarketing, direct mail marketing, or other marketing through electronic mail. Thus, even if a consumer fails to opt out of a financial institution's transfers, the credit card numbers, PINs, or other access codes cannot be sold, as they had been in some previous cases.

Fifth, certain types of pretexting were prohibited by the GLBA. Pretexting is the practice of collecting personal information under false pretenses. Pretexters pose as authority figures (law enforcement agents, social workers, potential employers, and so on) and manufacture seductive stories (that the victim is about to receive a sweepstakes award or insurance payment) to elicit personal information about the victim. The GLBA prohibits the use of false, fictitious, or fraudulent statements or documents to get customer information from a financial institution or directly from a customer of a financial institution; the use of forged, counterfeit, lost, or stolen documents to get customer information from a financial institution or directly from a customer of a financial institution; and asking another person to get someone else's customer information using false, fictitious, or fraudulent documents or forged, counterfeit, lost, or stolen documents.

GLBA's Implications for Exchange Messaging Environments

GLBA strictly limits the disclosure of personal information outside of a company or its immediate corporate affiliates. Exchange Server policies in regard to email can be set up to monitor communications for specific types of personal data or key phrases, restricting where it can be sent. Leveraging integrated technologies with Exchange Server 2013, an organization can set transport rules to look at message content in transit, assess whether the message has keywords to content that applies to GLBA protected information, and Exchange can be set to prevent, block, or flat the message so the management of the organization can take proactive actions to minimize violation of GLBA regulations.

Understanding Sarbanes-Oxley

Sarbanes-Oxley (commonly just referred to as SOX), named for the two senators who sponsored it, on the surface doesn't have much to do with information technology (IT) security. The law was passed to restore the public's confidence in corporate governance by making chief executives of publicly traded companies personally validate financial statements and other information.

President Bush signed the law in 2002. Initially, companies had to be in compliance by the fall of 2003, but extensions were granted with large corporations given until 2004 to meet the requirements of Sarbanes-Oxley, and smaller companies had to comply by 2005.

Congress passed the law in quick response to accounting scandals surrounding Enron, WorldCom, and other companies. Sarbanes-Oxley deals with many corporate governance issues, including executive compensation and the use of independent directors. Section 404 mandates that each annual report contain an internal control report, which must state the responsibility of management for establishing and maintaining an adequate internal control structure and procedures for financial reporting. It must also contain an assessment, at the end of the issuer's most recent fiscal year, of the effectiveness of the internal control structure and procedures for financial reporting. The auditor must attest to, and report on, the assessment made by the management of the issuer. It's hard to sign off on the validity of data if the systems maintaining it aren't secure. It is the internal IT systems that keep the records of the organizations. If the IT systems aren't secure, internal controls can also be questioned.

Sarbanes-Oxley doesn't mandate specific internal controls such as strong authentication or the use of encryption. However, if someone can easily get in to an organization's IT system, the security hole can establish a condition of noncompliance. Sarbanes-Oxley creates a link between upper management and the security operation staff on what is needed to ensure that proper and auditable security measures are in place. The executives who have to sign off on the internal controls have to ensure the security in their organizations is well established; otherwise, the executive could face criminal penalties if a breach is detected.

Sarbanes-Oxley's Implications for an Exchange Messaging Environment

SOX controls stipulate that data must be secured and audited to make sure that a third party cannot manipulate financial data. Exchange Server 2013 includes administrative controls that protect an organization from security breaches. In addition, SOX controls look to an organization to establish specific guidelines in regard to data retention and data transfer controls. These factors can be controlled using specific Exchange Server enterprise policies, such as mail retention policies, privacy policies, and confidentiality policies, as outlined in subsequent sections of this chapter.

Using Transport Agents in Exchange Server 2013

Transport agents are part of the core Exchange Server functionality provided to organizations that allow for policies to be enforced within the messaging platform. Microsoft designed these policies with built-in support for third-party add-ons. This allows other companies to build products that directly integrate with Exchange Server 2013 to scan mail and to run specific tasks on the mail that flows through the system.

Unlike Exchange Server 2010 where transport agents were specific to the Edge server role and the Hub Transport server role, in Exchange Server 2013, the transport pipeline has three separate pieces:

- Front End Transport service (FET)
- Hub Transport service (HT)
- Mailbox Transport service (MT)

At their core, transport agents in Exchange Server 2013 are just a programmatic method of performing tasks on mail based on a specified criterion. They can range in complexity from a simple "Forward a copy of all emails sent to this person to this particular email address" to "Apply this equation to this email message to determine whether or not it is spam."

Understanding the Role of Transport Agents in Policy Management

Transport agents are especially important for companies looking to bring their messaging platform into compliance with specific governmental regulations, as some of the default transport agents, such as journaling or mail retention policies, offer out-of-the-box functionality that is required by many of these regulations. For situations where built-in functionality might not suffice, the field of third-party add-ons to Exchange Server 2013 transport agents is increasing every day, so organizations can deploy a custom agent to perform a specific task.

Prioritizing Transport Agents

Exchange Server 2013 allows administrators to prioritize the order in which transport agents act on a message. As an SMTP message passes through the transport pipeline, different SMTP events are acted out. These events, with names such as `OnHeloCommand` and `OnConnectEvent`, happen in a specific order every time, and transport agents set to act upon a specific event will only fire when that event has occurred. After it occurs, however, the priority level can be set, determining which transport agent acts first at that particular juncture.

Changing priority on a specific transport rule is as simple as right-clicking on the rule in the details pane and choosing Change Priority.

Using Pipeline Tracing to Troubleshoot Transport Agents

Pipeline tracing with Exchange Server 2013 transport agents is a diagnostic tool that can be used to send a copy of the mail message as it existed before and after a transport rule went into effect. This copy is sent to a specific mailbox.

To enable pipeline tracing on an Exchange server and set a specific mailbox to be the pipeline tracing mailbox, run the following command from the Exchange Management Shell:

```
Set-TransportServer Server5 -PipelineTracingEnabled $True
-PipelineTracingSenderAddress zack@companyabc.com
```

where `Server5` is the name of the server and only mail from `zack@companyabc.com` is traced through the pipeline.

Pipeline tracing must be enabled on the Hub Transport service on all Mailbox servers and/or Edge Transport servers in the topology for it to be useful as a troubleshooting mechanism.

Outlining the Built-in Transport Agents in Exchange Server 2013

Exchange Server 2013 contains built-in support for a wide variety of transport agents. Some of these agents run off of Hub Transport services on Mailbox servers, and others run off of Edge Transport servers.

The Hub Transport services transport agents are as follows:

- Journaling agent
- AD RMS Prelicensing agent
- Transport Rule agent

The Edge Transport server role transport agents are as follows:

- Content Filter agent
- Sender ID agent
- Recipient Filter agent
- Connection Filtering agent
- Attachment Filtering agent
- Address Rewriting Outbound agent
- Address Rewriting Inbound agent

- Edge Rule agent
- Sender Filter agent
- Protocol Analysis agent

Understanding the Hub Transport Agents in Exchange Server 2013

As previously mentioned, a handful of the default transport agents in Exchange Server 2013 are designed to run on servers running the Hub Transport service in an Exchange Server organization. These agents are designed to run against internal traffic as well as the external traffic that is being routed inside the organization. These agents are the Transport Rule agent, the AD RMS Prelicensing agent, and the Journaling agent, each of which is described further in the following sections.

Working with Transport Rule Agents

Transport Rule agents is the generic term used to describe any server-side rule that is run on the Hub Transport service on a Mailbox server. These rules are very similar in design to Outlook rules, but they are run against the entire organization.

To create a simple transport rule to test these chapter concepts, perform the following tasks in Exchange Administration Center:

1. From the Exchange Administration Center (https://{servername}/ecp), click Mail Flow, Rules.
2. On the Rules page, click the + button to create a new rule.
3. From the New Rule page, enter a descriptive name for the rule (like `Capture Sensitive Information Emails`).
4. In the Apply This Rule If pull-down option, shown in Figure 10.1, select which conditions the rule will operate under. In this example, selecting The Subject or Body Includes will look for keywords you specify by clicking Enter Words, for example, "ProjectX", in the subject or body of the email.
5. In the Do the Following pull-down option, select which action to take, e.g., "Forward the Message for Approval To..." and select the recipients from the list.
6. If you want to enter in Exceptions or start the rule on a specific date, click More Options to choose other options.

NOTE

You may choose to select More Options by default when creating transport rules as the More Options includes both the primary rules as well as additional rules providing more options to choose.

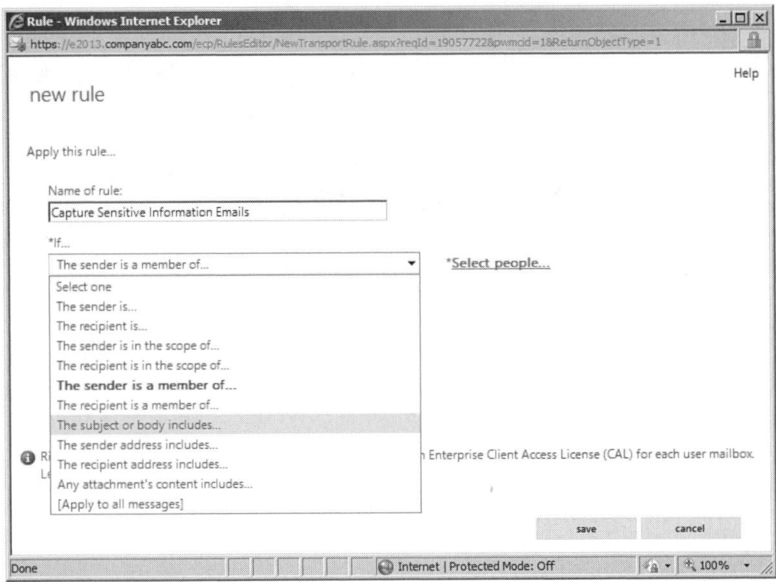

FIGURE 10.1 Creating a transport rule.

7. Click Save to save the policy.

CAUTION

Transport rules are very powerful, and improperly configuring a transport rule can result in the loss of mail data or other issues. Use caution when creating transport rules and always test them in a lab environment first.

Transport rules use Active Directory (AD) replication to replicate any changes made to specific rules. Each Hub Transport service queries AD once every 4 hours for changes made to transport agents, and then processes all new messages based on the changes made to the rules.

Transport agents are highly customizable, and it is wise to go through the wizards several times to determine what type of rule functionality is available and if your specific organization can take advantage of them.

NOTE

When a change is made to a transport rule, it can take multiple hours for that change to be enforced. This has to do with the fact that the change must be replicated over AD, which can be set to replicate slowly. In addition, the Hub Transport service uses a cache to avoid constantly asking AD for changes. This cache expires in 4 hours, so it is important to note how long it can take before a change is properly replicated.

Applying Rights Management Policies to a Transport Rule

One of the actions available in the More Options for transport rules is the ability to "Apply Rights Protection to the Message With." This option uses Microsoft Active Directory Rights Management Services (RMS) template policies to encrypt messages and their content in transit. RMS transit encryption is commonly applied to messages that are sensitive in nature (where the RMS template encrypts the message content). Other times, RMS transit encryption is applied to messages to either retain the message (preventing the message from being deleted for, say, seven years) or forcing a message to be deleted within 24 hours.

The RMS transport agent requires Microsoft Active Directory Rights Management Services to be implemented in the networking environment and the purchase of an Enterprise Exchange client access license (CAL). More on RMS is covered later in this chapter in the section titled "Utilizing Rights Management Services for Policy Enforcement."

Working with Journaling and Mail Retention Policies in Exchange Server 2013

Journaling in Exchange Server 2013 is a method by which all copies of emails sent to or from specific users are backed up and logged. Even if the original email is deleted, the journaling system has access to the original content in the email. Journaling is especially relevant to many organizations looking to comply with governmental regulations, such as SEC Rule 17A-4, SOX, GLBA, HIPAA, the Patriot Act, and NASD 3110.

Exploring the Journaling Licensing Differences

Journaling in Exchange Server 2013 goes beyond the capabilities present in the older versions of Exchange Server. Exchange Server now allows for three types of journaling:

- **Database journaling**—Database journaling is essentially the same journaling mechanism used since Exchange Server 5.5 Service Pack 1 (SP1). This form of journaling requires that journaling be turned on for all users in a specific database.
- **Transport journaling**—Taking advantage of the design change in Exchange Server 2010 where every message sent anywhere passes through the Hub Transport service, a transport rule can copy every message to a journaling mailbox. This method is particularly useful when combined with an email journal appliance or cloud service.
- **Premium journaling**—Premium journaling offers the capability of journaling "per user" within the organization.

For compliance, transport journaling is generally preferred over database journaling because it is much less resource intensive, especially when the journaling mailbox is outside of Exchange, and it is configured in one place for the entire organization, greatly lessening the chance of misconfiguration.

Premium journaling allows for the scope of the journaling to be performed to be specified. Options are to limit the scope to Internal, External, or Global. If the scope is not changed from Internal to External, journaling is not performed if the user sending the message is not remote.

NOTE

Premium journaling requires an Exchange Server Enterprise CAL to be purchased for each mailbox user.

Enabling Database Journaling

To initiate journaling of messages, database journaling needs to be enabled. It is done so as follows:

1. From the Exchange Administration Center (https://{*servername*}/ecp), click Servers, Databases.
2. Select the database whose mailboxes are to be journaled and then click Edit.
3. In the Database Properties Page, click Maintenance.
4. For Journal Recipient, click Browse.
5. Narrow the list by entering a search string if necessary, choose the journaling mailbox, and then click OK.
6. Click Save.

Creating a Transport Journal Rule

Transport journaling applies to all users within the organization. After being turned on, all messages for all users are journaled. To configure journaling for all mailboxes, perform the following steps:

1. From the Exchange Administration Center (https://{*servername*}/ecp), click Compliance Management, Journaling.
2. Click the + icon to open up the New Journal Rule page.
3. On the New Journal Rule page, enter in a name of the journal rule, such as "`Journal All Email Messages`."
4. For If the Message Is Sent To or From choose [Apply to All Messages].

5. For Journal the Following Messages, choose All Messages.
6. For Send Journal Reports To, enter the SMTP address where you want the messages sent.

CAUTION

The mailbox where "Send Journal Reports To" should be closely guarded and protected as all of the journaled messages from the databases will be stored there.

7. Click Save.
8. Click Yes to confirm that the rule applies to all messages.

Creating Journal Rules for Specific Users or Messages

Journal rules can be created to journal just specific users, just inbound messages, or just outbound messages. To set up a journal rule of this type, do the following:

1. From the Exchange Administration Center (https://{*servername*}/ecp), click Compliance Management, Journaling.
2. Click the + icon to open up the New Journal Rule page.
3. On the New Journal Rule page, enter in a name of the journal rule, such as "`Journal All Emails to/from the CFO`."
4. For If the Message Is Sent To or From, choose the name of the individual (in this case, Eva SooHoo, the CFO).

NOTE

If you need to journal messages from multiple users, create multiple individual rules.

5. For Journal the Following Messages, you can choose all inbound, all outbound, or just all messages.
6. For Send Journal Reports To, enter the SMTP address where you want the messages sent.
7. Review your settings similar to those shown in Figure 10.2.
8. Click Save.

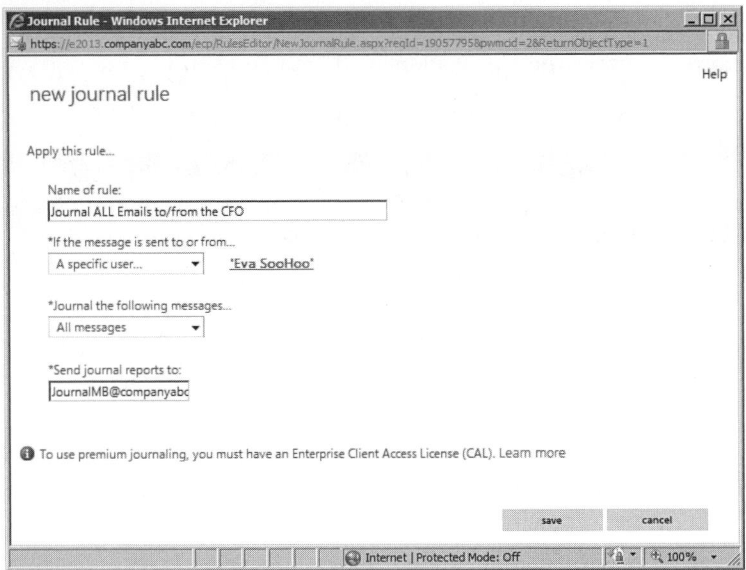

FIGURE 10.2 Enabling journaling on a database.

Setting Up Email Disclaimers

Email disclaimers have long been a desired feature in Exchange Server. In the past, complex SMTP event sinks or third-party products have provided this functionality, but Exchange Server 2013 now includes the built-in ability to apply a legal disclaimer to the end of all email messages. The transport rule topology is used for this mechanism.

To add a disclaimer to the Hub Transport service, do the following:

1. From the Exchange Administration Center (https://{*servername*}/ecp), click Mail Flow, Rules.
2. Click the + icon to open up the New Rule page.
3. Under Name of Rule, enter a descriptive name for the disclaimer (like `Standard Corporate Disclaimer`).
4. Click More Options.
5. In the Apply This Rule If pull-down option, select which conditions the rule will operate under such as [Apple to All Messages].
6. In the Do the Following pull-down option, select which action to take, select Apply a Disclaimer to the Message, and if you want it at the end of the message, choose Append a Disclaimer or if you want it at the start of a message, choose Prepend a Disclaimer.

7. Click Enter Text and type in or paste in what you want added to the message as well as choose the fallback action such as Wrap to word wrap text in the disclaimer message.
8. If you want to enter in Exceptions, click Add Exception and choose and configure the exception.
9. Scroll down and select any additional options available.
10. Review your disclaimer rule, as shown in Figure 10.3.

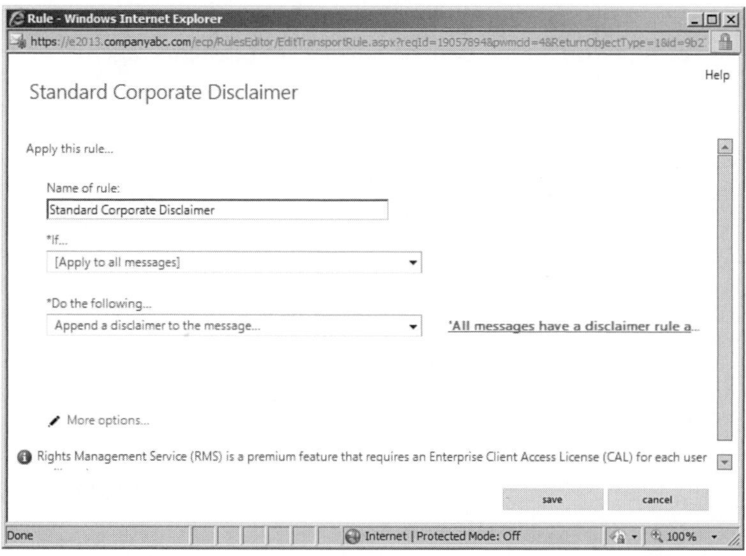

FIGURE 10.3 Creating a disclaimer rule.

11. Click Save.
12. Click Yes to confirm that the rule applies to all messages.

Understanding Transport Agent Policies on the Edge

The Edge Transport server role is vital in today's risk-fraught messaging environment as it is responsible for intercepting the onslaught of viruses and spam before they reach the internal network. Special transport rules have been created specifically for Edge servers in Exchange Server 2013. These transport rules include address rewriting policies and the like.

10

Understanding the Role of EdgeSync in Exchange Policy Management

The EdgeSync service runs as a special synchronization component that keeps specific information from the internal AD forest in sync with an external Active Directory Application Mode (ADAM) forest. It uses this information to determine if policies have changed. For more information on EdgeSync, see Chapter 11, "Exchange Edge Including Antispam/Anti-Malware Protection for Exchange."

Implementing Edge Rule Agents

Many of the transport rules in Exchange Server 2013 were designed to work on the Edge Transport role systems. This is especially true for services such as antivirus and antispam. Several other key pieces of functionality are run as policies on Edge Rule agents, as described in this section.

Setting Up Address Rewriting Policies

One of the Edge Transport rules available by default is the address rewriting policy. This policy allows internal email domains to be rewritten to a common external domain, or any other combination of domain rewriting as necessary.

Address rewriting cannot currently be performed from the graphical user interface (GUI)—it must be scripted. The following illustrates a sample script to set up a rewriting policy:

```
New-AddressRewriteEntry -name "marina@abc.internal to marina@companyabc.com"
-InternalAddress marina@abc.internal -ExternalAddress marina@companyabc.com
```

This sample policy rewrites any instance of `marina@abc.internal` to `marina@companyabc.com`.

To rewrite all email addresses in the domain companyabc1.com to companyabc2.com, enter the following command.

```
New-AddressRewriteEntry -name "Rewrite companyabc1.com to companyabc2.com"
-InternalAddress companyabc1.com -ExternalAddress companyabc2.com
```

Understanding Content Filtering Policies

Edge Server role systems have a built-in Content filter running to provide for antispam and antivirus functionality. This agent serves as a direct replacement for the Exchange Server 2003 Intelligent Message Filter (IMF). The agent works by assigning a Spam Confidence Level of 1–9 for an email. The higher the number, the more likely it is to be spam. Removing the junk messages at the edge is the best way to reduce the load that this type of environment has on the current messaging environment.

Creating Messaging Records Retention Policies

Messaging Records Management retention policies in Exchange Server 2013 allows organizations to create and enforce mailbox retention policies for their messaging environment. Retention policies are simply created and enabled so that messages, or in some terms legal records and evidence, is not accidentally or purposely deleted.

Content retention could be handled in two ways. One method is to just retain the content in Exchange logs so that information can be searched and discovered at a later date. The other option is to flag the content and even encrypt the content with a specific aging policy applied to it to prevent the content from being deleted.

Using Retention Policies to Retain Content

Exchange Server 2013 uses retention tags and retention policies to apply retention periods to messages. Messaging Records Management, or MRM, is flexible in its approach, as it allows for different policies to be set up for different types of messages.

Exchange Server 2013 provides a number of default retention tags; examples of some of the default retention tags are as follows:

- **1 month delete**—For this default retention tag, the tag is flagged as personal, which means the user can apply the policy themselves (or not), the default retention is 30 days, and after 30 days the message is deleted, and at that point the enterprise retention policy is applied whether the message is permanently deleted or searchable and recoverable by Exchange.
- **1 year delete**—For this default retention tag, the tag is flagged as personal, which means the user can apply the policy himself (or not), the default retention is 365 days, and after 365 days the message is deleted and at that point the enterprise retention policy is applied whether the message is permanently deleted or searchable and recoverable by Exchange.
- **Never delete**—For this default retention tag, the tag is flagged as personal, which means the user can apply the policy himself (or not); the default retention is unlimited.
- **Personal 1 year move to archive**—For this default retention tag, the tag is flagged as personal, which means the user can apply the policy himself (or not), the default retention is 365 days, and after 365 days the message is automatically moved to archive.

NOTE

The mere presence of retention tags does not cause any effect on mailbox content.

The step-by-step procedures for setting up this type of scenario are outlined in the following sections.

Creating Retention Tags

Retention tags are created in the Exchange Administrative Center. To create a retention tag, do the following:

1. From the Exchange Administration Center (https://{*servername*}/ecp), click Compliance Management, Retention Tags.
2. Click the + icon and choose whether the tag will be applied automatically to the entire mailbox of a user, applied automatically to a specific folder, or individually applied by users to items and folders as chosen by the user.
3. Under Name, enter a descriptive name for the retention tag (such as **`Delete After 60 days`**).
4. Choose to Delete and Allow Recovery, Permanently Delete, or Move to Archive, as shown in Figure 10.4.

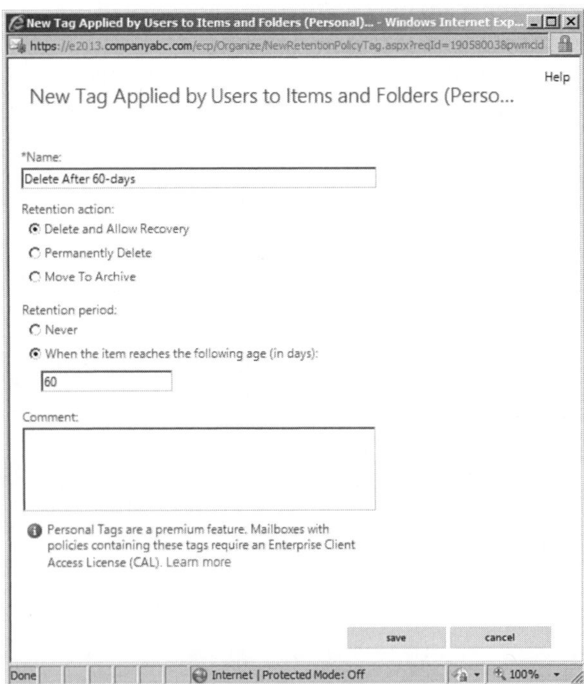

FIGURE 10.4 Choosing the retention action for a retention tag.

5. Choose the retention period (in this example, it'll be 60 days).
6. Click Save.

Creating Retention Policies for Retention Tags

The next step is to create retention policies for the retention tags so that the tags are grouped together and the organization can see that the policies are made available and applied automatically if appropriate. To create retention policies for retention tags, do the following:

1. From the Exchange Administration Center (https://{*servername*}/ecp), click Compliance Management, Retention Policies.
2. Click the + icon and enter the name of the retention policy you want to create (such as `Policy for SOX Retention`).
3. Under Retention Tags, click the + icon to add the retention tags you want to apply to this policy (in this case, if it is a SOX retention policy, then likely the policy will retain messages for a period of seven years).
4. Click Save.

Applying Retention Policies to Mailboxes

Finally, the retention policies need to be added to the mailboxes of the users you want the policies applied to. As an example, if there is a SOX Policy for seven-years retention of content, then the SOX policy needs to be applied to the mailbox of the CEO, CFO, and other executives to whom the policy applies. To apply the retention policy, follow these steps:

1. From the Exchange Administration Center (https://{*servername*}/ecp), click Recipients, Mailboxes.
2. Double-click a user to whom you want the policy applied to open the user's settings.
3. Click Mailbox Features.
4. Click Retention Policy and from the pull-down list of retention policies that you created in the previous section, choose the policy you want to apply, similar to what is shown in Figure 10.5.
5. Click Save.

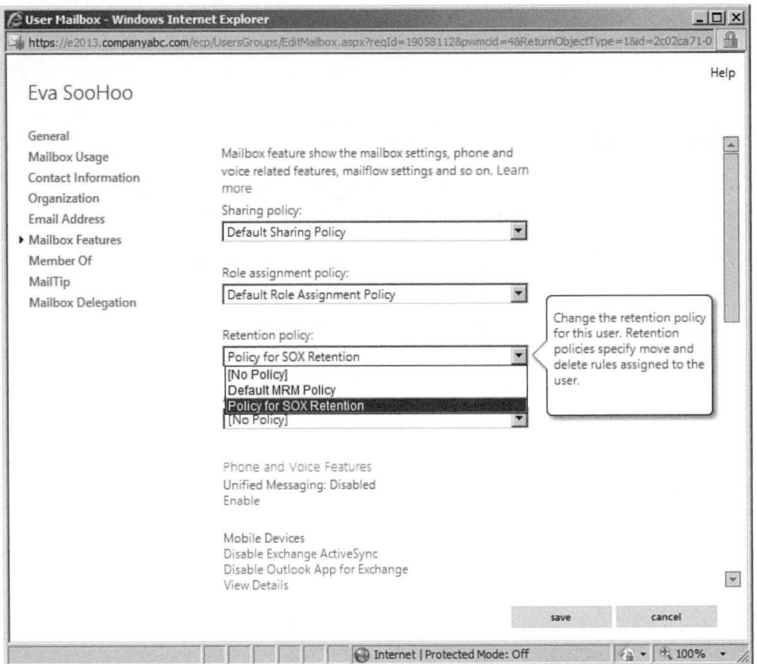

FIGURE 10.5 Applying a mailbox policy to a user's mailbox.

Utilizing Rights Management Services for Policy Enforcement

Another method of enforcing security policies to messages in Exchange is to leverage Microsoft's Active Directory Rights Management Services, or RMS. RMS provides the organization the ability to encrypt email messages and apply policies that limit who has access to the email, who can open an email, limit an email from being forwarded to unauthorized recipients, and expire an email along with several other policy-based message options.

How RMS Works

RMS is a Windows Server role that is installed on a server in an Active Directory environment. RMS utilizes Active Directory for username and password identification. In an environment where RMS has been installed, when a user is added to Active Directory, the user has an RMS account to immediately begin encrypting and protecting Exchange emails, Microsoft Word documents, Excel spreadsheets, and the like. When the user is terminated and his or her Active Directory account is disabled or deleted, the user no longer has access to any of his or her RMS-encrypted documents.

RMS can be configured for just internal users of Active Directory, or external users can participate in RMS-encrypted content access and sharing. There are several methods for noninternal users to access RMS documents, which includes providing the external user an Active Directory account, federating Active Directories together so that two (or more) organizations can share RMS content between one another, or there are services from companies (including Microsoft LiveID, Gigatrust, and others) where external individuals can subscribe to a service that interconnects with an organization so that the organization and the external user can interchange RMS-protected content.

In addition, although Microsoft provides "in-the-box" support for RMS-encrypted content in Office 2007 and above for Office documents, there are several third-party organizations that provide plug-ins to Windows, Apple iPhones, BlackBerry devices, and others to support RMS policies for non-Microsoft content (like Adobe Acrobat PDF files, AutoCAD drawing documents, JPG or TIF graphic files, MP3 and WMV audio and video content) as well as access to non-Windows-based endpoint devices.

Installing RMS in Active Directory

As noted previously, RMS is a Windows Server role that is installed on a server that will be called the RMS policy server. RMS has been supported since Windows Server 2003 and an organization can install the RMS role on an old Windows Server 2003 server; however, as an application server role, an organization can install RMS on the latest Windows Server 2012 server that is a member of an older Active Directory 2003, 2008, or 2008 R2 environment. Because Microsoft has added incremental features and functionality to RMS in more current versions of Windows, it is recommended to install the RMS role on the latest Windows server available, even if the organization's Active Directory is not necessarily the latest release of AD.

The RMS server role can be installed on existing servers, so for a small business, the RMS could be installed on a domain controller, a file server, or other utility server. When the organization has over 250 users that will be using the RMS server for content encryption and data protection, the organization should consider installing the RMS server role for the policy server on a member server of the domain that is not shared by other server services. This will help the organization add additional RMS servers, cluster the RMS server role for higher availability, and/or modify and update the server role without being tied to other server role functions installed on a system.

Assuming the organization is installing RMS on Windows Server 2012, from a member server of the domain, do the following:

1. Log on to the server that will become the RMS policy server with a domain administrator account.
2. From Windows Server 2012 Server Manager, click Manage in the upper-right side of the console, and select Add Roles and Features.
3. After the Add Roles Wizard loads, click Next to continue past the Welcome screen.
4. On the Select Installation Type page, select Role-based or Feature-based Installation, and then click Next.

5. On the Select Destination Server page, choose Select a Server from the Server Pool, which should have highlighted the server you are on, and then click Next.
6. On the Select Server Roles page, select the Active Directory Rights Management Services role, click Add Features to add the required features, and then click Next.
7. On the Select Features page, just click Next as you are not adding any new features beyond the RMS role and features.
8. On the Active Directory Rights Management Services Installation Welcome page, click Next.
9. When prompted to select role services, choose the default Active Directory Rights Management Server, and then click Next.
10. For the Web Services Roles (IIS) Welcome page, click Next.
11. For the Web Services Role Services page, click Next to choose the defaults.
12. On the Confirmation Installation Selections page, click Install.
13. Click Close when the Installation Wizard has completed.

NOTE

During any point of the installation where RMS fails to install with an error like "Attempt to configure Active Directory Rights Management Server failed" or "target of an invocation" or the like and you know no one is using RMS or have protected any content previously with RMS, many times an uninstall of RMS is required. Many organizations find when installing RMS that "someone" long ago tried to install RMS and some of the components still existing in the environment, specifically the Service Control Point (SCP), prevent RMS from being installed again. If an existing RMS installation exists, running an uninstall of that RMS installation will remove the server. Or in many cases, the RMS server does not exist anymore, just the SCP. To remove the SCP, install the RMS Toolkit that can be downloaded off the Internet (typically a 2006/2007 Service Pack 2 (SP2) release of the kit is the most current version of the kit). Run the `ADScpRegister unregisterSCP` that is in the ADSCPREGISTER folder installed with the toolkit. Once the SCP has been unregistered, proceed with installing RMS again. This SCP Unregister should be run if you need to uninstall RMS and reinstall RMS during your setup process.

Once the RMS role has been installed on the server, the next step is to configure the role service. In Service Manager (in Windows Server 2012) a yellow warning triangle appears on the Task Details option and by clicking on the warning, you will be prompted to choose to "Perform Additional Configuration," as shown in Figure 10.6.

By clicking the Perform Additional Configuration option, the AD RMS configuration will begin. In that wizard, perform the following steps:

1. At the RMS Configuration Welcome page, click Next.
2. When prompted to Create or Join an AD RMS Cluster, if this is the first RMS server, then you would choose Create a New Cluster, and then click Next.

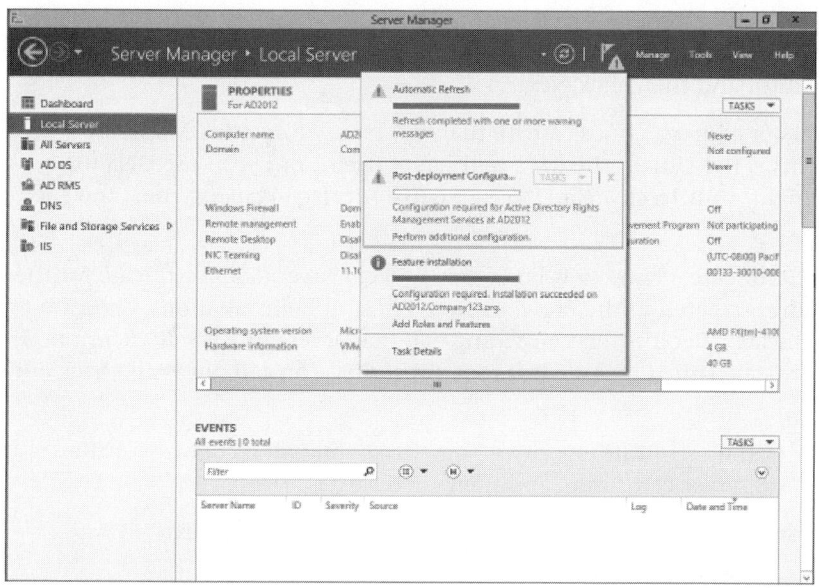

FIGURE 10.6 Notification to perform additional configuration tasks for the RMS installation.

NOTE

Even if you only plan to have one RMS server, they still call it an RMS cluster. It'll just be a single-node cluster. The good thing is if you want to add additional RMS nodes for high availability of RMS or if you have a lot of employees and need the scalability for more nodes, you can simply follow the steps to install a new RMS server, and then "join" the existing RMS cluster to add more nodes.

3. For the Configuration Database, if this is the only RMS server in your environment, choose User Windows Internal Database on This Server and click Next and it will install a local copy of SQL Express on the RMS server. If you choose to use an existing SQL server or you plan to have more than one RMS policy server, then choose the Specify a Database Server and a Database Instance (and enter in the information about the external SQL server you intend to use), and then click Next.

4. For the Service Account for RMS, enter in an unprivileged account (such as creating a simple user account in AD Users and Computers like "RMSAdmin" and using that account), and then click Next.

5. For Cryptographic Mode, choose Cryptographic Mode 2, and click Next.

6. For Cluster Key Storage, choose Use AD RMS Centrally Managed Key Storage unless you have a centralized cryptographic service provider, which you can then choose to store the key in your existing CSP. Click Next.

7. For the Cluster Key Password, enter in a password for your cluster, and then click Next.

8. For the RMS Cluster Website, choose a website that will be used as the main uniform resource locator (URL) for the RMS cluster (if this is just a single local RMS server, choose the default), and then click Next.
9. For the RMS cluster address, choose a URL that will be used for the RMS website (many times, this is the URL of the RMS web server itself), or if you use DNS for naming, you might want to create a DNS name like rms.{*yourdomain*}.com, and then click Next.
10. For the Server Certificate, choose a valid Secure Sockets Layer (SSL) certificate for the RMS cluster address created in the previous step. For simple installations, choose a self-signed certificate. If you will be providing external access to RMS, then you need to choose a certificate issued by a trusted root authority. You can always go back and add a certificate later. Click Next.
11. For the licensor of the certificate, specify a name that you will recognize for the backup of the RMS server certificate, and then click Next.
12. For SCP Registration, choose Register the SCP Now and then click Next.
13. Review the settings and click Install.
14. When the wizard completes, click Close.

NOTE

After installing the RMS role, while the server frequently will not prompt you to reboot the system, many times the policies and services are not working properly after installation; a reboot of the new RMS server will help make sure RMS is working after installation.

Testing RMS in Microsoft Word

When RMS has been installed in the environment, before creating policies and transport rules, a quick test of RMS will confirm that it is working. A quick way to validate whether RMS is working is to run a copy of Microsoft Word and see if you can manually apply an RMS policy to a document.

To manually apply a policy, do the following:

1. On the system you want to test RMS (e.g., a workstation, laptop, client system), log on as a user of the domain.
2. Go into Internet Explorer and add the URL of the RMS Cluster Address in the previous section to the Trusted Sites list. As an example, in Internet Explorer, choose Tools, Internet Options, Security, Trusted Sites, click Sites, under Add This Website to This Zone, add the URL of your RMS cluster (like https://rms.companyabc.com), click Add, click Close, and then click OK.
3. Launch Microsoft Word, and in Word 2010 or Word 2013, click File, Info, Protect Document, Restrict Permission by People, and choose Restricted Access.

4. If prompted, select Use a Microsoft Windows Account and then click OK.

5. When prompted for your username/password, enter in the username and password of the domain user that you logged on to the system.

NOTE

It is recommended that you enter RMS credentials to open or secure a document as the same credentials used to log on to the system so that the pairing of content access and logon are matched. When you log on with one logon name and open documents with another user account, the results are confusing and sometimes just don't work properly.

6. Select the Restrict Permission to This Document check box.

NOTE

If you've gotten to this point where the "Restrict Permission to This Document" shows up, that means your system has successfully communicated with the RMS server. You can fiddle with RMS policies to understand the options you have in locking down documents to View Only, Edit, Print, Expire, and so on. All of these settings can be set in a policy in the next section and applied in a more automated manner than having to click through all of the document option settings one by one.

7. When choosing recipients for document restrictions, enter the email addresses of individuals you want to only read or have the ability to read and change documents, similar to what is shown in Figure 10.7. Click the More Options button to choose other options, such as limit printing, setting expiration date on the content, and so on.

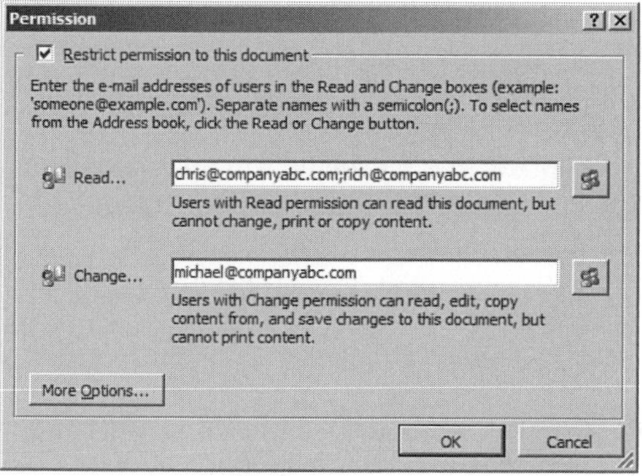

FIGURE 10.7 Choosing users who have access to read or change a document using RMS protection.

8. Click OK to apply the settings to the document.

Once the RMS document settings have been associated to a document, the document can be saved like a normal document, attached to an email, saved to a hard drive, saved to a USB thumb drive, or posted on a public document share site, and the only people who can open or modify the document are the individuals who have been given explicit rights to access and/or modify the document.

Creating an RMS Policy

Once you know that the RMS server is working and you can manually RMS protect a document, rather than having to manually apply permissions for each and every document each and every time, RMS provides the ability to create templates. A template predefines who has access to documents, the expiration of the document, whether the document can be read or read and written, and the like. By creating a template, a user simply selects a template when applying a policy, and all of the properties of the template are applied to the document. A common template is one where a document cannot be edited and is only accessible by authenticated users within the organization. An RMS policy of this type limits external users from accessing the content, and it ensures that the document remains in a form that is not modified.

To create an RMS policy, an administrator needs to create an RMS template. To create a template, the administrator does the following:

1. Log on to the RMS policy server with administrator rights to access the RMS administrator console.
2. From Server Manager (in the Tools pull-down), from the Start button (in Administrative Tools), from the Metro menu (in Administrative Tools), launch the Active Directory Rights Management Services administration tool.
3. If this is the first time you are running the RMS administration tool, you will be prompted to connect to your RMS cluster; otherwise, you will automatically be connected to your default RMS cluster. When in the RMS administration tool, click to expand the navigation tree.
4. Click the Rights Policy Templates container.
5. If this is the first time creating a policy template, first set the default template file location where templates will be stored. Do so by clicking the Change Distributed Rights Policy Templates File Location. Click Enable Export. Under Specify Templates File Location (UNC), type in a share name that users will have access to RMS templates (such as `\\RMSserver\templates`), and then click OK.
6. Click Create Distributed Rights Policy Template.
7. For Template Identification Information, click Add and choose the language(s) your RMS templates will support. This might include English. Click Add. Add additional languages if your documents include other languages. In addition, for name, this is important, enter in a name that describes this policy (might be "`ReadOnlyDocs`" or "`DeletesAfter3Days`" or "`ForCxOsOnly`"). Provide a description for the policy so that

when someone hovers over the policy, the description will provide more details. This configuration looks something similar to Figure 10.8. Click Next.

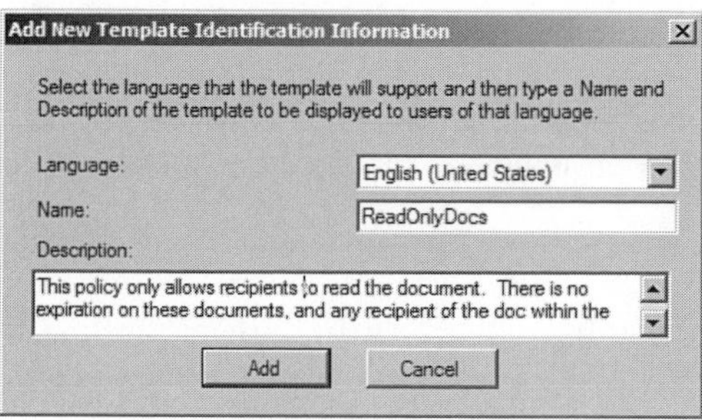

FIGURE 10.8 Creating and defining an RMS template.

8. For User Rights, choose what rights you want this template to support that includes specific users, group of users, or anyone as well as choose the file access privileges you want supported such as View, Edit, Save, and so on. Click Next.
9. For Expiration Policy, choose whether you want the policy to protect the document with no expiration, to expire on a specific date and time, or to expire after a specific number of days after the policy is applied to the document, and then click Next.
10. For Extended Policy, choose whether you want users to view the document through a browser add-in (which limits the users from not being able to download and store the document, but instead only view the document from a secured Web browser). In addition, choose whether you want the user to have to directly authenticate with the RMS security server every time he or she wants to access the document (meaning credential caching is disabled), and then click Next.
11. For Revocation Policy, choose whether you want to have the user automatically validate whether his or her credentials have been revoked to access the document content, and then click Finish.

Repeat the process of creating policies that meet the protection needs of the organization.

Pushing Templates Out to Users Through AD Group Policy

After policy templates have been created, the organization needs to push the templates out to users so that when they are in Word, Excel, Outlook, and so on, the users see the policy templates created and can choose one of the policies. Policies are pushed out by Microsoft Active Directory Group Policies by doing the following:

1. On a server in the domain, launch an Internet browser and search and download the Office ADM template file (a search under Microsoft ADM Group Policy download will usually net the download desire). Assuming you are running a 64-bit server, if prompted to download either the 32-bit or 64-bit version of the files, choose the

64-bit version. Run the downloaded file to expand out the ADM/ADMX file that will be used in a couple steps, and save the files to something like `c:\templates`.

NOTE

If you have multiple versions of Office (e.g., Office 2007, Office 2010, Office 2013), then you need to download the ADM/ADMX template files for all of the versions of Office. To support all of the versions of Office you have in your environment, make sure to install each of the corresponding ADM/ADMX files.

2. Repeat this process for all versions of Office you have (2007, 2010, 2013).
3. On a server in the domain, run the Group Policy Management Console.
4. Choose a policy such as the Default Domain Policy or create a new group policy and edit the policy to push RMS templates to users.
5. Expand the Computer Configuration, Policies and get to Administrative Templates.
6. Right-click the Administrative Templates and choose Add/Remove Templates.
7. Click Add and choose the directory where you downloaded and expanded the ADM template files you downloaded.
8. Select the files ending in .ADM for Active Directory 2003. Select the files ending in .ADMX for Active Directory 2008 or higher. Click Open, then click Add. Click Close.
9. In the Group Policy Management Console, click to expand the User Configuration, Policies, Administrative Templates, and click to expand the Microsoft Office 2013 folder (repeat this with Office 2007 and Office 2010 if in use).
10. Click the Managed Restricted Permissions folder.
11. Double-click the Specify Permission Path.
12. Click Enable, and for Enter Path to Policy Templates for Content Permission, specify the UNC of the templates folder created when configuring the RMS server (in my example, **`\\rms.companyabc.com\rmstemplates`**). This is all shown in Figure 10.9.
13. Click OK.

NOTE

To have the policy applied to end-user systems so they can see the templates, the group policy needs to be “pushed” to each domain attached system. The way policies are applied are either the endpoint system needs to be rebooted, the user needs to log out and log in to the system, 90 minutes needs to pass, or the end user needs to run `GPUpdate /Force` to have the policy applied.

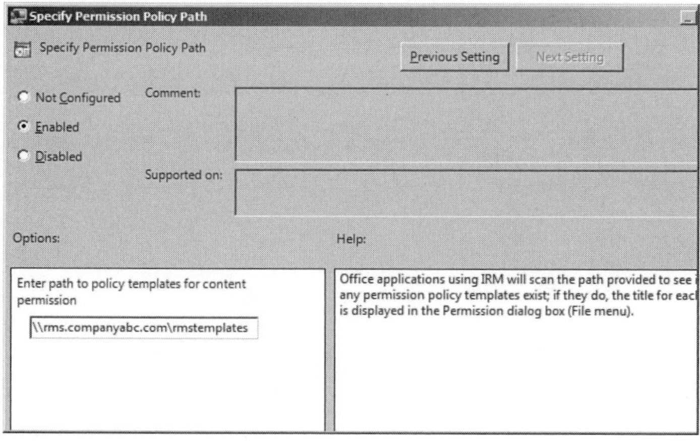

FIGURE 10.9 Enabling RMS policy distribution in group policies.

Applying an RMS Policy to Microsoft Office Content

After policy templates have been created, now instead of a user having to go through and click through all of the various options of protection for a document (View, Edit, Print, expiration, and so on), the user can just choose a policy and apply the policy directly to the document with all of the details of the policy applied to the document.

To apply a policy to Microsoft Office content, do the following:

1. Open Microsoft Outlook.
2. To protect an email message from being forwarded (as an example), as you are in the email message, click File, Info, Set Permissions, then click Do Not Forward.

NOTE

When a Do Not Forward policy is applied to an email, the sender will see a MailTip on the top of the email that'll note "Do Not Forward—Recipients Can Read This Message but Cannot Forward, Print, or Copy Content...." This will provide a warning or notification that an RMS policy has been applied to the message. This message is shown in Figure 10.10.

3. To apply an RMS policy to a Word document (or Excel spreadsheet or PowerPoint presentation document), open, for example, Microsoft Word.
4. Click File, Info, Protect Document, Restrict Permission by People.
5. Choose the RMS policy you want to apply to the message; you will now see policies that you had created and pushed out as part of the RMS templates, as well as the Active Directory group policy, as shown in Figure 10.11.

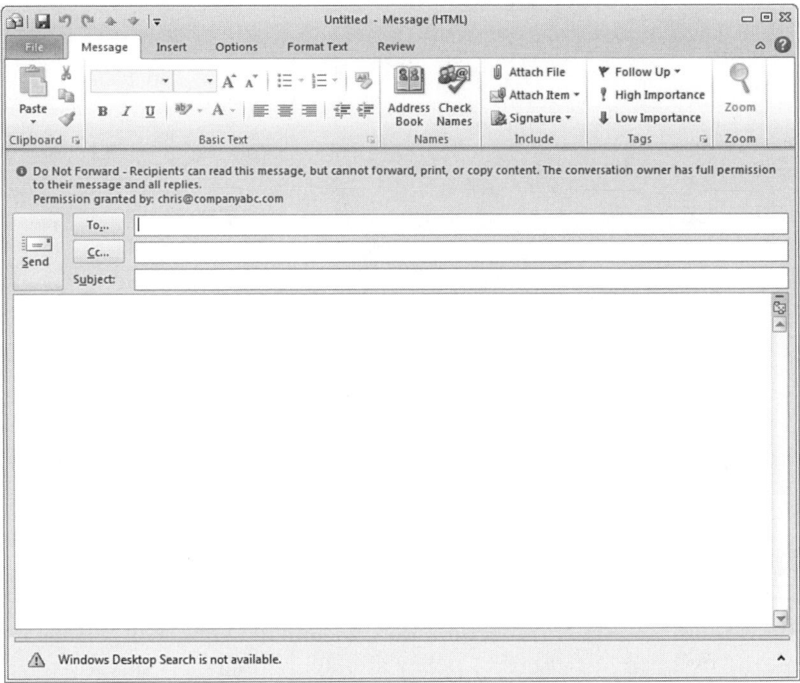

FIGURE 10.10 Sample Do Not Forward message applied in Outlook from an RMS template.

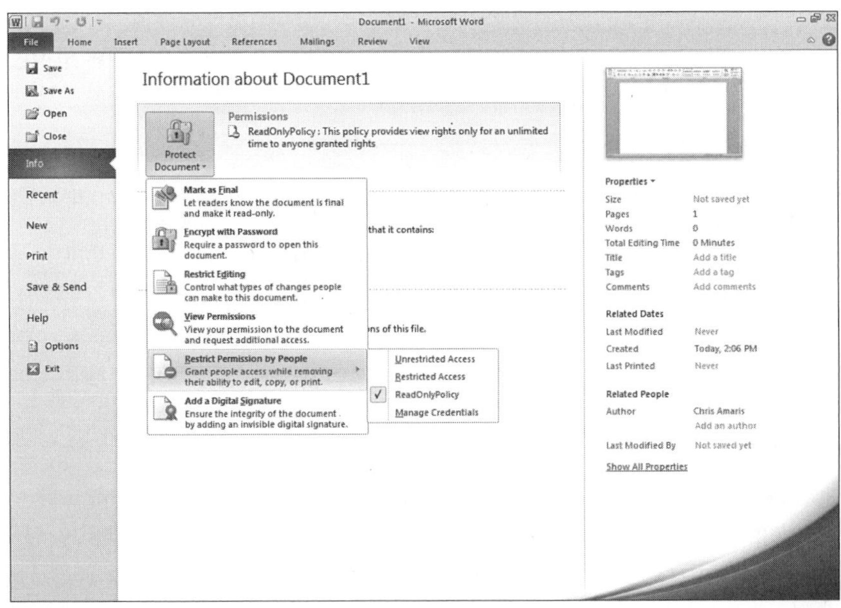

FIGURE 10.11 Seeing RMS templates and choosing the template to apply to this document.

6. Continue with writing the email or document as desired, and save and/or send the document or message as normal; however, the contents will be protected based on the policies devices in the RMS template.

Applying an RMS Policy to Messages in Transit in Exchange

Getting back to creating simplicity in security policies, as much as RMS can be used to manually apply policies to restrict access, or templates can be created and then pushed out to users to choose a policy to apply to content, an even easier process is to have content assessed by the Exchange server and an RMS policy applied to the content in transfer. This is done through Hub Transport policies in conjunction with RMS templates and allows for content to be assessed automatically by Exchange with RMS policies applied when a trigger is enacted for the message.

To integrate RMS into an Exchange Server 2013 environment, certain server configurations need to be done to grant rights and access between the two systems. For server configurations, perform the following steps:

1. On the RMS Server, open Windows Explorer and go to the `\Inetpub\wwwroot\_wmcs\certification` directory.
2. Right-click the `ServerCertification.asmx` file and select Properties.
3. Click the Security tab; by default, only the local SYSTEM account has rights to this certification file. You need to ensure Exchange servers and administrators have security rights.
4. Click Edit, then click Add, and add Exchange Servers as well as the RMS administrator that you define when installing RMS. Give them the default Read & Execute and the Read permissions, as shown in Figure 10.12. Click OK, and then click OK again to save the changes.
5. On the Exchange server, open the Exchange Management Shell and run the command `New-DistributionGroup "RMS_Super_Users"`.
6. Then in EMS, run the command `add-DistributionGroupMember -Member FederatedEamil* -Identity RMS_Super_Users`.
7. On the RMS server, in the Active Directory Rights Management Services console, expand the Security Policies into the Super Users option. Click Super Users and then click Enable Super Users.
8. For the Super Users option, you need to name the Super User Group you want to be a super user (which was created in the previous steps on Exchange). Click Change Super User Group.
9. For the Super User Group, click Browse. Choose RMS_Super_Users, click OK, and then click OK again.
10. Back on the Exchange server in EMS, run the command `set-IRMConfiguration -InternalLicensingEnabled:$true`.

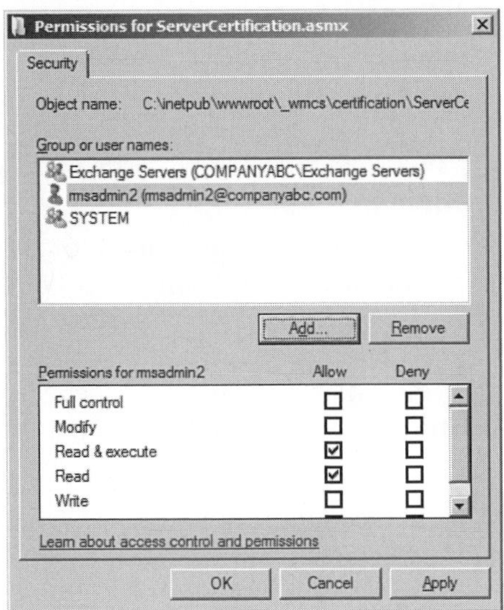

FIGURE 10.12 Giving Exchange Servers and the RMS administrator permissions for RMS management.

All the previous steps will get Exchange and RMS working together so that templates created in RMS are available as Transport Policy templates in Exchange.

NOTE

After completing the preceding steps, it might take upward of 24 hours to complete the connection between RMS and Exchange; however, real-world experience in a typical environment is just a few minutes. The key to test whether the RMS and Exchange integration is working is to view whether RMS templates show up in transport policies in the following set of steps. If your RMS policies do not show up, check and confirm configuration settings are set as noted and wait a little longer.

With RMS templates created and the integration between Exchange and RMS complete, the next step is to set transport policies that automatically apply an RMS policy to a message in transit if a rule is triggered. To create the in-transit policy management, do the following:

1. From the Exchange Administration Center (https://{*servername*}/ecp), click Mail Flow, Rules.
2. On the Rules page, click the + button to create a new rule.
3. From the New Rule page, click More Options at the bottom of the page to expand the RMS options within the pull-downs.
4. For Name of Rule, enter a descriptive name for the rule (like **`RMS Encrypt ProjectX Info`**).

5. In the Apply This Rule If pull-down option, select which conditions the rule will operate under. This may vary based on the rule you are building, but frequently it is If the Subject or Body Includes and enter in keywords like `ProjectX`, or `Project Confidential`, or the like. Alternatively, the message may be "If the Message Contains Sensitive Information..." where one of the built-in regulatory keywords are found.
6. In the Do the Following pull-down option, select the action Apply Rights Protection to the Message With and choose a policy that is an appropriate action, such as Do Not Forward or Encrypt and Set 1-Day Expiration or the like.
7. If you want to enter in Exceptions or start the rule on a specific date, choose the actions desired.
8. Review the settings, similar to what is shown in Figure 10.13.

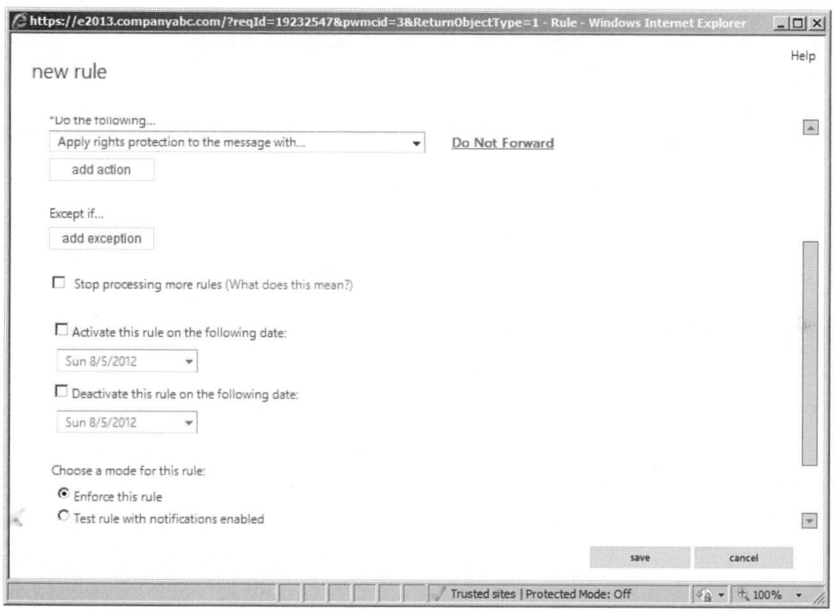

FIGURE 10.13 Creating an RMS in-transit rule.

9. Click Save to save the policy.

Testing an RMS In-Transit Policy

To test an RMS in-transit policy, simply create an email that would trigger the policy such as putting the word *ProjectX* in an email or the key phase "Confidential Do Not Forward." Do the following:

1. Open Microsoft Outlook.
2. Create an email message, but do not choose to manually protect the message with RMS.
3. Make sure a keyword is in the email that will trigger the in-transit rule to work.
4. Send the message.

NOTE

If the rule doesn't work as expected, work backward to determine where the problem resides. Create a message, manually apply the rule to the message, and confirm that the rule applies.

Exchange Server 2013 Client-Level Security Enhancements

As mentioned earlier, Exchange Server 2013 continues to add security features to enhance Exchange in protecting the integrity of messaging communications—especially when combined with Outlook 2010 and Outlook 2013. Some of these features include the following:

- **Minimizing junk email**—The Junk E-mail folder, first introduced in Outlook 2003, helps protect users from junk email. Utilizing the Outlook 2010/2013 Junk E-mail filter, Outlook can disable threatening links and warn you about possibly malicious content within an email message.
- **Antiphishing methods**—Exchange Server 2013 acts as the first scan on incoming email and works to determine the legitimacy of the message. If applicable, Exchange Server 2013 can disable links or URLs present in the message to help protect users.
- **Information Rights Management (IRM)**—Exchange Server 2013 can help control the distribution of corporate data by preventing recipients from forwarding, copying, or printing confidential email messages. In addition, expiration dates can be applied to messages, after which they cannot be viewed or acted upon. IRM functionality is based on AD RMS in Windows Server 2012, 2008 R2, and 2008.
- **Managed email folders**—Exchange Server 2013 helps organizations maintain compliance by applying a new approach to document retention. Utilizing managed email folders, users can see and interact with their messages in Outlook just as they would using regular mail folders, but the managed email folder applies retention, archive, and expiration policies defined by the administrator. Utilizing managed email folders, users and administrators can comply with regulations set by corporate policy or by external agencies.

In addition, Exchange Server 2013 continues to support several security technologies that were present in Exchange Server 2003, including the following:

- Support for MAPI (RPC) over HTTP or HTTPS, known as Outlook Anywhere, can be configured to use either SSL or NT LAN Manager (NTLM)–based authentication.
- Support for authentication methods, such as Kerberos and NTLM.
- Antispam features such as safe and block lists, as well as advanced filtering mechanisms to help minimize the number of unwanted emails that reach the end user.
- Protection against web beaconing, which is used by advertisers and spammers to verify email addresses and determine whether emails have been read.
- Attachment blocking by Exchange Server 2013 before it reaches the intended recipient.
- Rights management support, which prevents unauthorized users from intercepting emails.

Protecting Against Spam

Unsolicited email messages are often referred to as spam. These usually unwanted and often offensive messages are utilized as cheap advertising for unscrupulous organizations. In the past several years, the increase in spam traffic has surpassed even the most liberal estimates, and many studies have found that spam traffic accounts for up to 85%–90% of the messaging traffic on the Internet today.

Spam does not just affect your patience and productivity; it affects companies, Internet service providers, and anyone else who is hosting messaging services. The battle against spam is just beginning, and legal battles are well under way against both known spammers and companies that host the messaging services. In some cases, employees are suing employers on grounds that the employer has not taken adequate steps to protect them from offensive materials.

Exchange Server 2013 Antispam Features

Spammers are becoming increasingly more creative and cunning, frequently changing their email addresses, domain names, content, and more to get past a company's protective measures.

Microsoft has provided at least some basic form of antispam technologies in Exchange Server since version 5.5 and Outlook 98. For example, junk mail filters were provided to help identify messages that had either offensive material or other keywords indicating the message was spam. This form of spam prevention placed most, if not all, of the responsibility on the end user to block unwanted email messages.

Exchange Server 2013, when combined with Microsoft Outlook, provides several methods of reducing unwanted spam messages:

- Increase protection through integrated security technologies
- Improved email legitimacy assurance
- Distribution lists restricted to authenticated users
- Connection filtering
- Reputation service
- Outlook Junk E-mail filter lists aggregation

Protecting Against Web Beaconing

A common and very popular format for email messages is Hypertext Markup Language, or HTML. This format is popular because of the rich content that can be presented, including graphics, images, font formatting, and more. However, HTML-based messages can also present security problems and annoyances because of the ability to hide various codes and images within the message.

One such security problem is called web beaconing. Web beaconing is a term used to describe the method of retrieving valid email addresses and information on whether a recipient has opened a message. Advertisers, spammers, and the like utilize web beaconing to help them become more profitable and improve audience targeting. For instance, when an unsuspecting user opens an email message that contains a web beacon, the user's email address and possibly other information is sent to the solicitor, notifying the solicitor that he or she (a) has reached a valid recipient and (b) has reached a recipient who is willing to open the message before deleting it. The user is oblivious that his or her personal information has been given.

Microsoft Outlook can be used to block web beacons and, consequently, prevent the user's email address from ending up in the wrong hands. By default, if Outlook suspects that the content of a message could be used as a web beacon, it presents a pop-up window warning users that links to images, multimedia, or other external content have been blocked to help protect their privacy. The text content of the email message is viewable by the user, and the user is then presented with an option to unblock the content. This enables the user to make a conscious decision of whether to display all the contents of the message.

To change the default settings for automatic downloading of content in Microsoft Outlook, do the following:

1. Select File, Options, Trust Center, Trust Center Settings.
2. Click the Automatic Download tab. Select the desired settings from the available options. By default, all options are selected.

NOTE

If Automatic Picture Download is turned off, messages from or to email addresses or domain names on the Safe Senders and Safe Recipients lists are treated as exceptions and the blocked content is downloaded. Safe Senders and Safe Recipients lists are discussed in more depth later in this chapter.

Filtering Junk Mail

As mentioned earlier, junk mail filtering has been available in earlier versions of Exchange Server and Outlook. This feature has been improved with each new revision and is useful in minimizing the need for end users to configure junk mail filtering options. In fact, junk mail filtering is primarily controlled by Exchange Server administrators. However, some options can be configured by the users. With junk mail filtering, many unwanted messages can be segregated and set aside before they reach the user's Inbox.

Microsoft Outlook 2013 gives you the ability to change the level of protection provided by your Junk E-mail filter. On the Home tab in Outlook 2013 by clicking on Junk Mail Options, the user has a series of Junk Mail filter options.

Microsoft Outlook provides the following junk email protection options:

- **No Automatic Filtering**—Although the Junk E-mail filter does not perform any filtering on incoming mail, messages sent from the Blocked Senders list is still moved to the Junk E-mail folder.
- **Low (the default setting)**—Safe and block lists are consulted with this level of protection, but Outlook also searches for keywords and phrases in the message's subject and body.
- **High**—On this setting, the most aggressive filtering is performed. Although you can increase the amount of junk email captured by using this setting, there is the possibility of false positives, which can result in valid messages being mistakenly filtered out.
- **Safe Lists Only**—This setting is the most restrictive because it allows only messages from preapproved senders to be delivered to the Inbox.

Microsoft Outlook also offers you the additional option to Permanently Delete Suspected Junk E-Mail Instead of Moving It to the Junk E-Mail Folder. You should hesitate before using this option because you lose the ability to review the Junk E-mail folder to look for missing messages.

Outlook also gives you the following options to battle email phishing attacks:

- **Disable Links and Other Functionality in Phishing Messages (Recommended)**—Using this option disables links, the Reply feature, and the Reply All feature on suspected phishing email messages.

- **Warn Me About Suspicious Domain Names in E-Mail Addresses (Recommended)**—Using this option warns you when a message comes from a domain name (for example, @mlcrosoft.com) that uses certain characters to make it appear to be a well-known domain.

Filtering with Safe and Blocked Senders

Outlook allows users to create and manage their own Safe Senders and Blocked Senders. As the name implies, the Safe Senders list is made up of user-defined addresses or domains, and messages from these addresses or domains will never be treated as junk email. Conversely, the Blocked Senders list is made up of user-defined email addresses or domain names, and all messages from them will automatically be treated as junk email.

In addition, Outlook provides the option to configure a Safe Recipients list. This option is useful when you are a member of an emailing list or group. By adding the list or group to your Safe Recipients list, any messages sent to the email addresses or domain names on that list will not be treated as junk email messages, regardless of the sender.

Outlook also allows you the option to automatically treat anyone in your Outlook Contacts list as a Safe Sender. This option is enabled on the Safe Senders tab by selecting the Also Trust E-Mail from My Contacts check box. By default, this feature is enabled.

In addition, if there are people who are not in your Contacts list, but with whom you regularly correspond, you can select to Automatically Add People I E-Mail to the Safe Senders List. This option is also found on the Safe Senders tab.

To quickly add a sender, domain name, or mailing list to one of these lists, you can right-click the message, select Junk E-Mail, and choose the desired option.

Blocking Read Receipts

Microsoft Outlook enables users to request read receipts for the messages that they send. Read receipts tell the sender that the intended recipient has at least opened the email. Automatically sending these read receipts can offer spammers (or others) more insight into your mail reading habits than you might want to share.

By default, Outlook blocks the automatic sending of read receipts. Instead, the recipient is prompted with a message that asks him if he wants to send a response.

If you want, you can change this setting to Always Send a Response, or Never Send a Response. To change this behavior, do the following:

1. In Outlook, select File, Options, Mail.
2. On the Tracking section, you can select your desired setting relative to delivering a read receipt or not, and then click OK to save and exit the configuration.

Securing Outlook Web App

Outlook Web App (OWA) provides the interface for users to access their mail across the Internet utilizing a web browser. Over the years, Microsoft improved the OWA client until it was almost as powerful as the actual Microsoft Outlook client.

With OWA 2010 and OWA 2013, Microsoft has continued this trend, providing an improved user experience and enhanced security over previous versions.

Some of the security-related features in OWA include the following:

- Stripping of web beacons, referrals, and other potentially harmful content from messages
- Attachment blocking
- OWA forms-based (cookie) authentication
- Session inactivity timeout
- OWA infrastructure using IPSec and Kerberos
- Safe and block lists

There are a number of additional improvements in Outlook Web App to continue to improve security. These include the following:

- **Improved logon screen**—In OWA, when you connect from a trusted machine, your previous "private" selection (and your username) is remembered on subsequent connections.
- **Junk email management**—OWA has improved the capabilities of the Junk E-mail filter by allowing users to manage their junk email settings from within OWA.
- **Protection from harmful content**—If an OWA user clicks a link that is embedded in an email message, and the link uses a protocol that is not recognized by OWA, the link is blocked, and the user receives a warning stating "Outlook Web App has disabled this link for your protection."

Supported Authentication Methods

Client Access servers in Exchange Server 2010 and 2013 support more authentication methods than previous versions of Exchange servers did.

The following types of authentication are allowed:

- **Standard**—Standard authentication methods include Integrated Windows authentication, Digest authentication, and Basic authentication.
- **Forms-based authentication**—Using forms-based authentication creates a logon page for OWA. Forms-based authentication uses cookies to store user logon credentials and password information in an encrypted state.

- **Microsoft Threat Management Gateway (TMG) Server forms-based authentication**—By using TMG Server, administrators can securely publish OWA servers by using Mailbox server publishing rules. ISA Server also allows administrators to configure forms-based authentication and control email attachment availability.
- **Smart card and certificate authentication**—Certificates can reside on either a client computer or on a smart card. By utilizing certificate authentication, Extensible Authentication Protocol (EAP) and Transport Layer Security (TLS) protocols are used, providing a two-way authentication method where both the client and server prove their identities to each other.

Table 10.1 shows a comparison of authentication methods along with the security level provided relative to password transmission and client requirements.

TABLE 10.1 Authentication Methods for OWA Logon Options

Authentication Method	Security Level Provided	How Passwords Are Sent	Client Requirements
Basic authentication	Low (unless SSL is enabled)	Base 64-encoded clear text.	All browsers support Basic authentication.
Digest authentication	Medium	Hashed by using MD5.	Microsoft Internet Explorer 5 or later versions.
Integrated Windows authentication	Low (unless SSL is enabled)	Hashed when Integrated Windows authentication is used; Kerberos ticket Integrated Windows authentication includes the Kerberos and NTLM authentication methods.	Internet Explorer 2.0 or later versions for Integrated Windows authentication. Microsoft Windows 2000 Server or later versions with Internet Explorer 5 or later versions for Kerberos.
Forms-based authentication	High	Encrypts user authentication information and stores it in a cookie.	Forms-based authentication is now supported in Internet Explorer, Mozilla Firefox, Apple's Safari, and other browsers.

NOTE

When multiple methods of authentication are configured, Internet Information Services (IIS) uses the most restrictive method first. IIS then searches the list of available authentication protocols (starting with the most restrictive), until an authentication method that is supported by both the client and the server is found.

Disabling Web Beacons for Outlook Web App

As previously mentioned in this chapter, web beaconing is a method used to retrieve valid email addresses and recipient information. Web beaconing is often used by unscrupulous advertisers and spammers to improve the accuracy and effectiveness of their spamming campaigns.

Exchange Server 2013 allows the disabling of web beacons for OWA. Administrators can use the Exchange Management Shell to define the type of filtering that is used for web beacon content and enforce it for all users.

To use the Exchange Management Shell to configure web beacon filtering settings, perform the following command from the shell:

```
Set-OwaVirtualDirectory -identity "SERVERNAME\Owa (Default Web Site)"
-FilterWebBeaconsAndHtmlForms ForceFilter
```

This command configures the filtration of web beacon content in the Outlook virtual directory named OWA in the default IIS website. Possible values for the `FilterWebBeaconsandHtmlforms` setting are as follows:

- **`UserFilterChoice`**—Prompts the user to allow or block web beacons
- **`ForceFilter`**—Blocks all web beacons
- **`DisableFilter`**—Allows web beacons

Using Safe and Block Lists

OWA 2013 users can manage their Junk E-mail settings from within OWA. Users can enable or disable junk email filtering, create and maintain Safe Senders, Blocked Senders, and Safe Recipient lists, enter email domains or Simple Mail Transfer Protocol (SMTP) addresses, and elect to trust email from their contacts.

NOTE

The option to "always trust contacts" does not function if the user has more than 1,024 contacts. Although this limitation will not be reached for most users, those with an exceptionally large number of contacts should be aware of the limitation.

To access the Junk E-Mail settings in OWA, select Options from the upper-right corner of the screen, and then select Junk E-Mail on the left side of the page.

Summary

Organizations today are subject to any number of strict governmental and industry regulations in regard to messaging retention, email security, and policy enforcement. Fortunately, Exchange Server 2013 has unprecedented levels of policy enforcement built in to the application, helping organizations to become compliant with these regulations and positioning them to better control their messaging environment going forward.

Best Practices

The following are best practices from this chapter:

- Establish Messaging Records Management policies to control mailbox retention in Exchange Server 2013.
- Fully understand the implications of the various governmental regulations that apply to your organization, such as HIPAA, SOX, GLBA, and others.
- Use transport agents to control email traffic with well-defined policies. This includes Edge Transport server role transport agents and Hub Transport service on the Mailbox server role transport agents.
- Use Premium journaling when you are licensed with Enterprise Server CALs and when the need for journaling on individual mailboxes is required.
- Customize baseline security templates to reduce the attack surface of workstations and servers. However, implement adequate testing to ensure that required applications function as intended.
- Keep servers and client computers up to date with the latest service pack and security updates. Use automated processes whenever possible to ensure the timely application of updates.
- Implement antivirus software in a layered configuration, implementing gateway, server, and client-level antivirus solutions.
- Authenticate clients to the Exchange Server messaging infrastructure, using Kerberos whenever possible.
- Leverage RMS to create templates to simplify the implementation of policy-based security.
- Utilize transport policies integrating RMS templates to create in-transit policy management of messages.
- Combat spam by utilizing the protective features included in both Exchange Server and Outlook. Fortify these features with additional or third-party measures when necessary.
- Configure Outlook to always prompt you before sending a read receipt.
- Leverage built-in security in Outlook Web App to utilize built-in security components in Exchange Server 2013.

CHAPTER 11

Exchange Edge Including Antispam/ Anti-Malware Protection for Exchange

IN THIS CHAPTER

- Installing and Configuring the Edge Transport Server Components
- Utilizing the Basic Sender and Recipient Connection Filters
- Utilizing SenderID on an Edge Transport Server
- Using Content Filtering to Isolate Inappropriate Content
- Fine-Tuning Content Filtering
- Using Content Filtering to Allow and Reject Domain-Level Content
- Filtering Content in a Message Attachment
- Using Sender/IP Reputation to Filter Content
- Using Address Rewriting to Standardize on Domain Address Naming for an Organization
- Using EdgeSync to Synchronize Active Directory Information to the Edge Transport Server
- Implementing Safelist Aggregation for Microsoft Outlook
- Managing and Maintaining an Edge Transport Server
- Exchange Server-Level Security Features
- Forefront Online Protection for Exchange

The Edge Transport server role provides an important layer of security between the Internet and an organization's messaging environment. Rather than having messages go straight from the Internet directly into an Exchange server, messages first go to an Edge server and are assessed and filtered based on certain policies or rules. The Edge server analyzes messages and can identify spam, content, and connection trends and take the appropriate action to prevent delivery of potentially harmful content, spam, and other undesired messages. The Edge server plays an important role in the messaging infrastructure, protecting the organization from attack, data leakage, and the delivery of unnecessary email, which ultimately can save an organization's reputation, reduce administrative overhead, and increase productivity. Ensuring the delivery of legitimate messages is just as, if not more, important as filtering out unwanted messages. The Edge server addresses this need by providing advanced controls and configuration options to ensure the delivery of legitimate email and assist administrators in troubleshooting.

By default, Edge Services are not installed on an Exchange server in the organization, and an organization can choose to not have an Edge server and still have a fully operational Exchange Server messaging environment. However, by placing an Edge server in the network, the organization substantially improves its ability to eliminate unwanted messages. Edge servers must be deployed in a workgroup and not members of the Active Directory domain. Active Directory does, however, play an important role in the effectiveness of the Edge server's functionality.

This chapter focuses on the planning and implementation of Edge Services in an organization, along with critical configuration and tuning of Edge Services rules to further enhance the effectiveness of the Edge server in filtering messaging content.

Installing and Configuring the Edge Transport Server Components

The first thing that needs to be done is to determine how the Edge Transport server role will be implemented and configured in the Exchange Server environment. This involves planning and designing the placement of the Exchange Edge Transport server location, considering configuration options, and then actually installing the Edge Transport services onto a server in the network. This section defines the configurable items for the components available on an Exchange server when the Edge Transport server role is selected during installation. Several items are identified in this section specific to the appropriate configuration options to properly achieve a secure, effective, and stable Edge Transport server environment.

Planning the Implementation of the Edge Transport Servers in Exchange Server

The first item to consider when installing and configuring the Edge Transport Services is the desired end result of the email message or connection being processed by the Edge Transport server. Determining what type of email should always be rejected, quarantined, or tagged for end-user review or which connections should be blocked and for how long will help reduce the amount of false positives and allow for a moderately aggressive spam filtering policy the first time Edge Transport servers begin monitoring email for an organization.

Planning for the Message Processing Order of Edge Services

To assist with the planning for your Edge Transport server deployment, take a moment to become familiar with the order in which filtering agents analyze messages. Understanding the order in which messages are processed will help you determine where you should place filters and assign settings for messages you do or don't want to receive. The Edge Transport Antispam filtering order is as follows:

1. An email message is received from the Internet.
2. The IP Block and Allow Lists are checked for a match to the sending IP address.
3. The IP Block List Providers and IP Allow List Providers are checked for a match to the sending IP address.

4. The Sender Filtering agent checks the Blocked Senders list for a match.
5. The SenderID agent performs a Sender Policy Framework (SPF) record lookup against the sending IP address.
6. The Recipient Filtering agent checks the Blocked Recipients list for a match. This is also where messages addressed to nonexistent recipients get identified.
7. The Content Filtering agent analyzes the content contained inside the message. Using Safelist Aggregation, the Content Filtering agent also recognizes block and allow entries obtained from users' Outlook clients.
8. Attachments are analyzed by the Attachment Filter agent. Edge transport rules run against the message.
9. The message is either delivered to the Hub Transport service on the Mailbox server, rejected, deleted, sent to the spam quarantine mailbox, or placed in the user's Junk E-mail folder in the Outlook client.

NOTE

Messages can be identified for delivery or one of the blocking actions at any point in this process, depending on how the Edge Transport server agents have been configured.

TIP

Because most unwanted email delivered today is spam, it is recommended to scan for spam messages before performing virus scanning. This reduces the load placed on the server when it performs virus scanning because virus scanning requires more processing power. This best practice assumes other antivirus mechanisms are in place throughout the network.

TIP

The Microsoft Exchange Server TechCenter located at http://technet.microsoft.com/en-us/exchange/default.aspx contains a wealth of information, tools, tips, and virtual labs for Exchange Server administrators.

TIP

The Microsoft Exchange Team Blog located at www.msexchangeteam.com is a great place to stay current on Exchange Server news and communicate with other Exchange Server experts in the industry.

Installing Edge Transport Services on an Exchange Server

With a general concept of what the Edge Transport Services does, the next step is to install Edge Services on a system and begin configuring filters to test the results in your environment.

Unlike some server functions where you can test functionality in a lab environment, such as performance, features, and functions, testing Edge Services filtering is a little harder to do in an isolated setting. You need to have incoming messages, including spam and good messages, to filter to determine the effective results of the filters you create. The only way to truly measure the impact of Edge Services on an organization's email is on a production environment's mail flow.

Many organizations insert an Edge Services system into their network and set the filter settings low enough that no good messages are accidentally filtered. Then, the organization trends the effectiveness of the filters and tunes up the settings over time to be more and more restrictive, effectively increasing the filter catch rate. While the filtering is expanded, quarantine areas are monitored to look for false-positive messages ensuring that good messages are not being blocked unintentionally or unnecessarily filtered. This process can take an organization several weeks to work through; however, it provides tight control and oversight on the processing of filtered messages.

Another option that is frequently adopted is where an organization sets up a test network with a live connection to the Internet and creates a *honeypot*. A honeypot is an Internet-connected system that purposely attracts messages, including spam and other content, but is not connected to the production network. The process involves establishing a domain on the Internet, setting up an email server to the domain, and then signing up to be on mailing lists with an email account from this test domain. This might include going to the websites of established businesses such as retail stores, mail-order houses, and so on and signing up to receive emails about their promotions and regular newsletters. To get less desirable content, you could sign up to receive notification of events on sites with questionable reputations such as triple-X sites. Do note that it could take several weeks before your honeypot attracts enough messages to make the filtering effective.

TIP

Prior to deploying any email filtering controls, organizations should first clearly define all domains, subdomains, and email addresses it wants to ensure aren't inadvertently blocked because it could have a direct impact on business. The domains, subdomains, and email addresses identified should first be placed in the Safe Senders list on the Edge Transport server, with other filters put in place after.

As a caution, make sure that if you sign up on sites for the purpose of attracting spam that you are connected to an Internet connection, that you clearly understand that the incoming content might be inappropriate for professional organizations, and that you expose the external IP address and incoming ports to questionable content.

Preparing an Exchange Server to be an Edge Server for the Organization

With Exchange Server 2013, Microsoft supports the implementation of an Exchange Server 2010 Edge Transport server as the Edge system for the Exchange Server 2013 environment. As such, this chapter covers the implementation of the Edge Transport server role running on an Exchange Server 2010 Service Pack 3 (SP3) server for the Exchange Server 2013 environment. The Exchange Edge Transport server role needs to be installed on a computer running the 64-bit version of Windows Server 2008 Service Pack 1 (SP1) or Windows Server 2008 R2 Standard Edition operating system. Enterprise Edition does not provide any additional features typically required for an Edge Transport server. Because this server will be connected to the Internet, hardening the server for security is extremely important; therefore, it is even more important that the server system is properly configured and has the latest service pack and security updates installed.

Because the Edge Transport Server role is typically installed on a nondomain attached simple workgroup server, the installation is simply a base Windows server with a given name and IP address. The Edge Transport server is typically installed in the organization's demilitarized zone (DMZ) as it will be a point of connection to the public Internet to receive email messages.

Beyond the basic installation of Windows, make sure to add the domain name DNS suffix on the system that will be the Edge Transport server. To add the organization's domain name, do the following:

1. On the server that will be the Edge Transport server, click Start, Control Panel.
2. Double-click System.
3. Click Advanced System Settings.
4. Click the Computer Name tab.
5. Click Change.
6. On the Computer Name Change page, click More.
7. In the Primary DNS Suffix of This Computer, enter in the domain name for the Active Directory domain that this Edge Transport server will by communicating with, as shown in Figure 11.1.

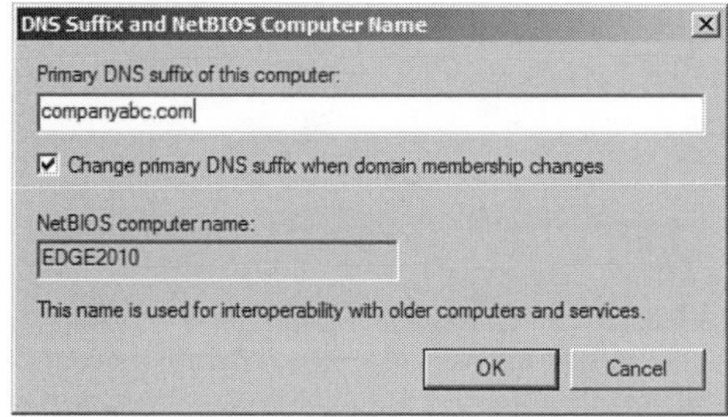

FIGURE 11.1 Setting the DNS suffix on the Edge Transport server.

8. Click OK, and then click OK again.
9. Click OK to confirm that you know you must restart your computer to apply these changes.
10. Click Close.
11. Click Restart Now to reboot the server.

Installing the Exchange Server 2010 Application on the Server

After the system has Windows Server 2008 R2 installed and is properly patched and updated, you can begin the installation of Exchange Server 2010. To install Exchange Server using the interactive installation process of Exchange Server, use the following steps:

1. Ensure all prerequisites for an Edge Transport server have been met before attempting to install Exchange Server 2010:
   a. Windows Server 2008 R2 or Windows Server 2008 R2 SP1
   b. Microsoft .NET Framework 3.5 SP1
   c. Windows PowerShell v2.0
   d. Active Directory Lightweight Directory Services (AD LDS)

TIP

To quickly and easily install the prerequisites on a Windows Server 2008 R2 system, launch PowerShell on the server and enter the following command. The Telnet Client isn't strictly a requirement, but it should be considered a necessary tool for troubleshooting and testing on any server that handles Simple Mail Transfer Protocol (SMTP).

```
Add-WindowsFeature NET-Framework,RSAT-ADDS,ADLDS,Telnet-Client -Restart
```

2. Insert the Exchange Server 2010 CD or DVD (Standard or Enterprise, for Edge Transport Services, the Standard Edition of Exchange Server 2010 is fine).
3. AutoRun should launch a splash screen with options for installing the prerequisites and application. (If AutoRun does not execute, select Start, Run. Then type **`[Drive]:\setup.exe`** and click OK.)
4. On the splash screen, click Step 4: Choose Exchange Language Option and typically select to install only those on the DVD.
5. Click Step 5: Install Microsoft Exchange.

NOTE

Before Microsoft Exchange Server 2010 can be installed, the Setup Installation Wizard will verify if the necessary prerequisites have been fulfilled. If the prerequisites have not been met, configure the prerequisites as recommended by the Configuration Wizard and run setup again.

6. `Setup.exe` copies the setup files locally to the server on which Exchange Server 2010 is being installed.
7. In the Microsoft Exchange Server Installation Wizard dialog box, on the Introduction page, click Next.
8. At the License Agreement page, click I Accept the Terms in the License Agreement, and click Next.
9. At the Error Reporting page, select whether to participate in the Exchange Error Reporting program by sending feedback automatically to Microsoft, and then click Next.
10. At the Installation Type page, select the Custom Exchange Server Installation option and click Next.
11. On the Server Role Selection page, select Edge Transport Role, as shown in Figure 11.2, and click Next.

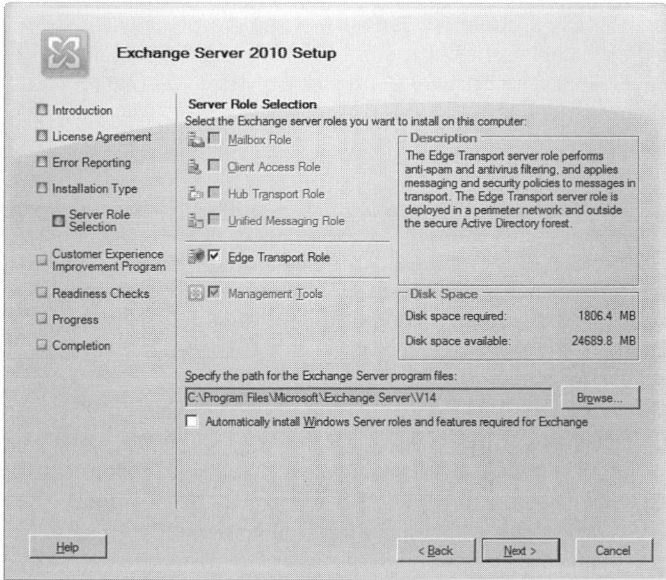

FIGURE 11.2 Server role selection of the Edge Transport role.

NOTE

If there is a need to change the installation folder, click Browse before proceeding and specify a path for the Exchange Server installation.

12. On the Customer Experience Improvement Program (CEIP) page, select one of the following two options: (1) Join the Customer Experience Improvement Program (CEIP) or (2) I Don't Wish to Join the Program at This Time. Most administrators choose option 2; after making your selection, click Next.
13. On the Readiness Checks page, the Installation Wizard is verifying that the appropriate Exchange Server prerequisites have been installed. View the status to determine if the organization and server role prerequisite checks completed successfully, and then click Install.

NOTE

If there are any errors returned or prerequisites not met on the Readiness Checks page, it is necessary to address these issues and retry the setup.

14. To complete the Exchange Server 2010 installation, on the Completion page, click Finish. The Exchange Management Console launches displaying the Exchange Server 2010 postinstallation tasks.

NOTE

The Verify Deployment and Secure the Edge Transport Server by Using the Security Configuration Wizard tasks should be completed after you have finished configuring the Edge Transport server filters and services. The Security Configuration Wizard can be found under Start, All Programs, Administrative Tools.

NOTE

The Exchange Best Practices Analyzer should be run after you finish configuring the Edge Transport server filters and services. This tool scans the Exchange Server configuration and provides recommendations based on the configuration of the server. The Exchange Best Practices Analyzer can be found in the Exchange Toolbox.

The Finalize Deployment Tasks, End-to-End Scenario tasks, and Post-Installation Tasks sections in the Exchange Management Console outline the recommended tasks for end-to-end email routing scenarios along with other Help topics. For example, the Configure the Spam Confidence Level (SCL) Junk E-mail Folder Threshold link provides steps for setting the SCL thresholds for delivery to the end user's Junk E-mail folder in Outlook. Details for configuring these options are covered throughout the balance of this chapter.

Understanding the Edge Transport Components in the Exchange Management Console

After the Exchange Server software has been installed on the server system that will become the Edge Transport server, launch the Exchange Management Console to begin the process of configuring filters and parameters. The Exchange Management Console can be launched by doing the following:

1. Click Start, All Programs, Microsoft Exchange Server 2010.
2. Choose the Exchange Management Console program.

With the Edge Transport server role being selected during the Exchange Server 2010 setup process, the Edge Transport object and Toolbox are the only items that will be available in the console tree of the Exchange Management Console. Selecting the Edge Transport object in the console tree of the Exchange Management Console populates the work pane similar to what is shown in Figure 11.3 with the configurable options for the Edge Transport server.

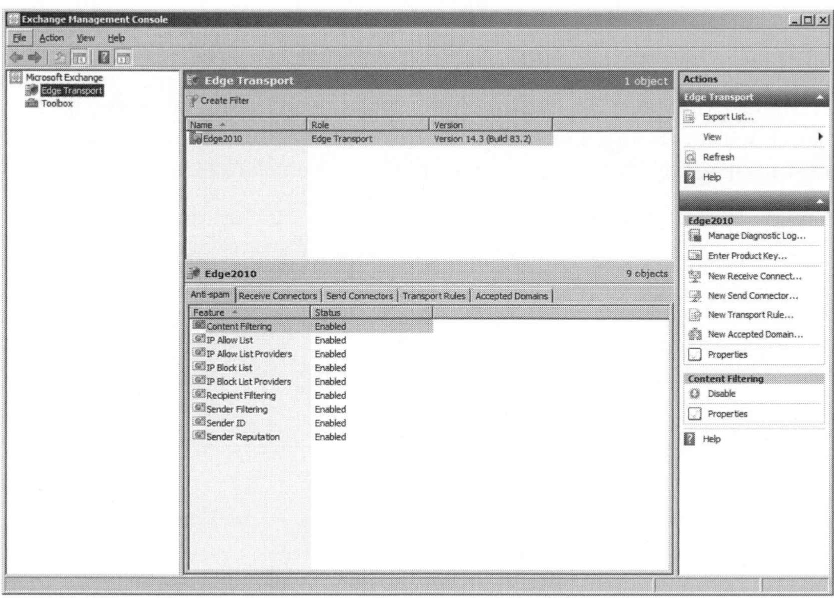

FIGURE 11.3 View of the Exchange Management Console.

NOTE

All filters, lists, and connector settings are enabled by default. As changes are made and applied, they will be in effect on the Edge Transport server. Careful attention to changes is necessary, especially in a live environment. It is recommended to design and configure the first Edge Transport server offline with the minimal configuration needed for email routing and moderate antispam filtering. In the future, the aggressiveness of the antispam filters can be increased and additional filters can be added or modified. This makes troubleshooting easier and helps ensure delivery of legitimate email, while retaining the benefit of blocking known spam or messages carrying a malicious payload.

Several tabs are displayed within the action pane, including the following:

- Anti-Spam
- Receive Connectors
- Send Connectors
- Transport Rules
- Accepted Domains

NOTE

For the Exchange Server 2010 Edge Transport server, there is the Accepted Domains tab that enables administrators to specify domains that they use for sending and receiving email. Accepted Domains can be authoritative, internal, or external mail relays.

The Anti-Spam tab is selected by default and includes all of the configurable filters, lists, and agents for effective spam filtering. Listed alphabetically, the following nine items are available under the Anti-Spam tab in the work pane:

- Content Filtering
- IP Allow List
- IP Allow List Providers
- IP Block List
- IP Block List Providers
- Recipient Filtering
- Sender Filtering
- Sender ID
- Sender Reputation

To the right of the Anti-Spam tab is the Receive Connectors tab. The Receive Connectors tab is used to configure email routing for messages received into the organization. From here, you can either create a new Receive Connector or modify the default Receive Connector labeled "Default internal receive connector <SERVERNAME>." This connector is enabled by default.

The tab to the right of the Receive Connectors tab is the Send Connectors tab. The Send Connectors tab is used to configure email routing for outgoing messages. From here, you can either create a new Send Connector or modify the default Send Connector labeled "Default internal send connector <SERVERNAME>."

NOTE

The Send Connector does not need to be configured if the Edge Transport server is subscribed to the Exchange Server 2013 organization and is receiving data from Active Directory through EdgeSync. See the "Using EdgeSync to Synchronize Active Directory Information to the Edge Transport Server" section later in this chapter for details on how to set up and configure EdgeSync.

The second to last tab in the action pane of the Exchange Management Console for Edge Transport servers is the Transport Rules tab. The Transport Rules tab allows for the creation of rules that should be applied to email messages passing through the Edge Transport server. Different conditions to check in email messages can be set for a rule.

The last tab in the action pane of the Exchange Management Console for Edge Transport servers is the Accepted Domains tab. The Accepted Domains tab enables for the creation of rules that specify which domains will be sending email to the Edge Transport server. For example, an organization would add any of its domains that are used for sending and receiving email in the Accepted Domains tab.

Take a few minutes to navigate through the different items in the Exchange Management Console to become familiar with the location and options for each Edge Transport server component and service.

Utilizing the Basic Sender and Recipient Connection Filters

Connection filtering combats spam by blocking and/or allowing email messages from specific networks, IP addresses, and IP ranges. Email that is routed through Receive Connectors is processed by the Connection Filtering agent. These messages are received from the Internet and travel inbound to the Edge Transport service for delivery to the recipient. The Connection Filter agent, that includes IP Block List, IP Allow List, IP Block List Providers, and IP Allow List Providers, are all enabled by default and can be configured using the Exchange Management Console or Exchange Management Shell.

An IP Allow List is a manual list of servers you trust to send email to your organization, more specifically those for which email communication cannot be disrupted. An IP Block List works in reverse, blocking email from specific email servers without further processing or retaining copies of the message. IP Block and Allow List Providers make it easier to stop email from known malicious entities or ensure communication continues for others. This is usually a free service and allows administrators to easily subscribe to these lists and benefit from them.

One example of a real-time block list provider is The Spamhaus Project at www.spamhaus.org. Spamhaus maintains the Spamhaus Block List (SBL) and provides it as a free service for anyone to use. Spamhaus records its block entries in the SBL domain name system (DNS) zone, and that list is updated at regular intervals and then mirrored to servers around the world with direct hourly feeds to major Internet service providers (ISPs).

NOTE

If the message matches an entry from the IP Allow List, the message is assigned a Spam Confidence Level (SCL) rating of 0 regardless of any matches from the IP Block List. SCLs are covered in more detail later in this chapter in the section, "Using Content Filtering to Isolate Inappropriate Content."

NOTE

Changes described in this section are applied only to the local system. This is important to know if you have more than one Edge Transport server in your environment because the change will need to be made locally on all other Edge Transport servers.

To disable the IP Block List, IP Allow List, IP Block List Providers, and IP Allow List Providers agents using the Exchange Management Console, right-click the appropriate agent icon in the action pane and select Disable.

To disable these same agents using the Exchange Management Shell, run the `set-< IPAllowListConfig, IPAllowListProvider, IPAllowListProvidersConfig, IPBlockListConfig, IPBlockListProvider,` or `IPBlockListProvidersConfig>` command with the `-Enabled $false` parameter. For example:

```
"set-IPBlockListConfig -Enabled $false"
```

When configuring an IP Block List or IP Allow List, entities to block must be entered manually by the administrator because these lists are created and maintained locally on the server. Unless specified otherwise by the organization, reject email messages received from addresses on IP Block Lists to avoid further processing, increased system overhead, and consumed disk space.

TIP

The IP Block List is administered by and applies only to the organization the Edge server is routing mail for. The IP Block List can be used to define IP addresses that consistently send virus-infected messages or unacceptable content to the organization, whereas an IP Block List Provider might not identify these messages, which can occur for several reasons.

Configuring an IP Allow List Using the Exchange Management Console

Email administrators can configure Allow Lists, also known as white lists, on an Edge Transport server to ensure messages from desired source mail senders or organizations are not filtered and blocked at the Edge server. Administrators can define single IP addresses, IP addresses and subnet masks, and/or IP ranges from which to allow email messages.

TIP

In addition to IPv4 support for filtering of addresses and ranges, Exchange Server 2010's Edge Transport role supports filtering using IPv6 addresses and ranges.

NOTE

In some organizations, the Edge Transport server might sit behind another SMTP server that receives email from the Internet. In scenarios like this, the SMTP address of each upstream email server must be added to the Transport Configuration object in an Active Directory forest before connection filtering can be used. The SMTP addresses listed in the Transport Configuration object in Active Directory are replicated to the Edge Transport servers via EdgeSync. See the "Using EdgeSync to Synchronize Active Directory Information to the Edge Transport Server" section on how to configure EdgeSync.

To configure an IP Allow List using the Exchange Management Console, do the following:

1. Launch the Exchange Management Console.
2. Select Edge Transport in the console tree.
3. Double-click the IP Allow List item in the action pane.
4. In the IP Allow List Properties window, select the Allowed Addresses tab.
5. Click the Add button or the down arrow and choose the IP address option to add a Classless Internet Domain Routing (CIDR) IP v4 or v6 address or range (for example, 192.168.1.10, 192.168.1.10/24, or 2001:DB8:0:C000::/54).
6. Click OK to add the IP address or address range.
7. The IP addresses or address ranges are shown in the IP Address(es) section of the Allowed Addresses tab in the IP Allow List Properties window.

NOTE

You must first obtain the IP address or address ranges of the email server or servers for those you want included in the IP Allow List.

8. Click Apply to save changes or click OK to save changes and close the window.

NOTE

Entries in an IP Allow List cannot be scheduled to expire.

Alternatively, an IP address and subnet mask, or IP address range can be defined for filtering. To define an allowed IP address and subnet mask, do the following:

1. In the IP Allow List Properties window, select the Allowed Addresses tab.
2. Click the down arrow and select IP and Mask.
3. In the Add Allowed IP Address – IP and Mask window, enter the IP address in the IP Address field (for example, `192.168.1.10`).
4. Enter the subnet mask of the IP address in the IP Mask field (for example, `255.255.255.0`).
5. Click OK to add the IP address and IP mask.

To define an allowed IP address range, do the following:

1. In the IP Allow List Properties window, select the Allowed Addresses tab.
2. Click the down arrow and select IP Range.
3. In the Add Allowed IP Address – IP Range window, enter the first IP address in the Start Address field (for example, `192.168.1.1`).
4. Enter the last IP address in the address range in the End Address field (for example, `192.168.255.255`).
5. Click OK to add the IP address range.

Any defined IP addresses, IP addresses and subnet masks, and/or IP address ranges are shown in the IP Address(es) section of the Allowed Addresses tab of the IP Allow List Properties window.

Several list providers are available; the criteria for being added to or removed from their databases along with how often those databases are updated are different. For example, Microsoft provides updates twice per week for its Intelligent Message Filter, which is used with content filtering and the heuristics rules specific to phishing attempts. To configure an IP Allow List Providers using the Exchange Management Console, complete the following steps:

1. Launch the Exchange Management Console.
2. Select Edge Transport in the console tree.
3. Double-click the IP Allow List Providers item in the action pane.
4. In the IP Allow List Providers Properties window, select the Providers tab.
5. Click the Add button to define an IP Allow List Provider.
6. Enter the name of the provider in the Provider Name field.
7. Enter the IP address or fully qualified domain name (FQDN) in the Lookup Domain field.
8. Select Match Any Return Code to Identify All Delivery Status Notifications (DSN) and respond to them accordingly.

9. Select Match Specific Mask and Responses to specify an IP address or subnet mask and respond accordingly or to list multiple IP addresses or subnet masks and respond accordingly.
10. Click OK when you are finished; the newly created provider entry will be displayed in the IP Allow List Providers Properties window.

Configuring an IP Block List Using the Exchange Management Console

The IP Block List is configured using the same procedures as the IP Allow List; however, an entry made in the IP Block List can be scheduled to expire, whereas an entry in the IP Allow List cannot. By default, new entries are set to never expire.

NOTE

You must first obtain the IP address or address ranges of the email server or servers that you want included in the IP Block List.

To configure an IP Block List using the Exchange Management Console, do the following:

1. Launch the Exchange Management Console.
2. Select Edge Transport in the console tree.
3. Double-click the IP Block List item in the action pane.
4. In the IP Block List Properties window, select the Blocked Addresses tab.
5. Click Add to make a new entry.
6. In the Add Blocked IP Address window, enter the CIDR information for the blocked addresses and select Block Until Date and Time.
7. Specify a date and time to expire the entry, and click OK.

Known spam servers and IP addresses sending malicious email should be double-checked for compliance before the expiration date comes due. Consider keeping maintenance logs or check entries frequently to avoid letting unwanted and previously blocked email messages (back) into your organization.

Configuring an IP Block List Provider Using the Exchange Management Console

The IP Block List Providers is configured in the same manner as the IP Allow List Providers filter; however, two different options are available in the IP Block List Providers properties that are not available when configuring an IP Allow List Provider.

The first difference can be found in the Add IP Block List Providers window when adding an IP Block List Providers on the Providers tab. A custom message can be specified or the default can be used for the Determine Error Message Returned when a Sender Is Blocked by a Provider option in the Return Status Codes section. To configure a custom error message, click the Error Messages button at the bottom of the window and select Custom Error Message in the IP Block List Providers Error Message window.

NOTE

A maximum of 240 characters can be entered into the Custom Error Message field.

The second difference between the IP Allow List Providers and IP Block List Providers filters is the ability to add exceptions. Exceptions to the IP Block List Provider's database can be configured on the Exceptions tab of the IP Block List Providers Properties window. On the Exceptions tab, you can add email addresses of recipients who should not be blocked in the Do Not Block Messages Sent to the Following E-Mail Addresses, Regardless of Provider Feedback field. Messages sent to addresses in this list will not be blocked if they trigger a match in the IP Block List Providers' database.

NOTE

You must first obtain the necessary DNS zone(s) or IP address(es) to query from the provider hosting the IP Block List being added.

Configuring IP Block and Allow Lists Using the Exchange Management Shell

Connection filtering can also be configured through the Exchange Management Shell. Each shell command has its own parameters you can set based on the action(s) performed by the command. There are four commands: `Get`, `Add`, `Remove`, and `Set`. Each command works with one or more IP Block and Allow List components.

The `Get-` command is used to retrieve the configuration of a component. For example, entering `Get-IPBlockListConfig` displays the IP Block List Configuration on the local system.

The `Add-` command can be used to add an IP Block or Allow List entry or list provider and to assign an expiration time to the entry. The following example adds an IP range to the block list with an expiration date and time (24-hour format):

```
Add-IPBlockListEntry -IPRange 192.168.0.0/16 -ExpirationTime "12/15/2013 11:30:00"
```

The `Remove-` command can be used to remove an IP Block or Allow List entry, list provider, or list entry. The following example removes a list provider using the name:

```
Remove-IPAllowListProvider -Identity Spamhaus
```

NOTE

Only static list entries can be removed using this command.

The `Set-` command allows an administrator to enable or disable the agent or modify the configuration of an IP Block or Allow List or list provider's configuration. The following example enables the Connection Filtering agent on email distributed internally:

```
Set-IPBlockListConfig -InternalMailEnabled $true
Test-IPBlockListProvider -Identity Spamhaus -Server EDGE2
```

NOTE

The status of the IP Allow or Block List Providers can be tested using the `Test-IPAllowListProvider` or `Test-IPBlockListProvider` commands, respectively.

You can test the configuration of the Block or Allow List Providers using the `Test-BlockListProvider` and `Test-AllowListProvider` Exchange Server shell commands, respectively.

Configuring Sender Filtering

Sender filtering allows an administrator to block email messages received from specific email addresses, domains, subdomains, and email messages that do not specify a sender. Email that is routed through Receive Connectors is processed by the Sender Filtering agent. These messages are received from the Internet and travel inbound to the Edge Transport server for delivery to the recipient. Sender filtering, for example, can be a very useful tool when someone in an organization is being harassed by an external person or ex-employee, receiving consistent nondeliverable reports (NDRs) or strange messages from the same source because of a virus or spam.

NOTE

Changes described in this section are applied only to the local system. This is important if you have more than one Edge Transport server in your environment.

The Sender Filtering agent is enabled by default and can be configured using the Exchange Management Console or Exchange Management Shell.

To disable the Sender Filtering agent using the Exchange Management Console, right-click the agent icon in the action pane and select Disable. To disable the Sender Filtering agent using the Exchange Management Shell, run `Set-SenderFilterConfig -Enabled $false`.

The General tab of the Sender Filtering Properties window displays a brief description of the feature and its capabilities, its current status, and the last time the agent's settings were modified.

To add email addresses to the Sender Filtering list, double-click the Sender Filtering agent in the action pane and select the Blocked Senders tab. From here, you can add, edit, or delete entries in the list. Checking the box at the bottom of the window enables the Block Messages that don't have the sender information option. If an email address isn't specified in the message received, it will be blocked. This is a fairly common trick used in spamming messages.

Click Add in the Add Blocked Senders window to do the following:

1. Add an individual email address to block.
2. Add a domain and subdomains (if applicable) to block.

NOTE

Limited wildcard usage is supported in these fields, specifically the asterisk (*). For example, you can add *@companyabc.com to the Individual E-Mail Address to Block field; however, it accomplishes the same result as adding companyabc.com to the Domain field. It is recommended to add the full email address to block.

The Action tab allows you to specify whether to reject or stamp messages with Blocked Sender and continue processing them if the address matches an entry in the list. If messages are rejected because of a match in the Sender Filtering agent, they are responded to with a "554 5.1.0 Sender Denied" SMTP session error message, and the session will also be closed. Stamping the message updates the metadata to indicate the sender was on the block list. This is taken into account by the content filter when it tabulates an SCL. The Sender Reputation filter agent uses the SCL rating when developing a sender reputation level.

Using the Exchange Management Shell to Add Blocked Senders

Sender filtering can also be configured through the Exchange Management Shell. Each shell command has its own parameters you can set based on the action(s) performed by the command. There are two commands: `Get` and `Set`.

The `Get-` command is used to retrieve the configuration of the Sender Filtering agent. For example, entering `Get-SenderFilterConfig` displays the Sender Filtering configuration on the local system.

The `Set-` command allows an administrator to enable or disable the agent and modify the configuration of the agent. The following example enables the Sender Filtering agent and rejects messages from blank senders on external SMTP connections.

```
Set-SenderFilterConfig -Enabled $true -Action Reject
-BlankSenderBlockingEnabled $true -ExternalMailEnabled $true
```

Configuring Recipient Filtering

Recipient filtering allows an administrator to block email delivery from the Internet to a specific email address. Email that is routed through Receive Connectors is processed by the Recipient Filtering agent. In addition, recipient filtering can prevent delivery of email messages to nonexistent accounts in Active Directory. This is extremely effective in stopping spam and virus-laden email to abused or commonly named email accounts (for example, `support@companyabc.com` or `domain@domain.com`).

NOTE

A maximum of 800 email addresses can be placed in this list.

The Recipient Filtering agent is enabled by default and can be configured using the Exchange Management Console or Exchange Management Shell.

NOTE

Changes described in this section are applied only to the local system. This is important if you have more than one Edge Transport server in your environment.

To disable the Recipient Filtering agent using the Exchange Management Console, right-click the agent icon in the action pane and select Disable. To disable the Recipient Filtering agent using the Exchange Management Shell, run `Set-RecipientFilterConfig -Enabled $false`.

The General tab of the Agent Properties window displays a brief description of the agent and its capabilities, its current status, and the last time the agent's settings were modified.

To add email addresses to the Recipient Filtering list, double-click the recipient Filtering agent in the action pane and select the Blocked Recipients tab, as shown in Figure 11.4. From here, you can add, edit, or delete entries in the list. You can also enable the Block messages sent to recipients that do not exist in the directory field. Enabling this feature prevents delivery of email messages to nonexistent accounts in Active Directory.

NOTE

For the Block messages sent to recipients that do not exist in the directory feature to work, you must first configure the EdgeSync process and Active Directory Lightweight Directory Services (AD LDS) for recipient lookup. See the "Using EdgeSync to Synchronize Active Directory Information to the Edge Transport Server" section of this chapter for more information.

TIP

Using the Block Messages Sent to Recipients That Do Not Exist in the Directory option can significantly help reduce the amount of email sent to commonly targeted addresses like `webmaster@companyabc.com`, `support@companyabc.com`, and `john@companyabc.com`.

This also reduces the spammer's ability to identify which email addresses are valid when no response or a response other than "nonexistent user" is returned in an NDR.

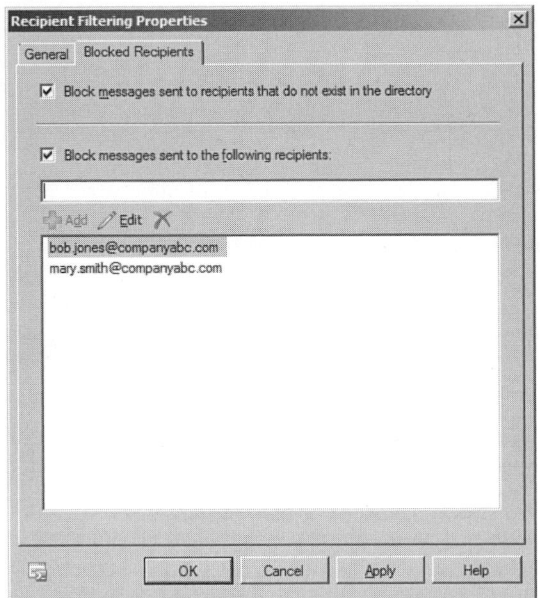

FIGURE 11.4 Blocked Recipients tab in the Recipient Filtering Properties dialog box.

Using the Exchange Management Shell to Add Blocked Recipients

Recipient filtering can also be configured through the Exchange Management Shell. Each shell command has its own parameters you can set based on the action(s) performed by the command. There are two commands: `Get` and `Set`.

The `Get` command is used to retrieve the configuration of the Sender Filtering agent. For example, entering `Get-RecipientFilterConfig` displays the Recipient Filtering configuration on the local system.

The `Set` command allows an administrator to enable or disable the agent or modify the configuration of the agent. The following example enables the Recipient Filtering agent and rejects messages to nonexistent recipients on external SMTP connections:

```
Set-RecipientFilterConfig -Enabled $true -ExternalMailEnabled $true
-RecipientValidationEnabled $true -BlockedRecipients
bob.jones@companyabc.com,mary.smith@companyabc.com
```

Utilizing Sender ID on an Edge Transport Server

Sender ID is a very effective defense mechanism against spam, phishing schemes, and mass-mailing computer viruses when an organization has its Sender ID information properly registered. One of the, if not the most, common tricks used by malicious email authors is the forging of fields in an email message's header information, specifically, the From address. This is often referred to as spoofing a sender's email address. Sender

ID processes inbound email from the Internet. These are the messages that are routed through the Receive Connector on the Edge Transport server.

Configuring Sender ID

The SenderID agent is installed and enabled by default when the Exchange Edge Transport server is installed on a Windows Server system. Because it is installed and enabled, the focus of this section is to identify the specific configuration tasks needed in configuring Sender ID using the Exchange Management Console or Exchange Management Shell.

> **NOTE**
>
> Changes described in this section are applied only to the local system. This is important if you have more than one Edge Transport server in your environment.

To disable the SenderID agent using the Exchange Management Console, right-click the agent icon in the action pane and select Disable. To disable the SenderID agent using the Exchange Management Shell, run `Set-SenderIDConfig -Enabled $false`.

The General tab of the Agent Properties window displays a brief description of the agent and its capabilities, its current status, and the last time the agent's settings were modified.

Malicious email crafters forge this field to hide their identity to avoid being discovered or direct any reply traffic to a specific or random domain, purposefully or not. Another reason this field is commonly forged is to trick the recipient into believing the message is from someone he or she knows, thus increasing the likelihood it will be read and actions such as opening an attachment or web page will be carried out.

Sender ID's primary purpose is validating that the server sending the message to your email server was authorized to do so for the domain specified in the From field of the message headers. When configured and maintained correctly, Sender ID can accurately eliminate malicious email without extensive analysis of the content contained inside. In this section, you learn how to create and look up SPF records, how to configure Sender ID, and how Sender ID Framework (SIDF) has merged these technologies together.

When configuring Sender ID, take into consideration which sending entities should always be allowed to deliver email messages to your organization, regardless of having a published SPF record. For example, in medium to large organizations a coordinated outreach to the other companies the organization does business with might be necessary to inform them of the impact Sender ID could have on email they send to your organization and how to mitigate that impact. Administrators should avoid automatically rejecting or deleting messages initially to help identify any senders that should be "white listed." Following this recommendation drastically reduces the impact the loss of legitimate email can have on an organization.

Sender ID is an invaluable tool that can combat more sophisticated spam attacks such as the Reverse NDR attack that delivers spam email to recipients using a forged From field and targeting accounts that obviously don't exist. The spam message is sent to bogus email addresses in an organization; however, the NDR is relayed to the address in the

From field—the target of the spammers campaign. This attack makes it appear to other systems that the organization sending the NDRs could be spamming and places the organization at risk of being placed on a block list. These types of NDRs are also referred to as backscatter.

There are two components to getting Sender ID functional on an Edge Transport server: the SenderID agent and SPF records. SPF records are not configured on the Edge Transport server, but are pieces of information that Sender ID is required to determine how to handle the message.

NOTE

Sender ID also works with the Sender Reputation agent to help the Sender Reputation agent compute a Sender Reputation Level (SRL) for the sending entity. The Sender Reputation agent is covered in the section "Configuring the Sender Reputation Agent Using the Exchange Management Console" later in this chapter.

Sender ID validates the sending email server by querying the DNS server providing name resolution for the Internet for the sending server's SPF record, provided the administrator of the sending system created and published one correctly. SPF is the "part" that makes Sender ID work. SPF is an open standard added to the SMTP protocol and was designed by Meng Weng Wong and Mark Lentczner to help combat unwanted email without the use of antispam engines or extensive content filtering. Extensive SPF record creation, supporting different SPF configurations and/or multiple domains, and advanced syntax use is beyond the scope of this text. This section outlines what SPF is, how it works, how it integrates with Sender ID, and how to create and activate a basic SPF record.

An SPF record, put simply, is a listing in DNS of what systems are authorized to send email for a specific domain or set of domains. Publishing an SPF record allows others to cross-reference the IP addresses of the mail servers in an organization against that organization's DNS entry for its domain, specifically a Mail Exchange (MX) record. This is also sometimes referred to as a reverse MX lookup.

The following is a sample SPF record for `CompanyABC.com`:

```
v=spf1 mx ip4:192.168.1.150 -all
```

The following is a sample SPF record for companyabc.com using multiple identifiers to include MX and A record lookup in DNS, and to allow email from another domain: Company123.org:

```
v=spf1 mx a:mail.companyabc.com include:company123.org -all
```

An SPF record can contain multiple domain mechanisms and domain modifiers to provide the correct identification and email handling or policy information when queried by other email systems running a Sender ID or SPF filtering configuration.

NOTE

More information regarding Sender ID and SPF can be found at http://www.ietf.org under Request for Comments (RFC) 4405, 4406, 4407, and 4408.

SPF only needs three pieces of information to work:

- The domain of the From address in the message headers
- The purported IP address of the email server that sent the message
- The HELO or EHLO parameter of the server that sent the message

Using this information, Sender ID can determine if the IP address was authorized to send email for the domain listed in the sender's email address.

SIDF is a combination of two similar technologies: SPF and Microsoft's CallerID for email.

Creating a Sender Policy Framework Record

This section walks you through setting up an SPF record using the Microsoft Sender ID Framework SPF Record Wizard located at http://www.microsoft.com/mscorp/safety/content/technologies/senderid/wizard/.

On the Microsoft Sender ID Framework SPF Record Wizard web page, first enter the domain for which you want to create a record (for example, `companyabc.com`) in Step 1 of 4: Identify Your Domain Field on the Website, and click Next. The website checks DNS information about the domain to see what records, including SPF, exist. If no records exist, you are taken to the next step, Step 2 of 4: Display Published DNS Records. Review the information provided to ensure its accuracy, and click Next when you are ready to proceed to Step 3: Create SPF Record.

In Step 3 of 4: Create SPF Record of the Microsoft Sender ID Framework SPF Record Wizard, seven sections can be configured to support the organization's email structure. On this page, you can create an SPF record to reflect the following:

- That the domain does not send email.
- That inbound email servers also send email for the domain.
- That outbound email servers are different from the domain's inbound email servers.
- That all reverse DNS records (PTR) resolve to the domain's outbound email servers.
- That a domain's outbound email is routed through another domain (outsourced).
- That the domain will send email from an IP address not listed in the SPF record being created.
- That the SPF record can be used to validate either the Purported Responsible Address (PRA) derived from the message headers, or from the MAIL FROM (or reverse-path) address derived from the SMTP protocol's MAIL command, or both. The PRA is the

[nonforged] IP address of the system responsible for sending the email message and the MAIL FROM tag (often forged) designates the email address the message is being delivered as.

NOTE

Some fields in the form might already contain data when the wizard queried DNS for information about the domain entered in Step 1.

For this example, you will create an SPF record in which `companyabc.com`'s SMTP server is running the Edge Transport server role and handles both incoming and outgoing email. No other domains or IP addresses should be allowed to route email for `companyabc.com`.

In the form, specify that the domain's inbound email servers can send email by selecting the check box of the same name in the Inbound Mail Servers Send Outbound Mail section of the form. Next, specify that the IP address of the outbound email server for `companyabc.com` is 192.168.2.150 by adding that IP address to the Outbound Mail Server Addresses field in the form. Accept the default of Discouraged to the question regarding whether legitimate email can or will originate from an IP address not included in this record, and allow the record to be used to validate both the PRA and MAIL FROM address in the message headers. Now that the information has been entered, you can proceed to Step 4 of 4: Generate SPF Record, where the record can be created so it can be reviewed and saved for later use.

The TXT record example for companyabc.com looks like one of the following:

```
v=spf1 mx ip4:192.168.1.150 -all
v=spf1 mx ip4:192.168.1.150 ~all
```

The `v=spf1` designates that this is an SPF record, and it is version 1. The portion `mx IP4:192.168.2.150` signifies the email server at 192.168.2.150 is authorized to send and receive email for `companyabc.com`. The `-all` closes the record by stating that no one besides the IP addresses in `companyabc.com`'s MX records is authorized to send email using a `companyabc.com` address and can be rejected. The difference between `-all` and `~all` is the `-all` is a soft fail with an intended action of reject, whereas the `~all` is a soft fail with an intended action of accept but mark. From here, you can copy the syntax, paste it into a Notepad or WordPad document, save the file in standard ASCII text (TXT) format, and add it to DNS so other organizations using Edge Transport servers or an implementation of SPF can look up `companyabc.com`'s SPF record.

NOTE

The SPF record must be published in DNS as a text file to be properly recognized. Beyond formatting of input on the form, the Sender ID Framework SPF Record Wizard does not test or validate the settings entered. After the wizard has finished creating your SPF record, take a moment to view it for accuracy before exporting it for use on the DNS servers.

More information about SPF—extensive SPF record creation, supporting different SPF configurations, multiple domains, and advanced syntax use—is beyond the scope of this text. More information can be obtained at the Microsoft website (http://www.microsoft.com/mscorp/safety/technologies/senderid/resources.mspx) or Sender Policy Framework (www.openspf.org).

So far, we've covered how Sender ID works, how to create and manage simple SPF records, and considered the impact Sender ID can have on legitimate email. At this point, the SenderID agent on the Edge Transport server(s) can be configured.

Configuring the SenderID Agent on the Exchange Edge Transport Server

The SenderID agent is enabled by default on Exchange Server 2010 Edge Transport servers. Configuration is quick and straightforward because Sender ID only relies on a couple of items to function properly. Sender ID like other spam-filtering technologies can impact legitimate email, but, as discussed earlier, there are ways to mitigate this impact while still identifying messages that don't have an SPF record.

To begin configuring Sender ID, do the following:

1. Launch the Exchange Management Console by doing the following on the Exchange Edge server. Click Start, All Programs, Microsoft Exchange Server 2010.
2. Choose Exchange Management Console.
3. Double-click the SenderID agent in the details pane.
4. Select the Action tab.

From here, you can change the action taken on messages if the Sender ID check fails. There are different actions to choose from. One action is to Stamp Message with Sender ID Result and Continue Processing. This is the default action and appends certain information to the message headers for further processing by the Content Filtering agent. The Content Filtering agent then takes this information into account when tabulating the overall spam score assigned to the message, also known as the Spam Confidence Level (SCL).

TIP

When you first implement Sender ID filtering, it is recommended to "stamp" messages to assist in filtering out false positives and generate a white list of legitimate senders and domains. After the organization is comfortable with the established white list, messages can be rejected.

Another option is to use the "exp" modifier in your SPF record and include a uniform resource locator (URL) to an Internet web page where others can retrieve information about your email policy, SPF records, and contact information. This helps offset false positives when rejecting email messages that fail to comply with SPF.

The actions available if a Sender ID check fails include the following:

- Reject the Message.
- Delete the Message.
- Stamp Message with Sender ID Result and Continue Processing.

Choosing to reject the message sends an error response to the sending server. The text contained in this error message corresponds to the Sender ID status derived from processing the SPF record of the message.

Choosing to delete the message sends a fake OK SMTP command to the sending server. The message is deleted and the sender is not notified.

Accepting the default action of Stamp Message with Sender ID Result and Continue Processing appends the Sender ID status derived from the SPF record lookup into the message headers for further processing by the Content/IMF filter. This information, often called metadata, is used by the Content/IMF filter to create the SCL.

Using the Exchange Management Shell to Configure Sender ID

One limitation of Sender ID is the inability to exclude recipients and domains from Sender ID filtering through the Exchange Management Console. Exclusion of recipients and domains from Sender ID filtering can only be accomplished using the Exchange Management Shell's `Set-SenderIdConfig` command. The following example enables the SenderID agent on external SMTP connections, bypasses checking one external domain, and sets the action on spoofed messages:

```
Set-SenderIdConfig -BypassedSenderDomains Microsoft.com -Enabled $true
-ExternalMailEnabled $true -SpoofedDomainAction Delete
```

The `Get-` command is used to retrieve the configuration of the Sender Filtering agent. For example, entering `Get-SenderIDConfig` displays the Sender Filtering configuration on the local system.

You can test the configuration of Sender ID using the `Test-SenderID` Exchange shell command. The following example tests to see if the SPF record resolves correctly:

```
Test-SenderId -IPAddress 192.168.1.150 -PurportedResponsibleDomain
mail.companyabc.com
```

Using Content Filtering to Isolate Inappropriate Content

Content filtering is not only effective for eliminating spam, but it can also be beneficial for identifying messages containing content deemed unacceptable to the organization, such as sexually derogatory remarks or racial slurs. The content filter processes messages that are routed through the Receive Connector on the Edge Transport server. The Content Filtering agent is enabled by default and can be configured using the Exchange Management Console or Exchange Management Shell.

NOTE

Changes described in this section are applied only to the local system. This is important if you have more than one Edge Transport server in your environment.

To disable the Content Filtering agent using the Exchange Management Console, right-click the agent icon in the action pane and select Disable. To disable the Content Filtering agent using the Exchange Management Shell, run `Set-ContentFilterConfig -Enabled $false"`.

The General tab of the Agent Properties window displays a brief description of the agent and its capabilities, its current status, and the last time the agent's settings were modified.

The content filter in Exchange Server 2010 builds on the Intelligent Message Filter technology that Microsoft developed and included in Exchange Server 2003. The Intelligent Message filtering technology, a proprietary message-analyzing filter developed by Microsoft, "learns" which messages are spam and legitimate by analyzing the characteristics contained in both. This filter is updated periodically through Microsoft Software Update Services.

After message analysis has occurred, the content filter assigns an overall score to the message that corresponds with an action you choose based on the needs of the organization. For example, all messages scoring an 8 or higher might be deleted while any message scoring a 3 or lower might be delivered. This message score is often referred to as the SCL. Messages are assigned a score ranging from 0 to 9, with 9 being the "most confident" score that the message is spam.

The content filter can leverage the end user's Safe Recipients List, Safe Senders List, or trusted contacts list in Outlook (2003 or later) by enabling Safelist Aggregation. Safelist Aggregation uses the entries inside of Outlook to help populate the list of legitimate senders so they can be safely bypassed by the Content Filtering agent. Configuring Safelist Aggregation is covered in the section "Implementing Safelist Aggregation for Microsoft Outlook" later in this chapter.

To begin configuring content filtering, launch the Exchange Management Console, and double-click the Content Filtering agent in the action pane. From here, you can customize the Custom Words list to block and allow certain words or phrases, add recipients to the exclusions list to exempt them from content filtering, and configure the actions to take on messages based on the messages' SCL. Some of these items are not available through the Exchange Management Console and can only be configured through the Exchange Management Shell.

The basic function of configuring the content filter on an Edge Transport server is performed as follows:

1. Enable the Content Filtering agent (default is enabled).
2. Designate and specify a quarantine mailbox for captured messages.
3. Enable and configure SCL thresholds and actions.
4. Enable or disable puzzle validation.
5. Specify recipient and sender exceptions.
6. Configure Allow phrases and Block phrases.
7. Set the rejection response.

These functions are covered in the balance of this section.

Configuring the Quarantine Mailbox for Captured Messages

Before configuring other content filtering components, it is advised that you first configure the mailbox that will store messages on which an action of "quarantine" was taken. This action is based on the corresponding SCL for the Quarantine Messages That Have an SCL Rating Larger or Equal To setting in the Exchange Management Console, or the `SCLQuarantineEnabled` and `SCLQuarantineThreshold` parameters of the `Set-ContentFilterConfig` Exchange Management Shell command.

To configure a mailbox for content filtering, complete the following steps:

1. Create a user account with a mailbox in Active Directory if the quarantine mailbox will reside on your internal Exchange servers. Creating mailboxes is covered in Chapter 13, "Administering an Exchange Server 2013 Environment."
2. To configure the mailbox using the Exchange Management Console, select the Action tab of the Content Filter and enter the email address of the mailbox.
3. To configure the mailbox using the Exchange Management Shell, run the `Set-ContentFilterConfig` with the `-QuarantineMailbox` parameter.
4. Then run the Exchange Management Console.
5. In the Content Filtering Properties window, select the Custom Words tab.
6. Enter the word or phrase you want to allow in the Messages Containing These Words or Phrases Will Not Be Blocked field. Email messages containing these entries will always be allowed to bypass content filtering.
7. Click Add to include the new entry.
8. To remove an entry, highlight it, and click the Delete button.
9. Click Apply to save your changes or OK to save changes and close the Content Filter dialog box.

Configuring Spam Quarantine

The spam quarantine holds messages that meet or exceed the SCL threshold set in the Content Filtering agent on the Edge Transport server. Messages marked for quarantine are sent to a quarantine mailbox where they can be reviewed and delivered, if necessary. Administrators who need to resend a quarantined message can use the Send Again feature of Outlook. For more information regarding Microsoft Outlook, refer to Chapter 21, "Getting the Most Out of the Microsoft Outlook Client."

For messages to be quarantined, an Active Directory user and corresponding mailbox must exist, solely for this purpose. If you are running multiple Edge Transport servers, you might consider having one spam quarantine mailbox per server. Although this might increase the amount of effort needed to find captured messages, it decreases the load expected of one Mailbox server. This can also help with troubleshooting configuration differences between Edge Transport servers. Depending on the size of the organization and the amount of Internet email received, the spam quarantine can grow substantially.

TIP

It is recommended to dedicate an Exchange Server database to the spam quarantine mailbox, configure an email retention policy or recipient policy to restrict the mailbox size, and set the duration for how long quarantined messages should be retained.

After a mailbox has been created for the use of quarantining spam messages, the spam quarantine mailbox must be specified on the Edge Transport server. The spam quarantine mailbox can only be specified on an Edge Transport server using the `Set-ContentFilterConfig` command with the `QuarantineMailbox` parameter.

```
Set-ContentFilterConfig -QuarantineMailbox anti-spam@companyabc.com
```

The `Set-ContentFilterConfig` command is covered in more detail in the section "Using the Exchange Management Shell to Configure Content Filtering" later in this chapter.

Configuring the Allowed Keyword or Phrases List

Content filtering varies from organization to organization, so Exchange Server 2010 Edge Services has exceptions to allow for keywords or phrases to not cause a message to be filtered or blocked. This is commonly used in the medical profession where the reference to certain drugs, body parts, or human activities is part of the field of business, whereas in other organizations, those references are commonly used in unwanted or unsolicited email messages.

To configure the Exchange Server 2010 Edge Transport server to allow keywords or key phrases, do the following from within the Exchange Management Console:

1. Select the Custom Words tab.
2. Enter the word or phrase you want to allow in the Messages Containing These Words or Phrases Will Not Be Blocked field. Email messages containing these entries will always be allowed to bypass content filtering.

3. Click Add to include the new entry.
4. To remove an entry, highlight it, and click the Delete button.
5. Click Apply to save your changes or OK to save changes and close the Content Filter dialog box.

NOTE

Messages containing an allowed word or phrase are given an SCL score of 0.

Configuring Keyword or Phrases List to Block Messages

The second section of the Custom Words tab allows you to define words or phrases in messages that should be blocked. There are two exceptions to this: use of the allowed word or phrase list and the exclusions list. Entries in this section result in the message being blocked, unless the word or phrase appears in the Messages Containing These Words or Phrases Will Not Be Blocked section or the recipient's email address is listed in the exclusions list.

For example, your organization might have an email policy that states any message containing racial slurs or derogatory terms should be blocked unless the message is sent to or from the organization's attorneys and senior management. To accomplish this, you would use the Block Messages Containing These Words or Phrases section to include the racially discriminatory language, the Messages Containing These Words or Phrases Will Not Be Blocked section could contain the lawyers' names, office names, addresses, and so forth of the law firm the attorneys work for, and the Exceptions tab would hold the email addresses of the company's executive staff. This would ensure any message not deemed appropriate would be blocked unless it contained information about the company's lawyers or were sent or copied to one of the organization's executives.

To configure blocked keywords or phrases, from within the Exchange Management Console, do the following:

1. Select the Custom Words tab.
2. Enter the word or phrase you want to block in the Block Messages Containing These Words or Phrases field. Email messages containing these entries will always be blocked unless they contain a word or phrase that is included in the allow list or are sent to recipients included in the Exceptions tab.
3. Click the Add button to include the new entry.
4. To remove an entry, highlight it, and click the Delete button.
5. Click Apply to save your changes or OK to save changes and close the Content Filter dialog box.

NOTE

Messages containing a blocked word or phrase are given an SCL score of 9.

As a recommendation from experience, get creative, but be precise! In the previous sample scenario, you could request the law firm to insert a particular code or phrase in messages sent to your company. This makes the message easier for your company to identify and entries in your content filter lists easier to manage, and increases the reliability of content filtering overall. Avoid entering words and phrases that are arbitrary. Instead choose keywords and phrases specific to why you are blocking the message and that won't be mistakenly identified in legitimate messages. This reduces the amount of false positives and processing power needed by the content filter.

Configuring the Exceptions List

The next item in the Content Filter Properties window is the Exceptions tab. The Exceptions tab is used to define email addresses for those you do not want to filter their messages by content. For example, a company might include the human resources', attorneys', or system administrator's mailbox because they might need to view these messages to fulfill the duties of their jobs, whereas the same is not true for the rest of the organization's employees. To configure exceptions, within the Exchange Management Console, do the following:

1. In the Content Filter Properties window, select the Exceptions tab.
2. In the Don't Filter Messages Sent to the Following Recipients field, enter the full email address of the account.
3. Click Add to include the entry in the list.
4. To remove an entry, highlight it, and click the Delete button.
5. To edit the email address of an entry, highlight it, and click the Edit button.
6. Click Apply to save your changes or OK to save changes and close the Content Filter.

NOTE

The exception list is restricted to a maximum of 100 entries.

Setting the Action Tab of the Content Filtering Agent

The last tab of the Content Filtering agent is the Action tab. The Action tab stores the configuration for what actions should be taken on a message based on the calculated SCL. The SCL can range from 0 to 9; 9 designates a high confidence level that the message is spam or contains a match to a block list and 0 designates a high confidence level the message is valid or contains a match to an allowed list.

In the Content Filtering agent, an action of Delete takes priority over the action of Reject, which takes priority over the action of Quarantine. For example, when all three actions are enabled with a threshold of Delete if SCL is 8 or higher, Reject if SCL is 6 or higher, and Quarantine if SCL is 4 or higher, a message with an SCL of 9 would get deleted even though it technically is higher than the other thresholds, and a message with an SCL of 5 would get quarantined. This hierarchy is by design. At least one but not all actions need to be enabled to use content filtering.

TIP

To avoid an impact on legitimate email (false positives), start with a more conservative approach leveraging either high SCL numbers as the threshold or quarantining most spam first. In addition, IP and sender blocking previously defined in this chapter also reduce the amount of false positives. The aggressiveness of the content filter can always be increased and messages that are quarantined can easily be delivered or retrieved.

Fine-Tuning Content Filtering

Content filtering can be used for more than just identifying the content of messages in reviewing whether content is considered spam or whether the content is appropriate for the users of an organization. The content filtering function can be used to delete, reject, or quarantine messages based on an SCL rating where the fine-tuning of the SCL helps keep unwanted messages out of the organization's email system, yet minimizes the potential of false positives where messages are deleted or quarantined even when they are being sent by legitimate senders. This section covers the fine-tuning of content filtering on an Edge Transport server.

Configuring Content Filtering Actions

Several options are available in the Content Filter properties that can be configured. The following goes through the configuration options and notes what the various settings do. To configure content filtering, do the following:

1. In the Content Filter Properties window, select the Action tab.
2. Check the Delete Messages That Have an SCL Rating Larger or Equal To option, and set the threshold appropriately. All messages with the respective SCL are deleted.
3. Check the Reject Messages That Have an SCL Rating Larger or Equal To option, and set the threshold appropriately. All messages with the respective SCL are rejected.
4. Check the Quarantine Messages That Have an SCL Rating Larger or Equal To option, and set the threshold appropriately. All messages with the respective SCL are quarantined.

NOTE

A quarantine mailbox must first be defined. A prompt appears if it is not and the action cannot be enabled. See the section "Configuring the Quarantine Mailbox for Captured Messages" earlier in this chapter for more information.

5. To disable an action, uncheck the box next to it.
6. To change the corresponding SCL threshold of an action, either enter a new number in the box or use the up/down arrows to change the value.
7. Click Apply to save your changes or OK to save changes and close the Content Filter.

Using the Exchange Management Shell to Configure Content Filtering

Content filtering can also be configured through the Exchange Management Shell. Each shell command has its own parameters you can set based on the action(s) performed by the command. There are four commands: `Get`, `Add`, `Remove`, and `Set`. Each command works with one or more content filtering components.

The `Get-` command is used to retrieve the configuration of a component. For example, entering `Get-ContentFilterConfig` displays the Content Filter configuration on the local system.

The `Add-ContentFilterPhrase` command can be used to add an acceptable or unacceptable word or phrase to the filter. The following example adds an unacceptable phrase:

```
Add-ContentFilterPhrase -Phrase "this is unacceptable" -Influence BadWord
```

The `Remove-ContentFilterPhrase` command can be used to remove a blocked or allowed keyword or phrase. The following example removes an unacceptable phrase:

```
Remove-ContentFilterPhrase -Identity "this is unacceptable"
```

NOTE

When replacing the `<String>` option with a phrase, the phrase must be enclosed with quotation marks and the phrase must be "influenced" so it gets added to the correct list.

The `Set` command allows an administrator to enable or disable the agent and modify the configuration of the content filter components. The following example enables the Content Filtering agent on email received on external SMTP connections, bypasses scanning of one domain, enables Microsoft Outlook postmark validation, sets the spam quarantine mailbox, and assigns the thresholds for the different actions:

```
Set-ContentFilterConfig -BypassedSenderDomains microsoft.com -Enabled $true
-ExternalMailEnabled $true -OutlookEmailPostmarkValidationEnabled $true
-QuarantineMailbox anti-spam@companyabc.com -SCLDeleteEnabled $true
-SCLDeleteThreshold 7 -SCLQuarantineEnabled $true -SCLQuarantineThreshold 4
-SCLRejectEnabled $false
```

Configuring Puzzle Validation for Content Filtering

Puzzle validation in Exchange Server works in conjunction with the Microsoft Outlook Email Postmark validation feature to lower the SCL of a message that was sent using the Outlook client. This helps reduce false positives in email messages exchanged between organizations running exclusively in Exchange Server and Microsoft Outlook messaging environments. Postmark validation is disabled by default.

NOTE

Puzzle validation can only be configured using the `Set-ContentFilterConfig` Exchange Management Shell command.

When Email Postmark validation is configured for Microsoft Outlook clients, and those clients send an email message, a presolved computational puzzle that an Exchange server running the Content Filtering agent with Puzzle Validation enabled will be able to "solve." If the message was marked as spam, but contains an Outlook Postmark Validation stamp and the Content Filtering agent was able to successfully resolve the inserted "puzzle," then the SCL of the message will be lowered because the sender's software has technically been validated making the message unlikely to be spam. If the message contains an invalid Email Postmark validation header or no Email Postmark validation at all, the SCL will remain unchanged.

To enable Puzzle Validation and Microsoft Outlook Email Postmark validation, run the following command in the Exchange Management Shell:

```
Set-ContentFilterConfig -OutlookEmailPostmarkValidationEnabled $true
```

To disable it:

```
Set-ContentFilterConfig -OutlookEmailPostmarkValidationEnabled $false
```

Using Content Filtering to Allow and Reject Domain-Level Content

At times, you might want to identify a specific email address or an entire domain on the Internet that is sending you messages that you either want to completely allow or specifically deny the receipt of messages from that source location. The content filtering function of Edge Transport Services enables you to create a white list that always allows content to be received from a user or domain, or specifically allows for the denial of messages from a user or domain.

Do note that each user can also allow and deny message communications, so the choice to allow or deny content at the server level should take into consideration that the communications are organizationwide and that making a setting at the Edge Transport server level will have a positive impact on the appropriate receipt of content to all users in the organization.

An example of a deny filter on a user address or entire domain would include a situation where a user or domain is sending inappropriate content to several users in the organization. Rather than having each user make a configuration to block content from a user or domain, it can be set at the server level.

Conversely, if users in an organization want to receive all messages from a user or domain, those names can be added to a white list that will always allow messages to be received by users or the entire domain in the organization.

Configuring the Content Filter Agent to Allow (White List) Specific Senders and Sending Domains

The Exchange Management Console allows you to exclude specific keywords, phrases, and recipients within your organization from content filtering checks; however, you can only exclude specific senders and sending domains from content filtering through the use of the Exchange Management Shell's `Set-ContentFilterConfig` command, using the `BypassedSenders` and `BypassedSenderDomains` parameters, respectively.

The `BypassedSenders` parameter allows you to specify up to 100 external email addresses to exclude from content filtering, with each entry separated by a comma.

```
Set-ContentFilterConfig -BypassedSenders fred@companyabc.com,heather@company123.org
```

NOTE

The entry must be the full SMTP address; wildcard (*) use is not supported. For example, you cannot exclude john*@companyabc.com, or john@companyabc.*.

When excluding a specific email address (for example, `user@companyabc.com`), consider whether it is safe to exclude the domain using the `BypassedSenderDomains` parameter instead (for example, `companyabc.com`). Not only does this save you time and message retrieval because of false positives, it also consumes fewer entries in your list, leveraging both lists and the allowed maximum of 100 more efficiently.

The `BypassedSenderDomains` parameter works similarly to the `BypassedSenders` parameter, allowing you to specify up to 100 external domains to exclude from content filtering, with each entry separated by a comma.

```
Set-ContentFilterConfig -BypassedSenderDomains *.companyabc.com, company123.org
```

NOTE

Wildcard use is supported to designate the exclusion of subdomains under the excluded domain, for example, *.companyabc.com.

Configuring the Content Filter's SMTP Rejection Response

The SMTP Rejection Response is inserted into an SMTP NDR that is sent in reply to a rejected message. The default message is Message Rejected Due to Content Restriction. This message can be changed using the `Set-ContentFilterConfig` command with the `-RejectionResponse` parameter. The SMTP Rejection Response cannot exceed 240 characters and must be enclosed in quotation marks.

NOTE

The SMTP Rejection Response cannot exceed 240 characters and must be enclosed in quotation marks.

```
Set-ContentFilterConfig -RejectionResponse "Message rejected,
an error has occurred. Contact your HelpDesk."
```

Filtering Content in a Message Attachment

The Microsoft Exchange Edge Transport server can also filter content within attachments of a message. There are times when an organization wants to prevent offensive or malicious content being stored in a Word document, Hypertext Markup Language (HTML) attachment, and so on from being transmitted to users in a network, so a filter can be configured to identify and handle incoming attachment messages.

Understanding Attachment Filtering Processing

A powerful tool in the fight against computer viruses and other malicious email attachments is the use of attachment filtering. Attachment filtering allows you to identify a specific filename or all files of a particular type using Multipurpose Internet Mail Extensions (MIME) recognition. Attachment filtering can be applied to both incoming and outgoing email. This allows you the flexibility of implementing attachment distribution that complies with business requirements or policy. For example, you can choose to block all executable file types (for example, `.bat`, `.exe`, `.scr`) on inbound email to help prevent the spread of new computer viruses or distribution of unacceptable content. On outbound connections, you could elect to block distribution of particular files by name (for example, `tradesecrets.doc`, `salaryinfo.xls`), which can help prevent proprietary information from being accidentally or purposefully distributed. SMTP Send and Receive Connectors can be included or excluded from attachment filtering.

NOTE

Changes described in this section are applied only to the local system. This is important if you have more than one Edge Transport server in your environment.

Planning Attachment Filtering Processing

One limitation to attachment filtering is that it can only be configured using the Exchange Management Shell. No attachment filtering options are available in the Exchange Management Console.

Exchange Server, Microsoft Outlook, and Active Directory's Group Policy can work together to orchestrate implementation of an organization's policy on email attachments. Microsoft Outlook includes an enabled default list of Level 1 attachments—attachments that will not be allowed. The Level 1 attachment list was derived from their known or potential ability to carry malicious code. Level 2 attachments are attachments that will initiate a prompt requiring the user first download the attachment prior to running it. This allows any locally installed antivirus product the opportunity to scan the attachment for viral code that might have bypassed email virus scanning, albeit a rare circumstance, but not impossible. By default, there are no Level 2 file types defined in Outlook.

There are over 70 Level 1 files included in Microsoft Outlook 2007, 2010, and 2013. Some examples of Level 1 file types are shown in the following list. For a complete list, refer to the Microsoft Outlook documentation.

- `asp`—Active Server Page
- `crt`—Certificate file
- `.hta`—Hypertext application
- `.msc`—Microsoft Management Console snap-in
- `.msh`—Microsoft Shell

Using Group Policy, an administrator can "open up" Level 1 attachments to users so they can choose whether to accept the attachment and/or make modifications to the Level 1 and Level 2 attachment lists. Alternatively, administrators can take full control of this functionality. This flexibility, unfortunately, can pose a security risk. To offset this risk, administrators can use the attachment filtering component on an Edge Transport server to block specific attachments, regardless of the configuration in place on internal email systems.

First, you need to determine what attachments and/or types of attachments you want blocked and in what direction(s) attachment filtering should take place: inbound, outbound, or both. If you will be blocking a specific attachment, implement the block using the filename. If you want to block all email attachments of a specific type, add the file extension so it can be identified by its MIME type, regardless of the filename.

After you have decided on which attached files or file types you want to identify in email messages, you also need to determine what you want to do with messages containing those attachments. The default action is to block the attachment and the message (Reject). The available actions you can take on messages and attachments defined in the attachment filter include the following:

- **Reject**—Stops delivery of the message attachments to the recipient and sends an undeliverable response to the sender.
- **Strip**—Delivers the message to the recipient, replacing the attachment in the message with a notification it has been removed. Any attachment not listed in the attachment filter will still be available to the recipient.
- **SilentDelete**—Similar to the Reject action in that the message and attachment aren't delivered; however, the SilentDelete action does not send an undeliverable notification to the sender.

Using the Exchange Management Shell to Configure Attachment Filtering

Attachment filtering, as previously mentioned, can only be configured through the Exchange Management Shell. Each shell command has its own parameters you can set based on the action(s) performed by the command. There are four commands: `Get`, `Add`, `Remove`, and `Set`. Each command works with one or more IP Block and Allow List components.

The `Get-` command is used to retrieve the configuration of a component. For example, entering `Get-AttachmentFilterEntry filename` displays the result of whether that file is being identified in messages.

The `Add-` command can be used to add an entry to the Attachment Filter agent. The following example adds a filename to be blocked:

```
Add-AttachmentFilterEntry -Name virus.exe -Type FileName
```

The `Remove-` command can be used to remove an attachment filter entry. The following example removes an entry by filename:

```
Remove-AttachmentFilterEntry -Identity FileName:virus.exe
```

The `Set-` command allows an administrator to modify the configuration of the attachment filter. In attachment filtering, it is primarily used to set the action. The following example configures the action and response options:

```
Set-AttachmentFilterListConfig -Action Reject -RejectResponse "Attachment type
not allowed."
```

Using Sender/IP Reputation to Filter Content

Sender Reputation when combined with the other antispam technologies in Edge Services can help reduce unwanted email very efficiently and effectively. Sender Reputation, simply put, allows administrators to answer the question, "Can I trust who sends us email, and if I can't, why should I process it?" The Sender Reputation agent answers this question for you by learning from values obtained in email messages to determine whether the source of the messages is legitimate or if it is sending junk.

Configuring Sender/IP Reputation

Email that is routed through Receive Connectors is processed by the Sender Reputation agent. These messages are received from the Internet and travel inbound to the Edge Transport server for delivery to the recipient. The Sender Reputation agent is enabled by default and can be configured using the Exchange Management Console or Exchange Management Shell.

NOTE

Changes described in this section are applied only to the local system. This is important if you have more than one Edge Transport server in your environment.

To disable the Sender Reputation agent using the Exchange Management Console, right-click the agent icon in the action pane, and select Disable. To disable the Sender Reputation agent using the Exchange Management Shell, run `Set-SenderReputationConfig -Enabled $false`.

The General tab of the Agent Properties window displays a brief description of the agent and its capabilities, its current status, and the last time the agent's settings were modified.

The Sender Reputation agent works by evaluating several items in an email message(s) and then assigns a score, known as the Sender Reputation Level (SRL). The SRL works very similarly to the SCL assigned to messages themselves. The SRL gets assigned to the IP address from which the email message(s) are originating. The Sender Reputation agent adds the IP address to the IP Block List when the SRL corresponds with the tolerance threshold you have set for this action. The SRL can be adjusted from 0 to 9. You can also configure the amount of time (in hours, 0 to 48) the flagged IP address should remain on your IP Block List.

The SRL for an IP address is derived from the following four items: an open proxy test, HELO/EHLO validation check, reverse DNS lookup, and SCL ratings derived from messages received from the sending IP address. The Sender Reputation agent takes the cumulative results of these items into account when composing the SRL.

An open proxy test determines whether the receiving Edge Transport server can communicate back to itself through the network on which the sending IP address resides. Open proxies are easy to establish and are commonly used by spammers to conceal the true identity of the server sending email. When email messages are routed through an open proxy, the information contained in the message changes to reflect that of the local host, that is, the network on the "other side" of the proxy server.

NOTE

Performing an open proxy test is enabled by default. This setting can be changed on the Sender Confidence tab of the Sender Reputation Properties window.

The HELO/EHLO SMTP commands are another item often forged by spammers. Their purpose is to provide the domain name or IP address from which the message originated. Spoofing the From address, using the same domain in the To and From fields, and forging the sending IP address are very common spam tricks.

A reverse DNS lookup is performed to determine if the domain name registered with the sending IP address is the same as that provided with the HELO/EHLO commands.

NOTE

Although similar, this is not the same as Sender ID and the use of SPF records.

The SCL of a message is the last item taken into account by the Sender Reputation agent when calculating an SRL for a particular IP address. The Sender Reputation agent tabulates SCL scores obtained from messages previously received from the same IP address.

Configuring the Sender Reputation Agent Using the Exchange Management Console

The Sender Reputation agent can be configured using the Exchange Management Console interface. To configure the sender reputation from EMC, do the following:

1. Launch the Exchange Management Console.
2. Select Edge Transport in the console tree.
3. Double-click the Sender Reputation agent.
4. The General tab provides a quick overview of the Sender Reputation agent along with the last time the agent's settings were modified.
5. The Sender Reputation tab allows you to enable (default) or disable the open proxy test. This typically remains enabled.
6. The Action tab allows you to set the block threshold for SRL on a scale of 0 to 9. (The default setting is 7.)
7. The Action tab also allows you to configure how long (0 to 48 hours) the IP address should remain on the Edge Transport server's IP Block List. (The default setting is 24 hours.)
8. Click Apply to save changes or click OK to save changes and close the window.

Configuring Sender Reputation Using the Exchange Management Shell

Sender Reputation can also be configured through the Exchange Management Shell. Each shell command has its own parameters you can set based on the action(s) performed by the command. There are two commands: `Get-` and `Set-`.

Entering `Get-SenderReputationConfig` displays the Sender Reputation configuration on the local system.

The `Set-` command allows an administrator to enable or disable the agent and modify the configuration of the agent. The following example enables sender reputation on email received on external SMTP connections, activates the open proxy detection test, and configures the blocking options:

```
Set-SenderReputationConfig -Enabled $true -ExternalMailEnabled $true
-OpenProxyDetectionEnabled $true  -ProxyServerName proxy1.companyabc.com
-ProxyServerPort  8080 -SenderBlockingEnabled $true -SenderBlockingPeriod 48
-SRLBlockThreshold 8
```

Using Address Rewriting to Standardize on Domain Address Naming for an Organization

Address rewriting was created by Microsoft to allow an organization to have all outbound or inbound email appear to be delivered from one domain when several mail-enabled domains could be sending messages through the same systems. This allows a company to provide a consistent appearance when communicating via email. Address rewriting is commonly used on outbound email when companies merge with or acquire other organizations. Address rewriting is also used on outbound email when an organization's network contains several other domains. Using address rewriting in these scenarios results in external recipients seeing email as originating from one domain name, even if it is coming from a domain with a completely different name.

NOTE

If you enable address rewriting on external messages, ensure you have enabled address rewriting on inbound messages as well, so that inbound messages will be delivered to the appropriate recipients.

Configuring Address Rewriting

As with many of the components for the Edge Transport server, address rewriting is enabled on inbound email messages so messages that were rewritten when sent externally can be routed back to the appropriate person. Address rewriting can also be beneficial when sending email between internal systems. For example, if an IT Department has multiple domains and the organization wants all email communication from the IT Department to internal departments (other than IT) to come from `*@it.companyabc.com`, then address rewriting would be used to accomplish this.

NOTE

Using address rewriting on your outbound email messages eases white-listing of your organization's email for external recipients and business partners by simplifying the answer to their question "What domain and systems can we expect to receive email from?"

NOTE

Changes described in this section are applied only to the local system. This is important if you have more than one Edge Transport server in your environment.

Some considerations to take into account when using address rewriting are items that will not be rewritten, end result of email addresses being combined, messages that have been secured, and rewriting in both directions.

Address rewriting will not modify messages that are attached to the message being rewritten and also will not modify the SMTP Return-Path, Received, Message-ID, X-MS-TNEF-Correlator, Content-Type Boundary=string headers, and headers located inside of MIME body parts. Message-ID, X-MS-TNEF-Correlator, Content-Type Boundary=string headers, and headers located inside of MIME body parts are used when securing email messages such as with encryption or Microsoft Rights Management and are, therefore, not rewritten purposely to ensure the message isn't modified to ensure delivery and integrity of the content.

To ensure messages (mainly responses to rewritten messages) get routed to the appropriate person, a few items need to be addressed. First, the end result of the email address must be unique between users so conflicts and incorrect delivery of messages does not occur; second, a proxy address must be configured on the mailbox that matches the rewritten address; and third, address rewriting must be configured on both the Send and Receive Connectors of the Edge Transport server.

To ensure the rewritten email address between domains will remain unique to the user, take into account how each domain creates its usernames. For example, domains that allow simple usernames like `rand@`, `chris@`, or `support@` may have more conflicts when using address rewriting than organizations that use more unique or defined usernames like `rand_morimoto@`, `chrisa@`, or `online-sales-support@`. If two domains used simple usernames in their email addresses and the organization wanted to use address rewriting, the end result could contain too many conflicts presenting the need to change email addresses at least in one domain. This could end up being quite an involved task depending on the number of users in each domain. For example, `CompanyABC.com` wants to have all email from domains like `infosec.companyabc.com`, `it.companyabc.com`, and `development.companyabc.com` leave the organization as `companyabc.com`. If two different users named Mike have the same email prefix (mike) in `it.companyabc.com` and `infosec.companyabc.com`, there will be a conflict as they would both be rewritten to `mike@companyabc.com`. This has more of an impact on replies to rewritten messages than it does to new outbound messages.

NOTE

The use of wildcards is supported in limited usage when rewriting addresses. For example, wildcards can only be used on internal domains. Partial wildcard use such as `john*@finance.companyabc.com` or `username@sales*.companyabc.com` is not supported, whereas username `@*.companyabc.com` is. One example of wildcard usage is rewriting `*@development.companyabc.com` and `*@software.companyabc.com` to `*@support.companyabc.com`.

Address rewriting can only be configured through the Exchange Management Shell. No address rewriting options are available in the Exchange Management Console. Each shell command has its own parameters you can set based on the action(s) performed by the command. There are four commands: `Get-AddressRewriteEntry`, `New-AddressRewriteEntry`, `Set-AddressRewriteEntry`, and `Remove-AddressRewriteEntry`. An example of each is shown later.

The `Get-` command is used to retrieve the configuration of address rewriting. For example, entering `Get-AddressRewriteEntry` displays the configuration settings on the local system.

The `New-AddressRewriteEntry` command can be used to add a new rewriting entry. Use of this command requires three parameters: `ExternalAddress`, `InternalAddress`, and `Name`. The following example rewrites all email addresses in both directions for `companyabc.com`:

```
New-AddressRewriteEntry -Name "Two-way Rewrite entry for companyabc.com"
-InternalAddress companyabc.com -ExternalAddress companydef.com
```

The `Set-` command allows an administrator to activate address rewriting or modify the existing configuration. The following example switches the internal and external domains given in our previous example and updates the description to reflect the change:

```
Set-AddressRewriteEntry -Identity "Two-way Rewrite entry for companyabc.com"
-ExternalAddress companydef.com -InternalAddress companyabc.com -Name "Two-way
Rewrite entry for companydef.com"
```

The `Remove-` command can be used to delete an address rewriting entry. The following example removes the entry created in the previous examples:

```
Remove-AddressRewriteEntry -Identity "Two-way Rewrite entry for companydef.com"
```

Using EdgeSync to Synchronize Active Directory Information to the Edge Transport Server

EdgeSync is a component of the Edge Transport server that allows replication of certain data from Active Directory to the Edge Transport server to support specific antispam and email filtering components. As an example, an organization might want a copy of its recipient email address list at the Edge Transport layer of its security system so that if an email comes in for a user who does not exist in the organization, the message can be purged immediately instead of taking up disk space to queue, route, or even manage unnecessary content.

Understanding the EdgeSync Process

The EdgeSync process runs on the Mailbox server in an Active Directory forest and replicates data to the Edge Transport server(s). The EdgeSync communication between the Hub and Edge Transport server is secure. For example, EdgeSync is required if you plan on recognizing and taking action on email messages that are sent to nonexistent recipients. See the Recipient Filtering section of this chapter for more information on stopping email to nonexistent recipients. EdgeSync is also required if you intend to recognize entries in Microsoft Outlook clients, also known as Safelist Aggregation, which is covered later in this section.

NOTE

AD LDS must be installed on the Edge Transport server before Exchange Server 2010 is installed because it is required to use EdgeSync. AD LDS works in conjunction with EdgeSync as a directory in which EdgeSync collects directory information. AD LDS can be used in conjunction with an organization's Active Directory in an extranet scenario where employees (in Active Directory) need mail routed through the Edge Transport server, but also nonemployees such as contractors or vendors would be populated in AD LDS and EdgeSync'd into the Edge Transport server system filter tables.

Using EdgeSync to Subscribe the Server to the Exchange Server 2010 Organization

EdgeSync is also used to subscribe the Edge Transport server to the internal Exchange Server 2013 organization. Subscribing the Edge Transport server in this manner automatically defines the Send Connectors on the Edge Transport server after they have been replicated to AD LDS on the Edge Transport server from a Mailbox server. The Mailbox server the Edge Transport server has subscribed with will now route all email from its domain addressed to Internet recipients through the subscribed Edge Transport server(s). Send Connectors must be configured manually if the Edge Transport server is not subscribed internally and utilizing EdgeSync Send and Receive Connectors.

NOTE

EdgeSync overwrites previously defined Send Connector configurations and disables the Send Connector configuration on the Edge Transport server after replication to the Edge Transport server has occurred, unless you deselect having Send Connectors automatically defined when you import the Edge subscription file on the Mailbox server.

Maintaining the EdgeSync Schedule of Replication

EdgeSync runs on a regularly scheduled basis with configuration data replicated every hour and recipient information replicated every 4 hours. In Exchange Server 2007's EdgeSync instance, a full replication took place at every interval, whereas with Exchange

Server 2010's EdgeSync instance, only changes are now replicated (deltas), significantly reducing bandwidth and time needed for replication. Also part of the Exchange Server 2010's EdgeSync process is the support of a customizable EdgeSync schedule. This ensures the information needed by the Edge Transport server is up to date. EdgeSync replicates the following items from Active Directory to the AD LDS instance on the Edge Transport server:

- Microsoft Outlook Safe Senders and Safe Recipients Lists (Blocked Senders are not replicated)
- Valid email recipients listed in AD (used by the Block E-Mail Sent to Non-Existent Recipients feature of the Recipient Filtering agent)
- Message classifications
- Accepted and remote domains
- Send Connector configuration
- List of Mailbox servers subscribed in Active Directory
- Transport Layer Security (TLS) Send and Receive Domain Secure lists
- Internal SMTP relay servers lists

Configuring EdgeSync on an Edge Transport Server

Configuring EdgeSync begins with exporting the Edge Transport subscription file for importing on a Mailbox server that communicates with Active Directory. The Edge Transport subscription file is in Extensible Markup Language (XML) format. This procedure must be repeated for each Edge Transport server with the process as follows:

1. Ensure communication through ports 25 and 50636 is available from the Mailbox server on Exchange Server 2013 to the Edge Transport server in the DMZ.

NOTE

Ports 25 (SMTP) and 50636 (Secure LDAP) were assigned at installation and cannot be changed on the Edge Transport server.

2. Open the Exchange Management Shell.
3. Enter the following command to export the Edge Transport subscription file:

```
New-EdgeSubscription -FileName "C:\temp\EdgeSubscriptionInfo.xml"
```

NOTE

You must include the full path to the file.

4. Copy the Edge subscription file to the Mailbox server.

Importing the EdgeSync Configuration File into the Exchange Server 2013 Environment

Once the EdgeSync configuration file has been generated by the Edge Transport server system, the XML file needs to be imported on the Exchange Server 2013 Mailbox server that will have the association with the Edge Transport server. This is done through the Exchange Management Shell (EMS) as follows:

1. On the Exchange Server 2013 Mailbox server that will be associated with the Edge Transport server, launch the Exchange Management Shell (EMS).
2. Run the following PowerShell script to import the XML configuration file into Exchange Server 2013, substituting the site name where the Hub Transport server is installed:

   ```
   New-EdgeSubscription -FileData ([byte[]]$(Get-Content -Path
   "C:\temp\EdgeSubscriptionInfo.xml" -Encoding Byte -ReadCount 0))
   -CreateInternetSendConnector $true - CreateInboundSendConnector
   $true -Site "Default-First-Site-Name"
   ```

3. The completion of the script should return something that looks like Figure 11.5.

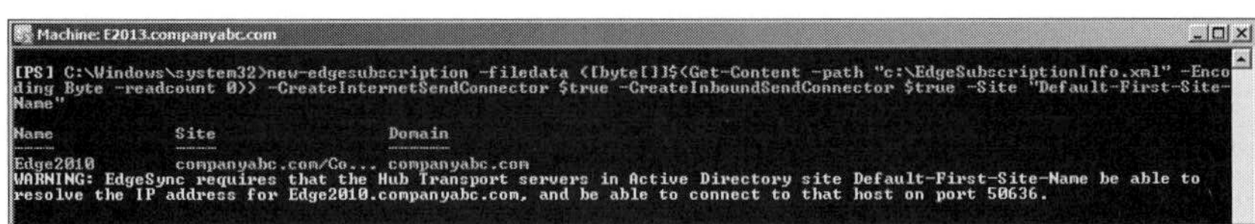

FIGURE 11.5 Importing the XML file into Exchange Server 2013 to create an EdgeSync association.

Adding DNS Records for the Edge Transport Server

The Edge Transport server needs to be in the DNS records that are resolved by the Exchange Server 2013 Mailbox server. It is easiest to just add the Edge Transport server to the organization's DNS record. To do so:

1. On the DNS server in the organization where the Exchange Server 2013 Mailbox server resides, launch the DNS administration tool.
2. Add an A record that corresponds to the fully qualified domain name of the Edge Transport server with the IP address of the Edge Transport server.
3. Confirm that the Exchange Server 2013 Mailbox server properly resolves the IP address of the Edge Transport server.

Starting EdgeSync Synchronization

Once EdgeSync has been configured, the EdgeSync server needs to be started. Edge synchronization can be started by running the `Start-EdgeSynchronization` command on any Exchange Server 2013 server joined to the Active Directory domain. Starting Edge synchronization comes in handy when you have added a new Edge server, want to test synchronization, or replicate changes immediately. The `Start-EdgeSynchronization` command initializes EdgeSync to all Edge Transport servers:

```
Start-EdgeSynchronization
```

Testing EdgeSync Synchronization

After configuring EdgeSync, it is important to test it for success. EdgeSync can be tested by running the `Test-EdgeSynchronization` command on any Exchange Server 2013 server joined to the Active Directory domain. Testing Edge synchronization comes in handy when you have added a new Edge server and want to validate the EdgeSync configuration and replication settings. The `Test-EdgeSynchronization` command produces a detailed report that can be used for troubleshooting. The `Test-EdgeSynchronization` command can be coupled with several different parameters. For example, the `VerifyRecipient` parameter validates that a single recipient was properly replicated to the Edge Transport server from Active Directory:

```
Test-EdgeSynchronization
```

The results of the EdgeSync test should show something similar to what is shown in Figure 11.6.

FIGURE 11.6 Testing Edge Synchronization.

Removing an EdgeSync Subscription

If at some point you want to remove the EdgeSync subscription, you run the `Remove-EdgeSubscription` command. This will unsubscribe an Edge Transport server from participating in EdgeSync. The following example removes an Edge subscription from Active Directory. This command is run on the Mailbox server. The identity specifies the Edge Transport server to be unsubscribed.

```
Remove-EdgeSubscription -Identity EDGE2010
```

NOTE

This unsubscribes the Edge Transport server from the synchronization process on the Mailbox server.

Implementing Safelist Aggregation for Microsoft Outlook

The Safelist Aggregation component of an Edge Transport server allows an administrator to obtain copies of end users' Safe Senders lists from Outlook 2003 or more current clients. Safelist Aggregation essentially provides a mechanism to respect the entries users have made in their Safe Senders lists, which reduces false positives when filtering for spam. By moving the user's safelist to the Edge Transport server, a rule or spam filtering process set up at the Edge won't delete email that a user has deemed desired.

Configuring Safelist Aggregation for Microsoft Outlook

As with all of the other Edge Transport rule processes, the Edge Transport server must be subscribed to the Exchange Server 2013 organization from which you want to retrieve Safe Senders list entries on Microsoft Outlook clients. Safe Senders are replicated to the Edge Transport server using EdgeSync. Safelist entries created by users and imported using Safelist Aggregation are recognized when the Content Filtering agent examines the message.

NOTE

You can only use Safelist Aggregation with the Content Filtering agent enabled and on an Edge Transport server that has a subscription with the organization's Mailbox server. Also, entries in the local Contacts list in Outlook and any external account the user sends email to are added to the user's safelist. These entries are replicated to the Edge Transport server and used with Safelist Aggregation. Outlook's safelist collection is composed of the Safe Senders, Recipients, Domains, and External Contacts. Each user can have a maximum of 1,024 entries in his or her safelist collection.

Safelist Aggregation can only be enabled with the Exchange Management Shell by running the `Update-SafeList` command against a user's mailbox on a server running under the Mailbox server role. That information must then be replicated to the Edge Transport server using EdgeSync.

To configure Safelist Aggregation, complete the following steps:

1. Use the `Update-Safelist` Exchange shell command on a server running under the Mailbox server role to aggregate and copy the safelist collection data from the user's mailbox to the user object in Active Directory.

```
Update-Safelist -Identity HeatherL -Type Both
```

NOTE

To run the `Update-SafeList` command against multiple mailboxes residing in a particular organizational unit, you must prepend its use with the `Get-Mailbox` command. This could also be useful when included inside of a script. At the end of the `Get-Mailbox` command statement, add the `update-safelist` command:

```
Get-Mailbox -OrganizationalUnit CompanyABC.com\Sales\Users |
Update-SafeList
```

2. Schedule the `Update-Safelist` command to run frequently.

```
AT 19:00 /every:M,T,W,Th,F,S,Su  cmd /c "C:\Temp\Update-SafeList"
```

NOTE

You must use the AT command to schedule Safelist Aggregation. The AT command can call to a batch file or script that includes the commands to run Safelist Aggregation.

3. Verify that EdgeSync is properly replicating from the Mailbox server to the Edge Transport server. See the section "Using EdgeSync to Synchronize Active Directory Information to the Edge Transport Server" earlier in this chapter for more information regarding EdgeSync.
4. Ensure the Content Filtering agent is enabled on the Edge Transport server on which you want to perform Safelist Aggregation.

Managing and Maintaining an Edge Transport Server

Managing and maintaining an Edge Transport server requires the same server hardware maintenance, Windows patching and updating, and ongoing system monitoring that is covered in Chapter 14, "Exchange Server 2013 Management and Maintenance Practices." However, there are a handful of things specific to the Edge Transport server, such as exporting the Edge Transport server configuration settings so that if the server needs to be recovered, you can more easily import in the settings after performing a server rebuild. In addition, you can view reports on messages and transport communications managed by the Edge Transport server. The details on how to perform these specific Edge Transport tasks are covered in this section.

Exporting and Importing Edge Transport Server Settings

Exporting the Edge Transport configuration from one server for use on another has two apparent benefits:

- Disaster recovery preparedness
- Cloning the configuration when multiple Edge Transport servers exist in an organization

This section focuses on exporting the Edge Transport configuration for use in these scenarios. For more information on disaster recovery for Exchange Server 2013, see Chapter 16, "Backing Up the Exchange Server 2013 Environment."

Utilizing the process described in this section of the chapter can help ease deployment of Edge Transport servers when a network will have more than one Edge Transport server or changes are frequently made.

NOTE

Exporting and importing the Edge Transport server configuration does not include the Edge subscription file used by a Mailbox server for EdgeSync replication. When importing the Edge configuration data to a new or restored server, ensure the Edge Transport server has a subscription on the Mailbox server and that EdgeSync is properly replicating. More information regarding EdgeSync can be found in the "Configuring EdgeSync on an Edge Transport Server" section of this chapter.

Exporting the Edge Transport server configuration requires the use of a script included with Exchange Server when the Edge Transport server role is selected during installation. The script exports the configuration to an XML file, which can later be used to restore the configuration to the same system or another. The name of this script is `ExportEdgeConfig.ps1` and is located in the `C:\Program Files\Microsoft\Exchange Server\V14\Scripts\` folder on the Edge Transport server. The `ExportEdgeConfig.ps1` script is executed through the Exchange Management Shell. For example, in the Exchange Management Shell on the Edge Transport server:

```
C:
CD "\Program Files\Microsoft\Exchange Server\V14\Scripts"
.\ExportEdgeConfig.ps1
```

Importing the Edge configuration data works in a similar manner, using the `ImportEdgeConfig` command. The name of this script is `ImportEdgeConfig.ps1` and is located in the `C:\Program Files\Microsoft\Exchange Server\V14\Scripts\` folder on the Edge Transport server. The `ImportEdgeConfig.ps1` script is executed through the Exchange Management Shell.

Exporting Edge Transport Server Configuration

Exporting the Edge Transport server configuration is a four-step process. The steps to export and import Edge Transport server configuration settings are shown next:

1. Copy the `ExportEdgeConfig.ps` file from the `C:\Program Files\Microsoft\Exchange Server\V14\Scripts\` folder to the root of your user profile on the Edge Transport server (for example, `C:\Documents and Settings\Administrator\ExportEdgeConfig.ps`).

2. Open the Exchange Management Shell and run the following commands:

   ```
   C:
   CD "\Program Files\Microsoft\Exchange Server\V14\Scripts"
   ./ExportEdgeConfig -cloneConfigData:"C:\temp\CloneConfigData.xml"
   ```

3. If the export is successful, a confirmation message appears showing the location of the exported file.

4. Copy the file to a location where it can be imported by an Edge Transport server.

NOTE

The `CloneConfigData.xml` is intended for use on a server with a clean installation of Exchange Server under the Edge Transport role—with the same name as the server from which the file was exported.

The following items are exported to file:

- Log paths for receive and send protocols, pickup directory, and routing table
- Message tracking log path
- Status and priority of each transport agent
- Send and Receive Connector information
- Accepted and remote domain configurations
- IP Allow and IP Block List information (Provider Lists are not included)
- Content filtering configuration
- Recipient filtering configuration
- Address rewrite entries
- Attachment filtering entries

Importing Edge Transport Server Configuration

After you've exported the Edge Transport server configuration information, you can store the information should you ever need to rebuild the Edge server again, or you might need to configure a secondary Edge server with the exact same configuration settings. The import process brings in the saved configuration settings to a freely installed Edge Server configuration.

To import the Edge Transport server configuration to a system, do the following:

1. Copy the `ExportEdgeConfig.ps` file from the `C:\Program Files\Microsoft\Exchange Server\V14\Scripts\` folder to the root of your user profile on the Edge Transport server to which you are importing the `CloneConfigData.xml` file (for example, `C:\Documents and Settings\Administrator\ExportEdgeConfig.ps`).
2. Copy the `CloneConfigData.xml` file you created during the export process to a location on the server (for example, `C:\temp\CloneConfigData.xml`).
3. Launch the Exchange Management Shell.
4. Run the `ImportEdgeConfig.ps1` script to validate the configuration file and create an answer file (`CloneConfigAnswer.xml`):

```
C:
CD "\Program Files\Microsoft\Exchange Server\V14\Scripts"
.\ImportEdgeConfig.ps1 -CloneConfigData:"C:\temp\CloneConfigData.xml"
-IsImport $false -CloneConfigAnswer:"C:\temp\CloneConfigAnswer.xml"
```

5. A confirmation message is displayed if the answer file was properly exported.
6. Open the `CloneConfigAnswer.xml` file that was created in the previous step. If the file is blank, the configuration is correct and no modification is necessary. If any

configuration items cause a discrepancy, they will be included in the answer file and must be modified for the correct configuration (for example, server name, invalid SMTP Connector IP address, log file path, and so on). Save your changes.

7. After you have reviewed and made any necessary modifications to the answer file, you must import both the `CloneConfigData.xml` file and the modified `CloneConfigAnswer.xml` file. The following syntax is for the `ImportEdgeConfig` command to accomplish this:

NOTE

If the answer file is blank, the configuration is correct and can be used and there is no need to import the answer file.

```
.\ImportEdgeConfig -CloneConfigData:"C:\temp\CloneConfigData.xml"
-IsImport $true -CloneConfigAnswer:"C:\temp\CloneConfigAnswer.xml"
```

8. After the XML file(s) have been imported, a message stating "Importing Edge Configuration Information Succeeded" appears.

9. Configure and run EdgeSync and ensure replication is occurring successfully.

Export the Edge Transport server configuration file and test importing it on a regular basis, especially when multiple changes have been made to the Edge Transport server and to ensure the configuration will work in the event of a disaster or outage. Network Load Balancing and other mechanisms can also help offset the impact of a disaster or system outage.

Viewing Antispam Reports Using Included PowerShell Scripts

The Edge Transport server includes several antispam reports that contain information about the top blocked items, such as IP addresses, domains, and senders, how frequently those items are blocked, how many times those items have been blocked, and who in the organization receives the most spam. The information contained in these reports can assist administrators in fine-tuning the spam filtering agents to achieve a higher level of spam detection while simultaneously reducing the number of false positives.

Antispam reports can only be generated using an Exchange Management Shell command. Each shell command will parse the logs files to create a report. The logs for each Antispam agent are stored in `C:\Program Files\Microsoft\Exchange Server\V14\TransportRoles\Logs\`.

To run any of the following scripts to generate the respective Antispam report, perform the following steps:

1. Launch the Exchange Management Shell on the Edge Transport server.

2. Change to the `C:\Program Files\Microsoft\Exchange Server\v14\Scripts\` folder using the command `cd $exscripts`.

3. Enter a `.\` and the name of the script for the Antispam report you want to review.

```
.\Get-AntispamTopBlockedSenderDomains
```

A handful of PowerShell scripts are included with Exchange Server to generate Antispam reports from the log files. Some of the default scripts are as follows:

- **`Get-AntispamFilteringReport`**—Generates a report displaying a summary of messages that have been rejected by connection, command, or filtering agent
- **`Get-AntispamSCLHistogram`**—Generates a report summarizing the amount of email identified with each SCL threshold (1 to 9 total)
- **`Get-AntispamTopBlockedSenderDomains`**—Generates a report summarizing how many times and how frequently a domain has been blocked
- **`Get-AntispamTopBlockedSenderIPs`**—Generates a report summarizing how many times and how frequently an IP address of a sending mail server has been blocked
- **`Get-AntispamTopBlockedSenders`**—Generates a report summarizing how many times and how frequently a sender's email address has been blocked
- **`Get-AntispamTopRecipients`**—Generates a report summarizing spam volume for recipients and the amount of spam messages received

Exchange Server-Level Security Features

As much as the first part of this chapter has referenced the Edge Server role, with Exchange Server 2013, Microsoft has included basic anti-malware functionality within the core Exchange server roles. So even if an organization chose to not implement an Edge Server or has other methods for protection for Exchange, there is some functionality built in to Exchange to support anti-malware.

In addition, Microsoft has other built-in protections that look for, identify, prevent, and manage common anti-malware activities. Again, without having to put in a specialty server, an organization has a basic level of protection built in to Exchange.

Exchange Server 2013 Antispam Measures

Exchange Server 2013 has integrated antispam measures built in to the Microsoft Exchange platform. These methods are especially effective when coupled with Microsoft Outlook. A few of these features are as follows:

- **Increased protection through integrated security technologies**—Exchange Server 2013 acts as the first line of defense on incoming email messages. The Exchange server determines the legitimacy of the message and is able to disable links or URLs to help protect the user community. In addition, Exchange Server 2013 offers anti-phishing capabilities to help to prevent emails of this nature from reaching your users in the first place.

- **Improved email legitimacy assurance**—Email legitimacy is managed through Email Postmark technology when you combine Microsoft Outlook and Exchange Server autoencryption. Outlook Email Postmark applies a token (actually a computational puzzle that acts as a spam deterrent) to email messages it sends. This token can be read by a receiving Exchange server to confirm the reliability of the incoming message.
- **Distribution lists restricted to authenticated users**—Using message delivery restrictions, you can configure a distribution list to accept mail from all senders, or specific senders or groups. In addition, you can require that all senders be authenticated before their message is accepted.
- **Connection filtering**—Improvements have been made in the configuration and management of IP Block Lists, IP Allow Lists, IP Block List providers, and IP Allow List providers. Each of these elements can now be reviewed and configured directly from the Exchange Management Console.
- **Content filtering**—Exchange Server 2013 includes the Exchange Intelligent Message Filter, or IMF, which uses the Microsoft SmartScreen patented "machine-learning" technology. This content filter evaluates inbound messages and determines the probability of whether the messages are legitimate, fraudulent, or spam.

  In addition, the IMF consolidates information that is collected from connection filtering, sender filtering, recipient filtering, sender reputation, Sender ID verification, and Microsoft Outlook Email Postmark validation. The IMF then applies an SCL rating to a given message. Based on this rating, an administrator can configure actions on the message based on this SCL rating. These actions might include the following:

  - Delivery to a user Inbox or Junk E-mail folder.
  - Delivery to the spam quarantine mailbox.
  - Rejection of the message and no delivery.
  - Acceptance and deletion of the message. The server accepts the message and deletes it instead of forwarding it to the recipient mailbox.
- **Antispam updates**—Exchange Server 2013 offers update services for its antispam components. The standard Exchange Server 2013 antispam filter updates every 2 weeks. The Forefront Security for Exchange Server antispam filter updates every 24 hours.
- **Spam quarantine**—The spam quarantine provides a temporary storage location for messages that have been identified as spam and that should not be delivered to a user mailbox. Messages that have been labeled as spam are enclosed in an NDR and are delivered to a spam quarantine mailbox. Exchange Server administrators can manage these messages and can perform several actions, such as rejecting the message, deleting it, or flagging it as a false positive and releasing it to the originally intended recipient. In addition, messages with an SCL rating that the administrator

has defined as "borderline" can be released to the user's Junk E-mail folder in Outlook. These borderline messages are converted to plain text to provide additional protection for the user.

- **Recipient filtering**—In the past, an email that was addressed to a specific domain would enter that domain's messaging service, regardless of whether it was addressed to a valid recipient. This not only utilized bandwidth, but also required Exchange servers to process the messages, create an NDR, and send that message back out. Now, by using the EdgeSync process on your Mailbox server, you can replicate recipient data from the enterprise Active Directory into the Exchange AD LDS instance on the Edge Transport server. This enables the Recipient Filter agent to perform recipient lookups for inbound messages. Now, you can block messages that are sent to nonexistent users (or to internal use only distribution lists).
- **Sender ID**—First implemented in Exchange Server 2003 Service Pack 2 (SP2), Sender ID filtering technology primarily targets forgery of email addresses by verifying that each email message actually originates from the Internet domain that it claims to. Sender ID examines the sender's IP address, and compares it with the sending ID record in the originator's public DNS server. This is one way of eliminating spoofed email before it enters your organization and uses your company resources.
- **Sender reputation**—The Sender Reputation agent uses patented Microsoft technology to calculate the trustworthiness of unknown senders. This agent collects analytical data from Simple Mail Transfer Protocol (SMTP) sessions, message content, Sender ID verification, and general sender behavior and creates a history of sender characteristics. The agent then uses this knowledge to determine whether a sender should be temporarily added to the Blocked Senders list.
- **IP Reputation Service**—Provided by Microsoft exclusively for Exchange Server customers, this service is an IP Block List that allows administrators to implement and use IP Reputation Service in addition to other real-time Block List services.
- **Outlook junk email filter lists aggregation**—This feature helps reduce false positives in antispam filtering by propagating Microsoft Outlook Junk E-mail Filter lists to Mailbox servers and to Edge Transport servers.

Built-in Anti-Malware in Exchange Server 2013

Exchange Server 2013 has built-in anti-malware capabilities, specifically methods for organizations to respond to malware and ways to provide notifications to Exchange administrators. The built-in anti-malware configuration is part of the Exchange Administration Center. To access and configure the integrated options, do the following:

1. As an Exchange administrator, log in to the Exchange Administration Center (EAC), going to https://{*domainname*}/ecp.
2. Click Protection and initially view and edit the default Anti-Malware policy (additional policies can be added at a future date).

3. In the Settings for the Anti-Malware policy, choose the Malware Detection Response (which includes "Block the Entire Message," "Delete All Attachments and Use Default Alert Text," or "Delete All Attachments and Use Custom Alert Text").
4. For Notifications, choose to "Notify Internal Senders," "Notify External Senders," or both. Many times, organizations choose to inform internal users so that internal users know messages are blocked, but external users are not informed so that an external violator is not provided information about attempts to prevent or block access.
5. For Administrator Notifications, choose who you want to notify when an anti-malware event is occurring, whether just the administrator or choose someone of your choice to get notified of an anti-malware event.
6. Once the preferred options have been set, click Save to save the settings and have them applied.

Additional Antispam Measures

In the battle against spam, passive measures protect your organization, but more aggressive measures can help lessen the problem overall. The following sections cover some suggestions of ways that your organization can help fight back.

Utilizing Blacklists

Many companies are unknowingly serving as open relays. Many spammers take advantage of this lack of security and utilize the organization's messaging system to send their unsolicited email. When a company or domain is reported as an open relay, the domain can be placed on a blacklist. This blacklist, in turn, can be used by other companies to prevent incoming mail from a known open relay source.

You can find some organizations that maintain blacklists or can check whether your organization is currently being blacklisted, visit the following addresses:

- **MX Toolbox**—http://www.mxtoolbox.com/blacklists.aspx/
- **What's My IPAddress**—http://whatismyipaddress.com/blacklist-check
- **Open Relay Database**—http://ordb.org

Report Spammers

Organizations and laws are getting tougher on spammers, but spam prevention requires users and organizations to report the abuse. Although this often is a difficult task because many times the source is undecipherable, it is nonetheless important to take a proactive stance and report abuses.

Users should contact the system administrator or help desk if they receive or continue to receive spam, virus hoaxes, and other such fraudulent offers. System administrators should report spammers and contact mail abuse organizations, such as those listed earlier in the "Utilizing Blacklists" section.

System administrators should use discretion before reporting or blocking an organization. For example, if your company were to receive spam messages that appeared to originate from Yahoo! or Hotmail, it wouldn't necessarily be in your best interest simply to block those domains. In that example, the cure might be worse than the disease, so to speak.

Third-Party Antispam Products

Although Microsoft has equipped users, system administrators, and third-party organizations with many tools necessary to combat spam, the additional use of a third-party product, or products, can provide additional protection. These third-party products can also provide a multitude of features that help with reporting, customization, and filtering mechanisms to maximize spam blocking, while minimizing false positives.

Do Not Use Open SMTP Relays

By default, Exchange Server 2013 is not configured to allow open relays. If an SMTP relay is necessary in the messaging environment, take the necessary precautions to ensure that only authorized users or systems have access to these SMTP relays.

NOTE

You can use the Exchange Best Practice Analyzer, or other tools such as Sam Spade (www.samspade.org/), to check your environment for open mail relays.

Protecting Exchange Server 2013 from Viruses

Exchange Server 2013 includes many improvements to assist organizations with their antivirus strategies. The product continues to support the Virus Scanning Application Programming Interface (VSAPI). In addition, Microsoft has made a significant investment in the creation of more effective, efficient, and programmable virus scanning at the transport level.

A few of the antivirus measures included in Exchange Server 2013 are listed as follows:

- **Transport agents**—Exchange Server 2013 improves upon the concept of transport agents that was introduced with Exchange Server 2007. Agents are managed software components that perform a task in response to an application event. These agents act on transport events, much like event sinks in earlier versions of Exchange Server. Third-party developers can write customized agents that are capable of utilizing the Exchange MIME parsing engine allowing extremely robust antivirus scanning. The Exchange Server 2013 MIME parsing engine has evolved over many years of Exchange Server development and is likely the most trusted and capable MIME engine in the industry.
- **Antivirus stamping**—Exchange Server 2013 provides antivirus stamping, a method of stamping messages that were scanned for viruses with the version of the antivirus software that performed the scan and the result of the scan. This feature helps reduce the volume of antivirus scanning across an organization because, as the message travels through the messaging system with the antivirus stamp attached,

other systems can immediately determine whether additional scanning must be performed on the message.

- **Attachment filtering**—In Exchange Server 2013, Microsoft has implemented attachment filtering by a transport agent. By enabling attachment filtering on your organization's Edge Transport server, you can reduce the spread of malicious attachments before they enter the organization.

NOTE

Although Exchange Server 2013 provides features to help minimize an organization's exposure to viruses, it does not have true, built-in antivirus protection, as Exchange Server does not actually scan messages or attachments to look for infection. However, continued support for the built-in VSAPI allows specialized antivirus programs to connect their applications to your Exchange Server environment to scan messages as they are handled by Exchange Server.

Forefront Security for Exchange Server

Designed by Microsoft specifically for Exchange Server, Forefront Security for Exchange Server is a server-based anti-malware product. Because Exchange and Forefront were designed to work together, Forefront integrates with Exchange Server 2013 to provide improved protection, performance, and centralized management.

Forefront Security for Exchange Server delivers the following:

- Advanced protection against viruses, worms, phishing, and other threats by utilizing up to five antivirus engines simultaneously at each layer of the messaging infrastructure
- Optimized performance through coordinated scanning across Edge, Hub, and Mailbox servers and features such as in-memory scanning, multithreaded scanning processes, and performance bias settings
- Centralized management of remote installation, engine and signature updating, reporting, and alerts through the Forefront Server Security Management Console

Although the client antivirus protection that is provided by Forefront Security for Exchange Server is language independent, the setup, administration of the product, and end-user notifications are currently available in 11 server languages. When Forefront Security for Exchange Server detects a message that appears to be infected with a virus, the system generates a notification message and sends it to the recipient's mailbox. This message is written in the language of the server running Forefront because the server is not able to detect the language of the destination mailbox.

Third-Party Antivirus Products for Exchange Server

In addition, there are many third-party antivirus vendors in the marketplace. Many mechanisms can be used to protect the messaging environment from viruses and other malicious code. Most third-party virus-scanning products scan for known virus signatures and provide some form of heuristics to scan for unknown viruses. Other antivirus products block suspicious or specific types of message attachments at the point of entry before a possible virus reaches the Information Store.

Antivirus products keep viruses from reaching the end user in two fundamental ways:

- **Gateway scanning**—Gateway scanning works by scanning all messages as they go through the SMTP gateway (typically connected to the Internet). If the message contains a virus or is suspected of carrying a virus, the antivirus product can clean, quarantine, or delete it before it enters your Exchange Server organization.
- **Mailbox scanning**—Mailbox scanning is useful to remove viruses that have entered the Information Store. For example, a new virus might make it into the Exchange Server environment before a signature file that can detect it is in place. These messages on the Information Store cannot be scanned by a gateway application; however, with an antivirus product that is capable of scanning the Information Store, these messages can be found and deleted.

NOTE

In the past half decade for Microsoft Exchange, the movement is away from scanning individual mailboxes and instead scanning at the "transport" layer. In Exchange Server 2013, *all* messages have to pass through the transport layer whether it is a message coming in from the Internet, going out to the Internet, or going from user to user, the message hits the mailbox. As such, scanning content "through" the mailbox ensures that all messages are scanned before a virus ends up in a user's mailbox. A periodic scan, say weekly or monthly, of the mailbox databases can validate that a virus had not slipped through, or possibly that a new strain of virus made it past the transport scan, but a mailbox scanner can clean up any slippage. However, less effort is paid these days in scanning mailboxes, thus minimizing the performance impact on Exchange for mailbox communications with scans to the mailboxes and the mailbox database.

Antivirus Outsourcing

Although an organization can put in place many gateway antivirus products to address antispam and antivirus issues, outsourcing these tasks has gained popularity in recent years. Companies specializing in antivirus and antispam are able to host your organization's MX records, scanning all messages bound for your company, and forwarding the clean messages to your organization. Although this removes a level of control from your administrators, many organizations are finding this outsourcing cost-effective, as they no longer have to maintain staff devoted strictly to these measures. One such provider is Microsoft Forefront Online Protection for Exchange (or FOPE) covered in the next section of this book.

Forefront Online Protection for Exchange

Managing and maintaining an Edge Transport server takes time and is vital to an organization's email security framework. Organizations can offset this responsibility (at a cost) to Microsoft using FOPE. FOPE is an email hygiene solution that exists in the cloud and is administered by Microsoft. Organizations can also choose to implement a hybrid approach, in which part of the messaging hygiene solutions are provided by Microsoft and some reside onsite. Both have distinct advantages and disadvantages. Off-loading spam and virus filtering to Forefront Online Security for Exchange Hosted Services can significantly reduce the amount of processing power and administrative overhead for the organization.

For regulatory compliance, corporate policy, technical limitations, or other reasons, not all organizations might take advantage of Forefront Online Security for Exchange Hosted Services; however, some of the same technologies used with Forefront Online Security for Exchange Hosted Services are built in to the Edge Transport server and Forefront Security for Exchange, so either way Microsoft customers get strong technologies for combating spam and malicious email.

The Forefront Online Security for Exchange Hosted Services utilizes the following anti-spam technologies to maintain a high level of spam detection and low level of false positives:

- Sender Reputation Analysis
- Recipient Validation
- Fingerprinting
- Content Filtering
- Rules-Based Message Scoring
- Custom Filtering Management

Using a Hybrid Solution for Messaging Hygiene

Implementing a hybrid solution where both a hosted and onsite solution is used to filter email provides the most flexibility and protection for the messaging infrastructure and is highly recommended if hosted services are going to be used at all. The most common implementation off-loads spam and malware filtering to the Forefront Online Security service while onsite malware scanning and other filtering rules are still used.

It is not uncommon for newer spam campaigns and malware messages to be identified by a cloud-based hosted service before the onsite solution because onsite solutions require periodic updates to be downloaded and installed before the malicious message reaches the network. This is because hosted solutions are updated first and typically on a much more frequent basis. In addition, hosted services handle mail for organizations around the globe making it possible for a new spammed piece of malware to go undetected in one country or region, and then get detected for all other parts of the world due to the nature of how the hosted service monitors mail and update the database used to identify unwanted messages.

An onsite solution, however, is necessary to add another layer of scanning should a message go undetected by the hosted service, and also to prevent against inside attacks, which would not be monitored by the hosted service. This applies more to malware and virus attacks than spam runs. Because both Forefront Online Security for Exchange Hosted Services and Forefront Security for Exchange utilize multiple scan engines, the attack surface is very low; however, no solution is 100% immune to attack.

Summary

The Edge Transport server provides an important layer of security between the general Internet and an organization's messaging environment. If set up properly, an Edge server can successfully filter unwanted content, such as spam, viruses, or inappropriate content. If not set up properly, an Edge server can filter desired content and accidentally eliminate critical messages of communications. The focus of this chapter was to provide guidance on implementing, configuring, and fine-tuning an Edge server to improve its impact on the filtering and management of information into a network.

Best Practices

The following are best practices from this chapter:

- Filter for spam before processing messages because spam accounts for the majority of mail messages transported on the Internet.
- When configuring an Edge server, configure it with minimal configuration rules and then add rules while testing a successful hit rate on filtration, and then fine-tune the filtering to be more restrictive.
- When first implementing filtration, consider stamping questionable messages with the word *Suspect* or something similar rather than deleting the message so you can track which messages might possibly be filtered when they otherwise shouldn't be.
- Configure Allow Lists to ensure messages from desired message senders or organizations are not filtered and that they are successfully received by the intended recipient.
- Configure custom Block Lists to ensure that messages from email senders or specific domains are not transmitted to users, but instead are blocked at the Edge server.
- Enable Safelist Aggregation that will collect users' safelists and add safelist users to the Edge server filters to allow content to be allowed instead of blocked by rule.
- Use message attachment filtering to assess the content of attachments as part of an appropriate content filtering process.

- Enable address rewriting when needed to standardize on domain address names used by the organization.
- When an Edge-based application utilizes directory content such as username and email address lists, use EdgeSync to propagate the directory information to the Edge server.
- Export Edge Transport server configuration information and store the information along with other server build documentation. The exported Edge Transport configuration information can be imported to a new system in the event of a server replacement or server failure scenario.

CHAPTER 12

Designing and Implementing Message Archiving, Retention, and eDiscovery

IN THIS CHAPTER

- Why Is Email Archiving and Retention So Important These Days?
- What Is Archiving, Retention, and eDiscovery?
- Archiving in Exchange Using Archive Mailboxes
- Creating and Using an Exchange Archive Mailbox
- Retention in Exchange Server 2013 Using Retention Policies
- Handling Legal Hold in Exchange
- eDiscovery and Searching for Content

When email was first introduced decades ago, the concept of sending information instantaneously instead of sending letters and documents through the postal system was an amazing concept. Email has had a major impact on the postal system where all forms of communications beyond just simple communications but also legal contracts, secured intellectual property documents, and confidential communications get sent every day over email.

However, with the transport of sensitive and legal communications comes the responsibility, obligation, and legal compliance requirements to protect the communications as *evidence*. As evidence, emails can no longer simply be deleted when an organization or an individual is being investigated for a crime. In terms of regulatory compliance and corporate governance, even government restrictions require email "paper trails" to be retained for months, years, or even the length of life of products or drug development in the case of the pharmaceutical industry in the United States.

Email archiving, retention, and the ability to discover (or eDiscovery) information is not just a request of information technology administrators and departments, but a legal obligation punishable by heavy fines and even imprisonment for not retaining information required by law.

Fortunately, Microsoft includes email archiving, retention, and eDiscovery functionality and tools right in the Exchange Server 2013 product that help organizations meet their legal and regulatory requirements.

Why Is Email Archiving and Retention So Important These Days?

Email archiving used to be as simple as a user who wanted to keep years of email messages, but couldn't keep them in his or her Inbox as the clutter of messages either made it hard to find active mail messages, or the organization had a policy to delete messages in the user's active mailbox, so users resorted to archiving old messages in a Personal Folder file (PST). PST files solved the problem at the user level, but created a bigger problem at the business level because the PST files that stored old archived emails of users commonly were not backed up and were subject to legal subpoena; however, the evidence could be easily lost. Further, PST files are very costly to collect and search when discovery is demanded.

For a while, lawyers were instructing their clients to eliminate emails every 60–90 days so that the organization *had* no retained messages. This was the best practice for most of the 1990s and 2000s with the thinking that if the organization had a policy to automatically delete messages, there was no obligation by the company to retain the information and, thus, no recourse for searching for and providing the evidence.

However, users continued to use PST files to archive old email messages without their employers knowing. Then came the introduction of iPads and mobile phones where content was stored and users didn't realize that old messages were being stored on their devices. While the organization was deleting messages on the back end, users were retaining information on a multitude of devices.

With the challenges of having a proper email archiving, retention, and eDiscovery process organizationwide, the best practice for organizations is to take a holistic approach to email and content management. Organizations are now allowing users to retain messages, and technology is being implemented in organizations to manage the content, including properly retaining content required by law and providing sophisticated methods for searching content when necessary.

What Is Archiving, Retention, and eDiscovery?

To be able to retrieve information for legal or official purposes, information must be properly retained so that the integrity of the information retrieved is valid. Lawyers will often request an audit trail to verify and authenticate the information by showing the chain of custody by whom and how the information was preserved and collected. As an example, if the Human Resources Department, Legal Department, or outside legal counsel wants to gather information, it's not good enough to just go into a user's mailbox and extract information because the information in a mailbox is considered fragile. It is fragile because a user can easily delete a key message or the user can even go in using the Microsoft Outlook client and *edit* a message. If someone opens a user's mailbox, the messages in the Outlook client can be tampered with and then the data is *not* considered valid evidence, even if the modification occurs accidentally.

In the past, Exchange Server 2007, Exchange Server 2003, or earlier required specific technologies and practices to protect the messages from tampering. The old way of doing things was to buy a third-party archiving product, such as Symantec Enterprise Vault, Iron Mountain/Mimosa NearPoint for Exchange, EMC EmailXtender, Zantaz EAS, or the like. The third-party tools required a separate server, typically a special agent to be installed on all Exchange servers and clients, and a relatively high expense to manage, maintain, and support the archiving server and services.

With Exchange Server 2007, Microsoft included email *journaling* that allowed a copy of any and all emails to be forwarded to a journaling server so that while a user's mailbox content might have been tampered with, the journaling server mailbox would have an unmodified version of the content. Legal review of the journal copy provided assurances that the copy had not been edited.

With the release of Exchange Server 2010 and the archiving capabilities built in to Exchange Server 2010, some mistakenly believed they must create an archive mailbox for all users to preserve data, which is not true. An archive mailbox creates a second mailbox store for a user to move content from his or her primary mailbox to the archive mailbox to get it out of the primary mailbox, but data retention can actually be done straight in Exchange Server 2010 simply by extending the deleted item retention period and enabling the Single Instance Recovery function of Exchange. In addition, Exchange Server 2010 introduced Legal Hold, a feature that prevents email from being purged from Recoverable Deleted Items for a period of time.

With Exchange Server 2013, Microsoft has further extended the capabilities of email archiving and eDiscovery with the enhancement of in-place discovery functionality. With several improvements in Exchange Server 2013, many organizations that were using third-party archiving and retention tools are simply using what Microsoft provides out of the box. It is easier to utilize the integrated tools; the integrated tools are just as sophisticated in storing and recovering content; and when the organization patches, updates, or migrates its mail, the organization doesn't have to spend extra time dealing with yet another third-party product and the integration and migration of the product and technology.

Archiving in Exchange Using Archive Mailboxes

The Archive Mailbox feature in Exchange Server 2013 simply allows a user (or the organization through rules) to move messages out of his or her primary mailbox to the archive mailbox to keep the primary mailbox small and the archive as large as the user (or organization) requires. The archive mailbox is an alternative to PST files that users have used for years to back up or archive their messages, but instead of being scattered across file systems, hard drives, USB drives, and other devices, archived mail can be kept in the user's archive mailbox for quick and easy search and access.

As noted at the start of this chapter, archiving is simply the storage of messages with the intent of having access to old messages in the future. Messaging retention, covered later in this chapter in the "Retention in Exchange Server 2013 Using Retention Policies" section, involves storing messages for a designated period of time, typically for legal purposes. An organization may choose to retain messages for three years or seven years due to a regulatory compliance reason. However, this section addresses just simple archiving, which is typically done for the purpose of splitting off active messages from old messages using a separate archive mailbox.

Using Outlook PST Files for Message Archiving

As mentioned at the start of this chapter, PST files were the method of email archiving for years, and to this day, it is common to find organizations with very strict email deletion policies that have executives with years of email messages stuffed in PST files. In enterprise organizations, PST files became prevalent when organizations started to enforce message deletion and placed mailbox size limits on users. Many times, the mailbox size limits were to prevent users from keeping old messages, but in addition, small mailboxes meant less data for the organization to store and, thus, small mailboxes were less expensive to store and manage old information.

In any case, users simply copied content off of their Exchange mailbox into PST files and stored the PST files on their laptops, desktops, or network servers, so ultimately, no disk space was typically saved, and the organization was still liable for the subpoena of PST files. The big challenge was when the organization was subpoenaed for content; the organization now had the responsibility to search the hard drives, USB drives, thumbsticks, network servers, and other storage mediums in the organization, making it even harder for the organization to now find the information it was trying to just make go away.

Using Exchange Server 2013 Archive Mailbox for Message Archiving

With archive mailboxes in Exchange Server 2010 and now in Exchange Server 2013, organizations can simply create a second online archive mailbox for a user, and the user can drag and drop messages from the primary mailbox to the secondary mailbox. As far as the user is concerned, the experience is identical to what the user was doing with PST files in that the archive mailbox is available for the user to drag and drop years of messages, calendar appointments, contacts, and other information into the archive mailbox.

The organization benefits from minimizing the user's primary mailbox size, which the organization would keep on highly available servers, backed up and replicated with high availability and disaster recovery in mind. However, the bulk of a user's mail data would be in the archive, which could be backed up less frequently because the loss of the archive server and subsequent restoral of the server and data could be done across days of time instead of instant minimal downtime as in the primary Mailbox server and data.

If an organization has different classifications of storage, such as can be the case when using storage area network (SAN)–based storage, there may be cost advantages to the organization to put the archive mailbox databases on lower-cost storage than is used for the primary mailbox databases. However, with the storage performance improvements that have been introduced in Exchange Server 2010 and further enhanced in Exchange Server 2013, there may not be any significant storage cost improvement that is possible by separating the archive mailbox databases onto separate storage.

One key advantage to the online archive mailbox is that it is not synchronized with the offline folders in Outlook, an important consideration when large mailbox quotas are provided. The thought of synchronizing a 25GB mailbox can be daunting, especially when it is necessary to perform an initial full synchronization, such as might happen when a computer is replaced or the Offline Storage (OST) file becomes corrupted. In addition, having a smaller primary mailbox and an online archive may improve Outlook performance, especially when performing I/O-intensive activities like searching a mailbox.

Organizations are able to buy and implement lower-cost server equipment for the archive server, the user can retain and access years of old messages, the organization can quickly search and access content in the case of litigation, and the organization can do away with the troublesome PST files.

Creating and Using an Exchange Archive Mailbox

Exchange archive mailboxes are a built-in function to Exchange Server 2013, and just as the organization creates a user and his or her primary mailbox, the administrator can simply go into the Exchange Control Panel (ECP) and create an archive mailbox for the user. The user ends up with two mailboxes; the organization can choose to put both mailboxes on the same server in the same database, but the organization most likely would put the archive mailbox on a lower-cost server and lower-cost storage subsystem (one of the main purposes of having a mailbox archive).

Creating an Exchange Archive Database

Before creating an archive mailbox for a user, the administrator first creates an archive database where he or she will store the archive mailboxes. As noted, the archive database is usually created on a separate, lower-cost server; however, if the organization doesn't have a less-expensive Exchange server on which to create the Exchange archive database, at a minimum, the administrator should create a new archive database.

To build the archive database, do the following:

1. Log on to the ECP with a user who has Exchange administration rights; the uniform resource locator (URL) is https://{*servername*}/ecp.
2. Click Servers in the left pane to view the various servers in the Exchange Server 2013 organization.
3. Click Databases at the top of the Servers screen, and then click the plus (+) button to create a new mailbox database.
4. Fill in the New Database page noting the name of the database, the Exchange server on which the archive database will be created, a database file path on that server (including the log folder path) where the database will be stored, and the file path where the logs will be stored, similar to what is shown in Figure 12.1.

FIGURE 12.1 Creating an Exchange database for the archive mailboxes.

NOTE

Despite the new database page requesting the database file path, it is looking for not only the path, but also the name of the file ending in EDB. So for the database path, it may end up being `c:\Program Files\Microsoft\Exchange Server\v15\Mailbox\ArchiveDB\ArchiveDB.edb` where the ArchiveDB is the name of the subfolder, and the archive database will be `archivedb.edb`.

5. Click Save.

The save time will take 30–60 seconds to complete; it is creating an Exchange EDB database for the archive and mounting the database for use.

Creating an Exchange Archive Mailbox

To create an archive mailbox, the user first needs to be created in Active Directory and have a primary mailbox created for the user. Basic Exchange user and mailbox creation is covered in Chapter 6, "Installing and Configuring the Basics of Exchange Server 2013 for a Brand-New Environment." With the basic user created, the creation of the archive mailbox is as follows:

1. Log on to the ECP with a user who has Exchange administration rights; the URL is https://{*servername*}/ecp.
2. Click Recipients in the left pane to view the list of the user mailboxes.
3. Click to select a user for whom you want to create an archive mailbox, and then click the Edit icon (depicted by a pencil) to edit the recipient.
4. Click Mailbox Features in the list of mail options.
5. Scroll down to the Archiving option and click Enable to enable the archiving for the recipient.
6. Browse and choose a database in which you want to place the archive mailbox (this will likely be selecting the archive database created in the last section), as shown in Figure 12.2, click OK to create the archive mailbox for the user, and then click Save to save the user setting.
7. Create the desired folders in the personal archive because it is created without any, except for the Deleted Items folder.

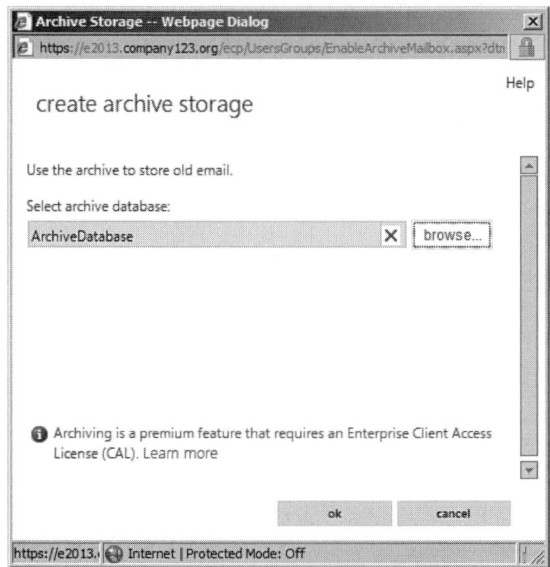

FIGURE 12.2 Creating an archive mailbox for a user.

Manually Dragging/Dropping Content to the Archive Mailbox

Once the archive mailbox has been created for the user, when the user logs in to Exchange, whether it is from an Outlook 2010 or Outlook 2013 client or from Outlook Web Access 2013, the user will now see a "Personal Archive" in his or her list of folders. The user can create subfolders in this personal archive; frequently users create folders based on the names of their clients, the names of their projects, or sometimes date ranges to designate messages organized by time. In any case, the personal archive is now available for the user to move content to the archive.

Moving content from the user's primary mailbox or even from a PST to the personal archive is simply selecting the message(s) and dragging and dropping the messages into folders in the personal archive.

To move content, you can choose from a handful of ways to manually get content into the personal archive, including the following:

- Drag messages one at a time (or hold down the Shift key or the Ctrl key to select multiple messages) and then drop the messages into a folder in the archive.
- Select messages one at a time (or hold down the Shift key or the Ctrl key to select multiple messages) and then right-click and select Move to move messages to the personal archive, as shown in Figure 12.3.

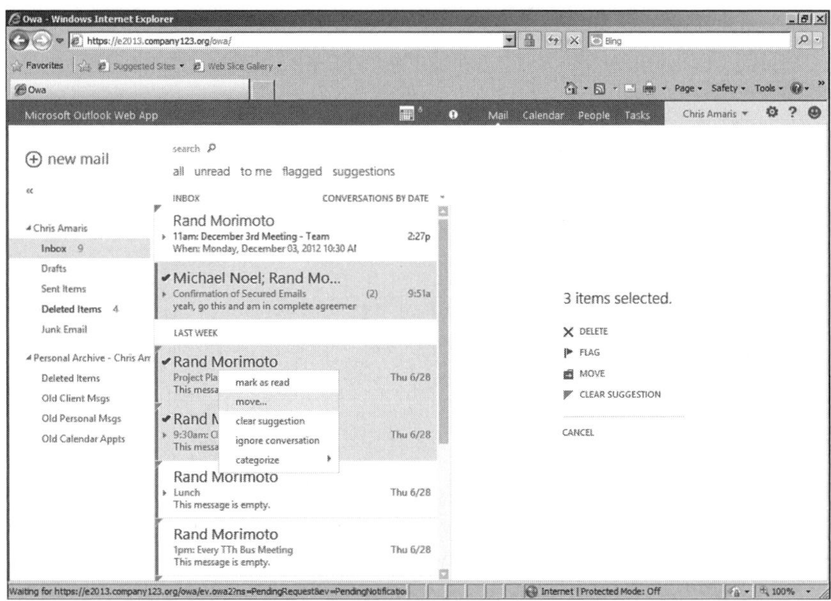

FIGURE 12.3 Moving messages to the personal archive.

Either method will result in the entire conversation thread (replies, forwards, and so on) being moved.

Manually Purging Content from the Archive Mailbox

Once the archive mailbox retains the messages that the user wants to get out of his or her primary mailbox, the user can easily go through the archive mailbox and delete messages. The Search function in Outlook can search a specific mailbox or a specific folder plus the subfolders under the mailbox. This can aid the user in searching for messages by keywords, even turning on Conversation view and purging messages that are no longer wanted or needed.

Retention in Exchange Server 2013 Using Retention Policies

As much as we've covered email archiving so far, archiving is *not* email retention. Archiving is simply moving messages out of the primary mailbox into another mailbox without any specific legal process of preserving the message during the archiving (moving) process. Retention is the ability of actually keeping messages, not just the content of the messages, but with the ability of preserving the integrity of the message so that if requested, the organization can show that the message was properly handled.

This section covers message retention and what is done in the industry and what can be done in the box in Exchange Server 2013 to address the retention of messages in Exchange.

Third-Party Solutions to Email Retention

Message retention in the past decade has for the most part relied on third-party solutions for the proper retention and ultimate eDiscovery of mail messages with solutions from Symantec, Iron Mountain, Zantaz, EMC, and the like as the mainstays in the industry. The third-party message archiving, retention, and eDiscovery tools all had different approaches to managing content, from pulling the messages out of Exchange completely and storing them on separate proprietary servers to just utilizing Microsoft's in-the-box functionality of Exchange message journaling or database recovery.

Although the third-party solutions worked extremely well at what they did, they were challenging to implement, taking weeks and months to get working, and the third-party solutions were notoriously difficult to maintain and manage between Exchange service pack upgrades and major version upgrades. Many organizations spent weeks and months planning and migrating archives during Exchange Server 2003 to Exchange Server 2007 migrations, so when Microsoft shipped message archiving and retention in Exchange Server 2010, organizations started to shift their usage to what Microsoft provided "in the box."

Less complicated to implement are cloud-based archives, which generally just require the simple configuration of a journal rule that forwards a copy of every message to the journal service's email address over the Internet.

With email archiving and email retention right within the Exchange architecture and base messaging implementation environment, service pack upgrades and version upgrades simply have archives and retention logs migrate along with the user's mailboxes.

Journaling in Exchange

Journaling in Exchange is the function where all messages going in and out of an Exchange server are captured and duplicated, with one copy continuing on to its destination, and another copy protected and stored in an Exchange journaling mailbox. Because each and every message in Exchange Server 2013 *has* to go through the Hub Transport service of a Mailbox server, whether the message is coming in from the Internet, going out to the Internet, or going from user to user within the organization, the Hub Transport service is the perfect place to fork the message and make an uneditable copy.

If content is ever requested to be validated, the organization could go to the user's mailbox to capture data, but because data within a user's mailbox is potentially subject to tampering, the organization is best off grabbing information off the journal server. Messages within a user's mailbox can be tampered with simply by having the user open the message, edit the message, and then press the Esc key and save the message back to Outlook. To any common reader, the message will appear authentic and can mistakenly be used as proof and evidence. With journaling, as long as there are security controls in place minimizing access to the journal server, the journal database, and the journaling mailbox, the organization can prove that the journal copy is indeed authentic and it can be used in any and all legal jurisdictions as evidence.

Implementing Journaling in Exchange

Journaling is easy to implement in an organization; effectively with journaling, a rule is created in the Exchange organization that says all messages get forwarded to a specific journal mailbox. The journaling mailbox is nothing more than a glorified user mailbox. Conceptually, journaling is like having every single email message cc'd to this journaling mailbox. The key to the success of the integrity of journaling is to ensure that no one has access to the journaling mailbox, database, and server so that no tampering can be implied or proved.

Best practice for journaling is to create a dedicated Exchange server that is a member of the Exchange organization, has a dedicated mailbox database on the server solely for the purpose of email journaling, and has a single journaling mailbox created on the server that will be the journaling mailbox. The server should be hardened and protected so that the normal Exchange administrators and the normal Windows Domain Administrators do not have access to the journal server. Commonly, two individuals share access to the server with logons, passwords, smart cards, and keys so that it takes two individuals to access the journal server.

By protecting the journal server, the organization can provide more proof that the server, database, and data on the server have not been tampered with.

Enabling Journaling in Exchange

To enable journaling in Exchange, the first thing that needs to be done is a journaling mailbox needs to be created as mentioned in the "Implementing Journaling in Exchange" section. The journaling mailbox is nothing more than a normal user mailbox placed on a server and database that is protected as best as possible in terms of security and integrity. For performance and data integrity, however, the journaling mailbox is generally created in a separate dedicated mailbox database, usually on separate physical disks. To create a journaling mailbox, do the following:

1. Log on to the ECP with a user who has Exchange administration rights; the URL is https://{*servername*}/ecp.
2. If there is not one already, create a journaling mailbox database using the same procedure you used to create the archive database.
3. Click Recipients in the left pane to view the list of the user mailboxes.
4. Click the plus (+) symbol to create a new mailbox.
5. Enter in a username (such as `JournalMB`), create a new user account for the mailbox, provide a secure password, and specify to put the mailbox on your protected server.
6. Select More Options; for Specify the Mailbox Database, click Browse and select the journaling mailbox database.
7. Click Save to create the journaling mailbox user and mailbox.

The next step is to create and email a journal rule that will automatically tell Exchange to send all messages to the journaling mailbox you just created. To create the rule, do the following:

1. Log on to the ECP with a user who has Exchange administration rights; the URL is https://{*servername*}/ecp.
2. Click Mail Flow in the left pane.
3. Click Journaling in the Mail Flow options.
4. Click the plus (+) button to add a new journal rule.
5. For the If the Message Is Sent To or From option, choose to journal for a specific user or for all users. Typically, organizations that do journaling journal for all users, and, thus, you would choose [Apply to all messages].
6. For the Journal the Following Messages option, typically organizations choose All Messages, although All Internal Messages or All External Messages can be selected.
7. For the Send Journal Reports To option, this typically goes to the journal administrator, the person in compliance who would want to receive reports on the status of journaling in the organization. The resultant screen looks similar to what is shown in Figure 12.4.
8. Click Save to save the journal rule, and then click Yes to confirm.

Now, all messages that are sent or received will be captured with a secured copy forwarded to the journaling mailbox that you created. When you want to extract information as evidence from the journaling mailbox, follow a very practical and well-documented approach with multiple personnel participating to ensure the integrity of the search and data extraction.

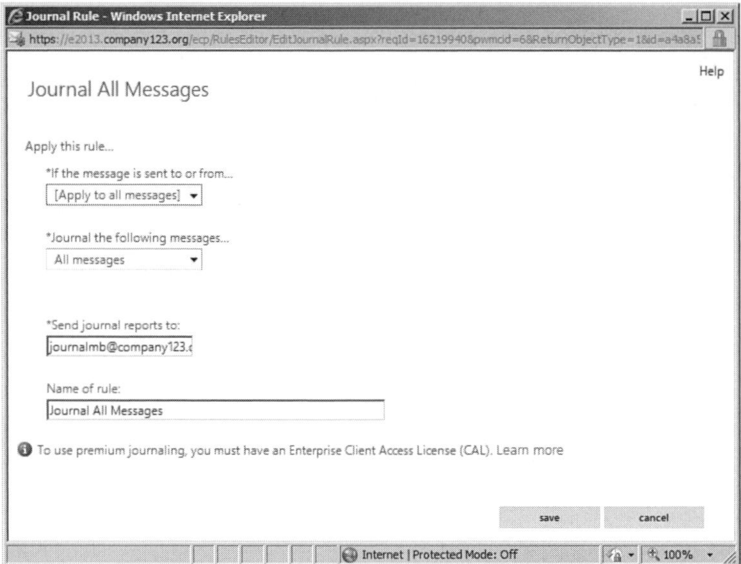

FIGURE 12.4 Creating a journal rule for message retention in Exchange Server 2013.

Viewing Journaled Information in Exchange

After journaling is enabled and messages are sent that should be captured by the journal rule, information out of the journaling mailbox can be reviewed. The journaling review process is as follows:

1. Make sure that proper controls are in place to document the journal review, validating who is logging in to the journal server, the access to journal content, and the validation that the journal information is acquired properly.
2. Log on to the journaling mailbox (in the previous section, we created a journaling mailbox with the name JournalMB) using Outlook Web App (OWA) or an Outlook client.
3. In the Inbox will be all of the journaled messages. The messages will have an attachment that has a captured copy of the original message sent between users as well as be time and date stamped with a unique message ID for the message, as shown in Figure 12.5.

"In-the-Box" Retention of Messages in Exchange

Although an organization can continue to buy third-party products as well as do journaling in Exchange Server 2013, an easy way of handling message retention and legal recovery and eDiscovery can be used by making setting changes right in Exchange Server 2013.

When a user deletes a message from a folder other than the Deleted Items folder, the message is not really deleted but instead moved to the Deleted Items folder and sits in

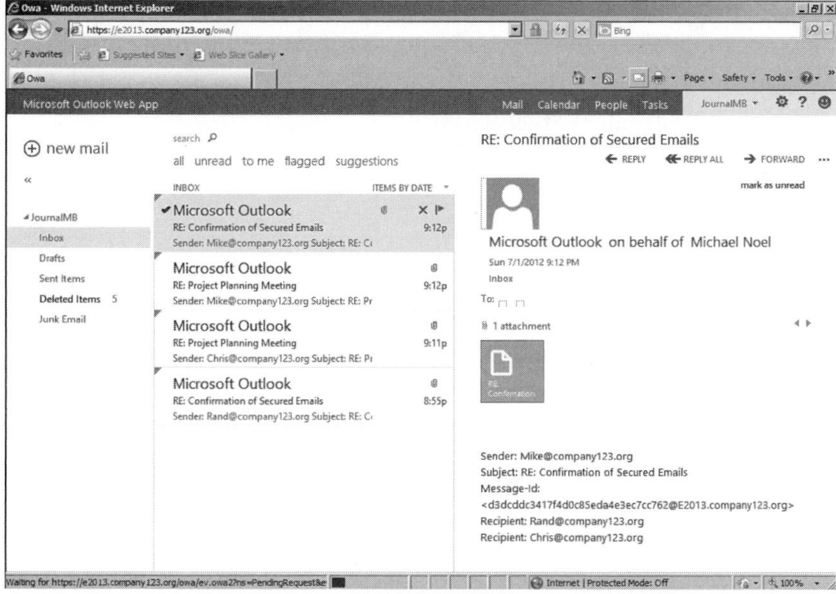

FIGURE 12.5 Viewing journaled mail messages in the journaling mailbox.

the Deleted Items folder until the message is fully deleted from the Deleted Items folder. When a user deletes an item from the Deleted Items folder or empties the Deleted Items folder, the message disappears from the Deleted Items folder and appears to be gone, but the message has actually just been moved to a hidden Recoverable Items folder, formerly known as the Dumpster in previous versions of Exchange. The Recoverable Items folder is hidden from the default view of Microsoft Outlook, OWA, and other email clients so the user no longer sees deleted messages, but the messages are still sitting in Exchange.

Items in the Recoverable Items folder are retained for the deleted item retention period configured for the user's mailbox or per database in Exchange. By default, the deleted item retention period is set to 14 days (or 30GB of storage per database, whichever comes first). This default retention period can be extended by the administrator to a longer period or even indefinitely. At any point, messages in the Recoverable Items folder can be retrieved by someone in the organization with Discovery role permissions.

An important point to note is that even though messages that are deleted by a user are retained on an Exchange Server 2013 server and hidden from the user, users have the ability to access their Recoverable Items/Deletions messages through Outlook 2010, Outlook 2013, and OWA. An Outlook user simply sits on the Deleted Items folder, selects the Folder tab in the ribbon, and clicks Recover Deleted Items, which shows messages that are stored in the Recoverable Items folder. The user can click to recover messages back into his or her Deleted Items folder or the user can click the Delete icon and messages are permanently deleted off the Exchange server.

However, the Exchange administrator can control message retention even for this permanent user deletion. For an Exchange administrator to control message retention, do the following:

1. Launch the Exchange Management Shell (EMS).
2. Run the command Set-Mailbox -Identity MAILBOX_NAME -SingleItemRecoveryEnabled $true.

This activates Single Item Recovery (SIR). SIR creates a Recoverable Items/Purges folder that is hidden from the user and is *not* accessible to the user at all.

By enabling SIR for a user's mailbox, messages that are edited and/or modified (and not necessarily deleted) are *also* now retained for the length of the deleted item retention period. Instead of ending up in a hidden Recoverable Items/Deletions folder for deleted messages, messages that are edited/modified end up in a hidden Recoverable Items/Versions folder. So for every edited version of the message, there is also a copy of the message prior to the modification or edit.

Therefore, all hard deleted or modified/edited messages are preserved for the default length of 14 days (or 30GB) or whatever the organization has set as the default retention period, whether that's 60 days, 90 days, a year, seven years, or forever.

To run the SIR on all mailboxes in a database, do the following:

1. Launch the EMS.
2. Run the command Get-Mailbox -Database <DatabaseName> | Set-Mailbox -SingleItemRecoveryEnabled $true.

NOTE

For organizations using Office 365 (in the cloud), per Microsoft's Office 365 administrator guide (http://help.outlook.com/en-ca/140/hh125820.aspx), "Single item recovery is enabled by default for new user mailboxes created in Exchange Online and for mailboxes migrated to Exchange Online from an on-premises Exchange organization." As such, there is nothing an Office 365 administrator needs to do; all message deletions, edits, and modifications are retained for the length of the organization's deleted item retention period. To extend the default 15- and 30-day retention policies set in Office 365, see http://help.outlook.com/en-us/beta/gg271153.aspx on Messaging Records Management (MRM).

For configuring deleted item retention and Recoverable Items quota for users, the administrator needs to be assigned either the following management role:

- Organization Management

or both of the following management roles:

- Recipient Management
- Records Management

For configuring the same settings on mailbox databases, the administrator must be assigned one of the following management roles:

- Organization Management
- Server Management

To configure administrative roles in Exchange Server 2013, do the following:

1. Log on to the ECP with a user who has Exchange administration rights; the URL is https://{*servername*}/ecp.
2. Click Roles in the left pane to view the list of roles.
3. Click Administrator Roles.
4. Select the Organization Management, Recipient Management, or Records Management role, according to the scope of responsibility you want to assign, and click the Edit icon to modify the role.
5. Scroll down to Members, click the plus (+) button, and add the administrator who you want to have the rights to configure deleted items retention and Recoverable Items quotas, and then click Save.

Once you set the administrative roles, then you can configure deleted items retention for a mailbox. To do so, do the following:

- As an example, to configure Rand Morimoto's mailbox to retain deleted items for 30 days, the PowerShell EMS command to run on the server is: `Set-Mailbox -Identity - "Rand Morimoto" -RetainDeletedItemsFor 30`

To configure Recoverable Items quotas for a mailbox, do the following:

- As an example, to configure Rand Morimoto's mailbox for a recoverable items warning quota of 16GB and a recoverable items quota of 20GB, the PowerShell EMS command to run on the server is: `Set-Mailbox -Identity "Rand Morimoto" -RecoverableItemsWarningQuota 16GB -RecoverableItemsQuota 20GB -UseDatabaseQuotaDefaults $false`

NOTE

To configure a mailbox to use different Recoverable Items quotas than the mailbox database in which it resides, you must set the `UseDatabaseQuotaDefaults` parameter to `$false`.

To configure deleted item retention for a mailbox database, do the following:

- As an example, to configure a deleted item retention period of 15 days for the mailbox database MDB4, the PowerShell EMS command to run on the server is: `Set-MailboxDatabase -Identity MDB4 -DeletedItemRetention 15`

To configure Recoverable Items quotas for a mailbox database, do the following:

- As an example, to configure a recoverable items warning quota of 20GB and a recoverable items quota of 25GB on a mailbox in database MDB4, the PowerShell EMS command to run on the server is: `Set-MailboxDatabase -Identity MDB4 -RecoverableItemsWarningQuota 20GB -RecoverableItemsQuota 25GB`

Handling Legal Hold in Exchange

Legal hold or litigation hold are terms used in the legal profession to designate that potential evidence is to be retained—specific to email, all email messages and attachments need to be preserved (i.e., prevent a user from deleting or modifying messages that might be used in a legal case).

As mentioned earlier in this chapter, with previous versions of Exchange, typically a third-party product needed to be purchased to retain content such as when a user's mailbox is put on legal hold. However, with Exchange Server 2013 using the deleted item retention process covered in this chapter, because all deleted and modified messages are automatically retained for a period of time, the only thing that needs to be done is make sure content is not automatically deleted after the default 14 days, by the user, or by some other full deletion process. Specifically putting a user's mailbox on legal hold ensures an indefinite retention on all content in the user's mailbox until the mailbox is removed from legal hold.

Configuring Exchange to Support Discovery Management

To put a mailbox on litigation hold, the person making that decision needs to be part of the Discovery Management role in Exchange if he or she does not have the Organization Management or Recipient Management role. To grant an individual (administrator, HR personnel, legal counsel) the rights to make litigation hold changes to mailboxes, do the following:

1. Log on to the ECP with a user who has Exchange administration rights; the URL is https://{*servername*}/ecp.
2. Click Roles in the left pane to view the list of roles.
3. Click Administrator Roles.
4. Select the Discovery Management role, and click to edit the role.
5. Scroll down to Members, click the plus (+) button, add the administrator who you want to have the rights to configure deleted items retention and Recoverable Items quotas as shown in Figure 12.6, and then click Save.

This individual (or individuals) now has the ability to proceed with actually putting a mailbox on litigation hold.

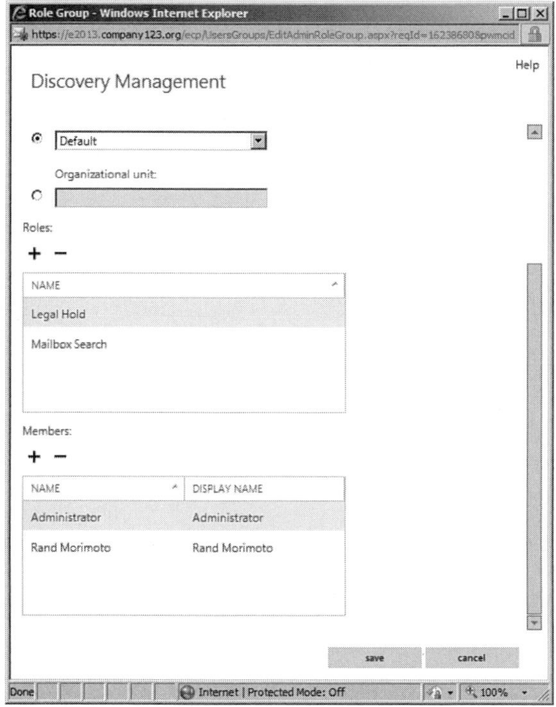

FIGURE 12.6 Adding an administrator to the Discovery Management administrative role.

Putting a Mailbox on Litigation Hold

To put a mailbox on litigation hold in Exchange Server 2013, an administrator needs to do the following:

1. Log on to the ECP with a user who has Exchange administration rights; the URL is https://{*servername*}/ecp.
2. Click Recipients to see a list of Exchange mailboxes.
3. Click the user you want to put on litigation hold.
4. Click to edit the recipient.
5. Click Mailbox Features and scroll down to Litigation Hold.
6. By default, the mailbox is set to Disabled for Litigation Hold; click Enable.

NOTE

When a mailbox is put on litigation hold, the administrator has the option of entering in a note and a URL in the area shown in Figure 12.7 where the user can be notified and/or provided more information that his or her mailbox has been put on litigation hold. It is not a requirement to notify the user as far as Exchange Server 2013 is concerned; however, the organization may choose to notify the user. Check with your legal counsel on the requested preference. If your legal counsel wants a notification to occur, the pop-up box will provide you an opportunity to enter in the note and notice as well as an optional URL that the user will receive.

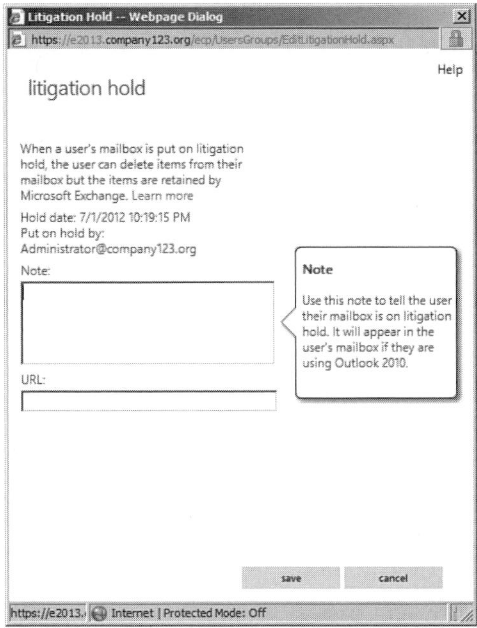

FIGURE 12.7 Putting a mailbox on litigation hold.

7. Click Save when done, and then click Save again to enable litigation hold on a user's mailbox.

NOTE

It may take up to an hour before litigation hold takes effect on a user's mailbox. This is because the policy needs to be enacted on all messages and folders in the user's mailbox and the policy needs to be replicated through Active Directory. You can see the status of litigation hold on a user's mailbox by going back and looking at the Mailbox Features and it may show Litigation Hold "Enable – Pending" when it is in the process of enabling litigation hold. When the mailbox is fully held, the Mailbox Features will simply show "Enabled."

With litigation hold enabled, all messages, regardless of the organization's retention policy, will be retained.

Once an employee is requested by legal counsel to be removed from legal hold, go back to the ECP for the recipient and select Disable for Litigation Hold, which will turn off litigation hold on the user's mailbox.

eDiscovery and Searching for Content

When searching for information, whether it is information actively in a user's mailbox, edited or modified by the user, deleted from his or her mailbox (but not yet purged off the Exchange servers), or held for litigation hold, information is all searched the exact same way. The only difference is the amount of information that may be found (i.e., mailboxes on litigation hold or for organizations that have cranked up the deleted item retention period to save information beyond the default 14 days—potentially indefinitely—will find more information because the information has not been automatically purged off the Exchange servers).

Choosing Search Words Carefully

The key to searching is to choose words, date ranges, and other key parameters to help you zero in on the information you are looking for, but not narrow down so tightly that your search doesn't find all the information you are looking for. As an example, if you simply search for information between Bob and Mary over a 30-day period, you might end up with 1,000 messages, which might be too much information to find what you are looking for. On the other hand, if you search for messages between Bob and Mary over the 30-day period with the key phrase "don't tell anyone," which might narrow down the search to say eight messages, if at any point during the email thread either Bob or Mary deleted or changed the "don't tell anyone" phrase in the email, those subsequent emails would not show up in your search results. This happens frequently as messages get really long, and users delete or truncate part of the message. Or if you only look for words in a Subject line but then one of the users changes the Subject line title—then your tight search may not result in what you were expecting to look for either.

TIP

It is recommended that you create a very small mailbox with only a dozen messages inside of it and try out the searching process to perfect your ability to look for (and ultimately find) information you are looking for before you try to look at a mailbox or several mailboxes with hundreds of thousands of email messages. Remember, this is a very specific search; it will find exactly what you are looking for. Unlike searching the Web with Google or Bing where the search finds information that "kind of" has the same words, or similar words and phrases, the eDiscovery search in Exchange will only find 100% exact matches to what you query.

Additionally, when you perform a multi-mailbox or eDiscovery search in Exchange, depending on your configuration, the results can show up in several different folders, including the following:

- The folder where the message currently resides
- The Deleted Items folder, which holds messages that have been deleted but not yet flushed from the Deleted Items folder
- The Recoverable Items/Deletions folder, which contains messages deleted from the Deleted Items folder
- The Recoverable Items/Purges folder, which is used for messages deleted while the mailbox is in litigation hold or Single Item Recovery
- The hidden Recoverable Items/Versions folder, which contains messages that were edited or modified

So you may find content for a single message that has been modified, edited, deleted, and attempted to be purged in four or five different locations!

In addition, the eDiscovery/multi-mailbox search capabilities in Exchange Server 2013 do not piece together the sequence of events for a message history, so while you may find a message in four or five different places dependent on the message status, you won't know the sequence where a message was deleted, modified, edited, or purged without manually going through and comparing time stamp properties for the messages.

Using Exchange Search

When you want to perform and eDiscovery to search for information—whether it is searching archives, searching retained messages, or searching mailboxes on litigation hold—the process breaks down to three steps.

eDiscovery Step 1: Assign Someone the Rights to Create a Search Query

This is a one-time step that needs to be performed to give someone the rights to create a search query. By default, *no one* in the organization, including the Exchange administrator, has the rights to create search queries. However, even though the Exchange administrator doesn't have the right to create a search query, the Exchange administrator can go into the Exchange Control Panel and give himself or herself (and anyone else) rights to create the query. So it's just one extra step for the Exchange administrator to assign himself or herself search query creation capabilities, or in large organizations, the Exchange administrator may assign the search query capability to someone in his or her internal legal counsel or Human Resources Department, as frequently the person who creates the query is someone "inside" the organization, whereas the person who has the rights to view the query results may be "outside" the organization.

To assign the rights to create a search query, do the following:

1. Log on to the ECP with a user who has Exchange administration rights; the URL is https://{*servername*}/ecp.
2. Click Roles in the left pane to view the list of roles.
3. Click Administrator Roles.

4. Select the Discovery Management role, and click to edit the role.
5. Scroll down to Members, click the plus (+) button, add the administrator who you want to have the rights to create a search query as well as be able to put a mailbox on litigation hold, and then click Save.

This individual (or individuals) now has the ability to go to step 2 to create and initiate a search query (and put someone's mailbox on litigation hold).

eDiscovery Step 2: Create and Initiate a Search Query

Once key individuals have been granted rights to create queries and review the results of the queries, the next step is to have the individual who has the right to create a query (the person in eDiscovery step 1) to actually create a query. The process is as follows:

1. Log on to the ECP with a user who has Exchange administration rights; the URL is https://{*servername*}/ecp.
2. Click Mail Flow in the left pane to view the list of roles.
3. Click In-Place Discovery & Hold.
4. Click the plus (+) button to create a new eDiscovery query.
5. Give the query a name, something that you would remember specific to the query, such as `Search for the word Litigation in Michael's emails`, and click Next.
6. Choose to search all mailboxes or just a specific user's mailbox. In this scenario, you are just looking at a specific user's mailbox, so make sure Specify Mailboxes to Search is selected and click the plus (+) button to add mailboxes to search.
7. Pick the mailbox in which you want to search, click OK, and then click Next.
8. Choosing to search all user mailbox content is typically not a good idea as that effectively dumps the entire user's mailbox to file, so choose the Filter Based on Criteria option and enter in the keyword(s) you want to search for.
9. Click any start and end date of the data you want to query as well as choose any specific From or To/cc senders and recipients similar to what is shown in Figure 12.8, and then click Next.
10. If the mailbox is not already on litigation hold, select the Place Selected Mailbox on Hold option and choose to hold the mailbox indefinitely until removed from hold or specify the number of days the box is being requested to be held, and then click Finish.

TIP

There is a Select Message Types option. By default, the option is to Search All Message Types Including One That May Not Be Listed Below so that *everything* is returned in the search results, including email messages, posts, calendar appointments, notes, tasks, and so forth.

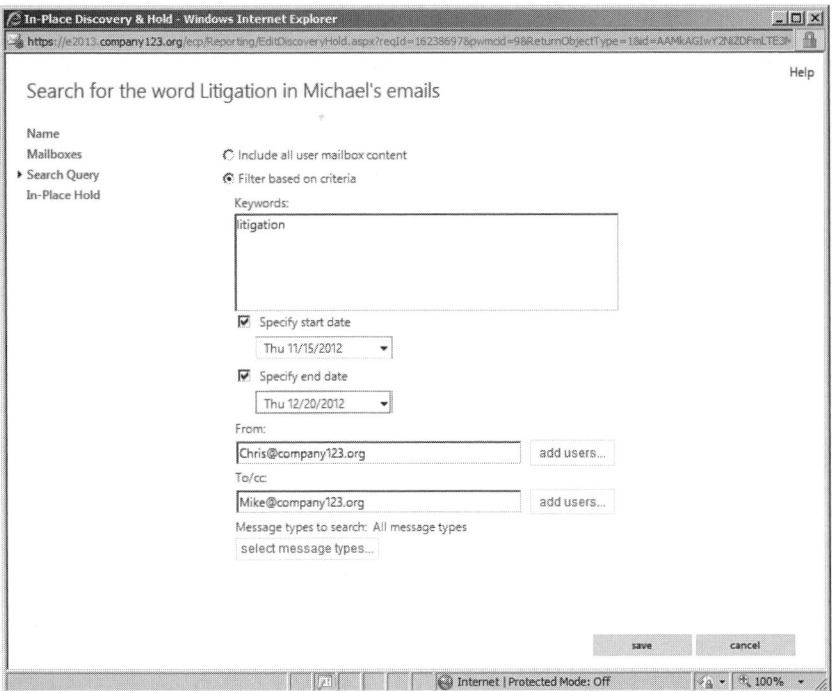

FIGURE 12.8 Creating a search query for eDiscovery.

The search (or estimate) will begin as soon as you click Save or Finish. Depending on how much information is being searched, this could take a few seconds or this could take an hour. On the In-Place Discovery & Hold page, you will see the search query noted. Remember, this is a web page, so the page won't automatically refresh with an update on the percentage of completion; click the Refresh icon periodically to see whether the search has completed or to see the percentage of completion.

NOTE

At any point, you can highlight the search query, click the Details option, and change the keywords on the query. Click the Start Search option to begin the new search, and remember to periodically click the Refresh icon to check the status.

Once the search has been successful, a user who has been set in eDiscovery will have the ability to see the search results. Proceed to eDiscovery step 3 to view the results.

eDiscovery Step 3: Review the Results of the Search Query

A person who has been given permission to view a search query will be able to view the results from a query initiated in eDiscovery step 2. To see the results, the individual would do the following:

1. Log on to the ECP with a user who has Exchange administration rights; the URL is https://{*servername*}/ecp.
2. Click Mail Flow in the left pane to view the list of roles.
3. Click In-Place Discovery & Hold.
4. Click the discovery/search item for which you want to review the results.
5. In the discovery preview in the far-right pane where the search has "succeeded," there is a Preview Results with an [open].
6. View the search preview of the information queried, as shown in Figure 12.9.

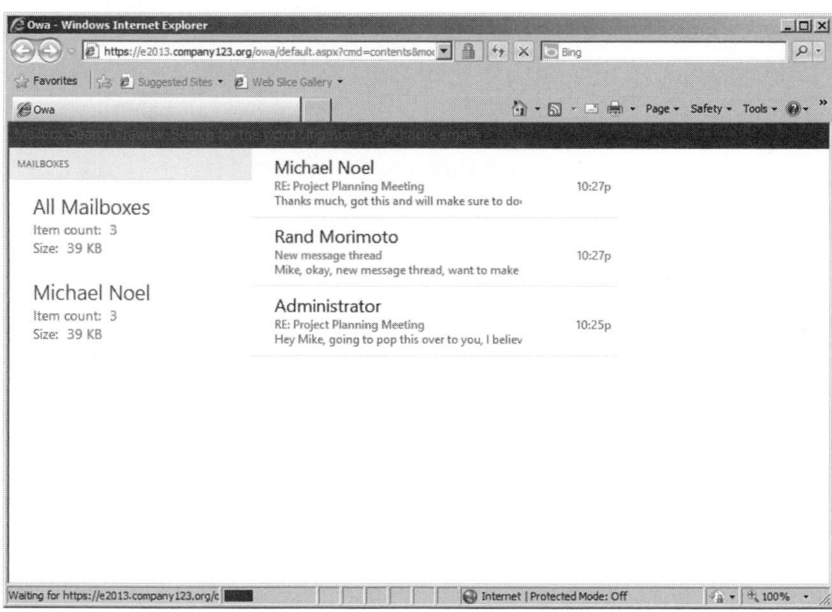

FIGURE 12.9 Viewing the results of an eDiscovery query.

The content in this search query can be exported to a PST file, or it can be left on the server. To export the content to a PST file, do the following:

1. In the ECP, click the discovery/search item for which you want to review the results.
2. Click the icon above the discovery/search item window that notes Export to PST, choose the file you want to export the messages to, and the PST file will be created.

In addition, a specific user account can be created in Exchange, and instead of dumping the contents in eDiscovery step 3 to a PST file, you can dump the search results to a dedicated mailbox and then give a user logon rights just to that "user account" where you dumped the eDiscovery results.

There are a number of variations on how information can be queried and reviewed. This chapter covered the most common functions; however, other variations can be made.

NOTE

Email retention and deletion policies are specific to messages in a mailbox (either an active or inactive mailbox). Mailboxes can be deleted, databases can be deleted, and information can get corrupt. Organizations need to protect the root storage of information from data loss that the mail handling policies noted in this document do not address.

Summary

Being able to successfully perform an eDiscovery and search for content depends solely on the ability to retain the information in a manner that has high reliability and integrity. An organization that needs to search for information for legal purposes but cannot prove the information as being reliable is no better off than having no information at all. Data integrity is key to the success of eDiscovery, and Exchange Server 2013 has the tools that help organizations properly retain content, lock the content down, and then search for the content being requested.

A key to note is that many people confuse email archiving with email retention. Email retention is the process of legally and temporarily holding content to prevent information from being accidentally or purposely deleted. In the case of email retention, the organization needs to have very clear policies and processes to ensure data is properly retained. However, if the organization merely wants to archive old messages and minimize the disk space taken up by old messages of a user, then using the very basic functions of personal archives in Exchange is all that is needed and is a *lot* easier to set up and implement.

Overall, Exchange Server 2013 provides tools and technologies to perform email archiving, retention, and eDiscovery, and an organization should evaluate the built-in functionality of Exchange Server 2013 before spending the time, effort, and cost to buy a complicated third-party tool that may not be needed for the organization.

Best Practices

The following are best practices from this chapter:

- If all the organization requires is the ability to archive messages and get messages out of the primary mail store, then personal archives in Exchange Server 2013 should be used.
- If the organization needs to have locked copies of content in a "journal," then Exchange Server 2013 journaling can be enabled for this functionality.
- When journaling content, the journal server, database, and mailbox should be protected to prevent a concern in data integrity of the journaled information.

- Viewing journaled information is as simple as viewing email messages out of OWA when OWA is used for the journal viewer.
- Mailboxes can be put on legal or litigation hold to prevent data from being accidentally or purposely deleted or modified.
- Choose words carefully when entering in search criteria for eDiscovery search.
- Test the query process with a sample mailbox with only a handful of messages, and perfect your skills on how to successfully enter in the right keywords and successfully search and find desired information.
- Assign administrative roles to individuals who need search and view permissions to content queried.

CHAPTER 13

Administering an Exchange Server 2013 Environment

IN THIS CHAPTER

Accompanying the many new features of Exchange Server 2013 is an updated set of administrative tools. These updated administrative tools provide Exchange administrators the capability to manage on-premises, online, or hybrid Exchange environments from a single administrative console, as well as from the command line.

Exchange Administration Center

One of the most noticeable changes to Exchange Server 2013 administration is the new Exchange Administration Center or EAC. In Exchange Server 2013, the Exchange Administration Center is a web-based management console that replaces the Exchange Management Console (EMC) by extending the Exchange Control Panel (ECP).

Features of the Exchange Administration Center

Some of the key features of the Exchange Administration Center include the following:

- **List view**—The List view in EAC offers a number of improvements over the earlier ECP tool. EAC provides the ability to display approximately 20,000 objects, which is a substantial increase from the ECP's limit of 500 objects. The EAC List view feature also adds a paging capability with a configurable page size, and allows results to be exported to a comma-separated value (CSV) file.

- **Column selection in the Recipient list view**—The Recipient list view allows the user to select only the desired columns and save these customized list views for future use.
- **Control external access to EAC administrative features**—The Exchange Administration Center gives administrators the ability to limit access to the Exchange Server 2013 management features. Administrators can allow or deny access to EAC from Internet or intranet locations while still allowing access to Outlook Web App configuration settings.
- **Manage public folders**—Exchange Server 2013 consolidates the Public Folder administrative tool from Exchange Server 2007 and Exchange Server 2010 into the Exchange Administration Center. A separate tool is no longer required to manage public folders.
- **Notification viewer**—The Exchange Administration Center includes a Notification viewer that provides a quick way to view the status of currently running processes such as mailbox moves. In addition, the Notification viewer can be configured to send an email message when a process completes.

Accessing the Exchange Administration Center

The Exchange Administration Center can be accessed through the default uniform resource locator (URL) https://<*servername*>/ecp. However, this URL is customizable, so the URL path may be different for your organization. To find the URL of the EAC virtual directory, open the Exchange Management Shell (EMS) and run the following command:

```
Get-ECPVirtualDirectory | Format-List Server,InternalURL,ExternalURL
```

The output of this command will be similar to the following:

```
[PS]C:\> Get-ECPVirtualDirectory | Format-List Server,InternalURL,ExternalURL
Server      : E15-CAS
InternalURL : https://mail.companyabc.com/ecp
ExternalURL : https://mail.companyabc.com/ecp
```

After running this command, open Internet Explorer and enter the value for the `InternalURL` attribute in the navigation bar to access the Exchange Administration Center. Enter a set of administrative credentials, as shown in Figure 13.1, and then click Sign In to continue.

NOTE

A warning screen will appear if the certificate that is used for Secure Sockets Layer (SSL) encryption on the Exchange Administration Center website is not trusted by Internet Explorer. If a self-signed or internal certificate is used, the certificate can be imported into the appropriate certificate category within Internet Explorer to remove the warning. Alternatively, the EAC website can be configured to use a third-party SSL certificate that can be verified back to a trusted public certification authority.

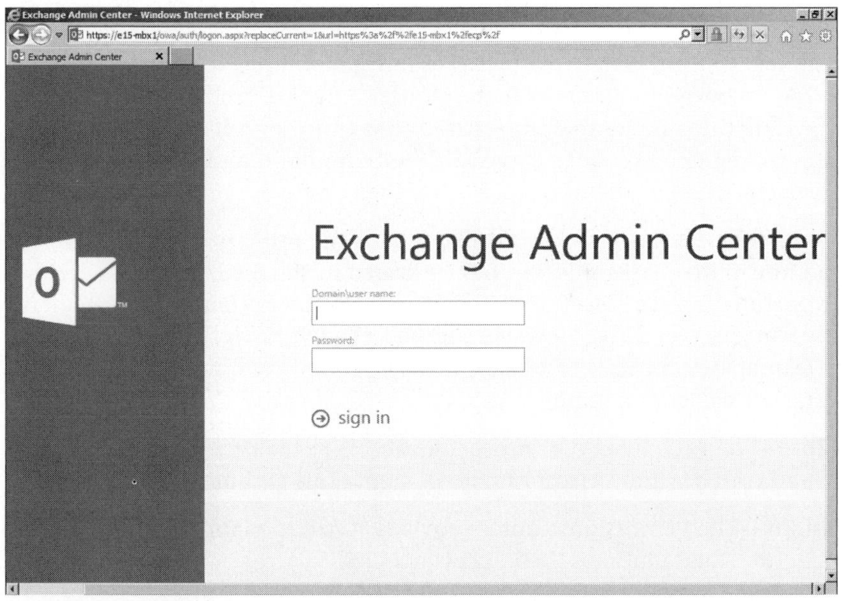

FIGURE 13.1 Sign-in screen for Exchange Administration Center.

Overview of the Exchange Administration Center

The initial view of the Exchange Administration Center is shown in Figure 13.2.

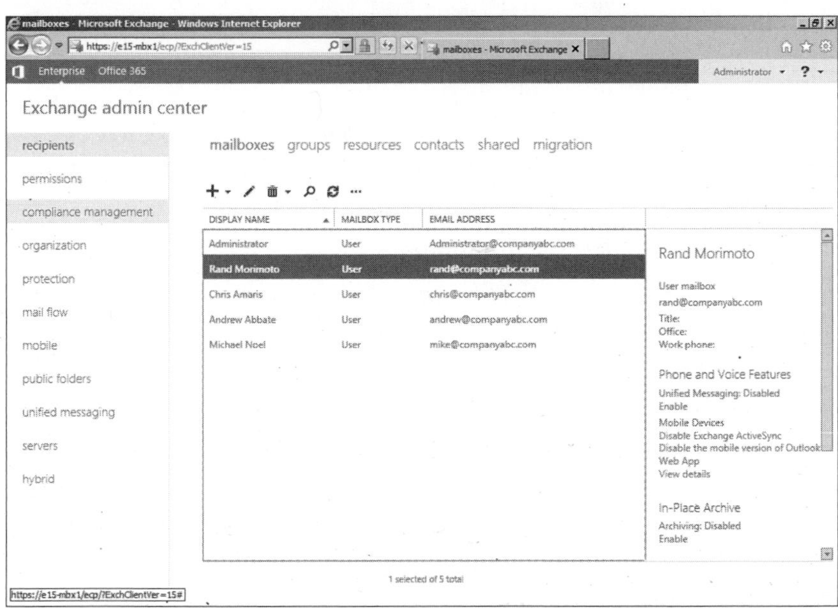

FIGURE 13.2 Initial view of the Exchange Administration Center.

Some of the features of the Exchange Administration Center include the following:

- **Cross-premises navigation**—The cross-premises navigation links in the upper-left corner of the EAC allow administrators to administer a hybrid Exchange Server 2013 environment. Using these links, an administrator can easily switch between administration of an on-premises Exchange Server 2013 environment and an Office 365 online environment.

- **Left navigation**—The left navigation control contains the primary categories for most of the administrative tasks that can be performed in the EAC. The left navigation pane is structured similarly to the console tree from the Exchange Management Console in Exchange Server 2010. However, in EAC, the left navigation control is organized by feature areas instead of server roles. The following list describes each of the items in the left navigation pane:

  - **Recipients**—The Recipients center provides access to manage mailboxes, groups, and contacts and perform mailbox migrations and moves.

  - **Permissions**—The Permissions center provides access to manage administrator roles, user roles, and Outlook Web Access policies.

  - **Compliance Management**—The Compliance Management center provides access to manage all settings related to Exchange compliance, including eDiscovery, in-place hold, auditing, data loss prevention, retention policies, retention tags, and journaling.

  - **Organization**—The Organization center provides access to manage tasks for the Exchange organization, including federated sharing, Outlook apps, and address lists.

  - **Protection**—The Protection center provides access to manage anti-malware settings for the Exchange organization.

  - **Mail Flow**—The Mail Flow center provides access to manage mail flow rules, delivery reports, accepted domains, email address policies, and Send/Receive connectors.

  - **Mobile**—The Mobile center provides access to manage mobile device access and policies for the Exchange organization.

  - **Public Folder**—The Public Folder center provides access to manage public folder settings. This removes the need for the Public Folder Management Console, which was used in Exchange Server 2010.

  - **Unified Messaging**—The Unified Messaging center provides access to manage Unified Messaging dial plans and IP gateways.

  - **Servers**—The Servers center provides access to manage Mailbox and Client Access servers, as well as databases, database availability groups, virtual directories, and certificates.

  - **Hybrid**—The Hybrid center provides access to manage settings for a hybrid Exchange Server 2013 environment with both on-premises and cloud-based components.

- **Tabs**—The Tabs area of the Exchange Administration Center provides a list of secondary categories for each of the primary categories listed in the left navigation center. When a primary task selection is made in the left navigation center, the secondary task selections in the Tabs area will change accordingly.
- **Toolbar**—The Toolbar element is present on most tabs containing icons that perform a specific action. Each tab has some subset of icons depending on the available functions for that tab. The following list describes each of the most common icons:
    - **New**—The Add icon is depicted by a + symbol and creates a new object. Some Add icons have a down arrow where there are additional types of objects that you can create. For example, in Recipients, Mailboxes, the Add icon's down arrow shows User Mailbox and Linked Mailbox as additional options.
    - **Edit**—The Edit icon is depicted by a pencil and allows you to make changes to an object's settings. Select the object in the List view and then click the Edit icon.
    - **Delete**—The Delete icon is depicted by a trash bin. Some Delete icons have a down arrow where there are additional options. For example, in Recipients, Mailboxes, the Delete icon's down arrow shows Delete and Disable as additional options.
    - **Search**—The Search icon is depicted by a magnifying glass. If you click the Search icon, a search field will display and you can type the search phrase for an object that you want to view.
    - **Refresh**—The Refresh icon is depicted by circular arrows. Click the Refresh icon to refresh the List view.
    - **More**—The More icon is depicted by an ellipsis, or three dots. Click the More icon to view more actions that you can perform for that tab's objects. For example, in Recipients, Mailboxes, the ellipsis shows Add/Remove Columns, Export Data to a CSV File, Connect a Mailbox, and Advanced Search.
    - **Up and down arrows**—The up arrow and down arrow allow you to move an object's priority up or down. For example, in Mail Flow, Email Address Policies, click the up arrow to raise the priority of an email address policy.
    - **Copy**—The Copy icon is depicted by a dot and allows you to copy an object in order to make changes to it without changing the original object. For example, in Permissions, Admin Roles, select an admin role from the List view and click Copy to create a new role group based on an existing role group. After clicking the Copy icon, an additional window appears where details can be entered for the new group.
- **List view**—The List view in Exchange Administration Center has been designed to remove limitations that existed in ECP. The viewable limit from within the EAC List view is approximately 20,000 objects in on-premises and 10,000 objects in Exchange Online Preview. In addition, paging has been added so that you can page to the results. In the Recipients list view, you can also configure page size and export to a CSV file.

- **Details pane**—The details pane allows the administrator to select an object in the List view and to view information about that object. In some cases, like with recipient objects, you can perform quick edit tasks. You can identify the quick edit tasks by the blue links. For example, in Recipients, Mailboxes, select a mailbox in the List view. In the details pane, you can enable an archive for that mailbox. You can also bulk edit quick tasks by holding down the Ctrl key and selecting objects. Selecting multiple mailboxes allows you to bulk update users' contact information, organizations, custom attributes, mailbox quotas, Outlook Web App settings, and Post Office Protocol 3 (POP) and Internet Message Access Protocol (IMAP) settings.
- **Notifications**—The Exchange Administration Center includes a Notification viewer to allow the administrator to view the status of long-running processes and provides notifications when the process completes. In addition, for particularly long-running processes, such as move requests, the administrator can opt in to receive email notifications.
- **Me tile and Help**—The Me tile allows the administrator to sign out of the Exchange Administration Center and sign in as a different user. From the Help drop-down menu, the following actions can be performed:
    - **Help**—This selection displays online help for Exchange Server 2013.
    - **Disable Help bubble**—The Help bubble was a feature available in the Exchange Control Panel. The Help bubble displays contextual help for fields when you create or edit an object. You can turn off the Help bubble or turn it on if it has been disabled.
    - **Performance console**—Click this link to view the Performance console.
    - **Copyright**—The Copyright link will display the legal information for Exchange Server 2013.

Exchange Management Shell

The EMS is the engine that powers all Exchange administrative tools. A powerful management tool in its own right, the EMS is also utilized by both the Exchange Management Console and the Exchange Control Panel to process actions initiated in their interfaces.

Introduced in Exchange Server 2007, the Exchange Management Shell is a command-line management interface. Administrators had been screaming for years for a command-line tool that was powerful enough to enable scripted changes of Exchange Server objects, and the Exchange Management Shell was well received.

Tasks that had to be done manually within the confines of the graphical user interface (GUI) management application in pre-2007 versions could now be scripted, allowing administrators increased flexibility for repetitive tasks. The Exchange Management Shell looks similar to the DOS command prompt (`cmd.exe`), in that it opens a window with a black background and a text interface. However, you notice immediately that certain commands and errors are highlighted in yellow or red text rather than the traditional monochromatic command prompt.

With the Exchange Management Shell, administrators can manage every aspect of Exchange Server, including the creation and management of new email accounts, the configuration of Simple Mail Transfer Protocol (SMTP) connectors and transport agents, or properties of database stores. In fact, every task that can be accomplished with the Exchange Management Console can be accomplished from the command line in the EMS, but the opposite is not true.

NOTE

When the EMS was first released, there were many commands that *had* to be performed in the shell because many configuration options were not available in the EMC. As much as administrators enjoyed the new capabilities of the command-line interface, they did not like being told "you have to use it all the time." Over time, more and more functionality was added back into the Exchange Management Console.

With the EMS, administrators have a powerful yet flexible scripting platform that is much easier to take advantage of than using Microsoft Visual Basic scripts—previously the only way to script changes in the Exchange Server environment. As described by Microsoft, "What once took hundreds of lines in Visual Basic scripts can now be accomplished easily with as little as one line of code."

The EMS uses an object model that is based on the Microsoft .NET platform. This enables the shell commands to apply the output from one command to subsequent commands when they are run.

Whereas Exchange Server 2007 used PowerShell 1.0, Exchange Server 2013 is built on PowerShell 3.0, which has several enhancements that distinguish it from the previous version.

Exchange Server 2013 also utilizes Windows Remote Management (WinRM) 2.0. Whether an administrator is connecting to a local server or one halfway around the world, EMS always connects to the desired Exchange Server 2013 server via a remote connection utilizing an Internet Information Services (IIS) virtual directory. This holds true even when administrators are running the PowerShell command against the server they are currently logged on to. Due to this capability, the ability to perform PowerShell-based Exchange Server management does not require Exchange Server binaries to be installed on the requesting client, so 32-bit clients that have PowerShell 3.0 with WinRM 2.0 installed can be used for remote PowerShell administration.

The supported client OS platforms include the x86 and x64 versions of Windows Vista, Windows Server 2008, Windows Server 2008 R2, Windows 7, Windows Server 2003, Windows Server 2003 R2, and Windows XP.

Exchange Management Shell Basic Concepts

The Exchange Management Shell has a number of command functions, support options, and customization features. The following is a list of some of the basic concepts administrators should be aware of:

- **Objects**—The collection of properties that represents each of the pieces that make up an Exchange Server environment. An object can refer to a user mailbox, a server, a connector, or one of many other configurable items.
- **Cmdlets**—A cmdlet, pronounced "command-let," is a specialized .NET class that performs a particular operation. Cmdlets are the smallest unit of functionality in the EMS. Similar in appearance to the built-in commands in other shells (such as the `DIR` or `CD` commands in a Microsoft command prompt), cmdlets can be run individually or combined in scripts. There are hundreds of cmdlets provided for Exchange Server–specific management tasks.
- **Parameters**—Parameters are elements that provide information to the cmdlet. Parameters can either identify an object or its attributes to act upon or can control how the cmdlet performs its task.
- **Restricted PSSession**—By implementing the Role Based Access Control (RBAC) model, the EMS can restrict available cmdlets and parameters to only those that the user has access to run. For example, if the user does not have the access to create new mailboxes, the `New-Mailbox` cmdlet will not be presented to them.
- **`Identity`**—`Identity` is a special parameter that can be used with most cmdlets to give access to the unique identifiers that refer to a particular object. By using the `identity` parameter, administrators can specify the particular object they want to retrieve, modify, or delete. To reduce unnecessary keystrokes, the `identity` parameter was created as a positional parameter. When running a cmdlet, the first argument is assumed to be the `identity` parameter, so running the command `get-mailbox -identity "linkin"` will produce the same results as `get-mailbox "linkin"`.
- **Pipelining**—Before the EMS, one of the biggest shortcomings of scripting in the Exchange Server environment was the lack of ability to take the output of one command and utilize it directly as the input for other commands. Within the EMS, pipelining allows exactly that. Administrators have the ability to string cmdlets together, using one cmdlet to gather data, passing the results to a second cmdlet that filters the data to a smaller subset, and then supplying the result to a third cmdlet to act on.
- **Object-oriented data handling**—Because the resulting output from any cmdlet in the Exchange Management Shell is an object, all output can be acted upon and processed by other commands with little to no changes. Commands that are intended to work together on particular feature sets accept the output from other commands in the same feature set.
- **Access `cmd.exe` commands**—Nearly all the commands available in the Windows command prompt (`cmd.exe`) are also available to the EMS, although there are

sometimes slight differences in syntax. Administrators can not only run these commands, but can also take the output from those commands and perform actions based on that output.

- **Trusted scripts**—Administrators have long been concerned that the ability to run scripts in an organization (especially when logged in with administrative credentials) could have disastrous results. To prevent this from happening, by default the Exchange Management Shell requires that all scripts be digitally signed before they are allowed to run. This feature is intended to prevent malicious users from inserting a dangerous or harmful script in the EMS. Before a script can be run, the administrator must specifically "trust" it, helping to protect the entire organization.
- **Profile customization**—The EMS provides a powerful, easy-to-use interface with the default installation, but administrators might want to customize the appearance of the interface, create shortcuts for commonly used commands, or specify specific commands to automatically run when the EMS starts. All these items can be configured using a customized Exchange Management Shell profile.
- **Tip of the day**—Although perhaps not as impressive as the preceding features, a welcome feature of the EMS is the display of a Tip of the Day each time the Exchange Management Shell is opened. The Tip of the Day offers advice on how to perform specific tasks within the shell, listing commands and proper syntax for their use.

Performing Common Tasks

With two different tools to choose from, determining which to use for a particular task is up to the person performing the task. The decision is based primarily on identifying which tool is most convenient for the task. If creating a new mailbox user, it might be easier to simply log on to the EAC through a browser and create the account, whereas creating 100 new accounts would be easier using a script in the EMS.

Some tasks can be performed in the EAC, and *all* tasks can be performed in the EMS—but for something as simple as changing the department for a single user, determining the PowerShell cmdlet and parameters might be more challenging than simply using the GUI or Web interfaces.

Creating User Mailboxes

The creation of a new user mailbox, either for an existing user or in conjunction with the creation of a new user, is an example of a task that can be accomplished from either the Exchange Administration Center or the Exchange Management Shell. This section shows how to perform the task using both tools.

Exchange Server 2013 allows for the creation of four different types of mailboxes:

- **User mailbox**—Owned by a user and used to send and receive messages. This mailbox cannot be used for resource scheduling.

- **Room mailbox**—Intended for room scheduling and not owned by a user. A user account is created with the mailbox, but the account is disabled.
- **Equipment mailbox**—Intended for equipment scheduling. Like the room mailbox, this is not owned by an active user. The associated user account that is created will automatically be disabled.
- **Linked mailbox**—Accessed by a user in a separate, trusted forest.

The following examples create a user mailbox for a new user named Oscar B. Hayve.

Creating a New User Mailbox in the Exchange Administration Center

Creating a new mailbox using the GUI interface of the EAC can be accomplished by following these steps:

1. Start the Exchange Administration Center.
2. In the left navigation control area, click Recipients.
3. In the center tab, click Mailboxes.
4. On the Toolbar, click the plus (+) symbol. The New User Mailbox dialog box appears, as shown in Figure 13.3.

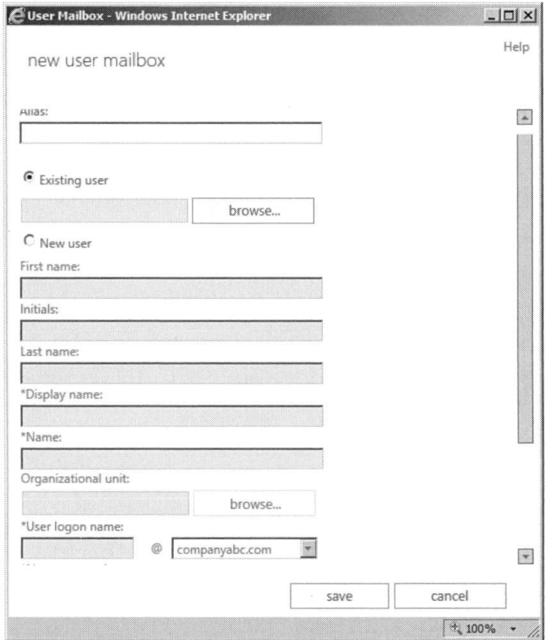

FIGURE 13.3 New User Mailbox dialog box.

5. Enter the user alias of `OBHayve`.

6. Because you are creating a new user as opposed to mailbox-enabling an existing user, click the New User option button and complete the following fields:

    - **First Name**—Type the first name of the user. This field is optional.
    - **Initials**—Type the initials of the user. This field is optional.
    - **Last Name**—Type the last name of the user. This field is optional.
    - **Display Name**—By default, this field is populated with the user's first name, initials, and last name, if entered. You can modify the name in this field or type one manually if no previous fields were populated.
    - **Name**—By default, this field is populated with the user's first name, initials, and last name, if entered. You can modify the name in this field or type one manually if no previous fields were populated.
    - **Organizational Unit**—Click the Browse button to select the organizational unit where the user should reside.
    - **User Logon Name (User Principal Name)**—This is the name that the user uses to log on to the mailbox. The user logon name consists of a username and a suffix. Typically, the suffix is the domain name in which the user account resides.
    - **Password**—Type the password that the user must use to log on to his mailbox.
    - **Confirm Password**—Retype the password that you entered in the Password field.
    - **User Must Change Password at Next Logon**—Select this check box if you want to require users to reset the password after their first logon (recommended).
    - **Specify the Mailbox Database**—Click the Browse button to display the list of available mailbox databases. Select the mailbox database for the user's mailbox and click OK.
    - **Manage Archive Storage**—Check the box labeled Create Local Archive Storage for This User, then click the Browse button to display the list of available archive storage databases. Select the location for the user's archive storage and click OK.
    - **Address Book Policy**—Choose a different policy if multiples are defined in your organization.

7. When finished, click Save to create the new user and his or her associated mailbox.

8. The procedure is complete at this point.

Creating a New Mailbox in the Exchange Management Shell

Creating a new mailbox from the EMS can be complicated because there are so many parameters to consider. However, by copying the EMS command created by the Exchange Administration Center in the previous steps, you can now paste that command into a text editor and modify the contents, allowing you to create your next test user.

Note that you must also remove the `Password System.Security.SecureString` and `ResetPasswordOnNextLogon $true` portions of the command because these were created in the EAC command to populate the password for the account.

You can create your new user, Yasmine B. Guud, by using the following command:

```
New-Mailbox -Name 'Yasmine B. Guud' -Alias 'YBGuud' -UserPrincipalName
'YBGuud@companyabc.com' -SamAccountName 'YBGuud' -FirstName 'Yasmine'
-Initials 'B' -LastName 'Guud'
```

After running the preceding command in the Exchange Management Shell, you are prompted for the password. Enter the desired password (carefully, there will not be an option to confirm it) and press Enter.

The password has to be a secure string, so with a little extra code you can pass an initial password as well by entering a command like the following. You can also add the `-Password` parameter to the `New-Mailbox` cmdlet.

```
Set-Mailbox -Identity 'YBGuud' -Password (ConvertTo-SecureString -String
"P@ssword1" -AsPlainText -Force)
```

NOTE

The user must have Reset Password management role for this cmdlet to work. Management roles are discussed a little later in this chapter.

Creating Multiple Mailboxes in the Exchange Management Shell

Given the complexity of creating a new mailbox in the EMS, why would anyone want to do so? Generally, they wouldn't. But what if your Human Resources Department handed you a list of 50 new employees and requested that you create new mailboxes for all of them? Doing so through the GUI interface of the EAC would not only take hours, but would also result in the increased likelihood that misspellings or mistakes might occur.

That's where the power of the EMS comes into play.

By putting the list of names in a `.csv` file, you can quickly create multiple accounts from only two lines of code. To do so, perform the following steps:

1. Create a text file called `newusers.csv` in a directory called (for our example) `c:\scripts`.
2. For this example, create several column names and populate the data, as shown in Figure 13.4. The columns to populate are Name, Alias, UPN, First, and Last.

Additional column names can be added, if desired, to populate more data in the user accounts.

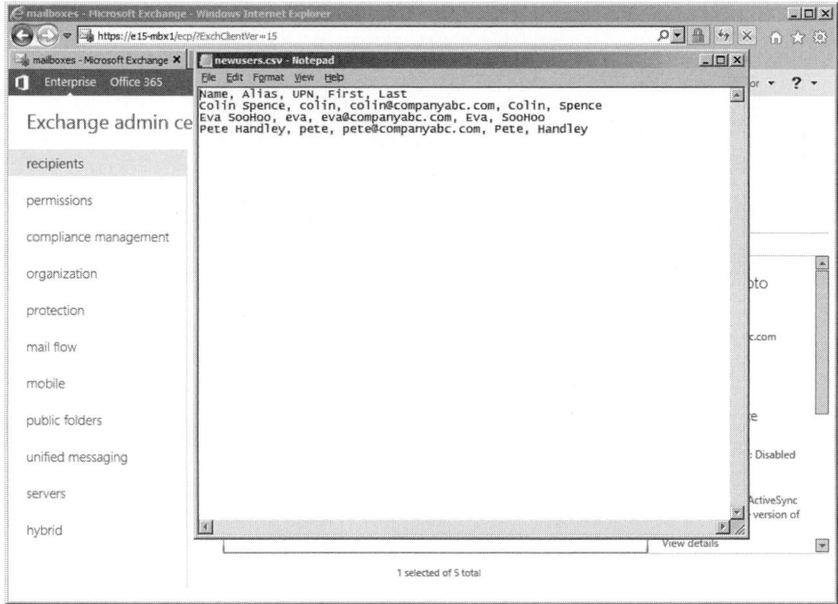

FIGURE 13.4 Creating the CSV file for multiple mailbox creation.

3. When the `.csv` file is complete, you are ready to begin. Each user account will be created with a default password, with the user required to reset the password when he or she first logs in. From the Exchange Management Shell, type the following command. (Type it word for word, do not attempt to enter the password yet.)

```
$Password = Read-Host "Enter Password" -AsSecureString
```

Press Enter. You will be presented with a prompt stating Enter Password. Type the password you want to apply to all your newly created users and press Enter. Your password will now be assigned to the variable `$Password` for use in your script.

4. Next, you run two cmdlets, piping the results of the first into the second, to create the new mailboxes from the `.csv` file. The syntax will be as follows:

```
Import-Csv "c:\scripts\newusers.csv" | foreach { New-Mailbox -name $_.Name
-alias $_.Alias -UserPrincipalName $_.UPN -FirstName $_.First -LastName
$_.Last -Password $Password
-ResetPasswordOnNextLogon:$true}
```

The result, as shown in Figure 13.5, is the creation of the new mailboxes. The existence can be confirmed by viewing the mailboxes in the Exchange Management Console. (Remember to refresh the screen if you already had it open.)

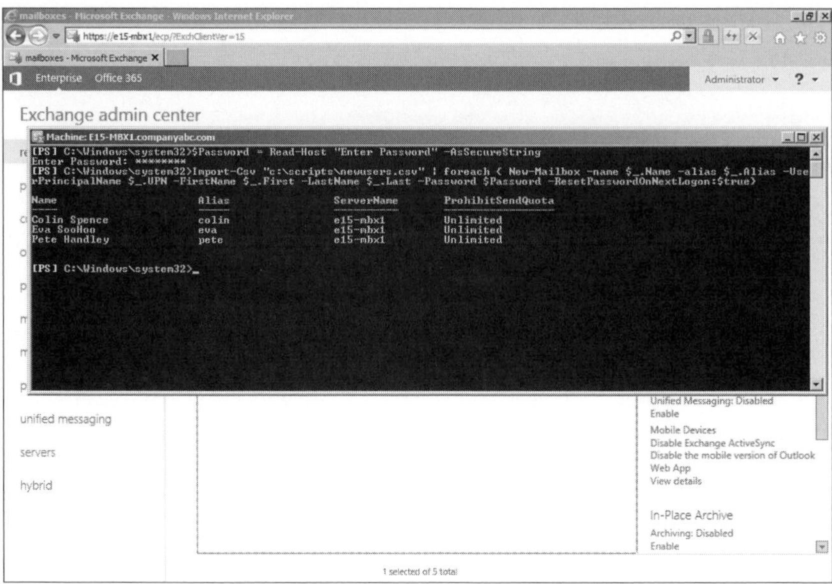

FIGURE 13.5 End result of multiple mailbox creation script.

Again—while this is a significant amount of work for three users, the same concept can be used to create 50 users (or 500) and can prove to be a valuable time-saver.

Introduction to Role Based Access Control

One of the administrative shortcomings of Exchange Server has been the ability to control precisely *who* can administer *what*. Granting a group of administrators the necessary permissions to create mailboxes anywhere in an Exchange Server environment might be practical for a small organization, but what about a large company with a worldwide presence? Do you actually want the support staff in one country to administer (and have access to) the mailboxes in another country? Do you actually want your tier 1 help desk personnel, staffed by junior administrators, to have the same access to Executive mailboxes as they do to Sales? And what about your user community? Just because an organization wants to allow its users to change their own phone numbers in the Global Address List (GAL), must they be allowed to change their display names as well?

By implementing RBAC, a feature first implemented in Exchange Server 2010, Microsoft has empowered organizations to not only dictate precisely *who* can access *what*, but also *where*.

With RBAC, the permission to perform tasks is assigned to specific *management* roles. Administrators and users are assigned to appropriate roles, and through their membership in the role, they acquire the necessary permissions to perform the desired task. This does not only apply to administrators; RBAC also controls the extent to which end users can self-administer their own accounts.

The RBAC permissions model consists of four components:

- **Management role group**—A special universal security group (USG) in Active Directory (AD) that can be composed of mailboxes, users, other USGs, and other role groups. All members of a role group are assigned the same set of roles, and members are added to a management role group to assign the desired permissions. Note that it is not absolutely necessary to define management role groups; management roles can be assigned directly to users, but this practice is discouraged because it is difficult to manage.
- **Management role**—A container that holds management group entries. Management roles define the actual tasks that can be performed by members of the associated role group. A *management role entry* is a cmdlet (a specialized command in the PowerShell environment) and its parameters that are added to a management role. This process grants rights to manage or view the objects associated with that cmdlet.
- **Management role assignment**—A designation that links a management role to a management role group. This grants the users assigned to the group the ability to perform the actions assigned to the role group.
- **Management role scope**—An entity that defines the scope of influence that a role assignment has. A management role scope can include servers, organizational units, filters on server or recipient objects, and more.

And thus, we achieve the ability to control *who* (via management role group and management role assignment) can do *what* (via management role and management role entries) and *where* (via management role scope). Exchange Server administration can now be as granular or as broad as the needs of the organization mandate, and with RBAC, organizations can more closely align the permissions assigned to users and administrators to the roles they actually hold.

Understanding Management Role Groups

A *management role group* is a universal security group that is part of the RBAC permissions model. A management role group simplifies the assignment of management roles to a user or group of users. Management roles are assigned to the entire role group, so all members of a particular role group share the same set of roles.

Role groups are assigned both administrator and specialist roles. These define the major administrative tasks in Exchange Server and enable an organization to assign a broader set of permissions to a group of administrators, specialists, or even end users.

Understanding Management Roles

As previously stated, *management roles* act as logical grouping of all the pieces that define what a user is allowed to do in an Exchange Server 2013 environment, whether he or she is a senior Exchange Server architect, a junior help desk employee, or an end user.

Microsoft has provided dozens of built-in management roles that meet the basic needs of most environments. These roles cannot be modified, nor can the management role entries that are configured for them, but the *scope* can be modified. Some examples of built-in management roles include the following:

- Reset Password
- Transport Rules
- Move Mailboxes

By adding users or groups of users to these management roles, the permissions needed to perform tasks can easily be assigned. So, if you want your tier 1 support staff to manage recipients and change their passwords, you would assign the Mail Recipients and Reset Password roles to the role group.

Although management roles can be directly assigned to users, it is recommended that role groups and role assignment policies are utilized to simplify the permissions model.

Run the cmdlet `Get-ManagementRole` to see the complete list.

Understanding Management Role Assignments

A *management role assignment* is the connector between a *role* and a *role assignee*. A *role assignee* can be a role group, role assignment policy, user, or universal security group. Before a role can take effect, it must be assigned to a role assignee.

By adding, removing, or modifying a role assignment, administrators can control what permissions are given to other administrators and users. This effectively enables (or disables) management capabilities for the user.

Role assignments come in two flavors: regular role assignments and delegating role assignments.

Regular role assignments enable the assignee to access the management role entries made available by the associated management role. Management role entries are aggregated (combined), so if an assignee has several role assignments, all of the associated management roles are given.

Delegating role assignments do not give access to manage features; instead, they give a role assignee the ability to assign the specified role to other role assignees.

Understanding Management Role Scopes

A *management role scope* enables administrators to define the specific range of impact or influence that a management role has once a management role assignment has been created. By applying a role scope, the role assignee can modify only the objects contained within the scope.

Every management role, whether built in or custom, is governed by its associated management role scope. Scopes can be inherited from the management role, specified as a predefined relative scope for a particular management role assignment, or created using custom filters and added to a management role assignment. Those that are inherited from management roles are called *implicit* scopes, whereas the predefined and custom scopes are called *explicit* scopes.

There are two types of management role scope:

- *Regular* role scopes are not exclusive. They determine where, in AD, objects can be viewed or modified by users assigned the associated management role. To put it simply, the management role dictates *what* objects a user can create or modify, and the management role scope dictates *where* the user can create or modify them. Regular scopes can be either implicit or explicit scopes.
- *Exclusive* role scopes behave similarly to regular scopes, except that they provide the ability to deny users access to objects if the users aren't assigned a role associated with the exclusive scope. All exclusive scopes are explicit scopes.

Shared Versus Split Permissions Models

Both AD and Exchange Server environments require administrators with specialized knowledge to administer them. In some organizations, the responsibility for managing these two environments is shared by the same personnel. Other organizations have separate departments for managing AD and Exchange Server.

Exchange Server 2013 enables organizations to use either a Shared Permissions or a Split Permissions model. By default, the Shared Permissions model is deployed.

Shared Permissions Model

Organizations that want to use a shared permissions model don't need to change anything because this is the default model used in Exchange Server 2013. There is no separation of the management of Exchange Server and AD objects from within the Exchange Server management tools: the Exchange Management Console, the Exchange Management Shell, or the Exchange Control Panel (introduced earlier in this chapter). Administrators using these tools can create security principles in AD *and* manage the configuration of those objects in Exchange Server.

Split Permissions Model

In the split permissions model, a distinction is made between the creation of security principals in AD (such as users and security groups) and the configuration of those objects. Proper implementation of a split permissions model allows organizations to minimize the risk of unauthorized access to the network by limiting the ability to create objects to a small group of authorized personnel.

Using this model, one group of administrators (AD administrators) can create security principals in AD, whereas another (Exchange Server administrators) can manage specific attributes on existing AD objects.

Organizations desiring to implement a split permissions model should give serious thought as to whether this model will truly work in the environment because it can be extremely difficult to implement correctly. Under this model, AD administrators need to create new users but *cannot* configure the Exchange Server attributes on the objects. Exchange Server administrators can configure the attributes but *cannot* create new accounts. Under the split permissions model, Exchange Server administrators can no longer use any of the following cmdlets:

- `New-Mailbox` or `Remove-Mailbox`
- `New-MailUser` or `Remove-MailUser`
- `New-MailContact` or `Remove-MailContact`
- `New-LinkedUser` or `Remove-LinkedUser`
- `Add-MailboxPermission`
- `Add-MailboxFolderPermission`

Exchange Server administrators can still create and manage Exchange Server–specific objects, such as transport rules, distribution groups, and so on. To implement a split-permissions model, the option Apply Active Directory Split Permissions Security Model to the Exchange Organization must be selected during Exchange 2013 setup.

The Benefits of RBAC

One of the goals that Microsoft worked toward with the design and creation of Exchange Server 2013 is the capability to decrease support costs. Early in the process, it realized that one way to significantly reduce the administrative overhead in an environment was to empower users to perform specific tasks for themselves, rather than go through the time-consuming and resource-intensive process of requesting assistance to complete relatively minor changes.

Granting users the administrative rights to perform certain low-level tasks, while still preventing them from accessing (and potentially damaging) configuration settings that could impact the entire organization was extremely difficult, if not impossible, using the access control list (ACL)-based model of previous Exchange Server versions.

Employees can now track the status of messages that they have sent, create and manage their own distribution lists, and update certain aspects of their account information, such as their Contact Location (address) and Contact Numbers (work, fax, home, and mobile phone numbers).

RBAC focuses on the effective and efficient distribution of administrative permissions. In previous versions of Exchange Server, granting help desk personnel (for example) the ability to create new mailboxes in one site gave them (by default) the ability to create new mailboxes anywhere in the environment. Locking down these permissions to one specific site was time consuming and complicated—and there are *many* different scenarios that had to be identified, evaluated, and resolved before administrators could be sure they had matched the appropriate personnel with the appropriate access.

Another example of the benefits of RBAC is in the area of eDiscovery—granting permissions to a group of users (such as members of the HR Department) to view the contents of a particular set of mailboxes (such as those located in the Marketing OU).

Using RBAC, administrators can grant the necessary access to allow the members of the HR Department to review the mailboxes of the Marketing users but *not* those in Sales (located in another OU).

These permissions can easily be delegated using RBAC for the duration of the discovery period and then removed until needed again.

NOTE

When creating a new OU in a Windows 2008 Active Directory environment, you might notice a new and welcome feature; when naming the OU, the option to Protect Container from Accidental Deletion is present and automatically selected. This places an explicit Deny permission on the object for the group "everyone," preventing accidental deletion of the object. To remove this (for intentional deletion), go to Active Directory Users and Computers; select View, Advanced Features; and then view the properties of the OU. On the Object tab, deselect the Protect Object from Accidental Deletion check box.

Understanding Journaling

Journaling and archiving are two concepts that are often confused for one another. Both have to do with the retention of data, but the purpose behind the concepts is the defining factor.

Journaling is the process of recording all inbound and outbound email communications in an organization to meet the email retention or archival strategy.

Archiving is the process of managing the size of an environment's data store by taking a backup copy of historical data, removing it from its native environment, and storing it elsewhere.

Each of these strategies can be used for meeting certain regulatory requirements, and journaling can often be used as a tool in an organization's archiving strategy.

The Benefits of Journaling

Over the past several years, there has been a significant increase in regulations requiring organizations to maintain records of communication—especially relating to the financial services, insurance, and health-care industries. In addition, many companies have found that maintaining accurate and complete records of employee communications can assist them in the legal arena, whether they are defending against or initiating lawsuits.

For example, a disgruntled former employee might file a lawsuit against a company for wrongful termination, stating that he had never been notified that his behavior or performance was unsatisfactory. If the organization has an email journaling solution in place, they could go through the historical data and show specific examples where the behavior problems were discussed with the employee. More and more courts are accepting, and often insisting on, historical corporate messaging data to determine culpability.

Some of the more well-known U.S. regulations that, in recent years, have specified requirements that might rely on journaling technology follow:

- **Sarbanes-Oxley Act of 2002 (SOX)**—One of the most widely known regulatory acts, the Sarbanes-Oxley Act is a U.S. federal law that requires the preservation of records by certain Exchange Server members, brokers, and dealers. This act was passed into law in response to a number of major corporate and accounting scandals that resulted in a decline of public trust in corporate accounting and reporting practices.
- **Security Exchange Commission Rule 17a-4 (SEC Rule 17a-4)**—This U.S. Security and Exchange Rule provides rules regarding the retention of electronic correspondence and records.
- **National Association of Securities Dealers 3010 & 3110 (NASD 3010 & 3110)**—The NASD details requirements for member firms that include the supervision of registered representatives, including inbound and outbound electronic correspondence with the public. In addition, the NASD details how long this information must be maintained and what conditions must be met.
- **Health Insurance Portability and Accountability Act of 1996**—More commonly known as HIPAA, this U.S. federal law provides rights and protections for participants and beneficiaries in group health plans.
- **Uniting and Strengthening America by Providing Appropriate Tools Required to Intercept and Obstruct Terrorism Act of 2001**—Better known as the Patriot Act, this U.S. federal law expands the authority of U.S. law enforcement for the stated purpose of fighting terrorist acts in the United States and abroad.

In addition, there are regulations imposed outside of the United States that organizations with a worldwide presence might need to adhere to, such as the following:

- **The European Union Data Protection Directive (EUDPD)**–A directive that standardizes the protection of data privacy for citizens throughout the European Union (EU) by providing baseline requirements that all member states must adhere to.
- **Japan's Personal Information Protection Act**—A law created and enforced by the Japanese government to regulate the collection, use, and transfer of personal information. The Personal Information Protection Act applies to government or private entities that collect, handle, or use personal information of 5,000 or more individuals.

Using journaling technology is one way that companies can work toward meeting these (and other) regulatory requirements.

The Journaling Agent

In an Exchange Server 2013 environment, all email is processed by at least one Hub Transport (HT) server. This includes messages that are sent to or received from external organizations, mail sent from a mailbox on one server to a mailbox on another server, or even mail sent between mailboxes located on the same server. All mail must pass through a Hub Transport server for delivery.

The *Journaling agent* is an agent that processes messages on HT servers and that is focused on compliance.

In Exchange Server 2013, there are two journaling options:

- **Standard journaling**—Standard journaling is configured on a mailbox database. It enables the Journaling agent (on the HT server) to journal all messages that are sent to or from any mailbox on that particular database. If an organization wants to journal all mail sent and received by all mailboxes in its environment, journaling must be configured on each mailbox database in the organization.
- **Premium journaling**—Premium journaling enables the creation and implementation of journaling rules that enable the Journaling agent to be more specific about what is and isn't journaled. Rather than capturing all mail to all mailboxes in a database, journal rules can be configured to only journal-specific mailboxes or the mailboxes of all members in a distribution group. The implementation of premium journaling requires an Exchange Enterprise client access license (CAL).

Journal rules are composed of three key components:

- **Journal rule scope**—The messages that are journaled by the Journaling agent
- **Journal recipients**—The SMTP address of the recipient to be journaled
- **Journaling mailboxes**—One or more mailboxes that are used for collecting journal reports

Journal Rule Scope

When configuring a journal rule, the scope of the rule defines what type of messages will be journaled. You can choose from the following three scopes:

- **Internal**—When journaling entries are based on the Internal scope, messages that are sent and received by mailboxes within the Exchange Server organization are journaled.
- **External**—When journaling entries are based on the External scope, messages that are sent to recipients outside the Exchange Server organization, or that are received from senders outside of the Exchange Server organization, are journaled.
- **Global**—When journaling entries are based on the Global scope, all messages that pass through a server with the Hub Transport server role are journaled.

NOTE

When the Global scope is selected, the Hub Transport servers journal *all* messages that pass through. This includes messages that might or might not have been journaled already by rules in the Internal and External scopes.

Journal Recipients

In addition to the journaling scopes just discussed, specific SMTP addresses can be targeted for journaling. This can be helpful when your organization has specific individuals or positions that are subject to regulatory requirements that are more stringent than other personnel in your organization. In addition, this feature can be extremely useful when an individual is investigated for a legal proceeding and your organization wants to track his or her messages to be used as evidence.

Because every journaled message takes up storage space, customizing your journaling environment to match the actual needs of your organization, rather than simply turning it on for everyone can go a long way toward minimizing your costs.

All messages sent to or from the journaling recipients specified in a journaling rule are journaled. If a distribution group (rather than an individual user) is specified in the rule, all messages to and from members of the group are journaled. If a journal rule recipient is not specified, all messages sent to or from recipients that match the criteria of the journal rule scope are journaled.

For organizations that also utilize Unified Messaging to consolidate their voice mail and fax infrastructure into their email system, they must evaluate if they want to journal their voice mail and missed call notifications as well. Voice mail messages can be significant in size, and costly in terms of disk space, so if there is no specific requirement for your organization to save these messages, you might not want to do so. However, messages that contain faxes and that are generated by a Unified Messaging server are always journaled, even if you disable journaling of Unified Messaging voice mail and missed call notifications.

When you enable or disable the journaling of voice mail and missed call notification messages, your change is applied to all Hub Transport servers in your organization.

Journaling Mailboxes

All of these journaled messages must reside somewhere if they are ever to be utilized; a journaling mailbox is one that is used only for collecting journal reports. In Exchange Server, you have the flexibility to create a single journaling mailbox to store all journal reports, or you can create separate journaling mailboxes for each journal rule (or set of journal rules) that you configure. This flexibility even enables you to configure multiple journal rules to use one specific journaling mailbox and then configure other rules to each use their own specific one. How you configure your journaling mailboxes depends on your organization's policies and regulatory and legal requirements.

It is important to note that journaling mailboxes collect messages that are sent to and from recipients in your organization, and that these messages might contain sensitive information, might be used as part of legal proceedings, or might be used to meet regulatory requirements. Various laws are in place that mandate that these messages remain tamper free if they are to be used by an investigatory authority. Administrators should work closely with the Legal Department in their organization (if one exists) to develop policies that specify who can access this data and security measures to ensure these policies are enforced. Access to the journaling mailboxes should be limited to those with the "need to know," so to speak. When a journaling solution is put in place, it should be reviewed and certified by your legal representatives to make sure it complies with all the laws and regulations that govern your organization.

Journal Rule Replication

When a journal rule is created, modified, or deleted on a Hub Transport server, the change is replicated to all Active Directory servers in the organization. All Hub Transport servers in the organization get these new configuration changes from AD and apply the new or modified rules to messages that pass through them. Every time the Hub Transport server retrieves a new journal rule, an event is logged in the security log of the Event Viewer.

By utilizing replication of journal rules throughout the organization, Exchange Server 2013 ensures a consistent set of rules are utilized throughout. All messages passing through the Exchange Server organization are subject to the same journaling rules.

NOTE

Journal rule replication relies on AD replication. Administrators should take link speeds and replication delays into consideration when implementing new or modified journal rules.

To reduce the number of requests that Hub Transport servers must make to AD, each one maintains a recipient cache that is used to look up recipient and distribution list information. This cache is updated every 4 hours, and the update interval cannot be modified. Changes to journal rule recipients might not be applied to journal rules until this cache is updated. To force an immediate update of the recipient cache, the Microsoft Exchange Transport service must be restarted on every Hub Transport server that you want to immediately update the cache.

Journal Reports

A journal report is the message that Exchange Server generates when a message is submitted to the journaling mailbox. Exchange Server 2013 supports envelope journaling only, which means that the original message matching the journal rule is included (unaltered) as an attachment to the journal report. The body of the journal report contains associated information such as the sender email address, message subject, message ID, and recipient address of the original message.

Creating a New Journal Rule

Unlike previous versions of Exchange Server, the Journaling agent is a built-in agent that is no longer visible in the Transport Agents tab in the EMC. It is also not included in the results when running the `Get-TranportAgent` cmdlet in the EMS. The Journaling agent is enabled by default in Exchange Server 2013, so administrators do not need to enable it before use.

To create a journal rule in the Exchange Management Console, follow these steps:

1. Open the Exchange Administration Center.
2. Click the Compliance Management tab.
3. Click the Journal Rules option.
4. Click the New (+) icon.
5. In the New Journal Rule dialog box, enter a name for your journaling rule.
6. For If the Message Is Sent To or From, select whether to journal mail sent to or from a specific user or all messages. If you choose to journal to or from a specific user, you will be presented with a dialog box where you can choose one or more users to journal.
7. For Journal the Following Messages, select whether to journal all, internal, or external messages.
8. In the Send Journal Reports to E-mail Address field, enter the email address of the recipient who is to receive the journal reports.
9. Click Save to save the rule.

Understanding Archiving

As previously stated, *archiving* is the process of managing the size of an environment's data store by taking a backup copy of historical data, removing it from its native environment, and storing it elsewhere.

By integrating archiving directly into Exchange Server, Microsoft has enabled organizations to store this historical data without the complex administration and (often significant) additional licensing costs that can come with the integration of third-party applications.

The Benefits of Archiving

As users send and receive messages, maintaining older messages for historical purposes results in the mailbox (and the associated database) to continue to grow in size. Where users once could function with mailboxes that were measured in the tens (or at the most, hundreds) of megabytes, Exchange Server 2013 provides users with a default mailbox size of 2 gigabytes (GB), and it is not unusual for users to fill this space completely and require more.

With the growing need for larger and larger mailboxes comes a need to systematically archive historical data, freeing up space inside the user's mailbox to enhance performance, while retaining access to the historical data when it is needed.

Archiving can also help organizations better address compliance and legal electronic discovery requirements by allowing the historical data to be easily managed and searched.

Users with an archive enabled can perform searches on both the primary mailbox *and* the archive mailbox at once—searching through all subfolders for the desired message.

Exchange Server 2013 now features new archiving capabilities that combine with additional enhanced mailbox management features that include the capability to perform advanced multi-mailbox searches and apply legal hold and granular retention policies for individual mailboxes.

Archiving in Exchange Server 2013 is composed of four main concepts:

- **Personal archive**—A personal archive is an additional mailbox that is associated with a user's primary mailbox. It appears beneath the primary mailbox folders in Outlook Web Access 2013 (similar to the way `.pst` archives were shown) and is labeled Online Archive – Username. This enables the user to have direct access to email within the archive just as he or she would with the primary mailbox. Users can drag and drop PST files into the personal archive, for easier online access and more efficient discovery by the organization. Mail items from the primary mailbox can also be off-loaded to the personal archive automatically, using retention policies, reducing the size and improving the performance of the primary mailbox. With a personal archive, users can now have access to their archived mail without having to have local access to a `.pst` file and can access the archived mail from anywhere in the world using Outlook Web Access.

NOTE

The personal online archive is not synchronized to a user's offline folders and is available online only.

- **Retention policies**—Retention policies are utilized to enable and enforce desired retention settings to specific items or folders in a mailbox. These policies are configured by the Exchange administrator and are displayed inside each email, along with a header stating the applied policy and delete date. Utilizing retention policies makes it easy for a user to identify when an email is set for expiration—and the user has the ability to apply a new expiration policy if the email needs to be retained for a longer period. Administrators can also set default policy that can move messages from the primary mailbox to the archive automatically, removing the responsibility for maintaining the archive from the user.
- **Multi-Mailbox Search**—In Exchange Server 2013, the ability to search for mailbox items across multiple mailboxes, including email, attachments, calendar items, tasks, contacts, and IRM-protected files, is a welcome addition to those who specialize

in eDiscovery. Multi-Mailbox Search searches both the primary and archive mailboxes for a user simultaneously and utilizes an easy-to-use control panel. Utilizing this feature, authorized personnel (such as HR representatives, legal, and compliance users) can perform searches as needed, without the extremely time-consuming involvement of your already overworked IT staff. Mail that is located through a mailbox search can be copied and moved to a specified mailbox or external store for further investigation.

- **Retention Hold**—Placing a retention hold on a mailbox temporarily suspends retention policies from applying to a mailbox for a designated period of time. When a mailbox is placed on retention hold, the administrator can optionally specify a retention comment that indicates that the mailbox is on retention hold. This comment can include the dates when the retention hold is scheduled to begin and end. These retention comments are visible in supported Outlook clients and can also be displayed in the preferred language of the user.

Enabling Archiving on a Mailbox

There are few things in the world that are simpler than enabling an archive for an Exchange Server 2013 mailbox. By navigating to the user mailbox (EAC, Recipients, Mailboxes), administrators can double-click the mailbox, select Mailbox Features, under Archiving select Enable, and then choose the archive mailbox database.

Administrators can, if they want, place a quota on the archive. The quota is enabled by selecting Edit Details under Archiving, and then entering the quota and warning sizes. This quota, placed on the archive mailbox, is completely separate from any quotas placed on the primary mailbox. Administrators can provide a name for the archive here, which will show up in Outlook as the folder name.

Accessing the Mailbox Archive

Archived messages are of little use to the end user if the end user cannot access them. With an Exchange Server 2013 archive, the user can view the contents (and search through the contacts) while connected to the network with Outlook 2013 or Outlook Web Access 2013. As the archive mailbox node is stored on the Exchange server, it is not accessible by offline users, even those in cached mode.

Because messages that are auto-archived retain the same folder structure in the archive that they had in the primary mailbox, users with complex folder structures are unable to maintain them, and searches can be conducted that span both the primary and archive mailbox at the same time.

Server Administration

In Exchange Server 2007, administrators were constantly reminded that to take advantage of the improvements in high-availability technology, there should only be one storage group per database. If having several databases in a storage group complicated high-availability scenarios and made single-database restores more complex, why bother having them at all? Apparently Microsoft agreed: In Exchange Server 2010 and 2013, the concept of the storage group is no more.

Creating a New Database

Creating a new mailbox database in Exchange Server 2013 is a straightforward process. To create a new database from the EMS, a sample command is shown here:

```
New-MailboxDatabase -Server E2013-1 -Name MDB2 -EdbFilePath D:\MDB2\MDB2.edb
-LogFolderPath D:\Logs\MDB2
```

To mount the newly created database, use the following command:

```
Mount-Database -Identity MDB2
```


Setting Limits on Databases

After you create a database, you can customize the maximum storage limits and deletion settings for mailboxes stored on that database. Although some organizations consider limits of these kinds to be draconian in nature, most understand that preventing users from storing unlimited amounts of archaic data and the regular automatic purging of deleted items helps to ensure a healthy and happy messaging system.

By default, these settings apply to all user mailboxes stored on that database. However, specific limits on individual mailboxes can be configured to override these databasewide settings. This can be useful when you want to set a limit for all users on a particular database, but you have one user who needs more (or less) restrictive settings. To configure these options, perform the following tasks:

1. Start the Exchange Administration Center.
2. In the left navigation control, click Servers.
3. Click the Databases tab.
4. Double-click the database that you want to configure.
5. Select the Limits tab.
6. Several limits are available to configure for the database. You can configure any of the following settings on the database:
    - **Storage limits**—The storage section limits enable you to configure restrictions on all mailboxes located within that database. The available storage limits options are as follows:
        - **Issue Warning At**—1.9GB. This is not a "hard" limit, but a warning threshold. When this limit has been exceeded, the user will get a message warning them.

- **Prohibit Send At**—2 GB. This is a "hard" limit. When a mailbox exceeds this threshold, the user is unable to send mail. This does not impact the user's ability to receive mail, ensuring the user does not miss any messages while scurrying to clean up his or her mailbox.
- **Prohibit Send and Receive At**—2.3GB. This is also a "hard" limit. When the mailbox exceeds this limit, the user can no longer send or receive messages. Incoming mail destined for this mailbox will be returned to the sender.

- **Deletion settings**—The deletion settings dictate how deleted items and mailboxes in the database will be dealt with. The available deletion settings options are as follows:
  - **Keep Deleted Items for (Days)**—By default, mailbox databases are configured to keep deleted items for 14 days.

NOTE

There is often some user confusion as to what messages can be recovered using the Tools, Recover Deleted Items option in Outlook. There are two types of deletion: hard deletion and soft deletion. When users delete an item, it goes to the Deleted Items folder and can be recovered simply by dragging and dropping it back into the Inbox. If a user goes to the Deleted Items folder, and again deletes the message, or if he or she selects Tools, Empty Deleted Items Folder, the item has been hard deleted and can be recovered using the Tools, Recover Deleted Items option. A user can also hard delete an item by using Shift+Delete. This recovery can be accomplished if it is initiated within the window set in the Keep Deleted Items for (Days) section field. However, if a user enters the Recover Deleted Items utility and selects to purge a message, or if the Keep Deleted Items for (Days) period has expired, the item is hard deleted and cannot be recovered without resorting to restore methods.

  - **Keep Deleted Mailboxes for (Days)**—In Exchange Server 2013, as it has been since Exchange Server 2003, disabling or removing a mailbox does not mean that the mailbox is permanently purged from the database immediately. The mailbox is flagged for deletion and can no longer be accessed by users. After the mailbox retention period controlled by this setting has been reached, the mailbox is then purged from the system. This option is extremely useful if a user deletion occurs that is the result of a mistake and enables the administrator to create a new user object (if necessary) and enable the deleted mailbox by connecting it to the user. By default, this setting is set to 30 days. It can be configured anywhere from 0 (immediate purge upon deletion) to 24,855 days. It is unlikely you will ever need the upper limit (equivalent to a little more than 68 years), but this setting can be adjusted to meet your organization's needs. Unless disk space becomes an issue, it is recommended that you do not disable the deleted mailbox retention feature.

- **Don't Permanently Delete Items Until the Database Has Been Backed Up**—This final setting is not enabled by default. By checking this option, you instruct Exchange Server to not delete items or mailboxes, even after the retention period has expired, until the database has been successfully backed up. By selecting this option, you ensure that you can recover critical items or mailboxes from backup media, even after the purge has been completed.

Summary

The Microsoft Exchange Server platform has grown over the years, becoming more and more powerful to meet the growing needs of organizations and the desire for more powerful, reliable, and feature-laden messaging systems.

The administrative tools available for managing the environment have improved with every revision, and things that would have been impossible a few revisions ago can now be done quickly and easily.

With the introduction of the RBAC security model, end users can now participate in the administration of the environment, albeit to a limited degree.

Changes in the way that databases are managed, the release of PowerShell 3.0 and the concept of remote PowerShell administration, the retirement of storage groups, the creation of the new PowerShell command log, new toolbox utilities—Exchange Server just keeps getting better and better.

Whether dealing with users and mailboxes, distribution groups, or monitoring and analyzing the environment for performance bottlenecks, Exchange Server 2013 has tools and utilities that give administrators more control over their Exchange Server environments than ever before.

Best Practices

The following are best practices from this chapter:

- Use the new Exchange Administration Center for daily administration tasks in Exchange 2013, but keep in mind that the automation capabilities of the Exchange Management Shell can save considerable time when performing tasks for multiple mailboxes.
- Use Role Based Access Control to grant permissions to perform Exchange Server administrative tasks. Consider delegating role assignments to allow role assignees to assign a role to other users, reducing administrative overhead.
- Implement storage limits on user mailboxes. Use the Issue Warning option to warn the users and the Prohibit Send option to enforce the limits.
- When configuring mailbox archiving in Exchange Server 2013, consider the use of archive quotas to limit the size of the archive.

- Implement the Prohibit Send and Receive option, even if you must configure it with a size that is three or more times your expected maximum mailbox size. Leaving mailboxes "open ended" can be dangerous.
- Keep deleted items for at least 14 days and deleted mailboxes for at least 30 days. Use the option to not remove the items permanently until the store has been backed up.

CHAPTER 14

Exchange Server 2013 Management and Maintenance Practices

IN THIS CHAPTER

- Proper Care and Feeding of Exchange Server 2013
- Maintenance Tools for Exchange Server 2013
- The Exchange Administration Center
- The Exchange Toolbox
- Auditing the Environment
- Best Practices for Performing Database Maintenance
- Prioritizing and Scheduling Maintenance Best Practices
- Postmaintenance Procedures
- Reducing Management and Maintenance Efforts

Organizations have become increasingly reliant on email as a primary method of communication and, as such, the messaging system in most environments has come to be considered a mission-critical application. Any messaging downtime results in frustrated calls to the help desk. For most organizations, gone are the days where the email system can be taken offline during business hours for configuration changes.

To ensure the dependability and reliability of any application, proper maintenance and upkeep is vital, and Exchange Server 2013 is no exception. By implementing and performing proper management and maintenance procedures, administrators can minimize downtime and keep the system well tuned. However, for organizations that have been performing structured and effective maintenance and management practices with previous versions of Exchange, the process is the same with Exchange Server 2013. The key is that many organizations have no structured process in maintenance and management, and it seems like patching and updating is only done on the operating system or on Exchange only when a problem occurs and a patch or update is required.

Exchange Server 2010 (and extended in Exchange Server 2013) has advanced the health of the messaging system through the introduction of continuous online defragmentation, compaction, and contiguity maintenance. This has eliminated the need for routine offline database maintenance, which dramatically reduces the need for planned downtime.

This chapter focuses on recommended best practices for an administrator to properly maintain an Exchange Server 2013 messaging environment.

Proper Care and Feeding of Exchange Server 2013

This section is not about how to perform common, albeit necessary, management tasks such as using the interface to add a database. Instead, it focuses on concepts such as identifying and working with the server's functional roles in the network environment, auditing network activity and usage, and monitoring the health and performance of your messaging system.

With each new iteration of Exchange Server, Microsoft has greatly improved the tools and utilities used to manage the environment. Exchange Server 2013 is no exception. Exchange Server 2013 management can be done locally or remotely. The administration can even be done through firewalls. There are primary management interfaces, the Exchange Administration Center (EAC) and the Exchange Management Shell (EMS).

Managing by Server Roles and Responsibilities

Key in Exchange Server 2013 is the concept of role-based deployment, allowing administrators to deploy specific server roles to meet the requirements of their environments. Exchange Server 2013 provides three distinct server roles: Edge Transport, Client Access, and Mailbox.

The Edge Transport Server Role

The Edge Transport server role is responsible for all email entering or leaving the Exchange Server organization. To provide redundancy and load balancing, multiple Edge Transport servers can be configured for an organization.

The Edge Transport role is designed to be installed on a standalone server that resides in the perimeter network. As such, it is the only Exchange server designed to *not* be a member of the Active Directory (AD) domain. Synchronization with Active Directory is provided through the use of Active Directory Application Mode (ADAM) and a component called EdgeSync.

Edge Transport servers can provide antispam and antivirus protection, as well as the enforcement of Edge Transport rules based on Simple Mail Transfer Protocol (SMTP) and Multipurpose Internet Mail Extensions (MIME) addresses, particular words in the subject or message body, and a Spam Confidence Level (SCL) rating. In addition, Edge Transport servers can provide address rewriting—an administrator can modify the SMTP address on incoming and outgoing messages.

It is possible for an organization to avoid the use of an Edge Transport server completely and simply configure a Hub Transport server to communicate directly with the Internet. However, this scenario is not recommended because it exposes your Hub Transport server to potential attack. The Edge Transport server has a reduced attack surface to protect against these external threats.

The Client Access Server Role

The Client Access Server (CAS) role is similar to the front-end server in Exchange Server 2000/2003. New to Exchange Server 2010 and 2013 is that all clients communicate through the CAS. This is different than in Exchange Server 2007, where Outlook clients using Messaging Application Programming Interface (MAPI) would access the mailbox servers directly. The CAS server mediates all client traffic, providing a single point of communication that can be monitored to ensure consistent compliance and security across all types of clients.

The Mailbox Server Role

The Mailbox role will be the most familiar to administrators with previous Exchange Server experience. As the name implies, the Mailbox role is responsible for housing mailbox databases, which, in turn, contain user mailboxes. The Mailbox server role also houses public folder databases if they are implemented in the environment.

The Mailbox server role integrates with the directory in the Active Directory service much more effectively than previous versions of Exchange Server allowed, making deployment and day-to-day operational tasks much easier to complete. The Mailbox server role also provides users with improved calendaring functionality, resource management, and Offline Address Book downloads.

For those familiar with Exchange Server 2007 and 2010, the Hub Transport role no longer exists as a separate role, but instead is embedded into the Mailbox server role as a Hub Transport service. The Hub Transport service is responsible for managing internal mail flow in an Exchange Server organization and is installed on a member server in the AD domain.

The Hub Transport service handles all mail flow within the organization, as well as applying transport rules, journaling policies, and delivery of messages to recipient mailboxes. In addition, Hub Transport agents can be deployed to enforce corporate messaging policies, such as message retention and the implementation of email disclaimers.

The Hub Transport service accepts inbound mail from the Edge Transport server(s) and routes them to user mailboxes. Outbound mail is relayed from the Hub Transport service to the Edge Transport server and out to the Internet.

The Unified Messaging server role is also now rolled in as a service in the Mailbox server role. The Unified Messaging service is responsible for the integration of Office Communication Server Voice over IP (VoIP) technology into the Exchange Server messaging system. When implementing Unified Messaging with Exchange Server 2013, users can have access to voice, fax, and email messages all in the same mailbox, and these messages can be accessed through multiple client interfaces.

Managing by User Roles

Exchange Server 2013 provides Role Based Access Control (RBAC) to the Exchange Server platform. This permissions model applies to the Mailbox and Client Access Server roles. RBAC has replaced the permission model used in Exchange Server 2007 and prior. RBAC is not used on the Edge Transport server role because the Edge Transport security is not integrated with the other roles and is based on the local Administrators group.

The role-based model enables administrators to easily assign staff to one of the predefined roles or to create a custom role that meets the organization's unique requirements. The RBAC permissions model is used by the Exchange Management Shell (EMS), and the Exchange Administration Center (EAC) (formerly known as the Exchange Control Panel and sometimes still referenced as the ECP).

There are 12 predefined administrative roles:

- Compliance Management
- Delegated Setup
- Organization Management
- Discovery Management
- Help Desk
- View Only Organization Management
- Recipient Management
- Hygiene Management
- Public Folder Management
- Server Management
- UM Management
- Records Management

There is a single initial user role called the Default Role Assignment Policy role. This default role includes default role assignments, including the following:

- MyContactInformation
- MyDistributionGroupMembership
- MyBaseOptions
- MyTextMessaging
- MyVoicemail
- MyTeamMailboxes
- MyDistributionGroups

The administrative and user predefined roles cannot be changed. However, new roles can be created to define precise or broad roles and assignments based on the tasks that need to be performed in a given organization. This is done through the RBAC User Editor.

Maintenance Tools for Exchange Server 2013

Several tools are available to administer and manage an Exchange Server 2013 environment. There are functions within the Exchange Administration Center, an automation and scripting shell, and several tools native to the Windows Server 2008/2012 operating systems.

What Happened to the Exchange Management Console?

For the past decade, Exchange has been administered through the Exchange Management Console or EMC. However, with Exchange Server 2013, the EMC is gone in favor of the web-based Exchange Administration Center. So the Exchange System Manager (ESM) of Exchange Server 2003 is gone, and the Exchange Management Console (EMC) is gone. A new era in Exchange administration and management has begun under the new EAC.

The New Exchange Administration Center

The Exchange Administration Center is the main administrative tool for Exchange Server 2013. From the Exchange Administration Center, an administrator can add users, add servers, add email routing, modify Exchange configuration settings, set up antispam rules, set up server transport rules, and so on. Effectively, everything that an Exchange administrator used to be able to do in the Exchange Management Console or Exchange System Manager is now done in the Exchange Administration Center, shown in Figure 14.1.

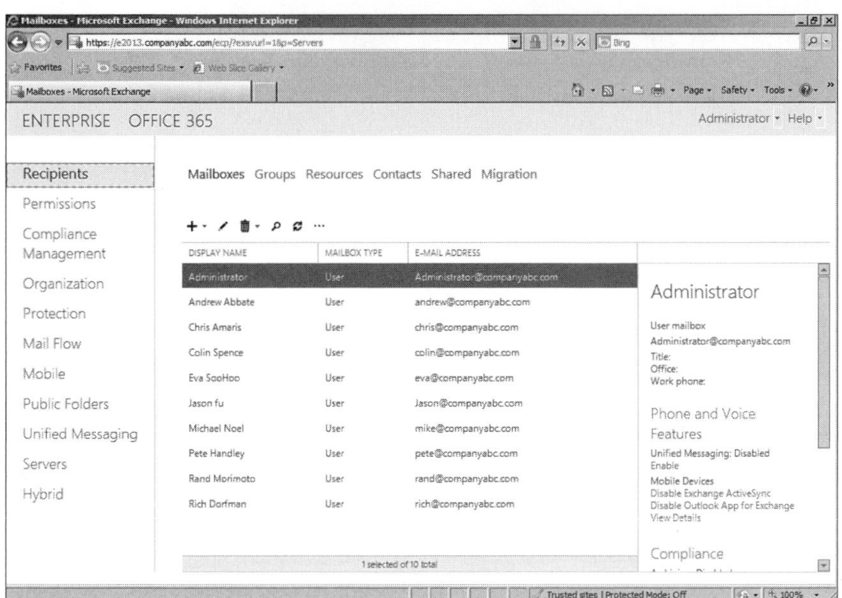

FIGURE 14.1 Exchange Server 2013 Exchange Administration Center.

More on the Exchange Administration Center is covered specifically in a section on the EAC in Chapter 13, "Administering an Exchange Server 2013 Environment."

The Exchange Management Shell

The second utility for managing an Exchange Server 2013 environment is an automation and scripting tool called the Exchange Management Shell (EMS), shown in Figure 14.2. This shell is a command-line management interface that can be used to administer servers in an Exchange Server 2013 organization. It enables administration of the Exchange Server 2013 environment without the Exchange management tools such as the EMC, albeit via a command-line interface. Built on Microsoft Windows PowerShell 3.0 technology, the Exchange Management Shell can perform any task that can be accomplished in the Exchange Management Console and a lot more. In fact, many configuration settings in an Exchange Server 2013 environment can only be accomplished using the Exchange Management Shell.

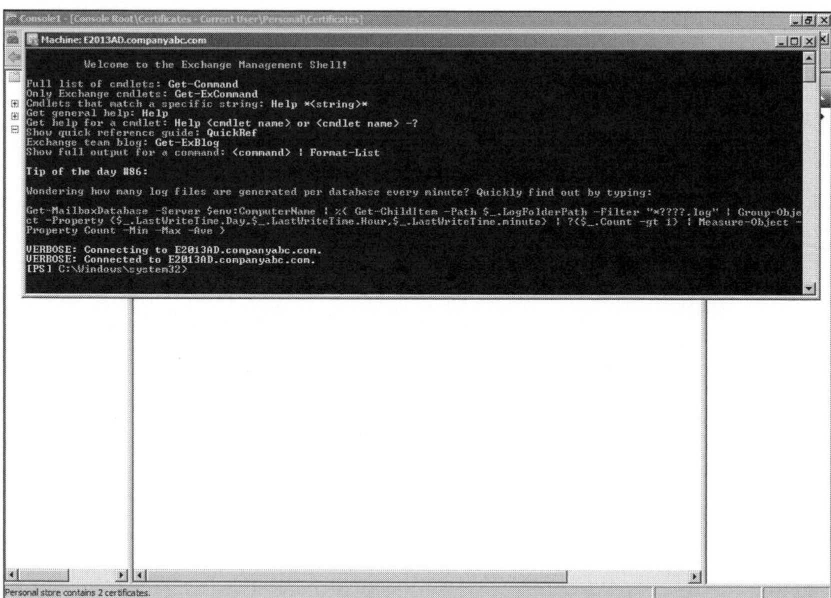

FIGURE 14.2 Exchange Server 2013 Exchange Management Shell.

Exchange Server has the ability to access all the familiar Exchange Server cmdlets remotely, leveraging the PowerShell 3.0 remote capabilities. This enables cmdlets and scripts to run across multiple servers in a single EMS instance. It also enables administrators to run the shell from their workstations and connect remotely to the Exchange Server 2013 servers. EMS can run on either 32-bit or 64-bit client systems and connect to 64-bit Exchange Server 2013 servers.

The EMS does not require Exchange Server binaries to be installed on the client, making deployment much easier.

Supported client OS platforms for the Exchange Management Shell are as follows:

- Windows Vista (32-bit or 64-bit)
- Windows 7 (32-bit or 64-bit)
- Windows 8 (32-bit or 64-bit)
- Windows Server 2008 (32-bit or 64-bit)
- Windows Server 2008 R2 (64-bit)
- Windows Server 2012 (64-bit)

The Exchange Administration Center

The Exchange Administration Center is an exciting new tool in Exchange Server 2013. The EAC is a browser-based management client for end users, administrators, and specialists. This provides a new way to administer a subset of Exchange Server features and is completely RBAC-integrated.

This new EAC web utility provides a great self-provisioning portal for administrators and a simplified user experience for common management tasks. It is accessible directly via a uniform resource locator (URL) just like email access is accessed by URL to Outlook Web App (OWA).

The EAC is AJAX based, deployed as a part of the Client Access Server role, and shares some code with OWA. However, the two are separate applications and sites.

The Exchange Administration Center can be used in a variety of scenarios. Administrators can delegate permissions using roles to support a variety of administrators, specialists, and users. These include the following types of scenarios:

- Administrators
- Help desk specialists
- Auditors
- End users
- Customers in a hosted environment

The scenarios are configured in the RBAC interface, which is based in the Exchange Administration Center.

Administrators would launch the EAC tool directly from the ECP link (https://*<servername>*/ecp) where *<servername>* is an Exchange Server 2013 CAS. Although administrators can switch between their OWA mailbox web page (https://*<servername>*/owa) and the EAC administration web page (https://*<servername>*/ecp), the security is integrated and provides separation between the user and administration roles.

The browser support for the EAC is the same as for OWA premium. Supported browsers are as follows:

- ▶ Internet Explorer
- ▶ Firefox
- ▶ Safari

The Exchange Administration Center is covered in detail in Chapter 13.

The Exchange Toolbox

All that remains of the Exchange Server 2010 Management Console is the tools, so the collection has been renamed the Exchange Toolbox and shows up in the Start menu with the Exchange Management Shell. The following sections describe the tools in the Toolbox.

Exchange Best Practices Analyzer

The Exchange Best Practices Analyzer (ExBPA) is included in Exchange Server 2013 and can be found in the Exchange Toolbox.

The ExBPA can be used to run health checks on an Exchange Server environment, and can also run performance checks, permissions checks, and connectivity tests to assist when troubleshooting problems.

The ExBPA should be run whenever a new server is added to an Exchange Server 2013 environment, or whenever configuration changes are made. More information on this utility can be found in Chapter 15, "Optimizing an Exchange Server 2013 Environment."

Remote Connectivity Analyzer

The Remote Connectivity Analyzer (RCA) is also found in the Exchange Toolbox in Exchange Server 2013. The RCA allows administrators to test services from outside their organizations. The tool essentially launches a browser to the website https://www.testexchangeconnetivity.com/ (shorthand https://exrca.com), shown in Figure 14.3. The website is maintained by Microsoft and is not technically a component of Exchange Server 2013, although the console has a link to it.

The tests that can be launched from the site include the following:

- ▶ Microsoft Exchange ActiveSync Connectivity Tests
- ▶ Microsoft Exchange Web Services Connectivity Tests
- ▶ Microsoft Office Outlook Connectivity Tests
- ▶ Internet E-Mail Tests

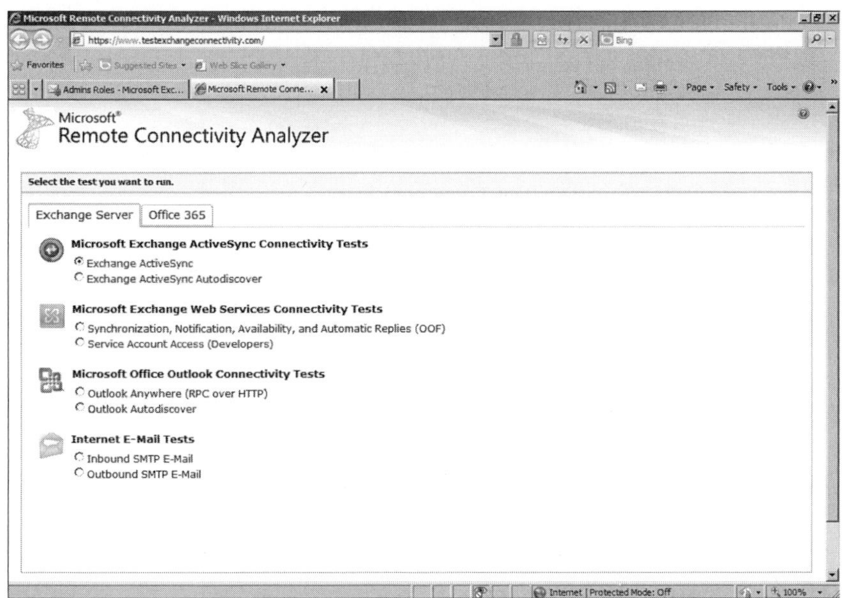

FIGURE 14.3 Remote Connectivity Analyzer website.

This site performs a valuable service by testing actual client access from a third party (that is, Microsoft). This simulates a client and exposes configuration or connectivity problems. For example, the Internet E-Mail Tests use SMTP to send email to a user, verifying the MX record, name resolution, SMTP, and if the gateway is an open relay. Another example is ActiveSync Provider AutoDiscover, which tests the notoriously difficult to test ActiveSync autodiscover services. As shown in Figure 14.4, the site prompts for email address, domain credentials, and verification. On clicking Perform Test, the site tests ActiveSync autodiscover and presents the results.

The tool does require domain credentials to test the various services, so security measures are built in to the product. The site uses the HTTPS protocol, so the confidentiality of the transmissions is protected by Secure Sockets Layer (SSL) encryption. The site prompts human verification, reading, and entering distorted text to ensure that the system is not hijacked by bots. And the site has a privacy statement indicating that the information collected is not retained after the tool is used. All that said, it is strongly recommended that dummy test accounts and credentials be used to execute the tests—and that those accounts be disabled or deleted following the tests.

Mail Flow Tools

The Mail Flow Troubleshooter is a utility that assists with troubleshooting common mail flow issues in an Exchange Server environment. Administrators can input the issues they are encountering, and the utility gathers information, diagnoses the environment, and presents a recommended plan of action.

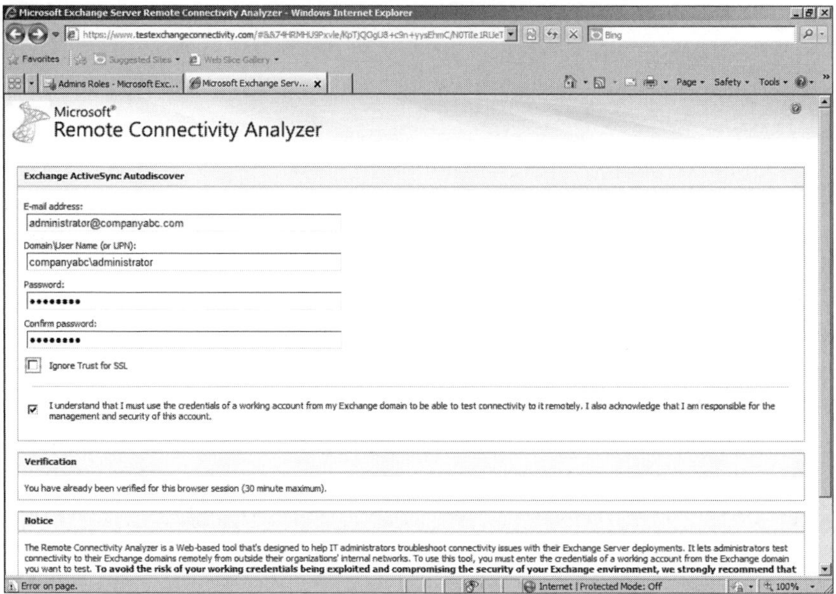

FIGURE 14.4 Remote Connectivity Analyzer ActiveSync Autodiscover Test setup.

The Tracking Log Explorer utility allows administrators to search for messages and track them through the Exchange Server environment. Message tracking can be extremely useful for determining where a message was delayed or "stuck" in the messaging environment.

Message Tracking, which once was part of the Mail Flow Tools is not part of the Exchange Administration Center message tracking section. The messaging tracking enables an administrator to search the mail store for messages that meet a certain criteria.

Exchange Queue Viewer

The Exchange Queue Viewer is another utility included in the Exchange Toolbox. The Exchange Queue Viewer is used to view the contents of the queues for each particular protocol on a server. Although this tool is more of a troubleshooting tool, it is important to periodically check protocol queues (for example, SMTP or X.400 queues) to ensure that no delivery problems exist.

Details Templates Editor

The Details Templates Editor is used to modify the graphical user interface for document templates for contacts, users, groups, mailbox agents, public folders, and search dialog boxes. When an organization wants to modify the default templates to add a custom field, change the size or type of an existing field, or modify the template form, it should use the Details Templates Editor.

Active Directory Database Maintenance Using ntdsutil

Exchange Server 2013 uses Windows Active Directory to store all its directory information. As a result, it is important to keep AD as healthy as possible to ensure that Exchange Server 2013 remains reliable and stable.

Windows Server automatically performs maintenance on Active Directory by cleaning up the AD database on a daily basis. The process occurs on domain controllers approximately every 12 hours. One example of the results of this process is the removal of tombstones, which are the "markers" for previously deleted objects. In addition, the process deletes unnecessary log files and reclaims free space.

The automatic daily process does not, however, perform all maintenance necessary for a clean and healthy database. For example, the maintenance process does not compress and defragment the Active Directory database. To perform this function, the ntdsutil command-line utility is needed.

CAUTION

To avoid possible adverse effects with the AD database, run ntdsutil in Directory Service Restore mode. Reboot the server, press the F8 key, and then select this mode of operation.

To use ntdsutil to defragment the Windows Active Directory database, perform the following steps:

1. Restart the domain controller.
2. When the initial screen appears, press the F8 key.
3. From the Windows Advanced Options menu, select Directory Services Restore Mode.
4. Select the Windows Server operating system being used.
5. Log on to the Windows Server system.
6. Click OK when the informational message appears.
7. At a command prompt, create a directory where the utility can store the defragmented file. For example, C:\NTDS.
8. At a command prompt, type **ntdsutil files**, and then press Enter.
9. At the file maintenance prompt, type **compact to <TargetDirectory>**, where *<TargetDirectory>* identifies the empty directory created in step 7. For example:

   ```
   compact to c:\ntds
   ```

   This invokes the esentutl.exe utility to compact the existing database and write the results to the specified directory.

10. If compaction was successful, copy the new `ntds.dit` file to `%systemroot%\NTDS`, and delete the old log files located in that directory.
11. Type **`quit`** twice to exit the utility.
12. Restart the domain controller.

This typically needs to be done only following a large migration or reorganization of the Active Directory forest, rather than on a routine basis.

Database Maintenance with the `eseutil` Utility

The `eseutil` utility is a database-level utility that is not application-specific. It can, for example, be used to maintain, test, and repair both AD and Exchange Server databases. More specifically, `eseutil` is used to maintain database-level integrity, perform defragmentation and compaction, and repair even the most severely corrupt databases. It is also the utility to use when maintaining Exchange Server 2013 transaction log files to determine which transaction logs need to be replayed or which log file the `Edb.chk` file points to.

CAUTION

Using the `eseutil` utility on an AD or Exchange Server database can produce irreversible changes.

It is best to restore a copy of a suspected corrupt database in a lab environment, and then run `eseutil` against that copy prior to any attempts to use it in a production environment.

NOTE

`eseutil` investigates the data that resides in the database table for any corruption or errors, which is why it is called a database-level utility. The `eseutil` options are shown in Table 14.1.

The `eseutil` tool repairs the mailbox and public folder databases (database files, tables, and indexes), whereas the `isinteg` tool repairs the contents of the mailbox and public folder databases (messages, links, and attachments).

TABLE 14.1 `eseutil` Syntax

Mode of Operation	Syntax
Defragmentation	`ESEUTIL /d <database name> [options]`
Recovery	`ESEUTIL /r <logfile base name> [options]`
Integrity	`ESEUTIL /g <database name> [options]`
Checksum	`ESEUTIL /k <filename> [options]`
Repair	`ESEUTIL /p <database name> [options]`

Mode of Operation	Syntax
File dump	`ESEUTIL /m[mode-modifier] <filename>`
Copy file	`ESEUTIL /y <source file> [options]`
Restore	`ESEUTIL /c[mode-modifier] <pathname> [options]`

NOTE

Because Exchange Server 2013 data is commonly replicated using database availability groups (DAGs) and subsequent copies of Exchange databases are available on the network, the `eseutil` is not used that frequently anymore. While database corruption may exist in one copy of the database, another copy of the organization's database may reside on another DAG copy without corruption. `Eseutil` should only be used when other alternatives for database repair do not exist, and `eseutil` is the last resort for data recovery.

Auditing the Environment

Various methods of auditing the Exchange Server environment exist to gather and store records of network and Exchange Server access and to assist with the monitoring and tracking of SMTP connections and message routing.

Typically used for identifying security breaches or suspicious activity, auditing has the added benefit of allowing administrators to gain insight into how the Exchange Server 2013 systems are accessed and, in some cases, how they are performing.

This chapter focuses on three types of auditing:

- **Audit logging**—For security and tracking user access
- **SMTP logging**—For capturing SMTP conversations between messaging servers
- **Message tracking**—For tracking emails through the messaging environment

Audit Logging

In a Windows environment, auditing is primarily considered to be an identity and access control security technology that can be implemented as part of an organization's network security strategy. By collecting and monitoring security-related events, administrators can track user authentication and authorization, as well as access to various directory services (including Exchange Server 2013 services).

Exchange Server 2013 relies on the audit policies of the underlying operating system for capturing information on user access and authorization. Administrators can utilize the built-in Windows Server event auditing to capture data that is written to the security log for review.

Enabling Event Auditing

Audit policies are the basis for auditing events on Windows Server systems. Administrators must be aware that, depending on the policies configured, auditing might require a substantial amount of server resources in addition to those supporting the primary function of the server. On servers without adequate memory, processing power or hard drive space, auditing can potentially result in decreased server performance. After enabling auditing, administrators should monitor server performance to ensure the server can handle the additional load.

To enable audit policies on a Windows Server 2008 or 2008 R2 server, perform the following steps:

1. On the server to be audited, log on as a member of the local Administrators group.
2. Select Start, Administrative Tools, and launch the Local Security Policy tool.

NOTE

For a Windows Server 2012 environment, press the Windows key to bring up the Metro desktop menu, type local (which will start to search for any application or utility that has the word local in it), and choose the Local Security Policy tool.

3. Expand Local Policies and select Audit Policy.
4. In the right pane, double-click the policy to be modified.
5. Select to audit Success, Failure, or both.
6. Click OK to exit the configuration screen, and then close the Local Security Policy tool.

Figure 14.5 shows an example of typical auditing policies that might be configured for an Exchange server.

These audit policies can be turned on manually by following the preceding procedure, configuring a group policy, or by the implementation of security templates.

NOTE

After enabling audit policies, Windows event logs (specifically the security log) will capture a significant amount of data. Be sure to increase the "maximum log size" in the security log properties page. A best practice is to make the log size large enough to contain at least a week's worth of data, and configure it to overwrite as necessary so that newer data is not sacrificed at the expense of older data.

Viewing the Security Logs

The events generated by the Windows Server auditing policies can be viewed in the security log in the Event Viewer.

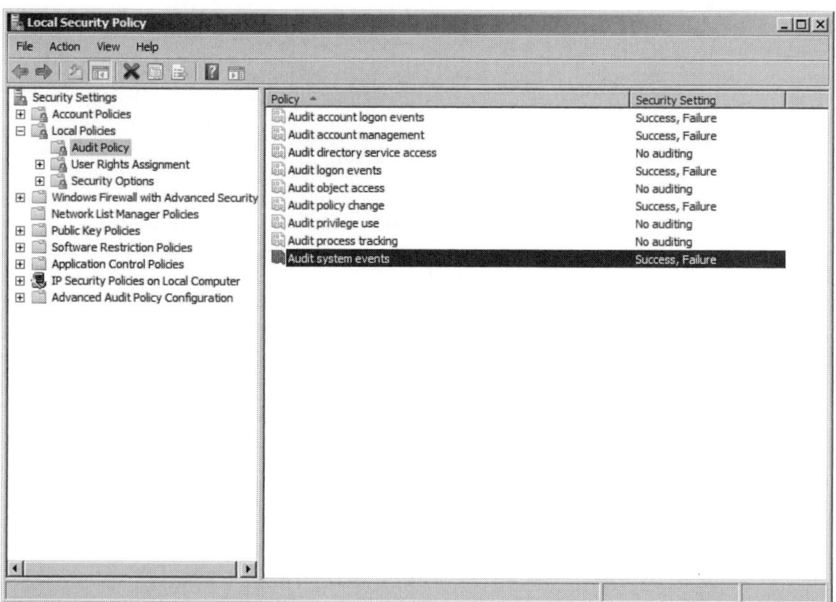

FIGURE 14.5 Windows Server 2008 audit policy setting example.

Understanding the information presented in the security log events can be a challenge. The event often contains error codes, with no explanation on their meaning. Microsoft has taken strides to make this easier by providing a link to the Microsoft Help and Support Center within the event.

When an administrator clicks on the link, the Event Viewer asks for permission to send information about the event to Microsoft. Administrators can select the option to always send information if they want, and can then click Yes to authorize the sending of the data. A connection is made to the Help and Support Center, and information about the Event ID is displayed. This information can be invaluable when trying to decipher the sometimes cryptic events in the security log.

Administrators can use the Filter feature (from the View menu) to filter the events based on various fields. In addition, when searching for a specific event within a specific time frame, administrators can select a specific window of time to filter on.

For an extensive list of security event IDs and their meaning in Windows Server 2008 R2, go to http://www.microsoft.com/en-us/download/details.aspx?id=21561 and for Windows Server 2008, go to http://support.microsoft.com/kb/947226.

The information supplied here on viewing security log Event IDs is intended to help administrators get a basic understanding of the topic. There is much more that can be learned on the subject of security auditing and event monitoring, and the Microsoft website is an excellent resource for doing so.

SMTP Logging

Logging SMTP protocol activity provides administrators with a powerful tool when troubleshooting issues with message delivery. By enabling SMTP logging, administrators can capture the SMTP conversations with email servers during message transport. Each Receive and Send connector in an Exchange Server 2013 environment has the capability of logging SMTP activity, providing information regarding messaging commands that a user sends to the Exchange Server 2013 server. This includes, but is not limited to, such information as IP address, bytes sent, data, time, protocol, and domain name.

To enable SMTP protocol logging, administrators must enable the feature on each Send and Receive connector on each Exchange Server 2013 server where logging is desired. By default, SMTP logging is disabled on all Send and Receive connectors.

Configuring SMTP Logging from the Exchange Administration Center

The configuration of SMTP protocol logging utilizing the Exchange Administration Center is limited to enabling or disabling the feature. To enable or disable SMTP protocol logging from the EAC, perform the following tasks:

1. Log on to the Exchange Administration Center (https://{*servername*}/ecp).
2. Click Mail Flow from the left window pane.
3. Choose either the Send Connectors or Receive Connectors option on which you want to enable logging.
    - **For Hub Transport Send connectors**—When you click Send Connectors and then click one of the Send connectors on screen, the "Logging" control is in the right pane.
    - **For Hub Transport Receive connectors**—When you click Receive Connectors, choose a server, and then click one of the Receive connectors on screen, the "Logging" control is in the right pane.
    - **For Edge Transport connectors**—On the Edge Transport server, select Edge Transport in the console tree. Select the appropriate server in the results pane, and then select the Receive Connectors or Send Connectors tab in the bottom half of the results pane. Select the desired connector from those displayed.
4. After you have selected the appropriate connector, click the Logging On or Off option, and a pop-up similar to what is shown in Figure 14.6 will appear to prompt you whether you want to turn on or turn off logging.

Changing the Protocol Log Path

Exchange Server 2013 allows administrators to specify the location of the Send and Receive log files. The log files for all Send connectors on a particular server are in one location, and the log files for all Receive connectors are in another.

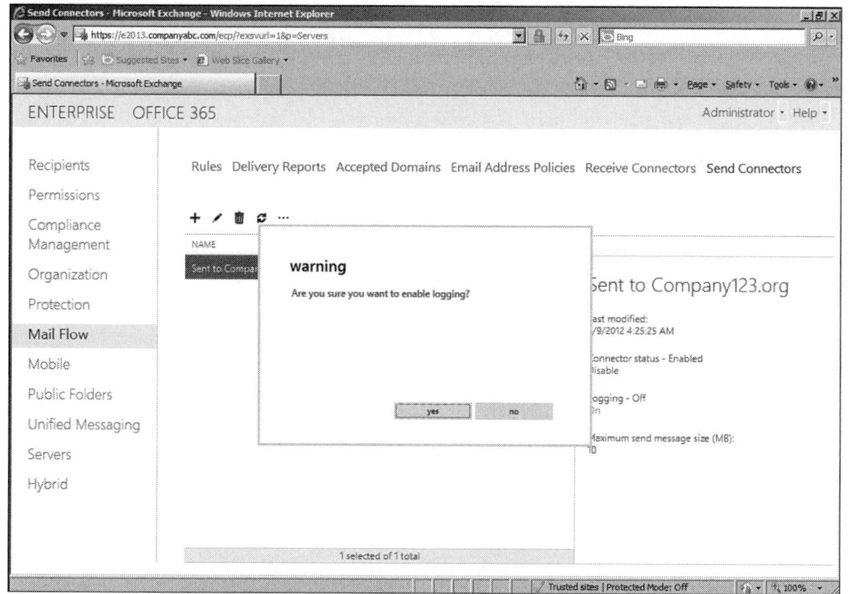

FIGURE 14.6 Changing logging in the Exchange Administration Center.

By default, these files are located in the following locations:

- **Receive log—** `C:\Program Files\Microsoft\Exchange Server\V15\TransportRoles\Logs\{Hub/Mailbox}\ProtocolLog\SmtpReceive`
- **Send log—** `C:\Program Files\Microsoft\Exchange Server\V15\TransportRoles\Logs\{Hub/Mailbox}\ProtocolLog\SmtpSend`

To change the default location for these log files, use the following commands in the Exchange Management Shell:

Change log file location for the Receive connectors:

```
Set-TransportServer <ServerName> -ReceiveProtocolLogPath <LogPath>
```

Change log file location for the Send connectors:

```
Set-TransportServer <ServerName> -SendProtocolLogPath <LogPath>
```

Sample command: To set the Receive SMTP protocol log path for all Receive connectors on Server1 to `C:\SMTP Receive Logs`, use the following command:

```
Set-TransportServer Server1 -ReceiveProtocolLogPath "C:\SMTP Receive Logs"
```

Configuring Log File and Log Directory Maximum Size

To prevent log files from growing so large that they deplete all available disk space, Exchange Server 2013 allows administrators to configure maximum log file and directory sizes. This configuration setting is a per-server setting and, by default, the maximum directory size is 250MB, whereas the maximum log file size is 10MB. When the maximum file size is reached, Exchange Server opens a new log file. When the maximum directory size is reached, Exchange Server overwrites the log files, starting with the oldest logs first.

To configure SMTP protocol log directory and file sizes, use the following commands in the Exchange Management Shell. Be aware, these commands must be performed for each server that you want to modify. The `<DirectorySize>` and `<FileSize>` arguments should be entered as a number followed by one of the following:

- B (bytes)
- KB (kilobytes)
- MB (megabytes)
- GB (gigabytes)
- TB (terabytes)

Change maximum size for Receive SMTP protocol log directory:

```
Set-TransportServer <ServerName> -ReceiveProtocolMaxDirectorySize <DirectorySize>
```

Change maximum size for Send SMTP protocol log directory:

```
Set-TransportServer <ServerName> -SendProtocolMaxDirectorySize <DirectorySize>
```

Change maximum size for Receive SMTP protocol log files:

```
Set-TransportServer <ServerName> -ReceiveProtocolMaxFileSize <FileSize>
```

Change maximum size for Send SMTP protocol log files:

```
Set-TransportServer <ServerName> -SendProtocolMaxFileSize <FileSize>
```

Sample command: To set the maximum size for the Receive SMTP protocol log directory on Server1 to 1GB, use the following command:

```
Set-TransportServer Server1 -ReceiveProtocolMaxDirectorySize 1GB
```

Configuring the Maximum Age for the SMTP Protocol Log

In addition to having the ability to configure the maximum file and directory sizes for SMTP protocol logs, administrators can also configure a maximum age for each SMTP protocol log file. The default age for all log files is set to 30 days, and any log files that exceed this age are deleted by Exchange Server.

To change the maximum age of SMTP protocol log files, use the following commands in the Exchange Management Shell. The `<Age>` argument is entered in the following format: DD.HH:MM:SS, for days, hours, minutes, seconds.

Change maximum age for the Receive SMTP protocol log file:

```
Set-TransportServer <ServerName> -ReceiveProtocolLogMaxAge <Age>
```

Change maximum age for the Send SMTP protocol log file:

```
Set-TransportServer <ServerName> -SendProtocolLogMaxAge <Age>
```

Sample command: To set the maximum age of the Send SMTP protocol log file on Server1 to 60 days, use the following command:

```
Set-TransportServer Server1 -SendProtocolLogMaxAge 60.00:00:00
```

or:

```
Set-TransportServer Server1 -SendProtocolLogMaxAge 60
```


Message Tracking

Of the auditing techniques available in Exchange Server, message tracking is by far the least resource intensive and will likely be the most commonly used by administrators. Because this feature has proven so valuable in previous versions of Exchange Server, Microsoft has enabled it by default in Exchange Server 2013. Previously, message tracking was disabled by default and had to be enabled on a server-by-server basis.

Administrators can use message tracking logs for message forensics, reporting, and troubleshooting, as well as analyzing mail flow in an organization.

Message tracking records the SMTP transport activity of all messages sent to or from any Exchange Server 2013 Hub Transport service, Edge Transport service, or Mailbox server.

To perform these procedures on a computer with the Hub Transport service or Mailbox server role installed, administrators must be logged on using an account that is a member of the Exchange Administrators group. The account must also be a member of the local Administrators group on that computer. For a computer with the Edge Transport server role installed, administrators must be logged on using an account that is a member of the local Administrators group on that computer.

Enabling or Disabling Message Tracking

As previously stated, by default, message tracking is enabled on all Exchange Server 2013 computers that deal with message transport. This includes Hub Transport service, Edge Transport service, and Mailbox servers. Message tracking can prove to be extremely useful, and administrators should avoid disabling the feature unless there are overwhelming reasons.

The message tracking is set via command line. All commands must be run from the Exchange Management Shell. As in other shell commands, the `<Identity>` argument is replaced by the server name. To enable the feature, use the `$true` argument, and to disable it, use `$false`.

To enable or disable message tracking on a Hub Transport service or Edge Transport server:

```
Set-TransportServer <ServerName> -MessageTrackingLogEnabled:[$true or $false]
```

To enable or disable message tracking on a Mailbox server:

```
Set-MailboxServer <ServerName> -MessageTrackingLogEnabled:[$true or $false]
```

Sample command: To disable message tracking on a Mailbox server named Server1, use the following command:

```
Set-MailboxServer Server1 -MessageTrackingLogEnabled:$false
```

Changing the Location of Message Tracking Logs

Exchange Server 2013 allows administrators to specify the location of the message tracking logs. The new location becomes effective immediately upon the completion of the command; however, any existing log files are not copied to the new directory—they will remain in the old directory.

By default, these files are located in the `C:\Program Files\Microsoft\Exchange Server\V15\TransportRoles\Logs\MessageTracking` directory.

When creating a new directory, the following permissions are required:

- **Administrator**—Full Control
- **System**—Full Control
- **Network Service**—Read, Write, and Delete Subfolders and Files

The location can be set on the properties of the Hub Transport service or Edge Transport server in the Exchange Administration Center using the procedure previously described. To change the default location for these log files via command line, use the following commands in the Exchange Management Shell:

Change message tracking log file location for a Hub Transport server or an Edge Transport server:

```
Set-TransportServer <ServerName> -MessageTrackingLogPath <LocalFilePath>
```

Change message tracking log file location for a Mailbox server:

```
Set-MailboxServer <ServerName> -MessageTrackingLogPath <LocalFilePath>
```

Sample command: To change the location of the message tracking log to `D:\Message Tracking` on an Exchange Server 2013 Hub Transport server named Server1, use the following command:

```
Set-TransportServer Server1 -MessageTrackingLogPath "D:\Message Tracking"
```

Configuring Message Tracking Log File and Log Directory Maximum Size

To prevent log files from growing so large that they deplete all available disk space, Exchange Server 2013 allows administrators to configure maximum log file and directory sizes. This configuration setting is a per-server setting and, by default, the maximum directory size is 250MB, whereas the maximum log file size is 10MB. When the maximum file size is reached, Exchange Server opens a new log file. When the maximum directory size is reached, Exchange Server overwrites the log files, starting with the oldest logs first.

To configure message tracking log directory and file sizes, use the following commands in the Exchange Management Shell. This cannot be done with the Exchange Administration Center. Be aware, these commands must be performed for each server you want to modify. The `<DirectorySize>` and `<FileSize>` arguments should be entered as a number followed by one of the following:

- B (bytes)
- KB (kilobytes)
- MB (megabytes)
- GB (gigabytes)
- TB (terabytes)

Change maximum size for message tracking log directory on a Hub Transport service or Edge Transport server:

```
Set-TransportServer <ServerName> -MessageTrackingLogMaxDirectorySize
<DirectorySize>
```

Change maximum size for message tracking log directory on a Mailbox server:

```
Set-MailboxServer <ServerName> -MessageTrackingLogMaxDirectorySize <DirectorySize>
```

Change maximum size for individual message tracking log files on a Hub Transport service or Edge Transport server:

```
Set-TransportServer <ServerName> -MessageTrackingLogMaxFileSize <FileSize>
```

Change maximum size for individual message tracking log files on a Mailbox server:

```
Set-MailboxServer <ServerName> -MessageTrackingLogMaxFileSize <FileSize>
```

Sample command: To set the maximum size for the message tracking log directory on a Hub Transport service server named Server1 to 500MB, use the following command:

```
Set-TransportServer Server1 -MessageTrackingLogMaxDirectorySize 500MB
```

Configuring the Maximum Age for the Message Tracking Logs

In addition to having the ability to configure the maximum file and directory sizes for message tracking logs, administrators can also configure a maximum age for each message tracking log file. The default age is set to 30 days, and any log files that exceed this age are deleted by Exchange Server.

To change the maximum age of message tracking log files, use the following commands in the Exchange Management Shell. This cannot be done with the Exchange Administration Center. The `<Age>` argument is entered in the following format: DD.HH:MM:SS, for days, hours, minutes, seconds.

Change maximum age for the message tracking log files on a Hub Transport service or Edge Transport server:

```
Set-TransportServer <ServerName> -MessageTrackingLogMaxAge <Age>
```

Change maximum age for the message tracking log files on a Mailbox server:

```
Set-MailboxServer <ServerName> -MessageTrackingLogMaxAge <Age>
```

Sample command: To set the maximum age of the message tracking log files on an Exchange Server 2013 Mailbox server named Server1 to 45 days, use the following command:

```
Set-MailboxServer Server1 -MessageTrackingLogMaxAge 45.00:00:00
```

Best Practices for Performing Database Maintenance

The Exchange Server storage system is a database and requires routine maintenance to perform efficiently and prevent failures. Exchange Server 2013 fully automates the routine maintenance tasks of defragmentation and compaction. Exchange Server 2013 has advanced the health of the messaging system through the introduction of the following:

- Continuous online database defragmentation
- Continuous online database compaction
- Continuous online database contiguity maintenance

These features eliminate any necessity for planned downtime to perform database maintenance.

As messaging environments have evolved from “nice to have” to “business critical,” database maintenance has evolved from “should be done” to “must be done.” Potential causes of database corruption include the following:

- Improper shutting down of the system, including unexpected power outages
- A poorly maintained disk subsystem
- Hardware failures
- Failure to use or review systems or operational management tools
- Manual modification of Exchange Server databases

Automatic Database Maintenance

Exchange Server 2013 automatically performs database maintenance procedures on a nightly basis during the scheduled maintenance window. Exchange Server 2013 performs two distinct activities: Online Maintenance (OLM) and Online Defragmentation (OLD). OLM starts by default at 1:00 a.m. every day, whereas OLD is continuous.

NOTE

This is different than in Exchange Server 2007, in which OLD ran during the OLM process, resulting in potentially poor performance during maintenance windows and the requirement to stagger maintenance schedules.

The following tasks are automatically performed by these processes (OLM and OLD):

- **Cleanup of deleted items and mailboxes**—Cleanup also happens during OLM. Cleanup is performed at runtime when hard deletes occur.
- **Space compaction**—The database is compacted and space is reclaimed at runtime. Automatically throttling performance demands avoids performance impact on end users.
- **Maintain contiguity**—The database is analyzed for contiguity and space at runtime and is defragmented in the background. Automatically throttling performance demands avoids performance impact on end users. The contiguity maintenance is integrated to Exchange Server 2013 and improves performance significantly.
- **Database checksum**—There are two options for the database checksum tasks, either run the background 24×7 (the default) or run during the OLM window. In both cases, the task runs against both active and passive copies of the database.

By default, the OLM maintenance schedule is set to run daily from 1:00 a.m. to 5:00 a.m. Because the maintenance cycle can be extremely resource intensive, this default schedule is intended to perform the maintenance during periods when most of an organization's mail users are not connected. Organizations might find the need to adjust these schedules when there are users connecting from other parts of the world or when there are 24-hour operations. Organizations should also take their Exchange Server backup schedules into consideration.

The OLD task runs continuously but is auto-throttled to prevent impact to the end user.

Taken together, the automatic maintenance regime is much more effective at keeping the database healthy and performing. In particular, the contiguity maintenance of Exchange Server 2013 reduces the I/O of the database immensely.

Prioritizing and Scheduling Maintenance Best Practices

Exchange Server 2013 is a very efficient messaging system. However, as mailboxes and public folders are used, there is always the possibility of the logical corruption of data contained within the databases. It is important to implement a maintenance plan and schedule to minimize the impact that database corruption will have on the overall messaging system.

This section focuses on tasks that should be performed regularly—on a daily, weekly, monthly, and quarterly schedule. Besides ensuring optimum health for an organization, following these best practices will have the additional benefit of ensuring that administrators are well informed about the status of their messaging environments.

TIP

Administrators should thoroughly document the Exchange Server 2013 messaging environment configuration and keep it up to date. In addition, a change log should be implemented that is used to document changes and maintenance procedures for the environment. This change log should be meticulously maintained.

Daily Maintenance

Daily maintenance routines require the most frequent attention of an Exchange Server administrator. However, these tasks should not take a significant amount of time to perform.

Verify the Online Backup

One of the key differences between disaster and disaster recovery is the ability for an organization to resort to backups of its environment if the need arises. Considering the potential impact to an environment if the data backed up is not recoverable, it is amazing to see how often backup processes are ignored. Many organizations implement a "set it and forget it" attitude, often relying on nontechnical administrative personnel to simply "swap tapes" on a daily basis.

NOTE

A "backup" in Exchange Server 2013 does not necessarily imply solely a backup to tape media as a backup would have been known by years ago. With Exchange Server 2013, a "backup" may be a replication of the database to another server, so the verification of the backup will be to confirm that the data has successfully replicated and is up to date on the secondary server.

Whatever method is used to back up an Exchange Server environment, daily confirmation of the success of the task should be mandatory. Although the actual verification process will vary based on the backup solution being utilized, the general concept remains the same. Review the backup program's log file to determine whether the backup has successfully completed. If there are errors reported or the backup job set does not complete successfully, identify the cause of the error and take the appropriate action to resolve the problem.

Some best practices to keep in mind when backing up an Exchange Server environment are as follows:

- Keep note of how long the backup process is taking to complete. This time should match any service level agreements that might be in place.
- Determine the start and finish times of the backup process. Attempt to configure the environment so that the backup process completes before the nightly maintenance schedule begins.
- Verify that transaction logs are successfully truncated upon completion of the backup.

Check Free Disk Space

All volumes that Exchange Server 2013 resides on (Exchange Server system files, databases, transaction logs, and so forth) should be checked on a daily basis to ensure that ample free space is available. If the volume or partition runs out of disk space, no more information can be written to the disk, which causes Exchange Server to stop the Exchange Server services. This can also result in lost data and the corruption of messaging databases.

Although it is possible to perform this process manually, it is easily overlooked when "hot" issues arise. As a best practice, administrators can utilize System Center 2012 Operations Manager (OpsMgr) or a third-party product to alert administrators if free space dips below a certain threshold.

For organizations without the resources to implement such products, the process can be accomplished utilizing scripting technologies, with an email or network alert being generated when the free space falls below the designated threshold.

Review Message Queues

Message queues should be checked daily to ensure that the mail flow in the organization is not experiencing difficulties. The Queue Viewer in the Exchange Toolbox can be accomplished for this task.

If messages are found stuck in the queue, administrators can utilize the Message Tracking and Mail Flow Troubleshooter to determine the cause.

Check Event Viewer Logs

On Exchange Server 2013 servers, the application log within the Event Viewer should be reviewed daily for any warning or error level messages. Although some error messages might lead directly to a problem on the server, some might be symptomatic of other issues in the environment. Either way, it is best to evaluate and resolve these errors as soon as possible.

Filtering for these event types can assist with determining if any have occurred within the last 24 hours.

Alternatively, if a systems or operational management solution (such as System Center 2012 Operations Manager) is utilized, this process can be automated, with email or network notifications sent as soon as the error is generated.

Verify Database Replication

Exchange Server 2013 leverages database replication for both redundancy and high availability, as such, verifying that database replication is occurring in the manner that the organization has set and expects replication to be working is critical.

In environments that have multiple DAG copies, administrators should ensure that the copy and replay queues are near zero, or at least not growing.

Weekly Maintenance

Tasks that do not require daily administrative input, but that still require frequent attention, are categorized as weekly maintenance routines. Recommended weekly maintenance routines are described in the following sections.

Document Database File Sizes

In an environment without mailbox storage limitations, the size of the mailbox databases can quickly become overwhelmingly large. If the volume housing the databases is not large enough to accommodate the database growth beyond a certain capacity, services can stop, databases can get corrupted, performance can get sluggish, or the system can halt.

Even with mailbox size limitations implemented, administrators should be aware of and document the size of databases so that they can determine the estimated growth rate.

By documenting the size of all mailbox databases on a weekly basis, administrators can have a more thorough understanding of the system usage and capacity requirements in their environments.

Verify Online Maintenance Tasks

Exchange Server 2013 records information in the application log about scheduled online maintenance processes. Check this event log to verify that all the online maintenance tasks are being performed and that no problems are occurring.

Using the filtering capabilities of the Event Viewer (View, Filter), administrators can apply a filter to search for specific events, and can specify a date (and time) range to search for these events. For example, it is easy to filter the events to view all events with an ID of 1206 that have occurred in the past week.

Alternatively, in the right pane of the Event Viewer, click the Event column to sort events by their ID number; however, this view is more challenging to read because you must then verify the dates of the events as well.

The following Event IDs should be regularly reviewed:

- **Event ID 1206 and 1207**—These IDs give information about the start and stop times for the cleanup of items past the retention date in Item Recovery.
- **Event ID 700 and 701**—These IDs indicate the start and stop times of the online database defragmentation process. Administrators should ensure that the process does not conflict with Exchange Server database backups and make sure that the process completed without interruptions.
- **Event IDs 9531–9535**—These IDs indicate the start and end times of the cleanup of deleted mailboxes that are past the retention date.

Analyze Resource Utilization

To keep any environment healthy, overall system and network performance should be regularly evaluated. An Exchange Server 2013 environment is no exception.

At a minimum, administrators should monitor system resources at least once a week. Primary areas to focus on include the four common contributors to bottlenecks: memory, processor, disk subsystem, and network subsystem.

Ideally, utilizing a monitoring utility such as Microsoft System Center 2012 OpsMgr to gather performance data at regular intervals is recommended because this data can be utilized to discover positive and negative trends in the environment.

Check Offline Address Book Generation

An Offline Address Book (OAB) is used by Outlook to provide offline access to directory information from the Global Address List (GAL) when users are working offline or in Cached Exchange mode. When a user starts Outlook in Cached Exchange mode for the first time, the user's Exchange Server mailbox is synchronized to a local file (an `.ost` file) and the offline address list from the Exchange server is synchronized to a collection of files (`.oab` files) on the user's computer.

An easy way to verify OAB generation and distribution is to look at the age of the OAB files on each Exchange server (in the `C:\Program Files\Microsoft\Exchange Server\V15\Client Access\OAB\`).

NOTE

If you are experiencing problems with OAB generation, enable diagnostic logging and review the application log for any OAB generator category events.

Monthly Maintenance

Recommended monthly maintenance practices for Exchange Server 2013 do not require the frequency of daily or weekly tasks, but they are, nonetheless, important to maintaining the overall health of the environment. Some general monthly maintenance tasks can be quickly summarized; others are explained in more detail in the following sections.

General tasks include the following:

- Install approved and tested service packs and updates.
- Schedule and perform, as necessary, any major server configuration changes, including hardware upgrades.

NOTE

With Exchange Server 2013, a periodic reboot or performing system patches and updates does not mean Exchange will experience a mail system outage. With the proper setup of high availability in Exchange Server 2013 (such as database availability groups for replicated databases, or redundant Client Access server roles), an organization can failover services to other servers, perform maintenance, and bring the updated system back online without service downtime.

Run the Exchange Best Practices Analyzer

Administrators should run the Exchange Best Practices Analyzer (ExBPA) health, permissions, and connectivity checks in their environments after making any significant changes to systems or settings to determine if there are any configurations or settings that are not in line with Microsoft recommended best practices. This utility and its configuration files are updated often with new and improved settings, and available updates are installed every time the utility is run.

The results of these scans can be saved and compared from month to month to determine when particular issues might have occurred.

Test System Performance with Performance Monitor

Periodically run Performance Monitor over a normal workday to monitor CPU, disk performance, and key Exchange counters to determine whether the server and storage are performing to standards. Compare the periodic results over time to detect any trends.

Test Uninterruptible Power Supply

Uninterruptible power supply (UPS) equipment is commonly used to protect the server from sudden loss of power. Most UPS solutions include supporting management software to ensure that the server is gracefully shut down in the event of power failure, thus preserving the integrity of the system. Each manufacturer has a specific recommendation for testing, and the recommended procedures should be followed carefully. However, it should occur no less than once per month, and it is advantageous to schedule the test for the same time as any required server reboots.

Quarterly Maintenance

Although quarterly maintenance tasks are infrequent, some might require downtime and are more likely to cause serious problems with Exchange Server 2013 if not properly planned or implemented. Administrators should proceed cautiously with these tasks.

General quarterly maintenance tasks include the following:

- Check mailbox and shared folder stores to verify database size, system performance, and overall operability of the servers in the environment.
- Evaluate the current rate of growth on server hard drives to ensure there is adequate space available on all volumes. This evaluation is based on the information gathered during the weekly maintenance tasks.

Validate Information Store Backups

As previously mentioned, the backing up of an environment's data is one of the most important steps an organization can take to ensure recoverability in the event of a disaster.

However, simply backing up the data, and assuming the ability to recover it is inadequate.

Backups should be regularly restored in a test environment or to a recovery database to ensure the recoverability of systems. By performing regular restores in a test environment, administrators are providing several services:

- Confirmation that the data is truly being backed up successfully
- Verification of the actual restore procedures
- Training for Exchange Server administrators, or practice for existing ones, in the steps needed to recover an Exchange Server environment

Organizations that do not implement regular testing of restore procedures often find that, in the time of actual need, restorations take significantly longer than necessary because of missing hardware, missing software, inadequate or inaccurate procedures, administrators unfamiliar with the process, or, worst of all, backup sources that had been reported good but are unable to be restored.

TIP

Backup and recovery procedures are one of the most critical documents in an Exchange Server organization. These procedures should be thoroughly tested and updated whenever changes to the process occur. And remember, it is not enough to store copies of this documentation electronically on network shares or (worse) within the messaging system. If these procedures can't be quickly accessed when they are most needed, they are practically useless.

Periodic Testing

For sites with offsite disaster recovery infrastructure, it is an excellent practice to periodically conduct a full test of the Exchange disaster recovery procedure to ensure that you can quickly recover Exchange service at the disaster recovery site. Testing of both planned site switchover and unplanned site failover procedures is optimal.

Postmaintenance Procedures

Postmaintenance procedures are designed to quickly and efficiently restore Exchange Server operations to the environment following any offline maintenance. Devising a checklist for these procedures ensures that the systems are brought back online quickly and efficiently, without time wasted because of minor errors. The following is a sample checklist for maintenance procedures:

1. Start all the remaining Exchange Server services.
2. Test email connectivity from Outlook, Outlook Web App, Outlook Anywhere, and ActiveSync.
3. Perform a full backup of the Exchange Server 2013 server(s).
4. Closely review backup and server event logs over the next few days to ensure that no errors are reported on the server.

Reducing Management and Maintenance Efforts

As you have seen throughout the chapter, numerous utilities are available with Exchange Server 2013 for managing, maintaining, and monitoring the messaging system. These utilities can often help administrators avoid problems, and can save time and energy addressing those that arise.

In any messaging environment, administrators should always attempt to develop processes and procedures that can reduce maintenance efforts while maximizing effectiveness and efficiency. Many management and maintenance procedures can be streamlined, or even automated, ensuring a maximum return for minimum time spent, resulting in a significant monetary savings for the organization. Equally important, proper upkeep of the Exchange Server environment ensures administrators are one step ahead of preventable issues, allowing more time for proactively managing the environment, and less time reacting to problems.

Using Microsoft System Center 2012 Operations Manager

Microsoft System Center 2012 Operations Manager is one tool that can be used to streamline and automate many of an administrator's messaging responsibilities. More specifically, the System Center management pack for Exchange Server provides the key features required to manage, maintain, and monitor the Exchange Server 2013 environment.

More details on System Center 2012 OpsMgr can be found in Chapter 17, "Using Microsoft System Center Operations Manager to Monitor Exchange Server 2013."

Key features to consider evaluating include, but are not limited to, the following:

- ▶ Provides monitors, rules, and scripts to track Exchange Server performance, availability, and reliability of all Exchange Server–related components, including Internet-related services, Extensible Storage Engine, System Attendant, Microsoft Exchange Information Store service, and SMTP
- ▶ Sends test synthetic emails to verify operations and measures actual delivery times
- ▶ Gathers Exchange Server data and provides technical reports on Exchange Server service delivery, traffic, storage capacity, and usage
- ▶ Alerts administrators when various thresholds are met, such as resource utilization statistics or capacity
- ▶ Provides performance baselining and continuous monitoring of system resources and protocols
- ▶ Provides trend analysis of usage and performance
- ▶ Contains a full knowledge base of Exchange Server–specific solutions tied directly to over 1,700 events
- ▶ Provides reporting on usage, problems, security-related events, and much more

Summary

Most organizations consider their email systems to be one of the most mission-critical applications in their environments. Message delays, nondeliveries, and unscheduled downtime are usually considered unacceptable, and administrators who cannot maintain their environments well enough to meet service level agreements and management expectations are often quickly out of a job.

For a messaging environment to perform well, remain reliable, and continue to provide full functionality, it must be properly managed and maintained. Exchange Server 2013 provides tools and utilities to assist in this endeavor, but they must be used properly and regularly to be effective.

Exchange Server 2013 brings some impressive advancements to the task of maintaining the Exchange Server environment, including the continuous online database maintenance features and the remote management tools. These advancements help the organization maintain a healthy environment.

With proper care and feeding, Exchange Server 2013 can meet and exceed the messaging needs for just about any organization.

Best Practices

The following are best practices from this chapter:

- Utilize the Exchange Best Practices Analyzer after making significant changes to the Exchange environment to evaluate and compare it with Microsoft recommended best practices.
- Audit the messaging environment using Windows auditing.
- Use Exchange Server 2013 protocol logging and diagnostic utilities for troubleshooting purposes.
- Install the Exchange Management Shell on an administrative workstation or server to remotely administer Exchange Server 2013.
- Never manually modify Exchange Server 2013 databases or transaction log files.
- Thoroughly document the Exchange Server 2013 messaging environment and configuration. Create and maintain change logs to document changes and maintenance procedures.
- Document the process of restoring Exchange Server 2013 databases thoroughly and completely. If documentation already exists, verify that the existing process has not changed. If it has changed, update the documentation.
- Store printed copies of the Exchange Server 2013 restoration process in an easy-to-access location.
- Create postmaintenance procedures to minimize time needed for restoration.
- Implement System Center 2012 Operations Manager with the available Exchange Server management packs to minimize administrative overhead for daily routines.

CHAPTER 15

Optimizing an Exchange Server 2013 Environment

IN THIS CHAPTER

As the latest version of Microsoft Exchange Server, Exchange Server 2013 offers several enhancements over previous versions of Exchange Server. These enhancements improve the messaging environment's reliability, availability, and scalability as well as give additional flexibility in how these improvements are utilized. To be able to make use of these features, however, you must carefully plan the deployment and implementation of Exchange Server 2013 with a strong understanding of your environment's needs. Any good implementation of Exchange Server 2013 includes an optimization phase. This involves baselining the performance of the "out-of-the-box" build and applying best practices and tweaks to improve the performance of the environment. Through careful analysis of capacity and testing with the available tools, a clever administrator can wring additional performance out of an Exchange Server 2013 environment.

Capacity analysis, stress testing, and performance optimization processes and procedures are, most often, low-priority tasks for most information technology (IT) organizations. This is frequently because productivity is regularly measured by what can be achieved now and not always what can be properly planned or designed. The benefits of capacity analysis and performance monitoring can be obtained in the short term, but they are more important when established over longer periods of time. As a result, the main focus of most IT Departments shifts to the more immediate and more tangible day-to-day processes and IT needs. Companies that focus on the performance optimization of their Exchange Server 2013 environments will find that it requires upgrades less often and it offers a better experience to the user community.

The results of capacity analysis and performance optimization save organizations of all sizes time, effort, and expenditures. This chapter is designed to provide best practices for properly and proactively performing capacity analysis and performance optimization so that IT personnel and end users can work more effectively and efficiently.

Examining Exchange Server 2013 Performance Improvements

Before delving into ways to tweak Exchange Server 2013 performance, it is useful to have an understanding of the performance improvements that have been made since its predecessors, Exchange Server 2007 and Exchange Server 2010. Although some of these performance improvements are more noticeable than others, Exchange Server 2013 has been designed to scale into the enterprise and beyond through architectural changes and through improvements to existing features.

Architectural Improvements

Exchange Server 2013 has undergone massive architectural changes to accommodate the new methodologies for providing better resiliency and better utilization of resources. The familiar roles of Client Access server (CAS), Mailbox server, Hub Transport server (HT), Edge Transport server, and Unified Messaging server (UM) have changed since Exchange Server 2010 in the way they are deployed and the functions they provide.

The Exchange Server 2013 architecture is in many ways simpler than the architecture in Exchange Server 2010. The typical approach now is that of a front-end array of CAS systems and a back-end cluster of Mailbox servers, with Edge Transport servers in the demilitarized zone (DMZ) to provide message hygiene. Conspicuous by its absence is the Hub Transport server, which doesn't really exist anymore.

In Exchange Server 2010, typically a hardware load balancer provided Layer 7 load-balancing services for CAS/HT/UM. The CAS/HT/UM servers provided authentication, proxy/redirect services, protocols, application programming interfaces (APIs), and business logic. Finally the Mailbox servers provided the mailbox assistants, the Information Store, and the content indexing. In Exchange Server 2013, the hardware load balancers provide Layer 4 load balancing, as there is no longer a need for session affinity. The CAS role provided authentication and proxy/redirect services. Protocols, mailbox assistants, APIs, business logic, Information Store, and content indexing are all provided by the Mailbox server role now.

By moving these functions to the typically much more powerful Mailbox servers, Exchange Server 2013 is able to better utilize the available resources.

Database Engine Improvements

Microsoft has continued to improve the JET database for Exchange. JET is the database used by Exchange Server 2013, as well as in previous versions of Exchange Server, to store mailbox data and public folder data. In the latest 64-bit version of JET offered by Exchange Server 2013, the JET engine is able to take advantage of the lift in restrictions on memory space and it allows JET to allocate significantly more cache for the Exchange Server store. This means that users have access to more cache and this greatly increases the likelihood that data requested by a user is already in memory and doesn't have to be read from disk. This results in quicker response times for the end users. The `store.exe` has been rewritten in managed code such that now each database runs under its own process. The redesign of JET has allowed additional reductions in I/O requirements for Exchange Server 2013. This is important because disks keep getting bigger but their I/O per second remains pretty much unchanged.

Exchange Server 2013 continues to offer what's called the personal archive. This functionality creates a folder within the mailbox that is actually located in a secondary mailbox. The functionality works very similarly to the concept of opening two mailboxes simultaneously, which is a fairly common situation for executive administrators or for IT members who monitor a common mailbox. By creating this secondary mailbox, Exchange Server 2013 is able to reduce the load on the more commonly accessed mailbox by allowing a user to off-load the bulk of his or her messages into an archive. The user is still able to access all the messages, but the loads are effectively separated from each other. Enabling this personal archive also prevents the user from creating personal folders or PST files, which can be a very useful control for IT Departments that need to control where potentially sensitive email information is stored. The primary mailbox is typically run in Cached mode, to result in a relatively small and manageable Offline Storage (OST) file on the client system. The archive mailbox, which can be located in the same database, a different database, or even a different server, is accessed in Online mode. This native archiving moves the work to the Exchange server for accessing or indexing archived content, but given the relatively infrequent access of this data, doesn't usually result in a significant impact on the servers.

Another change on the database side of things is in the way that public folders are stored. In all previous versions of Exchange, public folders were handled differently in terms of their replication. In Exchange Server 2013, the classic "public folder replication" goes away. Public folders are now stored in mailboxes and are replicated via the database availability group (DAG) functionality. In many ways, this is a godsend as public folders are no longer replicated as email messages and thus don't clog up the mail flow queues when large amounts of public folder data need to replicate. The potential drawback to this new public folder architecture is that public folders are no longer multimaster. At any given time, only one copy of a public folder is in a read/write state. This means that Exchange administrators need to pay careful attention to where various public folders live to provide for the best availability.

For example, in Exchange Server 2010, you might have a public folder called "Sales" with a replica in San Francisco (SF) and a replica in New York (NY). Exchange users needing to read or write to the "Sales" folder would attach to the closest replica based on Active Directory (AD) sites. In Exchange Server 2013, either the SF copy is active and the NY copy is a replica or vice versa. All users accessing the "Sales" folder will access the active copy, regardless of whether it's the closest replica, as it's the only active replica. It should come as no surprise that the "fix" for this behavior is to replace public folder functionality with SharePoint.

The other big database-level improvement is the switch from Exchange's search service to the FAST Search service, originally introduced in SharePoint.

Transport Pipeline Improvements

The transport pipeline refers to the collection of server roles as well as various queues, components, and connections within Exchange Server that work together to transport messages to the message categorizer in the Hub Transport server. The job of this categorizer is to deliver mail to the appropriate location within the Exchange Server environment. This process had been greatly improved in Exchange Server 2010 and was able to handle significantly more messages than earlier versions of Exchange Server and it provided the first iteration of Shadow Redundancy, to prevent the loss of messages when a server died with messages in flight.

Exchange Server 2013 eliminates the Hub Transport as a dedicated role and instead moves the transport functions to the Mailbox server. In Exchange Server 2013, the transport in the back end is broken into two components:

- **Hub Transport**—This transport is stateful and handles Simple Mail Transfer Protocol (SMTP) mail flow for the organization and performs content inspection.
- **Mailbox Transport**—This component combines mail submissions from the store and mail delivery from the Hub Transport service and is stateless.

Routing in Exchange Server 2013 recognizes both DAG boundaries and AD site boundaries. When delivering to Mailbox Transport, Exchange Server 2013 will queue messages per database and query the Active Manager to determine which Mailbox Transport to connect to, based on the active database location. When delivering to another Exchange Server 2013 Mailbox server, Mailbox Transport will queue per DAG and prefer closer Exchange Server 2013 Mailbox servers in the target DAG.

Exchange Server 2013 continues to support Transport Rules—these are now found in the Exchange Administration Center (EAC) in the Mail Flow section under Rules. Exchange Server 2013 continues to support Dynamic Signatures, which support hyperlinks and images as well as accessing fields in AD to populate the disclaimers. This is exceptionally useful for Exchange Server 2013 organizations that span multiple countries. For example, the European Union requires that email messages sent outside an organization must contain the physical address of the sending company's offices. In Exchange Server 2007, this required the creation of multiple disclaimers and required administrators to manage them such that they were attached to the members of the correct offices. In Exchange Server 2010 or 2013, a single disclaimer can be utilized that queries Active Directory to find the appropriate office address to use in the disclaimer.

For example:

```
<html>
<body>
<br><br>
Sent By: <b> %%Firstname%% %%Lastname%% </b><br>
%%Company%% <br>
%%department%% <br>
Telephone: %%Phone%% <br>
%%Street%% <br>
%%City%%, %%State%% <br><br><br>

If you received this message in error, please contact postmaster@companyabc.com and
delete the original message.
</body>
</html>
```

15

Exchange Server 2013 maintains moderated transport, which allows mail flow rules to enforce a workflow for various messages. This allows Exchange Server 2013 to provide process routing so that one or more parties would have to approve messages before they got to their final destination. This can be a very effective way to control the usage of managed distribution groups.

Shadow Redundancy, a feature introduced in Exchange Server 2010, serves to ensure that messages are effectively routed within an organization. When a message is sent, it isn't considered truly sent until there is a confirmation from the next hop that the message was passed along. This function has changed slightly to account for the changes to the mail transport architecture in Exchange Server 2013. For example, if a message leaves a Mailbox server and reaches its next hop, the Mailbox server doesn't consider the message sent until that next hop tells it that it was successfully sent to the hop after that. If, for example, the Mailbox server were to crash before it was able to pass the message along, the Mailbox server that activated the mailbox database copy would see that the original sending server never got a confirmation that the message left the mail transport and it would resend the message via its Mailbox Transport, and would wait for the next hop confirmation. This prevents messages "in flight" from being lost due to a hardware or storage failure.

Security Improvements

Exchange Server 2013 has expanded upon the Rights Management Services (RMS) integration that Exchange Server 2010 offered with Transport Rules through the introduction of native data loss protection (DLP). DLP in the context of Exchange Server 2013 is the ability to identify, monitor, and protect sensitive data via content analysis.

Exchange Server 2013 DLP provides out-of-the-box policy templates to help IT groups comply with regulations to prevent or at least detect sensitive data leaving the Exchange organization.

Exchange Server 2013 also supports granular control in the area of delegating permissions within the Exchange organization. The use of role-based administration will optimize the availability of Exchange by ensuring that only the appropriate members of IT have the ability to perform potentially impacting actions.

Accessibility Improvements

Not much has changed in the way of accessibility in Exchange Server 2013. Outlook Web App (OWA) continues to support multiple browsers as well as the usual "vision impaired" options to make the user interface more apparent. OWA still offers the Conversation view, which groups messages together as part of a logical conversation thread to prevent the need to scroll down and hunt for messages that are part of the same conversation.

Exchange Server 2013 EAC offers some accessibility improvements for navigating the user interface for administrators who might have issues operating a mouse, including the following:

- **Move between areas or between controls in the EAC**—Tab and Shift+Tab.
- **Move between items in drop-down menus in the EAC**—Up and Down arrow keys.
- **Move within lists from one item to another**—Up, Down, Home, End, Page Up, Page Down arrow keys.
- **Move within primary property pages from one item to another**—Up, Down, Home, End, Page Up, Page Down, Tab, Shift+Tab arrow keys. Use Enter or the Spacebar to activate your selection.
- **Move within secondary property pages from one item to another**—Up, Down, Home, End, Page Up, Page Down, Tab, Shift+Tab arrow keys. Use Enter or the Spacebar to activate your selection.

Monitoring Improvements

Exchange Server 2013 has improved on its ability to monitor itself through additional PowerShell scripts, which perform synthetic transactions within Exchange. By testing "end-to-end" communications rather than simply looking for process and port availability, Exchange Server 2013 is better able to determine if the application is operating correctly. The biggest difference in this area versus Exchange Server 2010 is that Exchange Server 2013 is much better about using these monitors to perform corrective actions. Exchange Server 2013 provides four key components to accomplish this:

- **Probes**—Synthetic transactions that perform tasks and look at performance counters and events
- **Monitors**—A process that initiates an action if certain criteria are met

- **Responders**—A process by which recovery or repair is performed (e.g., restarting a service, cycling an application pool, performing a failover)
- **Notifications**—A means by which the system or administrator can override a probe and trigger an immediate response

Much of this functionality was developed in Exchange Server 2010 in multitenant hosted services but was never released to on-premises Exchange Server 2010 customers.

Analyzing Capacity and Performance

Capacity and performance analysis for an Exchange Server 2013 environment requires a well-established understanding of the business and messaging needs of the organization and a well-documented outline of the organization's expectations of its messaging environment. The capacity of an Exchange Server environment is directly dependent on the expected level of performance. It is important to understand exactly what it is you are expecting from the system in terms of storage per user, level of responsiveness of the server, and room for anticipated expansion. When armed with these concepts, you can more accurately determine what your current capacity is.

The first step in capacity analysis is to grasp an understanding of these concepts and define performance expectations. This can be done by establishing policies and service level agreements (SLAs). It is in these policies and SLAs that an administrator can outline acceptable performance thresholds and more accurately gauge the capacity needs of Exchange Server 2013. These thresholds can also be used to accurately establish performance baselines from which to analyze the requirements against available resources.

To help develop the policies and SLAs, use questionnaires, interviews, business objectives, and the like along with performance measurements via the Performance Monitor, Exchange Best Practices Analyzer, or third-party analysis tools. This allows you to combine realistic expectations with concrete data to see where you are compared with where you want to be.

Establishing Baselines

The importance of establishing meaningful baselines of the messaging environment cannot be underscored enough. Baselines are particularly important in the sense that they are the measurable tools that can be used to balance what is required of Exchange Server 2013 with what resources are needed to fulfill those requirements. Achieving this balance can be made simpler if an administrator consults performance metrics, such as industry-standard benchmarks. By starting with an accurate baseline of system performance, you can quickly and easily test changes in the environment to see if they have made things better or worse. Accurate baselines are also very helpful when troubleshooting problems and you can quickly determine which subsystems are not performing the way they normally do. A clear baseline allows you to determine whether a server that "seems slow" really is slower than the way it usually runs.

NOTE

Use ExchDump to assist with baselining the environment. ExchDump exports a server's configuration, which can be useful to determine whether the build follows company standards. This is particularly important with Exchange Server clusters because each node in the cluster should be a replica of the other. Although not included with Exchange Server 2013, the downloadable version for Exchange Server 2010 works.

To establish an accurate baseline of Exchange Server 2013, a number of tools can help an administrator in this process. These tools are discussed in detail in the following sections. Some of these capacity analysis tools are built in to Windows Server 2008, and others are built in to Exchange Server 2013. Many third-party tools and utilities are also available for the careful measurement of Exchange Server 2013 capacity requirements and performance analysis.

Using the Exchange Best Practices Analyzer Tool

The Exchange Best Practices Analyzer (ExBPA) is a utility provided by Microsoft that analyzes an Exchange server's configuration and informs administrators on possible configuration changes that can be made to improve performance or mitigate problems. More specifically, ExBPA can be used to perform a health check, a health and performance check, a connectivity test, and a baseline test. This tool, which was a download in previous versions of Exchange Server, is now a built-in tool. To access the Best Practices Analyzer, perform the following steps:

1. Click Start, All Programs, Microsoft Exchange Server 2013, Exchange Toolbox.
2. If the left pane, select Toolbox.
3. In the center pane, double-click Best Practices Analyzer.
4. When the Best Practices Analyzer tool launches, check the Check for Updates on Startup check box, and click Check for Updates Now. Joining the Microsoft Customer Experience Improvement Program is optional.
5. If there are updates available, click Download the Latest Updates. This ensures you have the latest version of the tool and any of the latest updates to its configuration rules.
6. After being updated, the tool closes, and you have to click it again.
7. Choose Go to Welcome Screen.
8. Click Select Options for a New Scan.
9. Type the name of your closest global catalog, and click Connect to the Active Directory Server.
10. Enter a label for this scan, choose the systems you want to scan, choose Health Check, and click Start Scanning.
11. When the tool has finished, click View a Report of This Best Practices Scan.

When viewing the report, an administrator is able to see any critical issues, certain nondefault settings, or recent changes to the system. This quickly identifies configuration settings that might be detrimental to the overall performance of the system. Be sure to always update the Best Practices Analyzer before running it because Microsoft is constantly adding new information to this tool.

The Informational Items tab offers a convenient and consolidated view of information that is typically captured in Exchange Server documentation. Take advantage of this view when tracking the configuration of your Exchange Server 2013 servers.

The Best Practices Analyzer also allows administrators to run a multihour performance baseline that serves as an excellent way to track overall changes in the performance of servers. By looking at several hour blocks of time and running the tool at the same time on the same day of the week, administrators can get a very accurate view of how the loads on their servers are affecting performance.

Planning for Growth

One of the easiest ways to maintain the performance of an Exchange Server 2013 server is to plan ahead for the growth of the environment. Too many architects have a tendency to build an Exchange Server infrastructure that meets the storage and performance requirements of today but that fails to account for the growth of the company.

Typically, when designing an Exchange Server 2013 infrastructure, you should try to look ahead roughly three years to predict the size to which the company will grow. This is a good time to talk to groups such as Human Resources and Finance to see the rate at which the company has grown historically. This will give you a good idea of how many employees would be utilizing the Exchange Server environment in three years. This process should also uncover specific expansion plans for the company. For example, if the company were going to grow from 10,000 employees to 13,000 employees in three years, you would naturally consider that a 30% growth and would allow for an extra 30% capacity on servers. However, if the case were that 2,000 of those employees would be in a new facility in Australia that was going to be online in two years, it would really be a 10% growth across the enterprise and potentially a very large increase in capacity needs in the Asia/Pac region or perhaps an entirely new Exchange Server site in Australia.

Understanding these types of growth allows you to more easily plan for capacity growth and understand how the increase in user load will affect the performance of your Exchange Server 2013 servers in various sites.

The other thing to consider when planning for growth is the increases in usage of the Exchange Server environment. It is common to see companies increase the storage limits for users without changing the number of users on a server. When cloud-based email systems offer 25-GB mailbox quotas, perhaps it's time to start considering whether large quotas are feasible on the on-premises servers. There are also third-party technologies that might be in your three-year plan that will leverage Exchange Server 2013 as a storage or transport. Voice mail system, Structured Query Language (SQL), or Oracle implementations could quickly increase the loads placed on your Exchange Server 2013 servers.

The reason it is important to predict, as best you can, this anticipated growth is because it is often easier to account for these needs at the time of the Exchange Server 2013 design. Most companies are using storage area networks (SANs) or network attached storage (NAS) for the mailbox stores in Exchange Server. Although these systems do have the ability to resize their logical unit numbers (LUNs) to offer additional storage, this is a very time-consuming process, it directly impacts the users on the server, and NAS and especially SAN storage are usually significantly more expensive. Similarly, because these are usually shared storage devices, there is likely not enough spare capacity on the shelf or device to allocate more space to the Exchange servers. This results in the SAN or NAS administrator having to allocate additional space in a nonoptimal way, which can affect the performance of all the applications that attach to the NAS or SAN. That said, Exchange Server 2013 utilizing direct attached storage can generally be expanded easily by simply adding more disks, assuming the subsystem has room to allow for more disks. Based on this ability, administrators should consider avoiding deploying all 100 databases on a server from day one.

Optimizing Exchange Server 2013 Servers

Optimizing a Mailbox server is different from optimizing a Client Access server. The following sections address each of the roles in Exchange Server 2013 and how to optimize the performance of those roles.

Optimizing Mailbox Servers

Of all the servers in an Exchange Server 2013 environment, the Mailbox server role is the one that will likely benefit the most from careful performance tuning because more of the logic and heavy lifting has been moved to this role.

Mailbox servers' performance has traditionally been very dependent on the performance of the disk subsystem. Although the impact of this has decreased in Exchange Server 2013, it is important to understand that this change in disk behavior is very dependent on memory and can be skewed quite noticeably by the number of replicas of each database. As such, the general rule for performance on an Exchange Server 2013 Mailbox server is to configure it with as much memory as you can. For example, in Exchange Server 2003, if you had a load of 2,000 users that generated an average of 1 disk I/O per second and you were running a RAID 0+1 configuration, you would need 4GB of memory (the maximum) and 40 10k RPM disks each supporting 100 I/O per second to get the performance you'd expect out of an Exchange server. In Exchange Server 2013, the I/O load per user would be closer to 0.10 disk IOPS and you could reduce the number of disks required by roughly 90% if you increased the system memory to 12GB of memory. As you might imagine, that extra 8GB of RAM is a lot less expensive than 36 disks.

As you can see, with a Mailbox server, the trick is to balance costs against performance. In large implementations, it is less expensive to replace high-performance disks with memory. This makes direct attached disks a viable choice for Exchange Server 2013 Mailbox servers. In modern servers, configurations of 32GB are considered fairly baseline and systems with as much as 384GB of RAM are fairly common when supporting thousands of mailboxes. It should be pointed out, though, to be careful when virtualizing Exchange Server 2013 Mailbox servers to not use dynamic memory configurations. Exchange Server 2013 is very dependent on system memory to cache the databases, and a sudden drop in system memory due to load on another virtual machine (VM) will impact performance.

Another area where a Mailbox server benefits in terms of performance is the disk subsystem. Although you've just seen that the disk requirements are lower than previous versions of Exchange Server, this doesn't mean that the disk subsystem is unimportant. This is another area where you must create a careful balance between cost, performance, and recoverability. The databases benefit the most from large disks as generally with the demands of modern email users, the environment is likely more bound by space than by I/O performance. Exchange Server 2010 implemented several changes that specifically improve performance when utilizing SATA disks that are carried over into Exchange Server 2013. By altering the I/O pattern within Exchange Server, the disk writes are better spread out and are less "bursty" than in older versions. This makes SATA a very viable choice for Exchange Server 2013 as they provide large capacities with more than acceptable performance.

Another interesting performance benefit available in Exchange Server 2013 that was introduced in Exchange Server 2010 is the potential to eliminate Redundant Array of Inexpensive Disks (RAID) entirely on the Exchange Server 2013 server. When using database availability groups with three or more replicas of mailbox databases in the production data center, there is enough redundancy in the system as a whole to consider eliminating redundancy at the individual server level. If the 30-second "blip" in services is acceptable within your service level agreements, you could potentially remove all redundant disks, power supplies, and network interface cards (NICs) from their Exchange Server 2013 Mailbox servers. This would greatly reduce the number of disks that the server needs to be able to support, often resulting in the ability to deploy less-expensive servers and, thus, to deploy more of them. So while you aren't likely to save money in hardware, as there is a need to deploy additional disks, you can likely create a significantly more resilient environment for approximately the same cost. The easiest way to look at this idea of redundancy at the application level rather than redundancy at the server level is to think about Active Directory. In AD, if a domain controller (DC) fails, it's generally not a big deal so long as there are other DCs to take over the load. Rather than fixing a DC, you simply build a new one and let it replicate the directory. The same philosophy can apply to Exchange Server 2013 where if a DAG member fails, rather than restore it, you simply build a new one and let it replicate the data. Another DAG member would have already taken over for the failed node and services would not be significantly interrupted. For more details on creating and using DAGs, see Chapter 8, "Implementing and Supporting a Highly Availability Exchange Server 2013 Environment."

In a perfect world, the databases and logs are all on their own dedicated disks. Although this isn't always possible, it does offer the best performance. In the real world, you might have to occasionally double up databases or log files onto the same disk. Be aware of how this affects recoverability. When there is just one copy of a database, the best practice is to separate databases and log files onto separate physical drives to ensure that if either the database or log volume were to be lost, all data up to the failure can be recovered from the last backup. That said, in a DAG configuration with three or more replicas, placing both the database and the logs on the same physical disk is fairly common because, unlike in Exchange Server 2003 or Exchange Server 2007, the performance hit is insignificant.

Mailbox servers also generate a large amount of network traffic. Email messages are often fairly small and as a result, the transmission of these messages isn't always as efficient as it could be. Whenever possible, equip your Mailbox servers with Gigabit Ethernet interfaces. Consider running your network interfaces in a teamed mode to improve both performance and reliability. Microsoft has a strong commitment to NIC teaming and has even moved this function into the operating system in Windows Server 2012.

As Mailbox servers also hold the public folder stores, consider running a dedicated public folder Mailbox server if your environment heavily leverages public folders. Public folder servers often store very large files frequently accessed by users, so separating the load of those large files from the Mailbox servers can result in better overall performance for the user community.

For companies that only lightly use public folders, it requires some investigation of the environment to see if it is better to run a centralized public folder server or if it is better to maintain replicas of public folders in multiple locations. This is usually a question of wide area network (WAN) bandwidth versus usage patterns.

NOTE

Now that the public folder replication model has changed, it is more challenging to design a decentralized public folder infrastructure. Chapter 9, "Public Folders," describes the changes in more detail.

One optimization that cannot be stressed enough is the use of Cached mode on Outlook clients. Outlook can run in one of two modes, Online or Cached. In Online mode, Outlook basically opens each message as a unique event and when a message is closed, it's not cached in any way. If a user goes back and forth between the same messages, each event is unique and the contents are resent to Outlook. That said, those messages would have been cached in memory on the Exchange server, so the disk hit is lessened, but the network effort is the same for each message. In Cached mode, when Outlook is opened, all changes to the mailbox are downloaded locally and stored in an OST file. This means that anything that Outlook does is done against the local copy of the mailbox and changes are uploaded back to the Exchange server. As a result, disk-intensive tasks like indexing and searching are performed locally on the client, removing the load from Exchange. Similarly, large messages and attachments are downloaded locally before being presented to the user as available, so the user has the experience of attachments opening immediately, rather than having to be downloaded after trying to open them, the way Online mode would.

Now, when Microsoft gives guidance on server sizing, those numbers assume that users' primary mailboxes will be in Cached mode, as it greatly decreases the load on Exchange itself. Although archive mailboxes in Exchange Server 2013 or Exchange Server 2010 are always in Online mode, the fact that they are accessed much less often offsets much of the performance hit.

Optimizing Database Availability Groups

In a DAG configuration, mailbox data is replicated across multiple hosts. As such, it becomes less important to build in system-level redundancy when databases have many copies. Rather than have to struggle with the price versus performance trade-offs of RAID 5 versus RAID 0+1, administrators can consider just running basic disks with no redundancy whatsoever. This makes smaller servers viable as one isn't likely to need nearly as many disks in the chassis. This makes it even easier for administrators to move away from complex and expensive SANs back toward direct attached storage. In this case, optimizing doesn't always mean making things faster and more scalable, sometimes optimizing is about doing more with less.

When configuring a DAG, the best practice is to deploy a separate network for replication between servers in the same data center, but between data centers only when a separate physical network already exists. When there are just two servers in a DAG in the same data center, a crossover cable (or a straight-through cable as most modern NICs support Auto-NDIX capability) is sufficient and doesn't waste switch ports. DAGs offer the ability to configure the nodes to use a specific network for their replication traffic, which offers two potential benefits. Number one, in a LAN scenario, it means that clients aren't competing with replication traffic for access to their mailboxes over the LAN. In a WAN configuration, it means that if an environment has access to multiple networks, it can potentially move replication traffic to a lower-cost network. Consider a typical scenario where a large enterprise has its offices connected via a Multiprotocol Label Switching (MPLS) network. MPLS provides excellent bandwidth and performance but is generally somewhat expensive. Many of these large enterprises also have IPSec tunnels set up across an Internet connection to provide a secondary network to use in case of a failure of the MPLS links. These cheaper IPSec tunnels can be used to off-load the DAG replication. This reduces the load on the "production" network and, at the same time, saves money by utilizing a lower tier of bandwidth.

The other way to optimize DAG members is to balance the load across multiple DAG replicas. This was a concept that is new compared with Cluster Continuous Replication (CCR) in Exchange Server 2007. In Exchange Server 2010 and 2013, the replication is done at the database level rather than at the server level. This means that rather than running in active/passive pairs, one can effectively be active for one or more databases and passive for others on the same server. So a site might have three DAG members in a single location for redundancy and could run one third of the databases as "master" on node 1, one third on node 2, and the remaining one third on node 3, with replicas going to the other two nodes. Node 1 might be "master" for databases 1–5, the second priority for databases 6–10, and third priority for databases 11–15. This means that if a node failed, the load would double on the remaining two servers rather than tripling on a single node. This allows administrators to get the best performance out of their hardware by carefully planning out loads for both a "normal" and a disaster recovery situation. The optimization benefits of such a configuration are more modest than you might think, however, because the load placed on a passive database copy to copy and replay log files is not substantially less than that of an active database copy.

Optimizing Client Access Servers

CASs tend to be more dependent on CPU and memory than they are on disk. Because their job is to simply proxy requests back to the appropriate Mailbox servers, they don't need much in the way of local storage. The best way to optimize the Client Access server is to give it enough memory that it doesn't need to page very often. By monitoring the page rate in the Performance Monitor, you can ensure that the CAS is running optimally. If it starts to page excessively, you can simply add more memory to it. Similarly, if the CPU utilization is sustained above 65% or so, it might be time to think about more processing power.

Unlike Mailbox servers, Client Access servers are usually "commodity" class servers and commonly virtualized. This means that if they are physical, they aren't likely to have the capacity for memory or CPU that a Mailbox server might have. It is typical to increase the performance of the Client Access servers by simply adding more servers into a load-balanced group as they scale better that way than by adding CPU and memory.

Exchange Server 2013 utilizes the Client Access servers less than Exchange Server 2010 did because the new Exchange Server 2013 architecture no longer utilizes what was called MAPI on the Middle Tier in Exchange Server 2010. Outlook clients once again talk to the Mailbox server role. They initially talk to the Client Access server role and are proxied to the appropriate Mailbox server that holds the active copy of their mailbox database. Two reasons this change was made were to improve overall Exchange performance and to allow load balancing to be moved from Layer 7 to Layer 4. As with Exchange Server 2010, Exchange Server 2013 CAS roles are responsible for finding the active copy of a database. As such, Outlook merely needs to find an available Client Access server to make its connections.

Because CAS servers are less tied to the sites that host Mailbox servers, companies can often get away with fewer CAS servers in Exchange Server 2013 architectures. As long as Outlook clients can find a CAS server, often through DNS load balancing, they will make a connection and be proxied to their appropriate Mailbox server, regardless of whether it's in the same or a different site than the CAS server that was contacted.

Generally speaking, a Client Access server should run at least 2GB of memory, and 2GB per processor core is recommended. Client Access servers don't benefit much from having more than eight processor cores.

Another way in which the Client Access server role can be optimized is in the area of how users attach to it. One of the most common requests in Exchange Server from an OWA perspective is to configure things such that users don't have to remember the full uniform resource locator (URL) for connecting to OWA. For example, your users might need to type https://webmail.companyabc.com/owa to get to their OWA page, but many users will type https://webmail.companyabc.com instead. In the past, it was recommended to utilize a customized Active Server Pages (ASP) page to make the redirection. In Windows Server

2008, the redirection functionality is built in to Internet Information Services (IIS). When configuring IIS for Exchange Server 2013 CAS on Windows Server 2008 R2, be sure to include the HTTP Redirection feature. With this available, you can reconfigure the IIS site as follows:

1. Launch the IIS Manager.
2. Expand the left pane to Default Web Site.
3. Click the Features View and Group by No Grouping.
4. Double-click HTTP Redirect, as shown in Figure 15.1.

FIGURE 15.1 Choosing HTTP Redirect.

5. Check the box for Redirect Requests to This Destination, as shown as Figure 15.2, and set the destination to the /owa sub site.
6. Check both boxes under Redirect Behavior.
7. Click Apply.
8. Under Default Web Site, select the Autodiscover virtual directory.
9. Double-click HTTP Redirect.
10. Clear the Redirect Requests to This Destination check box, and then click Apply.
11. Repeat steps 8 through 10 for the ecp, EWS, Microsoft-Server-ActiveSync, OAB, owa, PowerShell, and Rpc virtual directories.

15

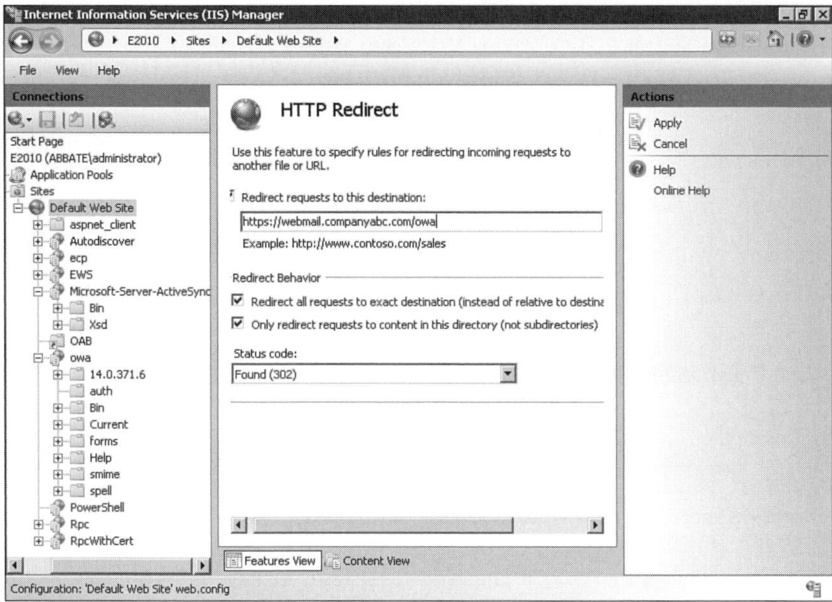

FIGURE 15.2 HTTP Redirect.

Optimizing Mailbox Transport Services

One of the big changes in Exchange Server 2013 is that the Hub Transport is no longer a dedicated Exchange role, having been moved to the Mailbox server and renamed Mailbox Transport.

Like the Hub Transport role it replaced, the goal of the Mailbox Transport service is to transfer data between different Exchange servers and sites. Its performance is based on how quickly it can determine where to send a message and send it off. The best way to optimize the Mailbox Transport service is via memory, CPU, and network throughput. The Mailbox Transport service needs ready access to a global catalog server to determine where to route messages based on the recipients of the messages. Placing an additional global catalog (GC) in the same site as a busy Mailbox server can be a good idea. Ensure that the Mailbox server has sufficient memory to quickly move messages into and out of queues. Monitoring available memory and page rate gives you an idea if you have enough memory. High-speed network connectivity is also very useful for this role.

Disk performance is potentially a concern in environments that send very high volumes of messages. The Mailbox Transport service maintains the SMTP queues on disk and the faster they can be processed, the faster mail can flow. In older versions of Exchange Server, it was recommended to run redundant disks for the SMTP queues. This was because if a Hub Transport lost the disks on which the SMTP queues lived, the messages would be lost. In Exchange Server 2013, the Shadow Redundancy feature protects against this type of message loss. Basically, when the Mailbox server hands a message to another Mailbox Transport, the Mailbox server doesn't consider the message as "sent" until the next hop reports back that it successfully handed the message off to someone else. This means that if the message were sitting on the second hop, awaiting a third hop and that second hop server failed, the originating Mailbox server would not have received a confirmation that the second hop sent to the third hop and it would re-queue the message, assuming that something had happened to it.

As was the case with older versions of Exchange, the SMTP queues associated with the Mailbox Transport are queued on disk as they await transfer. Making sure the disk the messages are cached on is of sufficient performance can be helpful in maximizing performance. The `EdgeTransport.exe.config` file contains the configuration used by the Mailbox Transport. It defines a `QueueDatabasePath` and a `QueueDatabaseLoggingPath`. By defining these queues on faster disks, you can improve the overall throughput of the Mailbox Transport service.

Optimizing Edge Transport Servers

At the time of this writing, Microsoft has not released the Exchange Server 2013 version of the Edge Transport server; however, they do support the Exchange Server 2010 Edge Transport performing message hygiene and directory-based filtering for an Exchange Server 2013 organization. As such, nothing has changed in the way that Edge Transport servers are optimized.

The Edge Transport server is very similar to the Exchange Server 2010 style Hub Transport server, with the key difference being that it is the connection point to external systems. As such, it has a higher need for processing power because it needs to convert the format of messages from SMTP to Messaging Application Programming Interface (MAPI) for internal routing. Edge Transport servers are often serving "double-duty" as antivirus and antispam gateways, thus increasing the need for CPU and memory. The Edge Transport role is one where it is very common to optimize the service by deploying multiple Edge Transport servers. This not only increases a site's capacity for sending mail into and out of the local environment, but it also adds a layer of redundancy.

To fully optimize this role, consider running Edge Transport servers in two geographically disparate locations. Utilize multiple MX records to balance out the load of mail coming into the company. Use your route costs to control the outward flow of mail such that you can reduce the number of hops needed for mail to leave the environment.

Keep a close eye on CPU utilization as well as memory paging to know when you need to add capacity to this role. Utilizing content-based rules or running message filtering increases the CPU and memory requirements of this role.

Generally speaking, an Edge Transport server should have at least 2GB of memory, and 1GB per processor core is recommended. Edge Transport servers must be workgroup members and not domain members.

Optimizing Unified Messaging Services

The Unified Messaging server that was introduced in Exchange Server 2010 has been integrated into the Mailbox server role in Exchange Server 2013. UM services allow Exchange to act as a voice mail system with automated attendants, voice-based access to mailbox content, and the ability to store voice mail in the users' mailboxes. Exchange's UM features even allow for the transcription of a voice message, resulting in a text-based preview of the voice mail. This is very convenient as it can allow a user who is checking a mobile device to see a preview of what a message contains to then make a decision on whether or not to listen to the full message.

As you might expect, to optimize this role, you must optimize the ability to quickly transfer information from one source to another. This means that the Unified Messaging service needs to have sufficient memory, CPU, and network bandwidth. To fully optimize Unified Messaging services, strongly consider running multiple network interfaces in the Unified Messaging server to allow one network to talk to the phone systems and the other to talk to the other Exchange servers. Careful monitoring of memory paging, CPU utilization, and NIC utilization allows you to quickly spot any bottlenecks in your particular environment.

Generally speaking, a Unified Messaging server should have at least 4GB of memory and the number of processor cores should be based mostly on the volume of voice mail messages. Exchange's UM functions require one full CPU per transcription conversation. Because UM features are now integrated into the Mailbox server role, the UM capacity will scale directly with the number of Mailbox servers. This is a welcome change as typically environments will have an abundance of Mailbox servers based on the DAG model, so these servers usually can provide enough capacity to keep the UM functions happy and help to provide redundancy for the Unified Messaging services.

General Optimizations

Certain bits of advice can be applied to optimizing any server in an Exchange Server 2013 environment. For example, the elimination of unneeded services is one of the easiest ways to free up CPU, memory, and disk resources. Event logging should be limited to the events you care about and you should be very careful about running third-party agents on your Exchange Server 2013 servers.

Event logs should be reviewed regularly to look for signs of any problems. Disks that are generating errors should be replaced, and problems that appear in the operating system should be addressed immediately.

You should regularly review the performance counters identified in this chapter to see how your systems are running compared with what you'd expect. Always investigate any anomalies to determine if things have been changed or if you are suffering a potential problem. By staying on top of your systems and knowing how they should run, you can more easily keep them running in an optimal manner.

The Security Customization Wizard should be run to ensure that correct network ports for Exchange Server 2013 roles are available. Although many administrators are tempted to simply disable the Windows Server 2008 R2 firewall, it is important to realize that the Windows Filtering Platform is still running and can potentially interrupt traffic. It is easier to install Exchange Server 2013 with the firewall already enabled than it is to turn on the firewall after the fact. This is because Exchange Server 2013 will create all the necessary firewall rules at the time of installation based on the roles installed.

Optimizing Active Directory from an Exchange Server Perspective

As you likely already know, Exchange Server 2013 is very dependent on Active Directory for routing messages between servers and for allowing end users to find each other and to send each other mail. The architecture of Active Directory can have a large impact on how Exchange Server performs its various functions.

When designing your Exchange Server 2013 environment, consider placing dedicated global catalog servers into an Active Directory site that contains only the GCs and the local Exchange servers. Configure your site connectors in AD with a high enough cost that the GCs in this site won't adopt another nearby site that doesn't have GCs. This ensures that the GCs are only used by the Exchange servers, which can improve the lookup performance of the Exchange server.

In the case of a large Active Directory environment, for example 20,000 or more objects, consider upgrading the domain controllers to run Windows Server 2003 64-bit or Windows Server 2008 64-bit. This is because a directory this large can grow to be larger than 3GB. When the Extensible Storage Engine database that holds Active Directory grows to this size, it is no longer able to cache the entire directory. This increases lookup and response times for finding objects in Active Directory. By running a 64-bit operating system on the domain controller, you can utilize the larger memory space to cache the entire directory. The nice thing in this situation is that you retain compatibility with 32-bit domain controllers, so it is not necessary to upgrade the entire environment, only sites that will benefit from it, particularly those containing Exchange servers.

It is also important to point out that Read-Only Domain Controllers are not supported in sites that contain Exchange servers of any version.

Monitoring Exchange Server 2013

A variety of built-in Microsoft tools are available to help an administrator establish the baseline of the Exchange Server 2013 environment. Among these, the Performance Monitor Microsoft Management Console (MMC) snap-in is one of the most common tools used to measure the capacity requirements of Exchange Server 2013. This MMC tool is built in to all modern versions of Windows Server.

Using the Performance Monitor Console

The Performance snap-in enables an in-depth analysis of every measurable aspect of the Exchange server. The information that is gathered using the Performance snap-in can be presented in a variety of forms, including reports, real-time charts, or logs, which add to the versatility of this tool. The resulting output formats enable an administrator to present a baseline analysis in real time or through historical data. The Performance snap-in, shown in Figure 15.3, can be launched from the Start, Administrative Tools menu.

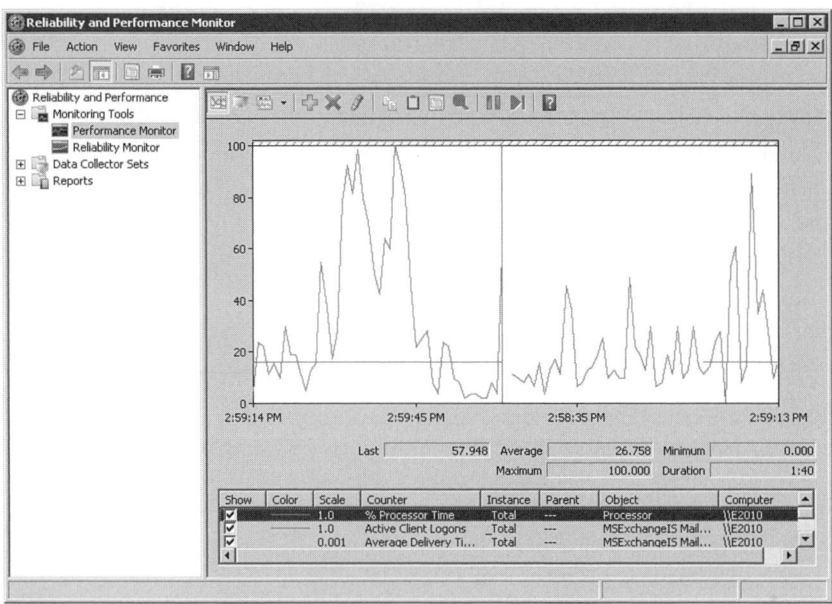

FIGURE 15.3 The Performance monitor snap-in.

Using Task Manager

Task Manager displays real-time performance metrics, so an administrator can quickly get an overall idea of how the Exchange Server 2013 server is performing at any given time. Its biggest downfall, however, is that it does not store any historical data, so it is not a suitable tool for capacity-analysis purposes. Task Manager is typically used as a quick check to see if anything is out of the ordinary. If a server appears to be running slow, using Task Manager and using the Processes tab allows you to sort the processes by CPU or memory use and quickly see if something is noticeably different from its baseline value. This is a quick way to spot common issues like an antivirus scanner taking up all the CPU time or an `lsass.exe` process using an excessive amount of memory.

Analyzing and Monitoring Core Elements

The capacity analysis and performance optimization process can be intimidating because there can be an enormous amount of data to work with. In fact, it can easily become unwieldy if not done properly. The process is not just about monitoring and reading counters; it is also an art.

As you monitor and catalog performance information, keep in mind that more information does not necessarily yield better optimization. Tailor the number and types of counters that are being monitored based on the server's role and functionality within the network environment. It's also important to monitor the four common contributors to bottlenecks: memory, processor, disk, and network subsystems. When monitoring Exchange Server 2013, it is equally important to understand the various Exchange roles to keep the number of counters being monitored to a minimum.

Memory Subsystem Optimizations

At the risk of sounding cliché, forget everything you knew about memory optimization in 32-bit Windows. Because Exchange Server 2013 is a 64-bit application, it requires a 64-bit operating system. 64-bit Windows Server 2008 and newer deal with memory in an entirely different way than Windows Server 2003 32-bit did. The concepts of Physical Addressing Extensions (PAE) have gone away, as there are now enough bits to natively address memory, and the old tricks such as `"/3GB"` and `"/USERVA=3030"` in the `boot.ini` files have gone away. Table 15.1 summarizes some of the key improvements in memory management that will greatly enhance the performance of Exchange Server 2013.

TABLE 15.1 Key Improvements in Memory Management with 64-bit Windows

Architectural Component	64-bit Windows	32-bit Windows
Virtual memory	16TB	4GB
Paging file size	512TB	16TB
Hyperspace	8GB	4MB
Paged pool	128GB	470MB
Non-paged pool	128GB	256MB
System cache	1TB	1GB
System PTEs	128GB	660MB

Virtual memory refers to the memory space made from a combination of physical memory and swap file space. Each process in Windows is constrained by this virtual memory size. In 32-bit Windows, this meant that the `store.exe`, traditionally the largest consumer of memory in Exchange Server, was limited to 4GB of address space. In 64-bit Windows, `store.exe` can access 16TB of address space. This gives `store.exe` 4,096 times as much memory space as before. This means Exchange Server 2013 can utilize significantly more physical memory and use the pagefile, consisting of much slower disks, less often. By being able to cache more of the Exchange Server database in this larger memory space, the requirements for disk I/O are greatly reduced. Moreover, because Exchange Server 2013 allows each database to run its own unique instance of `store.exe`, memory utilization can go even higher than before.

The pagefile refers to the disk space allocated for scratch space where the operating system will place "memory pages" when it no longer has room for them and they aren't being actively used. This increased value allows for the support of the greater virtual memory size.

Hyperspace is the special region that is used to map the process working set list. It is also used to temporarily map other physical pages for such operations as zeroing a page on the free list, invalidating page table entries in other page tables, and for setting up the address space of a new process.

Paged pool is the region of virtual memory that can be paged in and out of the working set of the system process. It is used by Kernel mode components to allocate system memory.

Non-paged pool is the memory pool that consists of ranges of system virtual addresses. These virtual addresses are guaranteed to be resident in physical memory at all times. Thus, they can be accessed from any address space without incurring paging I/O to the disks. This pool is also used by Kernel mode components to allocate system memory.

System cache refers to the pages that are used to map open files in the system cache.

System PTEs are the Page Table Entries that are used to map system pages. 64-bit programs use a model of 8TB for User and 8TB for Kernel, whereas 32-bit programs use 2GB for User and 2GB for Kernel.

With the Performance Monitor console, a number of important memory-related counters can help in establishing an accurate representation of the system's memory requirements. The primary memory counters that provide information about hard pages (pages that are causing the information to be swapped between the memory and the hard disk) are as follows:

- **Memory—Pages/sec**—The values of this counter should range from 5 to 20. Values consistently higher than 10 are indicative of potential performance problems, whereas values consistently higher than 20 might cause noticeable and significant performance hits. The trend of these values is impacted by the amount of physical memory installed in the server.

- **Memory—Page Faults/sec**—This counter, together with the Memory—Cache Faults/sec and Memory—Transition Faults/sec counters, can provide valuable information about page faults that are not committed to disk. They were not committed to disk because the memory manager allocated those pages to a standby list. Most systems today can handle a large number of page faults, but it is important to correlate these numbers with the Pages/sec counter as well to determine whether Exchange Server is configured with enough memory.

Improving Virtual Memory Usage

Calculating the correct amount of virtual memory is one of the more challenging parts of planning a server's memory requirements. While trying to anticipate growing usage demands, it is critical that the server has an adequate amount of virtual memory for all applications and the operating system. This is no different for Exchange Server 2013.

Virtual memory refers to the amount of disk space that is used by Windows Servers and applications as physical memory gets low or when applications need to swap data out of physical memory. Windows Server 2008 and up use a default page file sized to just barely fit a full memory dump, which for many systems is adequate. However, it is important to monitor memory counters to determine whether this amount is truly sufficient for that particular server's resource requirements. Another important consideration is the maximum size setting for the paging file. As a best practice, this setting should be at least 50% more than the minimum value to enable paging file growth, should the system require it. If the minimum and maximum settings are configured with the same value, there is a greater risk that the system could experience severe performance problems or even crash. Pagefiles can be very nonintuitive as you would think that by giving a system more memory, it would need less pagefile; however, pagefile isn't just there to provide storage when memory is exceeded, it's also there to allow information to be swapped into and out of memory. This means that very large memory transfers can require very large pagefiles.

The most indicative sign of low virtual memory is the presence of 9582 warning events logged by the Microsoft Exchange Information Store service that can severely impact and degrade the Exchange server's message-processing abilities. These warning events are indicative of virtual memory going below 32MB. If unnoticed or left unattended, these warning messages might cause services to stop or the entire system to crash.

TIP

Use the Performance snap-in to set an alert for Event ID 9582. This helps proactively address any virtual memory problems and possibly prevent unnecessary downtime.

To get an accurate portrayal of how Exchange Server 2013 is using virtual memory, monitor the following counters within the `MSExchangeIS` object:

- **VM Largest Block Size**—This counter should consistently be above 32MB.
- **VM Total 16MB Free Blocks**—This counter should remain over three 16-MB blocks.
- **VM Total Free Blocks**—This value is specific to your messaging environment.
- **VM Total Large Free Block Bytes**—This counter should stay above 50MB.

Other important counters to watch closely are as follows:

- **Memory—Available Bytes**—This counter can be used to establish whether the system has adequate amounts of RAM. The recommended absolute minimum value is 4MB.
- **Paging File—% Usage**—% Usage is used to validate the amount of the paging file used in a predetermined interval. High usage values might be indicative of requiring more physical memory or needing a larger paging file.

Monitoring Processor Usage

Analyzing the processor usage can reveal valuable information about system performance and provide reliable results that can be used for baselining purposes. Two major Exchange-related processor counters are used for capacity analysis of an Exchange Server 2013:

- **% Privileged Time**—This counter indicates the percentage of non-idle processor time spent in Privileged mode. The recommended ideal for this value is under 55%.
- **% Processor Time**—This counter specifies the processor use of each processor or the total processor use. If these values are consistently higher than 50%–60%, consider upgrade options or segmenting workloads.

Tracking these values long term, for trend analysis, makes it much easier to spot accountable anomalies, such as a processor time spike during the online defragmentation or interactions with other systems. Tracking a "weighted average" of these processor values allows you to predict the point in time at which a system needs to be upgraded or when an additional system needs to be deployed to share the load.

Monitoring the Disk Subsystem

Exchange Server 2013 relies heavily on the disk subsystem and it is, therefore, a critical component to properly design and monitor. Although the disk object monitoring counters are, by default, enabled in Windows Server 2008, it is recommended that these counters be disabled until such time that an administrator is ready to monitor them. The resource requirements can influence overall system performance. The syntax to disable and enable these counters is as follows:

```
diskperf -n (to disable)
diskperf -y [\\computer_Name] (to reenable)
```

Nevertheless, it is important to gather disk subsystem performance statistics over time.

The primary Exchange-related performance counters for the disk subsystem are located within the Physical and Logical Disk objects. Critical counters to monitor include, but are not limited to, the following:

- **Physical Disk—% Disk Time**—This counter analyzes the percentage of elapsed time that the selected disk spends on servicing read or write requests. Ideally, this value should remain below 50%.
- **Physical Disk—Avg. Disk sec/Read**—This counter monitors the read latency of a disk or disk subsystem. This value should average 20ms or less on database volumes and spike to 100ms or less.
- **Physical Disk—Avg. Disk sec/Write**—This counter monitors the write latency of a disk or disk subsystem. This value should average 10ms or less on log volumes, 20ms or less on database volumes, with spikes of 100ms or less on both.

- **Logical Disk—% Disk Time**—This counter displays the percentage of elapsed time that the selected disk spends fulfilling read or write requests. It is recommended that this value be 60%–70% or lower.
- **Current Disk Queue Length (Both Physical and Logical Disk Objects)**—This counter has different performance indicators depending on the monitored disk drive (Database or Transaction Log volume). On disk drives storing the Exchange Server database, this value should be below the number of spindled drives divided by 2. On disk drives storing transaction log data, this value should be below 1. When SAN storage is used, this counter may not be relevant, so consult with your SAN vendor.

If there appears to be an excessive load on the disks, consider adding more memory to the Exchange Server 2013 server. Improvements in cache in the Exchange Server database engine allow more information to be read and cached into memory. This decreases the workload on the disks and might alleviate the need to add more disks. For large Exchange Server 2013 servers, it is usually less expensive to add more memory than to add more disks to address this type of issue.

Of the values listed, the read and write latencies offer the best insight into the overall performance of the disks. Disk I/O ratings are actually given at 20ms of latency. This means that while a typical 15,000 RPM disk can offer 150 I/O per second, it's doing so at a latency of 20ms. This same disk might offer 200 I/O per second at a higher latency. 20ms of read or write latency is where Exchange server historically develops performance problems.

Monitoring the Network Subsystem

The network subsystem is one of the more challenging elements to monitor because so many components make up a network. In an Exchange Server messaging environment, site topologies, replication architecture, network topologies, synchronization methods, the number of systems, and more are among the many contributing factors.

To satisfactorily analyze the network, all facets must be considered. This most likely requires using third-party network monitoring tools in conjunction with built-in tools such as the Performance snap-in and Network Monitor. The current version of Network Monitor is 3.4 and can be downloaded from Microsoft at the following URL: http://www.microsoft.com/en-us/download/details.aspx?id=4865.

From a performance standpoint, always implement Gigabit Ethernet adapters in your Exchange Server 2013 servers. Given the amount of memory and disk likely to be in the server, it would easily saturate a 100-MB connection and in many situations can saturate even a single Gigabit connection with database replication, especially in the case of a large reseeding operation. If your server hardware offers it, consider using fault-tolerant configurations for your Ethernet connections that will not be participating in load-balanced groups. Most of the fault-tolerant configurations on the market today separate out input and output to different interfaces, resulting in better overall throughput for the network interfaces.

If you are connecting your storage via iSCSI, strongly consider running dedicated Gigabit Ethernet interfaces for the connection to the iSCSI network with an appropriate Device Specific Module (DSM) to support MultiPath I/O (MPIO). This separates the load of the iSCSI from the load for the users and results in better overall performance for the users.

Although in the past, Microsoft recommended against NIC teaming on Exchange Mailbox servers that were participating in a cluster, it is now fully supported and recommended. Microsoft has even gone as far as to move NIC teaming into the operating system in Windows Server 2012.

Properly Sizing Exchange Server 2013

Before delving into recommended configurations for Exchange Server 2013, it is essential to not only understand the fundamentals of this messaging system, but to also understand the dependencies and interactions those components have with the underlying operating system (that is, Windows Server 2008). Being a client/server messaging application, maximizing Exchange Server 2013 involves fine-tuning its entire core and extended components. Optimization of each of these components affects the overall performance of Exchange Server.

The core components of Exchange Server (for example, the Information Stores, connectors, transaction logs, and more) have a direct bearing on gauging resource requirements. The number of users in a messaging environment and the various Exchange Server functions are equally influential.

Expected User Loads

In Exchange Server 2013, you can predict with fair accuracy the load that will be generated by various types of users. Consider the following information when planning out CPU and disk configurations for an Exchange Server 2013 Mailbox server:

- **Light user—**5 receive/20 send—0.5 MCycles/user—0.04 IO/user/sec
- **Average user—**10 receive/40 send—0.9 MCycles/user—0.08 IO/user/sec
- **Heavy user—**20 receive/80 send—1.8 MCycles/user—0.15 IO/user/sec
- **Very Heavy user—**30 receive/120 send—2.7 MCycles/user—0.23 IO/user/sec

In this context, MCycles/user is the number of Mhz of processing time consumed by a user.

Mhz / MCycles per user × desired utilization = users

So a Light user consuming 0.5 MCycles/user means that a 1-Ghz (1,000 Mhz) CPU would support 2,000 light users at 100% CPU load. Similarly, it would only support 370 Very Heavy users at 100% CPU load. To put things into a more realistic perspective, a dual-core 3.0-Ghz processor would support:

2 × 3 × 1,000 = 6,000 Mhz / (1.8 MCycles per user) × 0.6 (desired 60% CPU utilization) = 2,000 users.

This formula is generally more accurate than a flat claim of "500 users per core" as it takes into account the fact that a 3.2-Ghz processor will support more users than a 2.0-Ghz processor.

Optimizing the Disk Subsystem Configuration

Many factors, such as the type of file system to use, physical disk configuration, database size, and log file placement, need to be considered when you are trying to optimize the disk subsystem configuration. The desire for performance must also be balanced with the requirements for redundancy and revocability.

Choosing the File System

Among the file systems supported by Windows Server 2008 and 2012, exFAT, and NTFS, only NTFS is supported for Exchange Server 2013 servers. NTFS provides the best security, scalability, and performance features. For instance, NTFS supports file- and directory-level security, large file sizes (files of up to 16TB), large disk sizes (disk volumes of up to 256TB), fault tolerance, disk compression, error detection, and encryption.

Choosing the Physical Disk Configuration

Windows Server 2008 and 2012, like their predecessors, support RAID technology. The levels of RAID supported by the operating system are as follows:

- RAID 0 (Striping)
- RAID 1 (Mirroring)
- RAID 5 (Striping with parity)

Other levels of RAID can be supported through the use of hardware-based RAID controllers. Only hardware RAID should be used with Exchange Server.

The deployment of the correct RAID level is of utmost importance because each RAID level has a direct effect on the performance of the server. From the viewpoint of pure performance, RAID 0 by far gives the best performance. However, fault tolerance and the reliability of system access are other factors that contribute to overall performance. The skillful administrator strikes a balance between performance and fault tolerance without sacrificing one for the other. The following sections provide recommended disk configurations for Exchange Server 2013.

NOTE

As mentioned earlier, various levels of RAID are available, but for the context of Exchange Server 2013, there are two recommended basic levels to use: RAID 1 and RAID 5. Other forms of RAID, such as RAID 0+1 or 1+0, are also optimal solutions for Exchange Server 2013. These more advanced levels of RAID are supported only when using a hardware RAID controller. As a result, only RAID 1 and 5 are discussed in this chapter.

Disk Mirroring (RAID 1)

In this type of configuration, data is mirrored from one disk to the other participating disk in the mirror set. Data is simultaneously written to the two required disks, which means read operations are significantly faster than systems with no RAID configuration or with a greater degree of fault tolerance. Write performance is slower, though, because data is being written twice—once to each disk in the mirror set.

Besides adequate performance, RAID 1 also provides a good degree of fault tolerance. For instance, if one drive fails, the RAID controller can automatically detect the failure and run solely on the remaining disk with minimal interruption.

The biggest drawback to RAID 1 is the amount of storage capacity that is lost. RAID 1 uses 50% of the total drive capacity for the two drives.

TIP

RAID 1 is particularly well suited for the boot drive and for volumes containing Exchange Server 2013 log files.

Disk Striping with Parity (RAID 5)

In a RAID-5 configuration, data and parity information is striped across all participating disks in the array. RAID 5 requires a minimum of three disks. Even if one of the drives fails within the array, the Exchange Server 2013 server can still remain operational.

After the drive fails, Windows Server continues to operate because of the data contained on the other drives. The parity information gives details of the data that is missing because of the failure. Either Windows Server or the hardware RAID controller also begins the rebuilding process from the parity information to a spare or new drive.

RAID 5 is most commonly used for the data drive because it is a great compromise among performance, storage capacity, and redundancy. The overall space used to store the striped parity information is equal to the capacity of one drive. For example, a RAID-5 volume with three 200-GB disks can store up to 400GB of data.

WARNING

Although RAID 5 has a significant performance penalty for disk activity that has a large percentage of writes, this can be mostly compensated for via caching on the RAID controller. This allows the writes to be done in cache and later be committed to disk. If you are going to utilize write caching on your RAID controller, ensure that the cache is protected by a battery. Otherwise a system failure could result in cached information never getting written to disk. This is a sure way to corrupt a database.

Hardware Versus Software RAID

Hardware RAID (configured at the disk controller level) is recommended over software RAID (configurable from within the Windows Server OS) because of faster performance, greater support of different RAID levels, support for caching, and capability of recovering from hardware failures more easily.

Database Sizing and Optimization

As mentioned throughout this book, Exchange Server 2013 is available in two versions: Standard and Enterprise. The Standard Edition supports five databases. The maximum Information Store (database) size is not limited with Exchange Server 2013, Standard Edition. The Enterprise Edition provides support for up to 100 databases per server, up to 16TB each, as limited by NTFS.

A key decision point in deciding the number of databases is to determine the maximum size of a database that can be restored from backup within the service level agreement. Of course, if your organization does not commit to restoring from backup or if your organization does not back up Exchange databases, as cloud-based email providers don't, then this criterion is not important.

The flexibility of Enterprise Edition is beneficial not just in terms of growth, but also in terms of performance and manageability. More specifically, the advantages for segmenting can include the following:

- Administrators can segment the user population on a single Exchange server.
- Multiple mailboxes can more evenly distribute the size of the messaging data and help prevent one database from becoming too large and possibly unwieldy for a given system.
- Multiple databases present greater opportunities for faster enumeration of database indexing.
- Multiple databases can be segmented onto different RAID volumes and RAID controller channels.
- Transaction logs can be segmented from other log files using separate RAID volumes.
- Failures such as database corruption affect a smaller percentage of the user population.
- If utilizing database availability groups, there is plenty of room to support replicas for other servers.
- Offline maintenance routines require less scheduled downtime, and fewer users are affected.
- More databases allow for smaller databases, which take less time to seed over a WAN.
- Smaller databases can be restored from backup in a more timely fashion when needed.

TIP

When using the Enterprise Edition, the recommended best practice is to keep database sizes in the 1–2TB range. This allows ESEUTIL to be run in a reasonable amount of time should they be needed. An administrator can use this guideline to gauge or plan for the number of users each database should optimally contain. This best practice is also useful in determining the appropriate number of Exchange Server 2013 Mailbox servers that are required to support the number of users in the organization.

If a deployment calls for a large number of databases, and there is some reason that each database and log volume be placed on its own LUN, it becomes necessary to use mount points rather than drive letters. This is most applicable where a SAN is utilized as most often the databases would live on unique LUNs within volumes to properly use the vendor's storage snapshot capabilities.

Optimizing Exchange Server Logs

Similar to the previous versions of Exchange Server, transaction log files should be stored on separate RAID volumes when there are fewer than three database copies in the DAG.

Sizing Memory Requirements

The recommended starting point for the amount of memory for an Exchange Server 2013 server is 5GB of RAM per server + 2MB of RAM per user. The specific memory requirements naturally vary based on server roles, server responsibilities, and the number of users to support. In addition, some organizations define certain guidelines that must be followed for base memory configurations. A more accurate representation of how much memory is required can be achieved by baselining memory performance information gathered from the Performance snap-in or third-party tools during a prototype or lab testing phase.

Another important factor to take into consideration is when the organization adds functionality to Exchange Server 2013 or consolidates users onto fewer servers. This obviously increases resource requirements, especially in terms of adding more physical memory. In these scenarios, it is recommended to use the base amount of memory (for example, 8GB) and then add the appropriate amount of memory based on vendor specifications. It is also important to consult with the vendor to determine what the memory requirements might be on a per-user basis. This way, the organization can plan ahead and configure the proper amount of memory prior to needing to scale to support a larger number of users in the future.

One of the big advantages to deploying Exchange Server 2013 on virtualized servers is the ability to quickly and easily add additional memory to a virtual machine. This allows IT groups to quickly reclaim unused resources and provision them to systems that can take better advantage of those resources.

Sizing Based on Server Roles

Exchange Server 2013 has dropped from five roles: Client Access servers, Mailbox servers, Hub Transport servers, Edge Transport servers, and Unified Messaging servers to only two roles: Client Access servers and Mailbox servers.

Mailbox Server Sizing

Table 15.2 shows the recommended resource requirements of Mailbox servers. It is important to note that these guidelines are minimum recommendations, and actual requirements might vary depending upon the organization.

TABLE 15.2 Recommended Minimum Mailbox Server Configurations

Resource	Description
RAM	5GB + 2–4MB/user
Processor	Xeon 5530 2.4GHz or higher processor with E64MT support or equivalent AMD processor
Hard disk	RAID 1 for Windows Server 2008 and Exchange Server 2013
	RAID 1+0 for mailbox data
Network	Gigabit Ethernet NIC(s)

Client Access Server Sizing

Table 15.3 shows the recommended resource requirements of Client Access servers. It is important to note that these guidelines are minimum recommendations, and actual requirements might vary depending upon the organization.

TABLE 15.3 Recommended Minimum Client Access Server Configurations

Resource	Description
RAM	2GB
Processor	Xeon 5503 2.0GHz or higher processor with E64MT support or equivalent AMD processor
Hard disk	RAID 1 for Windows Server 2008 and Exchange Server 2010
Network	Gigabit Ethernet NIC(s)

Monitoring Exchange Server with System Center Operations Manager

System Center Operations Manager (SCOM) is an application that can be used to actively monitor Exchange Server 2013. Employing SCOM in an Exchange Server messaging environment offers administrators the following benefits:

- SCOM has the capability of detecting even the smallest of problems that, if unnoticed, can lead to more complicated issues. Early detection of problems enables an administrator to troubleshoot the problem areas well in advance.
- SCOM can monitor all Exchange Server–related system health indicators.
- The Exchange Server 2013 Management Pack leverages all the new features of Exchange Server 2013.
- The Exchange Server 2013 Management Pack also includes the Microsoft Knowledge Base, which can be used for fast and reliable resolution of issues.
- SCOM can centrally manage a large number of Exchange Server 2013 servers over widely dispersed deployments.
- SCOM can actively monitor server availability by verifying that services are running, databases are mounted, messages are flowing, and users are able to log on.
- SCOM can actively monitor server health by monitoring free disk space thresholds, mail queues, security, performance thresholds, and more.
- SCOM provides detailed reports on database sizes, traffic analysis, and more.
- Alerts can be sent based on customized thresholds and events.
- SCOM can run synthetic transactions to mimic normal message flow to validate that the environment is not only up, but is performing tasks within an expected threshold of time.

In short, SCOM is an excellent tool that administrators can use to proactively monitor the Exchange Server environment from a centralized location.

Summary

Despite all the performance, reliability, scalability, and availability enhancements of Exchange Server 2013, capacity analysis and performance optimization are still a necessity. The techniques and processes described in this chapter not only help you determine how to size a server or tweak it to operate optimally, but they also reflect a methodology for continually monitoring a changing environment. By keeping one step ahead of the system, an organization can use resources more efficiently and effectively and in return save time, effort, and costs associated with supporting Exchange Server 2013.

Capacity must always be monitored and growth must be planned for. An efficient administrator will have a playbook built up for expanding the Exchange Server 2013 environment in a logical and effective manner. This includes plans for increasing capacity on existing servers, increasing capacity from a storage standpoint, and bringing up new Exchange Server 2013 sites when expansion requires it. By tying capacity expansion to company growth and expansion, Information Technology is able to stay in step with the needs of the business and fulfill its role as a business enabler rather than just being a support cost.

Best Practices

The following are best practices from this chapter:

- Begin capacity analysis and performance optimization sooner rather than later.
- Create performance baselines in which to gauge the changing requirements and performance levels of Exchange Server 2013.
- Use existing baselines to recognize changes in the performance or behavior of a server.
- Establish SLAs and other policies that reflect the business expectations of the messaging environment.
- Monitor counters that are pertinent to the server's configuration.
- Always monitor the four common contributors to bottlenecks: memory, disk subsystem, processor, and network.
- Run performance and stress tests in a lab environment prior to implementing in a production environment when servers are likely to be stressed in production.
- Set an alert for Event ID 9582 to proactively address any memory or virtual memory problems.
- Use enough physical memory in Mailbox servers to reduce the requirement on the disk subsystem.
- Choose hardware RAID over software RAID.
- Use separate, hardware-based RAID-1 volumes for system files and transaction logs unless running three or more copies of a mailbox database via DAG.

CHAPTER 16

Backing Up the Exchange Server 2013 Environment

IN THIS CHAPTER

Although the key to implementing technologies is to install the software in a production environment, making sure the new technology environment is properly backed up is just as important for the organization. This chapter covers the proper planning, implementing, testing, and support of a properly backed-up environment. Organizations should spend as much time planning and implementing their backup processes as they do implementing the core environment. This can ensure that if there are any problems with the systems, servers, and sites that a successful recovery process can be initiated.

Understanding the Importance of Backups

Through various improvements and changes in the JET database engine and storage, Microsoft Exchange Server 2013 offers the most stable and resilient database of any Exchange Server implementation to date. The database can recover from dirty shutdowns, hardware failures, and power outages. The database enables both users and administrators to recover recently deleted items. Exchange Server 2013 provides the replication option that results in up to 16 independent copies of mailbox data spread across the world (database availability group [DAG] replication). However, even with all this functionality, Exchange administrators need to determine where traditional backups fit into the organization and whether backups are required and for what purposes.

Just a few years ago, it would have been unheard of to even mention that servers would not be backed up; however, for organizations that have policies to delete all email within six months (unless a mailbox is on legal hold or content is required for archiving), with the ability for Exchange to replicate mail two, three, four times or more across multiple servers and sites, all data can remain on the replicated servers, and it's reasonable to consider whether tape can be eliminated. Having a tape that sits on a shelf for six months versus data sitting on a server in two separate geo-locations in the organization for six months has the same net result. And with the geo-replicated copies of Exchange, information can be recovered instantaneously, unlike tape backups that require the storage and management of tapes.

Traditionally, backups are performed and maintained for three primary purposes:

- Recovering deleted items past the retention period
- Offline extraction of messages
- Disaster recovery

In modern environments, a fourth common purpose would be legal discovery. Legal departments regularly need to access historic email for groups of users to utilize in legal proceedings. Because maintaining a deleted item retention of multiple years isn't realistic, it falls to the traditional backup to provide this data over the years. To support these functions, it is critical to not only perform the regular backups, but to also understand what it is you are backing up, how often you are backing it up, and exactly what recovery scenarios you can support. It is equally critical to ensure that a retention policy is clearly defined and that it is supported by both information technology and the legal departments within a company. The job of IT is to use technology to support and enforce the retention policies set forth by legal. This means not only ensuring that enough data is available, but also making sure that no data beyond that which is allowed is still resident in the environment. The goal of this chapter is to show an administrator how to develop a service level agreement (SLA) that includes the following:

- Evaluate the requirements for backup.
- Capture all the necessary information for disaster recovery.
- Properly document the environment.
- Design the backup strategy to support the SLA.
- Build policies and procedures around backup processes.
- Determine what data to back up.
- Determine how to take advantage of new backup technologies available in Exchange Server 2013.

The process of implementing a highly available Exchange environment with the ability to recover from a disaster is covered in Chapter 8, "Implementing and Supporting a Highly Available Exchange Server 2013 Environment."

NOTE

Exchange Server 2013 running on Windows Server 2008 R2 or Windows Server 2012 supports Volume Shadow Copy Service (VSS)–based backup technologies and can be backed up either with the native Windows Server Backup tool, through Microsoft's System Center Data Protection Manager (DPM) product, or through a third-party backup tool for Exchange Server 2013.

Establishing Service Level Agreements

The most common question from Exchange Server administrators is "How should I be doing my backups?" The answer to this question is quite simple. You should be doing them so that they support your service level agreements around recoverability and retention for Exchange Server services.

Based on this concept, it quickly becomes apparent that the first step in planning out your backups is to determine exactly what you've committed yourself to. This is commonly referred to as a service level agreement or simply an SLA.

Establishing a Service Level Agreement for Each Critical Service

Exchange Server 2013 is often deployed so that roles are distributed across multiple servers. This distribution of roles might vary from site to site. However, the SLAs will likely remain constant across the enterprise as the goal is actually to keep messaging alive and available to the end users.

It is important to understand the implication of SLAs for each aspect of Exchange Server 2013 because the SLA drives your design and must be considered up front and not as an afterthought to a deployed Exchange Server 2013 environment. Too often, IT groups implement Exchange Server and later go back to determine how quickly they can restore services or rebuild a failed system. The correct methodology is to determine recovery time objectives and uptime goals and then design the architecture to enable those goals.

Determining SLAs for Mailbox Servers

One of the most important aspects of Exchange Server 2013 is the Mailbox server. If the Mailbox server isn't up, users can't access their mail. This is usually the first thing that triggers the help desk phone to ring. Most companies start their SLAs around the Mailbox servers. In most environments, a 2-hour recovery for a mailbox database is acceptable. This means that if your database fails, you need to recover that data within 2 hours. If you know that your system is capable of restoring 100GB of data per hour, you know that, based on your backup process, you can support only 200GB per database.

If your SLA for an entire Mailbox server recovery is 4 hours and you know that it takes 2 hours to rebuild a new server with Exchange Server 2013, you have only 2 hours to restore data, which, based on the preceding example, means you can have only 200GB of data on the server. If you planned to allow users 2000MB of storage each, this limits the server to 100 users. If you want to support more users per server, you either need to alter the SLA or you need to change your backup strategy to allow you to restore more data in the same period of time. This is what enables you to safely support large numbers of users with good SLAs. This is where you have to balance the costs of the backup/restore system with the cost of adding additional servers.

Luckily Exchange Server 2013 offers technologies that enable you to run a significantly tighter SLA. For example, database availability groups enable a replica server to take over for a failed server automatically without users noticing.

Determining SLAs for Client Access Servers

Another major component of Exchange Server 2013 is the Client Access server (CAS). These are the systems that enable mobile devices and web browsers to access email. When determining SLAs for this server role, it is helpful to view the service and the servers as two entities. Although you likely want high availability on the service, you can likely worry less about the servers individually if they are designed with redundancy in mind. So, if you have at least one more Client Access server than you need for performance purposes, you have plenty of time to rebuild one server if it fails because there is already another that is taking up the load. Keep this in mind when designing your Exchange Server environment. Also keep in mind that the data on a CAS is mostly static. Building a new CAS from scratch in Disaster Recovery mode is usually faster than restoring an existing one because nearly all of the settings are in Active Directory.

Determining SLAs for Edge Transport Servers

For systems such as the Edge Transport servers in Exchange Server 2013, it is more useful to view the SLA for this role as being for the service as opposed to the servers themselves. In the case of Edge Transport servers, the service they provide is to send and receive external email to and from the Internet. In this sense, most companies try to enforce a fairly aggressive SLA on the service itself. For example, if Internet mail connectivity were to fail, they'd want the service restored within 1 to 2 hours. In most environments, this is fairly easy to accomplish because there is typically two or more Edge Transport servers to provide redundancy and minimize wide area network (WAN) traffic. In the case of the SLAs on the servers themselves, typically a 1-day recovery is acceptable. Because the Edge Transport servers don't store any data, they can easily be replaced if a failure occurs.

Remember that the Edge Transport service is dependent on the network itself. If the Edge Transport servers are running but the Internet connection is down, they can't do their job. One easy way to improve availability and thus support a tight SLA for Edge Transport is to have multiple entry points from the Internet. This can protect against Internet or Internet service provider issues by enabling Internet mail to enter from another location and simply ride the corporate WAN to reach the appropriate Exchange Server 2013 server. The simplest way to do this is to advertise multiple Mail Exchanger records (MX) in domain name system (DNS) on the Internet.

Determining SLAs for Hub Transport Services

The Hub Transport services of routing mail from one site to another connected site is now integrated in the Client Access server and Mailbox server, so the backup of either of those servers will back up the Hub Transport services. As such, when Hub Transport services fail, the site it served is effectively cut off from other sites. Moreover, because the architecture of Exchange Server 2013 requires that all messages first pass through a Hub Transport, if this role were unavailable in a site, users would not be able to send to each other even though they are hosted on the same Mailbox server. As such, a company would most likely want a fairly aggressive SLA on the Hub Transport servers. In most environments, the Hub Transport server role is combined with other roles because, in most cases, it won't justify being on an isolated server. As such, the SLA for recovery is often overwritten by the SLA for another role that it supports. As such, it is recommended that, when possible, two or more systems per site should host the Hub Transport server role.

Supporting Backups with Documentation

Performing trustworthy backups is a critical process in any Exchange Server environment. One of the simplest ways to ensure that your backups are done properly is to document your requirements and your processes.

A mechanism needs to be in place to track the success of backups and a process to follow if a backup fails. Sticking to this process and not conflicting with the set policies ensures that backups are valid and recoverable if a failure occurs.

Companies that are publicly traded follow a set of rules around documentation of processes and proof of following those processes. This is primarily dictated by Sarbanes-Oxley, or SOX. For privately held companies, although they are not legally required to follow SOX standards, they nonetheless serve as an excellent example of best practices around maintaining an IT environment and should be strongly considered.

Documenting Backup Policy and Procedures

When building your documentation around your backups, it is best to start with a policy that supports not only the SLAs for your Exchange Server environment, but one that also complies with any existing rules from your Information Security group or Regulatory Compliance group.

Management should review and approve your backup policies to ensure that they are in line with any established SLAs. Policies should include items such as the following:

- Frequency and type of backups
- Acceptable standards for offsite storage and retrieval
- Escalation path for failed backups
- Decision criteria for overrun jobs
- Clear statement of what is and isn't to be backed up
- Whether the backups are password protected
- Data retention periods

In this way, everyone knows what is and isn't covered by Exchange Server backups, and there are no surprises in the future. Having this policy documented is also helpful if you are required to pass any audits or verify regulatory compliance.

Maintaining Documentation on the Exchange Server Environment

Systems such as Exchange Server often outlast the employees who built them. This means that it's easy to lose track of exactly how systems are deployed, where various roles are located, and the specific needs of each participating system. For this reason, it is extremely important to maintain accurate documentation for the server configurations, the network, and the path of mail flow. In addition, you need to track the configuration of firewalls and switches that can potentially impact the overall Exchange Server environment if they were to fail and need to be replaced.

Server Configuration Documentation

Server documentation is essential for any environment regardless of size, number of servers, or disaster recovery budget. A server configuration document contains a server's name, network configuration information, hardware and driver information, disk and volume configuration, or information about the applications installed. This complete server configuration document contains all the necessary configuration information a qualified administrator needs if the server needs to be restored and the operating system cannot be restored efficiently. A server configuration document can also be used as a reference when server information needs to be collected.

The Server Build Document

A server build document contains step-by-step instructions on how to build a particular type of server for an organization. The details of this document should be tailored to the skill of the person intended to rebuild the server. For example, if this document were created for disaster recovery purposes, it might be detailed enough that anyone with basic computer skills could rebuild the server. This type of information can also be used to help information technology (IT) staff follow a particular server build process to ensure that when new servers are added to the network, they all meet company server standards.

Hardware Inventory

Documenting the hardware inventory of an entire network might not be necessary. If the entire network does need to be inventoried, and if the organization is large, the Microsoft System Center Configuration Manager can help automate the hardware inventory task. If the entire network does not need to be inventoried, hardware inventory can be collected for all the production and lab servers and networking hardware, including specifications such as serial numbers, amount of memory, disk space, processor speed, and operating system platform and version. By knowing all the hardware involved, the restore process becomes much simpler, especially in situations in which hardware needs to be replaced as part of the restoration.

Network Configurations

Network configuration documentation is essential when network outages occur. Current, accurate network configuration documentation and network diagrams can help simplify and isolate network troubleshooting when a failure occurs.

WAN Connection

WAN connectivity should be documented for enterprise networks that contain many sites to help IT staff understand the enterprise network topology. This document is helpful when a server is restored and data should be synchronized enterprisewide after the restore. Knowing the link performance between sites helps administrators understand how long an update made in site A will take to reach site B. This document should contain information about each WAN link, including circuit numbers, Internet service provider (ISP) contact names, ISP technical support phone numbers, and the network configuration on each end of the connection, and can be used to troubleshoot and isolate WAN connectivity issues.

A strong understanding of the network is also critical to the process of initially creating the backups. By understanding the implication of backups over the network or how bandwidth would be affected after replacing a failed database availability group replica, you can account for periods of time in which the environment might not have the normal level of redundancy that it was designed for and backups might potentially need to be altered to account for it.

For example, if an environment were using database availability groups to place replicas of mailbox data into two locations, administrators might feel that they were protected against system failures and combined with a 30-day deleted item retention period, they might only do traditional backups once a month. If a DAG replica failed and would take 2 days to reseed due to a total replacement of the failed replica, they would be at risk for those 2 days because only one copy of the mailbox databases would be available. During this period of time, administrators might alter their backup schedule to perform backups nightly until the additional replica was returned to service.

Router, Switch, and Firewall Configurations

Firewalls, routers, and, sometimes, switches can run proprietary operating systems with a configuration that is exclusive to the device. During a system recovery, certain gateway connections, configuration routing information, routing table data, and other information might need to be reset on the restored server. Information should be collected from these devices, including logon passwords and current configurations. When a configuration change is planned for any of these devices, the newly proposed configuration should be created using a text or graphical editor, but the change should be approved before it is made on the production device. A rollback plan should be created first to ensure that the device can be restored to the original state if the change does not deliver the desired results.

Updating Documentation

One of the most important, yet sometimes overlooked, areas around documentation is maintaining accuracy as changes are applied to server systems. Documentation is tedious, but outdated documentation can be worthless if changes have occurred to a server's software configuration since the document was created. For example, if a server configuration document were used to re-create a server from scratch but many changes were applied to the server after the document was created, the correct security patches might not be applied, applications might be configured incorrectly, or data restore attempts could be unsuccessful. Whenever a change will be made to a network device, printer, or server, documentation outlining the previous configuration, proposed changes, and rollback plans should be created before the change is approved and carried out on the production device. After the change is carried out and the device is functioning as needed, the documentation associated with that device or server should be updated.

Logging Daily Backup Results and Evaluation

When running regular backups of mission-critical systems, you need to monitor the process to ensure that backup jobs are running properly. You also need to ensure that the data backed up can actually be restored.

Tracking Success and Failure

Most third-party backup software packages have the capability to send a summary of the result of the backup job to the administrator. This is a critical function because failures or inconsistent results need to be immediately brought to the attention of the administrator who is responsible for backups.

The results of these nightly backups should be reviewed each day to ensure not only the success of the backup process, but also to sanity-check the results. For example, if your backup normally ran for 6 hours and filled up 800GB of space, you should be suspicious of a 16-hour job of the same size or a 1-hour job that backed up only 120GB of data. Because either of those results can show up as a successful run of the backup job, it is critical for an administrator to review the results.

If using a backup software package that doesn't send this level of information, you need to check the event logs each day on the Exchange Server 2013 Mailbox servers. The event log tracks any issues with the backup as the software in question must utilize the VSS application programming interface (API) to back up Exchange Server 2013. The old style legacy "streaming" backups are no longer supported in Exchange Server 2013.

Validating Your Backups

The benefit of backing up data to a remote location or media is the ability to recover the data at a later time. As such, you need to regularly validate that your backups are valid and can be successfully restored. It is recommended that you adopt a practice of randomly pulling backups and picking random databases to perform a restore to a nonproduction location. After the restore, verify that you can access the data successfully. This process helps ensure that your data can be restored if an emergency occurs.

There are many third-party utilities, such as NetApp's Single Mailbox Recovery Tool or Quest's Recovery Manager for Exchange Server, that enable an administrator to bypass the recovery storage group process and attach directly to an `.edb` file off disk or even directly off tape to recover individual mailbox items from a backup. This is a great way to test the restore process and to restore individual items without having to restore an entire database. Best of all, it doesn't require an Exchange server. That said, it is not a replacement for periodically practicing your disaster-recovery procedures.

NOTE

Exchange Server 2013 provides a restore process that only requires the mounting of a database, not the setup of an entire storage group. This process, known as the recovery database, simplifies the organization's ability to just mount a database and initiate a mailbox or mail items recovery straight from within the database.

Roles and Responsibilities

With any process that is likely to include more than one person, it is useful to clearly define the roles and responsibilities of those people. This ensures that the people involved know what is expected of them and they know who to go to in various situations.

Separation of Duties

A typical Exchange Server environment involves members from potentially many groups. For example, one group might be responsible for Exchange Server services and configuration, whereas another group might be tasked with management of Windows and security patches. Often, yet another group is responsible for performing backups of the systems. Each of these groups must be aware of what other groups are doing. For example, if the Windows group needs to install Windows patches on the Exchange servers, the backup group also needs to be aware of this because they might need to change the scheduling of the backup job. This type of interdependency must be taken into account when configuring the backup schedule.

Escalation and Notification

If a backup job fails, it is critical for the support staff to know what they are supposed to do and who they should contact. It is recommended to build a matrix of common issues and create an escalation path for various events. It is also quite useful to have those events automatically notify the responsible party. For example, the server monitoring group might be told that in the event of a backup failure, they should do the following:

- Contact the backup group to alert them of the failed job.
- Contact the Exchange Server group to alert them of the failed job.
- If neither group contacts you within 30 minutes, contact the IT manager.
- If the IT manager doesn't contact you within 60 minutes, contact the IT director.

By knowing who to call, it is easier to get a qualified party to look at the issue and potentially fix the issue in time to allow another backup job to be attempted before the backup window is expired.

Developing a Backup Strategy

Developing an effective backup strategy involves detailed planning around the logistics of backing up the necessary information or data via backup software, media type, and accurate documentation. To truly be effective, organizations should not limit a backup strategy by not considering the use of all available resources for recovery.

Along with planning and documentation, other aspects of a backup strategy include assigning specific tasks and responsibilities to individual IT staff members, considering the best person to be responsible for backing up a particular service or server and ensuring that documentation is accurate and current depending on his or her strengths and area of expertise.

What Is Important to Exchange Server Backups?

In general, the critical thing to capture in an Exchange Server backup is any unique data whose loss would impact users. This typically means that you need to back up the mailbox databases, public folder databases, and the log files that go with them. Files such as the operating system or the System State data are less important as that information can be easily recovered because it is stored in Active Directory (AD) or not needed for the mount and access to Exchange data. In the case of database availability groups, the backup of log files is less important because multiple copies of the databases and logs are in other locations that can take over if the primary replica fails. In these configurations, the primary purposes for the backups are to enable for long-term storage of data to protect against deletion and to truncate log files so that servers don't run out of space and shut down Exchange Server.

Creating Standard Backup Procedures

Creating a regular backup procedure helps ensure that the entire enterprise is backed up consistently and properly on a regular basis. When a regular procedure is created, the assigned staff members soon become accustomed to the procedure because they are given a guide that walks through each required step. If there is no documented procedure, certain items might be overlooked and not be backed up, which can be a major problem if a failure occurs. For example, a regular backup procedure for an Exchange Server 2013 server might back up the Exchange Server databases on the local drives every night, and perform a System State backup with Windows Server Backup Features once a month and whenever a hardware change is made to a server. These differences might be overlooked if no one is following regular change control and documented procedures.

TIP

It is a best practice to add documentation updates into standard server change control processes. This ensures that any modifications to server configurations also get added into server build documents.

Protecting Data If a System Failure Occurs

Server failures are the primary concern most organizations plan for because a complete system failure creates the most impact and, ultimately, a scenario in which data needs to be restored from backup tape. Server hardware failures include failed motherboards, processors, memory, network interface cards, disk controllers, power supplies, and, of course, hard disks. Each of these failures can be minimized through the implementation of RAID-configured hard disk drives, error-correcting memory, redundant power supplies, or redundant controller adapters. In a catastrophic system failure, however, it is likely that the entire data backup would need to be restored to a new system or repaired server.

Because data is read and written to hard drives on a constant basis, hard drives are frequently singled out as the most possible cause of a server hardware failure. To address this, Windows Server supports hot-swappable hard drives and RAID storage systems, enabling for the replacement of the drive without server downtime. However, this is only if the server chassis and disk controllers support such a change. Windows Server supports two types of disks: Basic disks, which provide backward compatibility, and Dynamic disks, which enable software-level disk arrays to be configured without a separate disk controller. Both Basic and Dynamic disks, when used as data disks, can be moved to other servers easily. This provides data or disk capacity elsewhere if a system hardware failure occurs and the data on these disks needs to be made available as soon as possible.

NOTE

If hardware-level RAID is configured, the controller card configuration should be backed up using a utility available through the vendor.

With most array controllers today, dynamic reading of the disk configuration can be done if the disks are placed into a new system using the same disk order. If this is not supported, the controller can be moved to the new systems, or the configuration might need to be re-created from scratch to complete a successful disk move to a new machine.

This process should always be tested, verified, and documented in a lab environment before being considered as a valid recovery option.

To protect against a system failure, organizations need to have a full image backup that can then be restored in its entirety to a new or repaired server system. This also requires completing and documenting these steps in advance to ensure that it can be completed and administrators understand the steps involved.

Protecting Data If a Database Corruption Occurs

Data recovery also is needed if a database corruption occurs in Exchange Server. Unlike a catastrophic system failure, which can be restored from the last tape backup, data corruption creates a more challenging situation for information recovery. If data is corrupt on the server system, a restore from the last backup might also contain corrupt information in its database, so a data restore needs to predate the point of corruption. This typically requires the capability to restore the database from an older full backup tape and then recover incremental data since the clean database restoral.

Providing the Ability to Restore a Message, Folder, or Mailbox

In other situations, an organization might need to recover a single message, folder, or mailbox rather than a full database. With most full backups of an Exchange server, the restore process requires a full restore of all messages, folders, and mailboxes. If an administrator needs to work with only a full image backup, typically a full restore must be performed on a spare server and information extracted from the full restore as necessary.

If message, folder, or mailbox recovery is required on a regular basis, the organization might elect to back up information in a format or process that provides an easier method of information recovery. This might involve the purchase and use of a third-party tape backup system, or a combination of various utilities available in Exchange Server 2013 to restore individual sets of information.

Assigning Tasks and Designating Team Members

Each particular server or network device in the enterprise has specific requirements for backing up and creating documentation around hardware and the service it provides. To make sure that a critical system is backed up properly, IT staff should designate a single individual to monitor that device and ensure the backup is completed and documentation is accurate and current at all times. Assigning a secondary staff member who has the same set of skills to act as a backup if the primary staff member is unavailable is a wise decision, to ensure that there is no point of failure among IT staff performing these tasks.

Assigning only primary and secondary resources to specific devices or services helps improve the overall security and reliability of the device and services provided to network users. By limiting who can back up and restore data—and even who can manage servers and devices—to just the primary and secondary qualified staff members, the organization can be assured that only competent, trained individuals work on systems they are assigned to manage. Even though the backup and restore responsibilities lie with the primary and secondary resources, the backup and recovery plans should still be documented and available to the remaining IT staff for additional training and a final means of support if needed.

Selecting the Best Devices for Your Backup

Each device used on any network could have specific backup requirements. As mentioned earlier, each assigned IT staff member should also be responsible for researching and learning the backup and recovery requirements of each device to ensure that all backups have everything that is necessary to also recover from a device failure.

As a rule of thumb for network devices, the device configuration should be backed up whenever possible—using the device manufacturer's configuration software whenever possible or just by documenting the configuration for use as a reference should a device require reconfiguration.

TIP

It is also a best practice to evaluate the hardware used in your environment to determine which areas might be the most likely points of failure. Having spare devices can reduce the overall downtime in case of a failure. When dealing with Exchange Server 2013 considerations, these spare hardware devices can be pieces such as hard drives to support a failed drive in a RAID configuration.

Understanding How Devices Affect Backups

Depending on how a given environment is architected, there might be several different options on how it will be backed up. Administrators lucky enough to have network attached storage (NAS) or storage area networks (SANs) for their Exchange Server 2013 servers might have significantly faster options for performing backups than administrators who use direct attached storage (DAS). Many times, the NAS or SAN devices can perform local snapshots, or the SAN might be backed up by a tape device that is plugged directly into the Fibre Channel fabric. This has great advantages when compared with backing up an Exchange Server 2013 server over the network. For example, Gigabit Ethernet enables 1Gb/sec of throughput. Fibre Channel not only offers speeds of 4Gb/sec to 8Gb/sec but also uses a more efficient protocol.

One way to drastically speed up backups performed is to use a faster media for the final destination. Although AIT and LTO tape technologies are very fast, they still can't compare to an array of hard drives for the destination. Technologies such as System Center Data Protection Manager can take regular snapshots of Exchange Server 2013 and store them on disks. Longer-term backups are made from the disk images to tape. Because this transfer from disk to tape happens on the backup server, it can be done during the day without impacting end users or interfering with the regular backups. Technologies exist for most backup software in the form of virtual tape libraries that are actually files within a set of disks that can enable you to retain the normal methodologies of traditional tape backup while taking advantage of the speed and size of modern hard drives to drastically shrink the backup window on network attached backups.

Determining Backup Speeds and Times

The time needed to perform a backup of Exchange Server is influenced mostly by the speed of the backup device. Although vendors quote values for MB per minute that their device can back up, this isn't always an accurate value when backing up an Exchange Server 2013 system. It is always recommended to perform test backups of Exchange servers to determine the speed at which they can be backed up. By knowing how long jobs take, an administrator can better select the backup window in which the backups occur. As Exchange servers grow in terms of the storage used by mail data, the backups take longer to occur. Pay careful attention to the network utilization and to the backup device utilization so that you can watch for bottlenecks that cause backup jobs to take too long.

TIP

Consider backing up Exchange Server 2013 to a backup server that uses disk media for the backup. This is typically the fastest media that you can utilize for "over the network" backups. Then take the locally stored backup and back that up to tape. Because you are backing up "cold" data, there is no concern about performing the backup during the day. This allows you to keep your backup window relatively short. The side benefit is that if you ever experience a failure that requires you to restore from the backups, you'll be doing a disk-to-disk restore, which is much faster than a tape-to-disk restore.

Validating the Backup Strategy in a Test Lab

Regardless of what methodology you choose for backups of your Exchange Server 2013 environment, it is critical to test the processes in a lab environment. The goal of this validation is not only to prove that data can be backed up and restored, but also to refine and document the exact steps used. It is much easier to figure out how to perform a restore in the lab than it is in production when hundreds or thousands of mailbox users are down. The goal of a production restore is to follow accurate, validated instructions and not have to figure out what you need to do on the fly.

What to Back Up on Exchange Servers

With the various roles available on Exchange servers, the process of backing them up is no longer a one-size-fits-all proposition. Different Exchange Server 2013 roles have different needs and different options on what to back up and how to back it up. This section highlights the needs of the various Exchange Server roles.

What to Back Up on Mailbox Servers

When planning backups for an Exchange server, you must first determine the critical data that is stored on that particular system. For a Mailbox server, the critical data present is as follows:

- Exchange database files—mailboxes
- Exchange database files—public folders
- Exchange transaction log files
- Content indexing information
- Free/busy information
- Offline address book

Of these items, the content index information, the free/busy information, and the offline address book can all be regenerated so that they do not need to be backed up. This leaves the databases and the transaction logs. If you use a certified Exchange Server 2013–compatible backup software product, you should back up the databases and the log files as logical devices.

If you should ever need to back up the databases or log files at a flat-file level, you must first stop all the Exchange Server services. These files can be found by running the Exchange Management Shell and typing the following:

```
Get-mailboxdatabase -server <server_name> | fl name,edbfilepath,logfolderpath
```

What to Back Up for Hub Transport Services

When planning for backups of Hub Transport services information, the critical data includes the following:

- Message tracking logs
- Protocol logs

The Hub Transport services logs are not critical for a restore of an Exchange Server 2013 environment; however, these logs might be useful for troubleshooting or for forensics and can be backed up at a file level. The logs are located in various locations identified in the following cmdlet:

```
Get-TransportService -Identity SERVERNAME | fl *logs*
```

What to Back Up on Client Access Servers

Generally speaking, there is no need to back up the Client Access server. This is because the CAS merely acts as a pass-through to get to Exchange Server data. This was also the case in previous versions of Exchange Server. Typically, multiple CAS servers are deployed for redundancy, so rapid restoration is rarely needed. Typically, if a CAS server fails, it would be rebuilt from scratch and would not need any data restored to it.

If there is only a single CAS server in the environment, it might be worthwhile to back up the POP/IMAP configuration stored in `\ClientAccess\PopImap`. Optionally, you can just document the Post Office Protocol (POP) and Internet Message Access Protocol (IMAP) settings and reset them if a CAS were rebuilt.

If your environment requires auditing of client or mobile device access to Exchange Server 2013, it might be of value to back up the IIS logs because they track this information.

On a related note, CASs can generate a large volume of IIS logs. Typically, these log files are forgotten about until they fill the drive they are on and cause an outage. Typically CASs are built with a single drive and the IIS log files default is stored on the C: drive. If the C: drive fills up, the Exchange Server services stop and stop serving clients. These log files can be pruned with a simple batch file that should be scheduled to run nightly:

```
FORFILES -p c:\inetpub\logs\logfiles\w3svc1 -s -m*.log -d -30 -c "CMD /C del @FILE"

-p = path
-s = include subdirs
```

```
-m = match filetype
-d = age in days (can also be set as an absolute date ie DDMMYYYY)
-c = command to execute
```

What to Back Up on Edge Transport Servers

When backing up the Edge Transport server, the unique protocol log data should be captured.

To back up the protocol logs on Edge Transport servers, it is the same as backing up the protocol logs of the Hub Transport services systems, which is backing up the logs, which, unless they were moved after installation, are located below the directory in which the Exchange Server code was installed in `\Transportroles\logs` (i.e., `c:\Program Files\Microsoft\Exchange Server\V15\TransportRoles\Logs\`).

What to Back Up for Unified Messaging Services

When planning for backups of the Unified Messaging services on a Mailbox server, the critical data located in the "Custom Audio Prompts" should be included in the backup.

This information is stored under the Exchange Server file structure in `\UnifiedMessaging\Prompts` (i.e., `c:\Program Files\Microsoft\Exchange Server\V15\UnifiedMessaging\Prompts\`) and is needed only on the system identified as the prompt publishing server. Not unlike a CAS server, its configuration is stored in Active Directory, and it acts as a pass-through to the `.wav` files stored in the users' mailboxes.

Directory Server Data

As was the case with the previous version of Exchange Server, Exchange Server 2013 stores the vast majority of its configuration information in Active Directory. This allows Exchange Server 2013 servers to easily read the configurations of other systems in the environment and provides an easy mechanism to restore the configuration of a rebuilt server. For this reason, it is critical to ensure that at least one domain controller in the root of the forest is backed up regularly.

To back up a Windows domain controller using Windows Backup, when logged in to a domain controller (in the following example from a Windows Server 2008 R2 domain controller), follow these steps:

1. Make sure the Windows Backup features have been installed (Server Manager, Features, Windows Server Backup Features).
2. Click Start, Program Files, Administrative Tools, Windows Server Backup.
3. Choose Action, Backup Once.
4. Choose Different Options, and then click Next.
5. Choose Custom, and then click Next.

6. Click Add Items, make sure your C: volume is selected and System State is selected, similar to what is shown in Figure 16.1, click OK, and then click Next.

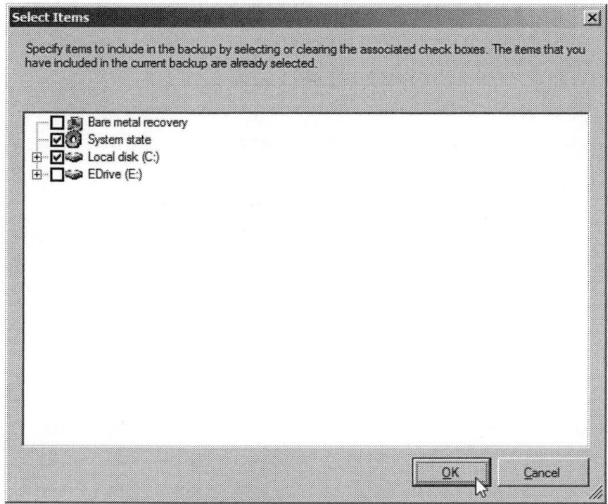

FIGURE 16.1 Choosing items for backup in Windows Server Backup.

7. Choose a remote shared folder or a local drive other than the C: that you are backing up from, and then click Next.
8. Choose the drive or path you want to save to. Typically also choose Do Not Inherit so that you can choose the authorized user(s) who can access the backup. Click Next.
9. Click Backup to begin.

Common Settings and Configuration Data

Be aware of any additional dependencies that would need to be backed up to fully restore the Exchange Server environment. This can include things such as the following:

- SSL certificates
- S/MIME certificates
- IIS metabase
- Custom Outlook Web Access pages
- Third-party applications

The Need for Backups with Database Availability Groups

Exchange Server 2010 introduced a new concept in backups for the databases due to the inclusion of database availability groups, or DAGs, which have continued to be included in Exchange Server 2013. This technology has drastically changed strategies for backup. DAGs are more thoroughly covered in Chapter 8. In short, a DAG is a real-time replica of a mailbox database that is replicated to up to 15 other Mailbox servers. As a result, if the master copy of a DAG goes offline, the next highest priority copy of the mailbox database becomes the master copy, and the users hosted on that mailbox database continue to function normally. Rather than restoring a failed DAG, you can simply rebuild the DAG replica and let the database replicate to it. This is similar to the situation you have with domain controllers in which the data replication effectively becomes a distributed backup. Not unlike in the case of domain controllers, the purpose of the backup shifts from being a tool for recovery to a tool for historic storage.

By maintaining a relatively long deleted item retention period, you can protect against the need to restore data from tape. Because up to 16 copies of a mailbox database are in a DAG, it is statistically unlikely that all 16 copies would fail simultaneously. This leaves relatively few reasons to need to perform backups:

- Reseeding
- Long-term storage for eDiscovery
- Truncating log files

Exchange Server 2010 introduced the ability to perform an incremental reseeding of a database that has gotten too far out of sync with the master copy. In earlier versions of Exchange Server, a database had to be copied in its entirety if it became too far out of sync. In Exchange Server 2013, only the deltas of the database need to be copied before normal log shipping can resume. Although this is a noticeable improvement, it does not help in a situation in which the delta is the entire database. Imagine a situation in which a new DAG replica is built and it asks to replicate copies of 10 different 100-GB databases. The delta in this situation is 1TB. This could take a long time to replicate over a WAN connection and would eat up a lot of bandwidth. In this situation, preseeding the database replicas via a backup/restore process would take a huge strain off the network and would potentially occur in a much shorter time frame. Something as simple as backing up the databases to an external hard drive and shipping the hard drive to the remote location would likely be accomplished in a single day whereas for the same amount of data to replicate over the WAN in 24 hours, you would need just under 100Mbps/sec of dedicated bandwidth.

Another situation involving DAG in which you would still need regular backups would be in the case of needing to store mail data for a period of time longer than what would be maintained in the deleted item retention period. This might be to protect against an accidental deletion of items or more commonly it might be to maintain a source of data for legal discovery. It is not unusual for a legal department to request all mailbox data for a set of users over a period of several months. If you weren't maintaining long-term backups, there would be no ability to recovery messages that had been deleted by the users when the deleted item retention period had been exceeded.

The last situation that is not obviated by the use of DAGs as a distributed backup is the need to truncate log files. Because you would not likely restore a DAG member, if you were comfortable that they had enough replicas of a mailbox database, the need to truncate log files could be addressed by enabling circular logging.

Backing Up Windows Server and Exchange Server 2013

As previously mentioned, the use of DAGs in Exchange Server 2013 mostly eliminates the need to perform backups of the Exchange servers because the data is already replicated to multiple locations. The individual identity of the Mailbox and Client Access servers becomes much less important because there is very little "unique" data stored on each server. This said, it is necessary to realize that not all environments will be large enough to justify the use of DAGs to provide protection against system failures. Smaller deployments will still need to be backed up to allow for recovery of failed systems.

The Windows Server operating system and the Exchange Server 2013 messaging system contain several features to enhance operating system stability, provide data and service redundancy, and deliver feature-rich client services. Windows Server continues to provide additional services such as VSS, which works to enhance backup capabilities when organizations use third-party backup products. Additional information about working with VSS is covered in the "Volume Shadow Copy Service and Exchange Server 2013" section later in this chapter.

Though other options have been mentioned, this section discusses ways to back up a Windows Server system, including key components of Exchange Server 2013.

By preparing for a complete server failure and using the information in this section, an organization is more likely to successfully recover from a failed server, restoring it to its previous state.

Volume Shadow Copy Service and Exchange Server 2013

Before discussing the backup process using Windows Server Backup, it is important for Exchange Server administrators to understand what Windows Volume Show Copy Service is used for. To back up Exchange Server 2013, the backup solution (like Windows Server Backup that comes with Windows) needs to support VSS because that is required to be able to back up Exchange Server 2013.

The Volume Shadow Copy Service is a server service in Windows Server and is available as part of the operating system. Alone, VSS is a service, but when combined with backup applications, VSS become a vital part of every organization's backup strategy and recovery plan.

What Role VSS Plays in Backup

Microsoft created VSS to provide application platforms and infrastructures to enhance functionality when working with Microsoft services such as Exchange Server 2013. The key to VSS is its capability to act as a go-between or coordinator for service providers (backup applications) and service writers (Exchange Server 2013 databases).

It is important to know that VSS does not function alone; VSS is designed to provide application developers a platform in which to build applications to create Exchange Server snapshots.

Shadow Copies and Snapshots

This capability enabled third-party backup applications to create shadow copies or mirrors of the Exchange Server database and enabled administrators to design more dynamic backup strategies and reduce the overall cost of restoring servers. Using Shadow Copies (Mirror Copies) and Snapshots (Point in Time Mirror Copies), daily backups can be much smaller and for vital messaging systems, snapshots can be taken several times a day.

VSS Requirements and Prerequisites

When looking at third-party products as an option for backups with VSS technology, you must evaluate the products to ensure that they are compatible with VSS. Compatibility is based on three specific areas:

- Backups of the Exchange Server 2013 database, logs, and checkpoint files must be completed by the application writer (Exchange Server 2013).
- The application must complete a full validation of the backup.
- When restoring data in Exchange Server, this must also be completed by the application writer (Exchange Server 2013).

VSS and third-party applications also require hardware compatibility. This is especially true when backing up to disk subsystems, such as NAS and SAN solutions. To verify this information, review the application vendor support pages and verify that the application and hardware meet all requirements.

TIP

For more information regarding Volume Shadow Copy Service, Microsoft published several articles over the years on the Microsoft web page. The most current content is at http://msdn.microsoft.com/en-us/library/exchange/aa579280(v=exchg.150).aspx.

Backing Up Specific Windows Services

Most Windows Server services that contain a database or local files are backed up with the System State but also provide alternate backup and restore options. Because the system restore from Windows Server Backup is usually an all-or-nothing proposition, except when it comes to cluster nodes and domain controllers, restoring an entire system might deliver undesired results if only a specific service database restore is required. This section outlines services that either have separate backup/restore utilities or require special attention to ensure a successful backup.

Disk Configuration (Software RAID Sets)

Disk is not a service but should be backed up to ensure that proper partition assignments can be restored. When Dynamic disks are used to create complex volumes—such as mirrored, striped, spanned, or RAID-5 volumes—the disk configuration should be saved. This way, if the operating system is corrupt and needs to be rebuilt from scratch, the complex volumes need to have only their configuration restored, which could greatly reduce the recovery time. Only a full system backup can back up disk and volume configuration.

Certificate Services

Installing Certificate Services creates a certificate authority (CA) on the Windows Server system. The CA is used to manage and allocate certificates to users, servers, and workstations when files, folders, email, or network communication needs to be secured and encrypted. In many cases, the CA is a completely separate secured CA server; however, many organizations use their Exchange server as a CA server. This might be because of a limited number of servers with several different roles and services installed on a single server, or because the organization wants to use Secure Sockets Layer (SSL) and forms-based authentication (FBA) for secured Outlook Web Access and to support encrypted connections from Outlook 2007 or higher to the Client Access servers, so they install Certificate Services on an Exchange server. Whatever the case, the CA needs to be backed up whether on the Exchange server or on any other server; if the CA server crashes and needs to be restored, it can be restored so that users can continue to access the system after recovery.

CAUTION

For security purposes, it is highly recommended that Certificate Services be enabled on a server other than the Exchange server. Definitely do not have the CA services on an Outlook Web Access server that is exposed to the Internet. The integrity of certificate-authenticated access depends on ensuring that certificates are issued only by a trusted authority. Any compromise to the CA server invalidates an organization's capability to secure its communications.

When the CA allocates a certificate to a machine or user, that information is recorded in the certificate database on the local drive of the CA. If this database is corrupted or deleted, all certificates allocated from this server become invalid or unusable. To avoid this problem, the certificates and Certificate Services database should be backed up frequently. Even if certificates are rarely allocated to new users or machines, backups should still be performed regularly.

Certificate Services can be backed up in three ways: backing up the CA server's System State, using the CA Microsoft Management Console (MMC) snap-in, or using the command-line utility `Certutil.exe`. Backing up Certificate Services by backing up the System State is the preferred method because it can be easily automated and scheduled. But using the graphic console or command-line utility adds the benefit of restoring Certificate Services to a previous state without restoring the entire server System State or taking down the entire server for the restore.

To create a backup of the CA using the graphic console, follow these steps:

1. Log on to the CA server using an account with local Administrator rights.
2. Open Windows Explorer and create a folder named `CaBackup` on the C: drive.
3. Select Start, Administrative Tools, Certification Authority.
4. Expand the Certificate Authority server, and select the correct CA.
5. Select Action, All Tasks, Back Up CA.
6. When the Backup Wizard launches, click Next.
7. On the Items to Back Up page, check the Private Key and CA Certificate check box and the Certificate Database and Certificate Database Log check box.
8. Specify the location to store the CA backup files. Use the folder created in the beginning of this process. The CA Backup screen would look similar to what is shown in Figure 16.2. Click Next to continue.

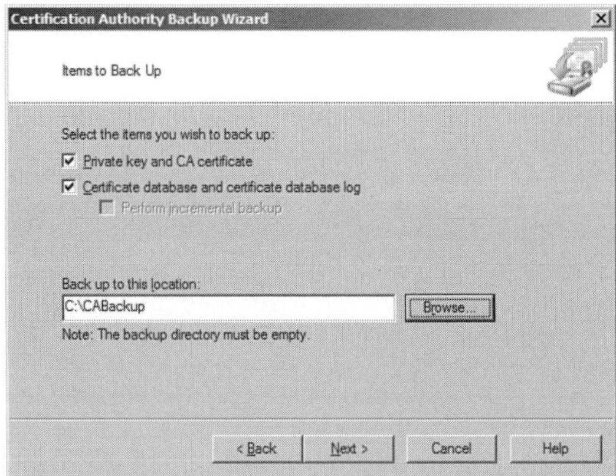

FIGURE 16.2 Backing up the Certification Authority server.

9. When the CA certificate and private key are backed up, this data file must be protected with a password. Enter a password for this file, confirm it, and click Next to continue.

NOTE

To restore the CA private key and CA certificate, you must use the password entered in step 9. Store this password in a safe place, possibly with the master account list.

10. Click Finish to create the CA backup.

Internet Information Services (IIS)

Internet Information Services (IIS) is the Windows Server web and FTP services that support websites like OWA. It is included on every version of the Windows Server platform. IIS stores configuration information for web and FTP site configurations and security, placing the information into the IIS metabase. The IIS backup methodology has changed quite a bit from IIS 6.0 that was built in to Windows Server 2003.

In the current versions of IIS, all the configuration data is stored in `%windir%/system32/inetsrv/config`. If you have a backup of that directory, the configuration can be restored by simply returning the files to this location. A more automated process can be performed by utilizing the `appcmd.exe` function.

To back up an IIS configuration, simply run `C:\Windows\System32\inetsrv\appcmd.exe add backup "IIS Backup"`.

To restore an IIS configuration, simply run `C:\Windows\System32\inetsrv\appcmd.exe restore backup "IIS Backup"`.

By creating and scheduling a batch file to perform the backup, you can take regular snapshots of the IIS configuration. This can be useful to perform right before making a change to IIS settings on a Client Access server so that if the changes cause any problems, the configuration can be quickly restored.

Backing Up Exchange Server 2013 with Windows Server Backup

Windows Server Backup is a good simple backup solution for backing up an Exchange Server 2013 system. With Exchange Server 2013, Microsoft includes a specific VSS plug-in that is automatically installed on every Exchange Server 2013 system when Exchange is installed on the system. The plug-in shows up in the Windows Services as Microsoft Exchange Server Extension for Windows Server Backup. This service is set by default as Manual and is automatically started when the Windows Server Backup begins backing up an Exchange Server.

The backup process is pretty straightforward in Exchange Server 2013 by following these steps on an Exchange server that has the Windows Server Backup Features installed:

1. Click Start, All Programs, Administrative Tools, Windows Server Backup.
2. In the right pane, click Backup Schedule.
3. When the wizard launches, click Next.

4. When prompted to select your backup configuration, choose Custom and click Next.
5. Select the volumes you want to back up and click Next.
6. Choose the time at which you'd like the backups to run and click Next.
7. Select the disk on which you want to store the backup. Click Next.
8. View the label of the destination disk and click Next.
9. Confirm the backup settings and click Finish. The backup begins and the Backup Progress is tracked, similar to what is shown in Figure 16.3. The Backup Progress runs until the backup is complete.

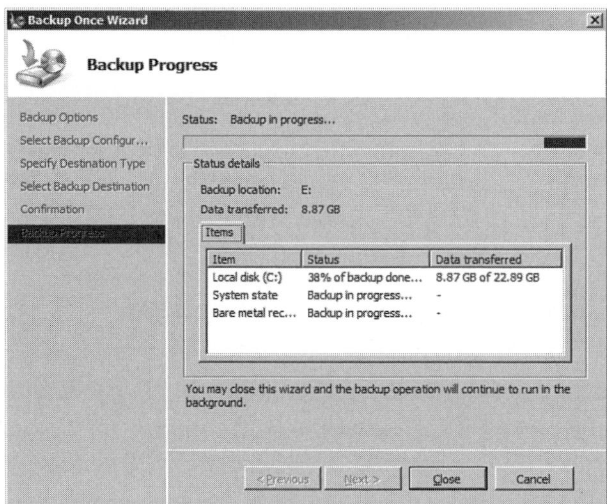

FIGURE 16.3 Backup Progress of an Exchange Server 2013 server.

Recovering Exchange Server Application and Exchange Server Data

To recover an Exchange server, there are several different ways of rebuilding the core Exchange server and restoring the Exchange Server data. In early releases of Exchange (i.e., Exchange Server 2003 and earlier), the restoration of Exchange Server databases had to be done to a server with the exact same server name as the original server from which the databases were backed up. Fortunately for Exchange Server 2013, there is a process that allows a database to be restored to a temporary storage location and *any* Exchange Server 2013 server can mount the database as a "recovery database" for an Exchange administrator to access the database content and recover a mailbox or even specific mail messages.

Recovering an Exchange Database Using Windows Server Backup

If an Exchange Server 2013 server was backed up using Windows Server Backup, the data from the backup can be restored, whether an entire Exchange server, specific Exchange database files and logs, configuration files for IIS, logs files, or the like. Windows Server Backup can be used to not only restore files to the original server, but to also restore data to any existing server in any target folder.

Because Exchange Server 2013 has the ability to mount a database to any Exchange Server 2013 server using the recovery database process, a database can be restored to an existing server anywhere that the server can access the file and the Exchange Server 2013 server can mount the database.

The first step is to restore the database from Windows Server Backup. The process is as follows:

1. Log on to the server using an account that has at least the privileges to restore files and folders. Backup Operators and local Administrators groups have this right, by default.
2. Click Start, All Programs, Administrative Tools, Windows Server Backup.
3. In the right pane, click Recover.
4. Choose the server for which to recover files and click Next.
5. Select the backup from which you want to recover and click Next.
6. When prompted to select a recovery type, choose Applications and click Next.
7. Select Exchange as your application and click Next.
8. When prompted to specify recovery options, choose to recover to another location. Click Browse to pick a location for the restored files. The screen will look similar to what is shown in Figure 16.4. Click Next.
9. Review the restore information and click Recover.
10. When the restore is completed, click Close.

To recover items from the restored database, you need to create a recovery database. The following are a couple of key points about the recovery database process in Exchange Server 2013:

- The source database used for recovering information must be an Exchange Server 2013 database; earlier versions of Exchange EDBs are not supported.
- The target database needs to be in the same Active Directory forest as the database being mounted as the recovery database.

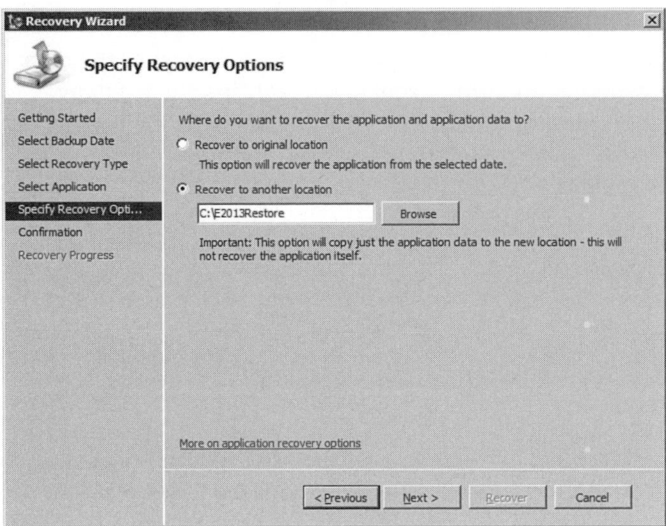

FIGURE 16.4 Preparing to restore Exchange databases to a folder.

The recovery database process uses the Exchange Management Shell for the recovery process. The process is as follows:

1. Launch the Exchange Management Shell (EMS) on the server that you will be creating the Exchange recovery database.
2. Run the command: `New-MailboxDatabase -Recovery -Name` *`{name of the DB you want to create}`* `-Server` *`{name of the server you want to create the DB on}`* `-EDBFilePath "directory and filename of the EDB you restored from backup" -LogFolderPath "directory where the backup has been restored to"`. So it'll look like `New-MailboxDatabase -Recovery -Name RDB1 -Server E2013 -EDBFilePath "c:\RestoredDirectory\RestoredDB.edb" -LogFolderPath "c:\RestoredDirectory"`. In my example, it will look like what is shown in Figure 16.5.

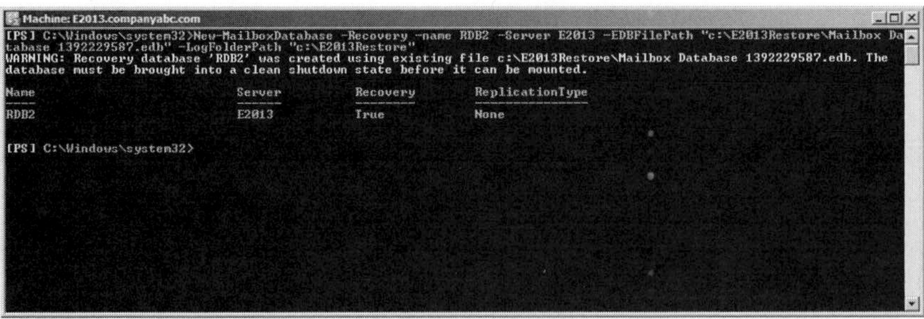

FIGURE 16.5 Creating a recovery database in Exchange Server 2013.

Once the recovery database has been created and database restored to a database, the next step is to make sure the recovered database is in a clean shutdown state so that it can successfully be mounted on the Exchange server. The command to bring the database to a clean state is the `ESEUtil /R` command. Do the following:

1. Run `cmd.exe` to launch a CMD prompt on the Exchange server that you just created the recovery database (Start, Run, **`CMD.exe`**).
2. Navigate to the directory where your Exchange recovery database has been created, such as in my previous example, `c:\e2013restore`.
3. Look for the file that starts with `e`, has 2 additional numbers following, and ends in `.log` in that directory, it'll typically be `e00.log`, or `e01.log`, or `e02.log`.
4. Run `eseutil /r E??`, where `E??` is either `e00`, `e01`, `e02`, and so on, as found in the previous step, so `eseutil /r e00`.

NOTE

If you get an error that an "Outstanding database attachment has been detected," you can run a `/i` (i as in indio) at the end of the `ESE` command, so `eseutil /r e00 /i` in the preceding example.

5. With the database restored as a recovery database and database integrity updated, you can now mount the recovery database using the EMS command `mount-database {databasename}`, so in the preceding example, `mount-database RDB2`.

NOTE

If your database still doesn't mount, frequently with an error "Active Manager operation failed," you can force a database repair and cleanup by running the `ESE` command `eseutil /p`. This is done by going into your directory where your recovery EDB is stored and run the DOS command `eseutil /p "DB file name"`, so in the example, it is `eseutil /p "RestoredDB.edb"`.

With the database successfully mounted, you can now restore data from the recovery database into a user's mailbox or archive. The recovery process is as follows:

1. Launch the EMS on an Exchange server in your environment.
2. To recover an entire user's mailbox, run the command: `New-MailboxRestoreRequest -SourceDatabase {DB} -SourceStoreMailbox "mailboxname" -TargetMailbox user@domain`. This would look something like: `New-MailboxRestoreRequest -SourceDatabase RDB2 -SourceStoreMailbox "Rand Morimoto" -TargetMailbox rand@companyabc.com`.

TIP

You can use the `Get-MailboxStatistics -Database DatabaseName` cmdlet to list the mailboxes present in the recovered database.

3. To recover a user's mailbox to an online archive, add `-TargetIsArchive` at the end, so it would look something like: `New-MailboxRestoreRequest -SourceDatabase RDB2 -SourceStoreMailbox "Rand Morimoto" -TargetMailbox rand@companyabc.com -TargetIsArchive`.
4. To recover a user's mailbox to a different mailbox, such as recovering a mailbox to search or query information, use the `-AllowLegacyDNMismatch` at the end, so it would look something like: `New-MailboxRestoreRequest -SourceDatabase RDB2 -SourceStoreMailbox "Rand Morimoto" -TargetMailbox randrestorebox@companyabc.com -AllowLegacyDNMismatch`. When this function is used, create the user and mailbox in the Exchange Administration Center first and logon in the mailbox first so that the mailbox is created in the database. Then run the mailbox restore request into this mailbox. After the mailbox restore process has been completed, you can log on as the restore user you created and access this mailbox.

NOTE

The `New-MailboxRestoreRequest` has additional switch commands that address message merging to restore and merge messages to a mailbox, or skip merging; commands that include and exclude folders; allow large items; and the like. The various switch command options can be viewed in EMS by running `help New-MailboxRestoreRequest -Full`.

Protecting Exchange Servers with System Center 2012 Data Protection Manager

Although the Windows Server Backup utility has the ability of simply backing up and recovering Exchange Server 2013 databases, organizations that have System Center 2012 implemented in the environment for things like Configuration Manager (patching and operating system deployment) and Operations Manager (for monitoring and alerting) could consider implementing the Data Protection Manager component that comes with the System Center 2012 suite. System Center 2012 Data Protection Manager, or DPM, uses the VSS backup process to back up and take incremental snapshots of Exchange; however, DPM has a number of functions that greatly enhance the backup and restore capabilities not included in Windows Server Backup.

In addition, DPM can be used to protect Exchange Server 2003 through 2013 systems from a single console as well as back up multiple Exchange servers simultaneously, so it is a good overall tool for backing up and recovering Exchange data. By using DPM, you can utilize its lossless recovery abilities to ensure that recoverable data includes not only last night's backup, but also the most recent transactions. To do this, a DPM protection agent performs a full backup (typically once a day) and uses the resulting VSS snapshot to identify what data has changed. Then, the agent synchronizes all of the changed blocks to the DPM server. Next, to ensure that administrators can recover Exchange data using DPM up to the latest recovery point (as often as 15 minutes), the protection agent performs an incremental VSS snapshot to copy committed sequential transaction logs to the DPM server. Lastly, during a recovery operation, DPM also has the ability to play back any other surviving Exchange transaction logs, thus ensuring as little data is lost as possible.

In addition to DPM's lossless abilities, its feature set also tackles the need to conduct single mailbox restores. In the past, if an individual mailbox had to be restored, either the entire database had to be restored, or administrators had to use third-party solutions. With DPM, administrators can select an individual mailbox and restore it to a recovery database (or recovery storage group depending on the version of Exchange Server being protected) and then use native Exchange tools to move the mailbox data back to a production database. To better illustrate DPM's ability to granularly recover Exchange data, a matrix of allowed data sources and the data that can be recovered is shown in Table 16.1.

TABLE 16.1 Exchange Server Data Sources and Recoverable Data

Exchange Server Version	Allowed Data Sources	Recoverable Data
Exchange Server 2003 Service Pack 2 (SP2)	Storage group	Storage group Database
Exchange Server 2007		Mailbox
Exchange Server 2010	DAG/database Database	Database Mailbox
Exchange Server 2013	DAG/database Database	Database Mailbox

How to Protect Exchange Databases

The steps used to protect Exchange Server 2013 databases using DPM are almost identical regardless of whether you are trying to only protect databases on a standalone Mailbox server or an entire DAG. For the purposes of this example, the following steps describe how to protect a DAG:

1. While logged on to the DPM server as a domain user account that is a member of the local Administrators group, open the DPM 2012 Administrator Console.
2. Next, ensure that all members of the DAG have the protection agent installed and the agent is reachable with a normal status.

NOTE

With DPM 2012, you can split the protection of DAG nodes between DPM servers. In other words, within a DAG that has five nodes, you can have one DPM server protect two nodes, and then have the other DPM server protect the other three nodes. However, for the purposes of these steps, all the nodes of the DAG are being protected by a single DPM server.

3. Now, click Protection on the navigation bar, and then click Create Protection Group in the actions pane.
4. Once the Create New Protection Group Wizard has started, click past the Welcome page, select the Servers Protection Group Type option, and then click Next.
5. On the Select Group Members page, use the interface to add the database copies that you want to protect into the protection group, as shown in Figure 16.6.

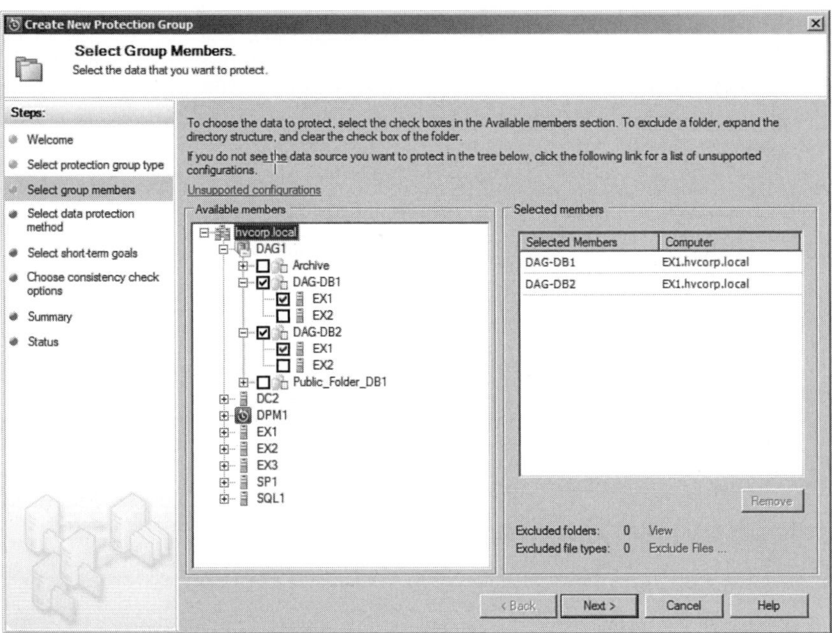

FIGURE 16.6 Adding database copies.

NOTE

In this example, you should notice that each of the two Mailbox servers that are part of the DAG named DAG1 are hosting a copy of the databases DAG1-DB1 and DAG1-DB2. However, only one copy of each database is being added into the protection group. Technically, this is all you need because individual databases in Exchange Server 2013 are not tied to a particular Exchange server. Therefore, you can recover a database by using backups from different database copies on different servers in the same DAG. Or, you can also add additional copies of the database into the protection group. Ultimately, the choice is yours as to how many protected copies you want of the same database and associated log files.

6. Once you have finished selecting the desired database copies, click Next.

7. On the Select Data Protection Method page, type a new name for the protection group in the Protection Group Name box, choose the desired protection methods, and then click Next.

8. On the Specify Exchange Protection Options page, choose if you want DPM to run the Exchange Server Database Utilities (`Eseutil.exe`) tool to check the integrity for both a database and its log files or just for its log files. For DAG servers, it is recommended that the ESEUTIL tool only be run for the log files.

NOTE

Before configuring the Eseutil integrity check option, you must first copy the `Eseutil.exe` and the supporting DLL (`ese.dll`) from an Exchange server to the DPM server (`c:\Program Files\Microsoft Data Protection Manager\DPM\bin`). In addition, the `Eseutil.exe` and `ese.dll` versions must be from the most recent edition of Exchange Server. If these files are updated on an Exchange server (either through an upgrade or by installing an update), you must then update these files on the DPM server as well.

9. Once you have finished selecting the desired Eseutil integrity check option, click Next.

10. On the Specify Exchange DAG Protection page, specify which database copies should be selected for a full backup and which copies should be selected for a copy backup. If you have selected multiple copies of a database to be protected by DPM, only one copy should be selected for full backup, as shown in Figure 16.7.

16

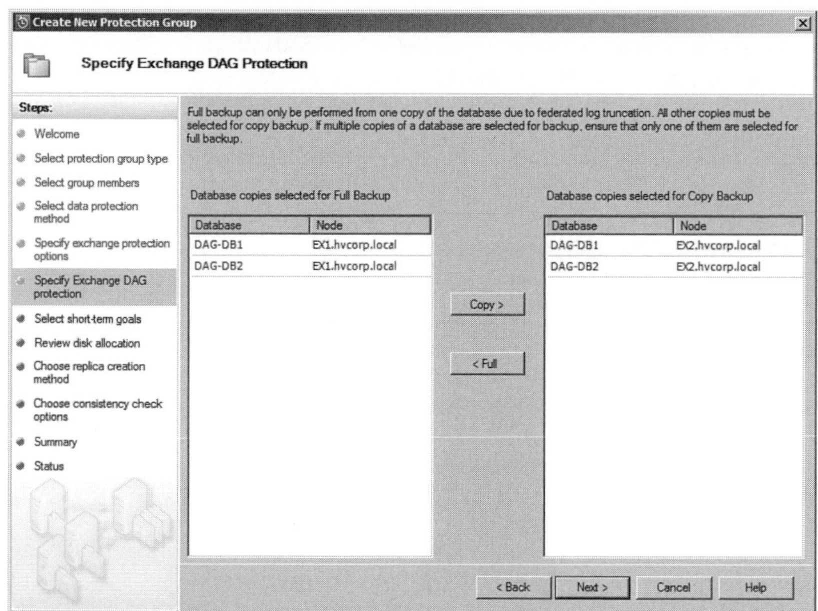

FIGURE 16.7 Specifying Exchange DAG protection.

11. Once you have finished configuring the desired DAG protection, click Next.
12. On the Specify Short-Term Goals page, specify your desired short-term protection goals, and then click Next.
13. On the Review Disk Allocation page, review the disk allocations that DPM recommends for the protection group, and then click Next.
14. If you have a tape device attached, the Specify Long-Term Protection page is shown. Use this page to specify your long-term protection goals, and then click Next.
15. Next, if you have a tape device attached, the Select Library and Tape Details page is also shown. Use this page to specify the library and configuration options for the backup tapes, and then click Next.
16. On the Choose Replica Creation Method page, use the Replica in DPM Server section to define how the initial replica of the protected data should be created, and then click Next.
17. On the Consistency Check Options page, specify the desired option for how the consistency check for the protection group will be handled, and then click Next.
18. On the Summary page, review the information about the protection group and then click Create Group.
19. Next, the status and results of the protection group creation process are shown on the Status page. Once the protection group has been created, click Close to exit the wizard.

NOTE

As a general rule, Exchange Server databases should not be configured to use circular logging when being protected by DPM. When using a VSS-enabled backup utility such as DPM in conjunction with circular logging, you can encounter backup and recovery issues.

How to Restore an Exchange Database

The steps used to recover an Exchange Server 2013 database using DPM differ depending on if you are trying to restore the database to the original location or to an alternate location. Use the following steps to restore a database to the original location, which is appropriate when the original database is lost or corrupted beyond repair. This option may result in a loss of data, so thoughtfully consider using it.

1. While logged on to a computer as a domain user account that is a member of the Exchange Organization Management and Server Management groups, open the EMS.
2. Next, execute the following command against the targeted database to allow restoring a database from a backup:

```
Get-MailboxDatabase -Identity <database name> | Set-MailboxDatabase
-AllowFileRestore $True
```

3. Next, open the DPM 2012 Administrator Console.
4. Once the console has loaded, click Recovery on the navigation bar.
5. Using either the Browse or Search tabs, find the most recent recovery point for the database that needs to be recovered, as shown in Figure 16.8.

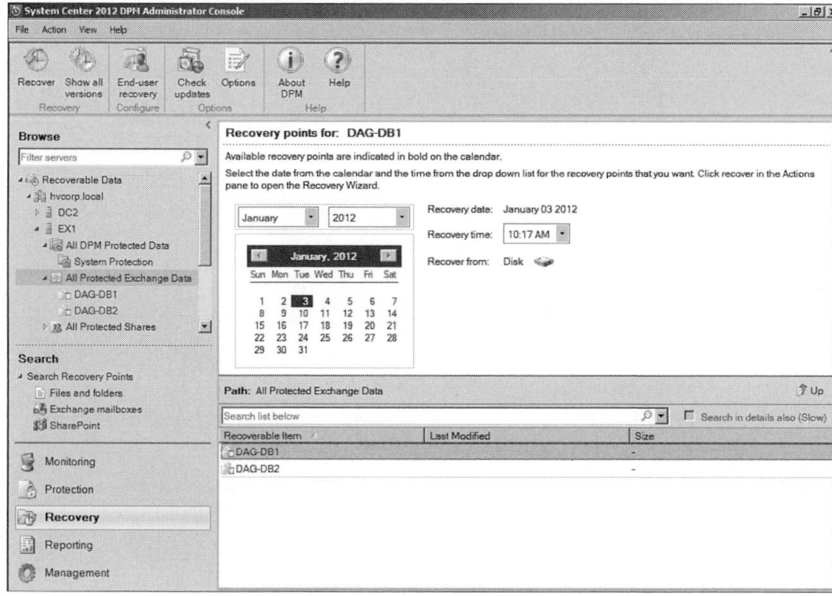

FIGURE 16.8 Choosing which Exchange database to recover.

6. Once you have selected the database to recover, click Recover in the actions pane.
7. After the Recovery Wizard has started, the Review Recovery Selection page is shown. Review the recovery selections and then click Next.
8. On the Select Recovery Type page, the Recover to Original Exchange Server Location option is already selected (as it is the only available option if the latest recovery point has been chosen); click Next to continue.
9. On the Specify Recovery Options page, ensure that the Mount the Databases After They Are Recovered option is selected, and then click Next.
10. On the Summary page, review the recovery settings, and then click Recover.
11. Next, the status and results of the recovery process are shown on the Recovery Status page, as shown in Figure 16.9. Once the recovery process has been completed, click Close to exit the wizard.

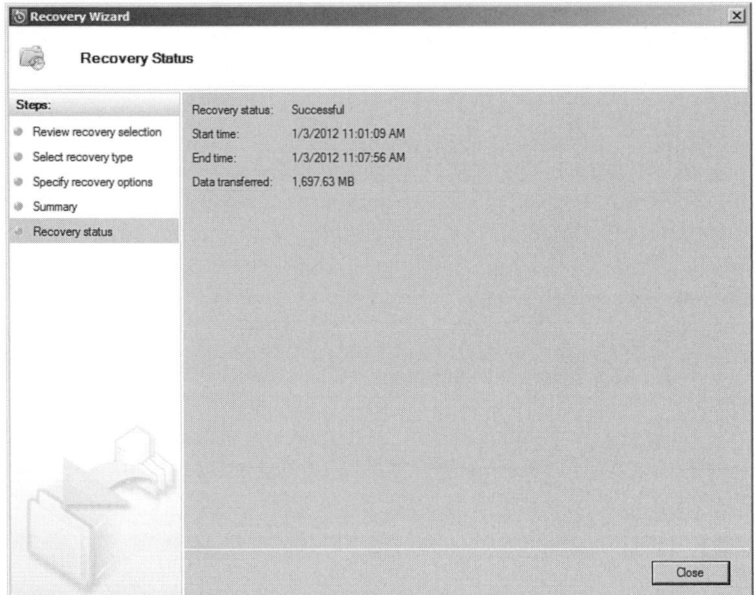

FIGURE 16.9 Exchange database recovery status.

12. Finally, execute the following EMS command against the recovered database to set the `AllowFileRestore` property to `False`:

```
Get-MailboxDatabase -Identity <database name> | Set-MailboxDatabase
-AllowFileRestore $False
```

In addition to being able to restore a database to its original location, you can also restore a database to any of the following alternate location options:

- **Recover to Another Database on an Exchange Server**—Use this option to recover the database to another Exchange server. This option might be used in scenarios where restoring to the original Exchange server is not feasible.
- **Recover to a Recovery Database**—Use this option to recover the database to a recovery database. Once recovered, you can then mount the database and extract data as part of a recovery operation to restore individual mailboxes or individual items in a mailbox.
- **Copy to a Network Folder**—Use this option to recover the database and its log files to a network location. This option is useful if you are trying to recover the database into a lab environment, if you are recovering to another Exchange server and want to bring the database to a clean shutdown, or if you are planning to do some form of forensic analysis on the database. However, keep in mind that the recovery destinations (network locations) available for this option can only be volumes or shares that are protected by DPM.

- **Copy to Tape**—Use this option to recover the database to a tape. This option is useful if you need to recover the database to a medium that can be shipped offsite.

NOTE

The alternate location options are not available if you use the latest recovery point to recover from. Instead, you must either choose an earlier recovery point or a database copy that is only being protected using a copy backup.

How to Restore a Mailbox

To recover a mailbox, the process is the same regardless of whether you are trying to recover a mailbox that is located in a DAG or in a single mailbox database. To complete such a recovery, complete the following steps:

1. While logged on to a computer as a domain user account that is a member of the Exchange Organization Management and Server Management groups, open the EMS.
2. Next, execute the following command to create a recovery database:

```
New-MailboxDatabase -Recovery -Name <new database name> -Server
<Exchange Server Name>
```

3. Now, open the DPM 2012 Administrator Console.
4. Once the console has loaded, click Recovery on the navigation bar.
5. Using either the Browse or Search tabs, find the mailbox that needs to be recovered, as shown in Figure 16.10.
6. Once you have selected the mailbox to recover, click Recover in the actions pane.
7. After the Recovery Wizard has started, the Review Recovery Selection page is shown. Review the recovery selections and then click Next.
8. On the Select Recovery Type page, select the Recover Mailbox to an Exchange Server Database option, and then click Next to continue.

NOTE

If needed, you can also choose to recover the mailbox to either a network folder or to a tape.

9. On the Specify Destination page, browse to the Exchange server that has the intended recovery database and then provide the recovery database name that was created in step 2, as shown in Figure 16.11.

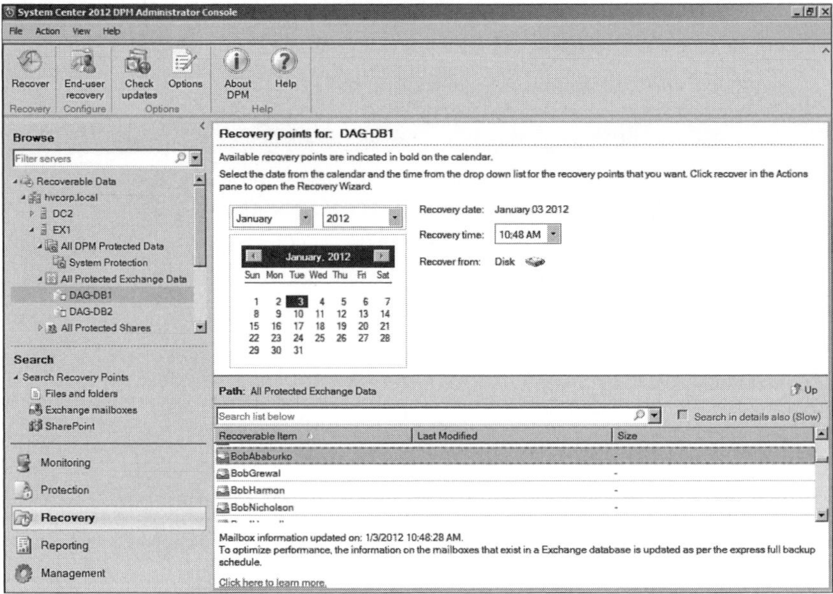

FIGURE 16.10 Choosing which mailbox to recover.

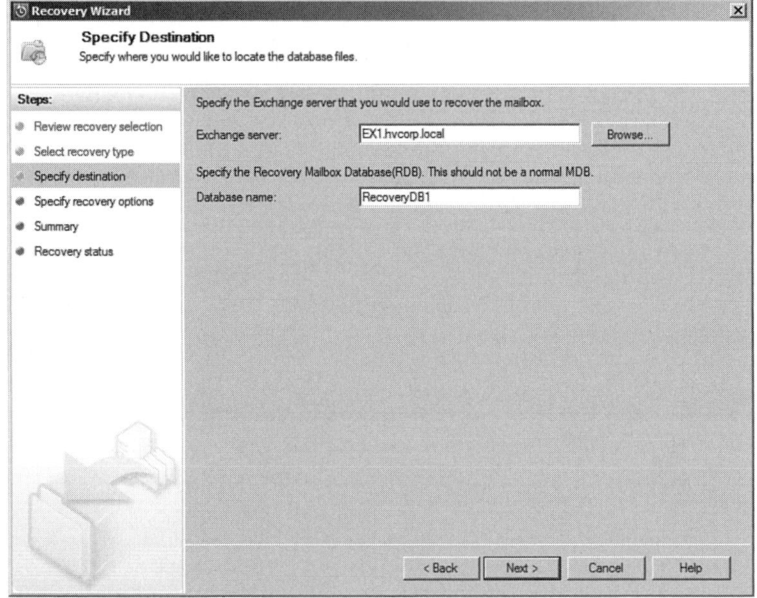

FIGURE 16.11 Specifying the recovery database information.

10. Once you have provided the recovery database information, click Next.
11. On the Specify Recovery Options page, click Next.
12. On the Summary page, review the recovery settings, and then click Recover.
13. Next, the status and results of the recovery process are shown on the Recovery Status page. Once the recovery process has been completed, click Close to exit the wizard.
14. Once the mailbox has been restored, use the following EMS commands to complete the recovery process:

```
Mount-Database -Name <recovery database name>
MailboxRestoreRequest -SourceDatabase {DB} -SourceStoreMailbox
"mailboxname" -TargetMailbox user@domain
```

Summary

While Windows Server Backup can do basic database backups and restores, other backup and recovery technologies like Microsoft's System Center 2012 Data Protection Manager or third-party packages such as NetBackup or CommVault utilize VSS with additional backup and recovery options for Exchange Server 2013. Microsoft introduced database availability groups in Exchange Server 2010 and continued support for DAGs in Exchange Server 2013 to drastically reduce the need for backups by making the data redundant across up to 16 servers. Backup has been deprecated from the role of primary disaster recovery to more of an historic storage of messages for purposes of eDiscovery. Depending on the needs of your environment and your regulatory compliance requirements, you might perform fewer backups than in the past. Depending on whether you build standalone Exchange Server 2013 servers or implement database availability groups has a huge impact on your backup strategy.

Exchange Server 2013 has taken a philosophy to improve the overall backup process by offering more scenarios in which you can restore or recover data without having to resort to restoring from tape. This means that Exchange Server 2013 administrators can put more faith into the stability and recoverability of Exchange Server 2013 by utilizing native retention functions, archiving, and data replication.

Although the backup mechanisms are mostly unchanged, this means that it is still easy to back up Exchange Server 2013 data to disk or tape for long-term storage if you implement a supported backup solution. VSS is still utilized for backups, and is the interface of choice for third-party backup applications as legacy style streaming backups are no longer supported. Advanced features such as backing up a "nonmaster" replica give administrators increased flexibility with the ability to back up Exchange Server 2013 mailbox databases during business hours with greatly reduced impact to end users. This can be especially helpful in situations in which a backup job fails and the administrator has to make a choice between impacting end users' performance or skipping a backup.

Backups continue to be the safety net that enables administrators to operate knowing that in any situation they can restore a message, a mailbox, or an entire server. Careful planning and regular verification of backups enable an administrator to sleep at night knowing his or her Exchange Server environment is safe.

Best Practices

The following are best practices from this chapter:

- When budget and bandwidth allow for it, implement database availability groups to replicate data to multiple locations to allow for near-instant recovery of failed services.
- Mailbox servers should be backed up often enough to meet any Recovery Point Objectives enforced by the environment.
- Always check the status of backup jobs to ensure they run properly.
- Maintain a list of who to contact if errors occur during the backup process.
- Always follow the documented process for performing backups. If the process changes because of a change in the environment or backup product, be sure to update the documentation.
- Always perform a full backup before making major changes to an Exchange server.
- Perform a weekly system backup of key systems to enable rapid restore in the case of a major failure if you are not running redundant CAS along with DAG for Mailbox servers.
- When possible, perform backups to disk for speed and spool them to tape during the day.
- Define your SLAs before determining your backup strategy because the SLA will heavily influence your choices.
- Clearly define the roles and responsibilities of the people who are involved in backups of Windows and Exchange Server.
- Always take your third-party Exchange Server 2013 applications into account when planning your backup strategy.
- Be sure to configure new databases for DAG if that is your backup strategy.
- Utilize Exchange recovery databases to restore mailboxes.
- Be sure to update your backup jobs when new databases are added.

CHAPTER 17

Using Microsoft System Center Operations Manager to Monitor Exchange Server 2013

IN THIS CHAPTER

- Exchange Server 2013 Monitoring
- Understanding How OpsMgr Works
- OpsMgr Architecture Components
- Securing OpsMgr
- Fault Tolerance and Disaster Recovery
- Understanding OpsMgr Components
- Putting It All Together in a Design
- Installing OpsMgr 2012
- Configuring OpsMgr
- Administering OpsMgr
- Exploring the Exchange Server 2013 Management Pack

System Center Operations Manager (OpsMgr) 2012 provides the best-of-breed approach to end-to-end monitoring and managing for Exchange Server 2013. This includes servers, applications, and devices. Through the use of monitoring and alerting components, OpsMgr helps to identify specific environmental conditions before they evolve into problems.

OpsMgr provides a timely view of important Exchange Server 2013 server and application conditions and intelligently links problems to knowledge provided within the monitoring rules. Critical events and known issues are identified and matched to technical reference articles in the Microsoft Knowledge Base for troubleshooting and quick problem resolution.

The monitoring is accomplished using standard operating system components such as Windows Management Instrumentation (WMI), Windows event logs, the extensive Exchange Server 2013 Health Manager event logs, and Windows performance counters, along with Exchange Server 2013–specific application programming interface (API) calls and scripts. OpsMgr-specific components are also designed to perform synthetic transaction and track the health and availability of network services. In addition, OpsMgr provides a reporting feature that allows administrators to track problems and trends occurring on the network. Reports can be generated automatically, providing network administrators, managers, and decision makers with a current and long-term historical view of environmental trends. These reports can be delivered via email or stored on file shares for archive to power web pages.

The following sections focus on defining OpsMgr as a monitoring system for Exchange Server 2013. This chapter provides specific analysis of the way OpsMgr operates and presents OpsMgr design best practices, specific to deployment for Exchange Server 2013 monitoring.

Exchange Server 2013 Monitoring

The Operations Manager 2012 monitoring is organized into management packs (MPs) for ease of installation and versioning. The Operations Manager 2012 includes some of the best MPs for monitoring and maintaining Exchange Server 2013.

To support Exchange, Operations Manager has a number of other management packs to monitor the operating systems, Active Directory, and other key supporting components. The management packs that should be used to monitor the supporting infrastructure in addition to the Exchange server itself include the following:

- Windows Server Operating System MPs
- Active Directory Server MPs
- Microsoft Windows DNS Server MPs
- Microsoft Windows DHCP Server MPs
- Microsoft Windows Group Policy MPs
- Microsoft Windows Hyper-V MPs
- Windows Server Internet Information Services MPs
- Windows Server Network Load Balancing MPs
- Windows Terminal Services MPs

Each of the preceding categories includes several different MPs to support monitoring, discovery, and libraries. These MPs were developed by the product groups and include deep knowledge about the product.

The features of the Exchange MPs for the following major systems are as follows:

- **Exchange Server 2013 Management Pack**—Monitors and alerts all the major elements that Exchange Server 2013 runs on, organized into Customer Touch Points, Service Components, Server Resources, and Key Dependencies. It gathers performance metrics and alerts on thresholds, as well as critical events.
- **Exchange Server 2013 Reports Library Management Pack**—Reports on the performance and availability of the Exchange Server 2013 infrastructure.

On all these elements, administrators can generate Availability reports to ensure that the servers and systems are meeting the service level agreements (SLAs) set by the organization.

The Reports Library MP includes a comprehensive set of reports that are specific to Exchange Server 2013. These include reports on performance, availability, events, and even configuration for the various Exchange Server 2013 roles. These reports can be generated ad hoc, scheduled for email delivery on a regular basis, or even generated into web pages for portal viewing. Figure 17.1 shows a Server Daily Mailflow Statistics Summary report for a server. The report shows the messages delivered, broken down by mailbox deliveries, internal routing, and to the Internet as well as failures.

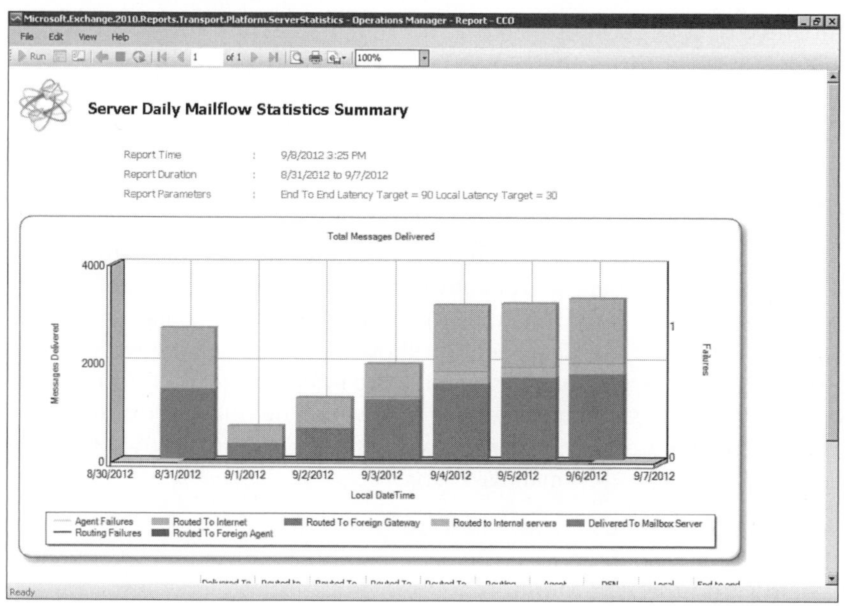

FIGURE 17.1 Server Daily Mailflow Statistics Summary report.

This kind of summary performance report showing trends, analysis, and color-coded problem areas is invaluable to reporting on the Exchange Server 2013 infrastructure and really ties together the low-level technical monitoring into a high-level view that support personnel can use.

Understanding How OpsMgr Works

OpsMgr is a sophisticated monitoring system that effectively allows for large-scale management of mission-critical servers. Organizations with a medium to large investment in Microsoft technologies will find that OpsMgr allows for an unprecedented ability to keep on top of the tens of thousands of event log messages that occur on a daily basis. In its simplest form, OpsMgr performs two functions: processing monitored data and issuing alerts and automatic responses based on that data.

The monitoring is accomplished using standard operating system components such as WMI and WS-Management, Windows and UNIX event logs, and Windows and UNIX performance counters, along with API calls and scripts. OpsMgr-specific components are also designed to perform synthetic transactions and track the health and availability of network services. In addition, OpsMgr provides a reporting feature that allows administrators to track problems and trends occurring on the network. Reports can be generated automatically, providing network administrators, managers, and decision makers with a current and long-term historical view of environmental trends. These reports can be delivered via email or stored on file shares for archiving or to power web pages.

The model-based architecture of OpsMgr presents a fundamental shift in the way a network is monitored. The entire environment can be monitored as groups of hierarchical services with interdependent components. Microsoft, in addition to third-party vendors and a large development community, can leverage the functionality of OpsMgr components through customizable monitoring rules.

OpsMgr provides for several major pieces of functionality, as follows:

- **Management packs**—Application-specific monitoring rules are provided within individual files called management packs. For example, Microsoft provides MPs for Windows Server systems, Exchange Server, SQL Server, SharePoint, domain name system (DNS), and Dynamic Host Configuration Protocol (DHCP), along with many other Microsoft technologies. MPs are loaded with the intelligence and information necessary to properly troubleshoot and identify problems. The rules are dynamically applied to agents based on a custom discovery process provided within the MP. Only applicable rules are applied to each managed server.
- **Monitors**—MPs contain monitors, which allow for advanced state-based monitoring and aggregated health rollup of services. There are monitors for events, performance, logs, services, and even processes. Monitors also provide self-tuning performance threshold monitoring based on a two- or three-state configuration.
- **Rules**—MP rules can monitor for specific event log data, collect performance data, or even run scripts on a timed basis. This is one of the key methods of responding to conditions within the environment. MP rules can monitor for specific performance counters. This data is used for alerting based on thresholds or archived for trending and capacity planning. A performance graph shown in Figure 17.2 shows processor and disk performance trends for an Exchange server.
- **Alerting and notification**—OpsMgr provides advanced alerting functionality, such as alert notifications via email, paging, Short Message Service (SMS), and instant messaging (IM). Alerts are highly customizable, with the ability to define alert rules for all monitored components.

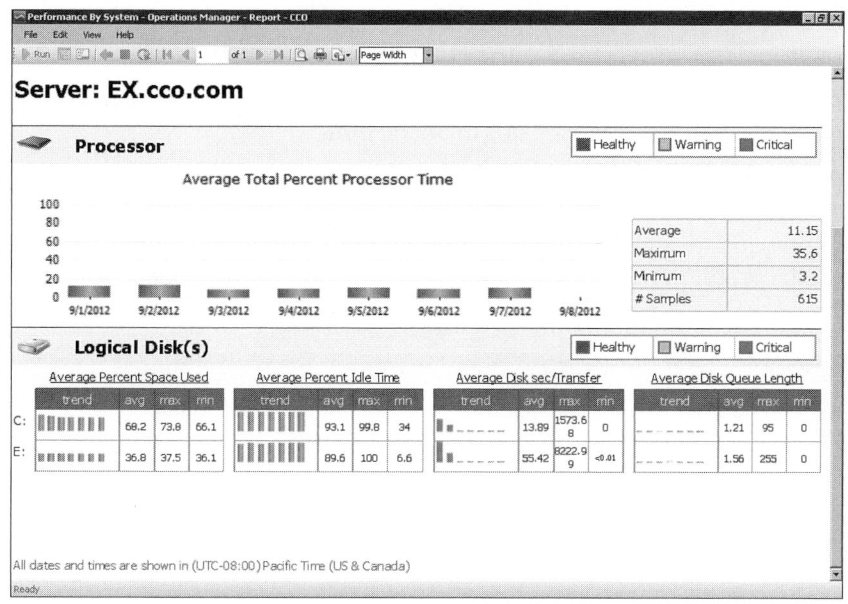

FIGURE 17.2 Operations Manager 2012 performance charts.

- **End-to-end service monitoring**—OpsMgr provides service-oriented monitoring based on System Definition Model (SDM) technologies. This includes advanced object discovery and hierarchical monitoring of systems, as well as synthetic transactions that confirm the health of the system from a client perspective. This includes uniform resource locators (URLs), ports, Active Directory, Lightweight Directory Access Protocol (LDAP), database access, and Exchange services.

Operations Manager 2012 can present the collected information in a variety of ways. The OpsMgr monitoring environment can be accessed through three sets of consoles: an Operations console, a Web console, and a command shell. The Operations console provides full monitoring of agent systems and administration of the OpsMgr environment, whereas the Web console provides access only to the monitoring functionality. The command shell provides command-line access to administer the OpsMgr environment.

Major OpsMgr components are as follows:

- **Consoles**—The main method for presenting information is the Operations console and the Web console. The Operations console is the full console and presents alert, event, and performance data in a highly scalable fashion. This allows an operator to drill into the information needed very quickly and effectively.

- **Notifications**—Notifications are generated from alerts and can be sent as email, SMS, or IM messages. There is also a generic command notification, which allows any command line or script to execute.

- **Reports**—Monitoring rules can be configured to send monitored data to both the operations database for alerting and the reporting database for archiving.
- **Dashboards**—Sophisticated dashboards can be configured to display alerts, performance, and state, both in the consoles and in SharePoint.
- **Service Level Dashboards**—The Service Level Dashboards Solution Accelerator leverages the Service Level Tracking feature of OpsMgr 2012 and the ubiquitous SharePoint to present a flexible view of how objects and applications are meeting defined service level objectives (SLOs), such as 99.9% uptime or other metrics.

NOTE

Service Level Dashboards are a Solution Accelerator and require Microsoft SharePoint. This is an add-on developed by Microsoft to leverage the functionality of Operations Manager, but is not really a part of the product.

Interestingly, the Service Level Tracking (SLT) feature of Operations Manager was developed expressly to enable Service Level Dashboards, although SLTs can be used completely independently using the Operations Manager reporting feature.

Processing Operational Data

OpsMgr manages Exchange Server 2013 infrastructures through monitoring rules used for object discovery, Windows event log monitoring, performance data gathering, and application-specific synthetic transactions.

Monitoring rules define how OpsMgr collects, handles, and responds to the information gathered. OpsMgr monitoring rules handle incoming event data and allow OpsMgr to react automatically, either to respond to a predetermined problem scenario, such as a failed hard drive, with predefined corrective and diagnostics actions (for example, trigger an alert, execute a command or script), or to provide the operator with additional details based on what was happening at the time the condition occurred.

Another key feature of OpsMgr is the capability to monitor and track service-level performance. OpsMgr can be configured to monitor key performance thresholds through rules that are set to collect predefined performance data, such as memory and CPU usage over time. Rules can be configured to trigger alerts and actions when specified performance thresholds have been met or exceeded, allowing network administrators to act on potential performance issues. Performance data can be viewed from the OpsMgr Operations console.

In addition, performance monitors can establish baselines for the environment and then alert the administrator when the counter subsequently falls outside the defined baseline envelope.

Generating Alerts and Responses

OpsMgr monitoring rules can generate alerts based on critical events, synthetic transactions, or performance thresholds and variances found through self-tuning performance trending. An alert can be generated by a single event or by a combination of events or performance thresholds. Alerts can also be configured to trigger responses such as email, pages, Simple Network Management Protocol (SNMP) traps, and scripts to notify you of potential problems. In brief, OpsMgr is completely customizable in this respect and can be modified to fit most alert requirements. A sample alert is shown in Figure 17.3. The alert shows that the health manager on EX02 has detected a problem with the Autodiscover service application pool.

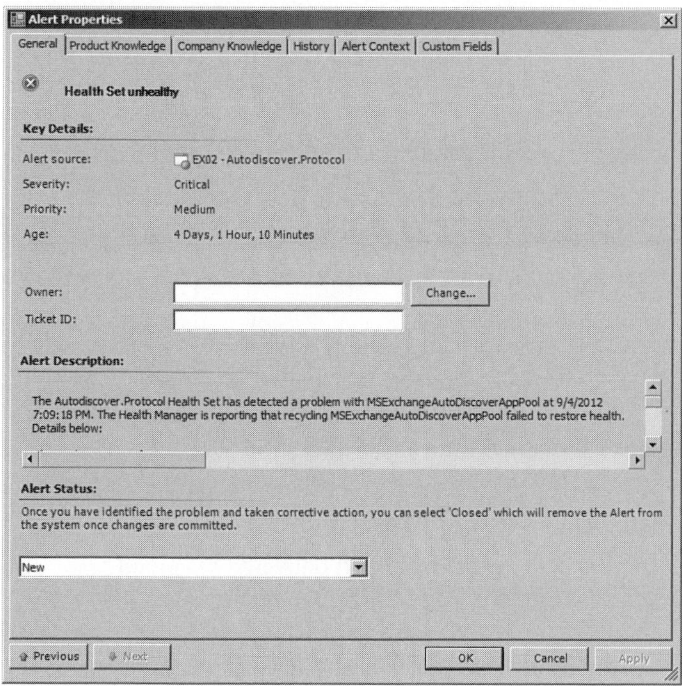

FIGURE 17.3 Operations Manager 2012 alert.

Reporting from OpsMgr

OpsMgr MPs commonly include a variety of preconfigured reports to show information about the operating system or the specific application they were designed to work with. These reports are run in SQL Reporting Services. The reports provide an effective view of systems and services on the network over a custom period, such as weekly, monthly, or quarterly. They can also help you monitor your networks based on performance data, which can include critical pattern analysis, trend analysis, capacity planning, and security auditing. Reports also provide availability statistics for distributed applications, servers, and specific components within a server.

Availability reports are particularly useful for executives, managers, and application owners. These reports can show the availability of any object within OpsMgr, including a server, a database, or even a service such as Windows Server 2012 Active Directory that includes a multitude of servers and components. The Availability report shown in Figure 17.4 is a custom Exchange Availability report for Exchange holistically, including all components that make up the Exchange service.

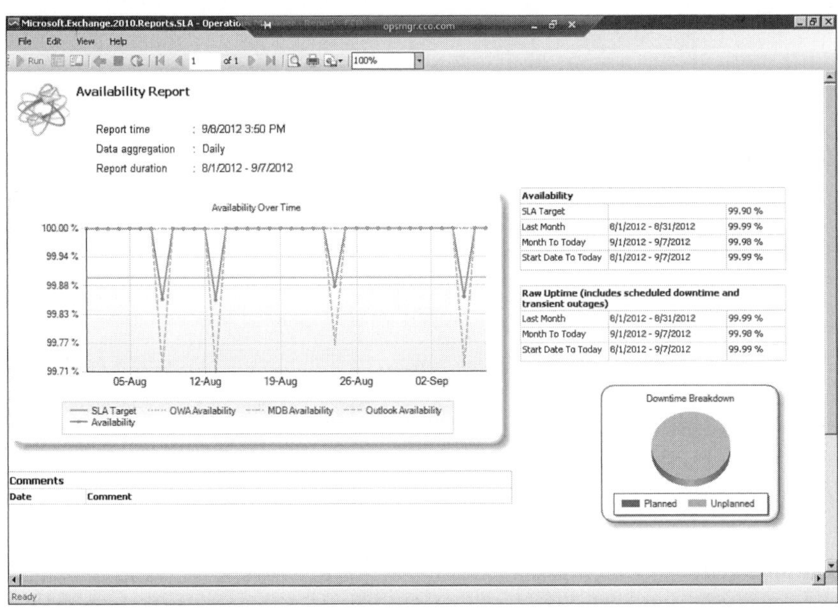

FIGURE 17.4 Availability report.

The reports can be run on demand or at scheduled times and delivered via email. OpsMgr can also generate Hypertext Markup Language (HTML)–based reports that can be published to a web server and viewed from any web browser. Vendors can also create additional reports as part of their MPs.

OpsMgr Architecture Components

OpsMgr is primarily composed of five basic components: the operations database, reporting database, management server, management agents, and Operations console. These components make up a basic deployment scenario. Several optional components are also described in the following bulleted list; these components provide functionality for advanced deployment scenarios.

The following list describes the different OpsMgr components:

- Agents
- Management server
- OperationsManager database
- Reporting data warehouse
- Reporting server
- Operations console
- Web console
- Command shell
- Gateway

OpsMgr was specifically designed to be scalable and therefore can be configured to meet the needs of any size company. This flexibility stems from the fact that all OpsMgr components can either reside on one server or can be distributed across multiple servers.

Each of these various components provides specific OpsMgr functionality. OpsMgr design scenarios often involve the separation of parts of these components onto multiple servers. For example, the database components can be delegated to a dedicated server, and the management server can reside on a second server.

The Operations Manager 2012 architecture is shown in Figure 17.5, with all the major components and their data paths.

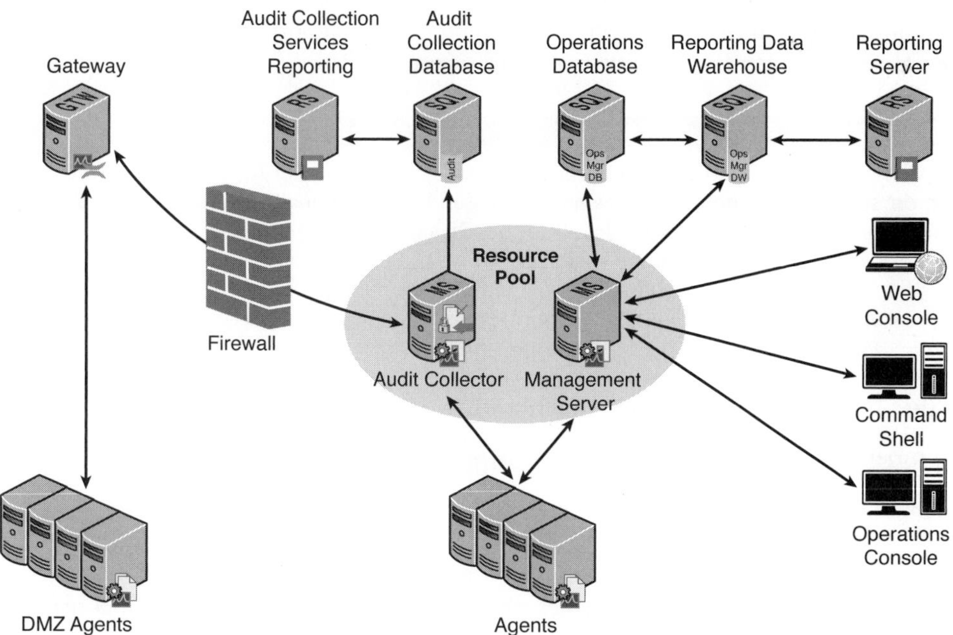

FIGURE 17.5 Operations Manager 2012 architecture.

The components are organized by two major architectural structures: the management group and resource pools. All the components are contained within a management group, which can contain only a single operations database and a single reporting database. The management group can contain multiple management servers and other components. For fault tolerance, management servers can be organized into resource pools. Management servers inherently provide fault tolerance for Windows servers, although they are also organized into a default resource pool.

In the next sections, each of the components is discussed in detail.

Understanding the Agent Component

Agents are installed on each managed system to provide efficient monitoring of local components. Almost all communication is initiated from the agent with the exception of the actual agent installation and specific tasks run from the Operations console. Agentless monitoring is also available with a reduction of functionality and environmental scalability.

Agents can report to more than one management group at the same time by using multihoming, allowing for different administration and bifurcation of operations. For example, an agent might report to one management group for operations monitoring and to another management group for security monitoring.

Windows computers can also be monitored as agentless, in which case the management server will perform the monitoring. No agent is deployed, but rather the management server makes remote procedure call (RPC) connections to the managed computer to poll the event and performance data. This places a tremendous load on the management server and the network, so agentless monitoring is not recommended.

NOTE

When virtual components are discovered, such as the virtual cluster machines, they are shown as separate monitored objects and are listed in the Administrative space in the Agentless node. The agents are deployed to the physical nodes, but not to the virtual node. These virtual systems are monitored by their physical nodes and not by the management server, thus there is no undue load placed on the management servers. These agentless virtual objects should not be confused with agentless managed computers.

Factors that impact the agent include the following:

- Number of MPs deployed
- Type of MPs deployed

The maximum supported number of agents in a management group is 10,000 agents; however, due to the impact of the consoles, that is with a maximum of 25 open consoles. If 50 consoles will be open (the maximum per management group), only 6,000 agents are supported. The maximum number of agentless managed computers per management group is 60.

The software requirements for the agent component are as follows:

- %SYSTEMDRIVE% must be formatted with the NTFS file system
- .NET Framework 3.5 Service Pack 1 (SP1)
- Windows Installer 3.1 or later
- Microsoft Core XML Services (MSXML) 6.0

Understanding the Management Server Component

Optionally, additional management servers can be added for redundancy and scalability. Agents communicate with the management server to deliver operational data and pull down new monitoring rules.

The management server in 2012 is similar to the Microsoft Operations Manager 2007 management server. It manages communication with managed agents and forwards events and performance data to the operations database. The management server also supports agentless monitoring of managed systems, and it provides support for audit collection. Management servers now write directly to the operations database and data warehouse, which eliminates the need to transfer data from one database to another. This arrangement enables near-real-time data for reporting.

Each management server runs the software development kit (SDK) and Configuration service and is responsible for handling console communication, calculating the health of the environment, and determining what rules should be applied to each agent.

Compared with Microsoft Operations Manager 2007, management server fault tolerance, performance, and scalability is generally improved. In OpsMgr 2007, all operational data passed through the Root Management Server (RMS), and it was also responsible for rollups and notifications. Thus, the RMS was a single point of failure unless clustered. Operations Manager 2012 eliminates the single point of failure by grouping management servers into resource pools in which all management servers share in the duties. The most important resource on a management server is the CPU; however, management servers do not typically require high-end hardware.

Factors that impact the management server include the following:

- Number of agents
- Configuration changes to agents
- Number of consoles

The maximum number of open consoles supported by a management group is 50, due to the load that the console places on the RMS SDK service and the database. Operations Manager can support a maximum of 3,000 Windows agents. The maximum number of agentless managed computers per management server is 10.

NOTE

The value of 10 for the maximum number of agentless monitored computers per management server is not a typo. Agentless managed computers place a huge load on the management server, which must gather and process all the workload of the rules, monitors, and other elements. This takes place over RPC, which has a heavy performance penalty on the network and the processor of the management server.

Because of the heavy load and abysmal scalability, agentless managed computers are not recommended.

OpsMgr does not have a hard-coded limit of management servers per management group. However, it is recommended to keep the environment to 10 or fewer management servers per management group.

The minimum supported hardware configuration for the management server component is as follows:

- 2.8GHz or faster x64 processor
- 2GB of RAM or more
- 20GB of available hard disk space (a minimum of 1GB on the OS drive)

The software requirements for the management server component are as follows:

- Windows Server 2008 R2 SP1

NOTE

At time of publication, OpsMgr 2012 does not support installation of server components on Windows Server 2012. Support for installation of OpsMgr 2012 components on Windows Server 2012 will be supported in the System Center SP1.

- .NET Framework 3.5 SP1
- .NET Framework 4.0
- MSXML 6.0
- Windows PowerShell version 2.0

Understanding the OperationsManager Database Component

The operations database (OperationsManager) stores the monitoring rules and the active data collected from monitored systems. This database has a seven-day default retention period.

The OperationsManager database is a Microsoft SQL Server 2008 database that contains all the data needed by Operations Manager for day-to-day monitoring. Because you can only have a single OperationsManager database, it is very important to ensure that it is sized appropriately. The most critical resource used by the OperationsManager database is the I/O subsystem, but the CPU and RAM are also important.

OpsMgr operates through a principle of centralized, rather than distributed, collection of data. All event logs, performance counters, and alerts are sent to a single, centralized database, and there can subsequently be only a single operations database per management group. Considering the use of a backup and high-availability strategy for the OpsMgr database is, therefore, highly recommended to protect it from outage.

Factors that impact the OperationsManager database include the following:

- Volume of data collection
- Configuration changes to agents
- Number of consoles open simultaneously

There is only one OperationsManager database per management group. The maximum number of open consoles supported by a management group is 50, due to the load that the consoles place on the OperationsManager database and the RMS SDK service.

It is recommended to keep this database with a 50-GB limit to improve efficiency and reduce alert latency.

The minimum supported hardware configuration for the OperationsManager database component is as follows:

- 2.8GHz or faster x64 processor
- 4GB of RAM or more
- 50GB of available hard disk space

The software requirements for the OperationsManager database component consist of the following:

- Windows Server 2008 Service Pack 2 (SP2) 64-bit or Windows Server 2008 R2 SP1

NOTE

At time of publication, OpsMgr 2012 does not support installation of server components on Windows Server 2012. Support for installation of OpsMgr 2012 components on Windows Server 2012 will be supported in the System Center SP1.

- SQL Server 2008 SP1 or higher
- SQL Server 2008 R2 or higher
- .NET Framework 3.5 SP1
- .NET Framework 4.0
- SQL Collation—SQL_Latin1_General_CP1_CI_AS

- %SYSTEMDRIVE% formatted with the NTFS file system
- SQL Server Full Text Search

Understanding the Reporting Data Warehouse Component

The reporting database (OperationsManagerDW) stores archived data for reporting purposes. This database has a 400-day default retention period.

Operations Manager 2012 uses Microsoft SQL Server Reporting Services 2008 (SRS 2008) for its reporting engine. SRS provides many enhancements to previous reporting solutions, including easier authoring and publishing. Operations Manager 2012 includes an easy-to-use graphical report designer as part of the Operations Manager 2012 console. Several new controls are also included to allow sophisticated reports and dashboards to be created. Most common reports are shipped as part of the MPs, so very little customization is needed to start working with best-practice reports.

Because Operations Manager 2012 inserts data into the Reporting data warehouse in near real time, it is important to have sufficient capacity on this computer that supports writing all data being collected to the Reporting data warehouse. As with the OperationsManager database, the most critical resource on the Reporting data warehouse is the I/O subsystem. On most systems, loads on the Reporting data warehouse are similar to those on the OperationsManager database, but they can vary. In addition, the workload put on the Reporting data warehouse by reporting is different from the load put on the OperationsManager database by Operations console usage.

NOTE

This requirement is relatively new to OpsMgr 2007 and later, because in earlier versions the data transfers from the OperationsManager database to the data warehouse database were batched. However, this caused reports to be out of date because of the lag in the transfer and also spikes in load when the transfers took place. Microsoft shifted to a real-time transfer, which improves reporting and increases performance, but it puts the data warehouse in the critical data path.

Factors that impact the Reporting data warehouse include the following:

- Volume of data collection
- Number of consoles generating reports
- Number of Service Level Dashboards open simultaneously

There is only one Reporting data warehouse per management group.

The minimum supported hardware configuration for the Reporting data warehouse component is as follows:

- 2.8GHz or faster x64 processor
- 4GB of RAM or more
- 100GB of available hard disk space

The software requirements for the Reporting data warehouse component consist of the following:

- Windows Server 2008 SP2 64-bit or Windows Server 2008 R2 SP1

NOTE

At time of publication, OpsMgr 2012 does not support installation of server components on Windows Server 2012. Support for installation of OpsMgr 2012 components on Windows Server 2012 will be supported in the System Center SP1.

- SQL Server 2008 SP1 or higher
- SQL Server 2008 R2 or higher
- .NET Framework 3.5 SP1
- .NET Framework 4.0
- SQL Collation—SQL_Latin1_General_CP1_CI_AS
- %SYSTEMDRIVE% formatted with the NTFS file system
- SQL Server Full Text Search

Understanding the Reporting Server Component

The Reporting Server component is installed on a Reporting Services instance and provides the extensions needed for the Operations Manager reports. The reports are generated from the Reporting data warehouse and can be generated ad hoc, exported, or scheduled for email delivery.

The reports are accessed via the Operations console and security is integrated with the Operations Manager roles.

Factors that impact the reporting server include the following:

- The size of the Reporting data warehouse database
- The number and complexity of reports being generated

The minimum supported hardware configuration for the Reporting Server component is as follows:

- 2.8GHz or faster x64 processor
- 2GB of RAM or more
- 20GB of available hard disk space

The software requirements for the Reporting Server component are as follows:

- Windows Server 2008 R2 SP1

NOTE

At time of publication, OpsMgr 2012 does not support installation of server components on Windows Server 2012. Support for installation of OpsMgr 2012 components on Windows Server 2012 will be supported in the System Center SP1.

- SQL Server Reporting Services 2008 SP1 or higher or SQL Server Reporting Services 2008 R2 or higher
- .NET Framework 3.5 SP1
- .NET Framework 4.0
- At least 1024MB free hard disk space on %SYSTEMDRIVE% drive
- SQL Collation: SQL_Latin1_General_CP1_CI_AS

Understanding the Operations Console Component

The Operations console is used to monitor systems, run tasks, configure environmental settings, set author rules, subscribe to alerts, and generate and subscribe to reports. The console automatically scopes to the objects that an operator is authorized to manage in his or her user role. This allows the OpsMgr administrator to grant application owners full operator privileges to the Operations console, but to a restricted set of objects. These restrictions are based on Active Directory security principles (users and security groups) and are respected by all consoles, APIs, and even the command shell.

Console performance can be a major issue to contend with in an OpsMgr infrastructure. The Operations console places a substantial load on the operations database, more so than any other factor. This manifests itself in slow console performance, including delays in presenting information, updating views, or switching between views. Because this is the end-user-facing component, this can generate frustration for operators and administrators.

Factors that impact the Operations console include the following:

- Disk latency on the OperationsManager database
- Number of consoles open simultaneously

There can be a maximum of 50 simultaneous open consoles on any management group, which includes the Operations console, the Web console, and the command shell.

The minimum supported hardware configuration for the Operations console component is as follows:

- 2.8GHz or faster processor
- 2GB of RAM or more
- 20GB of available hard disk space

The software requirements for the Operations console component are as follows:

- Windows Vista, Windows 7, Windows Server 2008 64-bit, or Windows Server 2008 R2 SP1

NOTE

At time of publication, OpsMgr 2012 does not support installation of server components on Windows Server 2012. Support for installation of OpsMgr 2012 components on Windows Server 2012 will be supported in the System Center SP1.

- .NET Framework 3.5 SP1
- .NET Framework 3.5 SP1 hot fix KB976898
- .NET Framework 4.0
- Microsoft Windows PowerShell 2.0
- Microsoft Report Viewer 2008 SP1 Redistributable Package
- File system: %SYSTEMDRIVE% must be formatted with the NTFS file system
- Windows Installer version: at least Windows Installer 3.1

Understanding the Web Console Component

The Web console is an optional component used to monitor systems, run tasks, and manage Maintenance mode from a web browser. The Web console is very similar to the Monitoring space in the Operations console, but the Web console has some limitations such as only a 24-hour view of performance data.

The Web console is an excellent choice for application administrators who need console access to the Operations Manager infrastructure, but don't want to go through the trouble of installing the full console.

Factors that impact the Web console include the following:

- Disk latency on the OperationsManager database
- Number of consoles open simultaneously

There can be a maximum of 50 simultaneous open consoles on any management group, which includes the Operations console, the Web console, and the command shell.

The minimum supported hardware configuration for the Web console component is as follows:

- 2.8GHz or faster x64 processor
- 2GB of RAM or more
- 20GB of available hard disk space

The software requirements for the Web console component are as follows:

- Windows Server 2008 R2 SP1

NOTE

At time of publication, OpsMgr 2012 does not support installation of server components on Windows Server 2012. Support for installation of OpsMgr 2012 components on Windows Server 2012 will be supported in the System Center SP1.

- .NET Framework 3.5 SP1
- .NET Framework 4.0
- Internet Information Services (IIS)
- ASP.NET

Understanding the Command Shell Component

This optional component is built on PowerShell and provides full command-line management of the OpsMgr environment. A wide array of PowerShell cmdlets are available that allow for viewing configuration and operations data, as well as setting operational parameters.

Factors that impact the command shell include the following:

- Disk latency on the OperationsManager database
- Number of consoles open simultaneously

There can be a maximum of 50 simultaneous open consoles on any management group, which includes the Operations console, the Web console, and the command shell.

The minimum supported hardware configuration for the command shell component is as follows:

- 2.8GHz or faster processor
- 2GB of RAM or more
- 20GB of available hard disk space

The software requirements for the command shell component are as follows:

- Windows Vista, Windows 7, Windows Server 2008, or Windows Server 2008 R2 SP1

NOTE

At time of publication, OpsMgr 2012 does not support installation of server components on Windows Server 2012. Support for installation of OpsMgr 2012 components on Windows Server 2012 will be supported in the System Center SP1.

- .NET Framework 3.5 SP1
- .NET Framework 4.0
- Microsoft Windows PowerShell 2.0

Understanding the Gateway Component

This optional component provides mutual authentication through certificates for nontrusted systems in remote domains or workgroups.

The gateway server is designed to improve management of devices in demilitarized zones (DMZs) or behind firewalls. The gateway server aggregates communication from agents and forwards them to a management server inside the firewall. The gateway server does not have direct access to the database, data warehouse, or Root Management Server. The most important resource on a gateway server is the CPU; however, gateway servers do not typically require high-end hardware.

Factors that impact the gateway server include the following:

- Volume of data collection

Operations Manager can support a maximum of 1,500 Windows agents or 100 UNIX/Linux agents per gateway server. OpsMgr does not have a hard-coded limit of gateway servers per management group.

The minimum supported hardware configuration for the gateway server component is as follows:

- 2.8GHz or faster processor
- 2GB of RAM or more
- 20GB of available hard disk space

The software requirements for the gateway server component are as follows:

- Windows Server 2008 R2 SP1

NOTE

At time of publication, OpsMgr 2012 does not support installation of server components on Windows Server 2012. Support for installation of OpsMgr 2012 components on Windows Server 2012 will be supported in the System Center SP1.

- .NET Framework 3.5 SP1
- .NET Framework 4.0 (for UNIX/Linux management)
- Microsoft Windows PowerShell 2.0
- MSXML 6.0

Securing OpsMgr

Security has evolved into a primary concern that can no longer be taken for granted. The inherent security in any information technology (IT) system is only as good as the services that have access to it; therefore, it is wise to perform a security audit of all systems that access information from servers. This concept holds true for management systems as well because they collect sensitive information from every server in an enterprise. This includes potentially sensitive event logs that could be used to compromise a system. Consequently, securing the OpsMgr infrastructure should not be taken lightly.

Role-Based Security Model

The Operations Manager infrastructure supports a role-based security model, which allows roles to be defined as profiles and assigned to Active Directory security principles.

NOTE

The built-in Operations Manager Administrator profile can only have group security principles assigned to it. Other built-in and custom profiles can have both group and user security principles assigned.

Seven different roles provide a range of authorization options:

- **Administrator**—The Administrator profile includes full privileges to Operations Manager. No scoping of the Administrator profile is supported.

NOTE

The local Administrators group is placed in the Administrator profile at installation by default. This means that all members of the local Administrators group are by default also Operations Manager administrators. Because the Domain Admins group is normally a member of the local Administrators group, all members of the Domain Admins group are also by default Operations Manager administrators.

This can be changed by changing the groups in the Administrator profile.

- **Operator**—The Operator profile includes a set of privileges designed for users who need access to alerts, views, and tasks. A role based on the Operator profile grants members the ability to interact with alerts, execute tasks, and access views according to their configured scope.
- **Advanced Operator**—The Advanced Operator profile includes a set of privileges designed for users who need access to limited tweaking of monitoring configuration in addition to the Operator privileges. A role based on the Advanced Operator profile grants members the ability to override the configuration of rules and monitors for specific targets or groups of targets within the configured scope.
- **Read-Only Operator**—The Read-Only Operator profile includes a set of privileges designed for users who need read-only access to alerts and views. A role based on the Read-Only Operator profile grants members the ability to view alerts and access views according to their configured scope.
- **Report Operator**—The Report Operator profile includes a set of privileges designed for users who need access to reports. A role based on the Report Operator profile grants members the ability to view reports according to their configured scope.
- **Author**—The Author profile includes a set of privileges designed for authoring of monitoring configuration. A role based on the Author profile grants members the ability to create, edit, and delete monitoring configuration (tasks, rules, monitors, and views) within the configured scope. For convenience, Authors can also be configured to have Advanced Operator privileges scoped by group.
- **Report Security Administrator**—The Operations Manager Report Security Administrator profile is designed to enable the integration of SQL Server Reporting Services security with Operations Manager user roles. This gives Operations Manager administrators the ability to control access to reports. This role cannot be scoped.

For each of the roles, a profile is created at installation that grants the role access across all objects. Additional profiles can be created for the Operator, Advanced Operator, Read-Only Operator, and the Author roles that narrow the scope of objects, allowing flexible access control to different users or groups of users.

NOTE

The access granted by profiles is cumulative. If a user is a member of two profiles, they will have the access granted by the combined profiles. There is no "deny" concept in the access controls within profiles.

The access is granted based on the user's account either directly or via group membership. The access controls are respected across all methods of access, including the Operations console, Web console, command shell, and even API access.

A key part of any Operations Manager design is developing the administrative model that will grant users the appropriate console access they need.

Securing OpsMgr Agents

Each server that contains an OpsMgr agent and forwards events to management servers has specific security requirements. Server-level security should be established and should include provisions for OpsMgr data collection. All traffic between OpsMgr components, such as the agents, management servers, and database, is encrypted automatically for security, so the traffic is inherently secured.

NOTE

In environments with high-security requirements, the organization could investigate the use of encryption technologies such as IPSec to scramble the Event IDs that are sent between agents and OpsMgr servers, to protect against eavesdropping of OpsMgr packets.

OpsMgr uses mutual authentication between agents and management servers. This means that the agent and management server must trust a common certificate authority, a simple requirement when the agents reside in the same forest as the management server. If the agent is located in a different forest or workgroup, client certificates can be used to establish mutual authentication. If an entire nontrusted domain must be monitored, the gateway server can be installed in the nontrusted domain, agents can establish mutual authentication to the gateway server, and certificates on the gateway and management server are used to establish mutual authentication. In this scenario, you can avoid needing to place a certificate on each nontrusted domain member.

Understanding Firewall Requirements

OpsMgr servers that are deployed across a firewall have special considerations that must be taken into account. Port 5723, the default port for OpsMgr communications, must specifically be opened on a firewall to allow OpsMgr to communicate across it.

Table 17.1 describes communication ports for this and other OpsMgr components.

TABLE 17.1 OpsMgr Communication Ports

From	To	Port
Agent	Management server	5723
Agent	Gateway server	5723
Agent (ACS forwarder)	Management server ACS collector	51909
Management server	Network device	161, 162
Gateway server	Management server	5723
Management or gateway server	UNIX or Linux computer	1270
Management or gateway server	UNIX or Linux computer	22
Management server	OperationsManager database	1433
Management server	Management server	5723, 5724

From	To	Port
Management server	Reporting data warehouse	1433
Management server ACS collector	ACS database	1433
Operations console	Management server	5724
Operations console (reports)	SQL Server Reporting Services	80
Reporting server	Management server	5723, 5724
Reporting server	Reporting data warehouse	1433
Web console browser	Web console server	51908
Web console server	Management server	5724

The firewall port for the agents is the port that needs to be opened most often, which is only port 5723 from the agent to the management servers for monitoring. Other ports, such as 51909 for ACS, are more rarely needed. Figure 17.6 shows the major communications paths and ports between OpsMgr components.

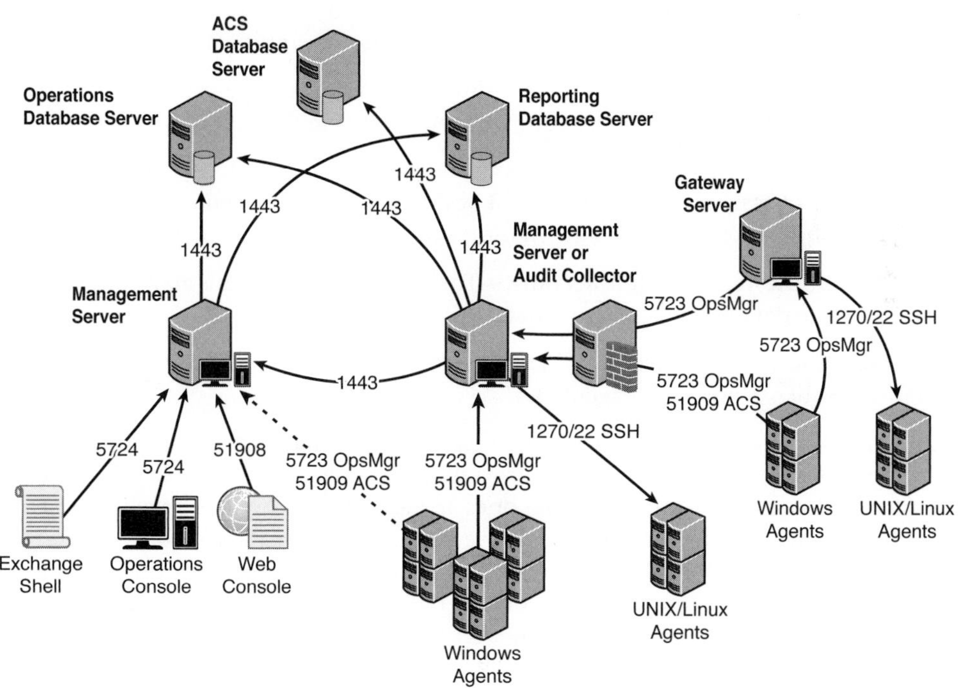

FIGURE 17.6 Communications ports.

NOTE

Note the directionality of the management server to UNIX/Linux arrow. This is because the management server collects information from the UNIX/Linux agents, rather than having the UNIX/Linux agents upload the information. This explains the lower scalability numbers for UNIX/Linux agents.

Action and RunAs Account Security

In addition to the aforementioned security measures, security of an OpsMgr environment can be strengthened by the addition of multiple service accounts and RunAs accounts to handle the different OpsMgr components and MPs. For example, the Management Server Action account and the SDK/Configuration service account should be configured to use separate credentials, to provide for an extra layer of protection in the event that one account is compromised:

- **Management Server Action account**—The account responsible for collecting data and running responses from management servers.
- **SDK and Configuration service account**—The account that writes data to the operations database; this service is also used for all console communication.
- **Local Administrator account**—The account used during the agent push installation process. To install the agent, local administrative rights are required.
- **Agent Action account**—The credentials the agent will run as. This account can run under a built-in system account, such as Local System, or a limited domain user account for high-security environments.
- **Data Warehouse Write Action account**—The account used by the management server to write data to the Reporting data warehouse.
- **Data Warehouse Reader account**—The account used to read data from the data warehouse when reports are executed.
- **RunAs accounts**—The specific accounts used by MPs to facilitate monitoring. Out of the box, Operations Manager provides a number of RunAs accounts and RunAs profiles, and you can create additional ones as necessary to delegate specific rights as defined in the MP documentation. These accounts are then assigned as RunAs accounts used by the MP to achieve a high degree of security and flexibility when monitoring the environment. New to OpsMgr 2012 is the ability to selectively distribute the RunAs account to just the agents that need them.

Various MPs have their own RunAs accounts, such as the Active Directory MPs and the Exchange MP. These allow accounts with specific elevated privileges to be assigned to execute MP scripts.

Securing DMZ Servers with Certificates

Servers in an organization's DMZ are usually not domain members and, therefore, cannot do automatic mutual authentication with the OpsMgr server. However, these servers are the most exposed in the organization and, thus, a critical asset to be monitored. Thankfully, there is a well-defined process for using certificates to handle the mutual authentication. Certificates on both the management servers and the agents are used to mutually authenticate their communications.

The certificates used for mutual authentication must do the following:

- Have the Name field match the computer name in the Computer Properties
- Be configured with server (1.3.6.1.5.5.7.3.1) and client (1.3.6.1.5.5.7.3.2) Object Identifiers (OIDs)
- Be marked as exportable
- Have their issuing CA trusted by the computer

The agent checks for these conditions at startup and will not use the certificate if these conditions are not satisfied.

Fault Tolerance and Disaster Recovery

The ability to recover from failures is critical to the proper function of any system, including Operations Manager. Although the two concepts are closely related, fault tolerance and disaster recovery are fundamentally different.

Fault tolerance is the ability to continue operating even in the event of a failure. This ensures that failures don't result in loss of service. Fault-tolerance mechanisms, such as clustering or load-balanced components, have activation times typically measured in seconds or minutes. These mechanisms typically also have high costs associated with them, such as duplicated hardware.

In contrast, disaster recovery is the ability to restore operations after a loss of service. This ensures that failures don't result in the loss of data. Disaster recovery mechanisms, such as backups or log shipping, have activation times typically measured in hours or days. Disaster recovery mechanisms generally have lower costs associated with them, though failover sites in backup data centers can be expensive.

As IT organizations mature, the monitoring systems such as Operations Manager become more critical and, thus, require investment in fault tolerance.

NOTE

Depending on the organization, Operations Manager is sometimes considered to be a non-business-critical system and therefore is not implemented with fault tolerance. The rationale for this is that if Operations Manager is down, business-critical systems would still be operational albeit without monitoring or alerting.

17

In addition to the scalability built in to OpsMgr, redundancy is built in to the components of the environment. Proper knowledge of how to deploy OpsMgr redundancy and place OpsMgr components correctly is important to the understanding of OpsMgr redundancy. The main components of OpsMgr can be made redundant through the following methods:

- **Management servers**—Management servers are automatically redundant, and agents will failover and fail back automatically between them. Simply install additional management servers into the resource pool for redundancy.
- **SQL databases**—The SQL database servers hosting the various databases can be made redundant using SQL clustering, which is based on Windows clustering. This supports failover and failback.

Figure 17.7 shows a fully fault-tolerant architecture.

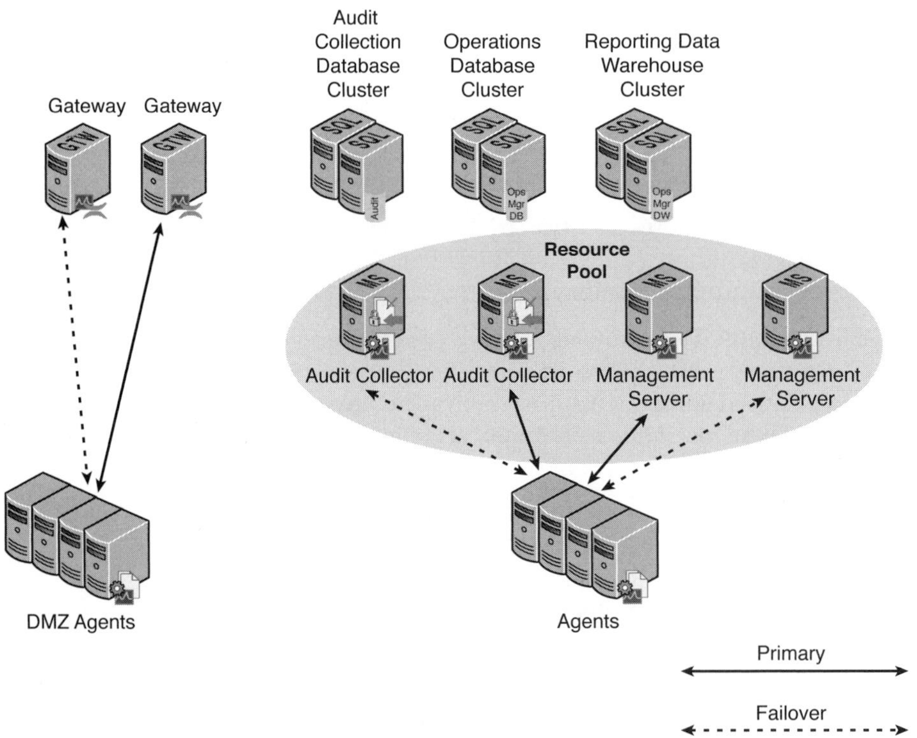

FIGURE 17.7 Operations Manager 2012 fault tolerance.

Management Group Redundancy

Having multiple management servers deployed across a management group allows an environment to achieve a certain level of redundancy. If a single management server experiences downtime, another management server within the management group will take over the responsibilities for the monitored servers in the environment. For this reason, it might be wise to include multiple management servers in an environment to achieve a certain level of redundancy if high uptime is a priority.

Resource Pools

Resource pools provide fault tolerance for the OpsMgr 2012 management group. However, they are used differently by different managed devices, such as Windows computers, UNIX computers, and network devices.

Windows computers work exactly as they did within OpsMgr 2007 and are assigned a primary management server. The difference with resource pools is that they will failover to management servers within the default resource pool, which is the All Management Servers Resource Pool. All management servers are members of this default resource pool and cannot be removed.

UNIX and Linux computers and network devices function differently. They can be manually assigned to resource pools and will failover between management servers within their resource pool. The OpsMgr administrator can create resource pools and assign management servers to those pools, allowing different devices to failover between different management servers.

Resource pools can also be used to control which management servers will send out notifications. The Notifications Resource Pool is created at installation and by default automatically includes all management servers. However, this resource pool can be converted to a manual resource pool, allowing the membership to be selected and thus controlling which management servers will send out notifications. Any management server within this group can send out notifications, allowing for fault tolerance.

Resource pools replace the RMS functionality, or limitations, present in OpsMgr 2007. The Root Management Server (RMS) component was a single point of failure and required complicated clustering to mitigate its loss. Resource pools in OpsMgr 2012 replace this functionality with an easily and automatically fault-tolerant service.

Clustering and Operations Manager

Because there can be only a single OpsMgr database and a single Reporting data warehouse per management group, the databases are a single point of failure and should be protected from downtime. Utilizing Windows Server 2008 R2 clustering for SQL databases helps to mitigate the risk involved with the OpsMgr and reporting databases.

NOTE

Geo-clusters (multisite clusters) are also supported; however, the maximum round-trip latency for the network heartbeat connection must be less than 500ms. This is a technology requirement for Microsoft Cluster Services (MSCS), but a violation of the requirement in an Operations Manager environment might result in inadvertent failover of components.

The following components can be clustered:

- Operations database
- Reporting data warehouse
- Audit collection database

Operations Manager only supports Microsoft Cluster Services quorum node clusters. The clusters should be single active-passive clusters dedicated to the respective components. This is the recommended cluster architecture.

Table 17.2 shows a sample cluster architecture with the components on separate dedicated clusters per recommended best practice.

TABLE 17.2 Sample Recommended Cluster Configuration

Component	Cluster	Node 1	Node 2
Operations database	CLUSTER01	Active	Passive
Reporting data warehouse	CLUSTER02	Active	Passive
Audit collection database	CLUSTER03	Active	Passive

The database components (operations database, Reporting data warehouse, and the audit collection database) can coexist on the same active node of an active-passive cluster. This could be all three or a combination of any two of the three database components. The cluster should be scaled up accordingly to avoid potential resource issues with having the multiple roles on a single node.

Other configurations are possible, but not recommended—for example, active-active SQL cluster configurations where there is a separate database component on each active node, such as the operations database on node 1 and the data warehouse on node 2. This is not recommended due to potential catastrophic performance issues when one of the nodes fails over. The concern is that if node 1 is running at 60% of resource utilization supporting the operations database and node 2 is running at 60% of resource utilization supporting the data warehouse, then when a node fails the single remaining node would suddenly be expected to be running at 120% of resource utilization supporting both components. This typically results in the failure of the second node in the cluster due to resource constraints.

NOTE

Management server clustering is not supported in OpsMgr 2012. This is a change from OpsMgr 2007, where clustering the RMS was the recommended approach to fault tolerance. Resource pools eliminated this need for clustering and are no longer supported.

Disaster Recovery

Disaster recovery in Operations Manager is critical to be able to recover in the event of the loss of any or all of the components. This includes the loss of a database, RMS, or a management server.

The critical items to back up in an Operations Manager infrastructure, that is, the items needed to recover the environment, include the following:

- **Operations database (OperationsManager)**—The OperationsManager database contains almost all of the Operations Manager environment configuration settings, agent information, MPs with customizations, operations data, and other data required for Operations Manager to operate properly.
- **Reporting data warehouse database (OperationsManagerDW)**—The OperationsManagerDW database contains all of the performance and other operational data from your Operations Manager environment. SQL Reporting Services then uses this data to generate reports, such as trend analysis and performance tracking.
- **Audit collection database (OperationsManagerAC)**—The Audit Collection Services (ACS) database, OperationsManagerAC, is the central repository for events and security logs that are collected by ACS forwarders on monitored computers.
- **Master database**—The master database is a system database, which records all of the system-level information for a Microsoft SQL Server system, including the location of the database files. It also records all logon accounts and system configuration settings. The proper functionality of the master database is key to the operation of all of the databases in a SQL Server instance.
- **MSDB database**—The MSDB database, Msdbdata, is a SQL system database, which is used by the SQL Server agent to schedule jobs and alerts and for recording operators. The proper functionality of the MSDB database is key to the operation of all the databases in a SQL Server instance.
- **Internet Information Services**—The IIS contains the custom settings for the Web console and the reporting database. Backing up the IIS 6.0 metabase in Windows Server 2003 or the IIS 7.x configuration in Windows Server 2008/R2 is necessary to restore the full functionality. Loss of this would require reconfiguring the Web console and the reporting database.
- **Override MPs**—These MPs contain the overrides that have been configured as part of tuning MPs. Loss of these MPs will reset the installed MPs to their default state and require all the overrides to be reentered.
- **Custom MPs**—These MPs contain all the custom development. Loss of these would require development to be redone.

Each of the components will have a different backup method and a different impact if the data is not recoverable. The most critical piece of OpsMgr, the SQL databases, should be regularly backed up using standard backup software that can effectively perform online backups of SQL databases. If integrating these specialized backup utilities into an OpsMgr deployment is not possible, it becomes necessary to leverage built-in backup functionality found in SQL Server. Table 17.3 lists the backup methods for each component.

TABLE 17.3 OpsMgr Component Backup Methods and Impacts

Component	Backup Method
Operations database (OperationsManager)	SQL backup
Reporting data warehouse database (OperationsManagerDW)	SQL backup
Audit collection database (OperationsManagerAC)	SQL backup
Master database	SQL backup
MSDB database	SQL backup
IIS 6.0 metabase or IIS 7.0 configuration	IIS backup
Override MPs	Operations console
Custom MPs	Operations console

The schedule of the backups is important. This is especially true because the databases can become quite large and the backup process time consuming, as well as expensive in terms of tapes and storage. The backup schedule suggested in Table 17.4 is based on a trade-off between the effort to back up and the impact of a loss.

TABLE 17.4 OpsMgr Component Backup Schedules

Component	Full Backup	Incremental Backup
Operations database (OperationsManager)	Weekly	Daily
Reporting data warehouse database (OperationsManagerDW)	Monthly	Weekly
Audit collection database (OperationsManagerAC)	Monthly	Weekly
Master database	Weekly	
MSDB database	Weekly	
IIS 6.0 metabase or IIS 7.0 configuration	Weekly	
Override MPs	Weekly and after changes	
Custom MPs	Weekly and after changes	

Given the volume of data in the Reporting data warehouse and the audit collection database, some organizations might choose to not perform backups of these components. The value of the long-term historical operational and security data might not be worth the storage requirements. Even if that is decided, the OperationsManager database should always be backed up to avoid loss of the valuable configuration, deployment, and tuning information.

TIP

The long-term operational, performance, and security information in the Reporting data warehouse and the audit collection database can be captured in reports as an alternative or supplement to database backups.

Reports that summarize key metrics and information can be scheduled automatically in SQL Reporting Services and stored in a file share, allowing for long-term access to summarized data.

Understanding OpsMgr Components

OpsMgr's simple installation and relative ease of use often belie the potential complexity of its underlying components. This complexity can be managed with the right amount of knowledge of some of the advanced concepts of OpsMgr design and implementation.

Each OpsMgr component has specific design requirements, and a good knowledge of these factors is required before beginning the design of OpsMgr. Hardware and software requirements must be taken into account, as well as factors involving specific OpsMgr components, such as the management server, gateway servers, service accounts, mutual authentication, and backup requirements.

Exploring Hardware Requirements

Having the proper hardware for OpsMgr to operate on is a critical component of OpsMgr functionality, reliability, and overall performance. Nothing is worse than overloading a brand-new server only a few short months after its implementation. The industry standard generally holds that any production servers deployed should remain relevant for three to four years following deployment. Stretching beyond this time frame might be possible, but the ugly truth is that hardware investments are typically short term and need to be replaced often to ensure relevance. Buying a less-expensive server might save money in the short term but could potentially increase costs associated with downtime, troubleshooting, and administration. That said, the following are the Microsoft-recommended minimums for any server running an OpsMgr 2012 server component:

- 2.8-GHz processor or faster x64 architecture
- 20GB of free disk space
- 2GB of RAM

These recommendations apply only to the smallest OpsMgr deployments and should be seen as minimum levels for OpsMgr hardware. More realistic deployments would have the following minimums:

- Two to four 2.8-GHz cores
- Windows Server 2008 R2 SP1 operating system
- 64-bit SQL Server
- 100GB of free disk space on RAID 1+0 for performance
- 4GB to 8GB of RAM

Operations Manager 2012 is one of Microsoft's most resource-intensive applications, so generous processor, disk, and memory are important for optimal performance. Future expansion and relevance of hardware should be taken into account when sizing servers for OpsMgr deployment, to ensure that the system has room to grow as agents are added and the databases grow.

Determining Software Requirements

OpsMgr components can be installed only on Windows Server 2008 R2 SP1, which is only available in x64 versions. The database for OpsMgr must run on a Microsoft SQL Server 2008 server. The database can be installed on the same server as OpsMgr or on a separate server, a concept that is discussed in more detail in following sections.

NOTE

At time of publication, OpsMgr 2012 does not support installation of server components on Windows Server 2012. Support for installation of OpsMgr 2012 components on Windows Server 2012 will be supported in the System Center SP1.

OpsMgr itself must be installed on a member server in a Windows Active Directory domain. It is commonly recommended to keep the installation of OpsMgr on a separate server or set of dedicated member servers that do not run any other applications that could interfere in the monitoring and alerting process.

A few other requirements critical to the success of OpsMgr implementations are as follows:

- Microsoft .NET Framework 3.5 SP1 and 4.0 must be installed on the management server and the reporting server.
- Windows PowerShell 2.0 must be installed on the management servers.
- MSXML 6.0 must be installed on all servers.
- Client certificates must be installed in environments to facilitate mutual authentication between non–domain members and management servers.
- SQL Reporting Services must be installed for an organization to be able to view and produce custom reports using OpsMgr's reporting feature.

Network Bandwidth Requirements

Each of the communications paths between OpsMgr components requires a certain minimum bandwidth to communicate properly.

Table 17.5 lists the communication bandwidth requirements between OpsMgr components.

TABLE 17.5 OpsMgr Minimum Communications Bandwidth

From	To	Minimum Bandwidth
Agent	Management server or gateway	64Kbps
Management server	Agentless	1024Kbps
Management server	OperationsManager database	256Kbps
Management server	Management server	64Kbps
Gateway server	Management server	64Kbps
Management server	Reporting data warehouse	768Kbps
Management server	Reporting server	256Kbps
Reporting server	Reporting data warehouse	1024Kbps
Operations console	Management server	768Kbps
Operations console	Reporting server	768Kbps
Web console browser	Web console server	128Kbps
ACS collector	ACS database	768Kbps

The values given are minimum requirements, but actual requirements will be based on load factors as well. For example, although the minimum bandwidth for a gateway server to a management server is given as 64Kbps, the actual bandwidth requirements will depend on the number of agents that the gateway is supporting and the workloads on the agents.

NOTE

The agentless bandwidth requirement clearly shows one of the issues with deploying agentless monitoring and why it does not scale. At 1024Kbps, the network requirement alone for agentless monitoring is 16 times that of an agent-based monitoring.

Figure 17.8 shows the communications bandwidth requirements graphically.

Sizing the OpsMgr Databases

Depending on several factors, such as the type of data collected, the length of time that collected data will be kept, or the amount of database grooming that is scheduled, the size of the OpsMgr database will grow or shrink accordingly. It is important to monitor the size of the database to ensure that it does not increase well beyond the bounds of acceptable size. OpsMgr can be configured to monitor itself, supplying advance notice of database problems and capacity thresholds. This type of strategy is highly recommended because OpsMgr could easily collect event information faster than it could get rid of it.

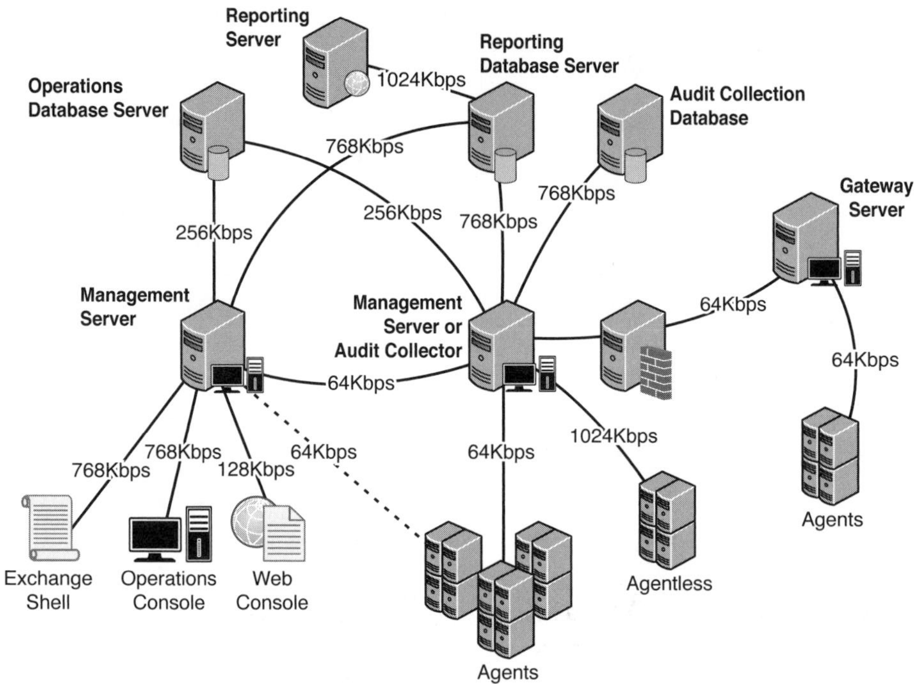

FIGURE 17.8 Communications bandwidth requirements.

The size of the operations database can be estimated through the following formula:

> Number of agents x 5MB x Retention days + 1024 Overhead = Estimated database size

For example, an OpsMgr environment monitoring 1,000 servers with the default seven-day retention period will have an estimated 36-GB operations database:

> (1,000 agents * 5MB / day per agent * 7 day) + 1024MB = 36024MB

The size of the reporting database can be estimated through the following formula:

> Number of agents x 3MB x Retention days + 1024 Overhead = Estimated database size

The same environment monitoring 1,000 servers with the default 400-day retention period will have an estimated 1.2-TB reporting database:

> (1,000 agents * 3 MB / day per agent * 400 days) + 1024MB = 1201024MB

The size of the audit collection database can be estimated through the following formula:

> Number of agents x 120MB x Retention days + 1024 Overhead = Estimated database size

This assumes that 4% of the servers are domain controllers (that is, 40 domain controllers for the 1,000 servers). At that ratio, the domain controllers are contributing 45% of the database size due to their high volume of events.

The environment monitoring 1,000 servers with the default 14-day retention period will have an estimated 1.6-TB audit collection database at steady state:

> (1,000 agents * 120MB / Agent per day * 14 days) + 1024MB = 1681024MB

Table 17.6 summarizes the estimated daily database growth for each database for each agent.

TABLE 17.6 Database Growth Estimates

Database	Daily Growth Estimate (MB)
OperationsManager database	5MB/day per agent
Data warehouse	3MB/day per agent
Audit collection database	120MB/day per agent

NOTE

It is important to understand that these estimates are rough guidelines only and can vary widely depending on the types of servers monitored, the monitoring configuration, the degree of customization, and other factors.

For example, more or fewer domain controllers will have a huge impact on the audit collection database and a large proportion of Exchange servers will have a similar impact on the OperationsManager database size.

Monitoring Non–Domain Member Considerations

DMZ, workgroup, and nontrusted domain agents require special configuration; in particular, they require certificates to establish mutual authentication. Operations Manager 2012 requires mutual authentication, that is, the server authenticates to the client and the client authenticates to the server, to ensure that the monitoring communications are not hacked. Without mutual authentication, it is possible for a hacker to execute a man-in-the-middle attack and impersonate either the client or the server. Thus, mutual authentication is a security measure designed to protect clients, servers, and sensitive Active Directory domain information, which is exposed to potential hacking attempts by the all-powerful management infrastructure. However, OpsMgr relies on Active Directory Kerberos for mutual authentication, which is not available to non–domain members.

NOTE

Workgroup servers, public web servers, and Microsoft Exchange Edge Transport role servers are commonly placed in the DMZ and are for security reasons not domain members, so almost every Windows Server 2008 R2 environment will need to deploy certificate-based authentication.

In the absence of Active Directory, trusts, and Kerberos, OpsMgr 2012 can use X.509 certificates to establish the mutual authentication. These can be issued by any Public Key Infrastructure (PKI), such as Microsoft Windows Server 2012 Enterprise CA.

Putting It All Together in a Design

To illustrate the concepts discussed in this chapter, three designs are presented. These design scenarios cover a range of organizations from small to medium to large. The profile of the three enterprises is as follows:

- **Small enterprise**—A total of 30 servers in three locations, a main office with a shared T1 to the branch offices, and 25% bandwidth availability
- **Medium enterprise**—A total of 500 servers in 10 locations, a main office with a shared 11-Mbps fractional T3 to the branch offices, and 25% bandwidth availability
- **Large enterprise**—A total of 2,000 servers in 50 locations, a main office with a shared 45-Mbps T3 to the branch offices, and 25% bandwidth availability

Based on these sizes, designs were developed.

In these designs, direct attached storage (DAS) was used as a design constraint, rather than a storage area network (SAN). This provides a more realistic minimum hardware specification. Performance could be further improved by using SANs in place of DAS.

Small Enterprise Design

The first design point is for a small enterprise consisting of the following:

- 30 servers
- Three locations, including a main office and two branch offices
- A shared T1 from the main office to the branch offices
- Approximately 25% bandwidth availability

For illustration and sizing, the numbers and types of servers at each location is listed in Table 17.7. Because the types of servers determine which MPs are loaded and determine database sizing, it is important to have some sense of the monitored servers.

TABLE 17.7 Small Enterprise Server Counts

Server Type	Central Office	Each Branch Office	Total
Windows servers	4	2	8
Exchange servers	5	0	5
SQL servers	5	0	5
IIS servers	4	2	8
Active Directory servers	2	1	4

Given the relatively small number of managed computers, a single-server design makes the most sense. The recommended design for the small enterprise is given in Table 17.8.

TABLE 17.8 Small Enterprise OpsMgr Design Recommendation

Server	Components	Processors	Memory	Disk
OM01	Operations database, Reporting data warehouse, reporting server, and management server	4 cores	8GB RAM	4-disk RAID-10 data 2-disk RAID-1 logs

For the server software, the recommendations are as follows:

- Windows Server 2008 R2 SP1, Standard Edition 64-bit

NOTE

At time of publication, OpsMgr 2012 does not support installation of server components on Windows Server 2012. Support for installation of OpsMgr 2012 components on Windows Server 2012 will be supported in the System Center SP1.

- SQL Server 2008 R2 Enterprise 64-bit

Given that the components are all on the same server, the single-server option can really use the SQL Enterprise performance improvements. Also, using the Enterprise version of SQL allows the database server to add processors in the future if resource utilization dictates it.

Figure 17.9 shows the architecture for the small organization.

The databases will grow to their steady state sizes proportional to the number of agents being monitored, all other things being equal. Table 17.9 lists the estimated database sizes for the small enterprise databases. These sizes are important for determining the drive sizes and sizing backup solutions.

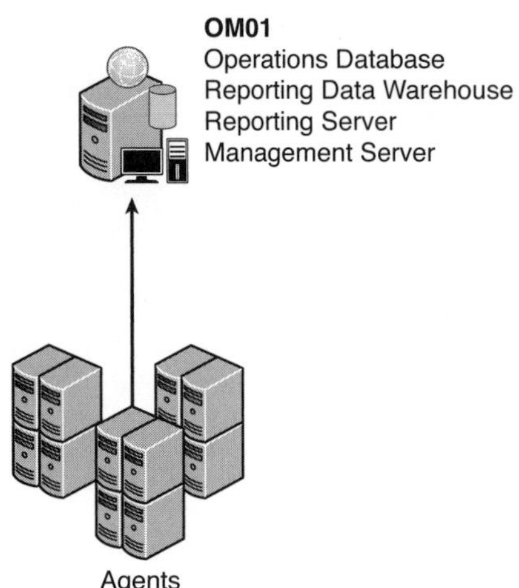

FIGURE 17.9 Operations Manager 2012 small enterprise architecture.

TABLE 17.9 Small Enterprise Estimated Database Sizes

Database	Agents	MB/Agent/Day	Retention	Database Size (GB)
OperationsManager	30	5	7	1.05
OperationsManagerDW	30	3	400	36

These sizes would be changed by adjustments to the retention periods, managed computer configuration, and MPs.

When determining the sizing of the disk subsystems, it is important to factor in the following:

- Database sizes
- Local backup overhead
- Log overhead
- Operating system overhead
- Application overhead

Typically, there should be a cushion of at least three to four times the database size to account for the overhead factors. The RAID types and number of disks would be changed to accommodate the storage needs.

Medium Enterprise Design

The second design point is for a medium enterprise consisting of the following:

- 500 servers
- 11 locations, including a main office and 10 branch offices
- A shared 11-Mbps fractional T3 from the main office to the branch offices
- Approximately 25% bandwidth availability

For illustration and sizing, the numbers and types of servers at each location are listed in Table 17.10. Because the types of servers determine which MPs are loaded and determine database sizing, it is important to have some sense of the monitored servers.

TABLE 17.10 Medium Enterprise Server Counts

Server Type	Central Office	Each Branch Office	Total
Windows servers	150	3	180
Exchange servers	10	1	20
SQL servers	50	1	60
IIS servers	185	3	215
Active Directory servers	5	2	25

Given the number of managed computers, a dual-server design makes the most sense. This would be a database server and a management server. The recommended design for the medium enterprise is given in Table 17.11.

TABLE 17.11 Medium Enterprise OpsMgr Design Recommendation

Server	Components	Processors	Memory	Disk
OM01	Management Server	2 cores	4GB RAM	2-disk RAID 1
OM02	Operations database, Reporting data warehouse, and reporting server	4 cores	4GB RAM	6-disk RAID-10 data 2-disk RAID-1 logs

These are minimum specifications for performance and storage requirements. They can be revised upward based on additional requirements, such as backup storage.

For the server software, the recommendations are as follows:

- Windows Server 2008 R2 SP1, Standard Edition 64-bit

NOTE

At time of publication, OpsMgr 2012 does not support installation of server components on Windows Server 2012. Support for installation of OpsMgr 2012 components on Windows Server 2012 will be supported in the System Center SP1.

- SQL Server 2008 R2 Enterprise 64-bit

Given that the database components are all on the same server, the database server can really use the SQL Enterprise performance improvements. Also, using the Enterprise version of SQL allows the database server to add processors in the future if resource utilization dictates it. Using 64-bit versions similarly allows memory to be added and utilized without having to rebuild servers.

Figure 17.10 shows the architecture for the medium-sized organization.

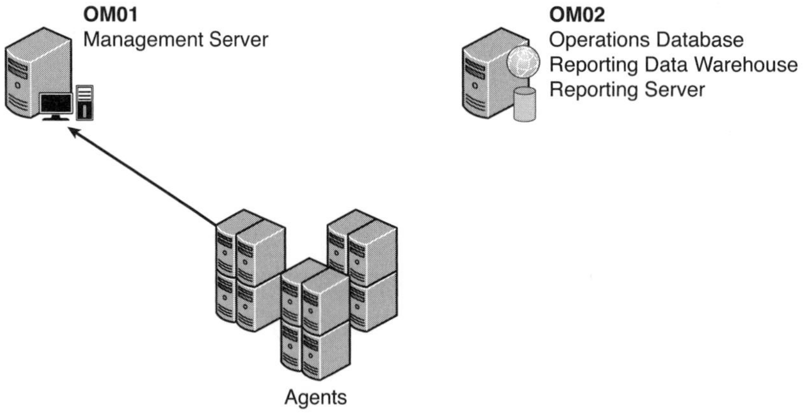

FIGURE 17.10 Operations Manager 2012 medium enterprise architecture.

The databases will grow to their steady state sizes proportional to the number of agents being monitored, all other things being equal. Table 17.12 lists the estimated database sizes for the medium enterprise databases. These sizes are important for determining the drive sizes and sizing backup solutions.

TABLE 17.12 Medium Enterprise Estimated Database Sizes

Database	Agents	MB/Agent/Day	Retention	Database Size (GB)
OperationsManager	500	5	7	17.5
OperationsManagerDW	500	3	400	600

These sizes would be changed by adjustments to the retention periods, managed computer configuration, and MPs.

When determining the sizing of the disk subsystems, it is important to factor in the following:

- Database sizes
- Local backup overhead
- Log overhead
- Operating system overhead
- Application overhead

Typically, there should be a cushion of at least three to four times the database size to account for the overhead factors. The RAID types and number of disks would be changed to accommodate the storage needs.

Large Enterprise Design

The last design point is for a large enterprise consisting of the following:

- 2,000 servers
- 51 locations, including a main office and 50 branch offices
- A shared 45-Mbps T3 from the main office to the branch offices
- Approximately 25% bandwidth availability

For illustration and sizing, the numbers and types of servers at each location are listed in Table 17.13. Because the types of servers determine which MPs are loaded and determine database sizing, it is important to have some sense of the monitored servers. This information can also be used with the System Center Capacity Planner tool.

TABLE 17.13 Large Enterprise Server Counts

Server Type	Central Office	Branch Office (Each)	Branch Offices (Total)
Windows servers	575	2	100
Exchange servers	15	2	100
SQL servers	300	2	100
IIS servers	600	2	100
Active Directory servers	10	2	100
Totals	1,500		500

Given the relatively large number of managed computers, a server per component design makes the most sense. This places each component on its own dedicated server, ensuring that there is no contention for resources between components. The recommended design for the large enterprise is given in Table 17.14.

TABLE 17.14 Large Enterprise OpsMgr Design Recommendation

Server	Component(s)	Processors	Memory	Disk
OM01	Management server	4 cores	12GB RAM	4-disk RAID 10
OM02	Operations database	4 cores	8GB RAM	8-disk RAID-10 data 2-disk RAID-1 logs
OM03	Reporting data warehouse	4 cores	8GB RAM	16-disk RAID-10 data 2-disk RAID-1 logs
OM04	Reporting server	2 cores	4GB RAM	2-disk RAID 1
OM05	Management server	2 cores	4GB RAM	2-disk RAID 10

These are minimum specifications for performance and storage requirements. The 8-disk RAID-10 subsystem for the OperationsManager database is driven mainly by performance considerations, whereas the OperationsManagerDW 16-disk RAID 10 is driven mainly by storage requirements. They can be revised upward based on additional requirements, such as backup storage.

NOTE

This configuration could really benefit from SAN storage to improve performance and scalability. At the very least, the database servers will require external drive enclosures to support the large number of disks.

For the server software, the recommendations are as follows:

- Windows Server 2008 R2 SP1, Standard Edition 64-bit

NOTE

At time of publication, OpsMgr 2012 does not support installation of server components on Windows Server 2012. Support for installation of OpsMgr 2012 components on Windows Server 2012 will be supported in the System Center SP1.

- SQL Server 2008 R2 Enterprise 64-bit

Given the scale of the infrastructure, the 64-bit platforms are needed to take advantage of the larger memory and to increase the performance of the SQL database servers.

Figure 17.11 shows the architecture for the large-sized organization.

The databases will grow to their steady state sizes proportional to the number of agents being monitored, all other things being equal. Table 17.15 lists the estimated database sizes for the large enterprise databases. These sizes are important for determining the drive sizes and sizing backup solutions.

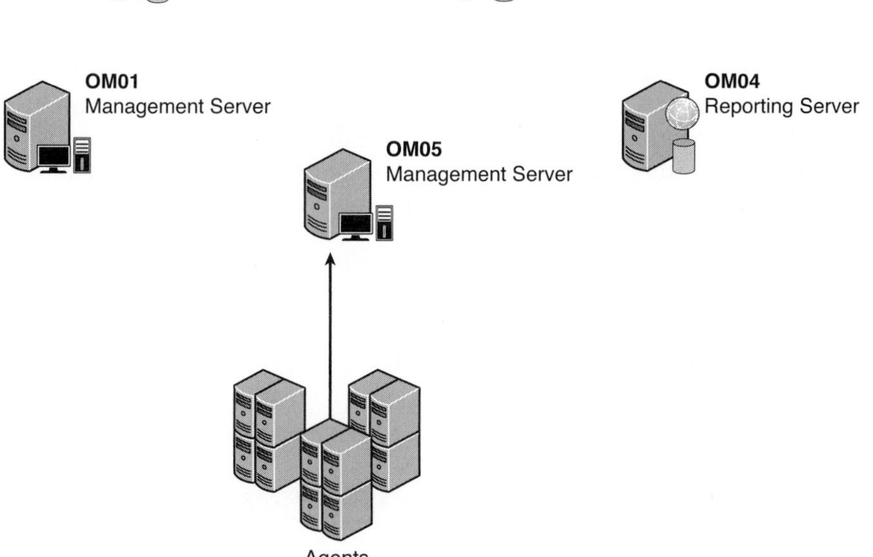

FIGURE 17.11 Operations Manager 2012 large enterprise architecture.

TABLE 17.15 Large Enterprise Estimated Database Sizes

Database	Agents	MB/Agent/Day	Retention	Database Size (GB)
OperationsManager	2,000	5	7	70
OperationsManagerDW	2,000	3	400	2400

These sizes would be changed by adjustments to the retention periods, managed computer configuration, and MPs.

NOTE

For these larger databases, larger drives can be used to reduce the number of spindles in the RAID-10 arrays. This reduces the performance but should not be a problem for the Reporting data warehouse and the audit collection databases.

When determining the sizing of the disk subsystems, it is important to factor in the following:

- Database sizes
- Local backup overhead

- Log overhead
- Operating system overhead
- Application overhead

Typically, there should be a cushion of at least three to four times the database size to account for the overhead factors. This is more difficult with large enterprise organizations and their correspondingly large data sets. The RAID types and number of disks would be changed to accommodate the storage needs, especially if online backup to tape or replication to an offsite recovery site might be used instead of local backup.

Installing OpsMgr 2012

Operations Manager 2012 is a multitier and multicomponent application that can be deployed in a variety of architectures. This allows OpsMgr to support scaling from a small organization to a very large enterprise.

Three different installations are performed in this section:

- A small organization install on a single server
- A small organization upgrade from a single server
- A medium-sized organization install on two servers

Single-Server OpsMgr 2012 Install

This section steps through the install of OpsMgr and reporting server on a single-server configuration. There will be a single server named OM1 with all the components. Figure 17.12 shows the architecture for the small organization build.

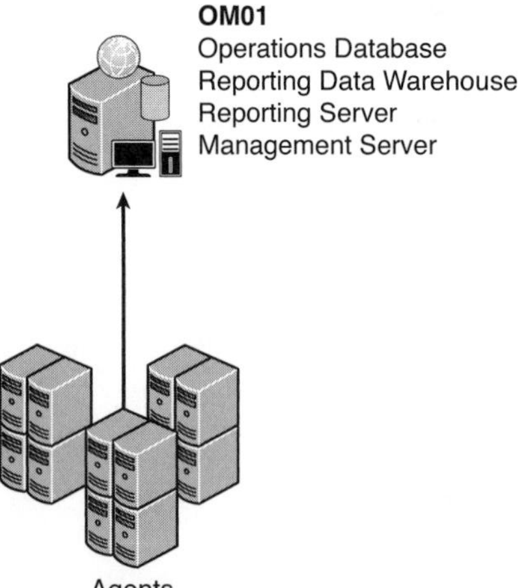

FIGURE 17.12 Operations Manager 2012 single-server architecture.

The specification for a single-server configuration of OM1 to support the small organization is as follows:

- 4 cores
- 8GB of RAM
- 4-disk RAID 10 for data and 2-disk RAID 1 for logs

These hardware requirements ensure that the system can perform to specification.

NOTE

If the configuration were to be virtualized on a Windows Server 2008 R2 Hyper-V host, a single-server configuration is not recommended. Instead, a two-server configuration is recommended and SQL Server 2008 R2 should be installed on the second server to balance the load. See the section "Multiserver OpsMgr 2012 Install" later in this chapter.

The steps in this section assume that the single server has been prepared with the following:

- Windows Server 2008 R2 SP1 operating system installed
- MSXML version 6.0
- Microsoft Report Viewer 2010 Redistributable Package
- Windows Remote Management enabled for the management server
- Web Server (IIS) role with the appropriate role services installed
- .NET Framework 3.5 SP1
- .NET Framework 4.0
- SQL Server 2008 SP1, SQL Server 2008 R2, or SQL Server 2008 R2 SP1 with Reporting Services installed
- SQL Collation: SQL_Latin1_General_CP1_CI_AS
- SQL Server Full Text Search required
- An OpsMgr service account with local administrator rights to the server and system administrator rights to SQL Server 2008

NOTE

It is recommended to install the IIS role before installing .NET Framework 4.0; otherwise, the ASP.NET 4.0 will need to be registered with IIS manually. To register ASP.NET 4.0 manually, execute the following command:

```
c:\windows\Microsoft.NET\Framework64\v4.0.30319\aspnet_regiis.exe -r
```

To support the OpsMgr 2012 Web Console role, the following Web Server role services are needed:

- Static Content
- Default Document
- Directory Browsing
- HTTP Errors
- HTTP Logging
- Request Monitor
- Request Filtering
- Static Content Compression
- ASP.NET
- Windows Authentication
- IIS 6 Metabase Compatibility

The first eight are selected by default when adding the Web Server role to Windows Server 2008; the other role services must be added manually.

This prepares the system for the install of OpsMgr 2012. Once the server meets all the prerequisites and is ready for installation, complete the following steps to run the install:

1. Log on with the OpsMgr service account.
2. Launch `Setup.exe` from the OpsMgr installation media.
3. Click Install Hyperlink.
4. Select the features to install; in this example, check all the boxes. These are Management Server, Management Console, Web Console, and Reporting Server.
5. Click Next.
6. Select the installation location and click Next.
7. The prerequisites will be checked. Remediate any issues or click Next to continue if passed.

NOTE

On the Prerequisites screen, the Review Full System Requirements link can be clicked to launch a browser window to see the full list of requirements for each component.

8. Type the management group name in the Management Group text box and click Next.

9. Accept the license agreement and click Next.
10. Enter the server name and the instance of SQL Server on which to install the Operations Manager 2012 operations database, and then click the Tab key to populate the database fields.
11. Leave the default database name OperationsManager and size of 1000MB. Change the data and log file locations if appropriate, and then click Next.
12. Enter the server name and the instance of SQL Server on which to install the Operations Manager 2012 data warehouse database, and then click the Tab key to populate the database fields.
13. Leave the default database name OperationsManagerDW and size of 1000MB. Change the data and log file locations if appropriate, and then click Next.
14. Choose the SQL Reporting Services instance and click Next.
15. Choose the Default Web Site to use for the Web console and click Next.
16. Leave the default selection Use Mixed Authentication and click Next.
17. Enter the account information for the Management Server Action Account, Data Reader Account, and Data Writer Account, and then click Next.

NOTE

If there is an action account warning pop-up, click OK to clear the warning.

18. At the Health Improve Operations Manager 2012 screen, check the appropriate options and click Next to continue.
19. At the Microsoft Update screen, select the recommended On option button.
20. At the Installation Summary screen, review the selections and click Install to continue.
21. Once setup is complete, click Close to exit the Installation Wizard.

Operations Manager 2012 is now installed in a single-server configuration. Although the small organization design was created for 30 servers, this configuration can manage up to 250 servers.

Multiserver OpsMgr 2012 Install

This section steps through the install of OpsMgr and reporting server on a two-server configuration to support a medium-sized organization. The infrastructure is designed to support up to 500 agent systems. There will be two servers, with the management server named OM1 and the database server named OM2. Figure 17.13 shows the architecture for the medium-sized organization build.

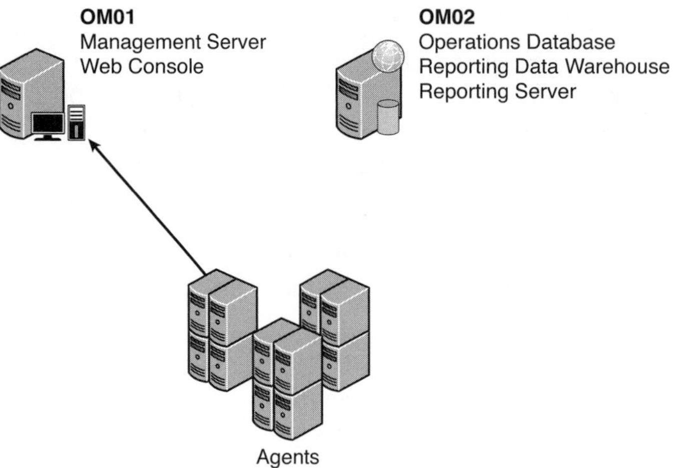

FIGURE 17.13 Operations Manager 2012 multiserver architecture.

The hardware specification for the management server OM1 configuration is as follows:

- 2 cores
- 4GB of RAM
- 2-disk RAID 1

The steps in this section assume that the management server OM1 has been prepared with the following:

- Windows Server 2008 R2 SP1 operating system installed

NOTE

At time of publication, OpsMgr 2012 does not support installation of server components on Windows Server 2012. Support for installation of OpsMgr 2012 components on Windows Server 2012 will be supported in the System Center SP1.

- MSXML version 6.0
- Web Server (IIS) role with the appropriate role services installed
- Microsoft Report Viewer 2010 Redistributable Package
- .NET Framework 3.5 SP1
- .NET Framework 4.0
- An OpsMgr service account with local administrator rights to the server and system administrator rights to SQL Server 2008

NOTE

It is recommended to install the IIS role before installing .NET Framework 4.0; otherwise, the ASP.NET 4.0 will need to be registered with IIS manually. To register ASP.NET 4.0 manually, execute the following command:

```
c:\windows\Microsoft.NET\Framework64\v4.0.30319\aspnet_regiis.exe -r
```

To support the OpsMgr 2012 Web Console role, the following Web Server role services are needed on the management server OM1:

- Static Content
- Default Document
- Directory Browsing
- HTTP Errors
- HTTP Logging
- Request Monitor
- Request Filtering
- Static Content Compression
- ASP.NET
- Windows Authentication
- IIS 6 Metabase Compatibility

The first eight are selected by default when adding the Web Server role to Windows Server 2008; the other role services must be added manually.

NOTE

The Web Console role requires that the Internet Server Application Programming Interface (ISAPI) and Common Gateway Interface (CGI) restrictions be allowed for ASP.NET 4.0. This can be done by selecting the web server in the IIS Manager tool and opening the ISAPI and CGI restrictions feature. Click the two ASP.NET v4.0.30319 options and select Allow for each one (as shown in Figure 17.14).

The hardware specifications for the database server OM2 configuration are as follows:

- 4 cores
- 4GB of RAM
- 6-disk RAID 10 for data and 2-disk RAID 1 for logs

These hardware requirements ensure that the system can perform to specification.

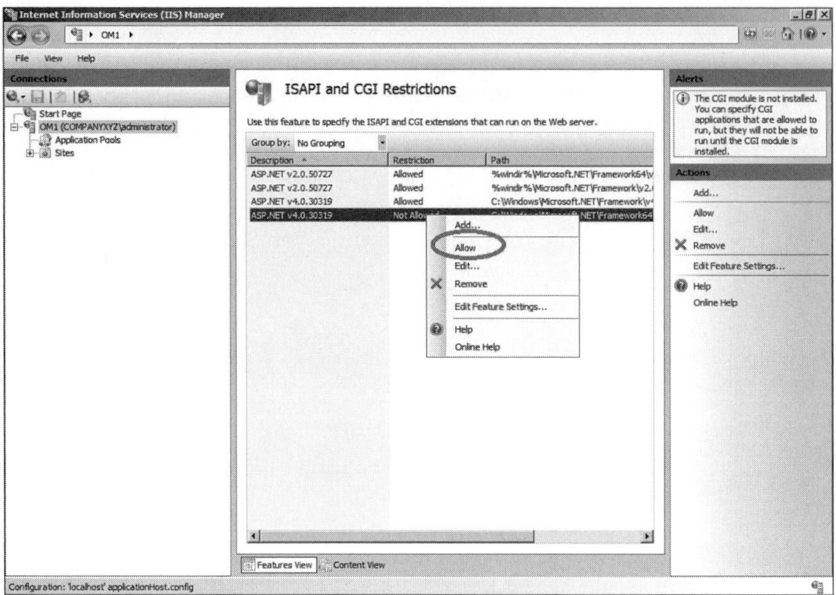

FIGURE 17.14 Allow ISAPI and CGI for ASP.NET 4.0.

The steps in this section assume that the database server has been prepared with the following:

- ▶ Windows Server 2008 R2 SP1 operating system installed

NOTE

At time of publication, OpsMgr 2012 does not support installation of server components on Windows Server 2012. Support for installation of OpsMgr 2012 components on Windows Server 2012 will be supported in the System Center SP1.

- ▶ SQL Server 2008 with Reporting Services installed
- ▶ SQL_Latin1_General_CP1_CI_AS Collation selected
- ▶ SQL Server Full Text Search installed
- ▶ .NET Framework 3.5 SP1
- ▶ .NET Framework 4.0
- ▶ An OpsMgr service account with local administrator rights to the server and system administrator rights to SQL Server 2008

This prepares the system for the install of OpsMgr 2012.

Because the install is on separate servers, this requires that the installations take place in a specific order. The order of installation is in two parts:

1. Management server, Management console, and Web console components. This will also install the operational database and data warehouse database components.
2. Reporting Server component. This will install the report engine that pulls data from the data warehouse database. This step must be run on the server that will hold the Reporting Server role.

The first part is to install the management server, Management console, and Web console components. Once the servers meet all the prerequisites and are ready for installation, the steps to run the install are as follows:

1. Log on to the management server (OM1 in this example) with the OpsMgr service account.
2. Launch `Setup.exe` from the OpsMgr installation media.
3. Click Install at the System Center 2012 Operations Manager splash screen, as shown in Figure 17.15.

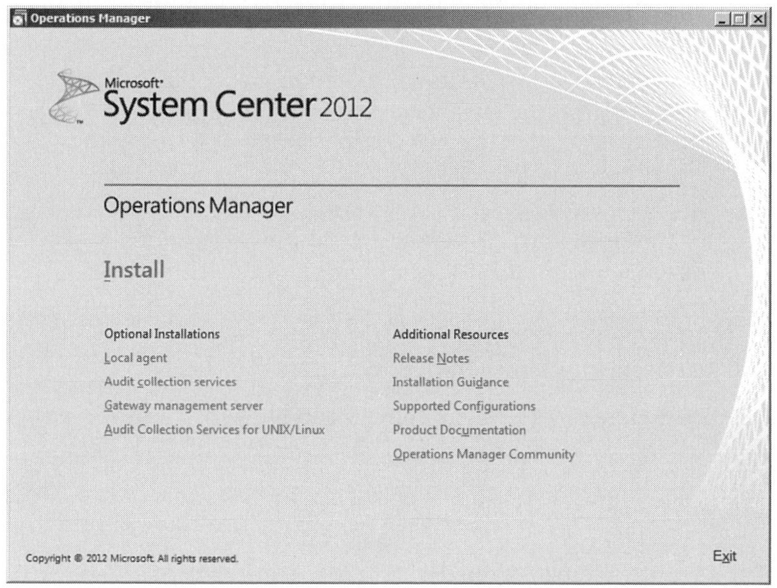

FIGURE 17.15 Operations Manager 2012 installation screen.

4. At the Select Features to Install screen, check off the options: Management Server, Management Console, and Web Console.
5. Click Next.

6. At the Select Installation Location screen, enter the installation location and click Next.
7. Verify the prerequisites have been met and remediate if necessary, and then click Next.
8. Enter a management group name, in this case **COMPANYABC**, and then click Next.
9. Accept the license agreement and click Next.
10. Enter the operational database server name and instance, in this case **OM2**. The wizard will automatically initiate a check of the target database server.
11. Leave the database name at the default OperationsManager. Change the data file and log file locations if necessary, and then click Next.
12. Enter the data warehouse database server name and instance, in this case **OM2**. The wizard will automatically initiate a check of the target database server.
13. Leave the database name at the default OperationsManagerDW. Change the data file and log file locations if necessary, and then click Next.
14. Leave the Default Web Site option selected and click Next.
15. Leave the Use Mixed Authentication option selected for the Web Console Authentication mode and click Next.
16. At the Configure Operations Manager Accounts screen, enter credentials for the Management Server Action Account, the Data Reader Account, and the Data Writer Account.
17. Click Next.
18. At the Help Improve Operations Manager 2012 screen, choose the Customer Experience Improvement Program and Error Reporting options.
19. Click Next.
20. At the Microsoft Update screen, check the On option button and click Next.
21. At the Installation Summary screen, review the choices and click Install to begin the installation.
22. Once setup completes, click the Close button to exit the Setup Wizard.

The first part of the installation has completed and the console will launch automatically. The second part is to install the Reporting components on the database server OM2. Complete the following steps to run the install:

1. Log on to the database server (OM2 in this example) with the OpsMgr service account.
2. Launch `Setup.exe` from the OpsMgr installation media.
3. Click Install at the System Center 2012 Operations Manager splash screen.

4. At the Select Features to Install screen, only check the Reporting Server option.
5. Click Next.
6. At the Select Installation Location screen, enter the installation location and click Next.
7. Verify the prerequisites have been met and remediate if necessary, and then click Next.
8. Enter a management server name, in this case `OM1`, and then click Next.
9. Choose the SQL Server instance for Reporting Services and click Next.
10. Enter the credentials for the Data Reader Account and click Next.
11. At the Help Improve Operations Manager 2012 screen, choose the Operational Data Reporting option and click Next.
12. At the Microsoft Update screen, check the On option button and click Next.
13. At the Installation Summary screen, review the choices and click Install to begin the installation.
14. Once setup completes, click the Close button to exit the Setup Wizard.

Operations Manager 2012 is now installed in a multiserver configuration. This configuration can manage up to 500 servers.

NOTE

The Operations console will need to be closed and reopened to see the newly installed reports in the console.

Importing Management Packs

After the initial installation, OpsMgr only includes a few core MPs. The MPs contain all the discoveries, monitors, rules, knowledge, reports, and views that OpsMgr needs to be able to effectively monitor servers and applications. One of the first tasks after installing OpsMgr 2012 is to import MPs into the system.

A large number of MPs are in the Internet catalog on the Microsoft website. These include updated MPs, MPs for new products, and third-party MPs. It is important to load only those MPs that are going to be used, as each additional MP increases the database size, adds discoveries that impact the performance of agents, and, in general, clutters up the interface.

The key MPs for a Windows environment are as follows:

- Windows Server Operating System MPs
- Active Directory Server MPs

- Windows Cluster Management MPs
- Microsoft Windows DNS Server MPs
- Microsoft Windows DHCP Server MPs
- Microsoft Windows Group Policy MPs
- Microsoft Windows Hyper-V MPs
- Windows Server IIS MPs
- Windows Server Network Load Balancing MPs
- Windows Server Print Server MPs
- Windows Terminal Services MPs
- SQL Server MPs (to monitor the OpsMgr database roles)

There might be other MPs that are appropriate for the environment, depending on the applications that are installed. For example, if the organization has deployed Exchange Server 2010 and HP Proliant server hardware, it would be good for the organization to deploy the Exchange MPs and the HP Proliant MPs.

For each of these MPs, it is important to load the relevant versions only. For example, if the environment includes Windows Server 2008 only, only load the Windows Server Core OS 2008 Management Pack. If the environment includes both Windows Server 2003 and Windows Server 2008, load both the Windows Server Core OS 2003 and the Windows Server Core OS 2008 Management Packs. In addition, a number of language packs don't need to be loaded unless those particular languages are supported by the organization at the server level.

Some collections of MPs require that all versions be loaded, but the Management Pack Import Wizard checks and warns if that's the case.

In versions of OpsMgr earlier than 2007 R2, the MPs had to be downloaded from the Microsoft website one by one, the MSI installed one by one, and the MPs imported one by one. Dependencies would not be checked unless additional steps were taken to consolidate the MP files prior to importing. This was a very labor-intensive process. Also, there was no easy way to check for updates to previously installed MPs.

In OpsMgr 2012, a new Management Pack Import Wizard was introduced. This wizard connects directly to the Microsoft MP catalog and downloads, checks, and imports MPs. It even does version checks to ensure that the MPs are the latest versions. This is a huge improvement over the old method of importing MPs.

To import the key MPs, follow these steps:

1. Launch the Operations console.
2. Select the Administration section.
3. Select the Management Packs folder.

4. Right-click the Management Packs folder and select Import Management Packs.
5. Click Add and select Add from Catalog.
6. Click the Search button to search the entire catalog.

NOTE

The View pull-down menu in the Management Pack Import Wizard includes four options: All Management Packs in the Catalog, Updates Available for Installed Management Packs, All Management Packs Released in the Last 3 Months, and All Management Packs Released in the Last 6 Months. The Updates option checks against the previously installed MPs and allows the download of updated versions of those.

7. Select the key MPs from the previous bulleted list and click Add for each of them. Each of the major MPs might include a number of sub-MPs for discovery, monitoring, and other breakdowns of functionality.

NOTE

Make sure to include the Exchange Server 2013 Management Pack in this step.

8. When done adding MPs, click OK.
9. The wizard now validates the added MPs, checking for versions, dependencies, and security risks. It allows problem MPs to be removed and dependencies to be added to the list.
10. Click Install to begin the download and import process. Progress is shown for each of the MPs being imported.
11. After all the MPs are imported, click Close to exit the wizard.

After the import completes, the MPs take effect immediately. Agents begin discovering based on the schedule specified in the MPs and monitors and rules begin deploying.

Deploying OpsMgr Agents

OpsMgr agents are deployed to all managed servers through the OpsMgr Discovery Wizard, or by using software distribution mechanisms such as Active Directory Group Policy Objects (GPOs) or System Center Configuration Manager 2012. Installation through the Operations console uses the fully qualified domain name (FQDN) of the computer. When searching for systems through the Operations console, you can use wildcards to locate a broad range of computers for agent installation. Certain situations, such as monitoring across firewalls, can require the manual installation of these components.

Generally, there are three ways to deploy agents: The first is using software distribution such as Microsoft System Center Configuration Manager or Active Directory GPOs, the second is manual installation using the product media, and the third and most common way is using the SCOM Discovery Wizard to search for and install agents on domain members by executing the following steps:

1. Launch the Operations console and select the Administration section.
2. At the bottom of the navigation pane, click Discovery Wizard.
3. Select Windows Computers and click Next.
4. Select Automatic Computer Discovery and click Next. This scans the entire Active Directory domain for computers.
5. Leave the Use Selected Management Server Action Account selected and click Discover. This starts the discovery process.
6. After the discovery process runs (this might take a few minutes), the list of discovered computers is displayed. Select the devices that should have agents deployed to them, as shown in Figure 17.16.

NOTE

The list only includes systems that do not already have agents installed. If a computer has an agent installed, the wizard excludes it from the list of devices.

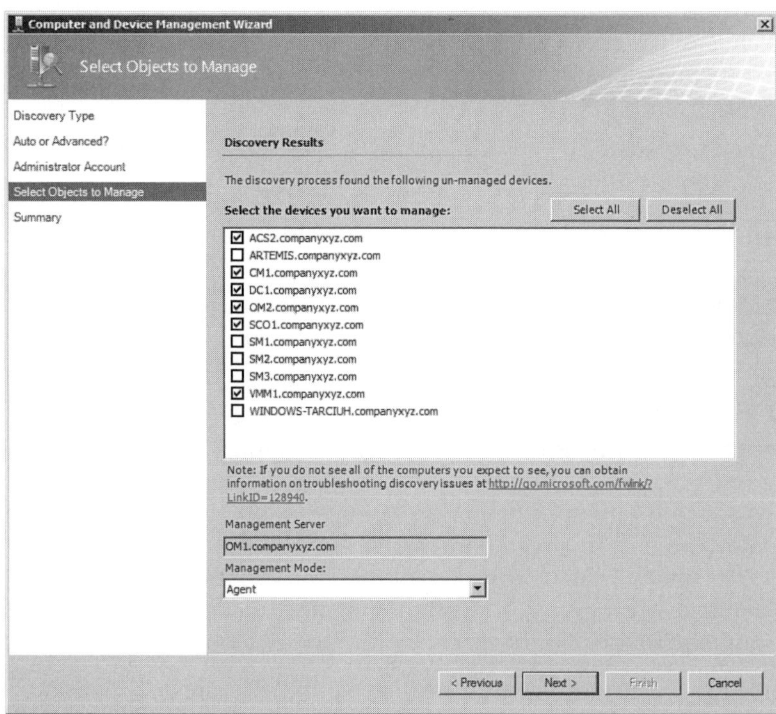

FIGURE 17.16 Discovered computers.

7. Click Next.
8. Leave the Agent Installation Directory and the Agent Action Account at the defaults, and then click Finish.
9. The Agent Management Task Status window opens, listing all the computers selected and the progress of each installation. As shown in Figure 17.17, the agent installation task started for the selected computers. The ACS2, CM2, and VMM1 agents have been installed successfully, and the others are in progress.
10. Click Close when the installation completes.

FIGURE 17.17 Agent installation progress.

Even if the window is closed before the installs complete, the results of the installs can be viewed in Task Status view in the Monitoring section of the Operations console.

The agent deployment is very efficient, and a large number of computers can be selected for deployment without any issues. The agents start automatically and begin to be monitored as they are discovered.

After installation, it might be necessary to wait a few minutes before the information from the agents is sent to the management server.

During the next few minutes after installation, the agent contacts the management server and establishes a mutually authenticated, encrypted communication channel with the assigned management server. If the agent was pushed through a software delivery system such as System Center Configuration Manager 2012, the agent determines the management server through command-line options or Active Directory–integrated discovery.

Figure 17.18 shows the state of the agents after deployment. The computers show the agent or management server state as Healthy. However, the Windows operating system state shows as Not Monitored. This is because there have been no additional MPs imported on this newly installed Operations Manager infrastructure. MPs must be imported and configured for OpsMgr to monitor additional objects like the Windows operating systems.

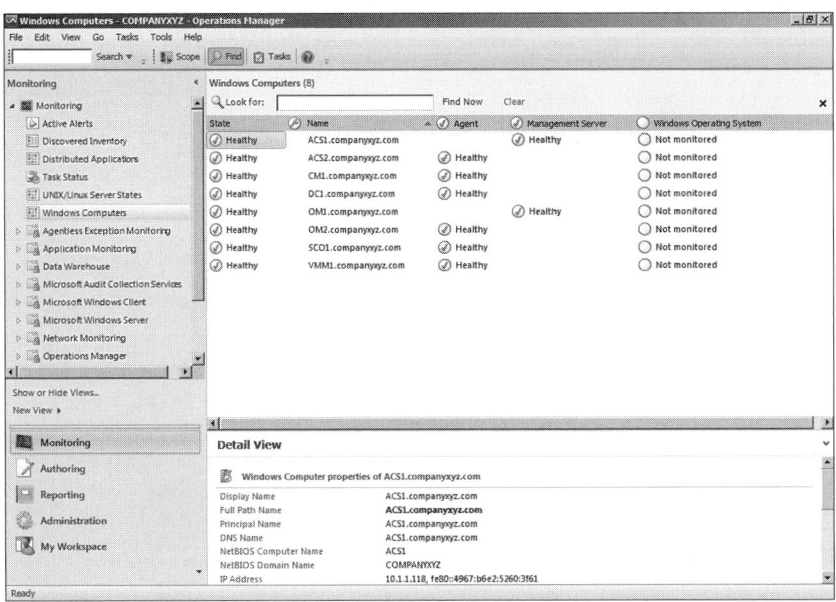

FIGURE 17.18 Agent state in a new infrastructure.

Once MPs are imported, the agent downloads rules to discover the various applications and components it's hosting, allowing the correct application-specific MPs to be applied.

This discovery process runs periodically to ensure the correct rules are always applied to the server.

Configuring OpsMgr

After installing the Operations Manager 2012 infrastructure, several configuration steps should be taken to have the system monitor properly, generate Active Directory synthetic transactions, and send out email notifications of alerts.

Management Group Settings

After the installation of the Operations Manager infrastructure, several settings need to be configured for the management group. These settings are called management group settings. They include a number of settings that control the security, data retention in the operations database, agent heartbeat interval, web addresses for alerts and consoles, and manual agent security. Figure 17.19 shows the Management Group Settings page.

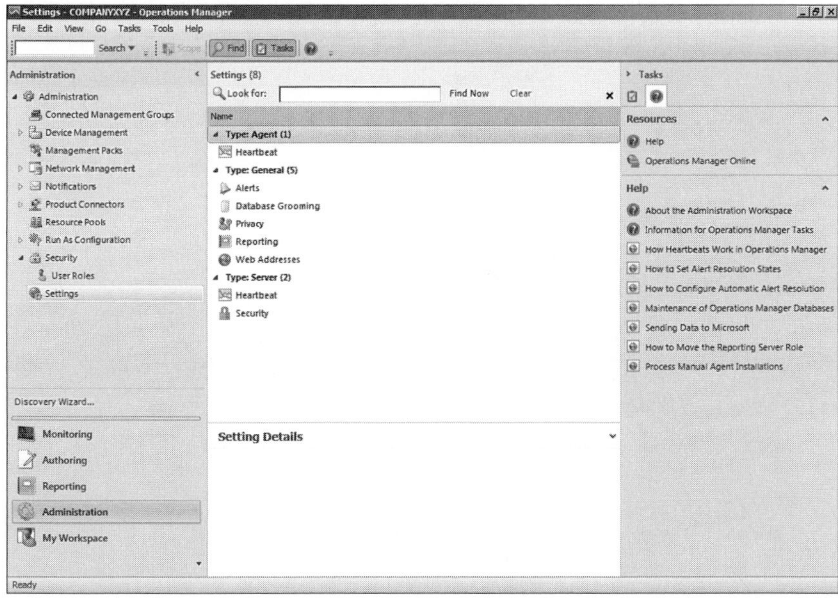

FIGURE 17.19 Management group settings.

The two key management group settings that need to be configured are as follows:

- ▶ Manual Agent Install Security
- ▶ Database Grooming

The manual agent install security controls how Operations Manager handles manual agent installations. If an agent is installed manually—that is, not pushed out from the console—the management servers will by default reject the agent. This is done to ensure that rogue computers are not connecting to the management infrastructure. In reality, this is a relatively low-probability threat. For most organizations, it is more convenient to have the manual agents be automatically accepted.

To configure the management group to accept manual agents, complete the following steps:

1. Launch the Operations console.
2. Select the Administration space.

3. Select the Settings folder.
4. Under the Type: Server section, right-click Security and select Properties.
5. Select the Review New Manual Agent Installations in Pending Management View option.
6. Check the Automatically Approve New Manually Installed Agents check box. Figure 17.20 shows how the settings should appear.

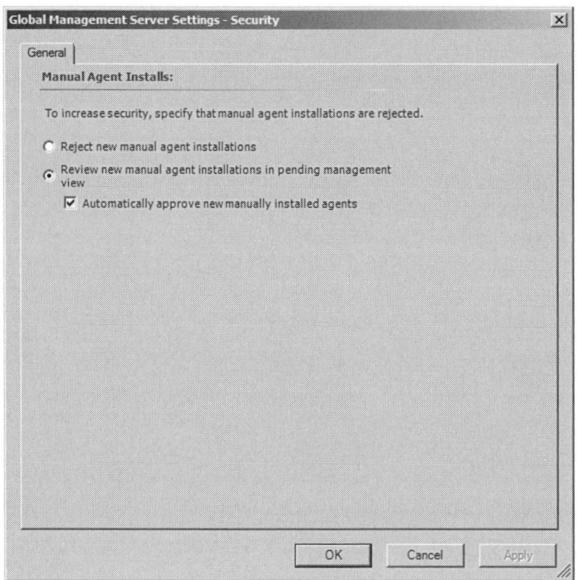

FIGURE 17.20 Manual agent install security.

7. Click OK to save the settings.

Now manual agents will be accepted automatically.

The database grooming controls how long data is retained in the operations database, which, in turn, dictates how much data is visible in the Operations console. Once the data retention period is reached, the data is groomed (that is, deleted) from the operations database. The default grooming settings are set for seven days, which means that after seven days the data is no longer available in the Operations console. However, the data is available in summarized form in the Reporting data warehouse for the retention period of that database, which is approximately a year. This data can then be viewed with the reports.

The biggest impact of the operations database grooming settings is that by default only a week of data is available. When troubleshooting problems using the console, it is important to have more than a week's worth of data. This allows for comparing data week to week to ascertain trends and catch longer-term problems.

However, the longer the grooming settings, the larger the size of the OperationsManager database. Therefore, it is important to balance the data retention against the size of the database.

The best-practice recommendation is to set the database grooming settings to 14 days to have two weeks' worth of data for troubleshooting without creating too large a database. These settings will essentially double the size of the OperationsManager database, which is manageable in most cases.

The settings to change are for the following records:

- Resolved Alerts
- Events Data
- Performance Data
- Task History
- Monitoring Job Data
- State Change Events Data
- Maintenance Mode History
- Availability History

WARNING

Do not adjust the Performance Signature grooming interval from the default of two days. This value is used to compute baselines. Changing it negatively affects performance baselines.

To adjust the Database Grooming settings, complete the following steps:

1. Launch the Operations console.
2. Select the Administration space.
3. Select the Settings folder.
4. Under the Type: General section, right-click Database Grooming and select Properties.
5. Select the record to change and click Edit.
6. Change the value to 14 and click OK.
7. Repeat for each of the remaining records. Do not change the Performance Signature record. Figure 17.21 shows how the configuration should look.
8. Click OK to save the configuration changes.

Now the data will be retained in the operations database for 14 days.

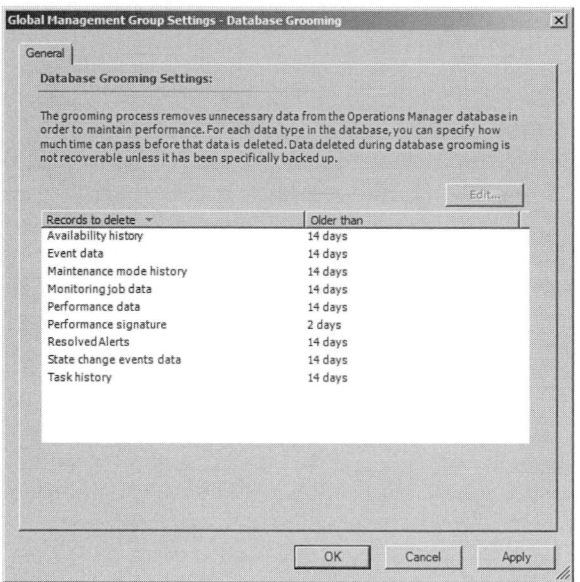

FIGURE 17.21 Database Grooming Settings.

Agent Proxy Configuration

Operations Manager 2012 has a variety of security measures built in to the product to prevent security breaches. One measure in particular is the prevention of impersonation of one agent by another. That is, an agent SERVER1 cannot insert operations data into the database about a domain controller DC1. This could constitute a security violation, where SERVER1 could maliciously generate fraudulent emergencies by making it appear that DC1 was having operational issues.

Although this is normally a good feature, this can be a problem if, in fact, SERVER1 is monitoring DC1 from a client perspective. The Operations Manager infrastructure would reject any information presented about DC1 by SERVER1. When this occurs, the system generates an alert to indicate that an attempt to proxy operations data has occurred. Figure 17.22 shows an example of the alert, where DC1.companyxyz.com is attempting to submit data for another computer. In the normal course of events, this alert is not an indication of an attack but rather a configuration problem.

To get around this problem, Agent Proxy can be selectively enabled for agents that need to be able to present operational data about other agents. To enable Agent Proxy for a computer, complete the following steps:

1. Open the Operations Manager 2012 console.
2. Select the Administration section.
3. Expand the Device Management folder and select the Agent Managed node.

4. Right-click the agent in the right pane, in this case SERVER1, and select Properties.
5. Click the Security tab.
6. Check the Allow This Agent to Act as a Proxy and Discover Managed Objects on Other Computers check box.
7. Click OK to save.

Repeat this for all agents that need to act as proxy agents.

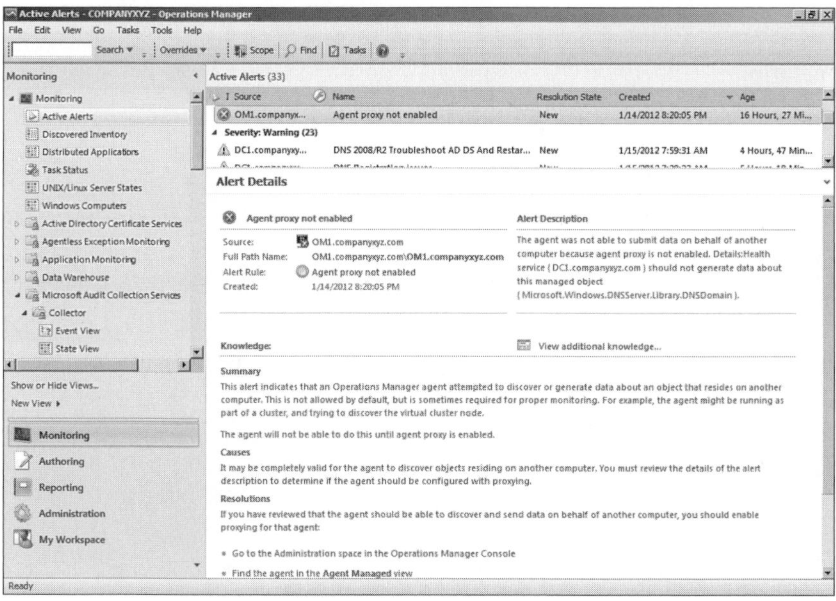

FIGURE 17.22 Agent Proxy alert.

NOTE

Because the alerts generated by this condition are rule based and not monitor based, the alert needs to be manually resolved by right-clicking on it and selecting Close Alert.

Agent Restart Recovery

Agents will heartbeat every 60 seconds by default, contacting their management server to check for new rules and upload data. On the management server, there is a Health Service Watcher corresponding to each managed agent. If the Health Service Watcher for an agent detects three missed heartbeats in a row (that is, 3 minutes without a heartbeat), the Health Service Watcher executes a pair of diagnostics:

- First, the Health Service Watcher attempts to ping the agent.
- Second, the Health Service Watcher checks to see if the Health Service is running on the agent.

An alert is then generated for each of the diagnostics if they failed. If the agent is reachable via ping but the Health Service is stopped, there is a recovery to restart the Health Service. This allows the agent to recover automatically from stopped agent conditions.

The Restart Health Service Recovery is disabled by default. To enable the functionality, an override can be created for the Health Service Watcher objects. To enable the recovery, follow these steps:

1. Open the Operations Manager 2012 console.
2. Select the Authoring space.
3. Expand the Management Pack Objects node.
4. Select the Monitors node.
5. Select View, Scope.
6. Click Clear All to clear the scope.
7. Type `health service watcher` in the Look For field and click the View All Targets option button.
8. Select the Health Service Watcher target. Don't pick the ones with additional information in parentheses.
9. Click OK.
10. Type `Heartbeat Failure` in the Look For field and click Find Now.
11. Right-click the Health Service Heartbeat Failure aggregate rollup node and select Overrides, Override Recovery, Restart Health Service, and For All Objects of Class: Health Service Watcher.
12. Check the Override box next to Enabled and set the value to True.
13. In the Select Destination Management Pack pull-down menu, select the appropriate override MP. If none exists, create a new MP named Operations Manager MP Overrides by clicking New and then following the prompts to create a new MP.

NOTE

Never use the Default Management Pack for overrides. Always create an override MP that corresponds to each imported MP.

14. Click OK to save the override.

Now if the Health Service is stopped on an agent, the management server automatically attempts to restart it.

Notifications and Subscriptions

When alerts are generated in the console, a wealth of information is available about the nature of the problem and how to troubleshoot and resolve it. However, most administrators will not be watching the console at all times. Operations Manager has a sophisticated notification mechanism that allows alerts to be forwarded to email, SMS, IM, or even a command-line interface. The most common method of alert notification is email.

However, Operations Manager generates a lot of alerts. If each one of these alerts were forwarded, this would overwhelm the average administrator's Inbox and prove totally useless. Operations Manager has two alert parameters to help categorize the alerts. Each alert has two parameters that help guide the notification process: severity and priority.

Alert Severity is the first and main parameter. There are three severity levels:

- **Critical (2)**—These alerts indicate that there is a problem that needs to be fixed immediately and is directly actionable (that is, something can be done).
- **Warning (1)**—These alerts indicate that there is a problem, but that it might not be immediately impacting the environment or might not be directly actionable.
- **Information (0)**—These alerts indicate that there is something that is good to know but might not be a problem nor is actionable.

By the nature of things, a lot more warning alerts are generated than critical alerts. In general, notifications should only be sent out for critical alerts. That is, an email should never be sent for a warning or informational alert.

Alert Priority is the second parameter that qualifies the alert status. The priority allows MP authors to make some alerts more important than others. There are three levels of priority, as well:

- High (2)
- Medium (1)
- Low (0)

In general, a high-priority, critical severity alert is very important. This includes events like an agent down or a security breach. A medium-priority, critical severity alert is important. Both are generally actionable.

The best practice is to create two Simple Mail Transfer Protocol (SMTP) channels to deliver the alert notification emails, which are as follows:

- **SMTP (High Priority)**—High-priority email to an SMTP gateway
- **SMTP (Normal Priority)**—Regular email to an SMTP gateway

Then, create two notification subscriptions that use the severity and the priority to select the emails to be sent:

- Notification for All Critical Severity High-Priority Alerts
- Notification for All Critical Severity Medium-Priority Alerts

This provides a configuration that delivers the very important alerts (high-priority, critical severity alerts) via high-priority email and important alerts (medium-priority, critical severity alerts) via regular email. All other alerts will be available in the console and no emails will be sent to notify of them.

The next sections set up the notification infrastructure described previously.

The first step is to set up a channel, that is, how the emails will be sent. To set up a channel, complete the following steps:

1. Launch the Operations Manager 2012 console.
2. Select the Administration space.
3. Expand the Notifications folder and select the Channels node.
4. Right-click the Channels node and select New Channel, E-Mail (SMTP).
5. Enter `SMTP Channel (High Priority)` for the channel name and click Next.
6. Click Add, enter the FQDN of the SMTP server, and click OK.
7. Enter a return SMTP address, such as `opsmgr@companyxyz.com`, and click Next.
8. Change the Importance to High and click Finish. Click Close to close the wizard.
9. Right-click the Channels node and select New Channel, E-Mail (SMTP).
10. Enter `SMTP Channel (Normal Priority)` for the channel name and click Next.
11. Click Add, enter the FQDN of the SMTP server, and click OK.
12. Enter a return SMTP address and click Next.
13. Leave the Importance at Normal and click Finish. Click Close to close the wizard.

The second step is to set up the subscriber, that is, to whom the emails will be sent. The steps are as follows:

1. Launch the Operations Manager 2012 console.
2. Select the Administration space.
3. Expand the Notifications folder and select the Subscribers node.
4. Right-click the Subscribers node and select New Subscriber.
5. Click the ellipsis (...) button and select a user or distribution group. Click OK.
6. Click Next.

7. Click Next to always send notifications.
8. Click Add.
9. Type `Email` for the address name and click Next.
10. Select the Channel Type as E-Mail (SMTP), enter the delivery email address, and then click Next.
11. Click Finish.
12. Click Finish again to save the subscriber. Click Close to exit the wizard.

NOTE

It is a best practice to use distribution lists rather than user email addresses for subscribers.

The last step is to set up the subscriptions, that is, what to notify on. To set up the subscriptions, complete the following steps:

1. Launch the Operations Manager 2012 console.
2. Select the Administration space.
3. Expand the Notifications folder and select the Subscriptions node.
4. Right-click the Subscriptions node and select New Subscription.
5. Enter `Notification for All Critical Severity High Priority Alerts` for the subscription name and click Next.
6. Check the Of a Specific Severity and the Of a Specific Priority check boxes.
7. In the Criteria Description pane, click the Specific Severity link, check the Critical check box, and then click OK.
8. In the Criteria Description pane, click the Specific Priority link, check the High check box, and then click OK.
9. Click Next.
10. Click Add, click Search, select the subscriber, click Add, and then click OK.
11. Click Next.
12. Click Add, click Search, select the SMTP Channel (High Priority) channel, click Add, and then click OK.
13. Click Next, click Finish, and then click Close.
14. Right-click the Subscriptions node and select New Subscription.
15. Enter `Notification for All Critical Severity Medium Priority Alerts` for the subscription name and click Next.

16. Check the Of a Specific Severity and the Of a Specific Priority check boxes.
17. In the Criteria Description pane, click the Specific Severity link, check the Critical check box, and then click OK.
18. In the Criteria Description pane, click the Specific Priority link, check the Medium check box, and then click OK.
19. Click Next.
20. Click Add, click Search, select the subscriber, click Add, and then click OK.
21. Click Next.
22. Click Add, click Search, select the SMTP Channel (Normal Priority) channel, click Add, and then click OK.
23. Click Next, click Finish, and then click Close.

Now, the subscribers will get email notifications for alerts based on the severity and priority. These severities and priorities are based on the judgments of the authors of the MPs, which might or might not be optimal for any given organization. Later in the chapter, the priority and severity of alerts are used to tune the MPs to reduce alert noise.

Administering OpsMgr

After Operations Manager 2012 has been installed and configured, ongoing work needs to be done to ensure that the product performs as expected. The two primary activities are to, first, tune the MPs to ensure that alerts are valid for the environment and that alert noise is reduced and, second, produce reports of the information that Operations Manager 2012 is collecting.

Dip Stick Health Check Tasks

Whenever a motorist is going for a drive, the conscientious driver goes through a set of basic automotive health checks, including the following:

- Check the oil level with the dip stick.
- Check the tire pressure.
- Check the gasoline level.

These are sometimes referred to as the "dip stick health checks" because the oil level is checked with a dip stick.

Like any other complicated technology, Operations Manager 2012 can have problems in a variety of ways, ranging from running out of disk space, to failing to send email notifications, to having agents stopped, and so forth. To make sure that Operations Manager is functioning properly, a set of dip stick health checks can be performed to make sure everything is running smoothly.

These are the health check tasks that the OpsMgr administrator should do every day to verify the health and proper operation of the OpsMgr infrastructure:

1. Verify that you have received notifications by email. Confirm that you are getting notifications within the normal range. Too many is a bad sign and too few (or none) is also a bad sign.
2. Review OpsMgr daily reports sent via email or in the console. If using the console, the reports are stored in the Favorites folder in the Reporting space.
3. In the Operations Manager console, review the Active Alerts view. This shows you new alerts.
4. In the Operations Manager console, review the All Alerts view. This shows you both new and closed alerts.
5. In the Operations Manager console, review the Agent Health State view in the \Operations Manager\Agent Details node. Investigate any Critical, Warning, or Not Monitored states.
6. In the Operations Manager console, review the Active Alerts view in the \Operations Manager\Agent Details node. Investigate any Critical or Warning alerts.
7. In the Operations Manager console, review the Management Server Health State view in the \Operations Manager\Management Server node. Investigate any Critical, Warning, or Not Monitored states.
8. In the Operations Manager console, review the Active Alerts view in the \Operations Manager\Management Server node. Investigate any Critical or Warning alerts.

After reviewing the results of these health check tasks, an administrator can be pretty confident that the Operations Manager 2012 infrastructure is functioning properly.

Health check task number 2 recommends reviewing the daily reports. The recommended Operations Manager health reports to review on a daily basis are as follows:

- **Alert Logging Latency report**—This report tells you the length of time between an event being raised to an alert being generated. This should be under 30 seconds.
- **Send Queue % Used Top 10 report**—This report tells you if agents are having trouble uploading their data to the management servers. These queues should be less than 1%.
- **Top 10 Most Common Alerts report**—This report analyzes the most common alerts that were generated and are good for identifying alert-tuning opportunities.
- **Daily Alert report**—This report gives you a complete list of all the alerts that were generated. This is very detailed, but is good for chasing down problems uncovered in other checks.

These health check tasks should give a good sense of the operational health of the OpsMgr infrastructure.

Management Pack Updates

Management pack updates are released periodically by Microsoft. The Operations console allows you to update installed MPs from the online catalog.

NOTE

Installing updates by definition changes the rules, alerts, and monitors that are deployed. This can have significant consequences on the alerts that are generated. Any updates should first be tested in a lab setting to ensure that there are no problems.

The online catalog should be checked for updates to the installed MPs on a monthly basis. To do this, complete the following steps:

1. Launch the Operations console.
2. Go to the Administration space.
3. Select the Management Packs node.
4. Right-click the Management Packs node and select Import Management Packs.
5. Click Add and select Add from Catalog.
6. In the View pull-down, select Updates Available for Installed Management Packs.
7. Click the Search button.
8. Review the results in the Management Packs in the Catalog pane.
9. Select the MPs to update and click Add to add them to the Selected Management Packs pane.
10. Click OK.
11. Review the select MPs, the version numbers, and any warnings or informational messages.
12. Click Install to download and import the MPs.
13. After download and import, click Close to close the Import Management Packs Wizard.

The MP updates take effect immediately.

Notification and Alert Tuning

After deploying Operations Manager 2012, there are frequently complaints about the number of alert notifications that get generated. This can cause organizations to decommission the product, ignore the emails, or generally complain about what a bad product it is. In reality, the Operations Manager alert notifications just need to be tuned.

The following process helps tune the MP quickly and effectively to reduce alert and email noise. This is done by adjusting parameters on the rules (Enable/Disable, Severity, and Priority) using overrides.

Alert Severity is the first parameter to be tuned. There are three levels:

- Critical (2)
- Warning (1)
- Information (0)

Alert Priority is the second parameter to be tuned. There are three levels of priority as well:

- High (2)
- Medium (1)
- Low (0)

There are two SMTP channels to deliver the emails:

- **SMTP Channel (High Priority)**—High-priority email to an SMTP gateway
- **SMTP Channel (Normal Priority)**—Regular-priority email to an SMTP gateway

NOTE

These channels were created earlier in the chapter.

There are two notification subscriptions that use the severity and priority to select the emails to be sent:

- Notification for All Critical Severity High-Priority Alerts
- Notification for All Critical Severity Medium-Priority Alerts

These channels and subscriptions automatically send email notifications for critical severity high- and medium-priority alerts.

NOTE

These notification subscriptions were created earlier in the chapter.

However, sometime the alerts that are generated are not appropriate for the environment. This is because the source alert is not appropriate or actionable, so the resulting email is not useful and can be considered noise.

When you get an email from an alert that you don't want, you need to tune the MP monitor or rule. The basic decision tree is as follows:

1. **Alert is noise?** If no, this means that the alert is appropriate and actionable. In this case, the underlying cause of the alert needs to be addressed.

2. **Alert not needed?** If yes, create an override to disable the rule for either the instance of the object, the class of objects, or a group of the objects. This prevents the alert from being generated, so no console alerts and definitely no emails are generated.

3. **Alert severity too high?** If yes, create an override to change the alert severity to warning. This keeps the alert in the console as a warning, but does not generate an email.

4. **Alert priority too high?** If yes, create an override to change the alert priority to low. This keeps the alert as a critical alert, but prevents an email from being generated.

Figure 17.23 shows the decision tree in a flowchart form.

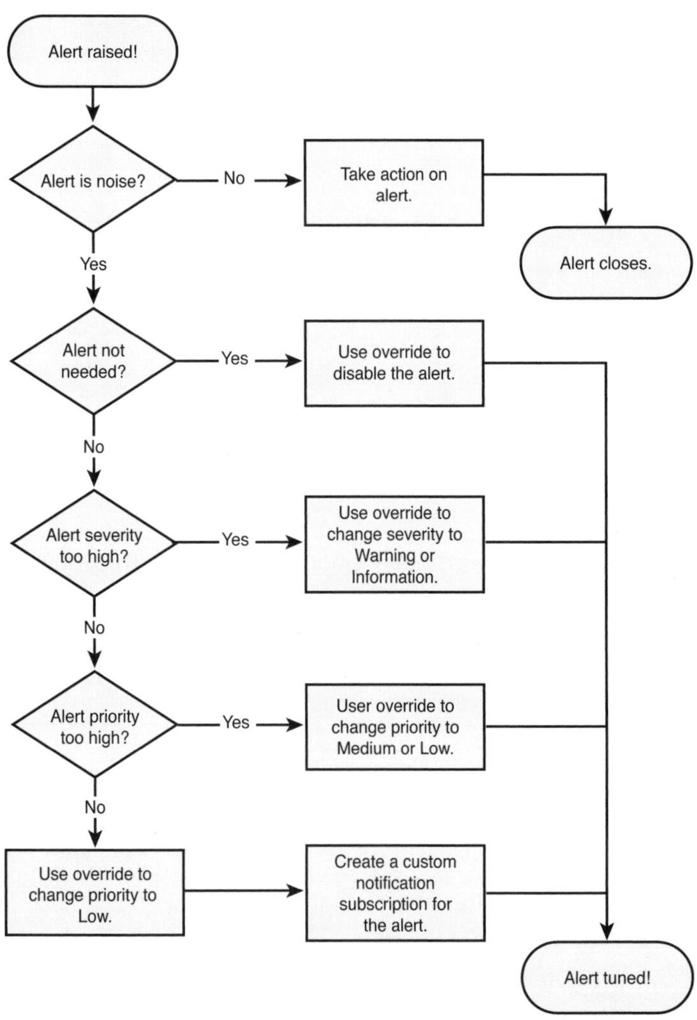

FIGURE 17.23 Alert tuning flowchart.

If these are not enough to narrow down the email notification behavior, a custom approach is needed. For example, if you want to get an email when mail flow alerts are generated but only after a couple are generated, do the following:

1. Change the alert priority to low using an override. This prevents the alert from generating a notification from the default subscriptions.
2. Create a notification subscription for the alert, but set an aging to longer than the test interval or whatever you want to wait before sending the email.

NOTE

When creating the custom notification subscription, make sure to have the With Specific Resolution State criteria checked and only New resolution states selected. If this is not done, the notification triggers after the aging. This is because even if the alert closes before the aging period is up, the Closed resolution state still triggers the notification.

This process takes care of the majority of cases and reduces spamming by the OpsMgr console.

These options can be taken for all objects of the target class, for just the specific instance that generated the alert, or for a group. The group would have to be created in advance and would have to contain objects of the type targeted by the monitor or rule generating the alert.

For example, let's say there is an Application of Group Policy critical alert that is occurring frequently in the environment. It is occurring on a number of Windows Server 2008 R2 servers and is generating a lot of email notifications. This alert is valid, but does not require immediate action. The alert needs to be tuned to change the severity from critical to warning. The steps to tune the alert are as follows:

1. Open the Operations Manager 2012 console.
2. Select the Monitoring space.
3. Select the Active Alerts view.
4. Locate and select the Application of Group Policy alert that is to be tuned.
5. Right-click the alert and select Overrides, Override the Monitor, and For All Objects of Class: Group Policy 2008 Runtime. This overrides the alert for all objects of that class.

NOTE

The alert is to be tuned for all objects, rather than any specific instances. If the alert is to be tuned for the specific instance that raised the alert, the For the Object option should be chosen. If it is a group of the objects, the For a Group option should be chosen. The group would have to be pre-created and be a group of the target objects.

6. Check the Override box next to Alert Severity and set the value to Warning.
7. In the Select Destination Management Pack pull-down menu, select the appropriate override MP. If none exists, create a new override MP named Group Policy MP Overrides by clicking New and then following the prompts to create a new MP.

NOTE

Never use the Default Management Pack for overrides. Always create an override MP that corresponds to each imported MP.

8. Click OK to save the override.

Now the next time the monitor triggers an alert, it will be of warning severity and will not generate a notification email. However, the alert can still be reviewed in the console.

This approach to tuning will address 90% of the noisy alerts that you get. To target the noisiest alerts, see the Most Common Alerts report. This helps identify the alerts that are responsible for the most noise. You'll frequently find that 50% of your alerts are coming from less than five rules or monitors. Tuning those gives you the most bang for your buck.

Exploring the Exchange Server 2013 Management Pack

The Exchange Server 2013 Management Pack for Operations Manager 2012 uses an extensive set of monitors, rules, scripts, and knowledge to manage the Exchange Server 2013 messaging environment. The management pack is one of the most sophisticated management packs produced by Microsoft.

Unlike the Exchange Server 2010 MP, the Exchange Server 2013 MP is refreshed and easier to use. This management pack provides monitoring on all facets essential to the overall health of the Exchange Server 2013 infrastructure.

Preparing to Install the Exchange Server 2013 Management Pack

In part due to the sophistication of the Exchange Server 2013 Management Pack, there are more preparation steps and requirements to installing it than for most management packs.

The prerequisites for the management pack are as follows:

- All Exchange Server 2013 servers must use the default LocalSystem as the agent action account.
- All Exchange Server 2013 database availability group (DAG) member servers must have agents.
- Agent proxy must be enabled for all Exchange Server 2013 servers.

These prerequisites are required for the management pack to operate properly, without which it might generate false alarms.

In addition, it is recommended that the following management packs be installed as well:

- Active Directory Management Pack
- IIS Management Pack
- DNS Management Pack
- Windows Server Management Pack

These management packs monitor supporting services, which can impact the overall health of the Exchange Server 2013 system.

Exchange Server 2013 Health Manager Logs

Rather than have an extensive set of event rules in the Exchange Server 2013 Management Pack, which would have to be kept in sync with the product, the Exchange Server 2013 product team instead incorporates all that management intelligence directly into the product and exposes it in the Exchange event logs, which is then simply captured by the management pack.

The Exchange Server 2013 component that manages these activities is the Microsoft Exchange Health Manager service. The service monitors, debugs, and remediates issues found in the Exchange Server 2013 server and reports its activities in the event logs.

Using the built-in monitoring and recovery via the Microsoft Exchange Health Manager service, Exchange Server 2013 does its own monitoring and recovery. The management pack simply consumes the results of those native activities in the form of event log entries.

NOTE

The Exchange Server 2013 Health Manager service eliminates the need for the Exchange Server 2010 Correlation Engine service that shipped with the Exchange Server 2010 Management Pack. The Health Manager service handles all the function that the correlation service managed, but it is installed natively on all Exchange Server 2013 servers rather than being a bolt-on service.

Largely overlooked in Exchange Server 2010, Exchange Server 2013 has a greatly expanded event logging infrastructure that the Exchange Server 2013 Management Pack leverages heavily. Located in the Event Viewer under the Applications and Services Logs\Microsoft\Exchange, there are 28 different logs organized into six major categories. The categories are ActiveMonitoring, HighAvailability, MailboxDatabaseFailureItems, ManagedAvailability, PushNotifications, and Troubleshooters.

The ActiveMonitoring category includes logs relating to maintenance activities, synthetic transactions, and infrastructure tests. The ActiveMonitoring logs consist of the following:

- MaintenanceDefinition
- MaintenanceResult
- MonitorDefinition
- MonitorResult
- ProbeDefinition
- ProbeResult
- ResponderDefinition
- ResponderResult

The HighAvailability category includes logs relating to replication, high-availability monitoring, seeding, and other high-availability logging. The HighAvailability logs consist of the following:

- AppLogMirror
- BlockReplication
- Debug
- Monitoring
- Network
- Operational
- Seeding
- TruncationDebug

The MailboxDatabaseFailureItems category contains logs relating to mailbox database issues and recoveries. The MailboxDatabaseFailureItems logs consist of the following:

- Debug
- Operational

The ManagedAvailability category contains logs relating to monitoring component health (health sets), automatic recovery operations, and startup notifications. The ManagedAvailability logs consist of the following:

- InvokeNowRequest
- Monitoring
- RecoveryActionLogs
- StartupNotification

The PushNotifications logs consist of the following:

- Analytics
- Debug
- Operational

The Troubleshooters log consists of the following:

- Operational

The contents of the event log messages are directly copied into the Operations Manager alerts.

Installing the Exchange Server 2013 Management Pack

The Exchange Server 2013 Management Pack can be downloaded directly from the catalog, making installation a simple task.

NOTE

The next steps can be skipped if the Exchange Server 2013 Management Pack was installed during the Operations Manager 2012 installation. If you are not sure, the user interface will show if the Exchange Server 2013 Management Pack was installed when it is selected for download.

To import the Exchange Server 2013 MP, follow these steps:

1. Launch the Operations console.
2. Select the Administration section.
3. Select the Management Packs folder.
4. Right-click the Management Packs folder and select Import Management Packs.
5. Click Add and select Add from Catalog.
6. Click the Search button to search the entire catalog.
7. Select the Exchange Server 2013 Management Pack from the previous bulleted list and click Add for each of them. Each of the major MPs might include a number of sub-MPs for discovery, monitoring, and other breakdowns of functionality.
8. When done adding the MPs, click OK.
9. The wizard now validates the added MPs, checking for versions, dependencies, and security risks. It allows problem MPs to be removed and dependencies to be added to the list.
10. Click Install to begin the download and import process. Progress is shown for each of the MPs being imported.
11. After all the MPs are imported, click Close to exit the wizard.

After the management pack is imported, discovery will be started and Exchange Server 2013 servers in objects will be discovered automatically.

Exchange Server 2013 Management Pack Views

Upon importing this management pack, a Microsoft Exchange Server sealed management pack folder will appear in the Monitoring view tree and in that folder will be an Exchange

2013 folder. The views are organized into folders by role, which helps control the number of objects within a given folder.

Included in the top-level views are the following:

- **Alerts view**—Details alerts that do not have a 255 resolution state for all systems discovered as part of the Exchange 2013 All Entities Group.
- **Event view**—Shows events related to the Exchange Server role.
- **Organization Health view**—Displays the state of the Exchange Server 2013 organization with summary states for each Exchange Server 2013 service.
- **Performance view**—Displays all the performance counters collected by the management pack. This allows Performance views across different counters for comparison and correlation.
- **Server Health view**—Displays the discovered role health, as shown in Figure 17.24 with the Service Components selected. The EX01 Transport role is in a critical state.

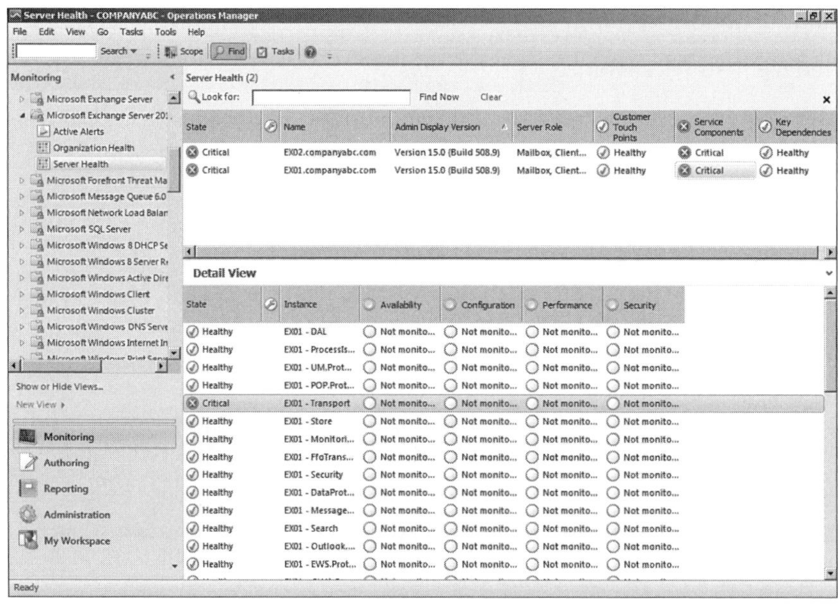

FIGURE 17.24 Exchange Server 2013 Server Health view.

- **Service State view**—Displays the state of all Exchange Server 2013 services, including individual instances.
- **Task Stats**—Shows the status of all Exchange-related tasks that have been run. This view is somewhat useless, as the Exchange Server 2013 Management Pack doesn't include tasks any longer.

For the Client Access role, the Client Access subfolder contains the following views:

- **Alerts view**—Displays alerts that do not have a 255 resolution state for all systems discovered with the role
- **Event view**—Shows events related to the role
- **Performance view**—Displays all the performance counters related to the role
- **State view**—Displays the state for all systems discovered with the role

Within the Client Access subfolder, a subfolder contains views related to the synthetic transactions:

- ActiveSync Connectivity
- ECP Connectivity
- IMAP4 Connectivity
- Outlook Client RPC
- Outlook Connectivity
- OWA Connectivity
- POP3 Connectivity
- Web Service Connectivity

Each of the folders contains Performance views of the synthetic transaction metrics (such as ActiveSync latency shown in Figure 17.25) and Event views of the scripts that generate the transactions.

The Outlook Client RPC subfolder under the Client Access subfolder contains the following Performance views:

- **Client: Latency > # secRPCs**—There are three Performance views that show the counts of client latency that are greater than 2 seconds, 5 seconds, and 10 seconds for each Mailbox server.
- **Client: RPCs Succeeded**—This is a Performance view that shows the number of successful RPC connections for each Mailbox server.

These views are very useful for understanding how the client response time is, but they require careful interpretation. The counters are counts since the last restart, so they will always be increasing. The different rates of increase or ratios are what are important. If there is a significant number of RPC latency over 10 seconds compared with 2 seconds, the system might be running below par. Or if the ratio changes in the wrong direction, that could be a sign of a problem.

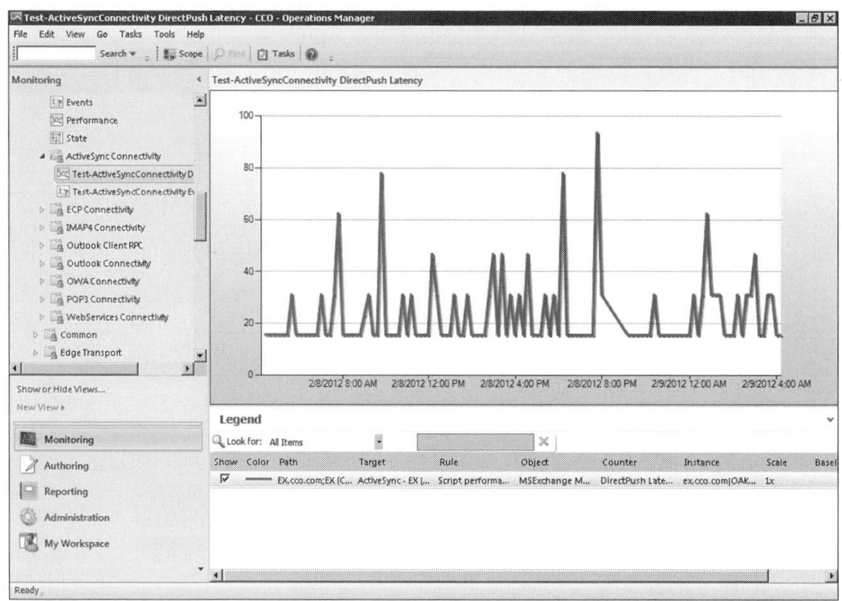

FIGURE 17.25 Exchange Server 2013 ActiveSync Connectivity view.

NOTE

A good ratio is something like 1:3:15 for 10 seconds to 5 seconds to 2 seconds RPC latency. In other words, a well-performing system will have an approximately 1:15 ratio of RPC request latency greater than 10 seconds to those greater than 2 seconds. Most RPC requests should be serviced in less than 2 seconds.

For the Edge role, an Edge Transport subfolder contains the following views:

- **Alerts view**—Displays alerts that do not have a 255 resolution state for all systems discovered as Exchange Server 2010 Edge Transport role
- **Event view**—Shows events related to the role
- **Performance view**—Displays all the performance counters related to the role
- **State view**—Displays the state for all systems discovered as Exchange Server 2010 Edge Transport role
- **Transport DSN view**—Displays performance counters for Delivery Status Notifications (DSNs)
- **Transport Queues view**—Displays performance counters for queues

In addition, an Agents subfolder under the Edge Transport subfolder contains the following Performance views that show metrics related to the antispam agents:

- Attachment Filter
- Connection Filter
- Content Filter
- Protocol Analysis
- Recipient Filter
- Sender Filter
- Sender ID

The Hub Transport service has a corresponding Hub Transport subfolder containing the following:

- **Alerts**—Displays alerts that do not have a 255 resolution state for all systems discovered as Exchange Server 2013 Hub Transport service
- **Event view**—Shows events related to the role
- **Performance view**—Displays all the performance counters related to the role
- **State**—Displays the state for all systems discovered as Exchange Server 2013 Hub Transport service
- **Transport DSN**—Shows the transport DSNs
- **Transport Queues**—Shows the transport queues

An Agents subfolder under the Hub Transport subfolder contains the following Performance views that show metrics related to the antispam agents:

- Connection Filter
- Content Filter
- Protocol Analysis
- Recipient Filter
- Sender Filter
- SMS
- Sender ID

The Mailbox role has a corresponding Mailbox subfolder containing the following:

- **Alerts**—Displays alerts that do not have a 255 resolution state for all systems discovered as Exchange Server 2013 Mailbox role
- **Database Service State**—Shows the state of all databases across the organization, including number of copies

- **Event view**—Shows events related to the role
- **Performance view**—Displays all the performance counters related to the role
- **State**—Displays the state for all systems discovered as Exchange Server 2013 Mailbox role

The Mailbox role has an Information Store subfolder containing two subfolders, Database and RPC, that contain Performance Metric views.

A Database subfolder under the Information Store subfolder contains Performance views related to database read/write performance per second and in averages such as I/O Database Reads Average Latency (shown in Figure 17.26).

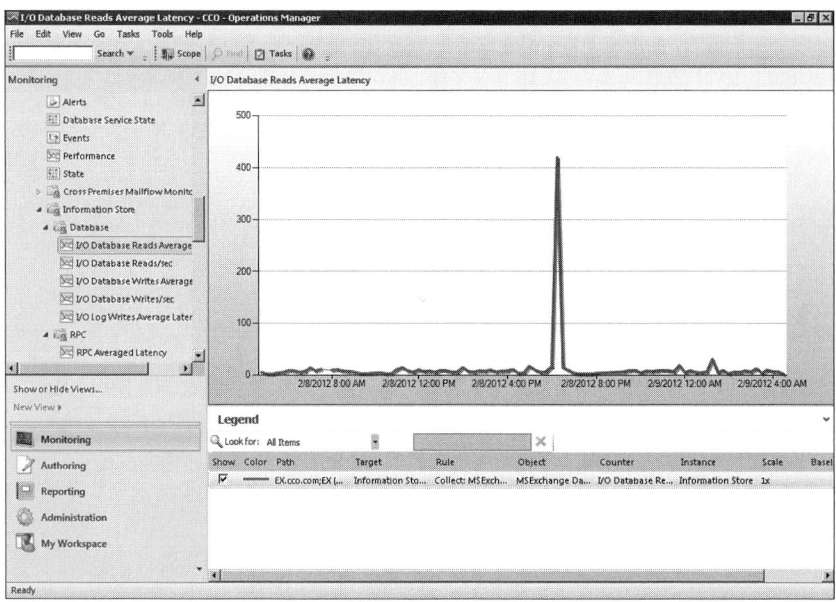

FIGURE 17.26 Exchange Server 2013 I/O Database Reads Average Latency view.

An RPC subfolder under the Information Store subfolder contains the following:

- RPC Average Latency
- RPC Requests

The Unified Messaging service subfolder contains the following:

- **Alerts**—Displays alerts that do not have a 255 resolution state for all systems discovered as Exchange Server 2013 Unified Messaging service.
- **Event view**—Shows events related to the role.

- **Performance view**—Displays all the performance counters related to the role.
- **Performance Reporting**—Contains all the UM performance counters collected. This is a legacy view that duplicates the Performance view.
- **State**—Displays the state for all systems discovered as Exchange Server 2013 Unified Messaging service.

After the Exchange Server 2013 Management Pack has been deployed, Exchange administrators heavily utilize the ExBPA, Active Alerts, and Server State views for daily health check status reports. The views are used as opposed to stating a green or healthy status based on the fact that an issue has not occurred before the morning health check.

In addition, the Exchange Server 2013 Topology view has been used for documentation. The Client Access CAS Synthetic Transaction State view can be used for an at-a-glance health check on client connectivity and mail flow, and the Edge performance counters under the Agents subfolder of Edge Transport can be used to tune the Edge server.

NOTE

If monitoring Exchange Server 2010 Edge Transport servers prior to the release of the Exchange Server 2013 SP1 with the new Exchange Server 2013 Edge Transport role, then the Exchange Server 2010 Management Pack will need to be installed to monitor the Exchange Server 2010 Edge Transport servers. If upgrading from Exchange Server 2010 to Exchange Server 2013, then the management pack is likely already loaded.

Exchange Server 2013 Management Pack Reports

The Exchange Server 2013 Management Pack ships with 17 reports, which are as follows:

- **CAS**—This report shows the Protocol Availability numbers.
- **Client Performance**—The Client Performance report (shown in Figure 17.27) shows the percentage of successful RPC client/server operations between clients (2003 and newer) and Exchange Server 2013 during the specified time period. Any operations that take less than or equal to 2 seconds are considered successful. The Client RPC Latency and RPC count columns are calculated from the data generated by clients and sent to the Exchange server.
- **Machine Level Capacity Trending**—The Machine Level Capacity Trending Report provides capacity utilization information at the server level.
- **Cross Premises Mail Flow Monitoring**—The Cross Premises Mail Flow Monitoring report is used to measure mail flow in a cross-premises topology where your organization uses both Outlook Live and on-premises Microsoft Exchange servers. The report shows latency between on-premises Internet egress sites and Outlook Live data centers and the status of test messages over the reporting interval.
- **Performance Counter View**—The Performance Counter View report graphs performance counters for a number of selectable metrics.

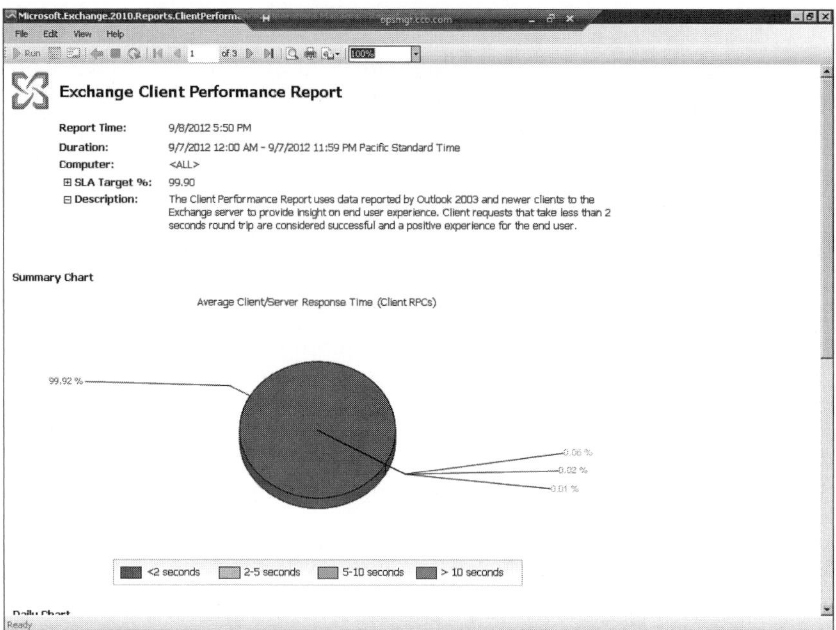

FIGURE 17.27 Exchange Server 2013 Client Performance report.

- **Performance Counter View Raw**—The Performance Counter View Raw report lists the performance counters data points for a number of selectable metrics.
- **Performance Nutrition**—The Performance Nutrition report shows the detailed % Processor Time, Private Bytes, and Working Set statistics for computers hosting a number of services.
- **Protocol Downtime Details**—The Protocol Downtime Details report shows daily downtimes and impacting alerts that affected protocol availability of service entities on a given day.
- **Remote PowerShell Service**—This report shows the availability numbers for the Remote PowerShell service.
- **Role Level Capacity Trending**—This report shows capacity trending for the various Exchange Server 2013 roles over the course of a month.
- **SLA**—This report shows the SLA availability numbers.
- **SMTP Availability**—The SMTP Availability report provides client SMTP submission availability data as measured by synthetic transactions.
- **Transport Platform Distribution Group Usage**—The Transport Platform Distribution Group Usage report provides usage data for distribution groups.

- **Transport Platform Hourly Server Statistics**—The Transport Platform Hourly Server Statistics report provides statistics from message tracking logs to provide information about mail flow latency, by the hour.
- **Transport Platform Server Statistics**—The Transport Platform Server Statistics report provides statistics from message tracking logs to provide information about mail flow latency, by the day.
- **Transport Platform Top Users**—The Transport Platform Top Users report provides usage data for the clients that send the most messages, receive the most messages, and experience the most failures.
- **UM Local Service**—This report shows the UM availability numbers.

Summary

System Center Operations Manager 2012 is key to managing Exchange Server 2013 environments, providing detailed performance monitoring, alerting, and reporting. The Exchange Server 2013 Management Pack provides out-of-the-box deep monitoring that allows administrators to easily understand how their Exchange Server 2013 systems are performing and quickly pinpoint any problems.

Understanding the components of Operations Manager, their interactions, and their constraints is critical to designing and deploying an effective infrastructure. This type of functionality is instrumental in reducing downtime and getting the most out of an OpsMgr investment.

Best Practices

The following are best practices from this chapter:

- Always create a design and plan when deploying Operations Manager, even if it is a simple one.
- Take future expansion and relevance of hardware into account when sizing servers for OpsMgr deployment.
- Keep the installation of OpsMgr on a separate server or set of separate dedicated member servers that do not run any other separate applications.
- Start with a single management group and add on additional management groups only if they are absolutely necessary.
- Use Windows Server 2008 R2 SP1 and SQL Server 2008 R2 together to gain maximum performance from both.
- Use SQL Enterprise when combining components on the same server.
- Use SQL Enterprise when scaling up Operations Manager.

- Allocate adequate space for the databases depending on the length of time needed to store events and the number of managed systems.
- Leverage the reporting database to store and report on data over a long period.
- Always create disaster recovery processes to restore in the event of a failure.
- Deploy fault tolerance (that is, clusters) only when needed.
- Size the disk subsystems to provide sufficient Input/Output Operations per Second (IOPS) to support the anticipated data flows.
- Use a dedicated service account for OpsMgr.
- Allocate adequate space for the databases depending on the length of time needed to store events and the number of managed systems.
- Monitor the size of the OpsMgr database to ensure that it does not increase beyond the bounds of acceptable size.
- Be sure to keep the MPs updated, as Microsoft routinely releases updates to the core MPs.
- When tuning, err on the side of fewer alerts. If nothing will be done about an alert, make sure it doesn't send a notification email.
- Configure OpsMgr to monitor itself.

CHAPTER 18

Documenting an Exchange Server 2013 Environment

IN THIS CHAPTER

Documentation is the cornerstone for building and maintaining a streamlined Microsoft Exchange Server 2013 environment. Documentation is not only an integral part of the installation or design of an Exchange Server 2013 environment, but it is also important for the maintenance, support, and recovery of new or existing environments.

Documentation serves several purposes throughout the life cycle of Exchange Server 2013 and is especially critical on a per-project basis. In the initial stages of a project, it serves to provide a historical record of the options and decisions made during the design process. During the testing and implementation phases, documents such as step-by-step procedures and checklists guide project team members and help ensure that all steps are completed. When the implementation portion of the project is complete, support documentation can play a key role in maintaining the health of the new environment. Support documents include administration and maintenance procedures, checklists, detailed configuration settings, and monitoring procedures.

In the discovery stages of the project, documentation serves to record the key elements of a successful implementation:

- Organizational goals and objectives
- Business requirements
- Technical specifications

It quickly becomes apparent how the documents become building blocks for the remaining documentation needs. By defining the organizational goals and objectives, the business requirements can be identified. After the business requirements are listed, the technical specifications are developed to support them.

This chapter is dedicated to providing the breadth and scope of documentation for an Exchange Server 2013 environment. Equally important, it provides considerations and best practices for keeping your messaging environment well documented, maintained, and manageable.

Benefits of Documentation

Although many of the benefits of Exchange Server 2013 documentation are obvious and tangible, others can be harder to identify. A key benefit to documentation is that the process of putting the information down on paper encourages a higher level of analysis and review of the topic at hand. The process also encourages teamwork and collaboration within an organization and interdepartmental exchange of ideas.

Documentation that is developed with specific goals, and goes through a review or approval process, is typically well organized and complete, and contributes to the overall professionalism of the organization and its knowledge base. The following sections examine some of the other benefits of professional documentation in the Exchange Server 2013 environment.

In today's world of doing more with less, the intangible benefits of good documentation can become a challenge to justify to upper management. Some key benefits of documentation include the following:

- **Collaboration**—Producing the documentation to support a good Exchange Server 2013 implementation requires input from departments across the organization. This teamwork encourages deeper analysis and more careful review of the project goals. With better base information, the project team can make more informed decisions and avoid having to go back to the drawing board to address missed objectives.
- **Historical records**—Implementation projects are composed of several different stages where goals are identified and key decisions are made to support them. It is important to make sure these decisions and their supporting arguments are recorded for future reference. As the project moves forward, it is not uncommon for details to get changed because of incomplete information being passed from the design stage onto the implementation stage.
- **Training**—Life is ever changing. That might sound a bit philosophical for a book on technology but when it comes to people, we know that some of them move on to other challenges. And that is when good documentation will become an invaluable tool to provide information to their replacement. This is equally true for the executive sponsor, the project manager, or the engineer building the Exchange server.

Knowledge Sharing and Knowledge Management

The right documentation enables an organization to organize and manage its data and intellectual property. Company policies and procedures are typically located throughout multiple locations that include individual files for various departments. Consolidating this information into logical groupings can be beneficial.

TIP

Place documentation in at least two different locations where it is easily accessible for authorized users, such as on the intranet, in a public folder, or in hard-copy format. Also consider using a document management system such as Microsoft SharePoint.

A complete design document consolidates and summarizes key discussions and decisions, budgetary concerns, and timing issues. This consolidation provides a single source of information for questions that might emerge at a later date. In addition, a document that describes the specific configuration details of the Exchange server might prove very valuable to a manager in another company office when making a purchasing decision.

All of the documents should be readily available at all times. This is especially critical regarding disaster recovery documents. Centralizing the documentation and communicating the location helps reduce the use of out-of-date documentation and reduce confusion during a disaster recovery. It is also recommended that they be available in a number of formats, such as hard copy, the appropriate place on the network, and even via an intranet.

Financial Benefits of Documentation

Proper Exchange Server 2013 documentation can be time consuming and adds to the cost of the environment and project. In lean economic times for a company or organization, it is often difficult to justify the expense of project documentation. However, when looking at documents, such as in maintenance or disaster recovery scenarios, it is easy to determine that creating this documentation makes financial sense. For example, in an organization where downtime can cost thousands of dollars per minute, the return on investment (ROI) in disaster recovery and maintenance documentation is easy to calculate. In a company that is growing rapidly and adding staff and new servers on a regular basis, tested documentation on server builds and administration training can also have immediate and visible benefits.

Financial benefits are not limited to maintenance and disaster recovery documentation. Well-developed and professional design and planning documentation helps the organization avoid costly mistakes in the implementation or migration process, such as buying too many server licenses or purchasing too many servers.

Baselining Records for Documentation Comparisons

Baselining is a process of recording the state of an Exchange Server 2013 system so that any changes in its performance can be identified at a later date. Complete baselining also pertains to the overall network performance, including wide area network (WAN) links, but in those cases it might require special software and tools (such as sniffers) to record the information.

An Exchange Server 2013 system baseline document records the state of the server after it is implemented in a production environment and can include statistics such as memory use, paging, disk subsystem throughput, and more. This information then allows the administrator or appropriate information technology (IT) resource to determine at a later date how the system is performing in comparison with initial operation.

Using Documentation for Troubleshooting Purposes

Troubleshooting documentation is a record of identified system issues and the associated resolution. This documentation is helpful both in terms of the processes that the company recommends for resolving technical issues and a documented record of the results of actual troubleshooting challenges. Researching and troubleshooting an issue is time consuming. Documenting the process and the results provides a valuable resource for other company administrators who might experience the same issue.

Exchange Server 2013 Project Documentation

An Exchange Server 2013 implementation is a complex endeavor that should be approached in phases. First and foremost, a decision should be made on how the project will be tracked. This can be done using a simple Microsoft Excel spreadsheet, but a tool like Microsoft Project makes mapping out the tasks much easier. Also, the first round of mapping out a project will most likely have at most 15–20 lines of tasks. Using a tool like Microsoft Project makes it easier to fill in more line items as you progress in the design and planning stages.

With the tracking method in place, you can move on to address the documents that are typically created for an Exchange Server 2013 implementation:

- Design and planning document
- Communication plan document
- Migration plan document
- Training plan document
- Prototype lab document
- Pilot test document
- Support and project completion document

This chapter examines each of these documents individually and focuses on their key elements.

Design and Planning Document

One of the concepts discussed earlier in the chapter was that of documents being used as building blocks. Continuing with that idea, the Exchange Server 2013 design and planning document is considered the foundation for all of the documentation created from this point forward. The design and planning document takes the original business requirements, matches them to the technical specifications, and then maps out how to produce the end product. It cannot be stressed enough the importance of a well-developed design and planning document.

The Exchange Server 2013 design and planning document is the outcome of the design sessions held with the subject matter expert (SME) and the technical staff within the organization. A standard Exchange Server 2013 design and planning document contains the following information:

- Executive Summary
  - Project Overview
- Project Organization
  - Resources
  - Costs
  - Risk Assessment
- Existing Environment
  - Network Infrastructure
  - Active Directory Infrastructure
  - Exchange Topology
  - Backup and Restore
  - Administrative Model
  - Client Systems
- Exchange Server 2013 Environment
  - Goals and Objectives
- Exchange Server 2013 Architecture
  - Server Placement
  - Exchange Version
  - Databases
  - Database Availability Groups
  - Recipient Policies
  - Connectors

- Global Catalog Placement
- Groups

Hardware Configuration and Capacity Planning

Client Access and Hub Servers

- Outlook Web Access
- Edge Services
- Unified Messaging Services

Exchange Server 2013 Security

- Exchange Roles and Advanced Security Delegation
- Edge Security
- Disabling Unnecessary Services/Protocols
- IPSec
- Antivirus/Antispam/Antiphishing

Project Plan

- Blackout Dates
- Vacation Schedules
- Additional Projects Overlap

Documentation Plan

- Design
- Plan
- Build Guides
- Migration Guides
- Administration Guides
- Maintenance Guides
- As-Builts
- Disaster Recovery Guides
- User Guides

Training Plan

- Users
- Administrators
- Migration Team

Communication Plan

Communication Plan Document

The detail of the communication plan depends on the size of the organization and management requirements. From the project management perspective, the more communication, the better! This is especially important when a project affects something as visible as the email system.

Mapping out the how, when, and who to communicate with allows the project team to prepare well-thought-out reports and plan productive meetings and presentations. This also provides the recipients of the reports the chance to review the plan and set their expectations. Once again, no surprises for the project team or the project sponsor.

A good communication plan should include the following topics:

- Audience
- Content
- Delivery method
- Timing and frequency

Table 18.1 gives an example of a communication plan. To make the plan more detailed, columns can be added to list for who is responsible for the communication and specific dates for when the communication is delivered.

TABLE 18.1 Communication Plan

Audience	Content (Message)	Delivery Method	Timing Stage/ Frequency
Executive sponsor	Project status	Written report	Weekly in email
Project team	Project status	Verbal updates	Weekly in meeting
IT department	Project overview	Presentation	Quarterly in meeting

Migration Plan Document

After the design and planning document has been mapped out, the project team can begin planning the logistics of implementing Exchange Server 2013. This document is a guide that contains the technical steps needed to implement Exchange Server 2013 from the ground up. However, depending on how the migration team is set up, it can also include logistical instructions such as the following:

- Communication templates
- Location maps
- Team roles and responsibilities during the implementation

In a large organization, a session or sessions will be held to develop the migration plan. An agenda for the development of the plan might look similar to the following:

- Goals and Objectives
- Migration Planning—E2013
    - New Exchange Organization Versus Upgrade
    - Exchange Server 2013 Directory Cleanup/One-to-One Mapping
    - Migration Tools
    - ForestPrep/DomainPrep
    - Rolling Migration
    - Special Considerations: Third-Party Add-ins (fax, voice mail, apps)
- Rollback Planning
    - Backup and Restore
    - Phased Migration Rollback
- Training
    - Users
    - Administrators
- Communications
    - Status Meetings
    - Open Issues Log
- Administration and Maintenance
    - Administration
    - Maintenance
    - Disaster Recovery
    - Guides
    - Periodic Schedules
    - Daily/Weekly/Monthly
    - Planned Downtime
    - Checklists
    - Test
- Project Management
    - Phased Approach
    - Phase I—Design/Planning
    - Phase II—Prototype

- Phase III—Pilot
- Phase IV—Implement
- Phase V—Support
- Timelines
- Resource Requirements
- Risk Management
- Interactive Refinement of Plan

Migration Planning—AD

- In Place Versus Restructuring
- Account Domains
- Resource Domains
- Active Directory Migration Tool (ADMT)
- DNS Integration
- Switching to Native Mode

Deployment Tools

- Scripting
- Built-in
- Third-Party

Building

- Normalize Environment
- Data Center First
- Branch Offices Second
- Deployment Strategies
- Staged Versus Scripted Versus Manual

Documentation

- Design
- Plan
- Build Guides
- Migration Guides
- Administration Guides
- Maintenance Guides
- As-Builts
- Disaster Recovery Guides
- User Guides

Training
    Users
    Administrators
    Migration Team
    Technical Experts
Communications
    Migration Team
    Executives and Management
    Administrators
    Users
    Methods
    Frequency
    Detail Level
Administration and Maintenance
    Administration
    Maintenance
    Disaster Recovery
    Guides
    Periodic Schedules
    Daily/Weekly/Monthly
    Planned Downtime
    Checklists
    Testing

Note that many of the agenda topics are stated in a way that facilitates discussion. This is a great way to organize discussion points and at the same time keep them on track.

Training Plan Document

When creating a training plan for an Exchange Server 2013 implementation, the first thing that needs to be identified is the target audience. That determines what type of training needs to be developed. Some of the user groups that need to be targeted for training are as follows:

- **End users**—If the implementation is going to change the desktop client, the end user must receive some level of training.
- **Systems administrators**—The personnel involved in the administration of the messaging systems must be trained.

- **Help desk**—In organizations where the support is divided among different teams, each team must be trained on the tasks they will be carrying out.
- **Implementation team**—If the implementation is spread across multiple locations, some project teams choose to create implementation teams. These teams must be trained on the implementation process.

After the different groups have been identified, the training plan for each one can be created. The advantage of creating a training plan in-house is the ability to tailor the training to the organization's unique Exchange environment. The trainees will not have to go over configurations or settings that do not apply to their network.

As a special note, if the systems administrators and implementation team members can be identified ahead of time, it is wise to have them participate in the prototype stage.

The implementation team can assist by validating procedures, and through the repetitive process can become more familiar with the procedures. After the prototype environment is set up, administrators and help desk resources can come in to do the same for the administrative procedures.

This provides the necessary validation process and also allows the systems groups to become more comfortable with the new tools and technology.

Prototype Lab Document

Going in to the prototype stage, experienced engineers and project managers are aware that the initial plan will probably have to be modified. This is because of a range of factors that can include application incompatibility, administrative requirements, or undocumented aspects of the current environment.

So, if it was important to start out this stage with a well-documented plan, the most important documentation goal for the prototype is to track these changes to ensure that the project still meets all goals and objectives of the implementation.

The document tool the project team will use to do this is the test plan. A well-developed test plan contains a master test plan and provides the ability to document the test results for reference at a later date. This is necessary because the implementation procedures might change from the first round of testing to the next, and the project team will need to refer to the outcome to compare results.

A prototype lab test plan outline contains the following:

Summary of what is being tested and the overall technical goals of the implementation

Scope of what will be tested

Resources Needed

Hardware

Software

Personnel

- Documentation
  - What will be recorded
  - Test Plan Outline
- Operating System
  - Hardware Compatibility
  - Install First Domain Controller
  - Test Replication
  - Install Additional Domain Controllers
  - Client Access
  - Role-Based Configuration
  - DNS
  - WINS
  - DHCP
  - IIS
  - Domain Controller
  - Exchange
  - Group Policy
  - GPMC
  - Antivirus
  - Password Policy
  - Security Templates
  - File Migration
  - Print Migration
  - DFS
  - Remote Assistance
  - Applications Testing
- Exchange Server 2013
  - Exchange Install and Configuration
  - Exchange Migration
  - OWA
    - Functionality
    - Forms-Based Authentication
  - Individual Mailbox/Message Restores
  - Database Restore

Antivirus

Exchange Management Console

Functionality

Backup and Restore

OpsMgr Agents

Administrative Rights

Each individual test should be documented in a test form listing the expected outcome and the actual outcome. This becomes part of the original test plan and is used to validate the implementation procedure or document a change.

A sample prototype lab test form is shown in Table 18.2.

TABLE 18.2 Sample Test Form

Test Name:	
Hardware Requirements:	
Software Requirements:	
Other Requirements:	
Expected Outcome:	
Actual Outcome:	
Test Name:	
Tester:	

Test Name:	
Date:	

At the end of the stage, it should be clearly documented what, if anything, has changed. The documentation deliverables of this stage are as follows:

- Test plan
- Implementation plan
- Pilot implementation plan
- Rollback plan

Pilot Test Document

Documenting a pilot implementation has special requirements because it is the first time the implementation will touch the production environment. If the environment is a complex one where multiple applications are affected by the implementation, all details should be documented along with the outcome of the pilot.

This is done by having a document similar in content to the prototype lab test plan form and tracking any issues that come up.

In extreme cases, the project team must put the rollback plan into effect. Before starting the pilot implementation, the team should have an escalation process along with contact names and phone numbers of the personnel with the authority to make the go-no-go decision in a given situation.

Support and Project Completion Document

An Exchange implementation should include a plan for handing off administration to the personnel who will be supporting the messaging environment after the implementation is complete—especially if the SMEs are brought in to implement the Exchange messaging infrastructure and will not be remaining onsite to support it.

The handoff plan should be included in the original project plan and have a timeline for delivery of the administrative documentation as well as training sessions if needed.

Exchange Server 2013 Environment Documentation

As the business and network infrastructure changes, it is common for the messaging infrastructure to change as well. Keep track of these changes as they progress through baselines (how the Exchange Server 2013 environment was built) and other forms of documentation, such as the configuration settings and connectivity diagrams of the environment.

Documents that map out the Exchange Server 2013 environment will prove to be an invaluable tool for maintaining, expanding, or troubleshooting the messaging infrastructure.

These documents should provide information on the physical setup of the network, such as server configuration and location, and also go over the logical elements such as mail flow.

Some of the key documents that are used for this include the following:

- **Network diagrams**—Network diagrams give a visual of the messaging infrastructure. This should show mail flow, location of front-end servers, site connectors, and WAN topology. A large or very complex organization might prefer to have this information mapped out in several different diagrams.
- **Server builds**—The server builds are guides that instruct on how to build the server from the ground up. These guides are key in ensuring standardized builds during an implementation as well as recovering from a major server crash or for use during a disaster recovery scenario.

Another document that is especially useful in larger organizations is the roles and responsibilities guide that outlines the administrative model used in the Exchange infrastructure.

NOTE

A great tool for examining the Exchange Server environment is the Exchange Best Practices Analyzer (ExBPA). The Exchange BPA produces reports on a variety of topics.

Server Build Procedures

The server build procedure is a detailed set of instructions for building the Exchange Server 2013 system. This document can be used for troubleshooting and adding new servers, and is a critical resource in the event of a disaster.

The following is an example of a table of contents from a server build procedure document:

- Windows Server Build Procedures
  - System Configuration Parameters
  - Configuring the Server Hardware
    - Installing Vendor Drivers
    - Configuring Storage
  - Installing and Configuring Windows Server
    - Using Images
    - Using Scripted Installations

Applying Windows Server Security

Using a Security Template

Using GPOs

Configuring Antivirus

Installing Service Packs and Critical Updates

Backing Up Client Configuration

Exchange Server 2013 Build Procedures

System Configuration Parameters

Configuring Exchange as a Mailbox Server

Creating Database Availability Groups

Creating Databases

Configuring Exchange as an Edge or Client Access Server

Configuration (As-Built) Documentation

The configuration document, often referred to as an as-built, details a snapshot configuration of the Exchange Server 2013 system as it is built or after the fact after it has been built. This document contains essential information required to rebuild a server.

The following is an Exchange Server 2013 server as-built document template:

Introduction

The purpose of this Exchange Server 2013 as-built document is to assist an experienced network administrator or engineer in restoring the server in the event of a hardware failure. This document contains screenshots and configuration settings for the server at the time it was built. If settings are not implicitly defined in this document, they are assumed to be set to defaults. It is not intended to be a comprehensive disaster recovery with step-by-step procedures for rebuilding the server. For this document to remain useful as a recovery aid, it must be updated as configuration settings change.

System Configuration

Hardware Summary

Disk Configuration

Logical Disk Configuration

System Summary

Device Manager

Windows Server TCP/IP Configuration

Network Adapter Local Area Connections

Security Configuration

  Services

  Lockdown Procedures (Checklist)

  Antivirus Configuration

Share List

Exchange Configuration

  Database Availability Groups

  Mailbox Databases

  Public Folder

  Virtual Directory Configuration

  SMTP Routing Configuration

  Edge Configuration

Topology Diagrams

Network configuration diagrams and related documentation generally include local area network (LAN) connectivity, WAN infrastructure connectivity, IP subnet information, critical servers, network devices, and more. Having accurate diagrams of the new environment can be invaluable when troubleshooting connectivity issues. For topology diagrams that can be used for troubleshooting connectivity issues, consider documenting the following:

- Internet service provider contact names, including technical support contact information
- Connection type (such as fiber, DS3, OC-12)
- Link speed
- Throughput
- Endpoint configurations, including routers used
- Message flow and routing

Exchange Server 2013 Administration and Maintenance Documents

The administrative documents are designed to provide information for the ongoing support and administration of the Exchange Server 2013 environment. Most of the diagrams and guides created to document the environment (discussed in the previous section) will also be used for reference in the day-to-day administration. These documents should address the basic administrative tasks, such as adding a user and troubleshooting documents.

It is a best practice to have one location where all of the documents are consolidated to make it easy to find any one of them. This also facilitates replication of the directory to a website or a share on another server for disaster recovery purposes.

Administration Manual

The administration manual is the main tool for the administrative group. All of the Exchange tasks are documented with the organization-specific details. A well-prepared administration manual can also be used for training new administrators.

Some of the documents that are typically consolidated into the enterprise Exchange Server 2013 administration manual are as follows:

- Exchange User Administrative Tasks
  - Creating a Mailbox
  - Creating a Shared Mailbox
  - Creating a Resource Mailbox
  - Modifying Mailbox Permissions
  - Moving an Exchange Mailbox
  - Reconnecting a Deleted Exchange Mailbox
  - Hiding and Unhiding a User
  - Setting Mailbox Quotas
- Contacts
  - Creating a Contact
  - Deleting a Contact
  - Modifying a Contact
- Distribution Groups
  - Creating a Distribution Group
  - Deleting a Distribution Group
  - Modifying a Distribution Group
- Outlook Administration
  - Recovering Deleted Items Using Outlook
  - Re-creating an Outlook Profile
  - Creating a Resource Account
- Message Tracking
- Exchange Server Administration Tasks
  - Creating a Mailbox Store in Exchange
  - Managing Database Copies
  - Managing Storage Usage

Testing and Refining Disaster Recovery Procedures

Configuring an Exchange Alert Notification

Monitoring Backups

Exchange Server Troubleshooting Tasks

Diagnosing Message Delivery Problems

Outlook Connectivity Diagnostics

Exchange Database Repair Procedures

Although the outline provided is a pretty complete example, some additional documents are outlined in more detail in the following sections.

Troubleshooting Guide

Troubleshooting documents are especially useful for larger organizations where multiple administrators are working together. Providing the information to all administrators can potentially shorten or avoid server downtime and user impact.

Procedural Documents

An important aspect of creating the administrative documentation is that it is mainly procedural. These are step-by-step guides that walk the administrator through any given task, and it is imperative that the documents are validated. This is a collaborative effort in which one person writes the document and another validates the procedures noting any differences so that they can be corrected. These are living documents that change along with the environment and updates to the documents should be routinely included as a part of changes or updates to the infrastructure or administrative model.

Exchange Server Maintenance

In most organizations, email is one of the most visible, if not number one, business applications. How to keep email up and running is the topic of many technical and business discussions. To keep the Exchange Server 2013 infrastructure up and running, the main goal of an Exchange administrator should be to be proactive. This is achieved by setting up a well-thought-out maintenance plan that checks all of the components of the Exchange infrastructure and addresses issues before they affect the email system causing downtime.

The maintenance plan should include daily, weekly, monthly, and quarterly tasks. The execution and status or outcome of the tasks should be documented and archived for historical reference. The best way to do this is by using checklists that can be easily followed and signed off on when the tasks are completed.

A standard maintenance schedule includes, but is not limited to, the following:

- Exchange Server Maintenance
- Exchange Status Monitor
  - Monitoring Tool
  - Monitoring Services with the Computer Management Console
- Daily Tasks
  - Examine Performance Counters
  - Monitor Services and Links
  - Check Server Mail Queues
  - Check SMTP Log Files
  - Check Daily Backup Logs
  - Check Available Disk Space
  - Verify the Alerter Service Is Running
  - Physical Server Check
- Weekly Tasks
  - Check Event Logs for Errors and Warnings
  - Check for Message Tracking Log File Buildups
- Monthly Tasks
  - Validate Exchange Backup
- Quarterly Tasks
  - Check Mailbox Usage
- Event Logs
  - Checking Event Log Events
  - Tools for Troubleshooting Event Log Messages
    - Microsoft Online TechNet Website

Disaster Recovery Documentation

Creating and maintaining a disaster recovery plan for the Exchange Server 2013 infrastructure requires the commitment of IT managers as well as the systems administrators in charge of the messaging systems. This is because creating a disaster recovery plan is a complex process, and after it is developed the only way of maintaining it is by practicing the procedures on a regular schedule. This, of course, involves the administrative personnel and should be worked into their scheduled tasks.

The initial steps of creating the disaster recovery plan involve determining the desired recovery times. Then, the team moves on to discuss possible disaster scenarios and maps out a plan for each one. The following table of contents outlines the different topics that are addressed when creating the disaster recovery plan:

Executive Summary or Introduction

Disaster Recovery Scenarios

Disaster Recovery Best Practices

  Planning and Designing for Disaster

Business Continuity and Response

  Business Hours Response to Emergencies

  Recovery Team Members

  Recovery Team Responsibilities

  Damage Assessment

  Off-Hours Response to an Emergency

  Recovery Team Responsibilities

  Recovery Strategy

  Coordinate Equipment Needs

Disaster Recovery Decision Tree

Software Recovery

Hardware Recovery

Server Disaster Recovery

Preparation

  Documentation

  Software Management

  Knowledge Management

Server Backup

  Client Software Configuration

Restoring the Server

  Build the Server Hardware

  Post Restore

Recovering Data

  Database Availability Group Replication

Exchange Disaster Recovery

  Disaster Recovery Service-Level Agreements

  Exchange Message/Mailbox Restore Scenario

  Complete Disk Failure

Network Operating System Partition Failure

Complete System Failure

NIC, Storage Controller Failures

Train Personnel and Practice Disaster Recovery

Disaster Recovery Planning

The first step of the disaster recovery process is to develop a formal disaster recovery plan. This plan, although time consuming to develop, serves as a guide for the entire organization in the event of an emergency. Disaster scenarios, such as power outages, hard drive failures, and even earthquakes, should be addressed. Although it is impossible to develop a scenario for every potential disaster, it is still helpful to develop a plan to recover from different levels of disaster. It is recommended that organizations encourage open discussions of possible scenarios and the steps required to recover from each one. Include representatives from each department because each department will have its own priorities in the event of a disaster. The disaster recovery plan should encompass the organization as a whole and focus on determining what it will take to resume normal business function after a disaster.

Backup and Recovery Development

Another important component of a disaster recovery development process is the evaluation of the organization's current backup policies and procedures. Without sound backup policies and procedures, a disaster recovery plan is useless. It is not possible to recover a system if the backup is not valid.

A backup plan does not just encompass backing up data to tape or another medium. It is an overarching plan that outlines other tasks, including advanced system recovery, offsite storage, testing procedures, and retention policies. These tasks should be carefully documented to accurately represent each backup methodology and how it's carried out. Full documentation of the backup process includes step-by-step procedures, guidelines, policies, and checklists.

Periodically, the backup systems should be reviewed and tested, especially after any configuration changes. Any changes to the system should be reflected in the documentation. Otherwise, backup documents can become stale and can add to the problems during recovery attempts.

Recovery documentation complements backup documentation. The primary purpose of the documented backup process is to provide the ability to recover that backup in the event of an emergency. Recovery documentation should outline where the backup data resides and how to recover from various types of failures, such as hard drive failure, system failure, and natural disasters. Just like backup documentation, recovery documentation takes the form of step-by-step procedures, guidelines, policies, and checklists.

Exchange Switchover and Failover Documentation

Exchange distinguishes between a database switchover, which is administratively initiated, and a failover, which is automatic. Database availability groups provide failover and redundancy capability for Exchange databases. When a system or database fails over, having fully tested and documented procedures help administrators quickly diagnose the problem and perform whatever recovery process might be required. Because these procedures are not used often, they must be thoroughly tested and reviewed in a lab setting so that they accurately reflect the steps required to recover each system.

Performance Documentation

Performance documentation helps monitor the health and status of the Exchange environment. It is a continuous process that begins by aligning the goals, existing policies, and service level agreements of the organization. When these areas are clearly defined and detailed, baseline performance values can be established, using tools such as the System Monitor, Microsoft System Center Operations Manager (OpsMgr), or other tools (such as Performance Monitor). These tools capture baseline performance-related metrics that can include indicators such as how much memory is being used, average processor use, and more. They also can illustrate how the Exchange Server 2013 environment is performing under various workloads.

After the baseline performance values are documented, performance-related information gathered by the monitoring solution should be analyzed periodically. Pattern and trend analysis reports need to be examined at least on a weekly basis. This analysis can uncover current and potential bottlenecks and proactively ensure that the system operates as efficiently and effectively as possible. These reports can range from routine reports generated by the monitoring solution to complex technical reports that provide detail to engineering staff.

Routine Reporting

Although built-in system monitoring tools log performance data that can be used in reports in conjunction with products such as Excel, it is recommended that administrators use products such as OpsMgr for monitoring and reporting functionality. OpsMgr can manage and monitor the Exchange systems and provide preconfigured graphical reports with customizable levels of detail. OpsMgr also provides the framework to generate customized reports that meet the needs of the organization.

Management-Level Reporting

Routine reporting typically provides a significant amount of technical information. Although helpful for the administrator, it can be too much information for management. Management-level performance reporting should be concise and direct. Stakeholders do not require the specifics of performance data, but it's important to take those specifics and show trends, patterns, and any potential problem areas. This extremely useful and factual information provides insight to management so that decisions can be made to determine proactive solutions for keeping systems operating in top-notch condition.

For instance, during routine reporting, administrators identify and report to management that Exchange Server processor use is on the rise. What does this mean? This information by itself does not give management any specifics on what the problem is. However, if the administrator presents graphical reports that indicate that if the current trends on Exchange Server processor use continue at the rate of a 5% increase per month, an additional processor will be required in 10 months or less. Management can then take this report, follow the issue more closely over the next few months, and determine whether to allocate funds to purchase additional processors. If the decision is made to buy more processors, management has more time to negotiate quantity, processing power, and cost instead of having to pay higher costs for the processors on short notice.

Technical Reporting

Technical performance information reporting is much more detailed than management-level reporting. It goes beyond the routine reporting to provide specific details on many different components and facets of the system. For example, specific counter values might be given to determine disk subsystem use. This type of information is useful in monitoring the health of the entire Exchange environment. Trend and pattern analysis should also be included in the technical reporting process to not only reflect the current status, but to allow comparison with historical information and determine how to plan for future requirements.

Security Documentation

Just as with any other aspect of the Exchange environment, security documentation also includes policies, configurations and settings, and procedures. Administrators can easily feel that although documenting security settings and other configurations are important, it might lessen security mechanisms established in the Exchange Server 2013 environment. However, documenting security mechanisms and corresponding configurations are vital to administration, maintenance, and any potential security compromise. Security documentation, along with other forms of documentation—including network diagrams and configurations—should be well guarded to minimize any potential security risk.

A network environment might have many security mechanisms in place, but if the information—such as logs and events obtained from them—isn't reviewed, security is more relaxed. Monitoring and management solutions can help consolidate this information into reports that can be generated on a periodic basis. These reports are essential to the process of continuously evaluating the network's security.

In addition, management should be informed of any unauthorized access or attempts to compromise security. Business policy can then be made to strengthen the environment's security.

Change Control

Although the documentation of policies and procedures to protect the system from external security risks is of utmost importance, internal procedures and documents should also be established. Developing, documenting, and enforcing a change control process helps protect the system from well-intentioned internal changes.

In environments where there are multiple administrators, it is very common to have the interests of one administrator affect those of another. For instance, an administrator might make a configuration change to limit mailbox size for a specific department. If this change is not documented, a second administrator might spend a significant amount of time trying to troubleshoot a user complaint from that department. Establishing a change control process that documents these types of changes eliminates confusion and wasted resources. The change control process should include an extensive testing process to reduce the risk of production problems.

Procedures

Although security policies and guidelines compose the majority of security documentation, procedures are equally as important. Procedures include not only the initial configuration steps, but also maintenance procedures and more important procedures that are to be followed in the event of a security breach.

Additional areas regarding security that can be documented include, but are not limited to, the following:

- Auditing policies including review
- Service packs (SPs) and Update Rollups (URs)
- Hot fixes for identified problems
- Certificates and certificate authorities
- Antivirus configurations
- Password policies (such as length, strength, age)
- Group Policy Object (GPO) security-related policies
- Registry security
- Lockdown procedures

Training Documentation

Training documentation for a project can be extensive and range from user training to technical training. The most important aspect of training documentation is to make sure that it meets the needs of the individual being trained. The two key documents created and used in organizations are focused for the benefit of end users, and technical documents are focused toward administrators.

End User

Proper end-user training is critical to the acceptance of any new application. Developing clear and concise documentation that addresses the users' needs is key in providing proper training. As discussed earlier, developing specific documentation goals and conducting an audience analysis are especially important to the development of useful training materials.

Technical

Administrators and engineers are responsible for the upkeep and management of the Exchange environment. As a result, they must be technically prepared to address a variety of issues, such as maintenance and troubleshooting. Training documentation should address why the technologies are being taught and how the technologies pertain to the Exchange environment. In addition, the training documentation should be easy to use and function as a reference resource in the future.

Summary

The development of documentation for the Exchange Server 2013 environment is important not only to establishing the environment, but also to the health, maintenance, and ongoing support of the system. After this documentation is developed, it must be thoroughly tested—preferably by a disinterested party—and maintained. Every change that is made to the environment should be changed in the documentation.

Best Practices

The following are best practices from this chapter:

- Determine the business needs for documentation.
- Determine the goals of each document.
- Determine the audience and the need for each document.
- Validate and test the documentation.
- Develop audience-level specific training materials.
- Establish a documentation update process.

CHAPTER 19

Designing and Configuring Unified Messaging in Exchange Server 2013

IN THIS CHAPTER

- Unified Messaging Features
- Unified Messaging Architecture
- Unified Messaging Installation
- Monitoring and Troubleshooting Unified Messaging
- Unified Messaging Shell Commands
- SIP Protocol

Microsoft Exchange Server 2013 Unified Messaging (UM) delivers voice messaging and email into a unified Inbox. These messages can be accessed from a telephone or a computer. Exchange Server 2013 Unified Messaging integrates with the telephony systems, operating fundamentally as a voice mail server using the Exchange Information Store as a repository for the messages.

Unified Messaging was initially launched in Exchange Server 2007. Exchange Server 2013 represents the natural evolution of the UM platform. This chapter focuses on the design and configuration of the Unified Messaging capabilities built in to Exchange Server 2013. This includes telephony concepts, server specifications, installation and configuration considerations, and monitoring of the Unified Messaging services.

Unified Messaging Features

Exchange Server 2013 extends the UM features first introduced in Exchange Server 2007. Unified Messaging seamlessly integrates voice messaging and electronic mail into a single Inbox. This frees up the user from having to manage separate accounts and Inboxes for these three types of messages. Exchange Server 2013 no longer has UM as a dedicated role and has rolled this functionality into the Mailbox server role. The Client Access server (CAS) role provides the UM Call Router service, which redirects calls to the appropriate Mailbox server.

Telephony Integration

With Unified Messaging, Exchange Server is integrated into the telephony world. This integration takes place between the Exchange Unified Messaging server and gateways or Private Branch Exchanges (PBXs).

In a classic set of telephony and electronic mail systems, shown in Figure 19.1, there are two separate networks that deliver voice messages and electronic messages (email). In the telephony system, there are separate components for the PBX, voice mail, external lines, and phones. As shown in the figure, calls from the Public Switched Telephone Network (PSTN) come into a PBX device. Typically, an incoming call is routed by the PBX to the telephone. If the phone does not answer or is busy, the call is routed to the voice mail system. Similarly, email from the Internet arrives at the Exchange messaging server. Note that in the classic system, there is no integration or connectivity between the telephony and electronic mail systems.

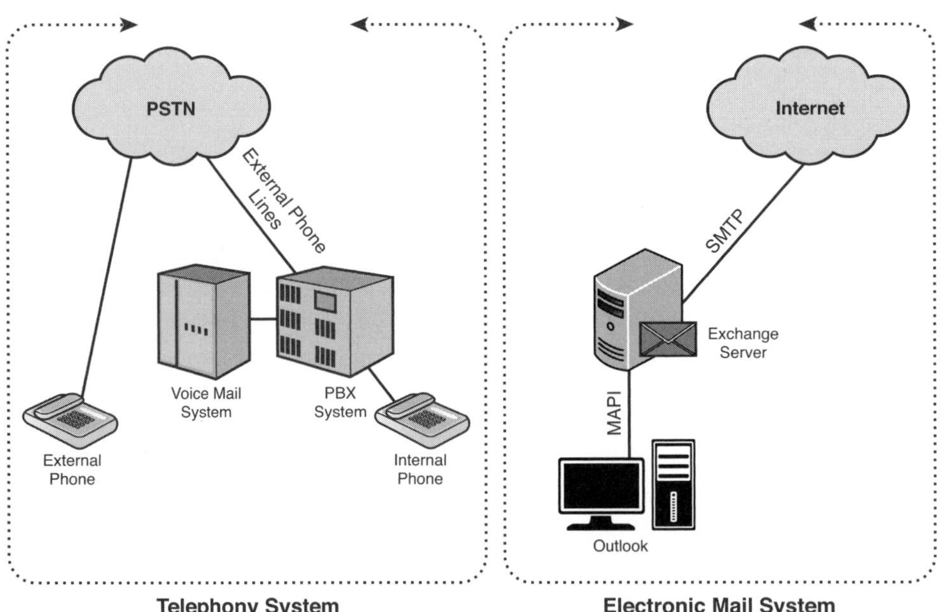

FIGURE 19.1 Classic telephone and electronic mail systems.

With Exchange Server 2013 and Unified Messaging, these two disparate systems are integrated, as shown in Figure 19.2. Although the UM server does not connect directly with a traditional PBX, it does integrate with PBXs via gateways or SIP (Session Initiation Protocol) trunks. The combination of the PBX and the Internet Protocol (IP) gateway can also be replaced by an IP-PBX, which provides both sets of functionality.

One such IP-PBX option is Microsoft Lync. Integrating these two Microsoft platforms provides a powerful enterprise voice solution that can replace most modern PBXs at a fraction of the cost.

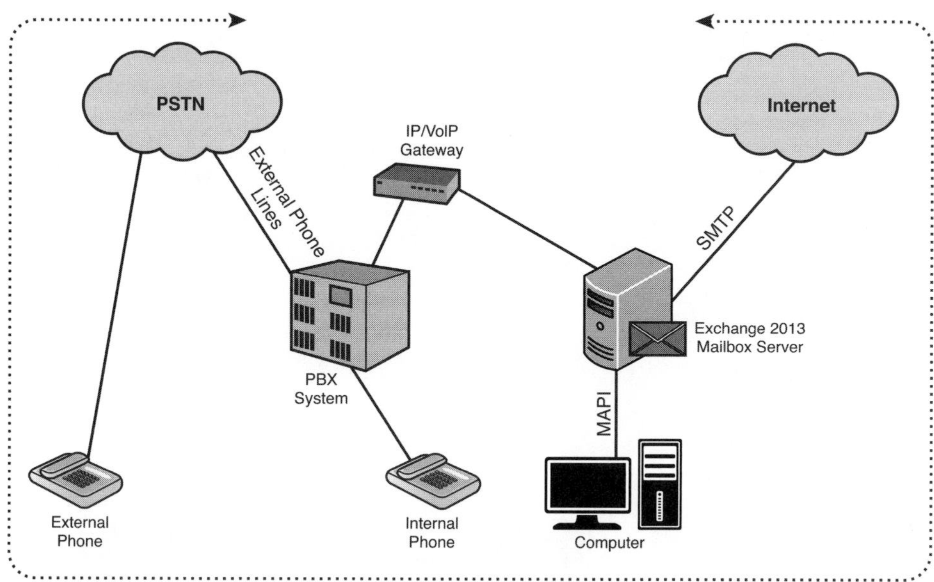

FIGURE 19.2 New integrated system.

Notice that, in effect, the Unified Messaging functionality has replaced the voice mail server in the classic system. The new Microsoft Exchange Server 2013 Unified Messaging service is a voice mail server as well as an automated attendant and voice-based access point for Exchange data.

The more detailed view with all the Exchange Server 2013 server roles is shown in Figure 19.3. This figure also includes the various ways that a user can interact with the integrated system.

This diagram is discussed in more detail in later sections of this chapter.

Single Inbox

The Unified Messaging server enables the true unification of email messages, voice mail messages, and fax messages into a single Inbox. Messages from all these disparate sources are stored in the user's Inbox and are accessible through a wide variety of interfaces, such as Outlook, a telephone, a web browser, or even a mobile PDA.

The Inbox can be managed just like a traditional email Inbox, with folders, Inbox rules, message retention, and so on. Exchange Server administrators can back up and restore Inboxes with all these forms of data just as they do with email data. This reduces the complexity and ease of use for both users and administrators.

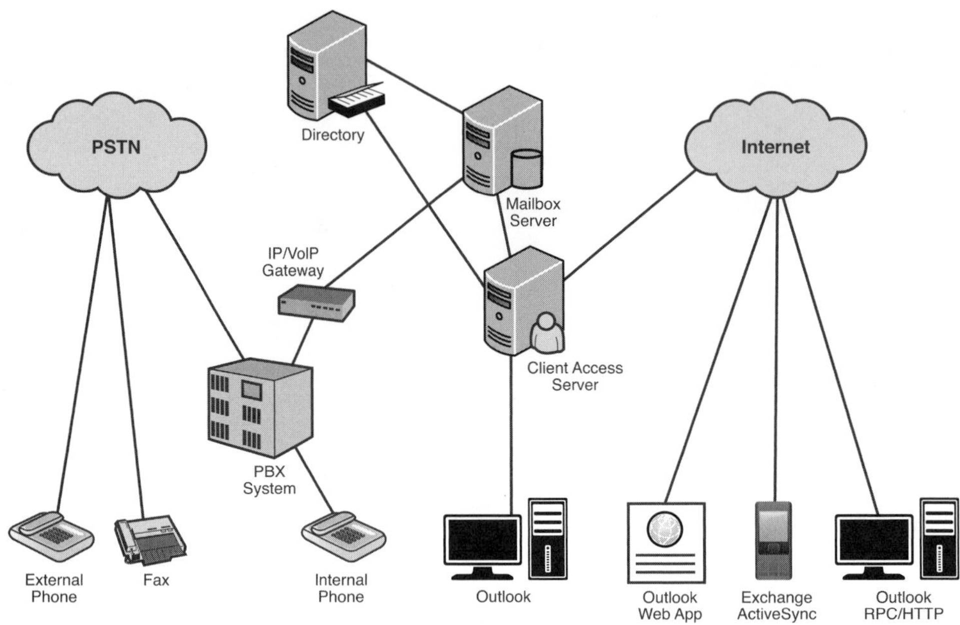

FIGURE 19.3 Detailed architecture diagram.

Call Answering

Call answering picks up incoming calls for a user who does not answer the phone. It plays a personal greeting, records voice messages, and converts the voice messages to an email message to be submitted to the user's Exchange Server mailbox. This is accomplished by forwarding unanswered calls to a hunt group, which terminates at Exchange UM. Exchange UM looks at the originally dialed number to determine the extension based on a dial plan. This is used to match up a phone number to a user so that the Auto Attendant settings can pick up the call and so that voice messages get associated and then routed to the correct user.

Fax Receiving

Although Exchange Server 2007 supported incoming Fax services, this was deprecated in Exchange Server 2010 and Exchange Server 2013. Fax Receiving would typically be intercepted by the gateway and routed as T.38 traffic to a third-party server or service.

Subscriber Access

The Subscriber Access feature allows a user to access his or her Exchange Server mailbox using a phone. This access mechanism is called Outlook Voice Access (OVA).

With Outlook Voice Access, a user can access his or her Exchange Inbox with the telephone to do the following:

- Listen to and forward voice mail messages.
- Listen to, forward, and reply to email messages.
- Listen to calendar information.
- Access or dial contacts.
- Accept or cancel meeting requests.
- Notify attendees that the user will be late.
- Set a voice mail out-of-office message.
- Set user security preferences and personal options.

This, in effect, gives the user working access to his or her Exchange Inbox while out in the field with only a telephone.

The system not only recognizes Dual Tone Multiple Frequency (DTMF) key presses from the phone, but also understands voice commands. The system guides the user through the prompts responding to voice commands, giving the user complete hands-free operation.

For example, a user might be on the freeway running late for a lunch meeting. Not remembering the exact time, the user calls into the subscriber access and says "Today's Calendar." The Unified Messaging system speaks the summary of the next meeting, which is at 12:00 p.m. Recognizing that the traffic will force him to be 20 minutes late, the user says "I'll be 20 minutes late for this appointment." The Unified Messaging system offers to reschedule the meeting. The user confirms and then Exchange sends a message to all the attendees to reflect the new meeting time.

The speech recognition is remarkably effective and able to recognize commands even over cell phones and with background noise.

Outlook Play on Phone

The Exchange Server 2013 Outlook Web App (OWA) client and the Outlook 2007 and later client both support a feature called Play on Phone. This feature allows users to play voice mail on a phone rather than through the computer. The user opens the voice mail message, selects the Play on Phone option, enters the number to play the message on, and clicks the Dial button.

This allows the user to send the audio stream of the voice mail message to a phone for more privacy or to allow a third party to hear the message. The system also provides prompts over the phone following the playback with message-handling options.

Outlook Voice Mail Preview

Outlook Voice Mail Preview is a feature carried over from Exchange Server 2010 Unified Messaging. Back in the days of Exchange Server 2007 UM, you would see caller information and message priority on an incoming voice mail. Exchange Server 2013, like Exchange Server 2010, kicks it up a notch with speech-to-text functionality. Before the voice mail message arrives in your Inbox, Exchange Server UM transcribes the voice mail and puts the text in the body of the email. Though not perfect, it's quite accurate. This is especially helpful for "spam" voice mail with "anonymous" caller information. Using this function, you can save time and frustration by deleting unwanted messages without listening to them with no fear of deleting a legitimate message. It's also an excellent way to preview a voice mail while in a meeting, allowing you to decide if it's important enough to excuse yourself from the room to listen to the full message.

Exchange Server 2013 takes advantage of the new Speech Engine 11.0 and UCMA 4.0 to improve overall accuracy of voice mail previews.

Call Answering Rules

Introduced in Exchange Server 2010, Exchange Server 2013 offers call answering rules. A user can configure basic call workflows using OWA or Outlook through rules similar to traditional message-based rules. By default, no call answering rules are configured. However, users can browse to the Phone tab and then select Voice Mail in the OWA options menu. See an example in Figure 19.4.

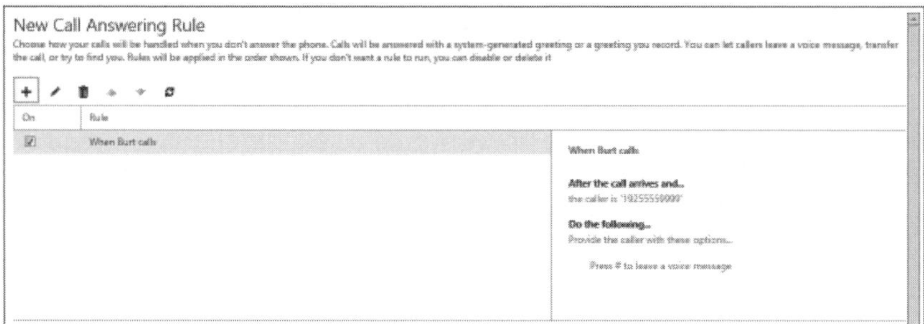

FIGURE 19.4 Call answering rules.

For example, suppose you want your kids to reach you anytime, but you don't want co-workers to reach you after 5:00 p.m. You could set a rule to allow calls from the numbers your children would call from to come through to Communicator and then also ring your mobile phone or another phone. You could also set a rule to force any calls from a business associate or co-worker to be forwarded directly to voice mail after 5:00 p.m. Or for that matter, force someone to only be able to leave you voice mail. The interface is reminiscent of Outlook Web App email rules and should be familiar to most users. Even after rules are created, they can be disabled or enabled through the Outlook Web App Voice Mail menu. Rules, by default, are created as enabled.

Intelligent call routing, a more generic term for Microsoft's call answering rules, was a frequently noted omission in Exchange Server 2007. Its inclusion in Exchange Server 2010 and 2013, and Exchange Server UM's tight integration with Lync offers a rich voice platform capable of being a full PBX replacement.

Auto Attendant

The Auto Attendant, as shown in Figure 19.5, is like a secretary, providing voice prompts to guide an external or internal caller through the voice mail system. The system can respond to either telephone keypad presses or voice commands. An Auto Attendant is typically used to answer a main office number and allow the caller to route either to an extension, to a user based on speaking his or her name, or to transfer to the operator for call routing.

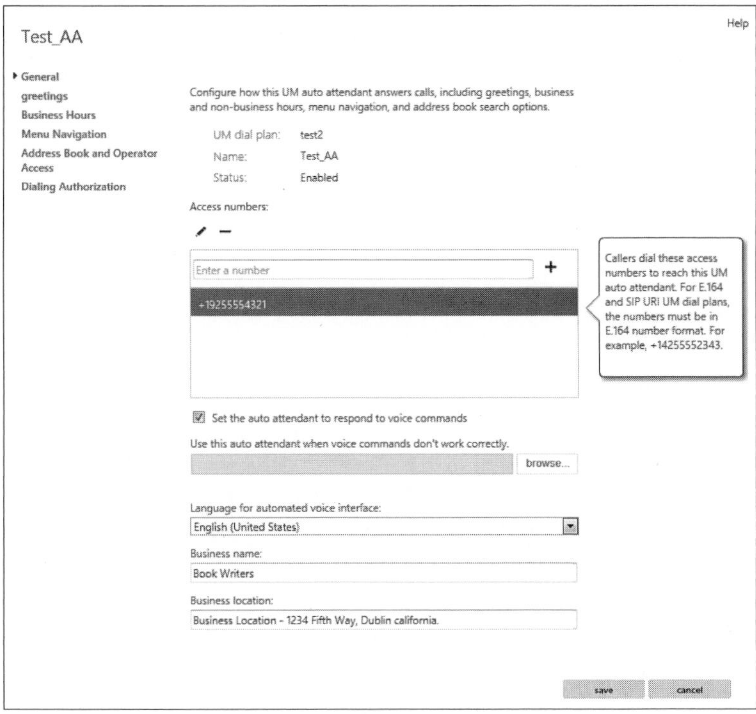

FIGURE 19.5 Auto Attendant menu.

The Auto Attendant features include the following:

- A customizable set of menus for external users
- Greetings for business hours and nonbusiness hours
- Hours of operation and holiday schedules
- Access to the organization's directory
- Access for external users to the operator

The voice prompts that provide the preceding information can be customized to suit the organization.

Unified Messaging Architecture

The Exchange Server 2013 Unified Messaging features and telephony integration bring a whole new set of concepts, terminology, and architectural elements to the Exchange Server platform. This section explores these different components, objects, protocols, and services.

Unified Messaging Components

The central repository for all the Unified Messaging components is Active Directory. The schema extensions that are installed as part of the Exchange Server 2013 prerequisites add a variety of objects and attributes that support the UM functionality. These objects are as follows:

- Dial plan objects
- IP gateway objects
- Hunt group objects
- Mailbox policy objects
- Auto Attendant objects
- Unified Messaging server objects

The objects and their relationships are illustrated in the example shown in Figure 19.6. The example consists of two locations, San Francisco (SFO) and Paris (PAR), with an integrated Exchange Server 2013 Unified Messaging infrastructure. The Unified Messaging objects are shown with a dotted line around them to separate them from the telephony objects.

When a UM hunt group is created manually, not only does the associated UM IP gateway and the associated UM dial plan get specified, but also a pilot identifier is specified.

This diagram is referenced in the subsequent sections describing the various Unified Messaging objects and components.

Dial Plan Objects

Dial plans are the central component of the Exchange Server 2013 Unified Messaging architecture. A UM dial plan essentially logically corresponds to PBX or subsets of extensions within a PBX. The UM dial plan objects can be found in the Exchange Administration Center on the Unified Messaging/UM Dial Plans page.

Different PBXs with an organization, such as between SFO and PAR in Figure 19.6, can have overlapping extensions. For example, a user in San Francisco might have extension 150 and a user in Paris might also have extension 150. Because the two users are on different PBXs, there is no inherent conflict. However, when Exchange Server 2013 Unified Messaging is deployed and the telephony infrastructure is unified in Active Directory, then there would be a conflict.

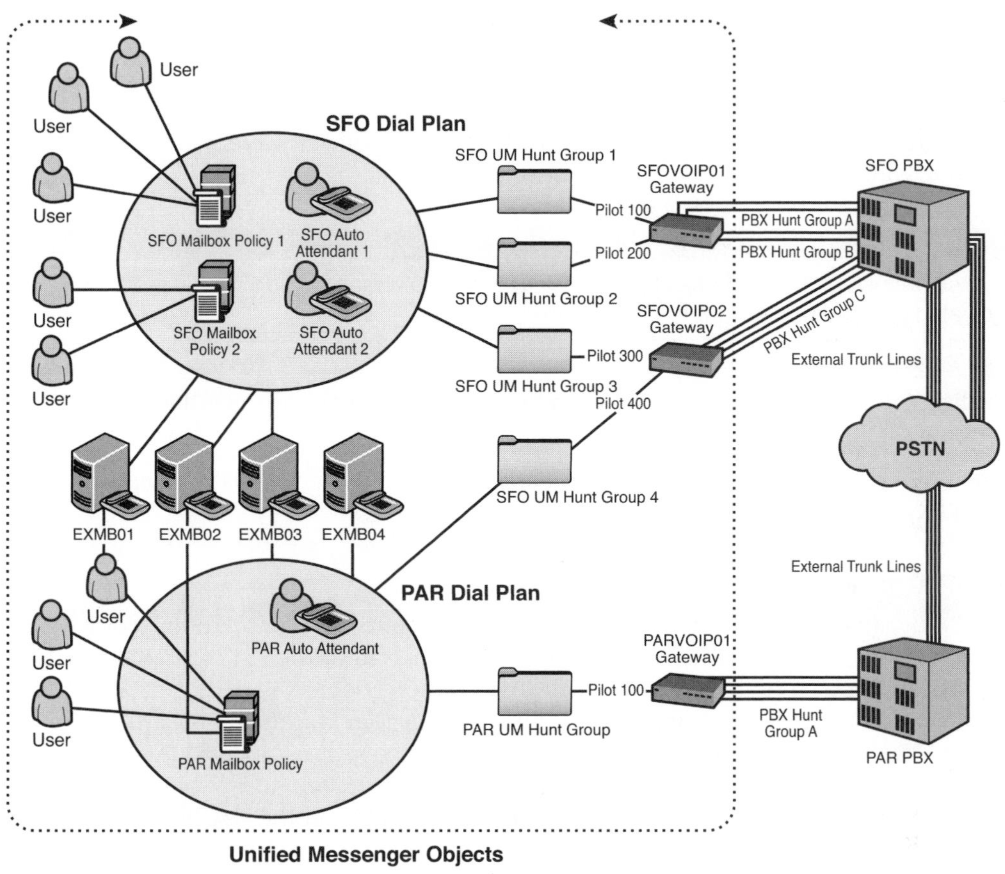

FIGURE 19.6 Unified Messaging objects and relationships.

Dial plans ensure that all extensions are unique within the architecture by mapping a dial plan to a PBX. Extensions within a dial plan must be unique. However, extensions between different dial plans do not have to be unique. A user can only belong to a single dial plan and will have an extension number that uniquely identifies him within the dial plan.

In the figure, there is one dial plan for each location. In the example, San Francisco is the large office with more users and Paris is smaller. There could be multiple dial plans per location.

Dial plans also provide a way to set up common settings among a set of users, such as the following:

- Number of digits in an extension
- Subscriber greetings
- Whom the caller can contact within the dial plan

- Users' call restrictions (international calls)
- Languages supported

These settings should not be confused with UM mailbox policies, which are covered in the "Mailbox Policy Objects" section later in this chapter.

NOTE

When a new UM dial plan object is created, a default UM mailbox policy object is also created and associated with the dial plan.

The dial plan also associates the extension for the subscriber access to Outlook Voice Access.

There can be multiple dial plans within an architecture and even associated with the same PBX.

UM IP Gateway Objects

The UM IP gateway object is the logical representation of the next hop in the Voice over IP (VoIP) chain. It can be either a media gateway connected to the PSTN, or a PBX such as Microsoft Lync Server 2010 or 2013. The UM IP gateway object is a critical component, in that it specifies the connection between the UM dial plan and the physical IP/VoIP gateway. The major configuration of the UM IP gateway object is the IP address of the IP/VoIP gateway device it represents and the associated dial plan. The UM IP gateway objects can be found in the Exchange Administration Center on the UM IP Gateway tab of the Organization, Unified Messaging container.

The UM IP gateway is created as enabled. The gateway can be disabled, either immediately (which disconnects any current calls) or by specifying to disable after completing calls. The latter mode disables the gateway for any new calls but does not disconnect any current calls.

If a UM IP gateway object is not created or is deleted, the Unified Messaging servers in the dial plan will not be able to accept, process, or place calls.

Within the same Active Directory, there can only be one UM IP gateway object for each physical IP/VoIP gateway, and it is enforced through the IP addresses. Multiple UM IP gateway objects with multiple IP/VoIP gateways might be defined within the Exchange Management Console for redundancy or advanced call routing.

UM IP gateway objects can be associated with multiple dial plans. This is accomplished by creating multiple hunt groups, as discussed in the following section.

Hunt Group Objects

In the telephony world, hunt groups are collections of lines that a PBX uses to organize extensions. The hunt group collections allow the system to treat the extensions as a logical group. Hunt groups are used for incoming lines, for outgoing lines, and to route calls to groups of users such as the Sales Department. The UM hunt group objects can be found in the Exchange Administration Center on the UM IP Gateway tab of the Organization, Unified Messaging container. They are listed under each of the UM IP gateways.

Calls with a hunt group can be routed using different methods or algorithms, such as the following:

- **Rollover**—The PBX starts with the lowest numbered line each time and increments until it finds a free line.
- **Round-robin**—The PBX rotates equally among all the lines when starting and then rolls over from that starting point. This ensures that the calls are distributed evenly within the hunt group.
- **Utilization**—The PBX tracks extension utilization and routes the call to the least utilized line first, and then rolls over to the next least busy line.

These algorithms basically encode what the organization deems the appropriate behavior for the routing.

Each hunt group has an associate pilot number, which is the extension that is dialed to access the hunt group. This is frequently the lowest numbered extension in the set of extensions because the most common implementation of a hunt group is rollover.

Within Exchange Server 2013, the UM hunt group object performs a different function. Essentially, the UM hunt group object maps the IP/VoIP gateway and an extension to a UM dial plan.

NOTE

If a default hunt group is created when the UM IP gateway object is created, that UM hunt group will not have a pilot extension associated with it. This creates call routing problems if you create additional hunt groups, so it is best to remove the default hunt group. When a new UM hunt group is created after that, the pilot identifier must be specified.

Additional UM hunt groups can be created to route different incoming extensions to different UM dial plans.

There is no limit to the number of UM hunt group objects that can be created. There must be at least one hunt group per UM IP gateway object for calls to be routed to a dial plan.

Mailbox Policy Objects

Mailbox policy objects control Unified Messaging settings and security for users. The UM mailbox policy objects can be found in the Exchange Administration Center on the UM Mailbox Policies tab of the Organization, Unified Messaging container.

These settings include the following:

- Maximum greeting duration
- Message text for UM generated messages to users
- PIN policies
- Dialing restrictions

Mailbox policies are created to control security and provide customized messages to users. For example, in Figure 19.6 the SFO Mailbox Policy 1 is a general user policy with default PIN settings that require a minimum of 6 characters. The second policy, SFO Mailbox Policy 2, is for executives with higher security requirements and more secure PIN settings that require a minimum of 10 characters.

A UM mailbox policy is associated with one and only one UM dial plan, but each dial plan can be associated with multiple mailbox policies. This allows the dial plan to be associated to the users associated with the mailbox policy. Each user will be associated with one and only one UM mailbox policy object, but many users can be associated with a single mailbox policy object.

There is no limit to the number of UM mailbox policy objects that can be created.

Auto Attendant Objects

The Auto Attendant provides an automated phone answering function, essentially replicating a human secretary. The Auto Attendant answers the incoming calls, provides helpful prompts, and directs the caller to the appropriate services. The UM Auto Attendant objects can be found in the Exchange Administration Center on the UM Auto Attendant tab of the Organization, Unified Messaging container.

The Auto Attendant supports both phone key press (DTMF) and voice commands. This sophisticated voice-recognition technology allows the caller to navigate the menus and prompts with nothing more than his voice if he wants to.

The Auto Attendant objects support the following configurable features:

- Customized greetings and menus for business hours and nonbusiness hours
- Predefined and custom schedule to specify business hours and time zone
- Holiday schedule for exceptions to the business hour schedule
- Operator extension and allowing transfer to operator during business and nonbusiness hours
- Key mapping to enable the transfer of callers to specific extensions or other Auto Attendants based on hard-coded key presses or voice commands

NOTE

Everyone has felt the frustration of moving through an automated call system and not being able to reach an operator or a live person. With Unified Messaging, the Exchange Server administrator now has control over that behavior.

The Auto Attendant can allow or disallow transfer to the operator by specifically allowing or disallowing transfer to the operator during business and nonbusiness hours.

The author's recommendation is to allow transfers to the operator at least during business hours to reduce caller frustration.

In the case of voice-based call transfer, administrators can define a fallback attribute to use in the case of multiple users with the same first and last name. For example, one could choose to use "Title" as this fallback attribute. A caller might ask for "Fred Thedog" and if there were two users with that name, it would ask "Did you mean Fred Thedog CEO?" allowing the caller to make sure she is getting the person she wanted.

Each Auto Attendant can be mapped to specific extensions to provide a customized set of prompts. For example, an organization could set up one Auto Attendant to support the Sales organization calls with specific prompts for handling calls to Sales. The organization could then set up a second Auto Attendant to support the Service organization with specific prompts for technical support and help. These would service different pilot numbers, depending on the number that the caller used.

A front-end menu can be created with key mapping and an Auto Attendant with customized prompts. This allows the organization in the previous example to create a top-level Auto Attendant that would prompt callers to "Press or say 1 for Sales or 2 for Service" and then perform the appropriate transfer. Figure 19.7 shows the key mapping configuration, which would be accompanied by customized prompts.

The initial greeting can be customized as well. There are two default greetings, one for business hours and a second for off-hours. By default, the system says "Welcome to Microsoft Exchange Server." In most implementations, you want to customize this to your company name and include other relevant information. Customized greetings must be in a specific format. They must be saved as PCM/16bit/8kHz/Mono `.wav` files. Each Auto Attendant can have a unique set of customized greetings and prompts.

There is no limit to the number of Auto Attendants that can be created in Active Directory. An Auto Attendant can only be associated with a single dial plan, though a dial plan can be associated with multiple Auto Attendants.

Unified Messaging Server Objects

In Active Directory, the Unified Messaging server object is a logical representation of the physical Exchange Server 2013 Mailbox server. Unlike Exchange Server 2010, Exchange Server 2013 no longer has a dedicated Unified Messaging server role. There are no additional installation steps needed in Exchange Server 2013 to make UM features available.

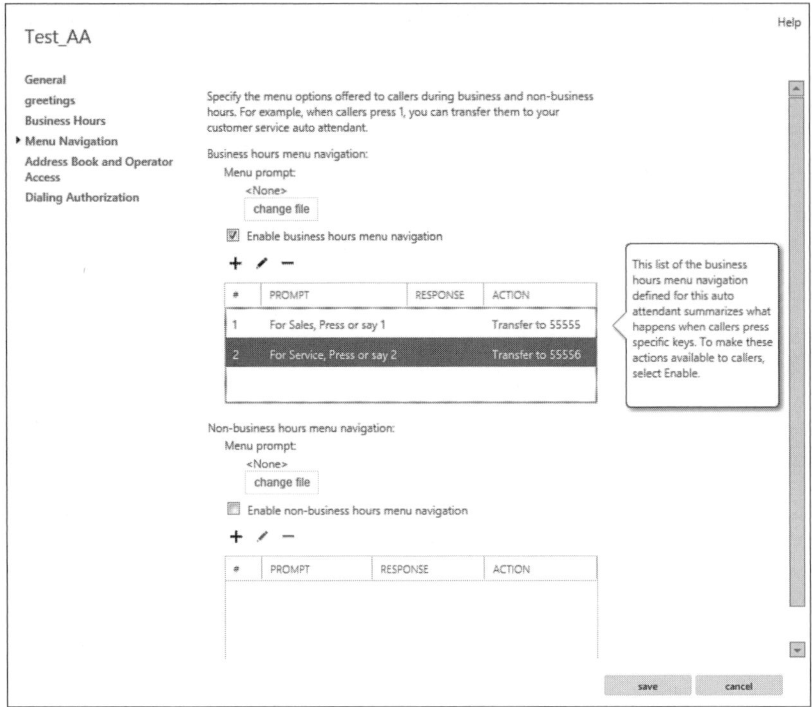

FIGURE 19.7 Key mapping example.

The Microsoft Exchange Unified Messaging service (`umservice.exe`) is the service that instantiates the Unified Messaging functionality that runs under the Local System account. It is dependent on the Microsoft Exchange Active Directory Topology service and the Microsoft Exchange Speech Engine service.

The major configuration task for the Unified Messaging server object is to specify the associated dial plans, of which there can be more than one. The Unified Messaging server must be associated with a dial plan to function. The other configurable parameters for the service are the maximum concurrent calls (default is 100) and maximum concurrent faxes (default is 100).

The Unified Messaging server checks for changes when the service is started and every 10 minutes thereafter. Changes take effect as soon as they are detected by the server.

After determining the dial plans for which it is associated, the server then locates and establishes communications with the appropriate IP/VoIP gateways.

Unified Messaging Users

There are not actually Active Directory objects for Unified Messaging users. Rather, the Unified Messaging properties are stored in the Active Directory user object and in the Exchange Server 2013 mailbox. Voice mail messages are stored in the user's mailbox.

These properties can be found in the Exchange Administration Center (EAC) in the properties of the user's account in the Recipient tab, under Phone and Voice Features. After navigating to the Unified Messaging feature, click the Edit Details link to access the feature properties.

When enabling a user for Unified Messaging, the associated UM mailbox policy and extension must be specified. The link to the mailbox policy provides a one-to-one link to the UM dial plan.

Because they are merely email messages with attachments, voice mails apply toward a user's storage limits. If the user's quota settings prevent the user from receiving email (that is, the user's mailbox is full), then callers attempting to leave a message will not be allowed to leave a message and will be informed that the user's mailbox is full.

NOTE

Interestingly, if a user's mailbox is almost full, a caller will be allowed to leave a message for the user even if that message will cause the mailbox to exceed its quota. For example, consider a user who only has 25KB before they exceed their quota and are prevented from receiving messages. A caller could leave a minute long 100-KB voice message. However, the next caller would be told the mailbox is full.

Exchange Server 2013 Unified Messaging includes a number of features to control the size of voice mail messages to help control the storage impacts. Also important to realize is that Exchange UM voice messages exist in only one place. So if a user deletes them either using the phone, Outlook, or OWA, the message is deleted from all perspectives. There is no need to manage voice mail separately from email the way it's typically handled in other solutions.

UM Web Services

A component that is not represented in Active Directory is the UM Web Services. This is a Web Service that is installed on Exchange Server 2013 servers that have the Mailbox server role, as that is where OWA and other web-based features have been moved.

The service is used for the following:

- Play on Phone feature for both Outlook 2010, Outlook 2013, and Exchange Server 2013 Outlook Web Access
- PIN Reset feature in Exchange Server 2013 Outlook Web Access

Users can access these features in OWA by selecting the Settings icon (depicted by a gear), Options, Phone, and then Options.

Audio Codecs and Voice Message Sizes

Codec is a contraction of coding and decoding digital data, the format in which the audio stream is stored. It includes both the number of bit rate (bits/sec) and compression that is used.

The codec that is used by the Unified Messaging server to encode the messages is one of the following four:

- **Windows Media Audio (WMA)**—16-bit compressed
- **GSM 06.10 (GSM)**—8-bit compressed
- **G.711 PCM Linear (G711)**—16-bit uncompressed
- **Mpeg Audio Layer 3 (MP3)**—16-bit compressed

The Exchange Server 2013 Unified Messaging default is MP3. This is a change from Exchange Server 2007 in which the default was WMA. Although using WMA results in slightly smaller file sizes, most people prefer the universal nature of MP3. This enables a much larger number of mobile devices to play voice mail messages. The Audio Codec setting is configured on the UM dial plan on the Settings tab.

CAUTION

A dirty little secret is that digital compression can result in loss of data. When the data is compressed and decompressed, information can be lost. That is, bits of the conversation or message can be lost. This is a trade-off that the codec makes to save space. This is why the G.711 codec is available, which doesn't compress data and doesn't lose data but at a heavy cost in storage.

These are stored in the message as attachments using the following formats:

- **Windows Media Audio Format** (`.wma`)—For the WMA codec
- **RIFF/WAV Format** (`.wav`)—For GSM or G.711 codecs
- **Mpeg Audio Layer 3** (`.mp3`)—For the MP3 codec

The choice of the audio codec impacts the audio quality and the size of the attached file. Table 19.1 shows the approximate size of data in the file attachment for each codec.

TABLE 19.1 Audio Size for Codec Options

Codec Setting	Approximate Size of 10 Sec of Audio
WMA	11,000 bytes
G.711	160,000 bytes
GSM	16,000 bytes
MP3	19,500 bytes

The G.711 audio codec setting results in a greater than 10:1 storage penalty when compared with the WMA audio codec setting. Although the GSM audio codec setting uses 45% more storage than the WMA codec setting, this comes at a cost of a 50% reduction in audio quality. MP3 provides similar audio quality to WMA at an acceptable file size. The ubiquitous nature of the MP3 codec makes it the preferred choice for Exchange Server 2013.

NOTE

The `.wma` file format has a larger header (about 7KB) than the `.wav` format (about 0.1KB). So for small messages, the GSM files will be smaller. However, after messages exceed 15 seconds, the WMA files will be smaller than the GSM files.

Supported IP/VoIP Hardware

Exchange Server 2013 Unified Messaging relies on the ability of the IP/VoIP gateway to translate time-division multiplexing (TDM) or telephony circuit-switched based protocols, such as Integrated Services Digital Network (ISDN) or Q Signaling (QSIG), from a PBX to protocols based on VoIP or IP, such as SIP or Real-Time Transport Protocol (RTP).

Although there are many types and manufacturers of PBXs, IP/VoIP gateways, and IP-PBXs, there are essentially two types of IP/VoIP gateway component configurations:

- **IP/VoIP Gateway**—A legacy PBX and an IP/VoIP gateway, such as a NET UX2000, provisioned as two separate devices. The Unified Messaging server communicates with the IP/VoIP gateway.
- **IP-PBX**—A modern IP-based or hybrid PBX such as a Cisco CallManager. The Unified Messaging server communicates directly with the PBX.

Table 19.2 lists some currently supported IP/VoIP gateways.

TABLE 19.2 Supported IP/VoIP Gateways for Exchange Server 2013 UM

Manufacturer	Model	Supported Protocols
AudioCodes	MediaPack 114, MediaPack 118	Analog with In-Band or SMDI
AudioCodes	Mediant 1000/2000/3000	T1/ or E1 with CAS—In-Band or SMDI, T1/E1 with Primary Rate Interface (PRI) and Q.SIG or Analog PSTN
Dialogic	1000/2000	T1/ or E1 with CAS—In-Band or SMDI, T1/E1 with Primary Rate Interface (PRI) and Q.SIG or Analog PSTN

Manufacturer	Model	Supported Protocols
NET	UX1000/2000	T1/ or E1 with CAS—In-Band or SMDI, T1/E1 with Primary Rate Interface (PRI) and Q.SIG or Analog PSTN Direct SIP

All these solutions must communicate with the Unified Messaging service via SIP over Transmission Control Protocol (TCP), Transmission Layer Security (TLS encrypted), and Secure Real-Time Transport Protocol (SRTP).

Telephony Components and Terminology

With the integration of Exchange Server 2013 into the telephony world, it is important for the Exchange Server administrator to understand the various components and terminology of a modern telephone system.

The following are some of the common components and terms that are critical to understand:

- **Circuit**—A circuit is a connection between two end-to-end devices. This allows the device to communicate. A common example of this is a telephone call where two people are talking, in which a circuit is established between the two telephones.
- **Circuit-switched networks**—Circuit-switched networks consist of dedicated end-to-end connections through the network that support sessions between end devices. The circuits are set up end-to-end through a series of switches as needed and torn down when done. While the circuit is set up, the entire circuit is dedicated to the devices. A common example of a circuit-switched network is the PSTN.
- **Direct Inward Dialing (DID)**—These are numbers provided by a carrier to a PBX to allow users of the PBX to receive calls from external PSTN networks.
- **Dual Tone Multiple Frequency (DTMF)**—The DTMF signaling protocol is used for telephony signaling and call setup. The most common use is for telephone tone dialing and is known as Touch-Tone. This is used to convey phone button key presses to devices on the network.
- **IP-PBX**—With the advent of high-speed ubiquitous packet-switched networks, many corporations have moved from legacy PBXs to modern IP-based PBXs known as Internet Protocol/Private Branch Exchange (IP-PBX). These devices come in myriad forms, including true IP-PBXs that only support IP protocols to hybrid devices that support both circuit-switched and packet-switched devices. A major advantage of the IP-PBXs is that they are typically much easier to provision and administer. Rather than having to add a separate physical line to plug a phone into, IP phones are simply plugged into the Ethernet jack. Rather than being provisioned by the physical line they are plugged into, the IP phones are provisioned by their own internal characteristics such as the MAC address. This allows for more flexibility.

- **IP/VoIP gateways**—Connecting legacy circuit-switched networks to packet-switched networks, IP/VoIP gateways provide connections between the new packet-switched VoIP protocols and the circuit-switched protocols. These gateways can connect the PSTN to an IP-PBX or a legacy PBX to VoIP devices. In the case of Exchange Server 2013 Unified Messaging, the IP/VoIP gateway connects the Unified Messaging server to the legacy PBX. This is not typically needed if the PBX that the Unified Messaging server is connecting to is an IP-PBX.
- **Internet Telephony Service Provider (ITSP)**—With the advent of SIP trunks as an alternative to PRIs, companies that resell SIP trunks with Direct Inward Dialing numbers attached to them are called ITSPs.
- **Packet-switched networks**—In packet-switched networks, there is no dedicated end-to-end circuit. Instead, the sessions between devices are disassembled into packets and transmitted individually over the network, then reassembled when they reach their destination. All sessions travel over the shared network. A common example of a packet-switched network is the Internet.
- **PBX/PABX**—In all but the smallest companies, there is a device that takes incoming calls from the circuit-switched telephone network and routes them within the company. This device is called a Private Branch Exchange or PBX (Private Automatic Branch Exchange [PABX]). In the old days, this was done by an operator who plugged in the lines manually. The PBX also routes internal outgoing calls, calls between internal phones, and calls to other devices such as the voice mail system.
- **Plain old telephone service (POTS)**—POTS is the original analog version of the PSTN. The term originally referred to Post Office Telephone Service, but morphed into the current definition when control of the telephone systems was removed from national post offices.
- **Public Switched Telephone Network (PSTN)**—The PSTN is the circuit-switched network to which most telephones connect. It can be analog, digital, or a combination of the two.
- **Time-division multiplexing (TDM)**—TDM is a digital, multiplexing technique for placing multiple simultaneous calls over a circuit-switched network such as the PSTN.
- **Voice over Internet Protocol (VoIP)**—VoIP is the use of voice technologies over packet-switched networks using TCP/IP transport protocols rather than circuit-switched networks like the PSTN. This takes advantage of and reflects the trend toward a single, ubiquitous packet-switched network. The local area network (LAN) and wide area network (WAN) are used not only for data traffic, but also for voice traffic. VoIP is not a single technology but rather a collection of different technologies, protocols, hardware, and software.

Unified Messaging Protocols

The Exchange Server 2013 Unified Messaging services use several telephony-related protocols to integrate and communicate with telephony devices. These protocols are discussed in the following list:

- **Session Initiation Protocol (SIP)**—SIP is the signaling protocol that is used to set up and tear down VoIP calls. These calls include voice, video, instant messaging, and a variety of other services. The SIP protocol is specified in RFC 3261 produced by the Internet Engineering Task Force (IETF) SIP Working Group. SIP is only a signaling protocol and does not transmit data per se. After the call is set up, the actual communications take place using the RTP for voice and video or T.38 for faxes.

NOTE

Exchange Server 2013 only supports SIP over TCP. SIP can be configured to run over User Datagram Protocol (UDP) or TCP. UDP is connectionless and does not provide reliability guarantees over the network. TCP is connection-oriented and provides reliability guarantees for its packets.

- **Real-Time Transport Protocol (RTP)**—RTP is a protocol for sending the voice and video data over the TCP/IP network. The protocol relies on other protocols, such as SIP or H.323, to perform call setup and teardown. It was developed by the IETF Audio-Video Transport Working Group and is specified in RFC 3550. There is not a defined port for the RTP protocol, but it is normally configured to use ports in the range 16384–32767. The protocol uses a dynamic port range, so it is not ideally suited to traversing firewalls.
- **T.38**—The Real-Time Facsimile Transport (T.38) protocol is an International Telecommunication Union (ITU) standard for transmitting faxes over TCP/IP. The protocol is described in RFC 3362. Although it can support call setup and teardown, it is normally used in conjunction with a signaling protocol such as SIP.

It is important to note that the Exchange Server 2013 Mailbox server, which provides Unified Messaging services, is also a Windows server, a web server, and a member of the Active Directory domain. There are myriad protocols, including domain name system (DNS), Hypertext Transfer Protocol (HTTP), Lightweight Directory Access Protocol (LDAP), remote procedure calls (RPC), and Simple Mail Transfer Protocol (SMTP), among others, that the servers uses to communicate with other servers in addition to the telephony communications.

Unified Messaging Port Assignments

Table 19.3 shows the IP ports that Unified Messaging uses for each protocol. The table also shows if the ports can be changed and where.

TABLE 19.3 Ports Used for Unified Messaging Protocols

Protocol	TCP Port	UDP Port	Can Ports Be Changed?
SIP-UM Service	5060		Ports are hard-coded.
SIP-Worker Process	5061 and 5062		Ports are set by using the Extensible Markup Language (XML) configuration file.
RTP		Port range above 1024	The range of ports can be changed in the Registry.
UM Web Service	Dynamic port above 1024		Ports are defined by the system.

Unified Messaging Installation

Unlike earlier versions of Exchange Server, Exchange Server 2013 no longer has UM as a dedicated server role. UM has been rolled into the Mailbox server role, so all implementations of Exchange Server 2013 will have UM available, regardless of whether one plans to utilize it.

Installation Prerequisites

Although the prerequisites for a Mailbox server are called out in another chapter, it is worthwhile to repeat that the UM services need the Unified Communications Managed API v.4.0, which provides the required Speech Server components as well as audio codecs.

Telephony Prerequisites

As the Exchange Server 2013 Unified Messaging service is a voice mail system, all the other components must be in place and operational before introducing it. This includes the following:

- **PBX**—The existing PBX must be configured with the appropriate hunt groups to route calls correctly.
- **Hunt groups**—The hunt groups and pilot numbers should be provisioned in the PBX. The Auto Attendant pilot numbers and the subscriber access pilot numbers should be part of a rollover group, so that if one number is busy, the call will roll over to the next line.

NOTE

Set up separate hunt groups and pilot access numbers on the PBX for the Auto Attendant and the subscriber access lines.

- **IP/VoIP gateway**—The IP gateway must be configured to route calls from the pilot extensions to the Exchange Server 2013 CAS IP address that will proxy to the appropriate Mailbox server. The gateway must also be configured to use SIP over TCP, rather than SIP over UDP. Some gateways will attempt UDP first and then try TCP, resulting in strange connection behavior such as delays in initiating calls.
- **Phones**—The phones must be provisioned and assigned to users. At the very least, at least two test phones should be available.
- **External lines**—External lines must be provisioned within the PBX.

The Early Media setting is not supported in Exchange Server 2013 Unified Messaging.

See the manufacturer's documentation for specific details of the configuration for each of the telephony components.

UM Configuration

After the server has the Mailbox server role installed, you need to complete several postinstallation configuration tasks for the use of Exchange UM:

- Create a UM dial plan.
- Associate subscriber access numbers.
- Create a UM IP gateway.
- Associate the UM server with the dial plan.
- Create a UM Auto Attendant.
- Create the hunt groups.
- Enable mailboxes for UM.
- Test functionality.

Performing these tasks results in a functioning Exchange Server 2013 Unified Messaging system. The remainder of this section details the installation steps for each task.

Creating a UM Dial Plan

The first task is to create the central organizing element of the Exchange Server 2013 UM infrastructure—the dial plan shown in Figure 19.8.

To create a dial plan, execute the following steps:

1. Launch the Exchange Administration Center.
2. In the left pane, click Unified Messaging.
3. Select the UM Dial Plans tab.
4. Click the + icon to create a new dial plan.

5. Enter the dial plan name, such as **SFO Dial Plan**.
6. Enter the number of digits in the PBX extensions, such as 5.
7. Select the dial plan type.

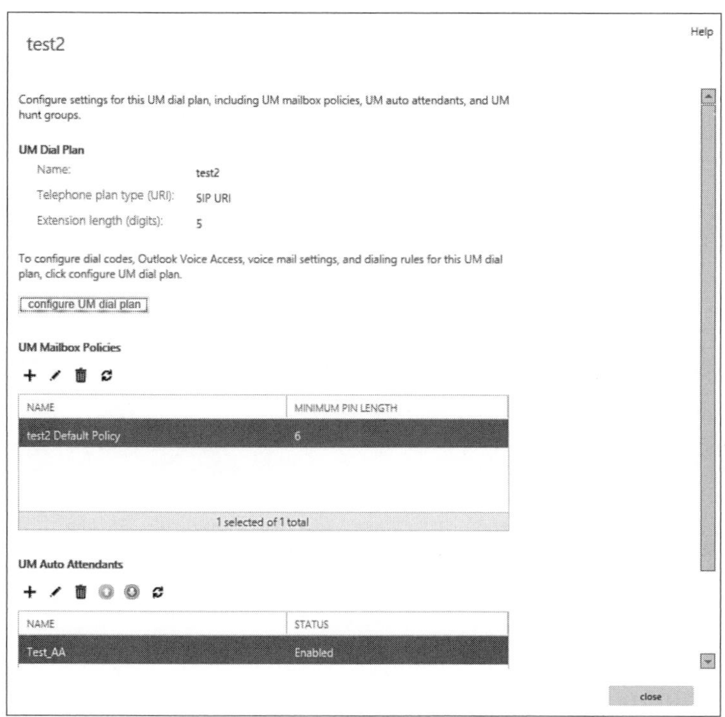

FIGURE 19.8 Viewing a dial plan.

NOTE

The dial plan type must be SIP URI if you are intending to associate a UM server with the dial plan.

19

8. Select the VoIP Security Mode. (SIP Secured is appropriate for a PBX like Lync.)
9. Select the Audio Language. (Be sure to use one you've installed.)
10. Enter the Country/Region code, such as 1 for the United States.
11. Click Save to create the UM dial plan. The newly created dial plan should be shown in the results pane.

Once created, the dial plan can be modified by selecting it and clicking Edit. This also shows the automatically created UM mailbox policy and allows administrators to see associated UM Auto Attendants and hunt groups. There are also additional settings that weren't part of the object creation that you can view and change by clicking Configure UM Dial Plan, including the following:

- **Dial Codes**—Configure dial codes for outside lines, international access, national prefix, and so on.
- **Outlook Voice Access**—Change the default greeting, add information announcements, and define the OVA access phone number.
- **Settings**—Choose the primary and secondary way of searching for names, define the audio codec, define the operator extension, and configure timeouts and retries.
- **Dialing Rules**—Create normalization rules to determine when and how to transform numbers from one format to another.
- **Dialing Authorization**—Determine which groups are allowed to call in country versus international.
- **Transfer & Search**—Configure permission for call transfers.

NOTE

Administrators familiar with Office Communications Server (OCS) or Lync may recognize many of these concepts. It is interesting to note that in Exchange UM, Dialing Rules don't use standard regular expressions. They use formats like 1925xxxxxxx rather than 1925(\d{7}).

Customizing the UM Mailbox Policy

While the UM mailbox policy is automatically created when a UM dial plan is created, it can still be customized based on the desires of the administrator. To customize the UM mailbox policy, follow these steps:

1. Launch the Exchange Administration Center.
2. In the left pane, click Unified Messaging.
3. Select the UM Dial Plans tab.
4. Select the UM dial plan associated with the UM mailbox policy you want to modify and click Edit.
5. In the Dial Plan page, select the UM mailbox policy and click Edit. From here, you can:
    - Limit the length of outgoing greetings.
    - Allow voice mail preview in text form.
    - Allow or disallow users to configure call answering rules (Personal Auto Attendant).

- Allow or disallow Message Waiting Indicator.
- Allow or disallow Outlook Voice Access.
- Allow or disallow missed call notifications.
- Allow or disallow Play on Phone for voice mail.
- Allow or disallow inbound faxes, which requires an external Fax service.

The Message Text page is where an administrator can configure messages to be sent to users when they're enabled for UM, when their PIN is reset, when they receive a voice message, or when they receive a fax. This can provide for a level of personalization or "branding" for a company for the services they are providing to the end users.

The PIN Policies page allows administrators to configure Minimum PIN length, enforce a PIN history, allow or disallow common PIN patterns, set a maximum PIN age, as well as define lockout policies based on bad PIN attempts.

The Dialing Authorization page controls users' ability to manage dialing groups and to allow Outlook Voice Access users to call or transfer to other users in various dial plans.

Protected Voice Mail allows administrators to restrict users' ability to listen to particular messages over their computers and forces them to listen to them via phone, to reduce the chances of those messages being overheard.

Associating Subscriber Access Numbers

For subscribers to access their mailboxes, one or more subscriber access numbers must be specified in the dial plan. This should be the pilot number for the PBX hunt group that the subscribers will use.

To associate a subscriber access extension to the dial plan, execute the following steps:

1. Launch the Exchange Administration Center.
2. In the left pane, click Unified Messaging.
3. Select the UM Dial Plans tab.
4. Select the dial plan in the results pane, such as SFO Dial Plan, and click Edit.
5. Under To Configure Dial Codes, click Configure.
6. In the left pane, click Outlook Voice Access.
7. Scroll down to Outlook Voice Access numbers.
8. Enter the number and click Add.
9. Click Save and then close the window.

The UM server will now recognize that subscribers will use the extension to access their mailboxes. This is the number that will appear in OWA when looking at Phone Options.

Creating a UM IP Gateway

Continuing the example so far, the next task is to create a UM IP gateway to link the dial plan with the IP/VoIP gateway and the PBX.

To create the UM IP gateway, execute the following steps:

1. Launch the Exchange Administration Center.
2. In the left pane, click Unified Messaging.
3. Select the UM IP Gateways tab.
4. Click New.
5. Enter a Name and an Address (FDQN or IP of the gateway).
6. Click Browse to select a UM dial plan to associate with the gateway and click OK.
7. Click Save.

The newly created UM IP gateway should be shown in the results pane. Once created, you can edit it to allow outgoing calls through the UM gateway or to enable/disable the message waiting indicator.

NOTE

If Lync is the IP gateway that will be used, you can run the `ExchUCUtil.ps1` script that is included with Exchange Server 2013 to automatically create the appropriate UM IP gateway object.

Associating the UM Server with the Dial Plan

The dial plan needs to be associated with the UM server that was installed in the first task. This eventually causes the UM server to register with the IP/VoIP gateway to receive calls.

To associate the UM server with the new dial plan, execute the following steps:

1. Launch the Exchange Administration Center.
2. In the left pane, click Servers, and then click the Servers tab.
3. Select the Mailbox server that will be associated with the dial plan and click Edit.
4. In the left pane, select Unified Messaging.
5. Click the + icon to add an associated dial plan.

NOTE

The dial plan type you select must be SIP URI.

6. Select the desired dial plan, click Add, click OK, and then click Save.

Repeat this task for each Mailbox server that will host the dial plan.

Creating a UM Auto Attendant

For the UM server to answer callers, a UM Auto Attendant must be created and associated with a dial plan. This allows incoming calls to be answered and directed to the appropriate voice mailbox. Auto Attendants are typically created to act as automated receptionists on office numbers where there is no human to answer the phone calls.

To create an Auto Attendant and associate it with a dial plan, follow these steps:

1. Launch the Exchange Administration Center.
2. In the left pane, click Unified Messaging and then click the UM Dial Plans tab.
3. Select an active UM dial plan and click Edit.
4. Scroll down to UM Auto Attendants and click New.
5. Enter a name for the UM Auto Attendant.
6. Check the Create the Auto Attendant as Enabled box.
7. If desired, check the Enable the Auto Attendant to Respond to Voice Commands box.
8. Enter an access number and click the + icon to add the access number.
9. Click Save.
10. Click Close to close the Dial Plan properties window. The newly created Auto Attendant should be shown in the results pane.

Creating the Hunt Groups

The default hunt group that is created with the UM IP gateway does not contain a pilot number. To have the system handle incoming calls correctly, the default hunt group should be deleted and new ones should be created for the caller and subscriber hunt groups.

NOTE

Dial plans of type SIP URI do not support hunt groups.

To accomplish the creation of the hunt groups, execute the following steps:

1. Launch the Exchange Administration Center.
2. In the left pane, click Unified Messaging and then click the UM Dial Plans tab.
3. Select an active UM dial plan and click Edit.
4. Scroll down to the UM Hunt Group section, select the Default Hunt Group and click Delete, and then click Yes to confirm.
5. Click New under UM Hunt Group to create a new hunt group.

6. Enter a name for the hunt group.
7. Click Browse and select the appropriate UM IP gateway.
8. Enter a Pilot Identifier; this is the number defined on the PBX for voice mail.
9. Click Save.
10. Click Close to close the Dial Plan properties window. The result of the configuration is shown in Figure 19.9, including the new hunt groups.

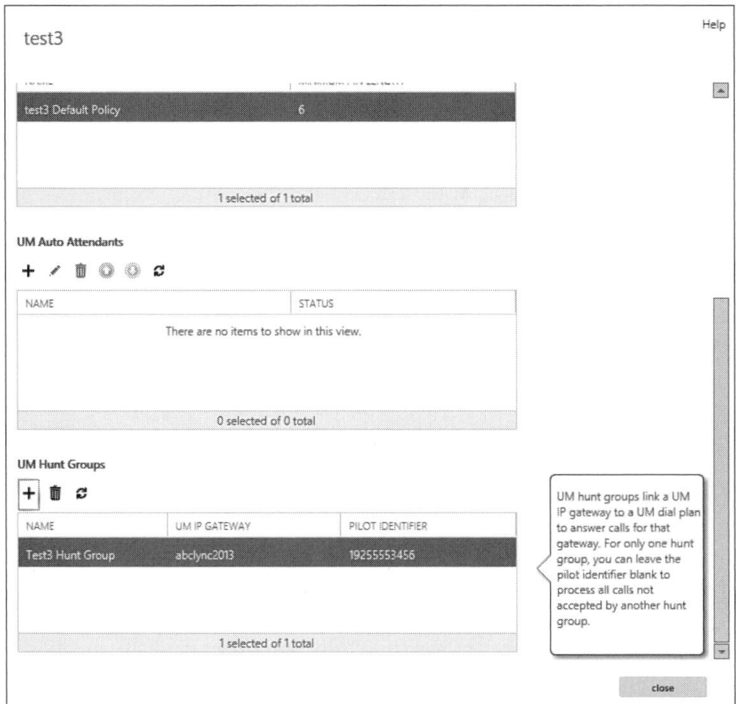

FIGURE 19.9 Creation of hunt groups.

The system is now configured and ready for the final configuration step in the basic configuration—the enabling of a user for Unified Messaging.

Enabling Mailboxes for UM

The last task is to enable a user's mailbox. This associates the user with a mailbox policy and, therefore, to the rest of the Unified Messaging infrastructure.

To enable a user, use the following steps:

1. Launch the Exchange Administration Center.
2. In the left pane, click Recipients.

3. Select a user in the middle pane and click Enable under Phone and Voice Features, Unified Messaging in the right pane.
4. Click Browse and select the UM mailbox policy you want to attach to this user and click Next.
5. Enter the extension for the user (this will autopopulate if the user is Enterprise Voice enabled in an integrated application like Lync), as shown in Figure 19.10.
6. Assign a PIN to the user and optionally require the user to change it at first sign in.
7. Click Finish.

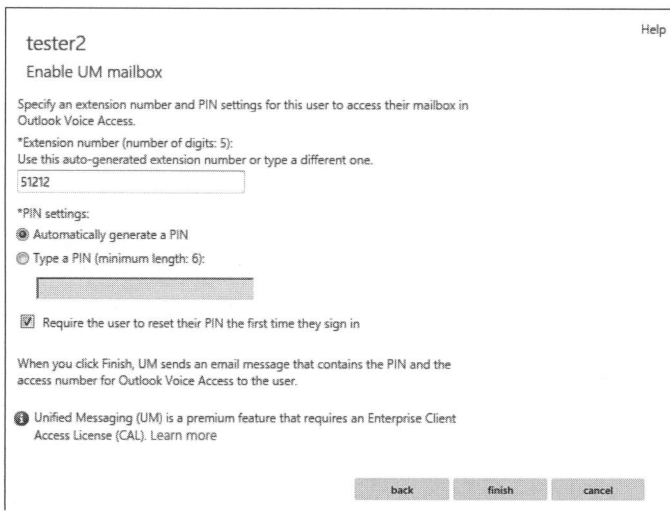

FIGURE 19.10 Enabling a user for Unified Messaging.

A simple welcome email message with the extension and a confidential PIN will be automatically sent to the Exchange Server mailbox. This message is customizable in the UM Mailbox Policy settings.

Testing Functionality

The final step is to make sure that it is all working. This could be the most difficult testing tasks for an average Exchange Server administrator, as he or she may be unfamiliar with the telephony elements of the infrastructure.

It is important to make sure that these critical functions be tested:

- The UM server is operating.
- The UM server can connect to the gateway and PBX.
- The UM server can be reached from an internal phone.
- The UM server can be reached from an external phone.

Figure 19.11 shows the paths of the critical tests.

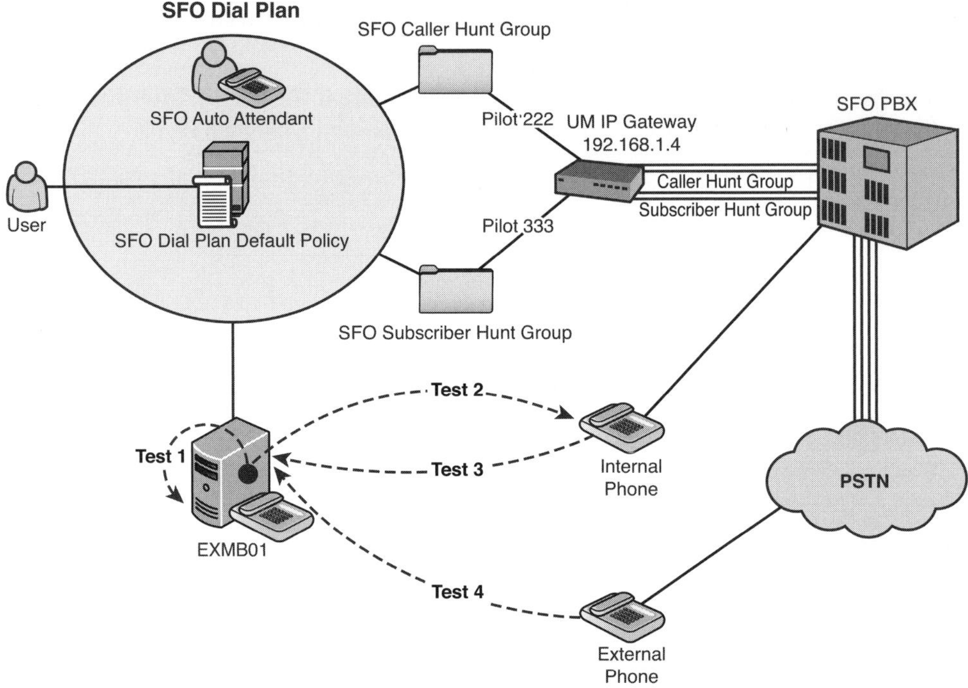

FIGURE 19.11 Paths of the critical tests for UM testing.

The specific commands and steps for testing are discussed in the following sections.

Testing Unified Messaging Server Operation

The Unified Messaging server operations test needs to run on the local UM server in the Exchange Management Shell. The shell command is:

```
Test-UMConnectivity
```

This command attempts a diagnostic SIP call and reports back on the success.

Testing Unified Messaging Server Connectivity

This test shows if the UM server can communicate with the PBX and access a phone. Specifically, it causes the internal phone to ring.

The command needs to be run from the Exchange Management Shell. The command syntax is:

```
Test-UMConnectivity -UMIPGateway "<IP Gateway Name>" -Phone <extension>
```

For example, the command might be:

```
Test-UMConnectivity -IPGateway "SFO IP Gateway" -Phone 10240
```

If successful, the phone at the extension should ring. If the test is successful, it will show that `"The call was disconnected by the other party"` at the end of the test.

To show the results of an unsuccessful test, enter the command:

```
Test-UMConnectivity -IPGateway "SFO IP Gateway" -Phone 104
```

This command specifies a nonexistent extension. This operation should fail.

Testing Unified Messaging Server with an Internal Phone

To test the Unified Messaging server from a phone, pick up a phone from within the dial plan and dial the pilot number.

For example, from the phone at extension 102, dial the pilot number 222. The Auto Attendant should pick up and prompt the caller.

Leave a message for a test user and then hang up.

Dial the pilot number for subscriber access (for example, extension 333) and check the message. Alternatively, check the message using Outlook or Outlook Web App.

Testing Unified Messaging Server with an External Phone

Use an outside line to call the company number that the PBX routes to the caller hunt group. Say the user's name. Press # to leave a message and leave a message for the user.

To verify the message was received, dial the external number for subscriber access and check the message. Alternatively, check the message using Outlook or Outlook Web App.

Data Storage in Unified Messaging

Unified Messaging stores data in several locations and formats. The different types of data include custom audio prompts, incoming calls, configuration, and setup.

It is important to understand where the data is stored, the relative importance of backing it up, and the method of restoring the data. Tables 19.4, 19.5, 19.6, and 19.7 list the relevant data storage information for each type of data.

The storage locations are the subdirectory under where Exchange Server 2013 was installed, which is `C:\Program Files\Microsoft\Exchange Server\V15` by default. The file paths shown are English (`...\en`); substitute the languages you support.

TABLE 19.4 Custom Audio Prompt Data

Data Type	Custom audio files (`.wav`) for UM dial plans and UM Auto Attendants Custom audio files (`.wav`) for telephone user interface (TUI) and Outlook Voice Access
Storage	File system in `\UnifiedMessaging\prompts\en`
Backup	File-level backup is only needed on the prompt publishing server
Restore	File-level restore is only needed on the prompt publishing server

TABLE 19.5 Incoming Call Data

Critical Data	Incoming calls: `.eml` and `.wma` files for each voice mail
Storage	File system `\UnifiedMessaging`\Temp
Backup	None
Restore	None

TABLE 19.6 Server Configuration Data

Critical Data	Server configuration data, including all objects and settings
Storage	Active Directory configuration container
Backup	Backup method is domain controller replication or Active Directory backup
Restore	This data is reapplied to the server during a setup `/m:recoverserver` restore

TABLE 19.7 Setup Data

Critical Data	Limited information is stored in the Registry by Setup that is not essential to server restore
Storage	`HKLM\SOFTWARE\Microsoft\Exchange` `HKLM\SYSTEM\currentcontrolset\Services`
Backup	Backup method is System State backup or Registry export
Restore	Restore method is System State restore or Registry import

Monitoring and Troubleshooting Unified Messaging

A number of tools are built in to the Exchange Server 2013 Unified Messaging platform to support the troubleshooting and monitoring of the services.

First and foremost, it is highly recommended that administrators deploy Microsoft System Center Operations Manager (SCOM) 2007/2012 to monitor the Exchange Server 2013 infrastructure. There is a management pack specific to the Exchange Server 2013 platform with a wealth of knowledge built in. See Chapter 17, "Using Microsoft System Center Operations Manager to Monitor Exchange Server 2013," for more details on SCOM and Exchange Server 2013.

That said, it is still important for the Exchange Server administrator to have a good knowledge and familiarity with the tools that are available to monitor Exchange Server 2013 Unified Messaging. These tools include the following:

- Exchange Management Shell test cmdlets
- Performance Monitor objects and counters
- Event log messages
- Removing the first UM server

These tools and techniques are covered in the next sections.

Active Calls

The system can provide information on active calls, which is very useful for monitoring and troubleshooting the Unified Messaging system. The `Get-UMActiveCalls` cmdlet returns information about the calls that are active and being processed by the Unified Messaging (UM) server. The syntax for the cmdlet is given in Table 19.8.

TABLE 19.8 `Get-UMActiveCalls` cmdlets

Syntax
Get-UMActiveCalls [-Server <ServerIdParameter>]
Get-UMActiveCalls -InstanceServer <UMServer>
Get-UMActiveCalls -DialPlan <UMDialPlanIdParameter>
Get-UMActiveCalls -IPGateway <UMIPGatewayIdParameter>

Connectivity

Connectivity to the IP/VoIP gateway can be one of the most troublesome aspects of the deployment and support of a Unified Messaging system. The `Test-UMConnectivity` cmdlet can be used to test the operation of a computer that has the Unified Messaging server role installed. The syntax for the cmdlet is given in Table 19.9.

TABLE 19.9 `Test-UMConnectivity` cmdlet

Syntax

```
test-UMConnectivity - [-ListenPort <Int32>]
[-MonitoringContext <$true | $false>] [-Secured <$true | $false>] [-Timeout <Int32>]
test-UMConnectivity -UMIPGateway <UMIPGatewayIdParameter> -Phone <String>
[-ListenPort <Int32>] [-MonitoringContext <$true | $false>]
[-Secured <$true | $false>] [-Timeout <Int32>]
```

This test was used in the installation section of this chapter to test the functionality of the UM server. See the section "Testing Functionality" earlier in this chapter for details of the command usage.

Performance Monitors

Unlike many applications, the Exchange Server 2013 Unified Messaging application is very well instrumented.

Tables of the counters for each of the monitored objects are noted in the balance of this section.

General Performance Counters for Unified Messaging

The counters listed in Table 19.10 are a subset of the performance objects found under the `MSExchangeUMGeneral` performance object and are useful for monitoring and troubleshooting general problems with the Exchange Server 2013 UM service.

TABLE 19.10 Counters for the `MSExchangeUMGeneral` Object

Performance Counter	Description
Total Calls	The number of calls since the service was started.
Total Calls per Second	The number of new calls that arrived in the last second.
Calls Disconnected by User Failure	The total number of calls disconnected after too many user entry failures.
Current Calls	The number of calls currently connected to the UM server.
Current Voice Mail Calls	The number of voice calls currently connected to the UM server.
Current Fax Calls	The number of fax calls currently connected to the UM server. Voice calls become fax calls after a fax tone is detected.
Current Auto Attendant Calls	The number of Auto Attendant calls that are currently connected to the UM server.
Current Play on Phone Calls	The number of outbound calls initiated to play back messages.

Performance Counter	Description
Current Unauthenticated Pilot Number Calls	The number of voice calls to the pilot number that have not yet been authenticated.
Total Play to Phone Calls	The total number of Play to Phone calls that were initiated since the service was started.
Average Call Duration	The average duration, in seconds, of calls since the service was started.
Average Recent Call Duration	The average duration, in seconds, of the last 50 calls.
User Response Latency	The average response time, in milliseconds, for the system to respond to a user request. This average is calculated over the last 25 calls. This counter is limited to calls that require significant processing.
Delayed Calls	The number of calls that experienced one or more delays longer than 2 seconds.
Call Duration Exceeded	The number of calls that were disconnected because they exceeded the UM maximum call length. This number includes all types of calls, including fax calls.
Current Prompt Editing Calls	The number of logged-on users who are editing custom prompts.
Current Subscriber Access Calls	The number of logged-on subscribers who are currently connected to the UM server.
OCS User Event Notifications	The number of OCS or Lync User Event notifications that have occurred since the service was started.

Call Answering Performance Counters for Unified Messaging

The counters listed in Table 19.11 are a subset of the performance objects under the `MSExchangeUMCallAnswer` performance object and are useful for monitoring and troubleshooting call answering problems with the Exchange Server 2013 UM service.

TABLE 19.11 Counters for the `MSExchangeUMCallAnswer` Object

Performance Counter	Description
Call Answering Calls	The number of diverted calls that were answered on behalf of subscribers
Call Answering Voice Messages	The total number of messages that were submitted because the calls were answered on behalf of subscribers
Call Answering Voice Messages per Second	The number of messages that were submitted because the calls were answered on behalf of subscribers
Call Answering Missed Calls	The number of times a diverted call was dropped without a message being left
Call Answering Escapes	The number of times a caller pressed the * key to connect to another user rather than leaving a message

Performance Counter	Description
Average Voice Message Size	The average size, in seconds, of voice messages left for subscribers
Average Recent Voice Message Size	The average size, in seconds, of the last 50 voice messages left for subscribers
Average Greeting Size	The average size, in seconds, of recorded greetings that have been retrieved by the UM server
Calls Without Personal Greetings	The number of diverted calls received for subscribers who did not have recorded greeting messages
Fetch Greeting Timed Out	The number of diverted calls for which the subscriber's personal greeting could not be retrieved within the time allowed
Calls Disconnected by Callers During UM Audio Hourglass	The number of calls during which the caller disconnected while Unified Messaging was playing the audio hourglass tones
Calls Disconnected by UM on Irrecoverable External Error	The number of calls that have been disconnected after an irrecoverable external error occurred
Diverted Extension Not Provisioned	The number of calls received for which the diverted extension supplied with the call is not a UM subscriber extension

Subscriber Access Performance Counters for Unified Messaging

The counters listed in Table 19.12 are a subset of the performance objects under the `MSExchangeUMSubscriberAccess` performance object and are useful for monitoring and troubleshooting subscriber access problems with the Exchange Server 2013 UM service.

The variety of counters in the subscriber access area is impressive and can really aid in the understanding of the behavior of the subscribers.

TABLE 19.12 Counters for the `MSExchangeUMSubscriberAccess` Object

Performance Counter	Description
Subscriber Authentication Failures	The number of authentication failures that have occurred since the service was started. This number is incremented once for every failed authentication. It's possible that a single phone call could generate several authentication failures.
Subscriber Logons	The number of UM subscribers who have successfully authenticated since the service was started.
Subscriber Logon Failures	The number of authentication failures since the service was started. This number is incremented once when all three per-call logon attempts fail.
Average Subscriber Call Duration	The average duration, in seconds, that subscribers spent logged on to the system. This timer starts when the logon completes.
Average Recent Subscriber Call Duration	The average length of time, in seconds, that subscribers spent logged on to the system for the last 50 subscriber calls.

Performance Counter	Description
Voice Message Queue Accessed	The number of times subscribers accessed their voice message queues using the telephone user interface.
Voice Messages Heard	The number of voice messages played to subscribers. This count is incremented as soon as playback starts. The subscriber does not need to listen to the entire message.
Voice Messages Sent	The number of voice messages sent by authenticated UM subscribers.
Average Sent Voice Message Size	The average size, in seconds, of voice messages that are sent. This size does not include any attachment data.
Average Recent Sent Voice Message Size	The average size, in seconds, of the last 50 voice messages that were sent.
Voice Messages Deleted	The number of voice messages that were deleted by authenticated subscribers.
Reply Messages Sent	The number of replies sent by authenticated subscribers.
Forward Messages Sent	The number of messages forwarded by authenticated subscribers.
Email Message Queue Accessed	The number of times subscribers accessed their email message queue using the telephone user interface.
Email Messages Heard	The number of email messages heard by authenticated subscribers.
Email Messages Deleted	The number of email messages deleted by authenticated subscribers.
Calendar Accessed	The number of times subscribers accessed their calendars using the telephone user interface.
Calendar Items Heard	The number of calendar items heard by authenticated subscribers.
Calendar Late Attendance	The number of messages sent to inform the organizer of a meeting to which the subscriber will be late.
Calendar Items Details Requested	The number of times a subscriber requested additional details for a calendar item.
Meetings Declined	The number of Meeting Declined messages sent by subscribers.
Meetings Accepted	The number of Meeting Accepted messages sent by subscribers.
Called Meeting Organizer	The number of times subscribers called the meeting organizer.
Replied to Organizer	The number of times subscribers sent reply messages to meeting organizers.
Contacts Accessed	The number of times subscribers accessed the Main Menu Contacts option using the telephone user interface.
Contact Items Heard	The number of times authenticated subscribers listened to directory details.
Launched Calls	The number of subscriber calls that resulted in an outbound call being placed.

Performance Counter	Description
Calls Disconnected by Callers During UM Audio Hourglass	The number of times callers disconnected while Unified Messaging was playing the audio hourglass tones.
Calls Disconnected by UM on Irrecoverable External Error	The number of subscriber calls that have been disconnected after an irrecoverable external error occurred.
Directory Accessed	The number of times subscribers accessed the Main Menu Directory option using the telephone user interface.
Directory Accessed by Extension	The number of directory access operations in which the user supplied the extension number.
Directory Accessed by Dial by Name	The number of directory access operations where the subscriber used the Dial by Name feature.
Directory Accessed Successfully by Dial by Name	The number of Dial by Name directory access operations that completed successfully on behalf of subscribers.
Directory Accessed by Spoken Name	The number of directory access operations in which the subscriber spoke a recipient name.
Directory Accessed Successfully by Spoken Name	The number of speech-recognition directory access operations that completed successfully on behalf of subscribers.

Unified Messaging Auto Attendant Performance Counters

The counters listed in Table 19.13 are a subset of the performance objects under the `MSExchangeUMAutoAttendant` performance object and are useful for monitoring and troubleshooting Auto Attendant problems with the Exchange Server 2013 UM service.

The variety of counters in the Auto Attendant area is impressive and can really aid in the understanding of the behavior of the callers, the menu choices they make, how long they stay in the system, and their preferred method of access to the menus.

TABLE 19.13 Counters for the `MSExchangeUMAutoAttendant` Object

Performance Counter	Description
Total Calls	The number of calls that have been processed by this Auto Attendant.
Business Hours Calls	The number of calls processed by this Auto Attendant during business hours.
Out of Hours Calls	The number of calls processed by this Auto Attendant outside of business hours.
Disconnected Without Input	The number of calls that were dropped without any input being offered to the Auto Attendant prompts.

Performance Counter	Description
Transferred Count	The number of calls that were transferred by this Auto Attendant. This number does not include calls that were transferred by the operator.
Directory Accessed	The number of directory access operations performed by this Auto Attendant.
Directory Accessed by Extension	The number of directory access operations in which the user supplied the extension number.
Directory Accessed by Dial by Name	The number of directory access operations in which the subscriber used the Dial by Name feature.
Directory Accessed Successfully by Dial by Name	The number of successful directory access operations in which the caller used the Dial by Name feature.
Directory Accessed by Spoken Name	The number of directory access operations in which the subscriber spoke a recipient name.
Directory Accessed Successfully by Spoken Name	The number of successful directory access operations in which the caller spoke a recipient name.
Operator Transfers	The number of calls that were transferred to the operator.
Menu Option 1 Used	The number of times that a caller has chosen option 1 from the custom menu. This value is always zero if no menu or option is defined.
Menu Option 2 Used	The number of times that a caller has chosen option 2 from the custom menu. This value is always zero if no menu or option is defined.
Menu Option 3 Used	The number of times that a caller has chosen option 3 from the custom menu. This value is always zero if no menu or option is defined.
Menu Option 4 Used	The number of times that a caller has chosen option 4 from the custom menu. This value is always zero if no menu or option is defined.
Menu Option 5 Used	The number of times that a caller has chosen option 5 from the custom menu. This value is always zero if no menu or option is defined.
Menu Option 6 Used	The number of times that a caller has chosen option 6 from the custom menu. This value is always zero if no menu or option is defined.
Menu Option 7 Used	The number of times that a caller has chosen option 7 from the custom menu. This value is always zero if no menu or option is defined.
Menu Option 8 Used	The number of times that a caller has chosen option 8 from the custom menu. This value is always zero if no menu or option is defined.

Performance Counter	Description
Menu Option 9 Used	The number of times that a caller has chosen option 9 from the custom menu. This value is always zero if no menu or option is defined.
Menu Option Timed Out	The number of times that the system has timed out waiting for a caller to select an option from the custom menu. This value is always zero if no menu is defined.
Average Call Time	The average length of time that callers interacted with the Auto Attendant.
Calls with DTMF Fallback	The total number of times a caller has been passed to the DTMF fallback Auto Attendant. This happens only for speech-enabled Auto Attendants.
% Successful Calls	% Successful Calls calculates the success rate of the Auto Attendant.
Calls Disconnected by UM on Irrecoverable External Error	The total number of calls disconnected after an irrecoverable external error occurred.
Average Recent Call Time	The average length of time, in seconds, of the last 50 Auto Attendant calls.
Calls with Speech Input	The total number of calls during which the caller is determined to have spoken at least once.
Calls with Sent Message	The total number of calls in which the caller has sent a voice message.
Calls with Spoken Name	The total number of calls to this Auto Attendant in which a caller has spoken a name at least once.
Custom Menu Options	The total number of times callers have selected custom menu options.
Disallowed Transfers	The number of times a caller was transferred to the operator because the user identified was configured to only accept calls from logged-on users.
Operator Transfers Requested by User	The number of times a caller to this Auto Attendant has asked to be transferred to an operator.
Operator Transfers Requested by User from Opening Menu	The number of times a caller to this Auto Attendant has asked to be transferred to an operator while at the opening menu.
Sent to Auto Attendant	The number of times a caller has used the custom menu to go to an Auto Attendant.
Ambiguous Name Transfers	The number of times that a caller was transferred to the operator because the name that they spelled or spoke was too common in the search results.

System Resources and Availability Counters for Unified Messaging

The counters listed in Table 19.14 are a subset of the performance objects under the `MSExchangeUMAvailability` performance object and are useful for monitoring and troubleshooting system resource and availability problems with the Exchange Server 2013 UM service.

TABLE 19.14 Counters for the `MSExchangeUMAvailability` Object

Performance Counter	Description
Directory Access Failures	The number of times that attempts to access Active Directory failed
Worker Process Recycled	The number of times a new UM worker process has been started
Total Worker Process Call Count	The total number of calls handled by this UM worker process
Incomplete Signaling Information	The number of calls for which the signaling information was missing or incomplete
Calls Disconnected by UM on Irrecoverable External Error	The number of calls disconnected after an irrecoverable external error occurred
Calls Disconnected on Irrecoverable Internal Error	The number of calls disconnected after an internal system error occurred
Spoken Name Accessed	The number of times the system retrieved the recorded name of a user
Name TTSed	The number of times the system used text-to-speech to create an audio version of the display name of a subscriber

Unified Messaging Performance Monitoring Counters

The counters listed in Table 19.15 are a subset of the performance objects under the `MSExchangeUMPerformance` performance object and are useful for monitoring and troubleshooting server latency problems with the Exchange Server 2013 UM services. These counters measure the time in number of seconds that server operations took. This is an important measure of the time that callers are waiting for the UM server to complete a task.

TABLE 19.15 Counters for the `MSExchangeUMPerformance` Object

Performance Counter	Description
Operations Between Two and Three Seconds	The number of all UM operations that took between 2 and 3 seconds to complete. This is the time during which a caller was waiting for UM to respond.
Operations Between Three and Four Seconds	The number of all UM operations that took between 3 and 4 seconds to complete. This is the time during which a caller was waiting for UM to respond.
Operations Between Four and Five Seconds	The number of all UM operations that took between 4 and 5 seconds to complete. This is the time during which a caller was waiting for UM to respond.
Operations Between Five and Six Seconds	The number of all UM operations that took between 5 and 6 seconds to complete. This is the time during which a caller was waiting for UM to respond.
Operations over Six Seconds	The number of all UM operations that took more than 6 seconds to complete. This is the time during which a caller was waiting for UM to respond.
Operations under Two Seconds	The number of all UM operations that took less than 2 seconds to complete. This is the time during which a caller was waiting for Unified Messaging to respond.

Event Logs

Event logs are important for troubleshooting Microsoft Exchange Server Unified Messaging. Each of the different aspects of a Unified Messaging server generates their own set of error messages. The tables of events show the errors and events that could be generated for each of the following categories:

- Call answering
- Call transfer
- Subscriber access
- Auto Attendant
- Active Directory
- Prompt publishing
- Outdialing
- Administrative
- Speech grammar
- System
- Performance

The event log messages are very detailed and specific to many conditions, making it very easy to understand, audit, troubleshoot, and instrument the Unified Messaging server.

Although there are hundreds of Event IDs related to Unified Messaging, a few common events are reviewed here for help in troubleshooting.

Call Answering

Unified Messaging generates call answering events to help troubleshoot call answering features and issues. A good example is when a call is directed to a user that is not enabled for Unified Messaging. Exchange Server UM logs an 1169 event in Event Viewer with the extension number of the affected user. To resolve this issue, enable the user for Exchange Server Unified Messaging.

Call Transfer

Unified Messaging generates call transfer events for actions related to call transfers in Unified Messaging. Event IDs 1025 and 1136 are often found together and relate to a failure in Exchange Server UM to transfer a call. Relevant information such as call ID and destination number are included in the body of the event logged in Event Viewer.

Subscriber Access

Exchange Server 2013 Unified Messaging generates events based on subscriber access behavior. This relates mostly to user-induced events such as Event ID 1012 that indicates a user has entered his PIN incorrectly more times than is allowed by the policy and has been locked out. Reset the user's PIN to allow him to log in again.

Another common event is ID 1080 that indicates the UM service could not process a message for a user because her mailbox is over quota. In this situation, the administrator can either raise the quota, or the user must delete messages from her mailbox to get under her allowed quota limit.

Auto Attendant

The Exchange Server 2013 Unified Messaging Auto Attendant is one of the most important functions within UM. It is almost always an external caller's entryway to the system. As such, any warnings or errors encountered should be taken seriously. Event ID 1128 indicates that an operator extension has not been defined. The UM service cannot forward a call to an operator. This means calls will simply be disconnected if they are not routed through the Auto Attendant. To resolve this issue, assign an operator extension using the UM portion of the Exchange Administration Center.

Active Directory

Every part of Exchange Server 2013 is tightly coupled with Active Directory, and Exchange Server 2013 Unified Messaging is no exception. If the UM service cannot contact Active Directory for lookup or authentication data, a warning or error is logged. If Active Directory is unavailable on startup of the UM service, the service fails to start.

Prompt Publishing

Exchange Server 2013 Unified Messaging enables for a number of custom prompts to be configured. Although this enables a lot of flexibility, it can also be a source of errors. The UM service logs alerts and errors for events related to custom prompts. Any update of custom prompts is logged. For example, Event ID 1100 indicates a successful publishing, whereas Event ID 1099 indicates that a failure occurred and provides information on where the failure happened.

Outdialing

Exchange Server 2013 UM enables users to dial out from the system dependent on policy. This includes the Play on Phone functionality. Most of the events in this section focus on the dialing rules set in Exchange Server UM. The dialing rules might be different depending if the next hop is a PBX or a media gateway. An example of a warning is Event ID 1076 that indicates the UM service cannot complete a Play on Phone request due to improperly configured dialing rules. To resolve the issue, review and make the appropriate changes to your dialing rules.

Administrative

The administrative events logged for Exchange Server 2013 Unified Messaging services are all administrative. They indicate actions such as enabling or disabling a user for Exchange Server UM or the changing of a PIN. They are often good to check when you make an administrative change if you suspect that change was not successful.

Speech Grammar

Exchange Server 2013 Unified Messaging has a built-in speech grammar file for understanding Automatic Speech Recognition (ASR) commands. If this file is not present or is malformed, a warning or error is logged. Event ID 1086, for example, indicates that the speech grammar files cannot be found, and ASR will be disabled. To resolve this issue, place a valid speech grammar file in the default location and restart the service.

System

The large majority of events logged for Exchange Server 2013 Unified Messaging fall under the System category. The events range from informational, such as when the UM worker process successfully starts, to significant failures, such as TLS certificate failures. Other events that are important are those related to the UM IP gateway, such as Event IDs 1124 and 1165 that indicate no IP gateways were found. To resolve this issue, ensure the UM server is configured to the correct IP gateway and the gateway is operational.

Performance

There are only two performance-related events for Exchange Server Unified Messaging. Event ID 1054 is informational and indicates the UM worker process was terminated because the startup time exceeded the maximum. Event ID 1089 is a warning and indicates the IP gateway did not respond promptly to a SIP request issued by the UM server.

Unified Messaging Shell Commands

Sometimes, just finding commands in the Exchange Management Shell can be a daunting task. In this section, each of the Unified Messaging commands is listed by verb.

For each of the commands, the detailed syntax can be obtained by executing the command `help cmdlet`. For example, to get help on the cmdlet `Add-ADPermission`, execute the command `Get-Help Add-ADPermission` in the Exchange Management Shell interface, as shown in Figure 19.12.

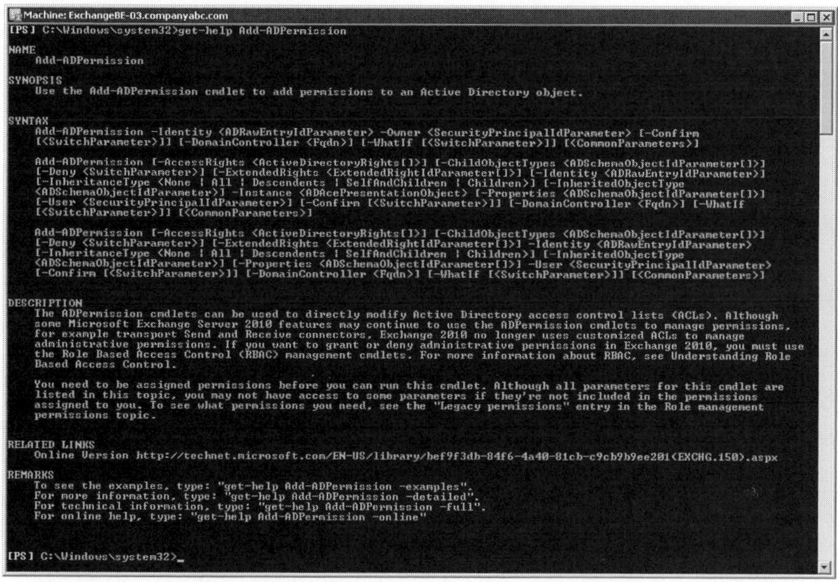

FIGURE 19.12 Exchange Management Shell help.

Add/Remove Verb Cmdlets

Table 19.16 lists all the Exchange Server 2013 Unified Messaging–specific add/remove verb cmdlets.

19

TABLE 19.16 Add/Remove Cmdlets

Verb	Noun	Cmdlet Name
Add	ADPermission	Add-ADPermission
Remove	ADPermission	Remove-ADPermission
Remove	UMAutoAttendant	Remove-UMAutoAttendant
Remove	UMCallAnsweringRule	Remove-UMCallAnsweringRule
Remove	UMDialPlan	Remove-UMDialPlan

Verb	Noun	Cmdlet Name
Remove	UMHuntGroup	Remove-UMHuntGroup
Remove	UMIPGateway	Remove-UMIPGateway
Remove	UMMailboxPolicy	Remove-UMMailboxPolicy

Get/Set Verb Cmdlets

Table 19.17 lists all the Exchange Server 2013 Unified Messaging–specific get/set verb cmdlets.

TABLE 19.17 Get/Set Cmdlets

Verb	Noun	Cmdlet Name
Get	ADPermission	Get-ADPermission
Get	UMActiveCalls	Get-UMActiveCalls
Get	UMAutoAttendant	Get-UMAutoAttendant
Get	UMCallAnsweringRule	Get-UMCallAnsweringRule
Get	UMCallDataRecord	Get-UMCallDataRecord
Get	UMCallRouterSettings	Get-UMCallRouterSettings
Get	UMCallSummaryReport	Get-UMCallSummaryReport
Get	UMDialPlan	Get-UMDialPlan
Get	UMHuntGroup	Get-UMHuntGroup
Get	UMIPGateway	Get-UMIPGateway
Get	UMMailbox	Get-UMMailbox
Get	UMMailboxConfiguration	Get-UMMailboxConfiguration
Get	UMMailboxPIN	Get-UMMailboxPIN
Get	UMMailboxPolicy	Get-UMMailboxPolicy
Get	UMPhoneSession	Get-UMPhoneSession
Get	UmServer	Get-UmServer
Set	EventLogLevel	Set-EventLogLevel
Set	UMAutoAttendant	Set-UMAutoAttendant
Set	UMCallAnsweringRule	Set-UMCallAnsweringRule
Set	UMCallRouterSettings	Set-UMCallRouterSettings
Set	UMDialPlan	Set-UMDialPlan
Set	UMIPGateway	Set-UMIPGateway
Set	UMMailbox	Set-UMMailbox
Set	UMMailboxConfiguration	Set-UMMailboxConfiguration
Set	UMMailboxPIN	Set-UMMailboxPIN
Set	UMMailboxPolicy	Set-UMMailboxPolicy
Set	UmServer	Set-UmServer

Test Verb Cmdlets

Table 19.18 lists all the Exchange Server 2013 Unified Messaging–specific test verb cmdlets.

TABLE 19.18 Test Cmdlets

Verb	Noun	Cmdlet Name
Test	SystemHealth	Test-SystemHealth
Test	UMConnectivity	Test-UMConnectivity

Enable/Disable Verb Cmdlets

Table 19.19 lists all the Exchange Server 2013 Unified Messaging–specific enable/disable verb cmdlets.

TABLE 19.19 Enable/Disable Cmdlets

Verb	Noun	Cmdlet Name
Enable	UMAutoAttendant	Enable-UMAutoAttendant
Enable	UMCallAnsweringRule	Enable-UMCallAnsweringRule
Enable	UMIPGateway	Enable-UMIPGateway
Enable	UMMailbox	Enable-UMMailbox
Enable	UMServer	Enable-UMServer
Disable	UMAutoAttendant	Disable-UMAutoAttendant
Disable	UMCallAnsweringRule	Disable-UMCallAnsweringRule
Disable	UMIPGateway	Disable-UMIPGateway
Disable	UMMailbox	Disable-UMMailbox
Disable	UMServer	Disable-UMServer

New Verb Cmdlets

Table 19.20 lists all the Exchange Server 2013 Unified Messaging–specific new verb cmdlets.

TABLE 19.20 New Cmdlets

Verb	Noun	Cmdlet Name
New	UMAutoAttendant	New-UMAutoAttendant
New	UMCallAnsweringRule	New-UMCallAnsweringRule
New	UMDialPlan	New-UMDialPlan
New	UMHuntGroup	New-UMHuntGroup
New	UMIPGateway	New-UMIPGateway
New	UMMailboxPolicy	New-UMMailboxPolicy

SIP Protocol

SIP is an application-layer signaling protocol for creating, modifying, and terminating sessions with one or more participants.

Given the importance of SIP in the Exchange Server 2013 Unified Messaging system, it is important to understand the protocol in some detail. This assists in troubleshooting integration problems between the Unified Messaging server and the IP/VoIP gateway, which is a frequent source of problems.

SIP Terminology

SIP uses specific terminology to define the elements and devices in a SIP call. Table 19.21 lists the various SIP terms and definitions.

TABLE 19.21 SIP Terminology

Term	Description
Methods	SIP commands and messages
Result codes	Responses to SIP methods indicating success, failure, or other information
User Agent	Endpoint devices that can issue or respond to SIP protocol methods (such as the UM server or IP gateway)
User Agent Client	Devices such as phones or PDAs
Server	An application that can accept or respond to SIP methods (for example, a UM server)
Term	Description
Gateway	A gateway that can convert SIP methods and result codes to another protocol (for example, an IP gateway)
Proxy server	A server that can make requests on behalf of other clients

SIP Methods

SIP uses a number of commands or methods within the protocol. Table 19.22 lists the methods that SIP uses.

TABLE 19.22 SIP Methods

Method	Description
`REGISTER`	Registers a user with a registrar.
`INVITE`	Invites a session setup request or media negotiation. Used also to hold and retrieve calls.
`CANCEL`	Cancels an in-progress transaction.
`ACK`	Acknowledges an `INVITE` transaction.

Method	Description
`BYE`	Terminates a session.
`OPTIONS`	Queries the capabilities of servers.
`INFO`	Used for mid-call signaling information exchange.
`SUBSCRIBE`	Requests notification of call events.
`NOTIFY`	Notifies of an event after a subscription.
`REFER`	Requests a call transfer.

This table can be useful when doing a protocol trace of a SIP session to determine what the session is doing.

SIP Response Codes

SIP uses a number of response codes, both informational and error related. Table 19.23 lists the response codes that SIP uses.

TABLE 19.23 SIP Response Codes

Response Code	Description
100	Trying
180	Ringing
181	Call is being forwarded
182	Call is being queued
183	Session progress
200	OK
302	Moved temporarily, forward call to a given contact
305	Use proxy: repeat same call setup using a given proxy
400	Bad Request
401	Unauthorized Request
404	Not Found
408	Request Timeout
486	Busy
5xx	Server Failure
6xx	Global Failure

Basic Call Example

The SIP protocol is used to set up calls and then hands the communication over to the RTP protocol. A basic call sequence for a SIP call setup and teardown in Unified Messaging looks like the example in Table 19.24.

TABLE 19.24 Basic SIP Call Example

IP Gateway	Direction	UM Server
INVITE	——>	
	<——	180 Ringing
	<——	200 OK
ACK	——>	
RTP	<——>	RTP
	<——	BYE
200 OK	——>	

Notice that after the IP gateway sends an SIP ACK method back to the Unified Messaging server, the call is handed off to the RTP protocol. After the call is complete, the Unified Messaging server sends a SIP BYE method to terminate the communication.

Summary

Exchange Server 2013 raises the bar yet again for Microsoft Unified Messaging. It builds on the rich feature sets of Exchange Server 2007 and 2010 UM and adds a host of new features. The interface and management should be familiar to seasoned Exchange Server professionals, making it easy to roll out new features in the course of an upgrade. For those who haven't worked with Exchange, the way the Exchange Server 2013 administrative interface is setup, the configuration is well organized to speed up the learning curve. If you are new to Exchange Server's telephony features, they might seem intimidating at first; however, by following the steps in this chapter, you can get the Exchange Server 2013 UM services up and running so that you can begin your testing of Unified Messaging in the new Exchange Server environment.

Best Practices

The following are best practices from this chapter:

- Allow transfers to the operator at least during business hours to reduce caller frustration.
- Be careful when implementing mailbox quotas because it can impact the ability of users to receive voice mail.
- Create a secondary Auto Attendant that is not speech enabled and configure the primary Auto Attendant to fall back to it.
- Create separate PBX hunt groups for the caller lines and the subscriber lines with separate pilot numbers.

- Have two test internal phones available for testing the new Unified Messaging system.
- Leave the audio codec setting on MP3 for small file sizes and playback on the largest number of mobile devices.
- Move users' mailboxes to an Exchange Server 2013 Mailbox server in advance of the Unified Messaging deployment.
- Remove the default hunt groups and create specific ones for maximum control over call routing.
- Use key mapping to create helpful front-end menus for callers.
- Use the disable after completing call feature when disabling UM IP gateways or UM servers.

CHAPTER 20

Integrating Exchange with SharePoint Site Mailboxes, Enterprise Search, and More

IN THIS CHAPTER

- Understanding the History of SharePoint Technologies
- Identifying the Need for SharePoint 2013
- Exploring Basic SharePoint Features
- Exploring End-User Features in SharePoint
- Enabling Site Mailbox Functionality in SharePoint 2013
- Customizing and Developing SharePoint Sites

Exchange Server is the messaging component of the Microsoft product stack; it focuses on providing tools for knowledge workers to communicate with each other using email and other Unified Messaging capabilities. Collaboration is not only limited to messaging, however, and many organizations are looking into document management and workflow solutions to provide for a higher degree of collaboration in their messaging environments.

The Microsoft product line that provides for a near-seamless integration of document management into a Microsoft Exchange Server 2013 environment is composed of several technologies collectively referred to as SharePoint. Indeed, direct integration between SharePoint and Exchange Server has been provided with the 2013 line of both products, with new capabilities such as the concept of a site mailbox, an Exchange shared mailbox that is accessed via Outlook but that resides on SharePoint servers. In addition, SharePoint allows for inbound email functionality, which turns a document library into an Exchange recipient, allowing for the automatic collection and indexing of emails and their attachments.

This chapter focuses on understanding what the latest SharePoint products, formally named SharePoint Server 2013 and SharePoint Foundation 2013, are and how they can integrate into an Exchange Server 2013 environment.

Understanding the History of SharePoint Technologies

SharePoint technologies have a somewhat complicated history. Multiple attempts at rebranding the applications and packaging them with other Microsoft programs have further confused administrators and users alike. Consequently, a greater understanding of what the SharePoint products are and how they were constructed is required.

SharePoint Foundation's Predecessor: SharePoint Team Services

In late 1999, Microsoft announced the digital dashboard concept as the first step in its knowledge management strategy, releasing the Digital Dashboard Starter Kit, the Outlook 2000 Team Folder Wizard, and the Team Productivity Update for BackOffice 4.5. These tools leveraged existing Microsoft technologies, so customers and developers could build solutions without purchasing additional products. These tools, and the solutions developed using them, formed the basis for what became known as SharePoint Team Services (STS), the predecessor of SharePoint Foundation (SPF).

With the launch of Office XP, SharePoint Team Services was propelled into the limelight as the wave of the future, providing a tool for non–information technology (IT) personnel to easily create websites for team collaboration and information sharing. Team Services, included with Office XP, came into being through Office Server Extensions and FrontPage Server Extensions. The original server extensions were built around a web server and provide a blank default web page. The second generation of server extensions provided a web authoring tool, known then as FrontPage, for designing web pages. Team Services was a third-generation server extension product, with which a website could be created directly out of the box.

Understanding the Original SharePoint Portal Server Tool

SharePoint Server 2013, as it is known today, is the enterprise-level entry of the SharePoint product, building on top of the base SharePoint Foundation functionality. SharePoint 2013 further extends the capabilities of SPF, allowing for multiple SPF sites to be indexed and managed centrally, providing for advanced Business Intelligence options, and giving users social-integrated features.

The first version of this software was known as SharePoint Portal Server 2001. The intent was to provide a customizable portal environment focused on collaboration, document management, and knowledge sharing. The product carried the "digital dashboard" Web Part technology a step further to provide an out-of-the-box solution. SharePoint Portal Server was the product that could link together the team-based websites that were springing up.

Microsoft's initial SharePoint Portal product included a document management system that provided document check-in/check-out capabilities, as well as version control and approval routing. These features were not originally available in SharePoint Team Services. SharePoint Portal also included the capability to search not only document libraries, but also external sources such as other websites and Exchange public folders.

Because the majority of the information accessed through the portal was unstructured, the Web Storage System was the means selected for storing the data, as opposed to a more structured database product such as Microsoft SQL Server, which was being used for SharePoint Team Services. The Web Storage System, incidentally, is the same technology that is used by Microsoft Exchange. Newer SharePoint implementations use the same SQL database as SPF does, however.

Outlining the Differences between the Two SharePoint Products

As SharePoint Team Services was available at no extra charge to Office XP/FrontPage users, many organizations took advantage of this "free" technology to experiment with portal usage. STS's simplicity made it easy to install and put into operation. Although functionality was not as robust as a full SharePoint Portal Server solution, knowledge workers were seeing the benefits of being able to collaborate with team members.

Adaptation of SharePoint Portal Server progressed at a slower rate. In a tight economy, organizations were not yet ready to make a monetary commitment to a whole new way of collaborating, even if it provided efficiency in operations. In addition, the SharePoint Portal interface was not intuitive or consistent, which made it difficult to use.

Having two separate products with similar names confused many people. "SharePoint" was often discussed in a generic manner, and people weren't sure whether the topic was SharePoint Portal or SharePoint Team Services, or the two technologies together. Even if the full application name was mentioned, there was confusion regarding the differences between the two products, and about when each was appropriate to use. People wondered why SharePoint Team Services used the SQL data engine for its Information Store, whereas SharePoint Portal Server used the Web Storage System. It appeared as though there was not a clear strategy for the product's direction.

Examining Microsoft's Next-Generation SharePoint Products: SharePoint Portal Server 2003 and Windows SharePoint Services (WSS) 2.0

Microsoft took a close look at what was happening with regard to collaboration in the marketplace and used this information to drive its SharePoint technologies. Microsoft believed that in the world of online technology and collaboration, people need to think differently about how they work. The focus was to develop a suite of products to better handle this collaboration.

In addition to looking closer at how people collaborate, Microsoft also analyzed what had transpired with its SharePoint products. The end result was that Microsoft modified its knowledge management and collaboration strategy. Microsoft began talking about its "SharePoint technology," with a key emphasis on building this technology into the .NET Framework, and, thus, natively supporting XML Web Services.

In 2003, Microsoft released the 2.0 generation of SharePoint Products. SharePoint Team Services was rebranded as Windows SharePoint Services (WSS) 2.0, the engine for the team-collaboration environment. Windows SharePoint Services included many new and enhanced features, some of which were previously part of SharePoint Portal

Server. Windows SharePoint Services was also included as an optional component to the Windows Server 2003 operating system at the same time.

SharePoint Portal Server 2001 was incrementally updated to SharePoint Portal Server 2003 and continued to be the enterprise solution for connecting internal and external sources of information. SharePoint Portal Server allowed for searching across sites and enabled the integration of business applications into the portal.

Unveiling the Third Wave of SharePoint: MOSS 2007 and WSS 3.0

As adoption of SharePoint technologies increased, Microsoft put more and more emphasis on the product line as collaboration functionality became increasingly important for organizations. Organizations were increasingly excited about the 2003 product line, but there were some functional disadvantages to the platform, which held many organizations back from a full deployment of the product or forced them to purchase third-party add-ons to the suite. Workflow, navigation components, and administration were all weaker than many organizations needed, and Microsoft began work on the 3.0 generation of SharePoint products.

Along with the new generation came another rebranding of the product. SharePoint Portal Server became Microsoft Office SharePoint Server (MOSS) 2007. Windows SharePoint Services retained the same name and simply incremented the version number to 3.0.

SharePoint 2007 and WSS 3.0 introduced several functional enhancements to SharePoint, including the following:

- **Integrated business process and Business Intelligence**—A significant portion of the development time for SharePoint was spent focused on improving the business workflow functionality of SharePoint. SharePoint 2007 introduced a multitude of business process and Business Intelligence improvements that allow organizations to increase the efficiencies in their tasks.

- **Consolidated administrative tools**—Previous versions of SharePoint proved to be a headache to administer, as administrative tools and interfaces were scattered throughout the product. SharePoint 2013 consolidates these administrative interfaces into a single location and provides for additional administrative tools as well.

- **Improved Office integration**—SharePoint 2007 further improved the tight integration between Office and SharePoint by allowing for advanced functionality, such as direct editing from Microsoft Excel, and offline capabilities in Microsoft Outlook and Groove.

- **Extranet and single sign-on enhancements**—SharePoint 2007 allowed for more secure and functional extranet deployment scenarios, so that internal SharePoint sites can be utilized from the Internet without compromising safety or violating governmental regulations.

Microsoft SharePoint Server 2010 and SharePoint Foundation

The "4.0" wave of SharePoint products and technologies was released as SharePoint Server 2010 (the MOSS was dropped) and SharePoint Foundation, the newly named version of WSS. The SharePoint 2010 line was wildly popular, introducing the following improvements:

- 64-bit only infrastructure, both on SharePoint and on the database back end
- Inclusion of the Office Ribbon for performing common Office tasks from within the browser
- Improved and consolidated administration from SharePoint Central Admin
- Improvements in business data tools
- Support for claims-based authentication models and extranet support

Microsoft SharePoint Server 2013

The latest wave of SharePoint technologies is the 2013 wave, which builds on the success of SharePoint 2010 and introduces the following new features and benefits:

- Greatly improved Business Intelligence
- Tightly integrated social-networking functionality
- A revamped UI, shown in Figure 20.1, that is more streamlined and mobile-device friendly

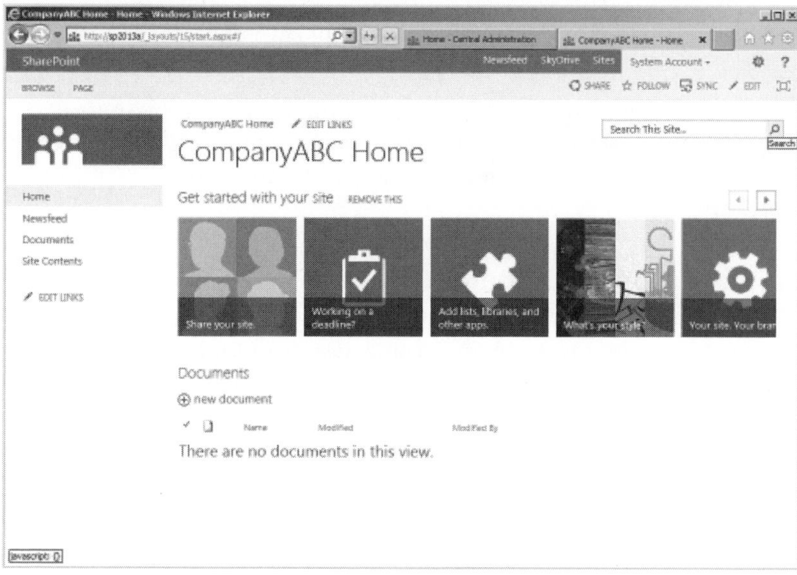

FIGURE 20.1 Viewing the SharePoint 2013 user interface.

- Search improvements and the inclusion of the highly powerful FAST Search features natively in all versions
- Cross-platform support for multiple browsers and content editors
- Tighter integration with Exchange Server 2013 with the inclusion of site mailboxes
- Multi-tenancy improvements and massive scalability options

For more information on the 2013 wave of SharePoint products and technologies, refer to the Sams Publishing title *SharePoint 2013 Unleashed.*

Identifying the Need for SharePoint 2013

SharePoint is one of those services that is greatly misunderstood. Much of the confusion over the previous branding of the product has contributed to this, but a fundamental shift in thinking is required to effectively utilize the platform. An understanding of what SharePoint is and how it can be fully utilized is an important step toward realizing the efficiency the system can bring.

Changing Methodology from File Servers to a SharePoint Document Management Platform

SharePoint expands beyond its origins as a web team site application into a full-fledged documentation platform with the new functionalities introduced. These capabilities allow SharePoint to store and manage documents efficiently in a transaction-oriented Microsoft SQL Server environment. What this means to organizations is that the traditional file server is less important, and effectively replaced, for document storage. Items such as Microsoft Word documents, Excel spreadsheets, and the like are stored in the SharePoint database.

Along with these document management capabilities comes the realization by users that their standard operating practice of storing multiple versions of files on a file server is no longer feasible or efficient. Using SharePoint effectively subsequently requires a shift in thinking from traditional approaches.

Enabling Team Collaboration with SharePoint

SharePoint has demonstrated how web-based team sites can be effectively used to encourage collaboration among members of a team or an organization. Content relevant to a group of people or a project can be efficiently directed to the individuals who need to see it most, negating the need to have them hunt and peck across a network to find what they need.

After being deployed, the efficiency and collaboration realized is actually quite amazing. A good analogy to SharePoint can be found with email. Before using email, it's hard to understand how valuable it can be. After you've used it, however, it's hard to imagine not having it. The same holds true for SharePoint functionality. Organizations that have deployed SharePoint have a hard time imagining working without it.

Customizing SharePoint to Suit Organizational Needs

If the default functionality in SharePoint is not enough or does not satisfy the specific web requirements of an organization, SharePoint can easily be customized. Easily customizable or downloadable Web Parts can be instantly "snapped in" to a site, without the need to understand Hypertext Markup Language (HTML) code. More advanced developers can use ASP.NET or other programming tools to produce custom code to work with SharePoint. Further enhancement of SharePoint sites can be accomplished using SharePoint Designer 2013 or other supported content editors, which allow for a great deal of customization with relative ease. In general, if it can be programmed to work with Web Services, it can interface with SharePoint.

Exploring Basic SharePoint Features

A SharePoint deployment can be used to create websites, manage documents, and provide other capabilities. Understanding and testing the features available in SharePoint is an important prerequisite step toward effectively using SharePoint, and a walk-through of those features should subsequently be performed.

Working Within the SharePoint Site

A SharePoint 2013 environment is composed of multiple SPF sites, illustrated in Figure 20.1, which are essentially individual workspaces that contain the knowledge worker content, such as document libraries, lists, document workspaces, and so on.

Understanding Document Libraries

Document libraries may well be the feature most often used, as it is the location where documents and folders can be stored and managed, and document libraries offer a number of features not available in a standard server file share.

The team members who are working on one of the documents in the document library can upload related items to this library for reference purposes. This eliminates the step of printing out copies of supporting documentation for an in-person meeting or emailing the actual files or hyperlinks via email.

NOTE

Alerts are an extremely powerful feature in SharePoint. A user can set an alert on an individual item stored in a SharePoint list, such as a document, so that if the document is changed, users receive an email letting them know of the change. Alternatively, an alert can be set for the whole document library, so if any items are changed, added, or deleted, users receive an email. The emails can be sent immediately, or in a daily or weekly summary. This is the primary way SharePoint pushes information to the users of its sites, enhancing the flow of information.

Other capabilities in the Shared Documents page include creating a new document, uploading other documents to the site, creating a new folder, filtering the documents, or editing the list in a datasheet.

Using Picture Libraries

A picture library can include a wide variety of file types, including JPEG, BMP, GIF, PNG, TIF, WMF, and EMF. Examples are photos of members of the team or screenshots of documents from software applications that might not be available to all users. For instance, a screen capture from an accounting application could be saved to the library in BMP format so that any of the users of the site could see the information.

Similarly, a Visio diagram or Project Gantt chart could be saved to one of these formats, or as an HTML file, and then saved to a picture library and thereby made accessible to users of the site who might not have these software products installed on their workstations. By providing a graphical image rather than the native file format, the amount of storage space required can be reduced in many cases, and there is no easy way for users to change the content of the documents.

Maps of how to find a client's office or digital photos of whiteboards can also be included. Some editing features are available using the Microsoft Picture Library tool (if Office 2013 is installed), which include brightness and contrast adjustment, color adjustment, cropping, rotation and flipping, red-eye removal, and resizing.

Pictures can be emailed directly from the library, or a discussion can be started about a photo as with other documents in libraries. Pictures can be sorted using the filter tool by file type, viewed in a slideshow format, and checked out for editing; the version history can be reviewed; or alerts can be set.

Although this type of library might not be useful in every collaborative workspace, it provides a set of tools that are well suited to newsletter creation, complex document publication, or less formal uses, such as company events.

Working with SharePoint Lists

Lists are used in many ways by SharePoint, and a number of the Web Parts provided in the default workspace site are, in fact, lists. Some of the list options available are listed as follows:

- **Links**—These lists can contain either internal or external uniform resource locator (URL) links, or links to networked drives.
- **Announcements**—These lists typically contain news that would be of interest to the employees accessing the site, and can be set to expire at predefined times.
- **Contacts**—Contacts can be created from scratch using the provided template or can be imported from Outlook. This type of list can help clarify who is involved with a particular project or site, what their role is, and how to contact them, and can contain custom fields.
- **Events**—Events can be created in the site complete with start and stop times, descriptions, location information, and its rate of recurrence. The option to create a workspace for the event is provided when it is created. Events can be displayed in list format or in a calendar-style view. Events can be exported to Outlook, and a new

folder will be added to the calendar containing the events. Note that this calendar will be read-only in Outlook.

- **Tasks**—Each task can be assigned to a member of the site and can have start/due dates and priority levels set, and the percentage complete can be tracked. These tasks do not link to Outlook, however, so they're specific to the SharePoint site.
- **Issue tracking**—Slightly different from tasks, issues include category references, and each receives its own ID number. Individuals assigned to an issue can automatically be sent email notification when an issue is assigned to them, and will receive emails if their assigned issue changes.
- **Custom list options**—If one of the template lists doesn't offer the right combination of elements, one can be created from scratch. This allows the individual creating the list to choose how many columns make up the list and determine what kind of data each column will contain, such as text, choices (a menu to choose from), numbers, currency, date/time, lookup (information already on the site), yes/no, hyperlink or picture, or calculations based on other columns. With this combination of contents available and the capability to link to other data contained in the site from other lists, a database of information that pertains to the site can be created that can get quite complex. For example, a custom list could include events from the Events list, tracking the cost of each event and which task corresponds to the event.
- **Data imported from a spreadsheet**—Rather than creating a list from scratch, data can be imported from a spreadsheet (ideally Excel). The data can then be used actively within the site without the file needing to be opened in Excel. It can then be exported for use in other applications.

After the list is displayed in Datasheet view, new rows can be added by either selecting this option in the toolbar, or by clicking in the row that starts with the asterisk. Totals of all columns can be displayed by clicking the Totals option.

Exploring End-User Features in SharePoint

The previous versions of SharePoint brought confusion to end users. The user interface was inconsistent, and it was difficult to maneuver between pages. For example, some pages had a Back button, some had menu items on the page that you could click and go back to, and some had nothing to get you "back," and you had to use the browser's Back feature or type in the URL to get back to where you wanted to go. In addition, there were some functions that had to be performed outside of SharePoint, some could only be done from within, and some could be done either way.

SharePoint 2013 has a better user interface, and also has tighter integration with Microsoft Office. A user working on a document in Microsoft Word can decide that collaboration is necessary and create a shared workspace, invite users to participate, and set up some milestone tasks without ever leaving the Office client.

SharePoint provides the end user with a much better set of features for customizing and personalizing sites. Users can create their own personal sites containing their own documents, their own links, and other content that is meaningful to them, as opposed to having to live with a generic website with generic content that might not be applicable to their position in the organization.

Some of the new and improved features available for enhancing the end-user experience are discussed in the following sections.

Expanding Document Management Capabilities

SharePoint 2013 has evolved into a complex enterprise document management and enterprise content management (ECM) solution, including features such as the following:

- Document check-in/check-out to ensure that one user's revisions are not overwritten by another user
- Ability to maintain versions of documents for tracking changes
- Ability to require approval when checking a document back in for quality control
- Ability to have multiple users edit a document simultaneously
- Improved document workflow capabilities

In addition to these features, SharePoint provides the user with the flexibility to create a structured document storage environment, as opposed to the relatively flat view of the document space. SharePoint is also more tightly integrated with SharePoint 2013, providing enhanced features available directly from the Office interface. Features in these areas include the capability to perform the following tasks:

- Create folders within a document library and view all documents in a library, including those in subfolders.
- Create a SharePoint document workspace directly from Word 2013, providing a means for easily setting up collaboration sites.
- Easily save and retrieve SharePoint documents from Office applications. Improvements in Microsoft Office and SharePoint make saving documents to a workspace as easy as saving them to a file share.
- Access document libraries in the same manner as file shares through WebDAV Folder support, preventing users from having to learn a whole new set of commands.
- View Office documents through the browser without having Office installed on the client computer. This enables the remote and mobile user to view documents stored in SharePoint when on the road from a client's computer, when sitting at an airport kiosk, or when having a cup of coffee at an Internet café.

Integrating SharePoint 2013 with Microsoft Office

A key design goal for SharePoint 2013 was to have it even more tightly integrated with Microsoft Office. Although SharePoint technologies support earlier versions of Office, such as Office 2007, improvements and enhancements in both SPF and in SharePoint 2013 provide a more efficient way for users to access shared document workspaces and team sites. This ease of use for accessing information encourages users to share, collaborate, and communicate together on projects, initiatives, or ideas. For example, instead of simply opening up a document in an older version of Office and working on the document, a user opening the same document off a SharePoint server with SharePoint 2013 is presented with not only the document, but also a new task pane that lists the members of the team site where the document is stored (showing presence information about the users), the status of the document, as well as any tasks and links associated with the document. Specifically, SharePoint 2013 integration means that

- The entire setup of the document workspace can be done from the Word 2013 interface. Using the Shared Workspace task pane, the document workspace can be created, users granted access, links pertaining to the document added, and tasks created.
- The document workspace is accessible through the task pane whenever the document is opened in Word 2013. The status of the members is displayed (such as whether they are online), messages can be sent to the members, links browsed to, and tasks viewed and updated.
- When a meeting is created using Outlook 2013, a SharePoint meeting workspace can also be created for storing content related to the meeting.
- SharePoint contacts can be viewed directly from Outlook 2013.
- Metadata and file properties are copied from Office documents to SharePoint libraries—therefore, file information doesn't have to be reentered into SharePoint if it has already been entered in Office.
- SharePoint documents can be attached to mail messages as shared attachments. When the user receives the message, there is a link to the workspace where the shared attachment can be accessed.
- SharePoint sites can be searched from the Office 2013 Research and Reference tool pane.
- Documents stored in SharePoint picture libraries can be edited with an Office 2013 picture editing tool.

Personalizing SharePoint 2013

SharePoint 2013 includes many ways in which users can personalize a SharePoint environment. Some forms of personalization can originate from Office 2013, and some features are accessed directly through SharePoint. The following list includes various ways in which users can personalize the SharePoint experience:

- Users can create private sites and private views with their own personalized look and feel, in a way that makes sense for the way they work. Changes to team sites are stored with the user's profile and will be applied each time the user visits the site.
- News can be targeted to users based on their audience affiliation. Considering the amount of information available, this is an efficiency feature that streamlines the content based on user interest.
- Users can be given the capability to create sites without involving IT personnel. A typical scenario in today's world, where the organization does not have a portal application such as SharePoint, might go something like this:
    - A user decides that a website would be helpful for collaborating on a project. The user presents the justification of the website to and obtains the approval of the department manager. The department manager submits a request to the IT Department to have the site created. The IT manager reviews the request and places it low on the priority list because it will take time to develop the site, and the users can collaborate in the current environment using email and shared network drives. By the time IT gets to the project, the users have already completed the work and no longer need the collaboration site.
    - If users can create shared sites and workspaces on their own, and don't have to wade through the red tape of getting IT personnel to create them, they will be more likely to use them and realize the benefits they can provide.

Using Lists with SharePoint

Each list in SharePoint can be viewed from a Web Part; therefore, they can be easily customized from the browser. Lists have been enhanced in many ways, including support for additional field types such as rich text, multivalued fields, and calculated fields. Field values can also be calculated. Field types can be changed after the list has been created, thus providing a means for accommodating data that is not particularly stable.

SharePoint also has many new options for viewing lists. Filtered list views can also be created based on a calculation. For example, all events within the next week can be viewed by setting up a filter based on the date being greater than the current date plus seven. Another new view is the Event Calendar view, which enables displaying any list that has a date and time field in it using the daily, weekly, or monthly Calendar view. Aggregated views enable totaling data into a number field and displaying the value. Totals can be based on the entire view or a subset of it. Group-by views enable grouping by one column, and then sorting within each group.

A picture library is a new kind of list. Graphics and photos can be stored in a picture library and optionally viewed as a filmstrip or as thumbnails in views automatically generated by SharePoint.

For Microsoft Office users, lists can be edited in Datasheet view. This option presents the data in spreadsheet style and provides spreadsheet types of editing features, such as copy and paste, adding rows, and fill options. Using the Datasheet view can be faster than the traditional SharePoint list editing style for some types of data entry and editing.

SharePoint includes security features for lists. Permissions can be applied to the list so that only specific people can change it. Also included is the capability for the list owner to approve or reject items that are submitted to the list.

Other new list features include the following:

- ▶ Users can create their own personal lists that are not visible to other users.
- ▶ Alert notifications for lists include the name of the user who made the change to the list and which item in the list was changed.
- ▶ Attachments can be added or removed from a list item dependent on whether the attachment is required or not.
- ▶ Recurring events can be set up on an event list when an event occurs on a regularly scheduled basis.

Improving on SharePoint Alerts

Alerts in SharePoint 2013 are what used to be called notifications in previous versions. Alerts have been improved to identify whether the alert was sent because content was changed or added, and now include the tracking of additional items. Prior versions of SharePoint tracked search queries and documents. In addition to these items, SharePoint alerts track the following:

- ▶ News listings
- ▶ Sites added to the site directory
- ▶ SharePoint lists and libraries
- ▶ List items
- ▶ Site users
- ▶ Backward-compatible document library folders

Microsoft Outlook 2013 can be used to view SharePoint alerts, and it includes rules to sort and filter them into special folders.

Exploring Additional New/Enhanced End-User Features

Many other new and enhanced features improve the end-user experience. These include the following:

- ▶ A site directory that lists all SharePoint sites.
- ▶ The capability for users to create a SharePoint site from the Sites Directory page, to indicate whether they want the site added to the directory, and whether they want

the site content to be indexed. This provides a level of security for protecting sensitive information, such as human resources data.

- Support for multiple file uploads. SharePoint supports multiple file uploads (such as an entire directory or folder). This is a great time-saver for organizations that are migrating large numbers of documents to SharePoint.
- The capability to select from one of several site templates when creating a new site. Organizations can also create their own site templates (such as with the organization logo and color theme) for providing a level of consistency among different types of sites within the site.
- The capability to create surveys and have the results automatically calculated and made available.
- Additional improvements in the survey process. The survey feature now supports responding to a question using a scale and the capability for users to select all answers that might apply to a survey question.
- A user presence menu that is available everywhere a member name appears in a SharePoint site. The presence menu can be integrated with Active Directory, Exchange Server 2013, and Lync Server 2013 for providing information such as office location and free/busy status. It can be used for scheduling meetings and sending email.
- Team discussions that can be expanded and collapsed.

Enabling Site Mailbox Functionality in SharePoint 2013

The tightest integration between Exchange Server 2013 and SharePoint 2013 comes in the form of site mailboxes, a new feature that allows a SharePoint site to serve as a repository for Exchange emails and documents. Users can simply copy the site mailbox when corresponding about a project and have all of the information within that email thread saved within the site and subject to the compliance policies set on the mailbox.

From Outlook 2013, users can also simply drag and drop documents and emails directly into the shared project space, at which point they are transferred within the SharePoint content databases. New emails and documents also show up directly within Outlook 2013 as new items, just as a new email message would in a user's Inbox.

Site mailboxes can be part of eDiscovery search scopes within Exchange, and their contents can also be put under legal hold. Retention policies set on the mailbox itself are enforced on the SharePoint site itself as well.

Essentially, site mailboxes become the preferred method for a group of people that are working together on a shared set of deliverables. It allows for all messages and documents related to that project to be stored in one managed location that is subject to Exchange policies and legal requirements. In a sense, it is a replacement for common public folder usage scenarios that involved documents, as public folders do not support multiauthoring or version management like a full-blown document management platform like SharePoint does.

Understanding the Prerequisites for Site Mailboxes

Enabling site mailbox functionality within an Exchange Server 2013 and SharePoint 2013 environment is no small task and involves several steps around creating the trust relationship between the two environments. In addition, several prerequisites must be in place before site mailbox functionality can be enabled. This includes the following:

- Both the Exchange and SharePoint servers must be part of the same domain.
- The user running the commands must be a local administrator on the Exchange server and must also be a member of the Organization Management role in Exchange.
- There must be a root site collection setup on the SharePoint farm.
- Both the SharePoint and Exchange sites need to be using SSL certificates that are fully trusted by each other. In other words, the SharePoint server(s) needs to trust the root certificate authority that issues the Exchange certificates, and vice versa.
- The User Profile Service Application (UPA) in SharePoint needs to be configured and working properly.
- Autodiscover in Exchange needs to be configured and working properly.
- Clients must access site mailboxes through either Outlook 2013 or through the SharePoint web interface. Outlook Web App does *not* currently support site mailboxes.

Installing the Exchange Web Services Managed API on SharePoint Farm Member(s)

The first step to enable site mailboxes is to install the Exchange Web Services Managed Application Programming Interface (API) 2.0 on all SharePoint 2013 servers in your farm. To do that, perform the following steps:

1. Download the Exchange Web Services Managed API version 2.0 from Microsoft (`EwsManagedApi.msi`).
2. Run the setup wizard for the EWS Managed API 2.0 on the SharePoint server, which will prompt you for a location to install the files. You can also install the files from the command prompt by using the following syntax:

   ```
   msiexec /i EwsManagedApi.msi addlocal=
   "ExchangeWebServicesApi_Feature,ExchangeWebServicesApi_Gac"
   ```

3. Run `iisreset /noforce` from the command prompt to reset Internet Information Services (IIS) on the SharePoint server after the installation.

20

Establishing SSL Trusts for Both SharePoint and Exchange

As mentioned earlier, both the SharePoint server(s) and the Exchange server(s) need to trust the root CA that issued both the Exchange SSL certificate and the SSL certificate for SharePoint (required for this configuration). If not, the following steps must be performed on both the SharePoint and the Exchange server(s):

1. Open Microsoft Internet Explorer and navigate to the SSL secured website on the other server (i.e., from SharePoint navigate to https://e2013a.companyabc.com/owa and from Exchange navigate to https://sp2013a.companyabc.com, or whatever URL is used).
2. On the Certificate Error: Navigation Blocked page, click Continue to This Website (Not Recommended), if prompted. If not prompted, the site is already trusted and the remaining tasks in this step can be skipped.
3. In the Security Status bar (next to the Address bar), click Certificate Error.
4. In the Untrusted Certificate box, click View Certificates.
5. Select Install Certificate and then select Place All Certificates in the Following Store.
6. Select to show physical stores.
7. Install the certificate to Trusted Root Certification Authorities, Local Computer.

Configuring SharePoint User Profile Sync

As previously mentioned, the SharePoint UPA must be enabled for the Site Mailbox feature to work properly. Setting up UPA is a complex task, and should be performed with care and with the aid of a SharePoint expert, as there are several different approaches to setting up UPA properly. If the UPA has already been set up, you can ignore the following steps. If not, the following process describes how to enable UPA.

To start the process of enabling UPA in SharePoint 2013 to support site mailboxes, first turn on the UPA by navigating to SharePoint Central Admin. Click System Settings, Manage Services on Server; click on User Profile Synchronization Service Application, click Start Service, and then enter the service account username and password. An IISReset will need to be performed on the server after this step is complete.

After enabling the UPA, start a full sync by navigating to SharePoint Central Administration, Application Management, Manage Service Application, User Profile Service Application, Start Profile Synchronization, Start Full Synchronization, as shown in Figure 20.2.

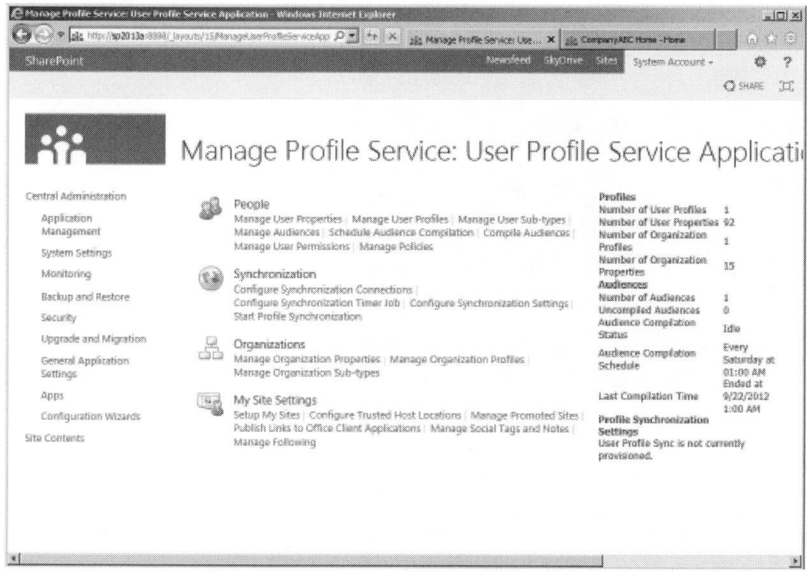

FIGURE 20.2 Starting a full sync of the UPA.

Once again, please note that UPA setup is a complex thing, and this example only illustrates a sample, very simple UPA setup. Talk to a SharePoint consultant or refer to Sams *SharePoint 2013 Unleashed* for more information on how to enable SharePoint 2013 User Profile Synchronization.

Configuring the Exchange Metadata Document as Trusted

The second step in the site mailbox process is to create a new Trusted Security Token Issuer for the Exchange Metadata document in SharePoint. To do this, type the following into the PowerShell prompt on the SharePoint server, as shown in Figure 20.3:

```
New-SPTrustedSecurityTokenIssuer -Name Exchange -MetadataEndPoint
https://e2013a.companyabc.com/autodiscover/metadata/json/1
```

(Replace the e2013a.companyabc.com with the name of your Exchange Client Access server [CAS] array.)

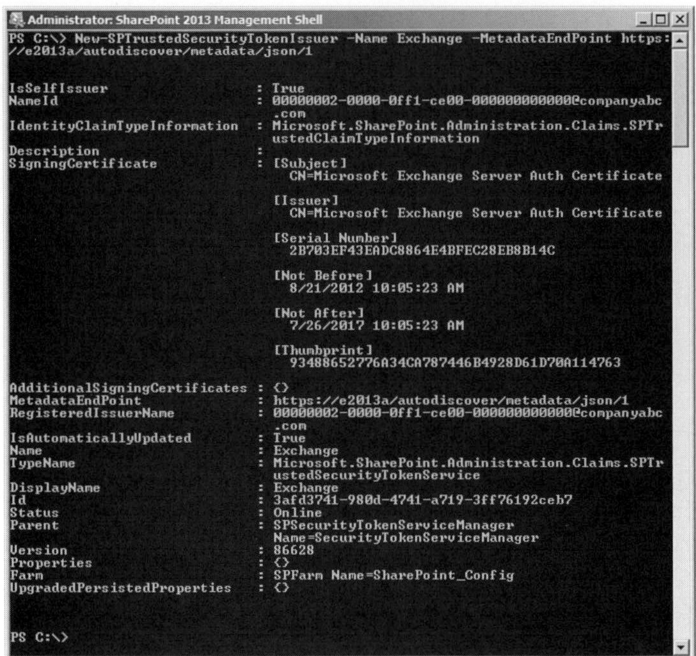

FIGURE 20.3 Configuring the Exchange Metadata document as trusted as part of a site mailbox configuration.

Granting the Exchange Service Principal Full Control to the SharePoint Site Subscription

The following PowerShell commands are required on the SharePoint server to allow the Exchange server to have full control over the SharePoint site subscription process. Perform them in order, as shown in Figure 20.4, and replace the sp2013a.companyabc.com parameter with the name of your SharePoint web application.

```
$exchange=Get-SPTrustedSecurityTokenIssuer
$app=Get-SPAppPrincipal -Site https://sp2013a.companyabc.com -NameIdentifier
$exchange.NameId
$site=Get-SPSite https://sp2013a.companyabc.com
Set-SPAppPrincipalPermission -AppPrincipal $app -Site $site.RootWeb -Scope
sitesubscription -Right fullcontrol -EnableAppOnlyPolicy
```

Enabling the Site Mailbox Feature on a SharePoint Web Application

Before it shows up as an installable app in SharePoint 2013, the Site Mailbox feature must first be turned on in the web application. To do this, type the following from the PowerShell prompt of the SharePoint server. It can be typed immediately after the above PowerShell steps are complete.

```
Enable-SPFeature CollaborationMailboxFarm
```

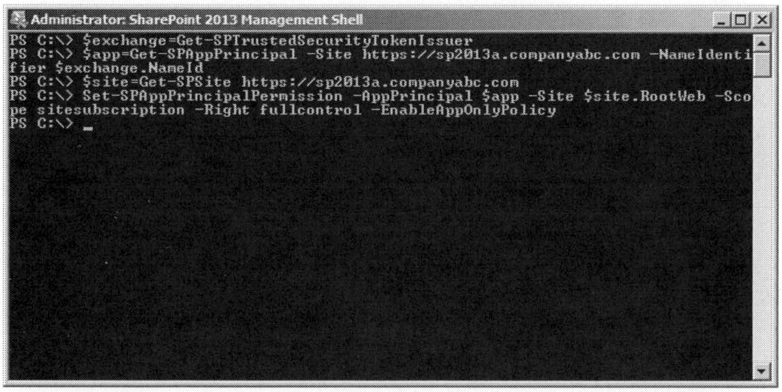

```
Administrator: SharePoint 2013 Management Shell
PS C:\> $exchange=Get-SPTrustedSecurityTokenIssuer
PS C:\> $app=Get-SPAppPrincipal -Site https://sp2013a.companyabc.com -NameIdenti
fier $exchange.NameId
PS C:\> $site=Get-SPSite https://sp2013a.companyabc.com
PS C:\> Set-SPAppPrincipalPermission -AppPrincipal $app -Site $site.RootWeb -Sco
pe sitesubscription -Right fullcontrol -EnableAppOnlyPolicy
PS C:\>
```

FIGURE 20.4 Granting the Exchange service principal full control to SharePoint site subscription as part of a site mailbox configuration.

Setting the Exchange Site Mailbox Target Domain for the Farm

The next step in the site mailbox process is to configure the Exchange Autodiscover domain on the SharePoint farm. Run the following commands one at a time from the command prompt of the SharePoint server, as illustrated in Figure 20.5 to accomplish these steps, replacing sp2013a.companyabc.com with the name of your SharePoint web application and companyabc.com with the Autodiscover name of your domain.

```
$webAppUrl=https://sp2013a.companyabc.com
$exchangeDomain="companyabc.com"
$exchangeServerName="E2013A"
$webApp=Get-SPWebApplication $webAppUrl
$webApp.Properties["ExchangeTeamMailboxDomain"] = $exchangeDomain
$webApp.Properties["ExchangeAutodiscoverDomain"] = $exchangeServerName
$webApp.Update()
```

FIGURE 20.5 Setting the Exchange site mailbox target domain as part of a site mailbox configuration.

Establishing the OAuth Trust on Exchange

The final command that must be run when enabling site mailbox functionality is run on the Exchange server and involves having Exchange download a file from the SharePoint server to establish the trust relationship. Use the following syntax to enable this functionality (replacing sp2013a.companyabc.com with the name of your SharePoint web application). Ensure that you are in the `C:\Program Files\Microsoft\Exchange Server\V15\Script` directory when running this PowerShell command, as shown in Figure 20.6:

```
.\Configure-EnterprisePartnerApplication.ps1 -ApplicationType Sharepoint
-AuthMetadataUrl https://sp2013a.companyabc.com/layouts/15/metadata/json/1
```

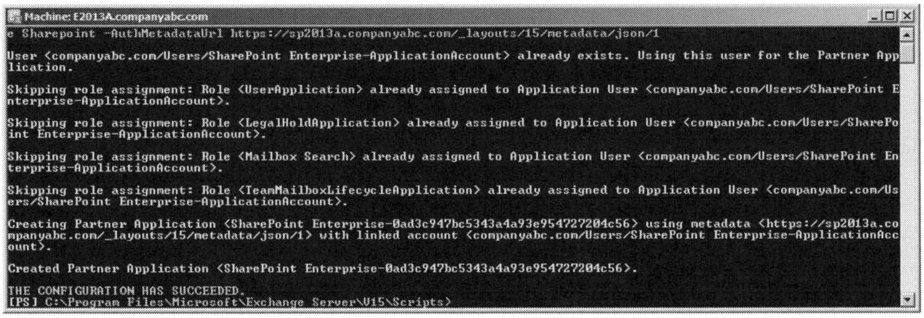

FIGURE 20.6 Creating the OAuth trust on Exchange as part of a site mailbox configuration.

Creating a Site Mailbox

After all of the prerequisite steps have been performed, the site mailboxes can be created through the following process:

1. Within a SharePoint site, install the Site Mailbox app by clicking on the Quick Launch menu, selecting More, choosing Add an App, and selecting Site Mailbox, as shown in Figure 20.7.

2. From the Quick Launch menu in SharePoint, click Site Mailbox.

3. Sign in to OWA with the user's credentials.

4. Enter an alias for the site mailbox and click Next.

5. Click Import to import the current users from the site.

6. Click Finish.

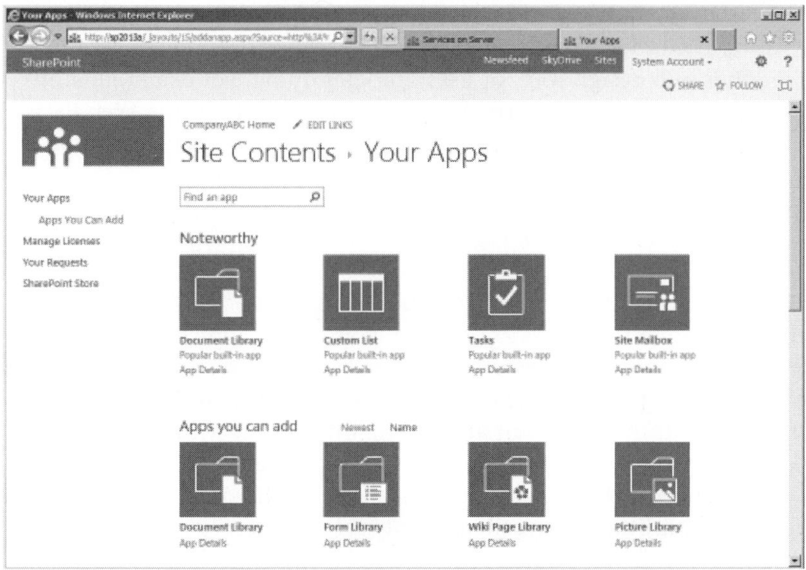

FIGURE 20.7 Adding a Site Mailbox app to a SharePoint site.

Customizing and Developing SharePoint Sites

SharePoint has many out-of-the-box new features that make it easier to customize using the browser interface. This provides nonprogrammers with a mechanism to create and customize sites to meet their needs.

For developers, the following provides an overview of the SharePoint technical structure. SharePoint is built on the .NET platform. Use of the .NET platform enables SharePoint to assimilate information from multiple systems into an integrated solution. ASP.NET contains many new features, and it is more responsible, secure, and scalable than ASP (Active Server Pages.) Using ASP.NET reduces the amount of code that needs to be written over similar ASP solutions.

In SharePoint, sites and lists can be saved as templates, stored in a Site or List template library, and then made available to all sites in the collection. There is also a library for Web Parts that can be shared across all sites in the collection.

Features such as these provide an environment for developing fully customized SharePoint solutions. Additional customization and development features are highlighted in the following section.

Development Enhancements for Site Templates

SharePoint includes multiple templates that can be used when you create a new site. Each template includes a set of features from SharePoint to satisfy a specific collaboration need.

If these templates don't satisfy the organization's requirements, customized templates can easily be put together using the browser-based customization features, using SharePoint Designer 2013 or some other web design tool, or using programming. For example, if an organization always put its company logo on the home page and used specific Web Parts that were unique to its organization, it could save the site as a template and then just duplicate the template when necessary to maintain consistency and security.

Summary

SharePoint Server 2013 is an excellent way to extend the capabilities of an Exchange Server 2013 messaging environment. Installation of SharePoint 2013 allows a server to become an enterprise-level document management and collaboration system, and allows users of Exchange to be able to take advantage of site mailbox features on the SharePoint server. Enhanced capabilities within SharePoint and strong integration with Office 2013 allow organizations to realize improvements in productivity and quality quickly. In addition, the scalability of SharePoint and its reliability on the robust Microsoft SQL database provide strong incentive to deploy and utilize SharePoint technologies.

Best Practices

The following are best practices from this chapter:

- Use document versioning sparingly in SharePoint document libraries to ensure that the SQL database does not grow too large.
- Keep SharePoint server up to date with all Windows Server and SQL Server patches and updates to reduce the risk of attacks or malfunctions.
- Deploy SharePoint server(s) to replace file servers for document storage to take advantage of the document management features SharePoint offers.
- Use site mailboxes in Exchange Server 2013 to be able to create a shared space for users to collaborate and/or as a replacement for shared public folders.
- Use an SSL certificate for SharePoint, especially when needing site mailbox functionality, as it is required for the trust relationship with Exchange.
- Consider using SharePoint for advanced Business Intelligence options.

CHAPTER 21

Getting the Most Out of the Microsoft Outlook Client

IN THIS CHAPTER

- Outlook over the Years
- Highlighted Features in Outlook 2013
- Security Enhancements in Outlook 2013
- Implementing Outlook Anywhere
- Deploying Outlook 2013
- Using Outlook 2013
- Leveraging Social Media in Outlook
- Using Cached Exchange Mode for Offline Functionality

Microsoft Outlook is likely the most familiar desktop productivity tool that business email and calendar users use on a daily basis. Many users spend more time in Outlook than other business software applications as Outlook provides email; calendaring; and access to contacts, notes, and other day-to-day information details.

Unlike Outlook Web App, which is discussed in Chapter 22, "Leveraging the Capabilities of the Outlook Web App (OWA) Client," the Outlook client is a full-fledged messaging client that runs locally on the user's workstation. It is packaged as part of the Microsoft Office Suite and is available in both a Microsoft Windows version as well as an Apple Mac version.

This chapter focuses on the current iterations of the product for Windows, Microsoft Outlook 2013. Users and administrators will be glad to hear that Outlook 2013 was designed specifically with Exchange Server 2013 in mind.

The whole focus of Outlook 2013 was to make a version of Outlook that is similar for Windows, Apple Mac, Web, tablet, and mobile phones so that regardless of the endpoint, the user will see the same look and feel out of Outlook. In short, there is no better client for accessing email located on an Exchange server because Outlook 2013 has been built from the ground up to work hand in hand with both Microsoft Exchange Server and Microsoft's Active Directory.

Outlook over the Years

As previously stated, Outlook has been built to work hand in hand with both Microsoft Exchange and Active Directory. This was not always the case.

In the early days of Microsoft, the developers of the client-side applications, such as Office and Outlook, did not work closely with the developers of the server-side applications, such as Exchange Server. The Office suite focused on individual productivity, whereas the server team focused on building software that facilitated collaboration.

Starting with Outlook 98, these two groups started to work more closely together and Outlook began to take on the characteristics of a collaboration tool, enabling users to more easily share information with one another. The results are self-evident with Outlook 2013 because Exchange Server and Outlook now have greater integration, enhanced functionality for the end user, and more improved collaborative tools than ever before.

The Evolution of a Messaging Client

Over the years, the developers at Microsoft have been listening attentively to their user community, and the Outlook client has evolved based on the recommendations of these users. Popular features have remained, and new ones have been added to support the ever-changing messaging needs of the business community.

Although the early versions of Outlook were focused almost entirely on messaging and calendaring, the later generations have added tools such as forms and rules to enhance the user's ability to manage his information. Microsoft has also developed the Outlook client to integrate closely with SharePoint, Microsoft's enterprise information portal, enabling organizations to create resources for collaboration in SharePoint and have the user community access these resources through the familiar interface of Outlook.

Microsoft has put a significant amount of effort into improving the security of its product as well. By implementing Information Rights Management, for example, users can create email messages that are restricted—helping to prevent them from being forwarded, printed, and having the information copied and pasted into new documents. In addition, documents created in Microsoft Office 2013 are automatically restricted when attached to a message with restricted permissions.

The look and feel of the Outlook product has evolved over the years as well. The interface has become less and less "cluttered" as the developers discovered ways of presenting more information with greater organization. Improvements have been made in the prioritizing of to-do items, the ability to create Internet calendars has been added, and enhanced search capabilities enable users to more easily locate messages in their mailboxes.

With each new version of Outlook, the underlying focus has been to streamline information, add new functionality, and make Outlook a more collaborative business tool.

The Basic Features of Outlook

The biggest improvement in the latest release of Microsoft Outlook is Microsoft's implementation of a common interface across all endpoints so that a user running Outlook

2013 will have the same interface when accessing emails from Outlook Web App on a browser and from a tablet or mobile phone. Outlook provides basic features of messaging, calendaring, and task tracking across all endpoint platforms. With a centralized client, users have access to all of the same content, including email archives, voice mail messages, and integrated shared content from the same look-and-feel interface.

Security in Outlook

Security has always been a concern for Information Technology (IT) departments, and Outlook 2013 offers cutting-edge security functions to help protect data from prying eyes. These functions range from support for Secure/Multipurpose Internet Mail Extensions (S/MIME) encrypted messaging to integrated antispam and antiphishing technologies. Outlook has always made an effort to reduce the exposure of the user by blocking Hypertext Markup Language (HTML) content and preventing embedded scripts from launching when messages are previewed. The past few versions of Outlook have prevented third-party applications from accessing it to help protect a user's email and the Exchange server itself.

Collaborating with Outlook

The word *collaboration* comes from the Latin word *collaborare* that means "labor together." Organizations have found that their users, when working together with tools that enable them to share information easily, can be more productive than individuals working alone. The ability for users to collaborate with one another by using Microsoft Outlook is a major reason companies leverage the client as their standard calendaring and messaging application. With each new version, the collaborative power of Outlook has grown, and although many tools are available for an Outlook user when partnered with an Exchange server, greater integration with Microsoft Office and Microsoft's SharePoint Server product has greatly increased the possibilities.

Other Enhancements in Outlook

Each new version of the Outlook client has introduced new or improved features to enhance functionality and enhance the end-user experience. By making the product faster, sleeker, and more intuitive, each version of Outlook has surpassed the previous one in usability and integration, not only with the Exchange Server product, but also with other applications. This chapter covers many of the most popular features available with Outlook 2013 and shows the user how to leverage some of the more powerful features of the product.

Highlighted Features in Outlook 2013

As previously mentioned, new versions of Outlook continue to provide new features and functionality, in addition to enhancing existing features. In this section, administrators can find information covering some of the new features that organizations might find beneficial, along with new tools for the end user.

Understanding the Outlook 2013 Interface

There is a lot of information kept in Exchange Server mailboxes these days, and the Outlook interface has changed to improve the organization and presentation of this data. In addition, the availability of large-screen monitors and high-resolution screens has become standard for the workforce, giving many users more "real estate" to work with.

In Outlook 2013, just as was the case in Outlook 2007 and 2010, Microsoft divided the Outlook view into four main sections: the folder pane, the message index pane, the reading pane (also sometimes called the preview pane), and the To-Do Bar, as shown in Figure 21.1.

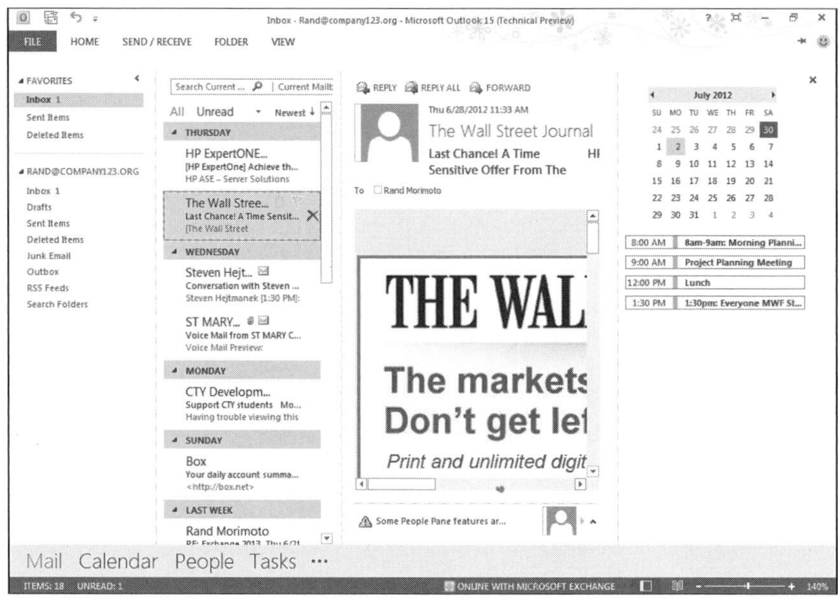

FIGURE 21.1 The Outlook 2013 interface.

The Folder Pane

The folder pane is primarily used to view, open, and manage individual folders that make up the user's mailbox. It enables the user to add or remove favorites, which are shortcuts to commonly accessed folders. There is also a shortcuts section, which allows single-click access to the various areas of the Outlook client. The navigation pane can be minimized or turned off completely. Under the View menu, click Folder Pane, and select either Normal, Minimized, or Off. Alternatively, the user can toggle through these choices by pressing the Alt+F1 keys.

The Message Index Pane

To the right of the folder pane is the message index pane. This display box shows a summary for each message contained in the folder that is currently viewed (the folder currently selected in the folder pane). This summary typically includes the sender's address, the date and time the message was received, and a portion of the information contained in the Subject line.

When a user clicks a message in the message index pane one time, he is selecting the message, and a preview of the message displays in the reading pane. When the user double-clicks a message instead, Outlook 2013 opens that message in a separate window.

The message index pane can be resized by hovering the mouse on the border of the pane until the pointer turns into a double-headed arrow. Click the left mouse button and hold it while dragging the border to the desired location.

The Reading Pane

The reading pane enables the user to preview the contents of a message without opening the message completely. In addition to the convenience of this method, there is a security-related benefit as well—potentially malicious scripts or attachments are not activated or opened automatically in the reading pane.

Users can also view attachments in the reading pane. After the user clicks the attachment in the reading pane, if a viewer add-on is installed in Outlook capable of rendering the view, the user will see a preview of the attachment. The user can double-click to launch and open the attachment in a full editing mode.

NOTE

For users to preview an attachment, they must have an application installed on their workstation that is capable of *viewing* the attachment. For example, to preview an Excel spreadsheet, users must have the Office viewer installed, which, by the way, is installed by default when Office/Outlook is installed on a system.

In addition to viewing attachments, the reading pane also enables users to follow embedded hyperlinks, use voting buttons, view follow-up information, and respond to meeting requests.

Outlook 2013 now has the ability for users to actively Reply, Reply All, and Forward a message right within the reading pane instead of clicking an icon in the ribbon, as shown in Figure 21.2. This is a very handy function where a user can quickly scan messages, see them in the reading pane, and click and reply to the message all right within the main Outlook 2013 window.

The reading pane can be enabled or disabled by clicking Reading Pane in the View menu. When enabled, the reading pane can be located to the right of the message index pane or underneath it. As with the preceding message index pane, the reading pane can be resized by dragging and dropping the borders to the desired location.

The To-Do Bar

On the right edge of the main Outlook page is the To-Do Bar. By default, the To-Do Bar displays a date navigator, which is a calendar of the current month. By clicking any date on the date navigator, the user is taken immediately to the selected date in his own calendar inside of Outlook. Below the calendar shows the user's next appointments and a list of outstanding tasks.

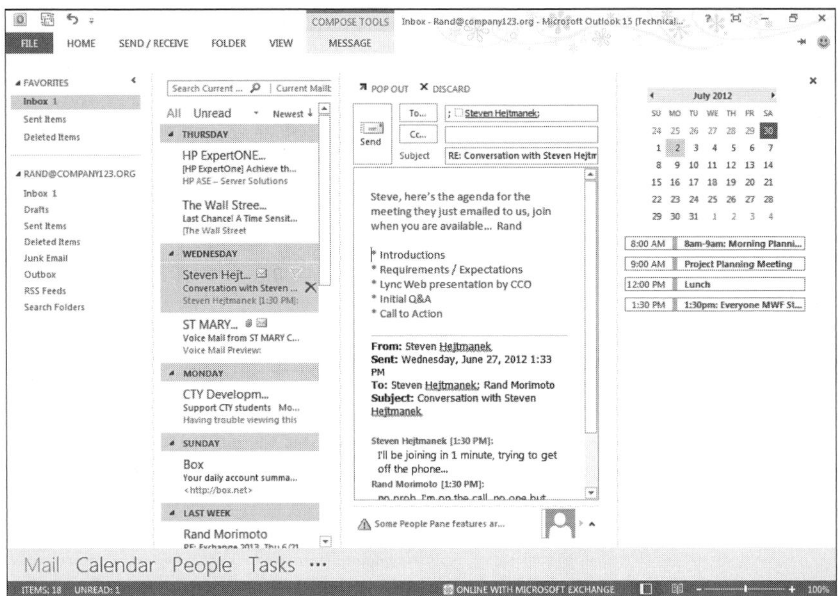

FIGURE 21.2 Replying to a message within the reading pane.

Any of these three features can be enabled and disabled, and the To-Do Bar can be minimized or turned off completely by going to the View menu and clicking the To-Do Bar.

Displaying the Ribbon

Microsoft introduced the "ribbon" at the top of Office applications where users can quickly and simply go to choose tasks. In Outlook, the ribbon includes options like Reply, Forward, Move, Categorize, High Importance, and the like. What's new in Outlook 2013 is the ability for the user to hide the ribbon. In the lower-right corner of the ribbon is an arrow that hides the ribbon. To unhide the ribbon, choose one of the menu items, such as View, then click the push pin that shows in the same location.

Common Mail, Calendar, People, Tasks Buttons

Although the ribbon at the top of Outlook provides quick access to features and functions in Outlook, at the bottom of Outlook are buttons for Mail, Calendar, People, and Tasks, which is new to Outlook 2013. These buttons are also present in Outlook Web App as well as Outlook for mobile devices. By choosing one of these buttons, a user can quickly switch between emails, calendars, contacts, and tasks. The ellipsis (the three dots ...) at the bottom allows access to Notes, Folders, and Shortcuts.

Similarities with Outlook Web App

As noted earlier, one of the goals of Exchange Server 2013 was to make the Outlook client identical in look and functionality as the web browser, tablet, and mobile device clients. The Outlook 2013 graphical user interface (GUI) is the same as the GUI for Outlook Web App users on an Exchange Server environment, such as viewing the Presence status of fellow employees and the MailTips feature. These features are discussed in the overview of Outlook Web App in Chapter 22.

Methods for Highlighting Outlook Items

Outlook helps users better organize and find messages. As email becomes a more and more common way of sharing information, the volume of mail received by end users continues to increase. With Outlook 2013, users are given methods for organizing, categorizing, and flagging messages when working with Outlook and Exchange Server.

Using Quick Flags to Tag Messages

Using quick flags in Outlook 2013, users can assign a colored flag to a message to help them organize messages. In Outlook 2013, flags can have some predefined meanings for follow-up tasks. Flags can be set for when a message must be dealt with and setting these flags results in a new entry in the Tasks area of the To-Do Bar.

To set quick flags in the Outlook 2013 client, complete the following:

1. Right-click an email message, and then choose Follow Up.
2. Choose the flag you want to use, whether a predefined or custom flag.

Flags can also be used to configure a reminder. The option for using reminders with flags allows users to configure information and a due date associated with each flag. To configure a reminder, complete these steps:

1. Flag the message.
2. Right-click an email message, and then choose Follow Up.
3. Click Add Reminder.
4. Choose the date and time for the reminder, similar to what is shown in Figure 21.3, and click OK when you are finished.

If you have the To-Do Bar enabled, you will now see your flagged message in the Tasks area, showing the flag, the category, and a bell to represent that there is a reminder set.

Using Categories to Color-Code Messages

In addition to flags, Outlook 2013 supports color-coded Categories that can be assigned to items. Categories have no predefined meaning, so users can implement them however they want. For example, a user might decide that the Yellow category references projects that are in danger, and Red refers to projects that are overbudget. By simply right-clicking the rounded square to the left of the flag, the user can tag the message with the desired color. In addition, multiple categories can be assigned to messages.

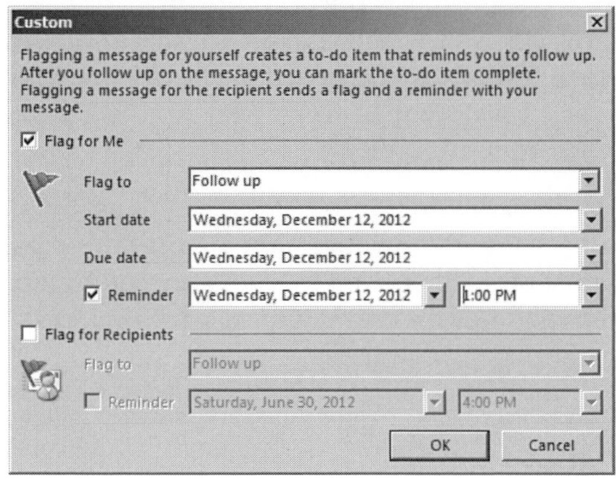

FIGURE 21.3 Setting a follow-up reminder for a message.

To categorize messages with color-coding in an Outlook 2013 client, complete the following:

1. Right-click an email message, and then choose Categorize.
2. Choose the color category you want to set, as shown in Figure 21.4.

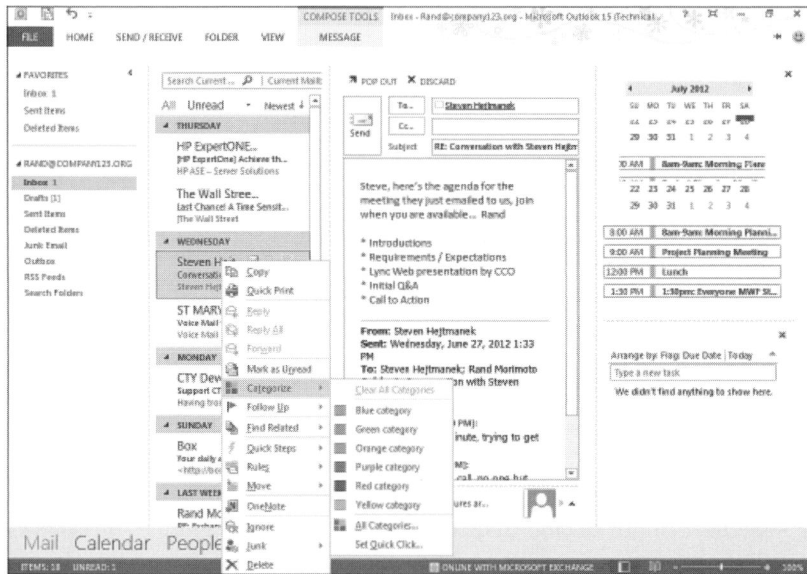

FIGURE 21.4 Choosing a color-coded category for a message.

NOTE

A flag with an associated reminder provides the end user a standard Outlook reminder pop-up balloon when the preconfigured reminder comes due.

Making Key Appointments Stand Out with Color

Using the Outlook 2013 calendar, this feature allows for the customization and organization of appointments using colors, allowing end-user appointments to stand out when viewing the calendar.

To choose a color and label an appointment, follow these steps:

1. Open the appointment in the calendar.
2. In the ribbon, select the multicolored button labeled Categorize. Alternatively, right-click the message in the Calendar view and select Categorize.
3. Choose the category you want to apply.
4. Close the calendar item.

The calendar item will now appear with the color you selected, similar to what is shown in Figure 21.5.

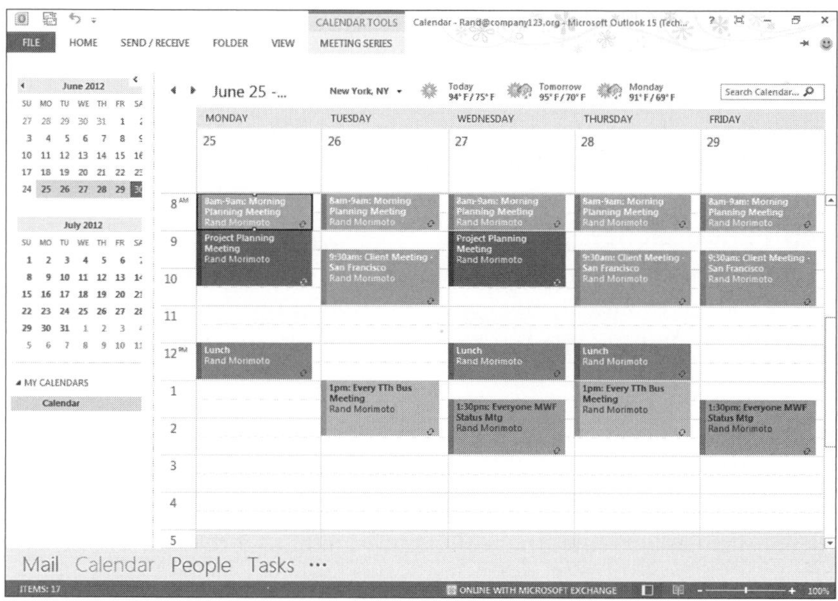

FIGURE 21.5 Calendar items with categories.

Creating Meetings Based on Time Zone

In early versions of Outlook (2003 and prior), users who travel often found it difficult to schedule meetings when their destination was in another time zone. Outlook (and most computers, email servers, and email clients) uses Coordinated Universal Time (UTC) for appointments and adjusts the time of the meeting based on the current time zone for the computer.

Users found that they would create a meeting while sitting in one time zone, for a date in the future when they would be in another time zone. At what time should they set the meeting? And if they change their time zone on their computer when they arrive, will it adjust the meeting time?

Outlook 2013 helps with this problem with the addition of a Time Zone option from within meeting requests. To utilize this feature, open new meeting request and complete the following:

1. Toward the right side of the main set of buttons, find the Globe icon labeled Time Zones.
2. Click the Time Zones icon and a new drop-down is created next to the start and end times.
3. Via the drop-down, select the time zone you want to use when choosing the meeting time.
4. Select the start and end time of the meeting.
5. Invite your attendees and click Send & Close when you are finished.

By selecting the time zone that the meeting will be held in when creating the meeting request, users find it much easier to set the appointments for the proper time.

Using the Search Functionality

Outlook 2013 makes it easier than ever to search through large mailboxes and calendars. Users can save searches that are commonly used and can leverage the flag and category functions mentioned earlier to provide very powerful ways of managing messages, appointments, or tasks.

Using the Search Bar

The Search Bar is easily accessible at the top of the message index pane (and below the ribbon). To perform a search, do the following:

1. Click inside the Search Bar and enter the word(s) to search for in the Search box.
2. Either click the search option that looks like a magnifying glass icon right next to the Search box to begin the search (or press the Enter key), or click to the right of the search option to choose something other than the Current Folder. Other options include searching Subfolders, Current Mailbox, and All Outlook Items. Click the X to clear the search criteria and view all items again.

Typing in the search area updates the results in near real time.

Additional Search Options

There are additional options when performing a search that includes repeating Recent Searches, choosing Advanced Find options, or adjusting Search Options. These options can be selected from the ribbon.

To access the ribbon and additional search options, do the following:

1. Click Search in the ribbon at the top of the Outlook screen.
2. Toward the right side of the ribbon, choose Recent Searches or Search Tools.
3. Select and modify changes as desired.

Managing Multiple Email Accounts from One Place

Outlook 2013 allows the end user to access multiple email accounts from the same Outlook client, including Internet Message Access Protocol (IMAP), Post Office Protocol 3 (POP3), and Hypertext Transfer Protocol (HTTP) mail accounts as well as additional Exchange accounts.

NOTE

Starting with Outlook 2010 (and continuing with Outlook 2013), multiple Exchange accounts can be accessed simultaneously from within an Outlook client. Prior to Outlook 2010, if a user wanted to access multiple Exchange accounts, the user had to create individual "Outlook Profiles" and then exit and enter Outlook with the applicable profile for the user desired. With Outlook 2013, a user can have multiple Exchange mailboxes open and accessible.

To configure Outlook to access multiple mailboxes for which you have rights, do the following:

1. From Outlook 2013, click File, and then click Add Account.
2. Enter the email account or click to choose Manual Setup settings for the mail account desired for access.
3. Restart Outlook.

Taking Advantage of the Trust Center

Outlook 2013 extends a function called the Trust Center that was part of Outlook 2007 and 2010. The Trust Center is a centralized location for the management of security-related functions in Outlook 2013. This includes the following:

- Trusted publishers
- Privacy options
- Email security

- Attachment handling
- Automatic download
- Macro settings
- Programmatic access

By placing these functions under a single interface, it is much easier to manage the security functions in Outlook 2013.

To configure Trust Settings, do the following:

1. From Outlook 2013, click File, and then click Options.
2. From the Outlook Options page, choose Trust Center at the lower left of the page.
3. Click Trust Center Settings to get to the Trust Center options.

Each of these areas is further addressed later in this chapter.

Out-of-Office Automatic Message Replies

Outlook 2013 provides users the ability to automatically respond and/or manage incoming messages. One of the most common automatic message rules is the Out-of-Office function. When an Outlook user is out of the office, possibly on vacation or even out on an appointment, Outlook can send a message to the sender of the message that the recipient is out of the office and not available.

To configure an Out-of-Office rule, do the following:

1. Within Outlook, click File and then choose Automatic Replies (Out of Office).

NOTE

The ability of having a different message whether inside or outside of your organization is extremely helpful so that you can let internal people know you are out and to have internal phone extensions or mobile phone numbers provided that you do not want external people to know. Or you may choose to just tell external people you are out and provide them with general contact information on how they can contact someone else for assistance.

2. Click Send Automatic Replies and on the Inside My Organization tab, enter in the reply you want the senders to receive when they send you a message and your out-of-office notification is enabled.
3. Select the Outside My Organization tab, select or clear the check box depending on whether you want to notify those outside your organization, and enter a message for outside recipients as appropriate.
4. Choose to Only Send During This Time Range if you want to prestage an out-of-office response to trigger for a specific time or date range you'll be out of the office.

NOTE

This Only Send During This Time Range is a great function that prevents users from having their out-of-office message still sending "I'm out of the office" weeks/months after they return from vacation. Instead of blanket sending the message "forever," this feature allows the notification to occur only during the time you know you'll be on vacation. Extremely helpful!

5. Click Rules in the lower left to add additional rules such as having external messages forwarded to an assistant or support person who will handle incoming messages from others while you are away. The rules can look for specific keywords like *Help* or *payroll* or *customer service* or the like keying in on keywords triggering an appropriate message forward destination. More on Rules can be found in the next section.

NOTE

Although out-of-office notifications are sent just once to each recipient during the out-of-office period, rules apply to all messages, not just the first.

6. Click OK to set the status of the Out-of-Office rule.

Outlook Rules and Alerts

Another type of automatic message process is Outlook Rules and Alerts. An Outlook Rule is a more generic form of Out-of-Office rule. Whereas an Out-of-Office rule typically triggers on each and every incoming message, an Outlook Rule can be set up to look for keywords, messages from specific individuals, or messages with specific content like an attachment.

When a message arrives in a user's mailbox, the rule parses the message, looks for key contact, and then triggers the rule. To set up the rule, do the following:

1. Within Outlook, click File and then choose Manage Rules & Alerts.
2. Choose E-mail Rules.

NOTE

An E-mail Rule looks for keywords, phrases, source, or other content and then triggers a response. An Alert is a specialized rule looking for incoming alerts from key alert sources that might include something like SharePoint or System Center with incoming alerts being received.

3. For E-mail Rules, click New Rule and build the rule you want. You'll notice you have several options, such as rules that move messages, play sounds, alert you through your mobile phone, or create your own unique rule.

4. Choose "who" you want to monitor incoming messages from and what you want the rule to do.

NOTE

By default, all emails from all users are monitored, and the trigger happens on each message. However if you want to just monitor messages from your manager, from the company CEO, or from members of your team, you can have Outlook look at specific users or groups of users and trigger based on those conditions.

5. Click Finish when the rule has been created, and then click to enable the rule to be active.

Security Enhancements in Outlook 2013

Microsoft announced its Secure Computing initiative in 2002 and has continued to improve the security of its products ever since. For Outlook 2013, this means the continuation of security and antispam features available when using the Outlook 2013 client partnered with Exchange Server. Similarly, security functionality is directly integrated within Outlook 2013 in the area of preventing unwanted viruses or malicious scripts from executing when a message is received or previewed. Microsoft continues to integrate advanced email security features such as digital signing of messages, mail encryption, and Information Rights Management.

Support for Secured Messaging

The Microsoft Outlook 2013 development team has taken the feedback from IT groups as well as from end users and has recognized the ever-increasing need for supporting industry standards. Outlook 2013 supports industry standards for secured messaging including S/MIME, digital signing, message encryption, and smart card support.

S/MIME Support, Digital Signatures, and Email Encryption

S/MIME has been supported in previous versions of Outlook, and Outlook 2013 provides support for the latest S/MIME functionality. Using S/MIME, email messages are encrypted by the recipient's public key and can be decrypted, and, therefore, made accessible, only with the recipient's private key. This private/public key exchange is critical for secure email correspondence.

Use of S/MIME support requires that the Outlook 2013 client have a certificate for cryptography on the client computer (and is stored locally either in the Microsoft Windows certificate store or on a smart card), and can be pushed through Registry settings or via Group Policy to easily implement S/MIME throughout an organization. This type of internal certificate use is usually performed via an internal Public Key Infrastructure (PKI). The creation of an internal PKI goes beyond the scope of this book; however, it is covered in the Sams Publishing book *Windows Server 2012 Unleashed.*

S/MIME support also includes digital signing. Digital signing allows for security labels and signed secure message receipts. This is a way for a message recipient to be sure that the message came from the person who claimed to send it. Using Outlook 2013, enterprise-wide security labels are enforced such as "For Internal Use Only" or labeling messages to restrict the forwarding or printing of messages through Information Rights Management. In addition, users can request S/MIME affirmation of receipt of a message. By requesting a receipt, the sender confirms that the recipient recognized and verified the digital signature because no receipt is received unless the recipient, who should have received the message, actually does receive the message. Only then does the sender receive the digitally signed read receipt. This allows email users to more safely trust the information they receive via email. This can be especially valuable when email is used for workflow or approval processes.

Setting Email Security on a Specific Message

Security such as payload encryption or digital signing can be set for an individual email using the options available when creating an email message. Clicking on the Options button opens the Message Options dialog box. There, the user can access the Security Properties page to set the security for the message. The user can choose to encrypt the message and/or add a digital signature, request S/MIME receipt, and configure the security settings.

To do this, follow these steps:

1. Open a new message.
2. Click the Options tab in the ribbon and click the arrow in the lower-right corner of the More Options box.
3. Click the Security Settings button.
4. Add security settings as desired, similar to the ones shown in Figure 21.6.

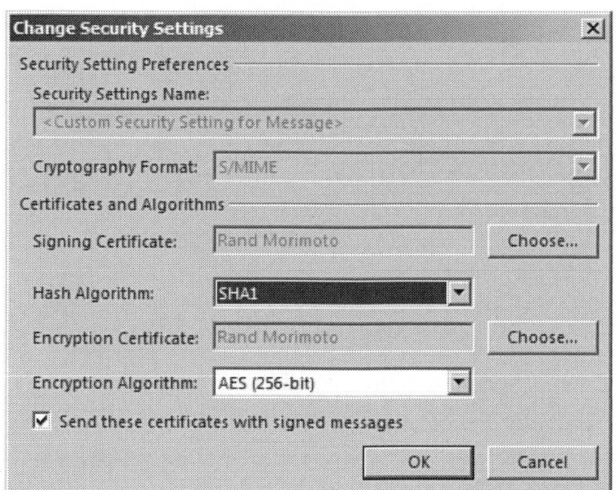

FIGURE 21.6 Security Properties page in Outlook.

5. Click OK when you are finished.
6. Continue composing the message as normal.

Setting Email Security on the Entire Mailbox

Security settings can also be globally configured for the entire mailbox so that they apply at all times.

To do this, follow these steps:

1. Go to File, Options, select Trust Center, and then Trust Center Settings.
2. Select E-mail Security from the left pane.
3. Enable the choices desired for security for the entire mailbox:
    - Encrypt Contents and Attachments for Outgoing Messages
    - Add Digital Signature to Outgoing Messages
    - Send Clear Text Signed Messages When Sending Signed Messages (picked by default). (This allows users who don't have S/MIME security to read the message.)
4. Request S/MIME Receipt for All S/MIME Signed Messages
5. For all choices (except the third choice) to work properly, the user must get a digital certificate provided by the administrator. This can be imported by clicking on the Import/Export button at the bottom of the window beneath Digital IDs (Certificates) or by clicking on Get a Digital ID.
6. After you import the digital certificate, the security functionality is complete.
7. Click OK when you are finished.

NOTE

More on PKI and certificates can be found in Chapter 5, "Integrating Certificate-Based Public Key Infrastructure (PKI) in Exchange Server 2013," in this book.

Leveraging Rights Management Services (RMS)

Security protection of email messages can be further enhanced in Outlook by leveraging Active Directory Rights Management Services (RMS). RMS provides the ability for a user to tag an email with an email header such as "Do not forward outside of the company" or "Confidential," and not only tag the notification, but have the policy extended to prevent the actual sending of the message outside of the organization. RMS policies can be configured on a message-by-message basis or for all messages sent from the system.

To configure an email for Rights Management Services policies, the organization first needs to implement RMS on a Windows server. RMS server and client configuration is covered in detail in Chapter 10, "Understanding Exchange Policy Enforcement Security." When the RMS server is implemented in a network environment, the user does the following to enable RMS policy protection:

1. Open a new message.
2. Click the Options tab in the ribbon and click Permission.
3. Click Permission from the Permission Options window.
4. Choose the RMS policy you want to apply to the message, as shown in Figure 21.7.

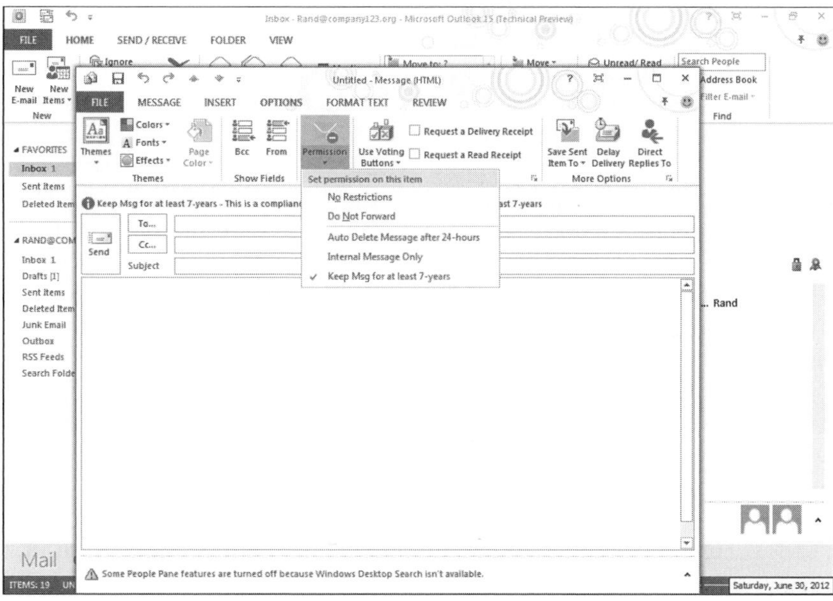

FIGURE 21.7 Applying an RMS policy to an email message.

NOTE

Policies need to be created on the RMS system, as covered in Chapter 10, before the policies will show up in the Set Permission on This Item pull-down menu.

5. Continue with writing the email as desired and send the message as normal.

Using Junk Email Filters to Reduce Spam

Antispam and phishing filters are integrated into Outlook 2013. With these features, the end user can configure the level of antispam filtering desired and control the level of restriction in which messages will be checked. These local functions work in tandem with antispam settings on the Exchange server.

In today's business environment, organizations often find that more than 90% of the mail coming into their environment is spam. Rather than burden the end user with the task of reviewing and deleting spam messages, Outlook 2013 is able to determine if a message is spam and prevent the user from having to deal with it. This can be especially helpful as spam messages are often infected with viruses or contain materials that would be inappropriate in the workplace. Occasionally, Outlook 2013 misses some messages that are actually spam, but the user has the ability to help improve the system when using Exchange Server. By tagging a message as spam, Exchange Server will be more likely to catch a similar spam message in the future. This can benefit an entire network when users tag spam messages in this way.

With the Outlook 2013 Junk E-mail filter, messages are reviewed when the client receives them to determine if the message should be treated as junk or valid email. To do this, the filter analyzes each message based on a class or criteria and imported spammer list. When Outlook is initially installed, the default setting is Low, which catches only the most obvious junk email. This setting is configurable by the end user and can be changed to increase the level of sensitivity on the junk email feature. This catches more unwanted email but increases the chance of false positives. False positives are valid messages that are mistakenly junked. It is important to occasionally check the Junk Mail folder to ensure that no valid messages were accidentally junked. Messages caught by the filter and determined to be junk mail are moved to a Junk E-mail folder in the Outlook 2013 client. The end user can and should review emails checking for false positive emails that were accidentally specified as junk. Optionally, the end user can configure the option to permanently delete junk email messages as they arrive and not save them to the folder at all. This setting should be used with caution.

To configure junk email filtering, follow these steps:

1. In Outlook 2013, select the Home tab in the ribbon and choose the pull-down Junk option.
2. From the Junk pull-down, choose Junk E-mail Options. On the Options tab shown in Figure 21.8, choose the level of blockage desired. Use caution when increasing the level of blockage because missing valid messages that are incorrectly categorized as spam can at times be more of a problem than removing a few spam messages per day from your Inbox.
3. Click OK when you are finished.

Utilizing the Safe Senders List

If the Outlook 2013 Junk E-mail filter incorrectly determines that a message is junk, the end user can add the sender's email address to a Safe Senders list. This list prevents the filter from identifying any new emails from that sender to be classified as junk mail. This function is also referred to as a "white list." The Safe Senders list supports both email addresses and wildcard domains for safe senders. So, a user could add `andrew@companyabc.com` to allow that individual to send him messages, or the user could add `@companyabc.com` to allow any user from companyabc.com to send him a message.

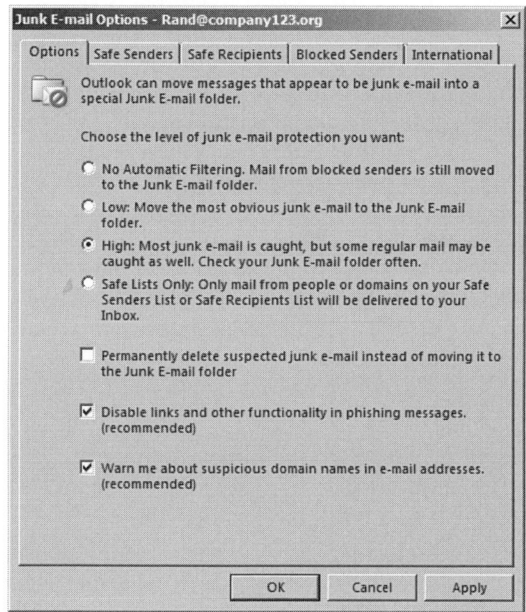

FIGURE 21.8 Junk E-Mail filtering options in Outlook.

The Safe Senders tab has two additional useful options. The first is "Also Trust Email from My Contacts" that ensures that messages sent from email addresses in the user's Contacts folder can bypass the Outlook antispam efforts. However, this useful feature can cause an often overlooked problem. Spammers rarely send out spam with a valid From address. They often *spoof* the address to match that of the person they are sending to—so a message sent *to* rand@companyabc.com will also appear to be *from* rand@companyabc.com. Now—if this user has a contact for himself in his Contacts folder and selects "Also Trust E-mail from My Contacts"—any mail with this address in the From field will be white-listed—including some of the most prevalent spam. When selecting this option, users should make sure they do not have a contact for themselves.

The other option, "Automatically Add People I E-mail to the Safe Senders List," is also useful. When users have more stringent settings in their Junk E-mail options, selecting this option builds a white list of anyone that the user sends an email to—working on the premise of "If you send to them, you probably want to receive from them."

Utilizing the Safe Recipients List

The Safe Recipients list performs a very similar function to the Safe Senders list. The Safe Recipients list allows the user to configure email lists or mail-enabled groups of which they are a member. Any messages sent from these email groups are automatically considered "safe" and bypass Outlook's antispam efforts.

Utilizing the Blocked Senders List

The opposite of the Safe Senders list is the Blocked Senders list. This concept is often referred to as a "black list." By entering email addresses or wildcard domains, a user can tell Outlook 2013 to automatically junk any and all messages received from the blocked senders. This tab is not useful when it comes to fighting spam, however, because the worst offenders change their email addresses (and usually domain names) with every round of messages.

TIP

It is important to understand that Blocked Sender rules are based only on the Reply To addresses given in the email. Reply To addresses are usually forged in an attempt to slip around antispam systems.

Utilizing the International Blocked Top-Level Domain List

Many organizations find unwanted spam messages originate from countries where the user would normally not receive a message. As an example, if a user gets a lot of spam from China and the user *never* expects to get emails from China, that person can go into the International Blocked Top-Level Domain List and select CN as a country from which the user does not want any messages to be received into his or her Inbox. In addition, the user can choose a language encoding list that the user does not want any messages from an email system with a language set, such as Arabic or Cyrillic, and all messages using that language set encoding will be blocked.

TIP

It is important to understand that doing blocking at the top-level country domain level or by language encoding set of the message can potentially block legitimate messages if the user does get emails from someone that was previously blocked. These are minute options; the administrator can try different variations to see what works best.

Populating the Lists

To add users to the Safe Senders, Safe Recipients, or Blocked Senders lists, users can do the following:

1. In Outlook 2013, select the Home tab in the ribbon and choose the pull-down Junk option.
2. From the Junk pull-down, choose Junk E-mail Options and choose one of the tabs (Safe Senders, Safe Recipients, Blocked Senders, or International), and then click Add to insert the user to the appropriate list.

3. Type in the SMTP email address of the sender (or his domain) in the following format: `rich@companyabc.com` or `@companyabc.com`.
4. Click OK when you finish.

Alternatively, any of these lists can be populated with an initial set of addresses by using a combination of Group Policy and the Office Outlook 2013 template. However, when added, administrators cannot *remove* an entry using GPO. If an invalid entry is distributed, it can be deleted by the user or the entire list can be overwritten by pushing another list via GPO.

Some organizations have been known to add their own domain to the Safe Senders list and push it out to all users. This can be a huge mistake because what the majority of the spam users are faced with will be spoofed with their own domain, and this setting leaves the door wide open.

TIP

Many services provide lists of junk senders for import into a Blocked Senders list. These lists are created based on known spammers. If your organization wants to provide the end users with a list of trusted or junk senders, the end user can easily import the list by clicking on the Import from File button. However, as previously stated, this option is of little value because the spammers change their addresses constantly.

Avoiding Web Beaconing

Web beaconing refers to the use of references to external content via email to identify a message as having been read. This allows a spammer to validate her list of addresses by identifying the messages that reached a valid user and were opened. When the end user opens the message or views it in the preview pane, the computer retrieves this external content. Outlook 2013 has the ability to block web beaconing, which can help reduce the chances of a user getting onto more spam lists.

To enable web beacon filtering, from Outlook 2013, do the following:

1. Click File on the ribbon, choose Options, click Trust Center, and then click Trust Center Settings.
2. Select Automatic Download in the left pane.
3. Make sure that the Don't Download Pictures Automatically in HTML E-Mail Messages or RSS Items check box has been selected.
4. Click OK when you are finished.

Implementing Outlook Anywhere

In Exchange Server 2013, the Outlook Anywhere feature (known long ago as RPC over HTTP) enables Outlook 2013 clients to connect to the Exchange server over the Internet by using the Remote Procedure Calls (RPC) over HTTP Windows networking component. By wrapping RPCs with an HTTP layer, the communication between the Outlook client and the Exchange server can go through network firewalls without requiring RPC ports to be opened. Users can have the benefits of direct connection to Exchange without having to utilize a virtual private network (VPN). In addition, as HTTP protocols were designed to function on networks with unreliable connectivity (such as the Internet), Outlook Anywhere enables users with higher latency to connect to Exchange.

With Exchange Server 2013 (as well as Exchange Server 2010), Microsoft did away with direct Messaging Application Programming Interface (MAPI) communications to the Exchange Mailbox server and instead, all client communications goes through a Client Access server (CAS). By simplifying end client communications to Exchange, Microsoft can better support remote connectivity into Exchange for both scalability as well as high availability.

Enabling Outlook Anywhere—Server Side

By default, Exchange Server 2013 servers are configured for Outlook Anywhere, which is effectively access to Exchange over HTTPS. When setting up an Exchange CAS system, a certificate is installed on the CAS system to provide certificate-based secured communications between the client and the server. More on configuring the basics of Exchange can be found in Chapter 6, "Installing and Configuring the Basics of Exchange Server 2013 for a Brand-New Environment."

Connecting to Outlook Anywhere with Outlook 2013

After the CAS server(s) in Exchange are set up, the Outlook client can be configured to connect to Exchange Server via Outlook Anywhere.

For Exchange Server 2013 to use Outlook Anywhere, the workstation needs to run Outlook 2007 Service Pack 2 (SP2) or higher. Outlook Anywhere has been supported since Outlook 2003; however, Exchange Server 2013 also requires support for Autodiscover to failover a client system across Exchange servers. This combination of Outlook Anywhere and Autodiscover is supported in Outlook 2007 SP2 and higher.

Normally, it should not be necessary to manually configure Outlook 2013 for Outlook Anywhere because Autodiscover should take care of it automatically. To manually configure the Outlook 2013 client for Outlook Anywhere access, complete the following:

1. In Outlook 2013, click File and then select Account Settings, Account Settings.
2. Highlight the Microsoft Exchange connection, and click Change.
3. On the Change Account screen, click More Settings.
4. Click the Connection tab.
5. Place a check mark in the Connect to Microsoft Exchange Using HTTP check box.
6. Click Exchange Proxy Settings.

On the Exchange Proxy Settings screen, configure the following:

1. For Connection Settings, enter the uniform resource locator (URL) of the Exchange CAS that has been configured as an RPC proxy server or the host name of the load-balanced virtual IP.

2. Select Connect Using SSL Only, select to connect using the name, and enter the certificate name followed by **msstd:**.

3. Select the two boxes to use HTTP as the first choice for both fast and slow connections, as shown in Figure 21.9, click OK, and then click OK again.

4. Click OK to accept the information box about restarting Outlook.

5. Click Next, click Finish, and then click Close.

6. Exit the Outlook application, and open it again to apply the new settings.

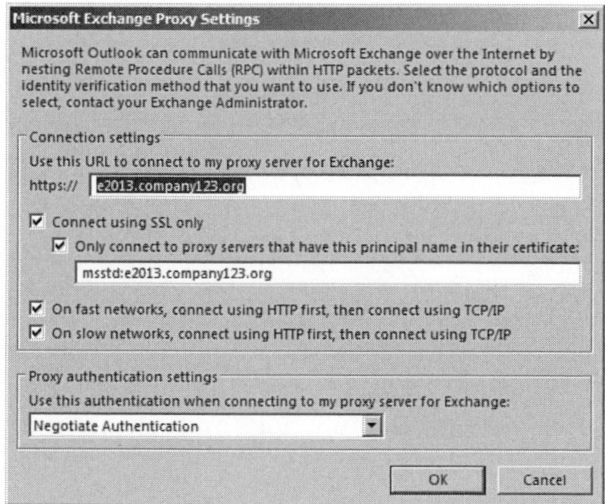

FIGURE 21.9 Outlook Anywhere client configuration.

TIP

To ensure that Outlook 2013 is now using RPC over HTTPS, hold the Ctrl key and right-click the Outlook icon in the taskbar. Select Connection Status, as shown in Figure 21.10. This screen shows you the connection type to the Exchange server, which should state HTTPS.

The most secure method of connecting uses the following settings, which are also the default settings when RPC over HTTP is first configured:

- Connect with SSL Only
- Mutually Authenticate the Session When Connecting with SSL
- Password Authentication Is NTLM

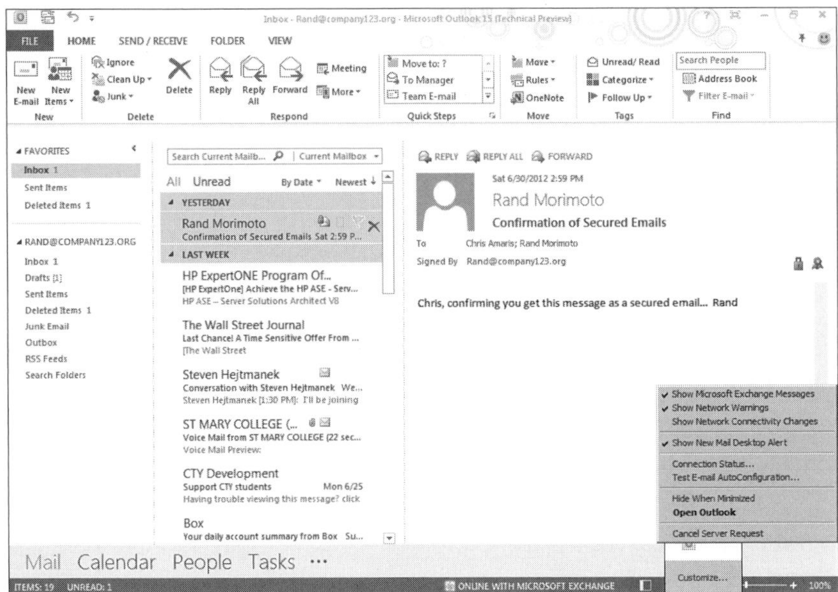

FIGURE 21.10 Selecting the Connection Status in the taskbar tray.

Deploying Outlook 2013

To take advantage of all the features of Outlook 2013, you need to deploy Outlook 2013 to your users. The deployment can be performed with many tools such as System Center Configuration Manager or though Group Policy Objects. This section focuses on how to preconfigure Outlook 2013 so that it will be deployed with the functions and settings that you need.

Utilizing the Office Customization Tool

The Office Customization Tool (OCT) is an application included in Office 2013. The OCT allows an administrator to preconfigure components and settings within the Office 2013 suite to simplify deployments of Office 2013 applications.

The OCT is accessed in the following manner:

1. Launch a command prompt.
2. Browse to the drive containing the Office install files.
3. Browse to the directory containing the `setup.exe` file.
4. Type **`Setup.exe /admin`**.

Running the OCT in this way allows you to either create a new setup customization file or to modify an existing one. If you are creating a new file, the OCT displays a list of the products available on the network installation point. You must select a single product that you want to customize.

After running the wizard, you can save your customizations in the Updates folder. Setup will look into this folder to find customizations when you run the setup.

Alternatively, you can save your customizations in another location and reference them during the install. For example:

```
Setup.exe /adminfile \\server\share\OCT\remoteusers.msp
```

This is an exceptionally powerful ability as you can create different custom settings for different types of users.

Taking Advantage of OCT for Outlook 2013

Although the OCT offers customizations for all Office 2013 components, this section examines some of the settings available specifically for Outlook 2013. Some of the more useful settings include the following:

- **Use Existing Profile**—This setting retains the existing profile or prompts the user to create a profile the first time Outlook is started.
- **Modify Profile**—This setting modifies the default profile or makes changes to profiles that you specify. If there isn't a default profile or no profile by the name that you specify, Outlook creates a profile based on settings you choose in the other areas of the OCT.
- **New Profile**—This setting creates a new profile and sets it as the default profile. If a profile already exists, it is not removed and is still available to the user. You need to enter a name in the Profile Name box, which appears in the E-Mail Accounts dialog box in Outlook. The new profile is created based on the options you choose in the other areas of the OCT.
- **Apply PRF**—This setting imports an Outlook profile (PRF) file to define a new default profile. You can use any profile created for Outlook 2013. Enter a name and path for the profile in the Apply the Following Profile (PRF File) field. If you created a PRF file for a previous version of Outlook, you can import it to Office 2013.
- **Do Not Configure Cached Exchange Mode**—This setting configures Outlook 2013 to only attach to the Exchange Server mailboxes directly from the Exchange server, as opposed to being cached on users' computers in an Offline Storage (OST) file.
- **Cached Exchange Mode**—This setting creates an OST file or uses an existing OST file. This results in users working with a local copy of their Exchange Server mailbox. When selecting Cached Exchange Mode, you can configure the following options.
    - **Download Only Headers**—Download copies of headers only from users' Exchange Server mailboxes.
    - **Download Headers Followed by the Full Item**—Download copies of headers from users' Exchange Server mailboxes, and then download copies of messages.

- **Download Full Items**—Download copies of full messages (headers and message bodies) from users' Exchange Server mailboxes.
- **On Slow Connections, Download Only Headers**—When a slow network connection is detected, download copies of headers only from users' Exchange Server mailboxes.
- **Download Public Folder Favorites**—Download the list of public folder favorites.

Using Outlook 2013

Like every evolution of Outlook, Outlook 2013 expands on the collaborative tools available to the end user when connecting to an Exchange server. This section covers many of these collaborative tools and new collaborative features available in the Outlook 2013 client.

Creating a Calendar Item and Appointment

One of the common tasks in Outlook is the ability to create a calendar item or appointment, effectively adding to the calendar.

To create a calendar item, do the following:

1. Click the Calendar option in Outlook.
2. In the ribbon at the top of the screen, click New Appointment.
3. Fill in the Subject, Location, and the Start and End Time.

NOTE

The Subject and Start and End times are the only mandatory fields that need to be included in an appointment. The user can also add in the location of the meeting as well as any body text that might be of interest or helpful. However, the basics are just the subject and times of the appointment.

4. To invite someone else to the appointment, click Invite Attendees from the ribbon and add in the email addresses of the attendees you want to have attend the meeting as well.
5. If the meeting will be an Online Meeting (such as a web conference or audio or video meeting) and the organization has Microsoft Lync installed, then click Online Meeting to enable the ability to have the meeting online.
6. If the meeting will happen more than once, such as the meeting will happen every Friday morning at 8:00 a.m., or the meeting will happen on the third Thursday of every month, then click Recurrence in the Options section and enter in the recurring meeting information.

NOTE

The meeting can also be scheduled with a different time zone; a reminder can be set to notify the attendees when the meeting is about to occur; the meeting can be set with high importance or low importance; the meeting can be set as private; and the meeting can have a color-coded category associated to it.

7. When you are finished, click Save (or Send in the case of a meeting where you are inviting others to attend) and the calendar appointment will be created.

Viewing Shared Calendars in Multiple Panes

Tracking appointments and setting meetings have quickly become high priorities for employees in today's business world. To simplify these types of functions, Outlook 2013 allows a user to view multiple Exchange Server calendars in a shared pane. In previous versions of Outlook, an additional calendar would be opened in a new window. In Outlook 2013, if a user has configured his calendar with View rights, other users can view those calendars as well as their own at the same time lined up side by side to view or compare them.

To open additional calendars, perform the following steps:

1. Choose File, Open & Export, Other User's Folder.
2. Choose the name of the user and select Folder Type: Calendar. The calendar opens in the main window and automatically both the mailbox owner's calendar and the other user's calendar are opened, as shown in Figure 21.11.

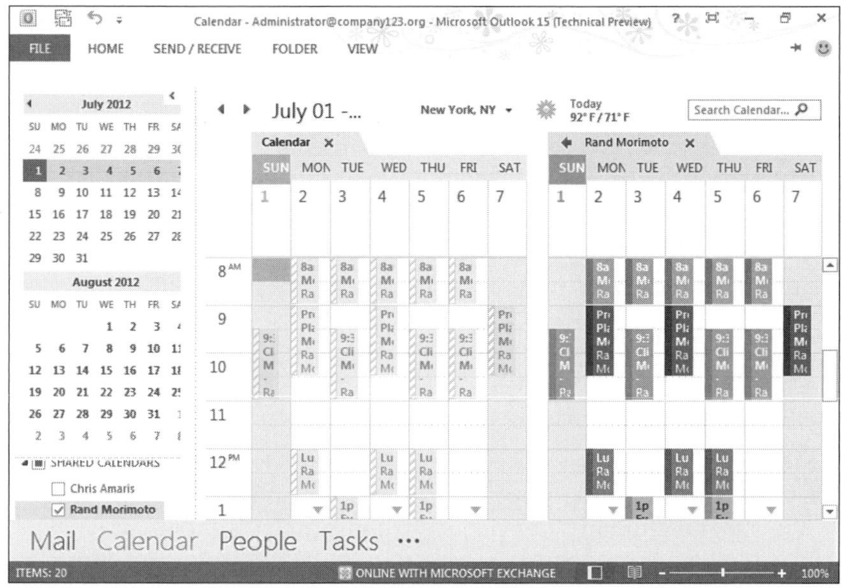

FIGURE 21.11 Viewing other person's calendar.

3. To open previously opened calendars, expand the left pane, and in the Shared Calendars location, a user can simply select (and deselect) calendars to view on screen.

TIP

When viewing multiple calendars, keep in mind that each additional calendar is shown in a different color; also note that the corresponding check box on the left is seen in the same color.

4. Continue to add the desired calendars, and click the check boxes to remove or add calendars to the view.
5. When you are finished, click the My Calendar check box, which will deselect all the additional calendars other than the individual's own calendar.

TIP

When in the Calendar view, you can click the Open a Shared Calendar hyperlink and you will be prompted to enter the name of the user whose calendar you want to view. Enter the name of the calendar to open and click OK. This automatically shows both the mailbox owner's calendar and the new calendar(s).

Enabling Calendar Sharing in Outlook 2013

By default, the full details of a user's calendar are not shared. Other users in the organization have the ability to view free/busy information, but that is all. If the calendar owner wants to allow others to view the full details of her calendar, or to write to her calendar, the default permissions must be modified.

To enable the mailbox owner's calendar to be shared, follow these steps:

1. From the Folder List view, right-click Calendar in the navigation pane, and click Share, Calendar Permissions. (If you don't see Calendar in the list, click the Folder List icon at the bottom of the navigation pane.)
2. From the Calendar Properties page, on the Permissions tab, click Add.
3. Browse or enter the name of the user who will get access to the calendar, and click Add.
4. Click OK when the users have been added.
5. The user must now specify what permissions are to be granted. Outlook provides predefined roles for permissions that appear in the Permission Level box. Clicking the drop-down menu and choosing a predefined permission level shows what permissions are being granted, making it easy to choose the desired permissions.

To create a unique set of permissions, choose an initial permission level and then check the check boxes and option buttons to assign the unique permissions, as shown in Figure 21.12.

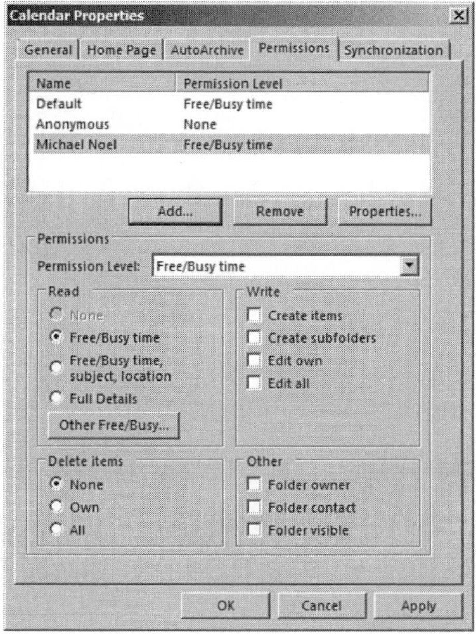

FIGURE 21.12 Changing calendar sharing permissions.

6. Click OK when finished. The user(s) specified will have those rights to the end user's calendar until the end user specifically removes them by going through the same process mentioned, and then clicking on the user or group with permissions to the calendar and choosing Remove.

NOTE

When you grant another user Read access to your calendar, that user will be able to read your calendar entries. They will not, however, be able to read calendar items that are marked as Private.

Sharing Other Personal Information

Outlook 2013 allows users to share their personal information (such as the Inbox, contacts, and tasks) with other users. This is done via the same method listed previously with the difference being that the permissions are set for the Inbox, Contacts, or Tasks folders.

To enable Inbox sharing, for example, follow these steps:

1. Right-click the Inbox in the Folder view and select Properties.
2. Choose the Permissions tab.
3. Add the users or groups and set their permissions as described previously in the "Enabling Calendar Sharing in Outlook 2013" section.

Creating Tasks and To-Do Items

Outlook has the ability of allowing users to create tasks and to-do items, which can be as simple as a shopping list, an action item list, or a project task list. Task and to-do items show up in the Tasks section of Outlook.

To create a task or to-do item, do the following:

1. Click Tasks in Outlook.
2. Click New Task in the ribbon at the top of Outlook.
3. Enter in the subject of the task.

NOTE

The subject is the only item that needs to be added to a task. It is optional for the user to enter in the time, date, status, or other information. Those details can be added for better clarity or for more information, but a task or to-do item can simply be just a single-line subject.

4. Choose to add in more details such as date, status, priority, % complete of the task, a reminder, recurrence, follow-up information, and importance priority of the task.
5. In addition, choose to assign the task to someone, which is similar to sending a calendar appointment, but instead of ending up in the recipient's calendar, the task ends up in the recipient's tasks list.
6. Click Save (or Send) to save and store the task or to-do item.

Viewing Tasks and To-Do Items

Once a task has been created, or a to-do item has been assigned, an Outlook user can go into Outlook, click Tasks, and see the tasks and to-do items in his task list. The items can be organized, status updated, assigned, modified, and changed as the user desires. Tasks and to-do items are very flexible; even OneNote messages can be associated, attached, and integrated into the task and to-do item. These items help a user better manage his information and actions.

Creating Notes

Outlook also has a Notes item, which is just like tasks, but instead of being task- and due date-oriented, notes are simply just notes or messages in freeform.

To create a note, do the following:

1. Click the ellipsis (the three dots [...] at the bottom of the page) and then Notes in Outlook.
2. Click New Note in the ribbon at the top of Outlook.
3. Enter in the body context of the note.

NOTE

Notes are very simple freeform text. There are no due dates, timelines, or subject names, nor are there any fancy formatting or styles available. Notes are simply like sticky notes—text is entered and saved.

4. Click the X at the top right of the note to close the note. Notes are automatically saved when closed.

Viewing Notes

Once a note has been created, an Outlook user can go into Outlook, click the ellipsis (the three dots [...] at the bottom of the page) and then Notes, and see the notes in his or her list. The user can open notes, modify notes, and delete notes, but that's about it. Notes are not too fancy—they are just simple items to enter in simple text of information.

Delegating Rights to Send Email "On Behalf Of" Another User

In some situations, such as when a user has an administrative assistant, the user might want to give someone the ability to send messages or meeting requests on his or her behalf. This results in a message that will come from "user B on behalf of user A." To enable a user to send email on someone else's behalf, follow these steps:

1. Go to File, Account Settings, and select Delegates Access.
2. Click Add.
3. Add the name of the user or group that needs the rights.
4. When finished, click OK.
5. Choose the permission level for each component of Outlook.
6. If desired, select Automatically Send a Message to the Delegate Summarizing These Permissions.
7. If desired, select Delegate Can See My Private Items.
8. Click OK when finished.

9. From the Options page, select how meeting requests should be delivered. The available options are shown in Figure 21.13. The default setting, "My Delegates Only, But Send a Copy of Meeting Requests and Responses to Me" is the recommended setting.

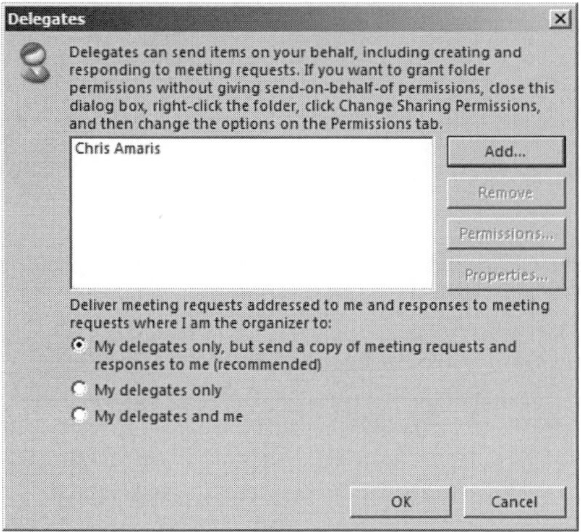

FIGURE 21.13 Adding permissions to delegates.

NOTE

Although Outlook does not have a predefined maximum number of delegates that can be assigned, typically a limit of no more than four delegates is suggested. Best practices recommend that users assign only *one* other user with Editor Permissions. Adding additional editors are a common cause of unpredictable behavior (e.g., calendar corruption) with meetings and appointments in Outlook.

Sharing Information with Users Outside the Company

Outlook 2013 also has the ability to extend Outlook information to users outside of an organization such as the ability to display a user's calendar for free/busy access. Much of the functionality available among users of the same Exchange Server environment can be made available across the Internet. This is a great enabler for users because it is now easier to collaborate with colleagues from other organizations.

Configuring Free/Busy Time to Be Viewed Via the Internet

Several years ago, specialized software and connectors were required to share free/busy information outside of an organization. Free/busy information is what tracks the availability of users in terms of having appointments, being in meetings, or having free time available. Exchange Server administrators and mailbox owners can publish this free/busy information outside of their Exchange Server environment to more easily set up meetings with other organizations. If this functionality is needed, this information can be published to a web server available to both organizations such as to a WebDAV server, or Microsoft provides a service for content sharing in Office Online. By publishing free/busy information to a shared website, users outside of the Exchange Server organization can view published free/busy information over the Internet. They can also use the same website to schedule meetings with recipients from the participating organizations.

To configure free/busy time to be displayed on the Internet using WebDAV, follow these steps:

1. Right-click the calendar to be shared and choose Share.
2. Choose Publish to WebDAV Server.
3. Enter the URL to which you will publish your information.
4. Choose the time frame you want to publish as well as the options and upload method.
5. Click OK.

To stop sharing this information on the custom server, complete the following steps:

1. Right-click the calendar to be (un)shared and choose Share.
2. Choose Publish to WebDAV Server.
3. Choose Remove from Server.
4. Click Yes.

To publish a calendar to Office Online, follow these steps:

1. Right-click the calendar to be shared and choose Share.
2. Choose Publish to Office Online.
3. Register for Office Online if you do not already have a Windows Live ID; if you have a Windows Live ID, click Sign-in.
4. Choose the time frame you want to publish and the options and upload method, similar to that shown in Figure 21.14.

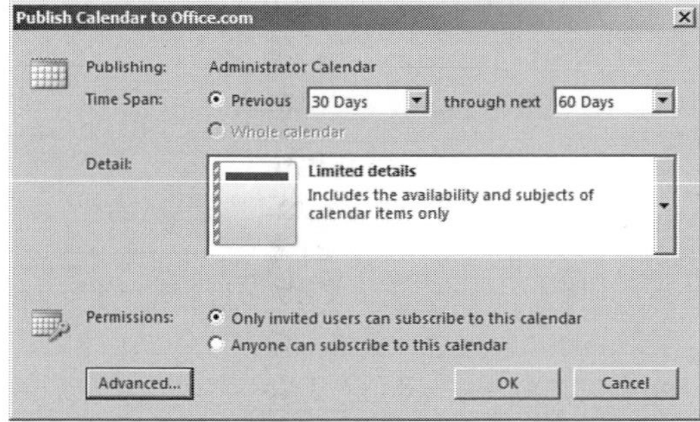

FIGURE 21.14 Publishing a calendar to Office.com.

5. Click OK and information will be published.
6. Optional: Send invites to contacts to share your information.

To stop sharing this information on Office Online:

1. Right-click the calendar to be (un)shared and choose Share.
2. Choose Publish to Office Online.
3. Choose Remove from Server.
4. Click Yes.

Sending Contact Information to Others

As the business world becomes more and more electronic, old customs such as the exchange of paper business cards are being replaced by more modern methods. Virtual business cards, or vCards, have greatly increased in popularity. These vCards enable an Outlook user to send anyone a small file containing his or her contact information. Because of the vCard format, this contact information can then be imported into the recipient's contact list. The vCard can contain common information such as the following:

- Name
- Address
- Phone numbers
- Email address
- Job title

Going beyond the concepts of a typical business card, a vCard can also include the following:

- A picture of the contact
- A public key for encryption or digital signing
- A link to Internet-published free/busy information

vCards can be emailed as attachments or they can be automatically attached to outgoing messages as part of a signature file.

To email a vCard, follow these steps:

1. In People or Contacts within Outlook, click once on a contact you want to share.
2. Either right-click the contact and choose Forward Contact, or choose Forward Contact in the ribbon.
3. Choose As a Business Card, As an Outlook Contact, or Forward as a Text Message.

NOTE

The As a Business Card option creates a business card looking graphic (JPG graphic format) as an email attachment along with an Outlook VCF file. The As an Outlook Contact option creates a vCard as an attachment. The Forward as a Text Message option uses the text messaging (SMS) option of Outlook to send a text message with the contact information.

4. Input in the recipient's information into the email and send the message.

When the user receives the card, he or she can open it and then select Save and Close to save the contact into his own contacts area.

To include a vCard in an autosignature, follow these steps:

1. Click File, Options.
2. Click the Mail tab and click the Signatures option.
3. Choose to edit an existing autosignature or create a new one.
4. In the toolbar above the text window, click the Business Card icon.
5. Select the business card from your contacts, and click OK.
6. Click OK.

Leveraging Social Media in Outlook

Starting with Outlook 2010, Microsoft enabled better integration with social media integration capabilities within Outlook, such as the ability to link Facebook, LinkedIn, SharePoint MySite, and other social connections to Outlook. Users of Outlook 2010's social connectors found the integration to be extremely helpful as the link allows users to commonly see a user's photo from within Outlook that the user may have posted on LinkedIn or Facebook. In addition, for users who have linked or friended with someone in a social media forum, feeds from the social connector become available, such as posted status, latest update, or latest social media change.

Enabling Social Network Connections

The first thing a user needs to do to set up social media network connections is to configure Outlook 2013 to acknowledge the user's social media accounts. It is these accounts that then query the social media providers to pull down photos, feeds, and other information associated with a user.

To create a social network account association, do the following:

1. Click File, Account Settings, Social Network Accounts.
2. Click Next through the social network account welcome page.

3. Click the check box to enable any of the existing social media account association pages, such as Facebook or SharePoint MySite, and type in your username and password for the social media service.
4. Click Connect to Another Social Network that will redirect you to Microsoft's page where other connects for Outlook are available (for things like Facebook, LinkedIn, Windows Live Messenger, Viadeo, Xing, and the like).
5. Click Connect and Finish when you are done selecting the social connectors desired.

Utilizing Social Network Connections

Once the social network connector has been set up, any time a user sends or receives an email from someone who has his email account associated with his social media account, his social media information will show up at the bottom of an Outlook message. As an example, as shown in Figure 21.15, the user has his Facebook account associated with his email address and, thus, his most recent Facebook "Wall" posts show up as available information. Likewise, information on LinkedIn, Windows Live Messenger, and so on show up as well.

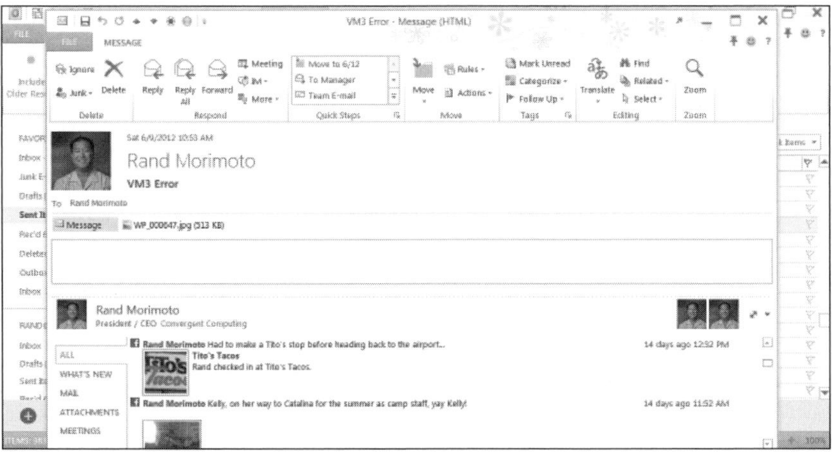

FIGURE 21.15 Social media information appears at the bottom of Outlook messages.

NOTE

Even though a user's associated business account may be connected to his LinkedIn business profile and a different, personal account is associated with his Facebook page, the social network profiles cross-link known accounts for users. As an example, if someone uses your business email address to connect with you on LinkedIn and someone else uses your personal email address to connect with you on LinkedIn, the LinkedIn service automatically associates your LinkedIn profile to *both* your business and personal email addresses. When your information shows up in someone's Outlook social connector, publicly available pictures and status updates will show up on the user's Outlook page for you.

Using Cached Exchange Mode for Offline Functionality

Outlook 2013 continues to support Cached Exchange mode. Cached Exchange mode, or Cached mode for short, refers to a configuration where Outlook is storing the messages and calendar items locally. Unlike the old Personal Folders file (PST) storage method, Cached mode utilizes an OST file. This file is synchronized with the Exchange server on a regular basis. This means that there are two copies of the mailbox at all times. One copy lives on the Exchange server and one copy lives on the Outlook client.

This configuration has many advantages in terms of performance and reliability. For example, imagine that a user is connecting to his or her Exchange server over a dial-up connection and isn't running Cached mode. The user receives a message with a large attachment. The user sees the new message and opens the attachment. Now, the message has to be downloaded to the user's computer. This takes several minutes because of the size of the file and the relatively slow link speed. This usually results in unhappy users because they had to wait several minutes between wanting to open the attachment and the attachment actually opening.

Now, let's view this same scenario with Cached mode. In Cached mode, the attachment is downloaded in the background when the message arrives, assuming the Outlook client is attached to the server. The message with the attachment doesn't appear in the mailbox until the contents have been downloaded and cached locally. Now, when the user sees the message appear in the Inbox, the files associated with the attachment are already on the local system. The user opens the attachment and it opens immediately. This results in a happier user.

The truth of the matter is that the download time of the message was exactly the same in both scenarios. However, the perceived difference is that the Cached mode situation was faster because the user doesn't know when the message was sent. This situation also takes great advantage of the idle time of the user. Most messages arrive and are fully downloaded to the client while the user is away from his or her system or doing other things. This means that when the user is actively working with email, there aren't any delays in moving data.

A key advantage of Cached mode is that a message with a large attachment is downloaded just once regardless of how many times the user clicks on it.

Because the data downloaded is only a mirror of the Exchange Server mailbox, the content available via Outlook Web App (OWA) is exactly the same. Similarly, if the user were to get another computer or a new computer, Outlook simply creates another copy of the data locally to keep in sync.

With the OST file locally stored, the user is able to work with the contents of his or her mailbox even when not connected to the Exchange server. Changes made locally will sync back to the Exchange server. Like most replication performed by Microsoft, the newest copy always wins and overwrites older changes. This allows a traveling user to reply to messages, organize folders, and create calendar entries while away from the office. Upon connecting to the Exchange server, the user's local changes get applied to the Exchange server copy. This is really an optimal configuration for traveling users and users who have limited connectivity.

The User Experience in Cached Exchange Mode

When the user is connected to the Exchange server, the phrase "Connected to Microsoft Exchange" appears in the lower-right corner of the Outlook 2013 window. The message "All Folders Are Up to Date" should also be displayed when synchronization is up to date.

When connectivity is lost, the message says "Disconnected" and gives the date and time the offline folders were last updated.

When connectivity is first restored, the message says "Trying to Connect." As connectivity is reestablished, the phrase "Connected to Microsoft Exchange" reappears, and to the left are updates informing the user what is automatically occurring to get the mailbox up to date.

These messages could be any of the following:

- Waiting to Update the Full Items in Inbox
- Sending Complete
- All Folders Are Up-to-Date

The user might occasionally find that people appear to be missing from the Global Address List (GAL). While running in Cached mode, Outlook 2013 no longer gets its GAL from the global catalog. The client downloads the offline address book (OAB). This is what allows the user to look up addresses while not connected to the network. The user can trigger a download of the OAB at any time. Important to realize is that, by default, Exchange Server only updates the OAB every 24 hours, and Outlook's own download schedule will cause the OAB to be updated somewhat later. As such, it's possible for a user to be added to Exchange Server after the OAB generation has occurred. Users not running in Cached mode would see the new user in the GAL but the Cached mode users wouldn't see them until the OAB was updated and they downloaded the latest copy.

Deploying Cached Exchange Mode

Cached Exchange mode is enabled by default when a user profile is created in Outlook 2013 for an Exchange Server environment. Default configuration settings are established, and the user's emails are automatically brought down to the local system upon setting up Outlook for a user.

In addition, Cached mode can be deployed by using the Office Customization Tool or through enabling this option using domain Group Policy. Be aware that setting it via Group Policy on a large number of users drastically increases network traffic to the Exchange server. Outlook in Cached mode has to download the entire mailbox. Environments where mailbox size limits aren't set are especially impacted by this. Imagine 200 users log on on Monday morning and a GPO sets their Outlook to Cached mode.

If each user had 100MB of mail in his or her mailbox, there would be 20GB of data being copied from the Exchange server. This could be especially impacting if some of those users were coming across wide area network (WAN) connections to get to Exchange Server.

Deploying Cached Exchange Mode Manually

When configuring a user's Outlook profile manually, it's possible to configure Cached mode at that time. Because Cached mode is enabled by default, this is when a user may choose to *not* implement Cached mode at time of installation of Outlook. This may be the preferred configuration when a user is working off a system that is not his or her default system or is a shared system where having an OST with email information is not preferred.

To configure Cached mode manually, do the following:

1. Begin configuring a user profile in the standard manner, typically launching Outlook 2013 for the first time on a system.
2. When the E-Mail Accounts page is reached, choose to either select the Use Cached Exchange Mode check box or deselect the check box to not have Cached mode enabled for the system.
3. Finish configuring the Outlook profile.

Deployment Considerations for Cached Exchange Mode

Because enabling Cached mode forces the end users to synchronize a full copy of their mailboxes to a local OST file as well as a full copy of the OAB, the demand on an Exchange server can be quite high. If a large number of users must be configured to use Cached mode at one time, the best choices for configuring Cached mode are as follows:

- Deploy Cached mode to groups of users at a time rather than to the whole enterprise.
- Encourage users to clean up their mailboxes prior to enabling Cached mode. Items in the Sent and Deleted items often account for 50% of the size of a mailbox.
- Deploy Cached mode sooner rather than later. The smaller the mailbox at the time of the OST creation, the less data needs to be moved.

Using Cached Exchange Mode

Because Cached mode acts somewhat differently from a traditional mailbox, an administrator might consider some additional user training for those with Cached mode. This helps users recognize those differences and should result in fewer calls to the help desk. Some of these differences are mentioned in the following sections.

The Send/Receive Button

For users in either Online or Cached mode, it is unnecessary to click the Send/Receive messages button regularly when synchronizing with the new Cached mode functionality.

This happens automatically and clicking Send/Receive doesn't accomplish anything in most environments as the Outlook mailbox keeps up to date on a regular basis.

An exception to this rule is if the user is looking for recipients who have not yet synchronized to the offline address book.

RPC Over HTTPS and the Cached Exchange Mode

It is recommended that users running RPC over HTTPS also run with Cached Exchange mode enabled. This is because Cached Exchange mode deals better with "slow links and disconnections" to Exchange Server. Because RPC over HTTPS accesses Exchange Server information via the Internet, these users are more likely to experience network latency and slowness.

Slow-Link Connection Awareness

Cached mode was originally designed to address the challenges associated with links 128Kbps or slower. When slow-link connection awareness is enabled, it automatically implements the following email-synchronization behaviors:

- OAB is not downloaded (neither partial nor full download).
- Mail headers only are downloaded.
- The rest of the mail message and attachments are downloaded when the user clicks on the message or attachment to open it.

Cached Exchange Mode and OSTs and OABs

Using Cached mode downloads a full copy of the user's mail to the OST file stored locally on the user's hard drive. However, administrators need to be aware of some considerations regarding OSTs and Cached mode to plan and make their configuration choices for these Exchange Server clients allowing optimal performance and efficient connectivity.

Cached Exchange Mode OST Considerations

OST files in Outlook 2013 use the new Unicode format. This allows them to go beyond the 2-GB limitation of the old American National Standards Institute (ANSI) format. However, be sure to account for the potential size of the OST file when planning your desktop or laptop images. The larger the user's mailbox, the more information the user will be "carrying around" with him in his OST.

Cached Exchange Mode and Outlook Address Book (OAB) Implications

When using Cached mode, it is possible to download a No Details Outlook address book. However, users in Cached mode should download the Full Details OAB. This is because they can experience significant delays when they access the OAB when the full details are not locally accessible. When this situation occurs, the user's workstation must contact the Exchange server to provide full data for the OAB. This results in delays for the user during the download.

When Cached mode is enabled, the OAB is synchronized every 24 hours, by default. If there are no updates to the server OAB, there will be no updates to the offline OAB. When there are changes to the OAB, only the differences are downloaded. This results in a faster update to the OAB for the Cached mode user.

Summary

Outlook has been around for years with Outlook 2013 being the latest rendition of the client software. Outlook 2013 takes advantage of the new features enabled by Exchange Server 2013 such as the common user interface across all endpoint devices.

Users can benefit from the powerful collaboration functions of Outlook 2013 and enjoy the improvements in the area of email access, calendar interaction, and people contact access. Sharing of calendars and contacts provides users both internal to a network as well as external to an Exchange environment access to common information.

Microsoft made the Search functionality more powerful while simplifying the use of the feature at the same time. Near-real-time searches of the entire mailbox are made possible through configurable search queries or filters, enabling users to find a particular message quickly and easily—even with today's larger and larger mailboxes. The search capabilities are further enhanced by enabling users' access to search information outside of Exchange.

As more and more unethical people attempt to assault us with spam and phishing attacks, Outlook 2013 fights back with integrated security capabilities, helping the user avoid these annoying and potentially dangerous email messages. By integrating with the message filtering functions of Exchange Server, Outlook 2013 allows the end users to do their part to help protect the company as a whole by acting as a secondary layer in the spam blocking by flagging messages that snuck through the primary filter.

Other security enhancements in Outlook 2013 include encrypted client-to-server communications by using RPC over HTTPS to connect to Exchange Outlook Anywhere. And the ability to add security to specific messages through Rights Management Services and the capability to set security for an entire mailbox give users a much more secured environment for enabling business processes.

Finally, a Cached mode method of access enables a user to access mail, calendar appointments, and other content within Outlook, regardless of whether he or she is connected to Exchange Server. Cached mode access provides remote and roving users an improved user experience by placing data local to their system making accessing large attachments significantly faster than if they were accessing them from the Exchange server.

All the powerful and useful features built in to Outlook 2013 make it the latest and truly greatest version of Outlook—until the next one.

Best Practices

- Quick flags should be used to flag messages that require follow-up or other attention.
- Key appointments can be categorized with colors to draw attention to appointments in user calendars.
- Using the enhanced search capabilities of Outlook 2013 can dramatically decrease the time it takes for a user to find messages or information within Outlook.
- Instead of establishing a VPN before accessing an Exchange server from a remote Outlook 2013 client, the RPC over HTTPS should be enabled to provide Secure Sockets Layer (SSL)–based 128-bit encrypted end-to-end communication from client to server.
- Outlook Anywhere provides the best performance on unreliable or high-latency links. However, it takes roughly twice the bandwidth to move the same amount of data. Take this into consideration when deploying Outlook Anywhere.
- Free/busy times can be configured to be viewable from the Internet, to provide external users access and views to appointment schedules.
- Cached mode can be used to support users accessing Exchange Server across WAN links, saving bandwidth for other network needs such as business application access.
- When deploying Outlook Anywhere, choose to enable Cached mode to simplify the roaming aspect of mail, calendar, and contact information.

CHAPTER 22

Leveraging the Capabilities of the Outlook Web App (OWA) Client

IN THIS CHAPTER

- Understanding Outlook Web App (OWA)
- Using Outlook Web App 2013
- Using the Calendar in OWA
- Using Tasks in OWA
- Using Contacts in OWA
- The Options Page
- Signing Out of OWA 2013

As email communication has become more entrenched in the daily business (and personal) lives of people throughout the world, the ability to *access* their email from alternative locations has stopped being a "want" for users and has become a "need."

Outlook Web App (OWA) has provided this functionality in one form or another since Exchange Server 5.0 and, with each new release, the product has improved in functionality, ease of administration, and ease of use.

The earliest versions of OWA were often criticized as providing a "watered-down" version of the Microsoft Outlook client. These criticisms were justified because these early releases were often lacking the functionality and polish of a full-blown email client. The later versions of OWA, however, have provided a user experience that rivals the full-blown Microsoft Outlook client.

With Exchange Server 2013, one of Microsoft's goals of this release was to provide a web experience that is identical to the full Outlook 2013 client available for Windows. With the release of Exchange Server 2013, Microsoft provides a unified interface in both look and feel as well as in feature parity among the full Outlook client, the web client available across multiple browsers, and client functionality provided to tablet and mobile phone users.

This chapter focuses on providing information for users on both the configuration and use of OWA 2013, including both basic and advanced features. For administrators who want to leverage the Outlook Web App capabilities of administration and management from within OWA, see Chapter 13, "Administering an Exchange Server 2013 Environment."

Understanding Outlook Web App (OWA)

With the release of Exchange Server 2013, Microsoft has attempted to implement new feature sets and functionality into the product, while keeping the interface of the application similar across both the Outlook 2013 installable release of the client as the web client. By maintaining a familiar "look and feel," Microsoft enables organizations to minimize the need to incur the costs of retraining users as they shift from desktop to laptop to kiosk to tablet and mobile phone.

By allowing organizations to provide a full-featured email client to web-based users, Microsoft can simplify the need of organizations in a Bring Your Own Device (BYOD) to work environment where users might not be able to install a client software on a personal system or might not want to install a corporate software application on their personal system.

The OWA 2013 interface is extremely intuitive. Those with any prior experience with OWA or Outlook feel right at home, and those with little to no experience with the product can quickly and easily take advantage of many of the capabilities of the product with little to no formal training.

Multi-Browser Support

Since Exchange 2000 Server, Microsoft has provided two different flavors of the OWA interface with each release of Exchange Server. The Premium user interface enabled clients with recent versions of Internet Explorer to connect with a user experience that was similar to the full Outlook email client in both usability and available features. The Light user interface was available for older versions of Internet Explorer and non-Microsoft browsers. Although the Light version improved with each new revision, it was always several steps behind the Premium version in functionality and was considered by many to be inadequate for regular use.

With the release of Exchange Server 2010, Microsoft made browser support for non-Microsoft browsers like Firefox, Safari, and Google Chrome supported for the Premium OWA experience. And now with Exchange Server 2013, the endpoint browser, regardless of the platform (Windows, Apple, and Linux) or browser type (Internet Explorer, Firefox, Safari, Chrome), provides the same end-user experience.

Leveraging a Common Interface

For those familiar with the full Outlook 2013 client, Outlook Web App in Exchange Server 2013 looks exactly the same, as shown in Figure 22.1.

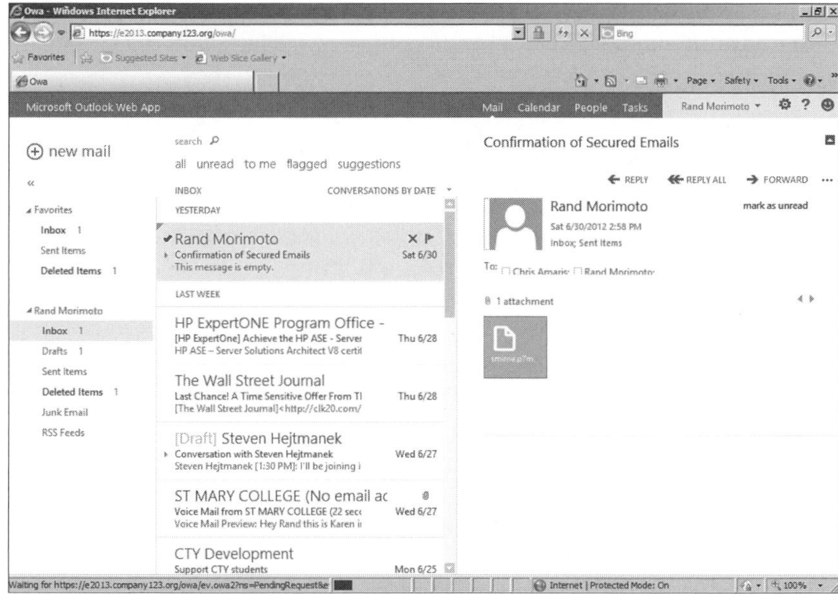

FIGURE 22.1 The Outlook Web App interface.

On the left side, the navigation pane lists the folders in the mailbox. At the top of the navigation pane, OWA 2013 has a Favorites section. The Favorites section is configurable, and users can add their most commonly accessed folders by simply right-clicking them and selecting Add to Favorites. Below the Favorites are the folders in the user's mailbox, things like Inbox, Drafts, Sent Items, and so on.

At the top of the screen are shortcut options to switch between Mail, Calendar, People, and Tasks. These shortcut options are identical to those found in all of the 2013 endpoint clients that allow users to quickly switch from screen to screen.

In the middle of the OWA screen is the view pane that shows the list of messages in the selected folder, collated in the new Conversation view. At the top of the view pane are options to view all messages, unread messages, flagged messages, and the like. This allows for quick and simple organization of messages within a view.

On the right is the reading pane. As with Exchange Server 2010, the reading pane is the place where users can simply view and read messages. However, with Exchange Server 2013, rather than having to double-click to open up a message in a separate web window, a user can preview the message and click Reply, Reply All, or Forward to respond to a message. This feature is common across Outlook 2013 and other versions of the endpoint client and makes managing emails easy for users.

Other common items on the OWA screen include the New Mail option on the far-left side of the screen that allows a user to create a new message. Also in the top middle is the Search function that allows a user to type in keywords and click the Magnifying Glass icon to search his or her mailbox for specific message content.

As with previous versions, the borders between each pane can be adjusted by hovering the mouse over the border until the double arrow appears and then clicking and dragging the border to the desired location.

Using Outlook Web App 2013

Outlook Web App provides a powerful and functional web interface that enables users to access email, calendar appointments, contacts, tasks, notes, and voice mail messages that are stored in their Microsoft Exchange Server mailbox.

Signing In to OWA

For a fresh installation, the uniform resource locator (URL) for OWA is https://*servername*/owa, in which *servername* is the name of the Client Access server (CAS) hosting OWA. The default authentication method, and the one most commonly used, is forms-based authentication (FBA).

Viewing Email Messages

After users sign in to OWA, the user will default to the Inbox folder of his or her mailbox and will see mail messages as well as previews of messages. The user can navigate up and down the mailbox, choosing to view, reply, or forward existing messages or create new messages. With the reading pane, the user no longer has to "open" a mail message in a separate window; instead, just by clicking on or arrowing up and down through messages, the preview of the message is shown.

Messages from other users that have been read have a normal font; messages that have not been read are in a darker, bold font.

Using the Conversation View

Added in Exchange Server 2010 and carried forward into Exchange Server 2013 is the Conversation view, which shows a user the threaded conversation of a message so that if there are several replies and responses to messages, the user does not have to search for the various messages—the user has access to all messages and responses from a single view.

Conversation view thread can also be expanded in the Inbox pane by clicking the arrow to the left of the Subject line. The expanded view, as shown in Figure 22.2, still shows the unread messages in a bold font in both the view and reading panes.

Because the entire conversation is grouped together and treated as a unit, the entire conversation can easily be moved to another folder, deleted, or ignored completely.

Ignoring a Conversation

Users can often find themselves involved in a message thread that no longer applies to or interests them. With the Conversation view, it is simple to opt out of the conversation and no longer view messages in that thread.

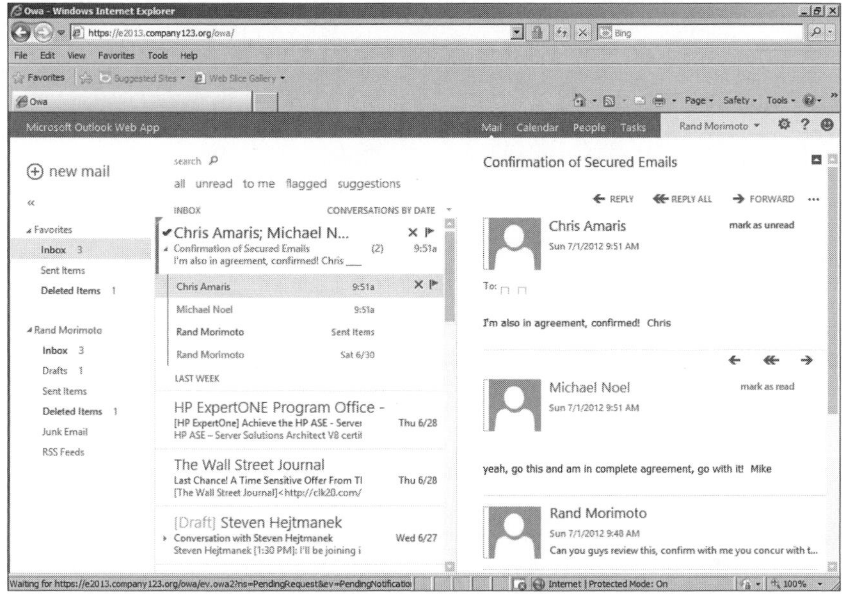

FIGURE 22.2 The Conversation view with thread expanded.

By right-clicking a message or thread and selecting Ignore Conversation, users can effectively elect to mute all messages within that thread. When a user chooses to ignore a conversation, they see a pop-up (as shown in Figure 22.3) notifying them that OWA will delete all the messages in that thread, except for the ones located in the user's Sent Items. Future messages from the thread will be automatically deleted upon receipt. Users might want to leave this check box unchecked, allowing OWA to remind them when they are deleting an entire conversation and not just a single message.

The messages remain in the user's Deleted Items folder, so if the user decides that he wants to review the messages, he can still see them there.

Canceling Ignore Conversation

Of course, there's always the possibility that the user's boss (or his boss's boss) will get involved in the thread and ask for his input. Should this happen, the user might need to get caught up on the previous messages in the thread quickly!

To unmute the message thread, the user can select one of the messages in the thread in his Deleted Items folder, right-click it, and select Stop Ignoring Conversation. This moves all the existing items in the conversation out of the Deleted Items folder and back into his previous location and stops the deletion of new items in the conversation thread.

Creating New Folders

Creating new folders to aid in the organization of mail is a basic task and is as simple as right-clicking on the folder that will house the subfolder, selecting Create New Folder, and naming the folder appropriately.

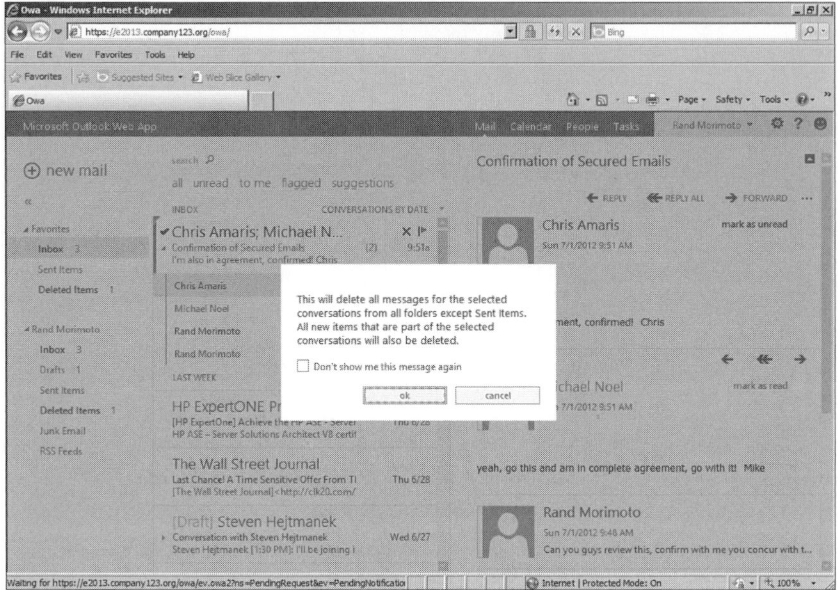

FIGURE 22.3 Warning about ignoring a conversation.

As basic as this sounds, with Outlook Web App, right-clicking is a common option for selecting options with Outlook Web App in Exchange Server 2013.

Customizing the Favorites Folder

The Favorites folder at the top of the navigation pane comes with shortcuts to three default folders: Inbox, Sent Items, and Deleted Items. Users can configure the Favorites shortcuts to suit their particular needs.

Want to add a new folder to the favorites? Right-click the desired folder and select Add to Favorites, or grab the folder and drag and drop it in the Favorites section.

Don't want a folder in the Favorites section? Right-click the folder and select Remove from Favorites.

Want the folders in the Favorites section to show in a different order? Grab the folder you want to move, drag it to the desired location, and drop it.

OWA remembers the user's Favorites, even when the user signs in from another computer. It should be noted that not all items can be added to the Favorites section. Notes, for example, do not have an Add to Favorites option.

Using Filters

OWA 2013 has default filters for viewing messages that include All, Unread, To Me, Flagged, and Suggestions. These filters are a single-click option that allows the user to view

All messages (by default) as well as click Unread messages to show messages that have not been read. This Unread message filter is helpful for users who have folders with a lot of messages and need to find messages that have not yet been read.

The filter "To Me" focuses on messages sent directly to a user, rather than where a user has been Cc'd or Bcc'd in on a message. Typically, messages sent directly to a user invoke the request of a response or are directly informational, but not always. It is a good start in trying to triage a mailbox.

Messages that have been Flagged or are Suggestions further filter messages as being messages that potentially invoke the need of a response.

Searching for Messages

The Search feature in OWA 2013 is very robust in that messages are indexed on the Exchange server and allow for quick lookup of messages for a user. Type the search criteria in the Search Inbox box and click the magnifying glass. If the user wants to change the parameters of the search, the user will find a series of search options that show up in the left pane of the OWA screen, as shown in Figure 22.4.

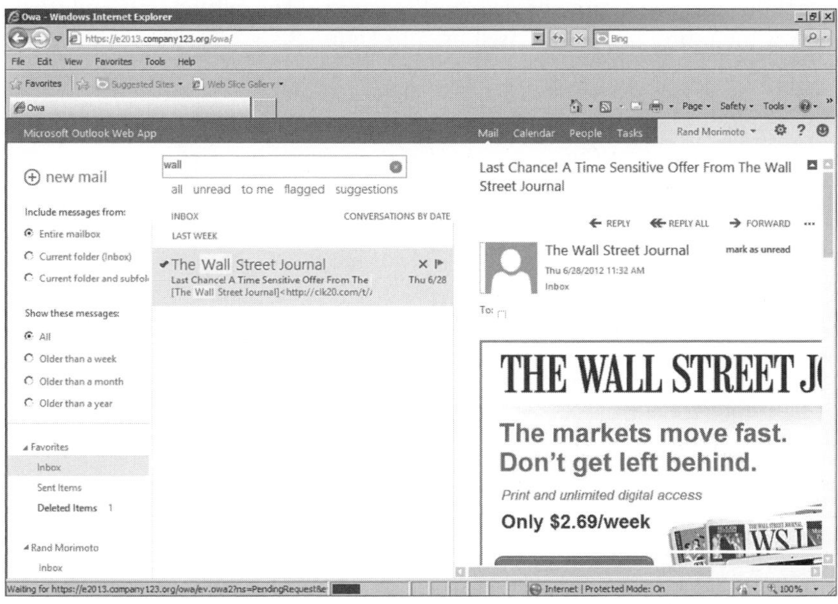

FIGURE 22.4 Searching for messages.

The options include the ability to expand the search to include the current folder and subfolders or the entire mailbox. There are also options to filter searches based on the age of the messages being searched.

Boolean arguments can be used for advanced searches as well—for example, if a user wanted to pull up emails with the words *server* and *specs* but *not CompanyABC*, the user could enter a search for `server +specs -companyabc`.

Using the combination of filters and the Search feature, users can quickly and easily locate messages that they might otherwise have to hunt for manually.

Creating an Email

To create a new email message, navigate to the Inbox view and click the New Mail option in the upper left of the OWA screen. If in the Calendar, People, or Tasks view, the New option on the top of the page creates a new calendar appointment, new contact, or new task.

When creating a new message, it appears in the reading pane. To open the message in its own window, click the Open as a New Window icon in the upper-right corner.

Addressing an Email

When creating a new message, by default, the To and Cc (carbon copy) fields are available for use. If a user wants to Bcc (blind carbon copy) a recipient, the user must click ... at the top of the message next to the Send, Discard, and Insert buttons, which will pull up a menu of other options, including Show Bcc, as shown in Figure 22.5.

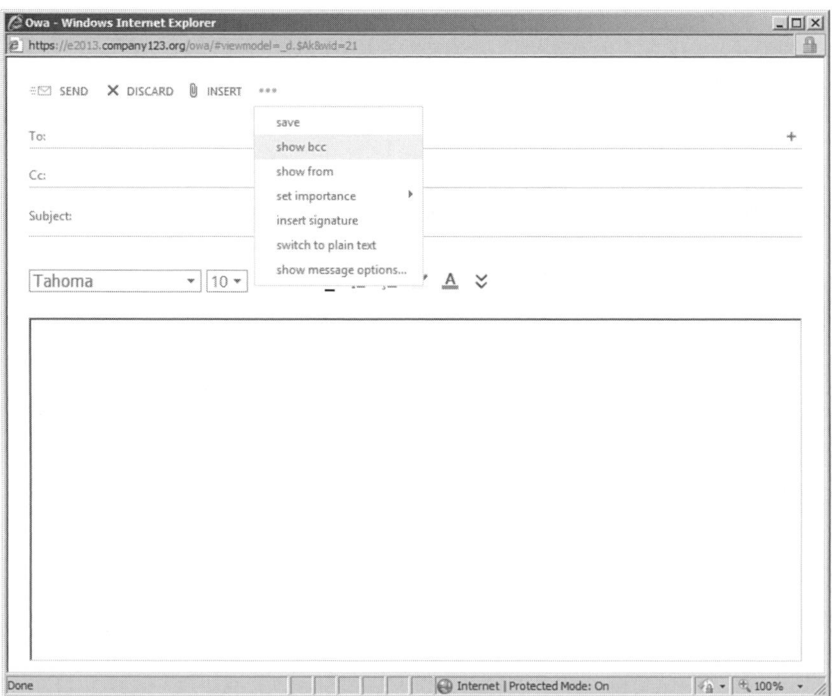

FIGURE 22.5 Adding a blind carbon copy (Bcc) to a message.

Commonly accepted email etiquette for addressing messages is shown here:

- If the message is being sent to only one person, use the To field.
- If the message is being sent to several people:
    - **Populate the To field with the primary recipients**—those to whom the message is directed, who have an action item in the email, or from whom you expect a reply.
    - **Populate the Cc field with secondary recipients**—those who are included for notification purposes only and from whom you do not expect a reply.
    - **Last**—utilize the Bcc field when you want someone to receive a copy of the message but you don't want the other recipients to *know* the person received a copy. If any of the recipients on the To or Cc lines reply to the message, the reply will *not* go to the originally Bcc'd user.

NOTE

Over the years, there have been some uncomfortable situations arising from the use of the Bcc feature. If a Bcc recipient has an auto reply set that is configured to reply to all messages, their mailbox might automatically reply to all the original recipients. Also, users receiving a message in which they were Bcc'd might not *realize* it and might reply to all users by mistake. Either of these situations could show all the users that the original sender had used the Bcc feature.

With the MailTips feature, if users are Bcc'd on an email message and they click Reply All, a MailTip warns users of the action they are about to take.

There are several ways to address an email message. The most basic is to enter the Simple Mail Transfer Protocol (SMTP) email address for the recipient. This is necessary when the user is not inside of your organization's Global Address List (GAL) or within your own Contacts list. The sender can also type in the display name or alias of a user in his organization or Contacts list. Multiple names can be entered into any of the To, Cc, or Bcc fields, as long as they are separated by a semicolon (`;`).

After names or partial names have been entered, the user can click the Check Names button to have OWA check against the GAL to find the closest match. If several matches are available, they will be displayed and the user can click the correct address.

When typing in the name of a previously used recipient, OWA provides a shortcut to the full name.

Adding a Recipient Using the OWA Address Book

With OWA 2003 and earlier, users trying to locate someone in the corporate GAL had to enter a name to search on. If the user did not know how to spell the recipient's name, finding her could be extremely challenging as there was no Browse feature.

Since OWA 2007 and thereafter, Microsoft provides the ability to browse the address book. In addition, it added additional features, such as showing the user's free/busy information in the search results. Prior to this feature, users had to open a new meeting request and add the recipient to the meeting request to view the free/busy information.

The address book can be accessed by opening a new mail message or meeting request and clicking on the To, Cc, or Bcc fields and then the + (plus) to the right of the field. The + opens a Search function that will search an individual's contacts or the global address book. Click the folder icon to the left to change the search scope.

An example of a GAL search in OWA 2013 is shown in Figure 22.6.

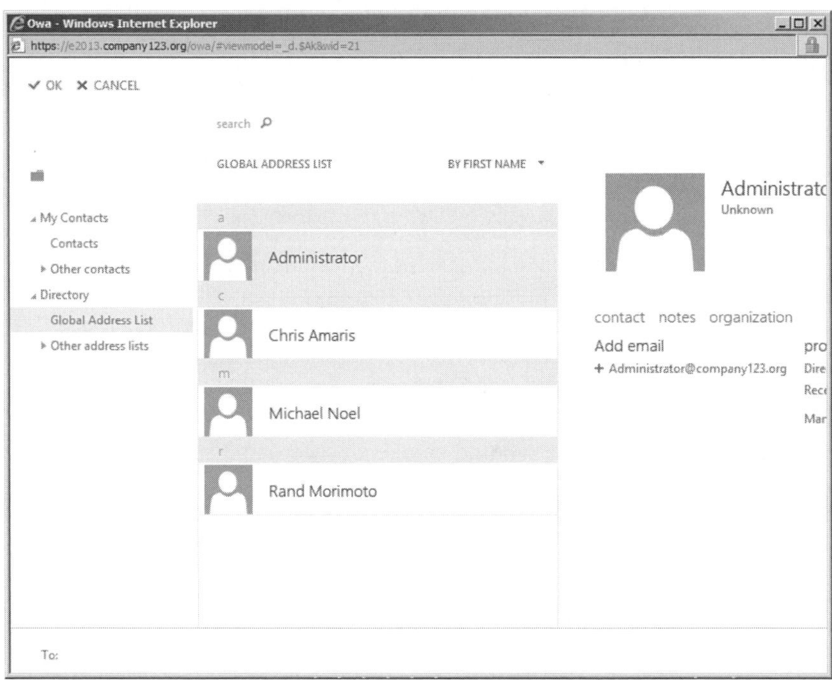

FIGURE 22.6 Searching the Global Address List.

Removing a User from the To, Cc, or Bcc Fields in a Message

If a user finds that he or she has accidentally added an incorrect recipient (or if the user changes his or her mind about a recipient), there is no need to cancel the message. A recipient can be removed from any of the three fields by right-clicking the recipient name or email address and selecting Remove from the available choices, or by highlighting the recipient's name and pressing the Delete key.

Adding Attachments

Email has proven to be an extremely effective tool for sharing documents, spreadsheets, photographs, and other files. By attaching them to email messages, users can distribute files to people anywhere in the world.

Attaching files to an email message is easy to do in OWA; however, users should realize that uploading the file from the local machine to the OWA client can take some time if the file is large, if the users connect via a slow link, or both.

Users should also be aware of any message or attachment size restrictions set by their organization. Also, the message must be smaller than the maximum receive size of the recipient's organization.

To attach a file, perform the following steps:

1. Click the Insert File icon (depicted by a paper clip) on the toolbar at the top of the new message and choose whether to add an attachment or picture inline in the message. The Attachment dialog box opens.
2. Browse to the file to be attached, highlight it, and then click Open.
3. To add additional attachments, click the Insert File icon (paper clip) again and select the desired files.

Configuring Message Options: Importance, Sensitivity, and Tracking Options

When creating a new message, additional options can be applied to the message. These options can be accessed when editing a new message by clicking the ... option to the right of the Send, Discard, and Insert buttons.

Clicking the ... button presents the user with several available settings.

Set Importance

The message can be sent with one of three levels of importance: Low, Normal, or High. By default, messages are marked as Normal. Configuring a message as Low importance causes a down-pointing blue arrow icon to appear to the left of the message when the recipient receives the message. Configuring an email message as High importance attaches a red exclamation mark (!) icon to the message that appears in the message list when the user receives the message.

Setting a level of importance has no impact on the delivery time of the message; it simply creates a visual indicator for the recipient that shows the importance of the message in the opinion of the sender.

Show Message Options

The message option shows sensitivity of the message such as Normal, Personal, Private, and Confidential. Adding a sensitivity setting to a message is a way for the sender to alert the recipient that the information provided in the email is not for general distribution. When a Sensitivity level is set for the message, a visual clue appears at the top of the message (above the Sent and To fields). The Sensitivity setting also appears in the reading pane when the message is highlighted.

As with the Importance option, setting a Sensitivity level is for information only and does not affect the message behavior in any way.

Also within the Show Message Options, the message can be set to Request a Delivery Receipt as well as Request a Read Receipt.

Both the Delivery Receipt and Read Receipt options are requests; both rely on the ability of the recipient's email system to actually generate the requested receipt. Some mail systems (and some users) elect *not* to send receipts of any kind, in effect ignoring the request.

Senders should note that receiving a read receipt does not necessarily ensure the message has been read, as some rules mark messages as Read even though the user has never laid eyes on them or the user might read them without acknowledging receipt.

Other Available Options

When composing an email in OWA, the user can change the font type, size, and color, and apply properties to the font, such as making the text **bold**, *italicized*, or underlined—or ***all of the above***. Users can add bullet points or numbered lists, insert a signature into the message, and perform several other available actions. There are several other options available in the formatting toolbar, and users familiar with Microsoft products will find most of them familiar.

All of the fonts and style options are right within the email message option to be selected when the message is being written.

Sending the Email

When the message has been addressed, the desired Subject line and body have been composed, and any files have been attached, the email can be sent by clicking the Send button at the top of the window. At this time, if there are any issues with the names in the To, Cc, or Bcc fields, OWA presents a dialog box highlighting the names to be resolved. Unresolved recipients can be modified or removed.

After all addresses are resolved, click Send and the message is sent.

Understanding MailTips in OWA

A feature added in Exchange Server 2010 and extended in Exchange Server 2013 is MailTips, as shown in Figure 22.7. A MailTip is automated or configurable information about a mailbox that can help senders decide if they want to send the message or not.

Some examples of an automated MailTip include the following:

- You are blind carbon copied (Bcc'd) on an email and you inadvertently click the Reply All button. MailTips notifies you that Your Address Was Hidden When This Message Was Sent. If You Reply All, Everyone Will Know You Received It.
- You're about to send a message to a fellow employee on a time-sensitive matter. When you enter his name in OWA, you receive a MailTip that this user is out of the office for the next two weeks and will not be checking email. Prior to MailTips, you needed to send the message and then you received an Out of Office reply *before* you knew this information.

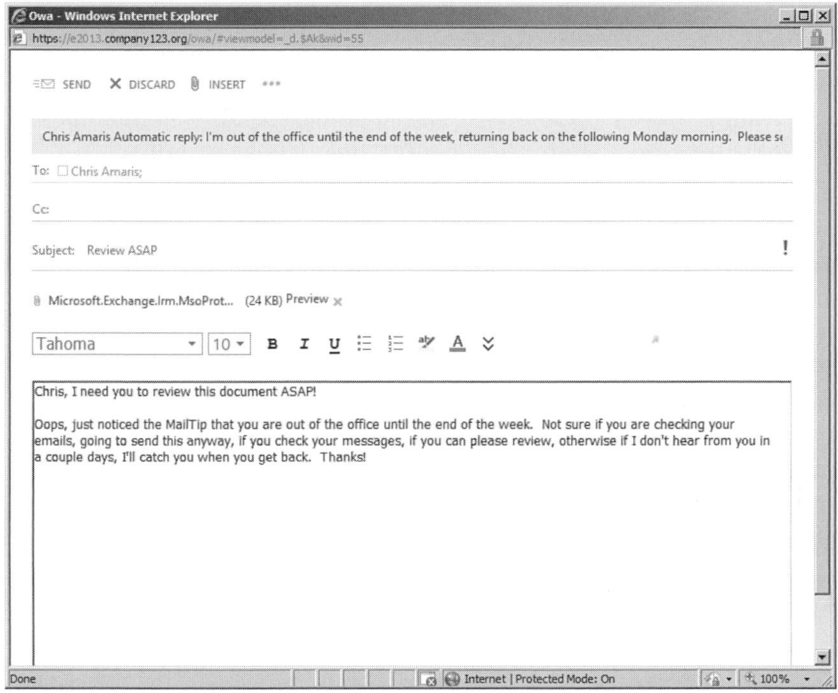

FIGURE 22.7 MailTips notification at the top of the message.

Some examples of a configurable MailTip include the following:

- ▶ You are about to send an email to a distribution list in your organization called SalesPeople@CompanyABC.com. However, you were not aware that this distribution list goes to 2,500 employees worldwide. If a MailTip has been configured for that distribution list, you could be notified of this before you inadvertently send your query to all those people.
- ▶ You are sending to John Doe and are selecting his name from the GAL. However, there are two users named John Doe in the company. When you resolve the name, you get a MailTip that states "I'm in New Orleans—if you want the John Doe in Albuquerque, you've got the wrong man."

These are only a few examples of the possible uses of MailTips in Exchange Server 2013.

NOTE

MailTips are an Exchange Server feature that can be used with Outlook 2010, Outlook 2013, and OWA. Older versions of Outlook (i.e., Outlook 2007 or prior) do not support MailTips.

Reading an Email

When a new message arrives in the user's mailbox, there are visual cues of message receipt. First, a New Message notification pops up and remains for 4 to 5 seconds. Second, the Unread Message Count is incremented, and third, the message appears in the Inbox view as unread (unless the user has rules in place to move the message elsewhere or mark it as Read). During this process, if the system is equipped with audio, an incoming message "chime" is heard.

OWA checks for new messages frequently, and the user does not have to refresh the screen to see them. If a new message arrives that Exchange Server or Outlook has classified as a junk email and placed into the Junk E-Mail folder, the new message pop-up window does not appear.

To read an email, users can select the message with the mouse and view it in the reading pane. Alternatively, users can click the message and in the preview window click the upper-right double box icon, which opens the message in its own window.

Replying to or Forwarding an Email

Users can reply to a message or forward it to other recipients. At the top of the message preview, several choices are available to perform these actions: Reply, Reply All, and Forward, as shown in Figure 22.8.

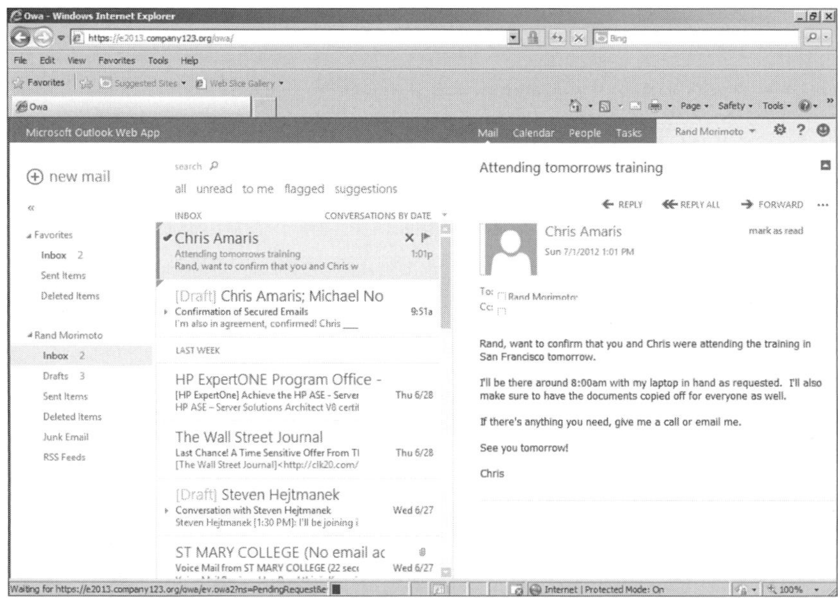

FIGURE 22.8 Reply, Reply All, and Forward options.

- Reply:
    - Represented by a single left-facing arrow.
    - A new email is generated that has the To field preaddressed with the address of the sender of the original message.
    - The original message is included in the body of the new email (at the bottom), and the Subject line is prepended with RE:.
    - Attachments sent in the original email are *not* included in a reply.
- Reply All:
    - Represented by a double left-facing arrow.
    - A new email is generated with the To field preaddressed with the sender of the original message *and* all recipients that were in the To field of the original message. The Cc field is preaddressed with recipients in the Cc field of the original message.
    - The original message is included in the body of the new email (at the bottom) and the Subject line is prepended with RE:.
    - Attachments sent in the original email are *not* included in a Reply All.
- Forward:
    - Represented by a single right-facing arrow.
    - A new email is generated, but no addressing fields are preaddressed.
    - The original message is included in the body of the new email (at the bottom), and the Subject line is prepended with FW:.
    - Attachments sent in the original email *are* included in the Forward.

All these options are also available by clicking a message and seeing the message in the view pane and selecting from the available items.

Marking Messages as Read or Unread

Some users choose to manage the Read status of messages to aid in their message organizing or to remind themselves to follow up on the message. For example, if a user reads a message from her boss stating, "Please contact me regarding this tomorrow," the user might want to leave the message marked Unread so the user can remember to look at it the next day.

To change the status of a message, simply right-click the message and choose Mark as Read or Mark as Unread. If the message is already read, the option to Mark as Unread appears. If the message is unread, the option to Mark as Read appears.

Viewing User Properties

When viewing a message, the recipient can click the sender's name in the Preview view to bring up some information about the sender, or right-click the name and select Details to bring up more information.

When the user Properties page appears, some of the information available includes contact information, email address, organizational information, and other information stored in Active Directory or in Contacts.

If the sender is a member of the user's organization, this information is pulled from Active Directory. If not, any available information is pulled from the user's Contacts list.

The user can be added to the recipient's Contacts by clicking Add. This adds the person to Contacts.

Deleting Email

Due to the implementation of the Conversation view in OWA, deleting a message can be a little trickier than before. Emails can be deleted from the navigation pane by selecting the message and clicking the Delete icon, represented by a big X. Expand the conversation to choose individual messages to delete.

Messages can be deleted from the reading pane as well. Click the ... option and select Delete from the Action menu.

Recover Deleted Items

Deleted items in OWA take on two separate meanings: one being a message that has been deleted from the Inbox or other folder and is sitting in the Deleted Items folder, or a message that has been deleted from the Deleted Items folder and appears to be permanently gone.

In the first case when a message has been deleted from a folder, the message is typically not permanently deleted, and in fact is merely sitting in the Deleted Items folder. By clicking on the Deleted Items folder, a user can see messages that can simply be dragged and dropped back into the Inbox or moved back into another active folder. When a message is moved out of the Deleted Items folder, the message is now available just like any other active message.

In the other case where a message appears to be more permanently deleted, such as the message has been deleted from the Deleted Items folder or the user held down the Shift key when deleting the message (which causes a "permanent" delete), these messages likely can still be recovered. Exchange has what is called a retention policy that enables messages permanently deleted from a user's mailbox to be recovered for a set period of time. The default retention period in Exchange is 14 days (or 30GB of storage)—whichever comes first. So even when a message appears to be permanently deleted out of Outlook and is no longer visible to the user, the message can (usually) be recovered.

To recover a "permanently" deleted message from Outlook Web App 2013, right-click the Deleted Items folder in the folder list (not the Favorites list) and choose Recover Deleted Items. When recovering these messages, users can recover them to a folder of their choice.

NOTE

An organization can change the default retention period, whether for a shorter period of time (so that a permanent deletion is truly permanent) or for a longer period of time (to protect accidental deletion of messages or use as a compliance-driven message retention system). More information is covered in Chapter 12, "Designing and Implementing Message Archiving, Retention, and eDiscovery."

Reading Attachments

When a message arrives with an attachment, the message displays with an Insert File icon (paper clip) next to the Subject line. In the reading pane or in an opened email, attachments appear shown next to the word *Attachments*.

Some attachments, such as executable programs, might be blocked by the security policies of your organization. In addition, some attachments might be removed or blocked by the organization's antivirus software. Bear in mind, these attachments might be blocked or stripped by the policies of the *sender's* organization as well.

Additional restrictions on attachments can be placed by the organization on OWA sessions from public computers. Because opening documents within OWA can potentially leave copies of the file in the accessing computer's pagefile or browser cache, some organizations limit the type of attachments that can be accessed from public computers.

There are several methods available to access attachments:

- **Open the attachment**—Clicking the attachment opens it as a preview. Clicking Download gives the user the option to open or save the attachment. If the user selects Open, OWA attempts to download the file and open it for viewing. For many proprietary file types (Microsoft Office Documents, Adobe .PDF files, and such), the computer must have an application associated with the file type that is capable of opening the attachment. For example, if you choose to open a Microsoft Word document, the computer must have Microsoft Word installed to open the attachment when it is downloaded.

- **Save the attachment**—Clicking Download also gives the option to save the attachment. This option enables the user to save the attachment to a drive on the computer accessing OWA. Users should be extremely cautious because downloading documents onto public workstations could put confidential intellectual property at risk. As previously mentioned, to view the attachment after it has been saved locally, the computer must have an application capable of opening the file.

- **Open as web page**—OWA enables many file types to be opened with a built-in feature called Office Web App. This feature enables OWA to convert supported document types into a viewable file and display them within a browser window. If the document type accessed is supported, beside the attachment name the user can see a link that says Open as Web Page. Clicking this link opens the supported attachment within a browser window for viewing.
- **View thumbnail**—A thumbnail of the attachment shows in the reading pane. For some types of attachments, this might be enough.

Using the Calendar in OWA

Outlook 2013 provides a fully functional calendar for managing personal meeting appointments, group appointments, and recurring events. The Calendar feature in OWA, shown in Figure 22.9, includes the same functionality as the Outlook client, including appointment views, meeting creation, and editing.

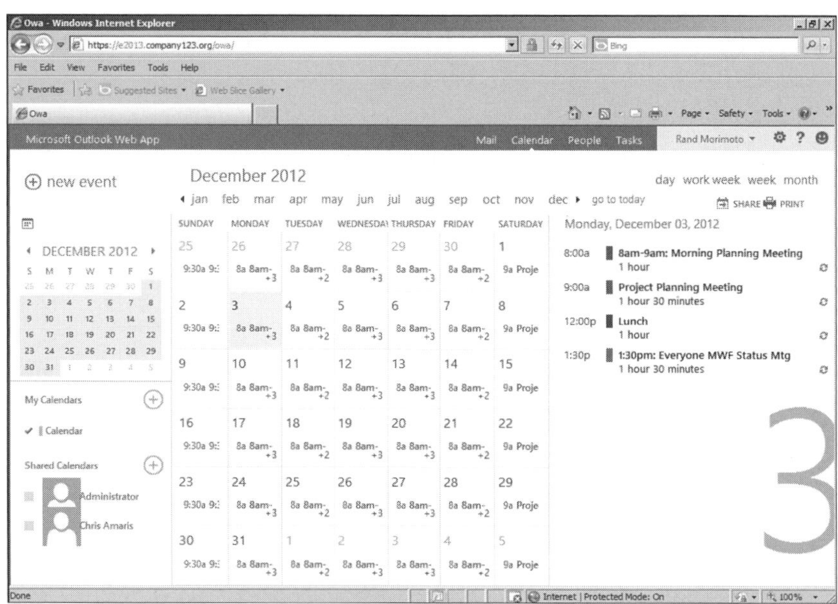

FIGURE 22.9 Viewing the calendar in OWA.

Sharing Your Calendar

OWA 2013 has the ability to share your calendar with others from within OWA. This capability has always been available in the full-blown Outlook client, but had limited support until Exchange Server 2010 and now full support in Exchange Server 2013.

From within the Calendar view, there is a button on the far right of the calendar that expands the Calendar navigation pane. At the bottom of the pane is the Shared Calendar option to open other calendars.

Opening a Shared Calendar

By clicking the + (plus) next to Shared Calendars, the user is prompted with the option to choose another user's calendar to open. When the calendar is selected, the user can see that user's calendar plus other user calendars. Simply clicking on the X button next to the user's name above the calendar, or deselecting the check box next to the user's name, removes the user's calendar from view. Clicking on the check box next to the user's name subsequently shows the user's calendar.

To remove a shared calendar, under Other Calendars, right-click the user's name and select Remove.

Sharing a Calendar

Selecting Share on the far-right side of the OWA screen opens up the option to share your calendar with other users. The user can type the name of the person with whom the user wants to share his or her calendar. By default, the person will share just free/busy information; however, by selecting the box below the name of the person you want to share your calendar with, you can choose Limited Details and Full Details as two additional options. When the Full Details option is selected, the following specifics are shared:

- **Share Availability Only**—Available times are clear on the calendar, but times that are busy are blocked off with no notation of what the individual is doing, other than something is on the calendar at that time slot.
- **Share Limited Details**—The subject of meetings is shown.
- **Share Full Details**—The subject and all information about the meeting are shown.

The recipient receives an email message that enables him to click an icon that states Add This Calendar. Upon clicking the icon, the sender's calendar will be added to the People's Calendar section for the recipient. When selected, the appropriate level of access is available.

Using Views

Users can view their calendars in several different ways. By selecting the appropriate icon in the toolbar, users can select either of the following:

- **Day**—The Day view displays one day at a time. Users can change the day they view by either selecting the desired day from the calendar in the left pane or by clicking the left and right (Previous and Next) arrows under the New icon.
- **Work Week**—The Work Week view displays a full week as defined in the user's Options, Settings, Calendar tab (for example, Mon–Fri).

- **Week**—The Week view displays one week at a time (Sun–Sat).
- **Month**—The Month view shows the entire month with brief information about each of the meetings in each day.

It might go without saying, but as the user changes from one view to the next, if more days are shown, less information about individual meetings might be shown. For the greatest detail, use the Day view and select the desired day from the calendar.

Scheduling Meetings in OWA

When scheduling meetings or appointments in OWA 2013, users can see that little has changed since Outlook 2007—another area where Microsoft already "had it right" and needed little improvement.

When scheduling a meeting, the familiar Scheduling Assistant is there to help. Users can add recipients and/or meeting rooms to their invitations, view the free/busy time for all people and resources, and select a recommended time for the meeting. Attendees can be marked as Required or Optional, which factors in to the attempt to find a free time that works for the largest number of people.

Suggested times are automatically displayed and tell the user how many of the invited people are free at that time (such as "3 of 3 free" or "2 of 3 free") and whether the rooms selected are available.

To schedule a meeting using the Scheduling Assistant, as shown in Figure 22.10, perform the following steps:

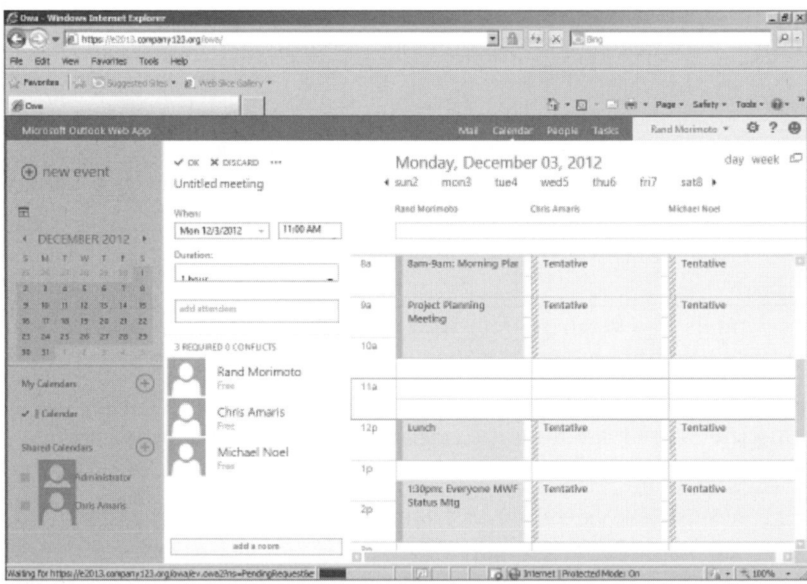

FIGURE 22.10 Using Schedule Assistant to schedule a meeting.

1. From OWA, click the Calendar button and then click the + (plus) button to create a new calendar appointment.
2. Click Invite Attendees and then click the Scheduling Assistant button.
3. Click Add Attendees to add individuals to the schedule.
4. Right-click the individual's name and choose Make Optional if the attendee is intended to be optional.
5. Choose a Suggested Time and Duration that best meets the requirements, and then click OK.
6. Enter the remaining meeting information, including Subject, Location, a Reminder time frame, any details as a body note you want the attendee to have, and so on, and then click Send.

Changing Meeting Times in OWA

To reschedule a meeting in OWA, users can edit the appointment, change the time in the appointment, and send an update. Alternatively, users can simply select the appointment and drag and drop it in the newly selected time slot. The appointment relocates and gives the user the option to Send Meeting Updates or Cancel. If the user selects Cancel, the meeting is returned to its former time.

Receiving Task and Calendar Reminders

Within Outlook Web App in Exchange Server 2013, a dialog box appears listing current reminders. Users can either double-click the item to open it in a new window or click one of the following buttons:

- **Dismiss All**—All reminders shown in the current window will be dismissed. No further reminders for these items will be displayed.
- **Dismiss**—Selecting this button will dismiss the highlighted (selected) item. No further reminders will be displayed for this item.
- **Snooze**—One other option is available. Under the statement Click Snooze to Be Reminded Again In, there is a drop-down box with various time frames. The user can select one of the time frames (the default is the ever-useful "5 Minutes Before Start") and click the Snooze button. Like the Snooze button on an alarm clock, this temporarily dismisses the reminder and allows it to pop up again 5 minutes before the appointment—just in time for the user to attend/dial in promptly.

Using Tasks in OWA

The Tasks option in OWA is like an electronic to-do list, enabling the user to track start dates, due dates, reminders, and associated notes. Tasks can be created, viewed, and organized. In addition, email messages with a Follow Up flag configured appear in the Tasks view as a visual reminder to address the issue.

The Tasks feature is one of the most underutilized of the Outlook and OWA features. Many users simply do not understand how helpful the feature can be and how easy it is to use.

Creating Tasks

Users can create tasks in OWA 2013 just as they do in Outlook. Tasks can remind users of jobs that must be completed by a certain date or time, to document the percentage of a task that has been completed, or to track billable hours and mileage driven for particular clients.

Users can also set reminders on tasks that generate a pop-up message in OWA.

To create a task, follow these steps:

1. Click Tasks from the top of the main OWA page.
2. Click the + New Task button.
3. Enter the subject of the task and populate desired fields such as Due Date or any notes about the task.
4. Click Show More Details to enter in other information about the task, such as completion dates, status, % complete, priority, repetition, and the like.
5. If desired, set a reminder on the task to enable a pop-up reminder in OWA.
6. When finished, click Save.

Task Views

Users can configure the Tasks page, electing to show All Tasks or only those that are Active, Overdue, or Complete. Tasks can be sorted by Due Date, Subject, or several other categories and can have categories assigned to them for easier identification.

In addition, emails that have been flagged for follow-up can be replied to or forwarded from within the Tasks view.

Using Contacts in OWA

The Contacts feature enables users to create a personal address book to keep track of people and their phone numbers, email addresses, physical address, and many other attributes. By entering users into the Contacts list, users can easily send emails and meeting requests to those contacts, populating their addresses in an email message by simply entering their names in the To field. Users can also create personal groups, a collection of recipients from inside and outside the organization.

Creating Contacts

Users can create contacts in OWA 2013 just as they do in Outlook. Contacts can be used at a later date to initiate an email to the person or look up phone numbers or other contact information.

To create a contact, do the following:

1. Click People from the top of the main OWA page.
2. Click the + New Contact button.
3. Enter the First Name and Last Name and click the + (plus) button next to any of the other attribute areas to add in email, phone, IM, work, address, notes, or other fields of information to add.

NOTE

When adding additional field information for phone, work, and so forth, additional fields will become available, such as for phone prompting for whether the phone number being added is a personal phone number, work phone number, mobile phone number or additional information for work would include job title, company, manager, assistant, and so on. Fill in the additional information as desired.

4. When finished, click Save.

Contact Views

Users can configure the People/Contacts page, electing to show all people, groups, personal contacts, Global Address List contacts, and the like. The options for filtering and showing different contacts show up in the left pane where additional directories are accessible.

The Options Page

Starting with Outlook Web Access 2007, Microsoft added an Options page that provided configuration settings and configuration options for OWA. With OWA 2013, the Options page is greatly expanded to include significantly more configuration options to provide similarity between Outlook 2013 and Outlook Web App 2013.

Clicking Options in the upper-right part of the OWA screen (which is exposed by clicking the Setting icon depicted by a gear) opens the Options page. The home view of the Options page is the Account tab.

The Account Tab

In the Account tab, users have access to view/edit their general account information. In addition, there are several shortcuts to other commonly used tasks.

Account Information

In the Account Information section, users can view their existing Display Name, Contact Location, and Contact Numbers. Users can also quickly and easily update particular aspects of their personal contact information, changing their Contact Location and Contact Numbers and storing the updated information in the GAL. This feature enables users to modify their information without requesting assistance from a help desk—a process that is time consuming and prevents the help desk from focusing on more critical tasks. Some of these fields are enabled by default, and modifying which fields are accessible can be accomplished by using the Role Based Access Control (RBAC).

NOTE

The ability of users to edit each of these fields is controlled by using the RBAC. Organizations that do not want users to edit their work phone number (for example) can disable this feature for some or all users.

Shortcuts to Other Things You Can Do

The Account tab also has shortcuts to some specific Help topics and several tasks that users often use.

The shortcut includes Help topics on learning how to connect your mobile phone or device to your account or connecting Outlook to your account, as well as a quick link to change your password, and the like.

The Organize E-Mail Tab

On the Organize E-Mail tab, the user is given the ability to create Inbox rules and configure automatic replies. In addition, users can now request delivery reports for messages that they have sent or received, placing a task in the hands of the user that previously would have required administrative intervention.

Inbox Rules

The first of the available Organize E-Mail utilities is the Organize Your Inbox with Rules link, OWA 2013's interface for creating, editing, enabling, disabling, or deleting mailbox rules.

The Rule Wizard is easy to use, and rules can be created that adhere to many situations. Many of the messaging fields are actionable, allowing rules to be written based on the sender or recipient address, specific words in the subject or body, if the message is marked urgent, if the message has an attachment, and several other options.

Various action items are available, including moving, copying, or deleting the message; marking the message as read; or forwarding or redirecting the message to other users.

Exceptions can be built in to the rule as well, allowing further specificity in the rule creation. The list of possible exceptions is as extensive as the list of previously mentioned possible actionable items.

Users should remember that rules are applied in order. An action item in the first rule might be negated by an action item in a later rule, unless the user has Stop Processing More Rules selected at the end of the rule creation. This was an option in previous versions of OWA but was hidden away under the Perform Other Actions screen and was *not* enabled by default. The default is still to be no enabled, but in Outlook 2013, the action item is shown in the actions screen.

NOTE

With Exchange Server 2013's capability to send and receive text messages, a user can even create a rule that says, "If the Incoming Message Meets These Certain Criteria, Send a Text Message to a Particular Phone Number," an extremely useful tool for users who are often away from their computers.

Automatic Replies

The next item in the Organize E-Mail tab is the Automatic Replies option, which is OWA 2013's version of the Out of Office Assistant. Users can configure automatic replies by either turning on the feature immediately or by configuring a period of time when the automatic replies should start and end.

Users have the option to reply only to senders from inside of their organization or to both internal and external senders. If electing to reply to external senders, there is the further option to reply to *all* external senders, or only those in the users' Contacts lists.

If the users decide to reply to both internal and external senders, the users can then create custom replies for each group. This can be helpful when there is information the users want to share with their co-workers during an absence (such as emergency contact information), but that they do *not* want to share with the rest of the world.

In the early days of automatic replies, administrators had to be on the alert for *mail storms* that could be created by dueling automatic replies. For example, UserA sends a message to 5 people (or 50 people). UserB, one of those recipients, has an automatic reply that replies to all recipients of the message, including UserC. UserC also has automatic replies enabled and sends the message back to UserB. UserB and UserC automatically replying to each other could potentially create thousands and thousands of messages, bringing the messaging system to its knees, before the problem was discovered and shut down.

To prevent this situation (and others like it), Exchange sends only one automatic reply per sender during each out-of-office period.

Delivery Reports

The Delivery Reports option was added to OWA in Exchange Server 2010 and has been a welcome addition. The Delivery Reports option enables users to search for delivery information on messages that they have sent or received during a previous time period.

Users can type the SMTP email address (user@companyabc.com), or click the I've Sent To or I've Received From fields, or choose the user from the GAL by clicking the Add Users button. Multiple addresses can be separated by a comma.

In addition, users can be more specific in their search by looking for messages with specific words in the Subject line.

The Groups Tab

Another area where users can utilize the new self-service tools built in to Exchange Server 2013 is in the Groups tab.

In keeping with Microsoft's concept of enabling users to self-manage basic tasks, the Groups tab enables users to see what Public Groups they are a member of, to join or leave Public Groups that already exist, and to create new Public Groups.

As shown in Figure 22.11, the Groups tab is split into two parts: the Public Groups I Belong To and Public Groups I Own. If the user doesn't have the rights to manage groups, then that column does not appear.

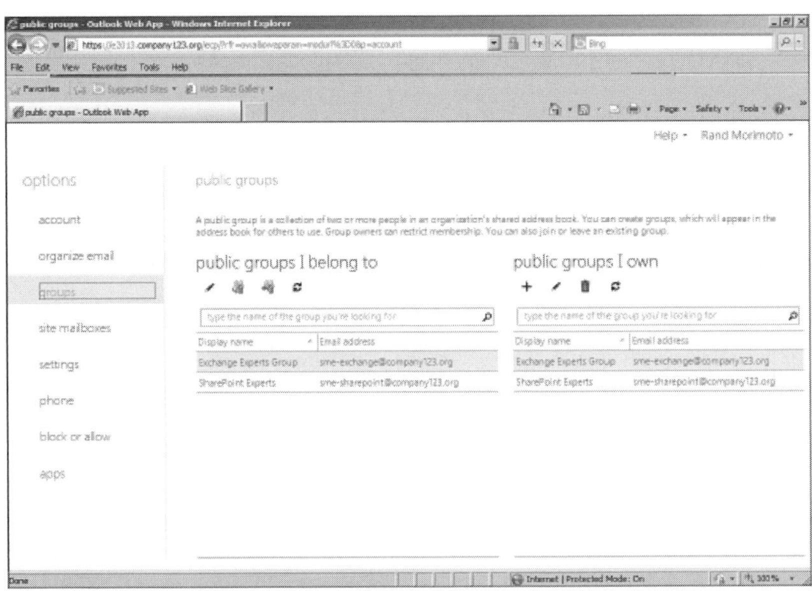

FIGURE 22.11 Public Groups management.

In the Public Groups I Belong To section, users can join or leave a group, search for a group, or view the details of a group.

In the Public Groups I Own section, users can create or delete a group that they own or view/change the details of a group that they own.

To create a new Public Group, do the following:

1. Click the + (plus) button.
2. Enter a Display Name for the group. This is the name that will appear in the GAL and will appear on the To line when an email is sent to the group. This name can be user-friendly so that people can identify the purpose of the group.

3. Enter the Alias. The alias will be part of the group's email address, so it must adhere to the RFC specifications for SMTP addresses. The alias can contain the following:

- Uppercase and lowercase English letters (a–z, A–Z)
- Digits 0 through 9
- Characters ! # $ % & ' * + - / = ? ^ _ ` { | } ~
- Character . (the period) if it is not the first or last character and does not appear two or more times consecutively

NOTE

When given free reign, users often begin their email addresses with a special character so that it appears at the top of the GAL. Of course, after a thousand users have done so, the benefit is lost. Administrators should develop a naming convention for email addresses and enforce it strictly.

4. Enter a description. The Description field can be seen by users when they double-click the alias in an email they are composing. Users should always enter a description that is accurate and thorough.

5. If necessary, modify the Ownership. By default, the creator of the group will be the owner. Users can add other users as owners of the group (and remove them after) if they want.

6. Confirm/modify the Group Membership. By default, group owners will be added as members of the new group. If this is not desired, remove the check mark for that selection. To populate the group with users, click the Add button. Members of the organization can be added to the group by searching and selecting them from the GAL. Alternatively, the group creator can leave the group empty and allow people to add themselves if they want.

7. Set the appropriate setting for Membership Approval. The available options follow:

- **Open**—Anyone can join this group without being approved by the group owners.
- **Closed**—Members can be added only by the group owners. All requests to join will be rejected automatically.
- **Owner Approval**—All requests are approved or rejected by the group owners.

8. Click Save to create the group.

After the group has been created, additional options can be configured. By looking in the Public Groups I Own section, selecting the group, and clicking to edit the group, owners can modify the preceding items or configure any of the following additional settings:

- **Delivery Management**—The default (empty) enables anyone to send to the group, regardless of whether they are members of that group. Users can elect to add individuals or other groups in this field, but only those users can send messages to the group. One common scenario is to select the name of the group; this enables only members of the group to send messages to the group.
- **Message Approval**—By placing a check mark in Messages Sent to This Group Have to Be Approved by a Moderator and adding a user (or users), the group becomes a moderated group in which messages are sent to the moderators for approval *before* being sent to the group members. In addition, when the group becomes moderated, there are three options for what should be done with messages that aren't approved:
    - Notify all senders when their messages aren't approved.
    - Notify senders in your organization only when their messages aren't approved.
    - Don't notify anyone when a message isn't approved.
- **MailTip**—The group owner can create a MailTip that will be displayed when people send email to the group. The MailTip will appear in the InfoBar of senders with Outlook 2010 or later. Although users can enter up to 492 characters in the MailTip field (including Hypertext Markup Language [HTML] tags), only 175 characters (including spaces) will appear in the InfoBar.

When a user addresses an email to the Public Group, he or she can double-click the group name to find out details about the group, including the current members.

NOTE

As with the ability for users to edit their own account information, the ability of users to create and edit Public Groups is managed utilizing the RBAC.

The Settings Tab

On the Settings tab, users can customize their mailbox configuration to suit their own preferences. There are many options available, some of which follow.

Mail

In the Mail section, users can assign an email signature, configure the message format, configure notifications or sounds for new messages, configure the behavior of the reading pane, and modify the behavior of the Conversation view.

Default Signature

Users can configure an email signature that can be manually entered when creating an email or added automatically to all emails the users send. Signatures usually provide personal information about the sender—such as name, company, title, and phone number—allowing the user to configure the information once and have it included in emails without typing it over and over. To configure an email signature, do the following:

1. In the E-Mail Signature area, enter the content of the signature utilizing the editing options available in the toolbar.
2. If desired, select the option to Automatically Include My Signature on Messages I Send.
3. Click the Save button in the lower-left corner.

If the Automatically Include My Signature on Messages I Send option is selected, the signature appears on any messages created from scratch, forwarded, or replied to. If that option is not checked, the user can add the signature on a message-by-message basis when composing an email. To add the signature manually, begin editing a message and then click the ... option and choose Insert Signature.

Message Format

Users can instruct OWA to always show the Bcc and/or From fields when creating a new email message. By showing the From field, users can elect to send the message as an account other than their own. The user *must* have Send As permissions to that other account for this option to work.

Users can also elect to compose new messages in HTML format (the default), or in plain text, and can select the default font they would like to compose messages in.

Message Options

Within Message Options, a user can choose whether a sound plays when a new item arrives, whether a notification is displayed when a new item arrives, whether to empty the Deleted Items folder when exiting Outlook, or to warn whether a sent message is missing an attachment.

Read Receipts

By default, OWA is configured to ask the user before sending a response to a read receipt request. Users can change this default behavior by selecting Always Send a Response to automatically respond to these requests, or Never Send a Response to stop prompting the user to determine if he or she wants to allow the read receipt to go out.

Reading Pane

The default behavior of the reading pane can be configured in this section, enabling users to select under what circumstances they want messages marked as Read.

If the user selects Mark the Item Displayed in the Reading Pane as Read, the user can then configure the default wait period that states how long the item must be viewed in the reading pane before being marked as Read.

Users can also elect to Mark the Item as Read When the Selection Changes, the default behavior in OWA. When users have a message in the reading pane and then change to another message, the one they were reading gets marked as Read.

Lastly, the user can elect to Don't Automatically Mark Items as Read. This option requires the user to manually mark the item as Read or the message will be marked as Read when the message is actually opened and viewed.

Conversations

The last of the configurable items in the Mail tab is the Conversations feature. Users can elect whether they want messages in the reading pane sorted with the Newest Message on Top (the default setting) or the Newest Message on Bottom.

Users can also select how to sort the messages in the List view in an expanded conversation: either Match the Sort Order of the Reading Pane (default) or Show the Conversation Tree.

Lastly, users can elect to Hide Deleted Items in the Conversation view.

Calendar

The appearance of the calendar can be modified here, including setting the days of the week and hours of the day that are the normal working hours for the user. Accurately setting these options helps ensure others will not schedule meetings during the user's regular time off.

Users can configure the behavior of their Reminders and the Automatic Processing of Meeting Requests here as well.

Two additional calendar option features include Text Messaging Notifications and a Calendar Troubleshooting utility.

Text Messaging Notifications

The user can elect to set up Text Messaging Notifications, which involves selecting the Locale (country or region that his mobile phone is registered in) and Mobile Operator (company that provides the user's cell phone service). Next, the user enters the telephone number for his or her cell phone, including area code.

A six-digit passcode will be generated and sent to the user's cell phone. Upon receipt, that passcode is entered into OWA to finalize the setup. After Text Messaging Notifications have been configured, the user can opt to receive SMS text messages when the calendar is updated, when meeting reminders are triggered, or when receiving messages that contain her daily calendar agenda.

Calendar Troubleshooting Utility

There are as many different ways to use the calendaring capabilities of Exchange Server as there are users. With so many available options, sooner or later many users find their calendar is not acting as they feel it should. With the Calendar Troubleshooting utility, OWA can access the users' calendar logs. Users can enter the subject of the meeting they have a question about and click Send My Calendar Logs, and Exchange Server will locate the logs associated with that meeting request and contact the users when complete.

Regional Settings

In the Regional Settings section, users can configure their preferred language, date format, time format, and current time zone. As remote users travel to different regions, they can easily update their configuration with their current time zone, displaying message delivery times and calendar items in the appropriate time for their location.

Password

In the Password section, as you would expect, users are presented with the option to change their password.

Changing the password requires three common steps. The user enters his old (current) password, enters a new password, and then enters the new password a second time to confirm the new password. By typing the password twice, the chance that the user mistyped the password is greatly reduced.

Click Save to update the password.

The Phone Tab

Under the Phone tab, the user can manage mobile devices that are configured to synchronize with Exchange Server via ActiveSync and configure text messaging.

Mobile Phones

In the Mobile Phones section, users can view the devices that are configured to synchronize with their Exchange Server account, delete configured devices, display their recovery password, or initiate a remote device wipe or a block on a misplaced phone.

The page also displays the Last Synch Time and Status of the mobile device. The status includes information such as the date and time when the first sync occurred, the date and time of the last successful sync, the Device ID, and the User Agent.

Text Messaging

In the Text Messaging section, users can turn on notifications for enabled devices and configure Calendar and E-Mail Notifications.

Calendar Notifications

The configurable options in this section include sending notifications by text message, whether to send messages only during working hours, notifications of meeting reminders, and when daily calendar agendas should be sent.

New Inbox Rule Notifications

The E-Mail Notifications page enables the user to configure rules to send text notifications when certain messages arrive using Inbox rules.

The Block or Allow Tab

On the Block or Allow tab, users can configure their Junk E-Mail settings. Users can elect to disable their junk email filtering altogether by selecting Don't Move Mail to My Junk

E-Mail Folder; with unsolicited bulk e-mail (UBE) constantly on the rise, few users are likely to elect to do so.

When the Automatically Filter Junk E-Mail option is selected (which is the default), users can add email addresses or domains to the Safe Senders and Recipients section, formerly known as the Safe Senders list. Configuring this option enables messages from the listed senders to bypass the junk email filters. This practice is also known as *whitelisting*.

There is also the option to Trust E-Mail from My Contacts. When this option is selected, emails from addresses in the user's Contacts list are automatically whitelisted and bypass the junk email filters.

Users can also add email addresses or domains to the Blocked Senders list. Configuring this option automatically sends mail from the listed senders straight to the Junk E-Mail folder, regardless of the content. This practice is also known as *blacklisting*.

Lastly, there is a check box that states Don't Trust E-Mail Unless It Comes from Someone in My Safe Senders and Recipients List or Local Senders. This option is the most restrictive of the Junk E-Mail options. With this option selected, only mail from local senders and trusted senders will be processed. All other messages go directly to the Junk E-Mail folder.

Apps

New to Exchange Server 2013 are apps that are add-ins to Exchange Server 2013. These apps enhance the Exchange Server 2013 experience for users such as embedding Bing Maps, dictionaries, social media connectors, and the like. The apps extend the out-of-the-box capability of Exchange to support functionality not embedded in Exchange. As an example, the Bing Maps app provides an integrated mapping function so that when someone opens a contact with an address and wants to map the location of the contact and possible directions on how to get to the contact's location, Exchange Server 2013 along with the Bing Maps app can help facilitate that need directly within Exchange.

The Office.com app store has apps being added for support of Exchange Server 2013 being developed as third-party applications.

Getting Help

As with all Microsoft applications, information on how to use the product is available by clicking the Help button. The Help button is a question mark (?) and is located in the upper-right portion of the Mailbox page or is a link and drop-down on the Options page.

The Help feature is a web-based feature and delivers information through a pop-up window. Users might need to make adjustments to their Internet Explorer settings to use the feature. Adding http://help.outlook.com to the allowed sites in the pop-up blocker (if enabled) and adding http://help.outlook.com as a trusted site within Internet Explorer should do the trick.

The Help pages provide information on features and step-by-step instructions for performing tasks, such as Create a Message, Search for an Item, and Learn About Inbox Rules.

Opening Another User's Inbox or Mailbox

There are several reasons why one user might need access to the data stored in another mailbox: Administrators who are troubleshooting delivery issues, administrative assistants who are gathering information for their bosses, or even a user accessing a "shared" team mailbox.

Opening Another User's Mailbox

As in OWA 2007 and 2010, OWA 2013 enables users who have the appropriate permissions to open another user's mailbox, granting access to his Inbox, calendar, deleted items, and so on.

To open another user's mailbox with OWA, perform the following steps:

1. In the primary OWA window, in the upper-right corner, click the display name to bring up the Open Another Mailbox window.
2. Type the display name, alias, or SMTP email address of the mailbox that is to be opened and press Enter to resolve the name. Ensure the name has resolved successfully (the font will change colors and become underlined), and then click Open.

NOTE

If the user has not been granted the appropriate permissions, the user receives an error. See the upcoming "Granting Full Access to a Mailbox" section. Also, the browser window will open the requested mailbox, granting access to all of the target folders.

Granting Full Access to a Mailbox

Before a user can access another user's mailbox from within OWA, that user must be granted Full Access to the target mailbox. By granting Full Access, the user can open and read the contents of the target mailbox but cannot send as the mailbox without additional permissions.

To grant Full Access, an Exchange administrator needs to go into the Exchange Administration Center to delegate full access permission to a user's mailbox. To do so, follow these steps:

1. As an Exchange administrator, log on to the Exchange Administration Center (https://{*servername*}/ecp).
2. Click the recipient for which you want to give someone else access to this recipient's mailbox.
3. Click Edit to edit the recipient.
4. Click Mailbox Delegation.
5. Scroll to the bottom of the page and under Full Access Permission, click the + (plus) button.

6. Enter the name of the individual to whom you want to give full access permission to this mailbox, and then click OK.
7. Click Save.

To grant Full Access from the Exchange Management Shell, do the following:

1. Run the following command to add the Full Access permission directly to the mailbox:

   ```
   Add-MailboxPermission "Mailbox" -User "Trusted User" -AccessRights FullAccess
   ```

   Mailbox is the alias for the mailbox modified and Trusted User is the alias for the user being granted full access.

   Example:

   ```
   Add-MailboxPermission "chris" -User "rand" -AccessRights FullAccess
   ```

   would grant user "rand" full access and the ability to open mailbox "chris."
2. View the results in the Exchange Management Shell and ensure Full Access permissions were granted.

Signing Out of OWA 2013

Just as users sign in to OWA instead of log on, they now sign out instead of log off. The Sign Out link is located at the upper-right corner of the screen, revealed by clicking the name of the Signed In user.

After clicking Sign Out, a screen appears to remind the user to close all browser windows. Users should be trained to always close all browser windows when they finish with an OWA session.

Summary

Exchange Server 2013 Outlook Web App is the most powerful and capable OWA client to date. With each new version, Microsoft adds capabilities that improve collaboration and make the product easier to use, and OWA 2013 is no exception.

Exchange Server 2013 supports Google Chrome and Mozilla Firefox with full functionality as the standard default option. With better cross-platform and cross-browser support for various endpoints, OWA is positioned to meet the needs of more and more users. In addition, there are enhancements in OWA 2013 that make the product, in ways, more powerful than prior versions of Outlook.

Best Practices

The following are best practices from this chapter:

- Modify the Options settings for turning on or off the Conversation view, reading pane, email notifications, and other functions to suit your needs.
- Customize the favorites pane to quickly access folders that are of most interest and used on a day-to-day basis.
- Get familiar with the Scheduling Assistant. Proper use makes scheduling meetings significantly easier.
- Take advantage of the MailTips feature and apply MailTips to large distribution lists, lists that contain external members, and users with similar names to show where they are located.
- Use the preview pane to quickly reply and forward messages instead of having to always open a separate message window for accessing messages.
- Take advantage of email retention policies to keep (or truly permanently delete) messages off Exchange.
- Use the Tasks feature for quick and simple reminders, notes, or to-do items.

CHAPTER 23

Mobility and Mobile Device Support in Exchange Server 2013

IN THIS CHAPTER

- Understanding Mobility Enhancements in Exchange Server 2013
- Enabling ActiveSync in Exchange Server 2013
- Securing Access to ActiveSync with Secure Sockets Layer (SSL) Encryption
- Enabling Offline Outlook Web App (OWA) in Exchange Server 2013

Microsoft Exchange Server 2013 was specifically designed to expand beyond the traditional boundaries that previously defined the messaging experience. No longer are users limited to receiving and responding to messages while in the office. Today's fast-paced information society requires more immediate capabilities of gaining access to mail data, enabling information workers to get anytime, anywhere access to their messages.

Exchange Server 2013 greatly enhances the capabilities of information workers to stay in touch, through enhancements to the ways that they receive and respond to emails. Exchange now allows for an unprecedented seamless integration between handheld mobile devices such as iPhones, iPads, Android devices, and Windows Phone, through an improved Exchange ActiveSync application and through the addition of features such as Offline OWA support and new Outlook Web App (OWA) graphical user interfaces (GUIs) that provide a more appropriate level of visible columns based on the type of device: one column for smartphones, two columns for tablets, and three columns for mouse-based user interfaces.

This chapter covers the details of deploying Microsoft Exchange ActiveSync with Exchange Server 2013 and Windows Phone devices. Step-by-step examples of ActiveSync deployments are outlined, and varying approaches are compared.

Understanding Mobility Enhancements in Exchange Server 2013

Microsoft Exchange ActiveSync is a technology that allows information workers to gain access to their messaging data, calendaring, and other information from a handheld device. ActiveSync works by tunneling the data over Hypertext Transfer Protocol (HTTP), the same one used for web traffic on the Internet.

Using ActiveSync in an Exchange Server 2013 environment gives organizations unparalleled control over the management of the remote devices and over their security, allowing for lost or stolen devices to be wiped and enforcing policies that require encryption of data and passwords to be used.

Outlining the History of Exchange Mobility Enhancements

ActiveSync was originally released as an add-on product to Exchange 2000 Server known as Mobile Information Server (MIS). MIS was the first foray Microsoft had into syncing handheld devices and saw limited deployment.

Exchange Server 2003 was the first release of the Exchange messaging platform that included built-in ActiveSync functionality, though it had to be enabled in a separate step. The first versions of the software in 2003 did not support automatically pushing emails out to the handhelds, with the exception of a concept called Always Up to Date that would notify the device via a short message service (SMS) text message. The device would then dial in and sync. This was time and battery consuming and costly.

Service Pack 2 (SP2) for Exchange Server 2003 introduced the concept of Direct Push technology, similar to BlackBerry style technology, where messages were automatically pushed out to a handheld as they were received. This improvement was warmly received.

At the same time, Windows Mobile, the handheld operating system formerly known as Windows CE and Pocket PC, was evolving. The Messaging Security and Feature Pack (MSFP) for Windows Mobile 5.0 allowed for built-in, file-level encryption for the devices, and integrated them with 2003 SP2's abilities to provision and deprovision devices over the air.

Exchange Server 2013 expands even further beyond the original ActiveSync technology, allowing for other improvements, such as the ability to automatically configure a handheld, encrypt connections, reset passwords, view file data, and integrate more seamlessly with non-MS ActiveSync devices such as iOS and Android devices.

In addition, Exchange Server 2013 greatly expands on Outlook Web App (OWA) access on mobile devices through the use of OWA in Offline mode, which allows for users to access their email on HTML5-enabled browsers on mobile devices and to view and respond to older messages while offline, syncing the changes back up to the server.

Exploring Exchange ActiveSync

Exchange ActiveSync is a service that runs on a Client Access server (CAS) in an Exchange Server 2013 topology. It uses the same website that other HTTP access methods to

Exchange use, such as Outlook Web App and Outlook Anywhere. As is the case with those services, it uses its own virtual directory, named Microsoft-Server-ActiveSync.

Because it uses the HTTP/HTTPS protocol, which is the same as OWA does, ActiveSync can be designed using the same CAS considerations that OWA and Outlook Anywhere do. In most cases, it is deployed as an ancillary service to these offerings. In any case, when it is deployed, it becomes a vital service to the organization.

Enabling ActiveSync in Exchange Server 2013

In Exchange Server 2013 ActiveSync, the application itself has become more integrated with the rest of Exchange functionality. After the CAS role has been installed on a server, the server supports ActiveSync. That said, several configuration steps can be taken to improve and streamline ActiveSync access, per Microsoft best practices.

Working with ActiveSync Settings in the Exchange Administration Center

Many of the ActiveSync settings and other mailbox settings can be modified within the Exchange Administration Center (EAC), as shown in Figure 23.1. The console allows for ActiveSync to be enabled, disabled, or for individual ActiveSync settings to be modified on individual mailboxes.

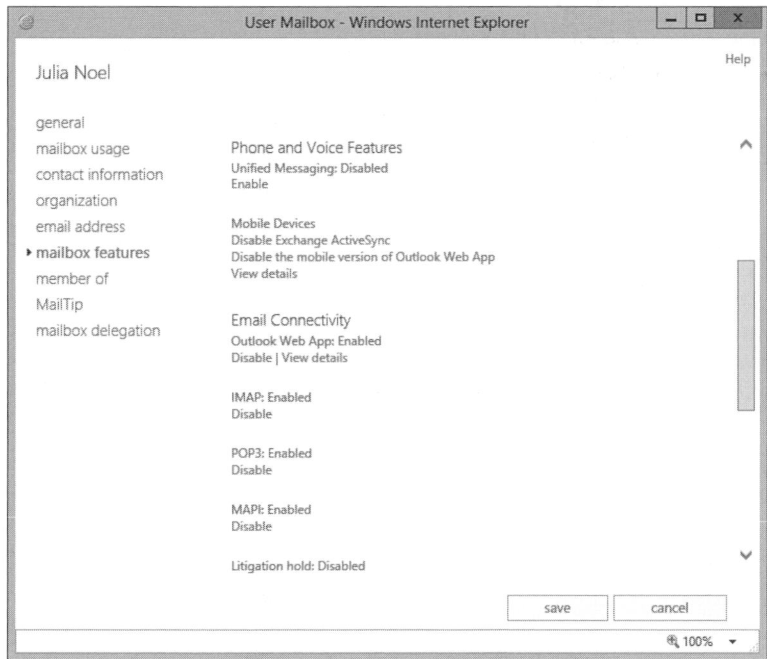

FIGURE 23.1 Administering mailbox settings for ActiveSync.

Configuring Per-User ActiveSync Settings

Individual mailbox settings can be configured for ActiveSync in the Mailboxes tab under Recipients in Exchange Admin Console in the console pane, shown in Figure 23.1. Enabling and disabling ActiveSync on an individual mailbox can be controlled from here, as well as the ability to add a mailbox to a specific ActiveSync mailbox policy.

Selecting an individual mailbox and choosing Edit invokes the Properties dialog box. Choosing the Mailbox Features tab allows for Exchange ActiveSync to be enabled or disabled for that particular mailbox.

Securing Access to ActiveSync with Secure Sockets Layer (SSL) Encryption

Exchange Server 2013 ActiveSync by default uses the more secure transport protection mechanism known as Secure Sockets Layer (SSL) encryption.

SSL provides a form of authentication that can be sent across the Internet, as it is encrypted using Public Key Infrastructure (PKI) certificates, which work through the principle of shared-key encryption. PKI SSL certificates are widely used on the Internet today, any website starting with an https:// uses them, and the entire online merchant community is dependent upon the security of their systems.

For ActiveSync, the key is to install a certificate on the server so that the traffic between the device and the server is protected from prying eyes. There are effectively two options to this approach as follows:

- **Use a third-party certificate authority**—A common option for many organizations is to purchase a certificate for ActiveSync (and other Exchange HTTP access methods such as OWA) from a third-party trusted certificate authority (CA), such as VeriSign, Thawte, or others. These CAs are already trusted by a vast number of devices, so no additional configuration is required. The downside to this option is that the certificates must be purchased and the organization doesn't have as much flexibility to change certificate options.
- **Install and use your own certificate authority**—Another common approach is to install and configure Windows Server 2003/2008/2012 Certificate Services to create your own CA within an organization. This gives you the flexibility to create new certificates, revoke existing ones, and not have to pay immediate costs. The downside to this approach is that no browsers or mobile devices will recognize the CA, and error messages to that effect will be encountered on the devices unless the certificates are trusted.

Each of these options is outlined in the subsequent sections of this chapter.

Installing a Third-Party Certificate Authority for ActiveSync Certificates

If a third-party certificate authority will be used to enable SSL on a CAS, a certificate request must first be generated directly from the CAS. After this request has been generated, it can be sent to the third-party CA, who will then verify the identity of the organization and send it back, where it can be installed on the server.

When deciding which CA to use, keep in mind that most mobile devices automatically trust the certificate authorities of the following organizations:

- VeriSign
- Thawte
- GTE CyberTrust
- GlobalSign
- RSA
- Equifax
- Entrust.net
- Valicert
- Go Daddy

If an internal CA will be utilized, this section and its procedures can be skipped, and you can proceed directly to the subsequent section titled "Using an Internal Certificate Authority for OWA Certificates."

To generate an SSL certificate request for use with a third-party CA, you can create a certificate from the Exchange Management Shell using the New-ExchangeCertificate applet, or you can create the request directly from the Exchange Administration Center Certificate Generation Wizard. Both options allow for the creation of Subject Alternative Name (SAN) entries in the certificate, allowing the Exchange server to impersonate multiple fully qualified domain names (FQDNs), such as mail.companyabc.com, autodiscover.companyabc.com, activesync.companyabc.com, and so on.

After the certificate request has been generated, the text file, which will look similar to the one shown in Figure 23.2, can then be emailed or otherwise transmitted to the certificate authority via its individual process. Each CA has a different procedure, and the exact steps need to follow the individual CA's process. After an organization's identity has been proven by the CA, it will send back the server certificate, typically in the form of a file, or as part of the body of an email message.

The certificate then needs to be installed on the server itself. If it was sent in the form of a `.cer` file, it can simply be imported easily via the wizard or PowerShell. If it was included in the body of an email, the certificate itself needs to be cut and pasted into a text editor such as Notepad and saved as a `.cer` file. After the `.cer` file has been obtained, it can be installed on the CAS using the Get-ExchangeCertificate applet.

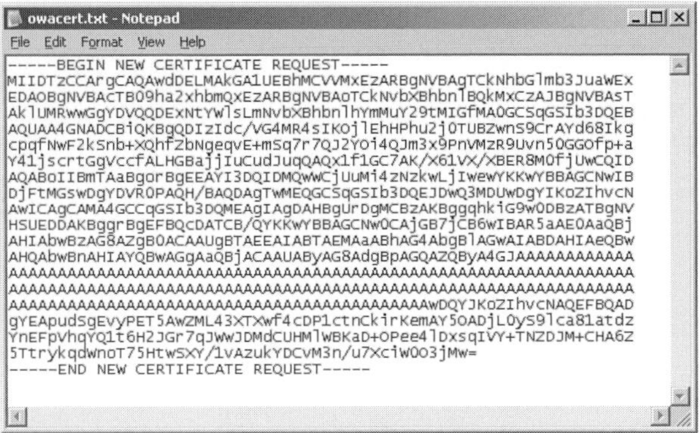

FIGURE 23.2 Viewing a certificate request file.

Using an Internal Certificate Authority for OWA Certificates

If a third-party certificate authority is not utilized, an internal CA can be set up instead. There are several different CA options, including several third-party products, and it might be advantageous to take advantage of an existing internal CA. Windows Server 2008 also has a very functional CA solution built in to the product, and one can be installed into an organization.

CAUTION

Proper design of a secure PKI is a complex subject, and organizations might want to spend a good amount of time examining the many factors that can influence CA design. This sample scenario assumes a very basic design, with an enterprise CA installed directly into a domain. Most enterprise CAs will want to consider a standalone root CA and a second or even third tier of intermediate and issuing enterprise CAs, depending on the organization.

The following types of CAs are available for installation:

- **Root CA**—An enterprise root CA is the highest level CA for an organization. By default, all members of the forest where it is installed trust it, which can make it a convenient mechanism for securing OWA or other services within a domain environment. Unless an existing enterprise root CA is in place, this is the typical choice for a homegrown CA solution in an organization. Best practice dictates that this server be installed on a Workgroup member server, rather than a domain-joined one, and that the server be shut down when not in use.
- **Subordinate CA**—An enterprise subordinate CA is subordinate to an existing root CA and must receive a certificate from that root CA to work properly. In certain large organizations, it might be useful to have a hierarchy of CAs, or the desire might exist to isolate the CA structure for OWA to a subordinate enterprise CA structure. A subordinate CA can also be made to be an enterprise CA, which allows it to automatically distribute certificates to users and computers, via a process called autoenrollment. Enterprise CAs are typically domain-joined systems.

After the internal CA is in place, the Exchange environment can automatically use it for generation of certificates. After being placed on a server, SSL encryption will be made available on the CAS. If the enterprise CA was installed in an Active Directory domain, all of the domain members will include the internal CA as a trusted root authority and connect to OWA via SSL with no errors. External or nondomain members, however, will need to install the enterprise CA into their local trusted root authorities. This includes Windows Mobile devices as well.

Installing a Root Certificate on a Mobile Device

If a third-party or self-generated certificate authority is used for ActiveSync, the mobile device must be configured to trust that CA. If the mobile device is not configured like this, it will error out as it will not trust the CA that issued the certificate.

For Windows desktops and laptops, this task is relatively straightforward, and involves simply installing the enterprise root CA for this third-party certificate into the Trusted Root Certificate Authority group for the machine. For other mobile devices, however, the enterprise root certificate must first be exported to a `.cer` file, which then needs to be copied physically to the device, either via a memory card or with ActiveSync. To export out the root certificate to a file that can be distributed to end users to be trusted, use the following procedure:

1. Click the Details tab.
2. Click the Copy to File button.
3. In the Certificate Export Wizard, click Next on the Welcome screen.
4. Select to export the certificate into a DER encoded binary form. Click Next to continue.
5. Enter a filename for the `.cer` file, and click Next.
6. Click Finish upon completion of the wizard.

Creating ActiveSync Mailbox Policies

Creating a new ActiveSync mailbox policy in Exchange Server 2013 is not a complex task. To do so, follow these steps:

1. From the Exchange Administration Center, expand Mobile, and then click Mobile Device Policies.
2. Click the Plus (+) symbol to add a new policy.
3. Enter a descriptive name for the policy, such as **`Manager's ActiveSync Mailbox Policy`**. Set password settings, such as that shown in Figure 23.3, select the settings needed, and click Save.
4. Click Finish.

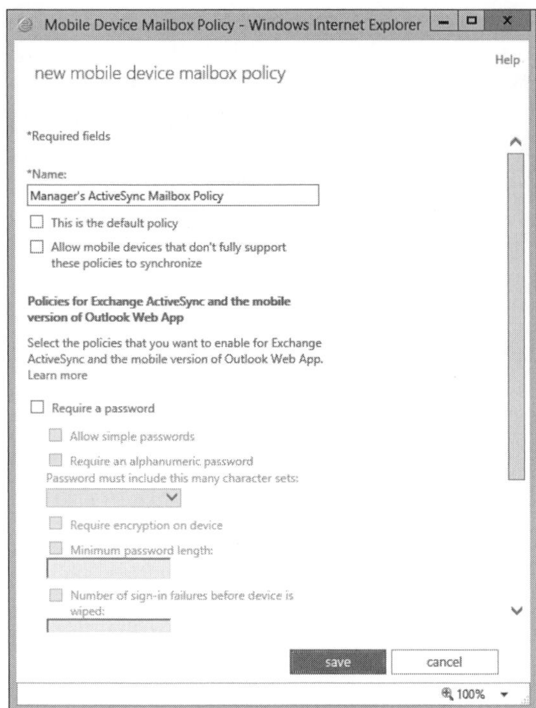

FIGURE 23.3 Creating an ActiveSync mailbox policy.

Applying Mailbox Policies to Users

After a specific policy has been created, it can be added to mailboxes, either during the provisioning process or after the mailbox has already been created. For existing mailboxes, perform the following steps:

1. From the Exchange Administration Center, click on Recipients, select the Mailboxes tab, select the recipient, and then click the Edit icon.
2. Click on Mailbox Features.
3. Under Mobile Devices, click View Details.
4. Click the Browse button and select the desired ActiveSync policy, which should then display something similar to what is shown in Figure 23.4.
5. Click Save to save the changes.

Adding multiple mailboxes to a specific mailbox policy is best done from the PowerShell console.

Wiping and Resetting ActiveSync Devices

One of the advantages to Exchange Server 2013's ActiveSync is the optimized management capabilities available. With ActiveSync and a supported mobile client, passwords can be reset remotely, and devices can be wiped clean of data in the event that they are lost or stolen. This concept allows an organization to deploy ActiveSync without fear of data compromise.

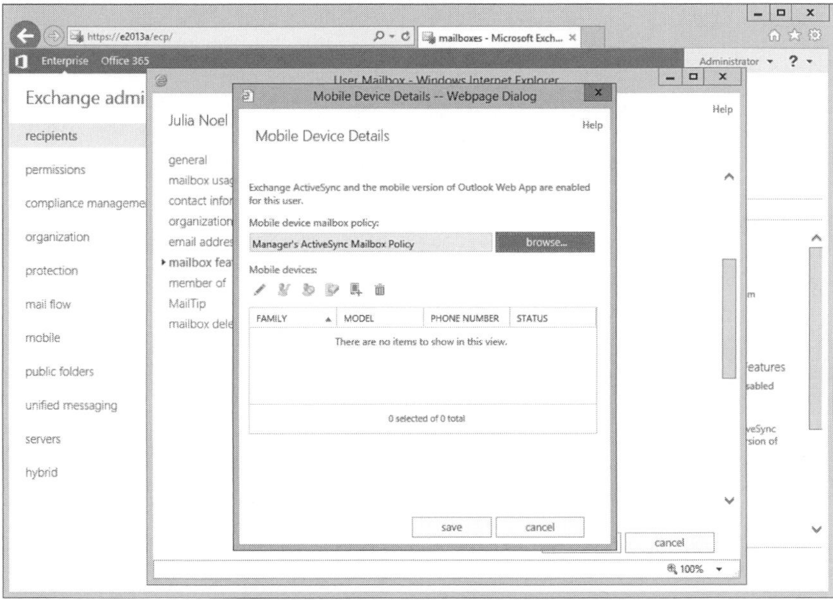

FIGURE 23.4 Applying an ActiveSync mailbox policy to a mailbox.

Configuring a Mobile Device

You can very easily connect nearly all ActiveSync devices to an Internet-facing Exchange Server 2013 CAS server by simply entering their email addresses and a username and password into the appropriate mail configuration settings on the devices. If Autodiscover is enabled, the device should automatically determine what the FQDN of the ActiveSync environment is (e.g., owa.companyabc.com). If Autodiscover is not in place, you may need to provide instructions for users on how to manually enter the ActiveSync server name.

The phone will then begin syncing with the ActiveSync server and will automatically keep mail, calendar, and tasks items in sync.

Enabling Offline Outlook Web App (OWA) in Exchange Server 2013

The most significant upgrade to the mobile browsing experience within Exchange Server 2013 is the addition of offline access to OWA. Offline access allows all clients, mobile or otherwise, to be able to access, respond to, and update mail information while offline. This allows for scenarios such as those where email access on airplanes and remote locations without connectivity is desired.

Understanding the Prerequisites for Offline OWA

Offline OWA requires a modern browser that understands the latest in HTML5 technologies, which currently includes the following minimums:

- Internet Explorer 10
- Chrome 16
- Safari 15

If the proper browser version is not supported, the option to enable Offline OWA simply won't appear.

In addition, the mailbox used for Offline OWA must be on an Exchange Server 2013 server and must be using an Exchange Server 2013 CAS server.

Limitations with Offline OWA

It is important to note the following limitations when using Offline OWA:

- Only the last several days of messages in the Inbox, Drafts, Sent Items, and any other folder viewed when offline within the past few days.
- Only the previous month and upcoming year in the active calendar are synched.
- Offline OWA only shows limited amount of upcoming calendar appointments.
- Offline OWA synchs all items in the Contacts folder, plus commonly emailed people from the Global Address List.
- Search is not available when offline.
- The personal archive mailbox is not accessible when offline.

Enabling Offline OWA on a Mailbox

There is no back-end step to enable Offline OWA; it is enabled at the browser level. It is also important to note that it must be enabled for each computer and for each browser used, and that it stores sensitive mail information in the local cache, so care should be taken to encrypt the device properly.

To enable Offline OWA on an Exchange Server 2013 mailbox, perform the following steps:

1. From a supported browser, while logged into OWA, click on the Settings icon (depicted by a gear) and select Use Mail Offline, as shown in Figure 23.5.
2. Click Yes when prompted for the warning that asks if you are the only person who uses the computer, as shown in Figure 23.6.
3. Click Add to Favorites when prompted to add OWA to the Favorites of the browser. This immediately turns on Offline OWA for that particular browser.

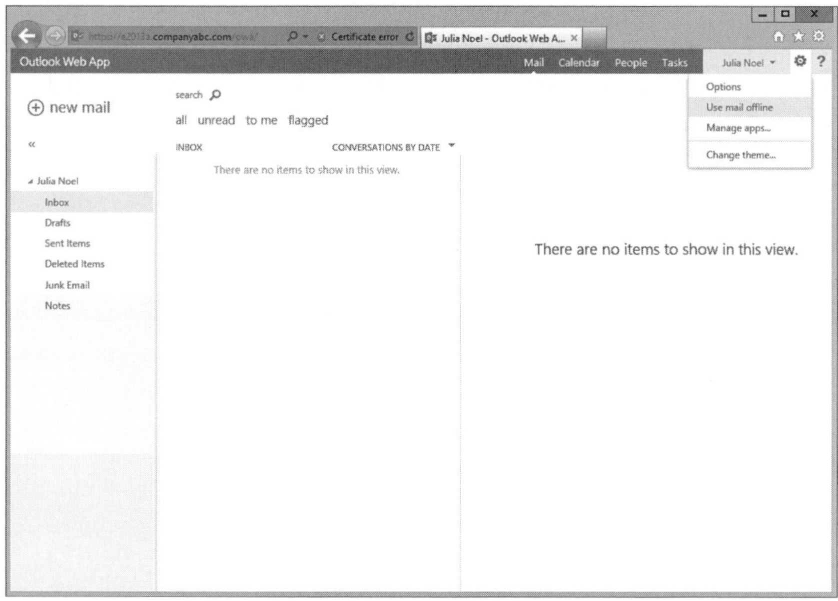

FIGURE 23.5 Enabling offline access on a mailbox for OWA.

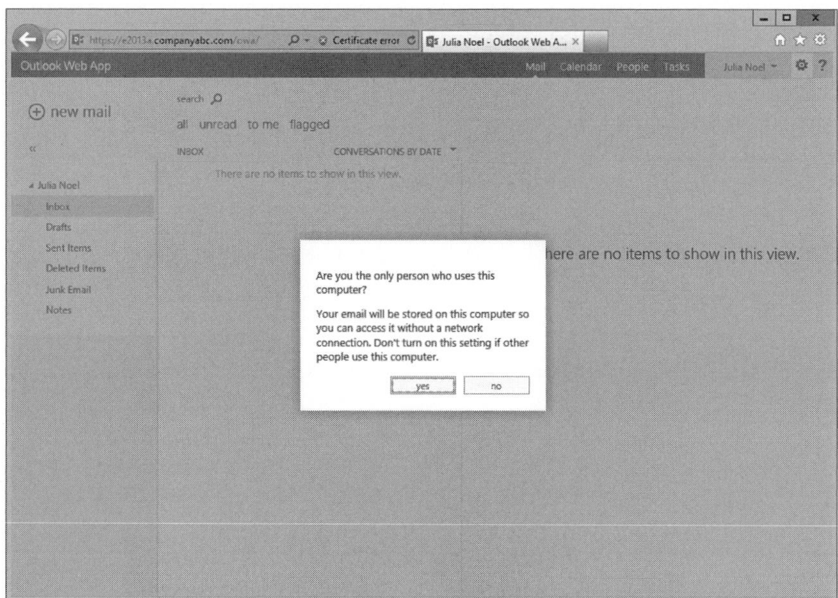

FIGURE 23.6 Warning box when enabling Offline OWA.

Working with Offline OWA

When enabled, Offline OWA will store a cached copy of the most recent messages and calendar appointments, and the page should remain responsive at all times, even if the network connection goes down. Once the network connection is back online, simply refreshing the page or performing any task is enough to put it back into Online mode.

To turn off Offline OWA mode, simply click on the Settings icon (depicted by a gear) again and select Stop Using Offline. The local cache will then be immediately purged.

Summary

The concept of the "office without walls" is fast becoming a reality, as information workers now have a myriad of options available to connect with their co-workers using Exchange Server 2013 technologies such as ActiveSync. ActiveSync in Exchange Server 2013 also allows for unprecedented management and security capabilities, allowing organizations to take advantage of the improved productivity these devices give, but without sacrificing security in the process. In addition, a greatly improved OWA interface that provides for offline support and improved GUIs that are different for each type of device allow for new access mechanisms that further improve the mobility possibilities of the platform.

Best Practices

The following are best practices from this chapter:

- Always use SSL encryption with ActiveSync technologies.
- Use ActiveSync mailbox policies to gain granular control over password and encryption settings of the mobile devices.
- Use a third-party trusted root CA for SSL with ActiveSync to avoid having to manually install a certificate on every mobile device.
- Use Offline OWA for mobile devices when on the road and needing access to mailboxes, though be sure to encrypt the device for security reasons.
- Secure the ActiveSync HTTP traffic to CAS systems by implementing a reverse web proxy device.

Index

Symbols

A

B

C

D

E

F

G

H

I

J

K

L

M

N

O

P

Q

R

How can we make this index more useful? Email us at indexes@samspublishing.com

S

How can we make this index more useful? Email us at indexes@samspublishing.com

T

How can we make this index more useful? Email us at indexes@samspublishing.com

U

V

W

X - Z

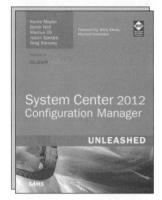

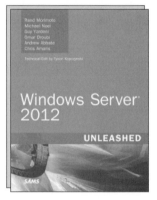

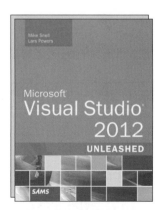

SAMS
REGISTER
THIS PRODUCT
informit.com/register

informIT.com
THE TRUSTED TECHNOLOGY LEARNING SOURCE

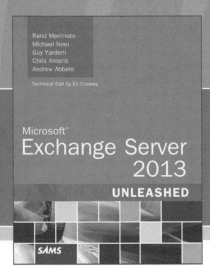